THE
SECOND
SEX

THE
SECOND
SEX

SIMONE DE BEAUVOIR

TRANSLATED AND EDITED BY

H. M. PARSHLEY

INTRODUCTION TO THE VINTAGE EDITION BY

DEIRDRE BAIR

VINTAGE BOOKS
A DIVISION OF RANDOM HOUSE, INC.
NEW YORK

Vintage Books Edition, September 1989

Introduction copyright © 1989 by Deirdre Bair

Copyright 1952 by Alfred A. Knopf, Inc.
Copyright renewed 1980 by Alfred A. Knopf, Inc.

Library of Congress Cataloging in Publication Data
Beauvoir, Simone de, 1908–1986
The second sex.
Reprint of the 1953 ed. published
by Knopf, New York.
Translation of Le deuxième sexe.
1. Woman.   I. Title.
[HQ1208.B352   1974]   301.41'2   74-4241
ISBN 0-679-72451-6 (pbk.)

Manufactured in the United States of America
10 9 8 7 6 5 4 3 2 1

Translator's Preface

A SERIOUS, all-inclusive, and uninhibited work on woman by a woman of wit and learning! What, I had often thought, could be more desirable and yet less to be expected? When I was asked, some three years ago, to read Mlle Simone de Beauvoir's *Le Deuxième Sexe*, then appearing in two successive volumes in France, and to offer my opinion on the advisability of its publication in English, I was not long in realizing that the unexpected had happened. My opinion, I need hardly say, was favorable, for the work displayed unique qualities of style and content which, I thought, would make it a classic in its often worked but far from exhausted field. And when, a little later, I ventured to undertake the arduous task of translation—not from any pretension to linguistic scholarship but because I had long been concerned with certain scientific and humanistic aspects of the subject (not to mention the subsidiary inducements of wealth and fame)— the ensuing more intimate acquaintance served to confirm and, indeed, to heighten my first impression of the work.

Much, in truth, has been written on woman from more or less restricted points of view, such as the physiological, the cynical, the religious, the psychoanalytical, and the feministic—some of it written even by women; but it has remained for Mlle de Beauvoir to produce a book on woman and her historical and contemporary situation in Western culture, which is at once scientifically accurate in matters of biology, comprehensive and frank in its treatment of woman's individual development and social relations, illuminated throughout by a wealth of literary and scientific citation, and founded upon a broadly generous and consistent philosophy. "Feminine literature," the author remarks, "is in our day animated less by a wish to demand our rights than by an effort toward clarity and understanding." Her work is certainly a good example of this tendency, and if, in addition, it sometimes may provoke dissent and give rise to controversy, so much the better. Mlle de Beauvoir is in general more concerned to explain than to reform, but she does look forward to better things and, portraying with approval the independent woman of today, in the end gives persuasive expression to her vision of the future.

The author's philosophy is, as I say, a broad one, drawn from the many sources familiar to a former teacher of the subject; but, as she is at pains to point out in her Introduction, her "perspective is that of existentialist ethics": her philosophy is focused in the existentialism of Sartre.[1] In the same passage, to which the reader is referred, she states in general how certain existentialist concepts—which, it may be remarked, in themselves command intellectual and ethical respect—apply to woman's situation, and throughout the book she shows in multifarious detail that these basic concepts serve to define problems and to suggest solutions. This is no place to go more deeply into existentialism, and Mlle de Beauvoir's book is, after all, on woman, not on philosophy; the reader who is indifferent to existentialism or even in opposition to it will nevertheless gain pleasure and profit in plenty. In any case the serious reader will find that the occasionally recurring passages of existentialist thought and terminology will tend to lose their strangeness, and their meaning will take shape in his mind as his reading progresses. Whatever the fate of existentialism as a philosophical and literary movement may be, the chief concepts used by Mlle de Beauvoir in the present work and referred to above have general validity, and therefore they could be—and doubtless most of them have been—expressed more or less adequately in quite other terms.

Mlle de Beauvoir is a Frenchwoman, and though by no means lacking in first-hand acquaintance with the United States and other foreign countries, she naturally draws heavily upon French life and customs in her detailed account of woman's past and contemporary situation. Her account of female upbringing and education may strike English and American readers as in some ways peculiar; but however familiar we may be, say, with little girls in football helmets and blue jeans playing a rough game against little boys on a plane of approximate equality, or with young girls roving the streets at night or freely taking bicycle and automobile trips without benefit of masculine

---

[1] The interested reader will do well to ignore the more or less sensational journalistic accounts of the Parisian café "existentialists" (lately repudiated quite unequivocally by Sartre) and consult, say, the excellent, brief exposition of existentialism in its various forms available in Marjorie Grene's *Dreadful Freedom: A Critique of Existentialism* (University of Chicago Press, 1940). Reference may also be made to Sartre's *Existentialism* (Philosophical Library, 1947), in which certain aspects of the philosophy are set forth, and, for readers of French, to R. Campbell's pamphlet *Expliquez-moi l'existentialisme* (published by Foucher in Paris), in which the various schools are described and the existentialist terminology is explained.

guardianship, we still do not have to look very far into the past, or, indeed, very widely around us, to perceive parallels in plenty for almost or quite all the conditions Mlle de Beauvoir describes and deplores. Here as in France and elsewhere, despite changes in educational technique and with comparatively few exceptions, the vast majority of girls are still more or less explicitly directed toward predatory coquetry and consequent masculine support in marriage or otherwise as a prime aim in life, in contrast to boys, who are commonly schooled in violence and initiative and urged toward a life of productive activity. Thus the perceptive reader will constantly recognize the familiar in more or less foreign guise, and this is because the author's picture is fundamentally valid for our Atlantic civilization as a whole.

The central thesis of Mlle de Beauvoir's book is that since patriarchal times women have in general been forced to occupy a secondary place in the world in relation to men, a position comparable in many respects with that of racial minorities in spite of the fact that women constitute numerically at least half of the human race, and further that this secondary standing is not imposed of necessity by natural "feminine" characteristics but rather by strong environmental forces of educational and social tradition under the purposeful control of men. This, the author maintains, has resulted in the general failure of women to take a place of human dignity as free and independent existents, associated with men on a plane of intellectual and professional equality, a condition that not only has limited their achievement in many fields but also has given rise to pervasive social evils and has had a particularly vitiating effect on the sexual relations between men and women. Genuine exceptions are doubtless becoming at present more numerous than formerly, but the commonly cited facts that many henpecked husbands exist, that many women exert a considerable influence upon men in positions of authority, and that especially in the United States a large proportion of wealth and property is held in women's names can easily be shown to uphold rather than to disprove the author's contentions, however serviceable such facts may be in jocose and superficial assertions regarding woman's dominance of American life.

In the United States, to be sure, perhaps more frequently than in some other countries, a good many women do succeed in attaining positions of professional independence, and some of them nevertheless

marry sooner or later—and even have children—without lessening
their competence or disrupting their careers. But their paths are still
beset with peculiar difficulties of one kind or another. It is a scarcely
noted fact, for example, that such married women, especially in academic communities, often become uncomfortably aware of the existence of a more or less subtly expressed prejudice against them on
the part not only of the nonprofessional and homebound wives of
their male colleagues, but also—for different though equally understandable reasons—on the part of their unmarried female colleagues.
This prejudice is possibly to be attributed in part to jealousy and more
or less conscious resentment—"They are having their cake and eating
it, too!"—but however that may be, it certainly testifies to the strength
and persistence of the traditional feeling that if a woman has a home
her place is in it. Similarly, successful businesswomen are often conscious of the fact, noted by the author, that neither men nor women
commonly enjoy working under feminine direction, which again indicates the weight of tradition—in this case to the effect that the boss
should be a man.

The traditional belief that man should be the provider has remained strong, especially in middle-class circles, in spite of the fact
that in the United States, for example, some twenty millions of
women—half of them married and many with children—are gainfully
employed outside the home; and the social and psychological problems involved, many of which are referred to in Mlle de Beauvoir's
pages, seem to occupy an increasing place in the press, in radio pro-
grams, in discussion groups, and in other more or less efficient agen-
cies of public enlightenment. The situation, with its attendant problems, is not new, since it originated in the industrial revolution, the
rise of the factory system, and the entrance of women into business
mostly on lower levels of employment; but it has gained new interest
and importance from, on the one hand, wartime demands for woman's
participation in ever widening fields of activity, and, on the other, a
growing realization of the bearing of home atmosphere upon the psychological development of children and their ultimate welfare as
adults. Yet in the still existing traditional situation all this extensive
employment of women has little to do with the author's ideal of the
independent woman, for the vast majority of unmarried workers entertain the hope—often enough illusive—that marriage will release
them from work in which they have no real interest and which they re-

gard as a temporary burden, and the married ones gain no real independence through work done only to supplement the perhaps temporarily inadequate earnings of their "providers."

It is only the highly trained professional woman and the highly placed woman in business—both genuine existents with a profound and permanent interest in their work and projects—who can attain under present circumstances the position of independence and equality envisaged by Mlle de Beauvoir as the one firm basis for ideal human relations between men and women. To refer here to only one relevant matter of perennial discussion, the question of whether women's higher education should be different from that of men in its greater emphasis on "domestic science," marriage problems, and the like, with consequent loss of rigor in professional training, can have but one answer in the light of the author's analysis.[2] She would approve the bold determination of the founders of a number of American colleges for women to provide an education identical with that of men, and she would deplore any departure from that ideal. It is just such differences in training, at whatever age level, that in the author's view are to be held largely accountable for the weaknesses of "femininity." In any case, whatever study of marriage problems may seem desirable in higher education is surely needed as much by men as by women.[3]

In Le Deuxième Sexe Mlle de Beauvoir, a practiced writer, employs a style which, while often in a sense informal, is for the most part precise and sometimes elevated and poetic; and I have conceived it my duty as translator to adhere faithfully to what she says and to maintain to the best of my ability the atmosphere she creates. Thus my intention has been in general to avoid all paraphrasing not required by language differences and to provide a translation that is at once exact and—with slight exceptions—complete. At the publisher's request I have, as editor, occasionally added an explanatory word or two (especially in connection with existentialist terminology) and provided a few additional footnotes and bibliographic data which I thought might be to the reader's interest; and I have also done some cutting and condensation here and there with a view to brevity, chiefly in reducing the extent of the author's illustrative material,

---

[2] See especially Book II, Ch. xxv.

[3] This point is strongly argued by Dr. A. Stone in A Marriage Manual (Simon & Schuster, new edition, 1952).

especially in certain of her quotations from other writers. Practically all such modifications have been made with the author's express permission, passage by passage; and in no case do the changes involve anything in the nature of censorship [4] or any intentional alteration or omission of the author's ideas.

In conclusion I must express my gratitude to all who have helped me in one way or another. I am indebted in particular to Professors Vincent Guilloton and Newton Arvin of Smith College, to Sabine Bass of Mount Holyoke College, to the publisher, and in less degree to still others, all of whom, I trust, are aware of my appreciation. In spite of such assistance, errors will no doubt be found in my work, and for these I claim sole responsibility.

H. M. PARSHLEY

Smith College
Northampton, Massachusetts

---

[4] Except for a few short passages, mostly referring to persons now living, which have been omitted on the advice of legal counsel.

Contents

BOOK ONE: *FACTS AND MYTHS*

BOOK TWO: WOMAN'S LIFE TODAY

Introduction to the Vintage Edition

"ONE IS NOT BORN, but rather becomes a woman," Simone de Beauvoir declared boldly in *The Second Sex*. The book startled readers when it was first published in her native France in 1949; more than forty years later, it continues to provoke spirited response in women and men alike throughout the rest of the world. In over 700 pages of analysis, Beauvoir scrutinizes the facts and myths of women's lives, using the disparate methodologies of (among others) literature, history, biology, and philosophy to examine not only the problems women encounter but also the possibilities open to them. Elizabeth Hardwick, who reviewed the first American translation of *The Second Sex* in 1953, probably spoke for many readers when, exhausted by the originality of its thesis and the intensity of its argument, she called it "madly sensible and brilliantly confused."

From the very beginning, *The Second Sex* was controversial. "How courageous you are [to have written it]," one of Beauvoir's friends said. "You're going to lose a lot of friends!" Twenty-two thousand copies were sold the first week, as the French "read, as it were, with averted eyes." Beauvoir described what happened next in her memoirs:

> I received—some signed and some anonymous—epigrams, epistles, satires, admonitions, and exhortations addressed to me by, for example, "some very active members of the First Sex." Unsatisfied, frigid, priapic, nymphomaniac, lesbian, a hundred times aborted, I was everything, even an unmarried mother. People offered to cure me of my frigidity or to temper my labial appetites; I was promised revelations, in the coarsest terms but in the name of the true, the good and the beautiful, in the name of health and even of poetry.[1]

The American writer Nelson Algren, visiting Beauvoir in Paris at the time, was outraged by the hostility in which she was "cartooned, ridiculed, sometimes made gentle fun of and, at other times, reviled with no restraint." By 1960, when he was next in Paris, Algren noted a striking difference:

There was no more laughter: she was feared. She had broken through the defenses of the bourgeoisie, of the church, the businessmen, the right-wing defenders of Napoleonic glory, and the hired press. She was, at once, the most hated and the most loved woman in France. It had become plain: she *meant* it.[2]

And all of this because Simone de Beauvoir, a French writer who until 1949 was better known as Jean-Paul Sartre's companion of more than twenty years than as the author of several well-received novels, decided to write a book about women in order to learn more about herself.

She said in her memoirs that the book originated "by chance." For several years, she had wanted to write about herself but had not yet identified autobiography as the genre in which to do so. Intending to write a nonfiction essay couched in the philosophical framework of existentialism, the theory Sartre had propounded in *Being and Nothingness* (1943), she soon realized that she would first have to describe the condition of women in general. As she later told a French interviewer: "One day I wanted to explain myself to myself . . . and it struck me with a sort of surprise that the first thing I had to say was 'I am a woman.' "[3]

Beauvoir claimed to have "spent two years" on the research and writing of *The Second Sex*, from October 1946 to June 1949.[4] In actuality, it took fourteen months once she had decided upon the book's form. However, the process from initial conception to final manuscript was much longer and might have actually begun as far back as 1935–36. She was then a philosophy teacher in a Rouen *lycée*, or high school, where her life-long friend, the feminist writer and political activist Colette Audry, was a fellow teacher.

In Rouen, the two women often spoke of their lot in life, and from the beginning they were surprised by how differently they perceived their situations. Audry, whose primary interest was politics, chafed at the fact that French women could not vote (they were not granted suffrage until 1947) and cited this fact as her primary reason why, as a woman, she could not participate fully in French society: "No matter how kindly, how equally men treated me when I tried to participate in politics, when it came right down to it, they had more rights, so they had more power than I did."[5]

But in the mid-1930s, Simone de Beauvoir was happy with the status her relationship with Sartre ensured and was puzzled by Audry's frustration, claiming she felt none at all, Audry recalled, "precisely because she had an egalitarian relationship with a man":

It was enough for her [that] all Sartre's friends treated her exactly as they treated him. [Within] her family, she was trained from the beginning to have a career, so there, too, she did not suffer the frustration of many women of her class who wanted a career but were prevented from having it by that false comfort, the security of their family's money and position.

In 1936, Audry actually began to keep notes for a book about women, but eventually she lost interest in it. The project became a running joke between her and Beauvoir on the infrequent occasions when they met throughout the next decade. When, on a chance encounter in a Paris café in 1948, Beauvoir told Audry that she was going to write such a book, Audry believed it was because the friend who had always insisted her "life as a woman was as free and equal as any man's" had probably "encountered some serious obstacle that made her change her mind."

It was not so much one serious obstacle as a succession of experiences that led Beauvoir to write *The Second Sex* in the form we now have before us. Arriving at the point where her original idea—for only an essay—evolved into the book she actually wrote was a long, drawn-out process, at times haphazard and unfocused. The actual composition was begun in the fall of 1946, after she finished the philosophical essays published as *The Ethics of Ambiguity*. She thought she would write another essay that would be a continuation of the book, and a "sort of credo" of herself as "both woman and Existentialist."[6]

This was the period during which Sartre was under sustained verbal attack in Paris by those who disagreed with his politics and philosophy, and because of their relationship, Beauvoir was also the frequent brunt of gossip and insult. She believed she could defend Sartre's positions as well as their unmarried liaison by writing an essay in which she defined herself personally as a woman and philosophically as an existentialist. Her intention was to relate them both to Sartre's system, which she had accepted unquestioningly as her own, but as in all her writing to this date, there was a strong, if still unfocused autobiographical element involved. In order to defend what she believed were Sartre's universal principles, she had to begin with the specific and the individual, which in this case was her role within his system.

One idea began "to emerge with some insistence, with clarity," from her thinking. It brought her to "the very profound and astonishing realization" that she was different from Sartre "because he was a man and I was only a woman." In a 1982 conversation she explained what she meant by "only":

I had not yet settled on the idea of woman as the other—that was to come later. I had not yet decided that the lot of woman was inferior to the allotment of men in this life. But somehow, I was beginning to formulate the thesis that women had not been given equality in our society, and I must tell you that this was an extremely troubling discovery for me. This is really how I began to be serious about writing about women—when I fully realized the disparity in our lives as compared to men. But [in 1947], none of this was clear to me.

These thoughts were interrupted that year when she went to the United States for the first time, sent by the French government to lecture in American colleges and universities on contemporary French literature. In the course of her travels, she began to think about enlarging her "essay about women" into a book that would be a comparative analysis of the situation of women in the United States and France. This time she intended it to be grounded solidly in existentialism but with a political cast "not . . . Marxism *per se*, but certainly . . . the politics of the Left."

Whenever she had the opportunity to talk to American women she asked questions about the differences between their culture and her own. When she returned to France she asked French women to tell her the story of their lives, intending to use them as case histories in her book. Listening to these stories made her realize that she owed a great deal of her success and independence to the good fortune of having chosen Sartre as her first and most enduring male companion.

She abandoned the idea of a comparative study of women in the two cultures shortly after she returned to France, and instead wrote a series of impressions about American life, collected in book form as *America Day by Day*. By mid-1947 she was envisioning "a long chapter on women," and planning to model it on *America Day by Day* as a series of independent, purely reportorial articles about the situation of contemporary women. It was not until the fall of that year that all her formerly haphazard ideas coalesced into the form that became her long, serious, and sustained examination of the condition of women throughout history.

"Sexuality and socialization" became Beauvoir's "poles of analysis and reflection"[7] as she turned first to the lost or missing history of women. She began "at the beginning, with biology," then continued with history, mythology, politics, and gender. She decided to divide her research into two parts, which ultimately appeared as two separately published volumes in French and as Books One and Two in the English translation.

Book One is a historical overview that she called "Facts and Myths" about women. These she divided further into three separate sections called "Destiny," "History," and "Myths," all of which are further divided into individual chapters. "Destiny" discusses the condition of women through biology, psychoanalysis, and historical materialism. "History" follows women through nomadic societies, as early tillers of the soil, and from the time of the patriarchs and classical antiquity through the Middle Ages, the Enlightenment, the French Revolution, and the granting of French suffrage in 1947. In "Myths" she speaks of dreams, fears, and idols, then follows the mythical woman created by five different male authors. Four are French: Montherlant, Claudel, Breton, and Stendhal; the fifth is English, D. H. Lawrence. She follows this with a discussion of "Myth and Reality."

In the second volume, or Book Two, she deals with "Woman's Life Today," which, following form, she also divides into three sections: "The Formative Years," "Situation," and "Justifications." These are followed by a conclusion called "Toward Liberation." Here she is both contemporary and personal, as she writes of childhood, adolescence, maturity, and old age. She also describes sexual initiation and various expressions of sexuality from lesbianism to heterosexual marriage as she deals with the idea of love in its many forms, from narcissism to mysticism. Her conclusion is optimistic, as she defines both a way of being and a model for action by women of future generations.

As Beauvoir filled in the details of her ambitious outline, the word "other" became increasingly important in her vocabulary.[8] She defined white men in Western civilizations as being the central figures in their societies, and according to this definition, not only women were

"other," but also anyone whom she considered barred from empower-
ment by color or sexual preference. To her, the next logical step seemed
"the need to define what these 'others' were in relation to white men,
then to study the historical situations which made such alterity possible
in the first place and what circumstances made it legitimate."

Nelson Algren, with whom she carried on an almost fifteen-year
long-distance love affair, was responsible for giving a particularly American slant to *The Second Sex.* He suggested that she conduct her study
of women along the lines of the experience of black Americans in a
segregated society and introduced her to the writings of Gunnar and
Alva Myrdal, among many others, and introduced her to his black
American friends in Chicago, urging them to share their experiences
with her. She adopted Algren's view in part because of her own friendship with the black American writer Richard Wright and his white wife,
Ellen. Seeing the problems they encountered as a couple convinced her
that white men had succeeded in relegating both black men and all
women into positions of "alterité" or "otherness." Algren also insisted
that she read American literature of the 1920s and 1930s, with its strong
political and social content. When he was in Chicago and she in Paris
their correspondence often contained discussions about such writers as
James T. Farrell, John O'Hara, John Dos Passos, Frank Conroy, Tess
Schlessinger, Maridel LeSeur, and others.

From reading fiction and sociology, she turned to history to ascertain
women's role in it. She discovered that in general there was none, for
they were seldom mentioned, if at all. She found support for her views
in the French writer Poulain de la Barre, whom she called "a little-
known feminist of the seventeenth century." She shared his belief that
"All that has been written about women by men should be suspect, for
the men are at once judge and party to the lawsuit."9

Beauvoir's citation of Poulain to prove a point is only one example
of the scope of her research and methodology. She was also inquisitive
about contemporary scholarship and incorporated much new information from developing disciplines into her book. Using anthropology, she
was an early practitioner of gender theory as she sought ways to extract
and define common characteristics among women from within studies
that only mentioned them as figures in the larger background. Although
she held a life-long distrust of psychology, she nevertheless attended
some of Jacques Lacan's lectures, hoping again to find patterns and
trends common among women.

She drew upon earlier feminist writers, among them Virginia Woolf, to develop still another perspective. Woolf's view of the relationship between economic independence and intellectual freedom had long been her own. She also used the documentation of women themselves, as she studied, evaluated, and formed theories about letters, diaries, personal psychoanalytic histories, autobiographies, essays, and novels. In many ways she deserves credit for focusing the attention of later generations of scholars upon these heretofore neglected areas that are now valued as important sources for revising history to include the participation and contribution of women.

These are only several examples of the scope of her research and methodology. The global influence of the book is all the more extraordinary when we realize that it was written by a French woman of a specific social and intellectual background who had very little firsthand knowledge of previous feminist movements, writings, or ideas within France itself to guide her initial explorations, and almost no knowledge of feminist activity elsewhere in the world. Yet she was able to go unfailingly to the important documents, sources, and writings in many fields, and to synthesize all this information within her self-imposed framework of existential philosophy.

The book that resulted has been many things to many readers in the years since it was published and translated into more than twenty-six different languages. One of the fairest assessments is by British scholar Terry Keefe, who called it "one of the most important and far-reaching books on women ever published," but who also noted that

> This highly ambitious project leaves a good deal to be desired, for the book cannot be said to be very carefully composed, or even, on the whole, particularly well-written. . . . While almost every section contains some fertile ideas and valuable insights, argument of the highest quality is rarely sustained for long.[10]

Criticism of the book was quick in coming and has continued ever since, even though it is generally praised for having changed how "official anti-feminist and feminist discourse have been carried on [since] the Middle Ages."[11] One of the most sustained criticisms has been that Beauvoir is guilty of unconscious misogyny, that having written about women, she has taken great care to separate herself from them. The French writer and political activist Francis Jeanson accused her of writing as someone who understood the feminist condition only because she herself had escaped from it.[12] A similar charge was made by the British poet and novelist Stevie Smith: "She has written an enormous book about women and it is soon clear that she does not like them, nor does she like being a woman."[13] Another oft-repeated criticism is British scholar C. B. Radford's, that she has been "guilty of painting women in her own colors" because *The Second Sex* is

> primarily a middle-class document, so distorted by autobiographical influences that the individual problems of the writer herself may assume an exaggerated importance in her discussion of feminity.

Radford recognized, however, that though

> her image of woman may be distorted: it is nevertheless sincere. In all her work she is motivated by the honest conviction that her own solution is the best . . . that accounts for the exaggeration and even the violence of her work.[14]

The debate grew stronger when the first English translation appeared in the United States in 1953.

Blanche Knopf, wife of the publisher Alfred A. Knopf, deserves credit for discerning that *The Second Sex* would be an important book worthy of translation but not for the reason she first assumed: that the book "was a modern-day sex manual, something between Kinsey and Havelock Ellis." Mrs. Knopf bought the book on a trip to France because she thought the popularity of existentialism among college-age Americans would result in healthy sales. Her husband wanted an expert's judgment before agreeing to publish it, and because the book was purported to be a study of female sexuality, he asked H. M. Parshley, a professor emeritus of zoology at Smith College, to provide one.

Professor Parshley was not as unlikely a candidate to evaluate it as many critics of his translation have since charged. He was considered an expert on human reproduction and collaborated frequently on translations from the French of works of a scientific nature. In choosing him the Knopfs believed they had carefully selected the most trustworthy candidate to provide them with the expert judgment such a work demanded, and it was because of Parshley's perceptive analysis and strong belief in it that *The Second Sex* was translated so early on in its long publishing life. In his initial report Parshley called it "a thoughtful and well-written work which throws new light on an old question." He continued:

> A book on women by an intelligent, learned, and well-balanced woman is, I think, a great rarity, and this is indeed such a book. It is not feminist in any doctrinaire sense, nor is it an attack on the male sex; and it does not belong to the category of ululations about the "lost sex," etc., of which we have plenty. . . . The book is a profound and unique analysis of woman's nature and position, eminently reasonable and often witty; and it surely should be translated. . . . It should pay for itself, and in any case will be a credit to the publisher.[15]

Alfred Knopf had a slightly different opinion:

> [Beauvoir] certainly suffers from verbal diarrhea—I have seldom read a book that seems to run in such concentric circles. Everything seems to be repeated three or four times but in different parts of the text, and I can hardly imagine the average person reading the whole book carefully. But I think it is capable of making a very wide appeal indeed and that young ladies in places like Smith who can afford the price, which will be high, will be nursing it just as students of my generation managed somehow to get hold of Havelock Ellis.[16]

From the beginning it was clear that the unwieldy French text had to be cut and condensed. Also from the beginning, Beauvoir refused to cooperate on the translation. After several frustrating years, Blanche Knopf told Parshley regretfully that nothing could be done about "la Beauvoir," as they had dubbed her, as she refused even to give them her address in Paris, insisting that all communication be sent through her agent. "I think you will simply have to carry on as you did [thus far]," Mrs. Knopf concluded.

Parshley worked diligently to keep as much of the text and to compose as faithful a translation as possible in the four years, from 1949 to 1952, during which he worked on the book. Difficulties arose because many of Beauvoir's sources were French, to be found only in France, and were thus unavailable to him. Also, she used terms that had a particular meaning in existential philosophy; without Beauvoir's explanations and despite Parshley's trying to read as widely as possible in Sartre and his precursors, Hegel and Heiddeger, many philosophers believe he has either misconstrued or misused much philosophical terminology.

Because Parshley received no suggestions from Beauvoir about cutting the massive manuscript, he had to make decisions on his own. One of the most extensive cuts was in the "History" section, where he deleted fully half the chapter and the names and histories of seventy-eight women. Since there is no note to indicate these deletions, much of Beauvoir's subsequent analysis of nineteenth-century European and American suffrage movements is seriously impaired, as is her treatment of the development of socialist feminism in France. She was upset to learn that any cuts had been made at all, but was furious about the "History" section, because, as she noted to her agent, "the detailed studies . . . make my writing vivid and convincing." Shortly after, she "agreed in principle to the idea of cuts," but only if they were submitted to her for approval first. Unfortunately, she lost interest in the project and her comments and suggestions were few and haphazard. All she really wanted from publication in the United States was "lots of dollars," so she made no further protest about changes in her text. When Mrs. Knopf sent her a copy of the finished book, Beauvoir replied insincerely via her agent that she found the book "superb" and the translation "excellent." She added that she hoped Mrs. Knopf (with whom she had never cooperated, and whom she had simply never liked) would return to Paris so she could tell her personally "how much I appreciate Mr. Parshley's work and the appearance of my book."[17]

One day a new, uncut translation of *The Second Sex* will no doubt be done. The book has become a classic and should therefore be available to readers exactly as its author wrote it, no matter how repetitious, unwieldy, or awkward the text. In the meantime, however, until we have a "definitive" text before us, this one will serve to alert readers to the remarkable variety and richness of Simone de Beauvoir's thesis and its continuing importance. It remains, as one of the first reviewers noted, "more than a work of scholarship; it is a work of art, with the salt of recklessness that makes art sting."[18]

In another instance, I tried to assess Simone de Beauvoir's contribution to our time, and I concluded:

Only one thing is certain: there has been no other woman in contemporary literature who has been so completely associated with the major events, causes and actions of her society. . . . Considered separately, most if not all of her remarks make splendid sense; seen together they create a crazy quilt kaleidoscope of image and reality, opinion and fact. Feminist ideology cannot ignore Simone de Beauvoir; her importance should be unquestioned and is undeniable. The real question will be how to assess her contribution, and what use to make of it in the future.[19]

I believe we would do well to start with *The Second Sex.*

—DEIRDRE BAIR

NOTES

1. Simone de Beauvoir, *Force of Circumstances* (New York and London: Penguin Books, 1978).

2. Nelson Algren, *Who Lost an American?* (New York: Macmillan, 1963), p. 97 ff.

3. Madeleine Chapsal, "Une interview de Simone de Beauvoir," *Les Ecrivains en personne* (Paris: Julliard, 1960), pp. 17–37; reprinted in Claude Francis and Fernande Gontier, *Les Ecrits de Simone de Beauvoir* (Paris: Les Editions Gallimard, 1979), p. 385. My translation.

4. Beauvoir, *Force of Circumstance*, p. 196.

5. Interview with Colette Audry, March 5, 1986, Paris. All subsequent comments by Audry are from this interview.

6. These remarks are taken from a series of interviews I conducted with Simone de Beauvoir from 1981 to 1986 in Paris and New York for the book *Simone de Beauvoir: A Biography* (New York: Summit Books, 1990). Hereafter, any unattributed remarks by Simone de Beauvoir are taken from these interviews and conversations.

7. Christine Fauré, "The Twilight of the Goddesses, or The Intellectual Crisis of French Feminism," translated by Lillian S. Robinson. *Signs* 7, 1 (Autumn 1981):82. This article was originally published as "Le Crépuscule des déesses, ou La Crise intellectuelle en France en milieu féministe," *Les Temps Modernes* 414 (January 1981):1285–91.

8. Throughout the composition of the book, when people asked Beauvoir what she was writing, she usually said "just something about the other sex." She had no title until she was almost ready to publish. Then, during a night of friendly drinking and conversation, her friend and Sartre's, Jacques-Laurent Bost, made a scatological joke calling homosexuals "the third sex, and that must mean women come in second." She decided to call her book *The Second Sex*.

9. François Poulain de la Barre (1647–1725), *De l'égalité des deux sexes (On the Equality of Both Sexes)*, (1673), (Paris: Librairie Arthème Fayard, 1984).

10. Terry Keefe, *Simone de Beauvoir: A Study of Her Writings* (Totowa, N.J.: Barnes & Noble Books, 1983), p. 111.

11. Elaine Marks and Isabelle de Courtivron, eds., *New French Feminisms* (Amherst: Univ. of Michigan Press, 1980), introduction, pp. 6 and 7.

12. Francis Jeanson, *Simone de Beauvoir ou l'entreprise de vivre* (Paris: Editions du Seuil, 1966), p. 253.

13. Stevie Smith, "The Devil's Doorway," review of *The Second Sex, The Spectator*, no. 6543 (November 20, 1953): 602–603.

14. C. B. Radford, "Feminism's Friend or Foe?," *Nottingham French Studies* 6, 2 (October 1967): 89.

15. H. M. Parshley, "Report on *Le Deuxieme Sexe* by Simone de Beauvoir, Vol. I," courtesy of Mrs. Elsa Parshley Brown.

16. Alfred A. Knopf to H. M. Parshley, November 27, 1951.

17. Simone de Beauvoir, quoted in Blanche Knopf's letter to H. M. Parshley, January 8, 1953.

18. Brendan Gill, "No More Eve," *The New Yorker* 29, 2 (February 28, 1953): 97–99.

19. Deirdre Bair, "Simone de Beauvoir: Politics, Language, and Feminist Identity," *Yale French Studies*, no. 72, 1986, p. 162.

Introduction

FOR a long time I have hesitated to write a book on woman. The subject is irritating, especially to women; and it is not new. Enough ink has been spilled in the quarreling over feminism, now practically over, and perhaps we should say no more about it. It is still talked about, however, for the voluminous nonsense uttered during the last century seems to have done little to illuminate the problem. After all, is there a problem? And if so, what is it? Are there women, really? Most assuredly the theory of the eternal feminine still has its adherents who will whisper in your ear: "Even in Russia women still are *women*"; and other erudite persons—sometimes the very same—say with a sigh: "Woman is losing her way, woman is lost." One wonders if women still exist, if they will always exist, whether or not it is desirable that they should, what place they occupy in this world, what their place should be. "What has become of women?" was asked recently in an ephemeral magazine.[1]

But first we must ask: what is a woman? "*Tota mulier in utero,*" says one, "woman is a womb." But in speaking of certain women, connoisseurs declare that they are not women, although they are equipped with a uterus like the rest. All agree in recognizing the fact that females exist in the human species; today as always they make up about one half of humanity. And yet we are told that femininity is in danger; we are exhorted to be women, remain women, become women. It would appear, then, that every female human being is not necessarily a woman; to be so considered she must share in that mysterious and threatened reality known as femininity. Is this attribute something secreted by the ovaries? Or is it a Platonic essence, a product of the philosophic imagination? Is a rustling petticoat enough to bring it down to earth? Although some women try zealously to incarnate this essence, it is hardly patentable. It is frequently described in vague and dazzling terms that seem to have been borrowed from the vocabulary of the seers, and indeed in the times of St. Thomas it was considered an essence as certainly defined as the somniferous virtue of the poppy.

---

[1] *Franchise,* dead today.

But conceptualism has lost ground. The biological and social sciences no longer admit the existence of unchangeably fixed entities that determine given characteristics, such as those ascribed to woman, the Jew, or the Negro. Science regards any characteristic as a reaction dependent in part upon a *situation*. If today femininity no longer exists, then it never existed. But does the word *woman*, then, have no specific content? This is stoutly affirmed by those who hold to the philosophy of the enlightenment, of rationalism, of nominalism; women, to them, are merely the human beings arbitrarily designated by the word *woman*. Many American women particularly are prepared to think that there is no longer any place for woman as such; if a backward individual still takes herself for a woman, her friends advise her to be psychoanalyzed and thus get rid of this obsession. In regard to a work, *Modern Woman: The Lost Sex*, which in other respects has its irritating features, Dorothy Parker has written: " I cannot be just to books which treat of woman as woman. . . . My idea is that all of us, men as well as women, should be regarded as human beings." But nominalism is a rather inadequate doctrine, and the antifemininists have had no trouble in showing that women simply *are not* men. Surely woman is, like man, a human being; but such a declaration is abstract. The fact is that every concrete human being is always a singular, separate individual. To decline to accept such notions as the eternal feminine, the black soul, the Jewish character, is not to deny that Jews, Negroes, women exist today—this denial does not represent a liberation for those concerned, but rather a flight from reality. Some years ago a well-known woman writer refused to permit her portrait to appear in a series of photographs especially devoted to women writers; she wished to be counted among the men. But in order to gain this privilege she made use of her husband's influence! Women who assert that they are men lay claim none the less to masculine consideration and respect. I recall also a young Trotskyite standing on a platform at a boisterous meeting and getting ready to use her fists, in spite of her evident fragility. She was denying her feminine weakness; but it was for love of a militant male whose equal she wished to be. The attitude of defiance of many American women proves that they are haunted by a sense of their femininity. In truth, to go for a walk with one's eyes open is enough to demonstrate that humanity is divided into two classes of individuals whose clothes, faces, bodies, smiles, gaits, interests, and occupations are manifestly

different. Perhaps these differences are superficial, perhaps they are
destined to disappear. What is certain is that right now they do most
obviously exist.

If her functioning as a female is not enough to define woman, if we
decline also to explain her through "the eternal feminine," and if
nevertheless we admit, provisionally, that women do exist, then we
must face the question: what is a woman?

To state the question is, to me, to suggest, at once, a preliminary
answer. The fact that I ask it is in itself significant. A man would
never get the notion of writing a book on the peculiar situation of the
human male.[2] But if I wish to define myself, I must first of all say:
"I am a woman"; on this truth must be based all further discussion.
A man never begins by presenting himself as an individual of a certain sex; it goes without saying that he is a man. The terms *masculine* and *feminine* are used symmetrically only as a matter of form, as
on legal papers. In actuality the relation of the two sexes is not quite
like that of two electrical poles, for man represents both the positive
and the neutral, as is indicated by the common use of *man* to designate human beings in general; whereas woman represents only the
negative, defined by limiting criteria, without reciprocity. In the
midst of an abstract discussion it is vexing to hear a man say: "You
think thus and so because you are a woman"; but I know that my
only defense is to reply: "I think thus and so because it is true,"
thereby removing my subjective self from the argument. It would be
out of the question to reply: "And you think the contrary because you
are a man," for it is understood that the fact of being a man is no
peculiarity. A man is in the right in being a man; it is the woman who
is in the wrong. It amounts to this: just as for the ancients there was an
absolute vertical with reference to which the oblique was defined, so
there is an absolute human type, the masculine. Woman has ovaries,
a uterus; these peculiarities imprison her in her subjectivity, circum-
scribe her within the limits of her own nature. It is often said that she
thinks with her glands. Man superbly ignores the fact that his anatomy also includes glands, such as the testicles, and that they secrete
hormones. He thinks of his body as a direct and normal connection

---

[2] The Kinsey Report [Alfred C. Kinsey and others: *Sexual Behavior in the
Human Male* (W. B. Saunders Co., 1948)] is no exception, for it is limited to
describing the sexual characteristics of American men, which is quite a different
matter.

with the world, which he believes he apprehends objectively, whereas
he regards the body of woman as a hindrance, a prison, weighed down
by everything peculiar to it. "The female is a female by virtue of a
certain *lack* of qualities," said Aristotle; "we should regard the female
nature as afflicted with a natural defectiveness." And St. Thomas for
his part pronounced woman to be an "imperfect man," an "incidental" being. This is symbolized in Genesis where Eve is depicted as
made from what Bossuet called "a supernumerary bone" of Adam.

Thus humanity is male and man defines woman not in herself but
as relative to him; she is not regarded as an autonomous being. Michelet writes: "Woman, the relative being. . . ." And Benda is most
positive in his *Rapport d'Uriel:* "The body of man makes sense in itself quite apart from that of woman, whereas the latter seems wanting in significance by itself. . . . Man can think of himself without
woman. She cannot think of herself without man." And she is simply
what man decrees; thus she is called "the sex," by which is meant
that she appears essentially to the male as a sexual being. For him she
is sex—absolute sex, no less. She is defined and differentiated with
reference to man and not he with reference to her; she is the incidental, the inessential as opposed to the essential. He is the Subject,
he is the Absolute—she is the Other.[3]

The category of the *Other* is as primordial as consciousness itself.
In the most primitive societies, in the most ancient mythologies, one
finds the expression of a duality—that of the Self and the Other. This
duality was not originally attached to the division of the sexes; it was
not dependent upon any empirical facts. It is revealed in such works

---

[3] E. Lévinas expresses this idea most explicitly in his essay *Temps et l'Autre*.
"Is there not a case in which otherness, alterity [*altérité*], unquestionably marks the
nature of a being, as its essence, an instance of otherness not consisting purely and
simply in the opposition of two species of the same genus? I think that the feminine represents the contrary in its absolute sense, this contrariness being in no
wise affected by any relation between it and its correlative and thus remaining
absolutely other. Sex is not a certain specific difference . . . no more is the sexual
difference a mere contradiction. . . . Nor does this difference lie in the duality
of two complementary terms, for two complementary terms imply a pre-existing
whole. . . . Otherness reaches its full flowering in the feminine, a term of the
same rank as consciousness but of opposite meaning."

I suppose that Lévinas does not forget that woman, too, is aware of her own
consciousness, or ego. But it is striking that he deliberately takes a man's point of
view, disregarding the reciprocity of subject and object. When he writes that
woman is mystery, he implies that she is mystery for man. Thus his description,
which is intended to be objective, is in fact an assertion of masculine privilege.

as that of Granet on Chinese thought and those of Dumézil on the East Indies and Rome. The feminine element was at first no more involved in such pairs as Varuna-Mitra, Uranus-Zeus, Sun-Moon, and Day-Night than it was in the contrasts between Good and Evil, lucky and unlucky auspices, right and left, God and Lucifer. Otherness is a fundamental category of human thought.

Thus it is that no group ever sets itself up as the One without at once setting up the Other over against itself. If three travelers chance to occupy the same compartment, that is enough to make vaguely hostile "others" out of all the rest of the passengers on the train. In small-town eyes all persons not belonging to the village are "strangers" and suspect; to the native of a country all who inhabit other countries are "foreigners"; Jews are "different" for the anti-Semite, Negroes are "inferior" for American racists, aborigines are "natives" for colonists, proletarians are the "lower class" for the privileged.

Lévi-Strauss, at the end of a profound work on the various forms of primitive societies, reaches the following conclusion: "Passage from the state of Nature to the state of Culture is marked by man's ability to view biological relations as a series of contrasts; duality, alternation, opposition, and symmetry, whether under definite or vague forms, constitute not so much phenomena to be explained as fundamental and immediately given data of social reality." [4] These phenomena would be incomprehensible if in fact human society were simply a *Mitsein* or fellowship based on solidarity and friendliness. Things become clear, on the contrary, if, following Hegel, we find in consciousness itself a fundamental hostility toward every other consciousness; the subject can be posed only in being opposed—he sets himself up as the essential, as opposed to the other, the inessential, the object.

But the other consciousness, the other ego, sets up a reciprocal claim. The native traveling abroad is shocked to find himself in turn regarded as a "stranger" by the natives of neighboring countries. As a matter of fact, wars, festivals, trading, treaties, and contests among tribes, nations, and classes tend to deprive the concept *Other* of its absolute sense and to make manifest its relativity; willy-nilly, individuals and groups are forced to realize the reciprocity of their relations. How is it, then, that this reciprocity has not been recognized

---

[4] See C. Lévi-Strauss: *Les Structures élémentaires de la parenté.* My thanks are due to C. Lévi-Strauss for his kindness in furnishing me with the proofs of his work, which, among others, I have used liberally in Part II.

between the sexes, that one of the contrasting terms is set up as the
sole essential, denying any relativity in regard to its correlative and
defining the latter as pure otherness? Why is it that women do not
dispute male sovereignty? No subject will readily volunteer to become
the object, the inessential; it is not the Other who, in defining himself
as the Other, establishes the One. The Other is posed as such by the
One in defining himself as the One. But if the Other is not to regain
the status of being the One, he must be submissive enough to accept
this alien point of view. Whence comes this submission in the case
of woman?

There are, to be sure, other cases in which a certain category has
been able to dominate another completely for a time. Very often this
privilege depends upon inequality of numbers—the majority imposes
its rule upon the minority or persecutes it. But women are not a minority, like the American Negroes or the Jews; there are as many
women as men on earth. Again, the two groups concerned have often
been originally independent; they may have been formerly unaware
of each other's existence, or perhaps they recognized each other's autonomy. But a historical event has resulted in the subjugation of the
weaker by the stronger. The scattering of the Jews, the introduction
of slavery into America, the conquests of imperialism are examples in
point. In these cases the oppressed retained at least the memory of
former days; they possessed in common a past, a tradition, sometimes
a religion or a culture.

The parallel drawn by Bebel between women and the proletariat is
valid in that neither ever formed a minority or a separate collective
unit of mankind. And instead of a single historical event it is in both
cases a historical development that explains their status as a class and
accounts for the membership of *particular individuals* in that class.
But proletarians have not always existed, whereas there have always
been women. They are women in virtue of their anatomy and physiology. Throughout history they have always been subordinated to
men,[5] and hence their dependency is not the result of a historical
event or a social change—it was not something that *occurred*. The
reason why otherness in this case seems to be an absolute is in part
that it lacks the contingent or incidental nature of historical facts. A
condition brought about at a certain time can be abolished at some

---

[5] With rare exceptions, perhaps, like certain matriarchal rulers, queens, and
the like.—TR.

other time, as the Negroes of Haiti and others have proved; but it might seem that a natural condition is beyond the possibility of change. In truth, however, the nature of things is no more immutably given, once for all, than is historical reality. If woman seems to be the inessential which never becomes the essential, it is because she herself fails to bring about this change. Proletarians say "We"; Negroes also. Regarding themselves as subjects, they transform the bourgeois, the whites, into "others." But women do not say "We," except at some congress of feminists or similar formal demonstration; men say "women," and women use the same word in referring to themselves. They do not authentically assume a subjective attitude. The proletarians have accomplished the revolution in Russia, the Negroes in Haiti, the Indo-Chinese are battling for it in Indo-China; but the women's effort has never been anything more than a symbolic agitation. They have gained only what men have been willing to grant; they have taken nothing, they have only received.[6]

The reason for this is that women lack concrete means for organizing themselves into a unit which can stand face to face with the correlative unit. They have no past, no history, no religion of their own; and they have no such solidarity of work and interest as that of the proletariat. They are not even promiscuously herded together in the way that creates community feeling among the American Negroes, the ghetto Jews, the workers of Saint-Denis, or the factory hands of Renault. They live dispersed among the males, attached through residence, housework, economic condition, and social standing to certain men—fathers or husbands—more firmly than they are to other women. If they belong to the bourgeoisie, they feel solidarity with men of that class, not with proletarian women; if they are white, their allegiance is to white men, not to Negro women. The proletariat can propose to massacre the ruling class, and a sufficiently fanatical Jew or Negro might dream of getting sole possession of the atomic bomb and making humanity wholly Jewish or black; but woman cannot even dream of exterminating the males. The bond that unites her to her oppressors is not comparable to any other. The division of the sexes is a biological fact, not an event in human history. Male and female stand opposed within a primordial *Mitsein*, and woman has not broken it. The couple is a fundamental unity with its two halves riveted together, and the cleavage of society along the line of sex is impossible.

[6] See Part II, ch. viii.

Here is to be found the basic trait of woman: she is the Other in a totality of which the two components are necessary to one another.

One could suppose that this reciprocity might have facilitated the liberation of woman. When Hercules sat at the feet of Omphale and helped with her spinning, his desire for her held him captive; but why did she fail to gain a lasting power? To revenge herself on Jason, Medea killed their children; and this grim legend would seem to suggest that she might have obtained a formidable influence over him through his love for his offspring. In *Lysistrata* Aristophanes gaily depicts a band of women who joined forces to gain social ends through the sexual needs of their men; but this is only a play. In the legend of the Sabine women, the latter soon abandoned their plan of remaining sterile to punish their ravishers. In truth woman has not been socially emancipated through man's need—sexual desire and the desire for offspring—which makes the male dependent for satisfaction upon the female.

Master and slave, also, are united by a reciprocal need, in this case economic, which does not liberate the slave. In the relation of master to slave the master does not make a point of the need that he has for the other; he has in his grasp the power of satisfying this need through his own action; whereas the slave, in his dependent condition, his hope and fear, is quite conscious of the need he has for his master. Even if the need is at bottom equally urgent for both, it always works in favor of the oppressor and against the oppressed. That is why the liberation of the working class, for example, has been slow.

Now, woman has always been man's dependent, if not his slave; the two sexes have never shared the world in equality. And even today woman is heavily handicapped, though her situation is beginning to change. Almost nowhere is her legal status the same as man's,[7] and frequently it is much to her disadvantage. Even when her rights are legally recognized in the abstract, long-standing custom prevents their full expression in the mores. In the economic sphere men and women can almost be said to make up two castes; other things being equal, the former hold the better jobs, get higher wages, and have more opportunity for success than their new competitors. In industry and politics men have a great many more positions and they monopolize the most important posts. In addition to all this, they enjoy a traditional

---

[7] At the moment an "equal rights" amendment to the Constitution of the United States is before Congress.—Tr.

prestige that the education of children tends in every way to support, for the present enshrines the past—and in the past all history has been made by men. At the present time, when women are beginning to take part in the affairs of the world, it is still a world that belongs to men—they have no doubt of it at all and women have scarcely any. To decline to be the Other, to refuse to be a party to the deal—this would be for women to renounce all the advantages conferred upon them by their alliance with the superior caste. Man-the-sovereign will provide woman-the-liege with material protection and will undertake the moral justification of her existence; thus she can evade at once both economic risk and the metaphysical risk of a liberty in which ends and aims must be contrived without assistance. Indeed, along with the ethical urge of each individual to affirm his subjective existence, there is also the temptation to forgo liberty and become a thing. This is an inauspicious road, for he who takes it—passive, lost, ruined—becomes henceforth the creature of another's will, frustrated in his transcendence and deprived of every value. But it is an easy road; on it one avoids the strain involved in undertaking an authentic existence. When man makes of woman the *Other*, he may, then, expect her to manifest deep-seated tendencies toward complicity. Thus, woman may fail to lay claim to the status of subject because she lacks definite resources, because she feels the necessary bond that ties her to man regardless of reciprocity, and because she is often very well pleased with her role as the *Other*.

But it will be asked at once: how did all this begin? It is easy to see that the duality of the sexes, like any duality, gives rise to conflict. And doubtless the winner will assume the status of absolute. But why should man have won from the start? It seems possible that women could have won the victory; or that the outcome of the conflict might never have been decided. How is it that this world has always belonged to the men and that things have begun to change only recently? Is this change a good thing? Will it bring about an equal sharing of the world between men and women?

These questions are not new, and they have often been answered. But the very fact that woman *is the Other* tends to cast suspicion upon all the justifications that men have ever been able to provide for it. These have all too evidently been dictated by men's interest. A little-known feminist of the seventeenth century, Poulain de la Barre, put it this way: "All that has been written about women by men should

be suspect, for the men are at once judge and party to the lawsuit."
Everywhere, at all times, the males have displayed their satisfaction in
feeling that they are the lords of creation. "Blessed be God . . . that
He did not make me a woman," say the Jews in their morning prayers,
while their wives pray on a note of resignation: "Blessed be the Lord,
who created me according to His will." The first among the blessings
for which Plato thanked the gods was that he had been created free,
not enslaved; the second, a man, not a woman. But the males could
not enjoy this privilege fully unless they believed it to be founded on
the absolute and the eternal; they sought to make the fact of their
supremacy into a right. "Being men, those who have made and com-
piled the laws have favored their own sex, and jurists have elevated these laws into principles," to quote Poulain de la Barre once
more.

Legislators, priests, philosophers, writers, and scientists have striven
to show that the subordinate position of woman is willed in heaven
and advantageous on earth. The religions invented by men reflect this
wish for domination. In the legends of Eve and Pandora men have
taken up arms against women. They have made use of philosophy and
theology, as the quotations from Aristotle and St. Thomas have
shown. Since ancient times satirists and moralists have delighted in
showing up the weaknesses of women. We are familiar with the savage
indictments hurled against women throughout French literature.
Montherlant, for example, follows the tradition of Jean de Meung,
though with less gusto. This hostility may at times be well founded,
often it is gratuitous; but in truth it more or less successfully conceals
a desire for self-justification. As Montaigne says, "It is easier to accuse
one sex than to excuse the other." Sometimes what is going on is clear
enough. For instance, the Roman law limiting the rights of woman
cited "the imbecility, the instability of the sex" just when the weakening of family ties seemed to threaten the interests of male heirs. And
in the effort to keep the married woman under guardianship, appeal
was made in the sixteenth century to the authority of St. Augustine,
who declared that "woman is a creature neither decisive nor constant," at a time when the single woman was thought capable of
managing her property. Montaigne understood clearly how arbitrary
and unjust was woman's appointed lot: "Women are not in the wrong
when they decline to accept the rules laid down for them, since the
men make these rules without consulting them. No wonder intrigue

and strife abound." But he did not go so far as to champion their cause.

It was only later, in the eighteenth century, that genuinely democratic men began to view the matter objectively. Diderot, among others, strove to show that woman is, like man, a human being. Later John Stuart Mill came fervently to her defense. But these philosophers displayed unusual impartiality. In the nineteenth century the feminist quarrel became again a quarrel of partisans. One of the consequences of the industrial revolution was the entrance of women into productive labor, and it was just here that the claims of the feminists emerged from the realm of theory and acquired an economic basis, while their opponents became the more aggressive. Although landed property lost power to some extent, the bourgeoisie clung to the old morality that found the guarantee of private property in the solidity of the family. Woman was ordered back into the home the more harshly as her emancipation became a real menace. Even within the working class the men endeavored to restrain woman's liberation, because they began to see the women as dangerous competitors—the more so because they were accustomed to work for lower wages.[8]

In proving woman's inferiority, the antifeminists then began to draw not only upon religion, philosophy, and theology, as before, but also upon science—biology, experimental psychology, etc. At most they were willing to grant "equality in difference" to the *other* sex. That profitable formula is most significant; it is precisely like the "equal but separate" formula of the Jim Crow laws aimed at the North American Negroes. As is well known, this so-called equalitarian segregation has resulted only in the most extreme discrimination. The similarity just noted is in no way due to chance, for whether it is a race, a caste, a class, or a sex that is reduced to a position of inferiority, the methods of justification are the same. "The eternal feminine" corresponds to "the black soul" and to "the Jewish character." True, the Jewish problem is on the whole very different from the other two —to the anti-Semite the Jew is not so much an inferior as he is an enemy for whom there is to be granted no place on earth, for whom annihilation is the fate desired. But there are deep similarities between the situation of woman and that of the Negro. Both are being emancipated today from a like paternalism, and the former master class wishes to "keep them in their place"—that is, the place chosen for

---

[8] See Part II, pp. 115–17.

them. In both cases the former masters lavish more or less sincere eulogies, either on the virtues of "the good Negro" with his dormant, childish, merry soul—the submissive Negro—or on the merits of the woman who is "truly feminine"—that is, frivolous, infantile, irresponsible—the submissive woman. In both cases the dominant class bases its argument on a state of affairs that it has itself created. As George Bernard Shaw puts it, in substance, "The American white relegates the black to the rank of shoeshine boy; and he concludes from this that the black is good for nothing but shining shoes." This vicious circle is met with in all analogous circumstances; when an individual (or a group of individuals) is kept in a situation of inferiority, the fact is that he *is* inferior. But the significance of the verb *to be* must be rightly understood here; it is in bad faith to give it a static value when it really has the dynamic Hegelian sense of "to have become." Yes, women on the whole *are* today inferior to men; that is, their situation affords them fewer possibilities. The question is: should that state of affairs continue?

Many men hope that it will continue; not all have given up the battle. The conservative bourgeoisie still see in the emancipation of women a menace to their morality and their interests. Some men dread feminine competition. Recently a male student wrote in the *Hebdo-Latin*: "Every woman student who goes into medicine or law robs us of a job." He never questioned his rights in this world. And economic interests are not the only ones concerned. One of the benefits that oppression confers upon the oppressors is that the most humble among them is made to *feel* superior; thus, a "poor white" in the South can console himself with the thought that he is not a "dirty nigger"—and the more prosperous whites cleverly exploit this pride.

Similarly, the most mediocre of males feels himself a demigod as compared with women. It was much easier for M. de Montherlant to think himself a hero when he faced women (and women chosen for his purpose) than when he was obliged to act the man among men —something many women have done better than he, for that matter. And in September 1948, in one of his articles in the *Figaro littéraire*, Claude Mauriac—whose great originality is admired by all—could [9] write regarding woman: "We listen on a tone [*sic!*] of polite indifference . . . to the most brilliant among them, well knowing that her wit reflects more or less luminously ideas that come from *us*." Evi-

---

[9] Or at least he thought he could.

dently the speaker referred to is not reflecting the ideas of Mauriac himself, for no one knows of his having any. It may be that she reflects ideas originating with men, but then, even among men there are those who have been known to appropriate ideas not their own; and one can well ask whether Claude Mauriac might not find more interesting a conversation reflecting· Descartes, Marx, or Gide rather than himself. What is really remarkable is that by using the questionable *we* he identifies himself with St. Paul, Hegel, Lenin, and Nietzsche, and from the lofty eminence of their grandeur looks down disdainfully upon the bevy of women who make bold to converse with him on a footing of equality. In truth, I know of more than one woman who would refuse to suffer with patience Mauriac's "tone of polite indifference."

I have lingered on this example because the masculine attitude is here displayed with disarming ingenuousness. But men profit in many more subtle ways from the otherness, the alterity of woman. Here is miraculous balm for those afflicted with an inferiority complex, and indeed no one is more arrogant toward women, more aggressive or scornful, than the man who is anxious about his virility. Those who are not fear-ridden in the presence of their fellow men are much more disposed to recognize a fellow creature in woman; but even to these the myth of Woman, the Other, is precious for many reasons.[1] They cannot be blamed for not cheerfully relinquishing all the benefits they derive from the myth, for they realize what they would lose in relinquishing woman as they fancy her to be, while they fail to realize what they have to gain from the woman of tomorrow. Refusal to pose oneself as the Subject, unique and absolute, requires great self-denial. Furthermore, the vast majority of men make no such claim explicitly. They do not *postulate* woman as inferior, for today they are too thoroughly imbued with the ideal of democracy not to recognize all human beings as equals.

In the bosom of the family, woman seems in the eyes of childhood

---

[1] A significant article on this theme by Michel Carrouges appeared in No. 292 of the *Cahiers du Sud*. He writes indignantly: "Would that there were no woman-myth at all but only a cohort of cooks, matrons, prostitutes, and bluestockings serving functions of pleasure or usefulness!" That is to say, in his view woman has no existence in and for herself; he thinks only of her *function* in the male world. Her reason for existence lies in man. But then, in fact, her poetic "function" as a myth might be more valued than any other. The real problem is precisely to find out why woman should be defined with relation to man.

and youth to be clothed in the same social dignity as the adult males. Later on, the young man, desiring and loving, experiences the resistance, the independence of the woman desired and loved; in marriage, he respects woman as wife and mother, and in the concrete events of conjugal life she stands there before him as a free being. He can therefore feel that social subordination as between the sexes no longer exists and that on the whole, in spite of differences, woman is an equal. As, however, he observes some points of inferiority—the most important being unfitness for the professions—he attributes these to natural causes. When he is in a co-operative and benevolent relation with woman, his theme is the principle of abstract equality, and he does not base his attitude upon such inequality as may exist. But when he is in conflict with her, the situation is reversed: his theme will be the existing inequality, and he will even take it as justification for denying abstract equality.[2]

So it is that many men will affirm as if in good faith that women *are* the equals of man and that they have nothing to clamor for, while *at the same time* they will say that women can never be the equals of man and that their demands are in vain. It is, in point of fact, a difficult matter for man to realize the extreme importance of social discriminations which seem outwardly insignificant but which produce in woman moral and intellectual effects so profound that they appear to spring from her original nature.[3] The most sympathetic of men never fully comprehend woman's concrete situation. And there is no reason to put much trust in the men when they rush to the defense of privileges whose full extent they can hardly measure. We shall not, then, permit ourselves to be intimidated by the number and violence of the attacks launched against women, nor to be entrapped by the self-seeking eulogies bestowed on the "true woman," nor to profit by the enthusiasm for woman's destiny manifested by men who would not for the world have any part of it.

We should consider the arguments of the feminists with no less suspicion, however, for very often their controversial aim deprives them of all real value. If the "woman question" seems trivial, it is because

---

[2] For example, a man will say that he considers his wife in no wise degraded because she has no gainful occupation. The profession of housewife is just as lofty, and so on. But when the first quarrel comes, he will exclaim: "Why, you couldn't make your living without me!"

[3] The specific purpose of Book II of this study is to describe this process.

masculine arrogance has made of it a "quarrel"; and when quarreling one no longer reasons well. People have tirelessly sought to prove that woman is superior, inferior, or equal to man. Some say that, having been created after Adam, she is evidently a secondary being; others say on the contrary that Adam was only a rough draft and that God succeeded in producing the human being in perfection when He created Eve. Woman's brain is smaller; yes, but it is relatively larger. Christ was made a man; yes, but perhaps for his greater humility. Each argument at once suggests its opposite, and both are often fallacious. If we are to gain understanding, we must get out of these ruts; we must discard the vague notions of superiority, inferiority, equality which have hitherto corrupted every discussion of the subject and start afresh.

Very well, but just how shall we pose the question? And, to begin with, who are we to propound it at all? Man is at once judge and party to the case; but so is woman. What we need is an angel—neither man nor woman—but where shall we find one? Still, the angel would be poorly qualified to speak, for an angel is ignorant of all the basic facts involved in the problem. With a hermaphrodite we should be no better off, for here the situation is most peculiar; the hermaphrodite is not really the combination of a whole man and a whole woman, but consists of parts of each and thus is neither. It looks to me as if there are, after all, certain women who are best qualified to elucidate the situation of woman. Let us not be misled by the sophism that because Epimenides was a Cretan he was necessarily a liar; it is not a mysterious essence that compels men and women to act in good or in bad faith, it is their situation that inclines them more or less toward the search for truth. Many of today's women, fortunate in the restoration of all the privileges pertaining to the estate of the human being, can afford the luxury of impartiality—we even recognize its necessity. We are no longer like our partisan elders; by and large we have won the game. In recent debates on the status of women the United Nations has persistently maintained that the equality of the sexes is now becoming a reality, and already some of us have never had to sense in our femininity an inconvenience or an obstacle. Many problems appear to us to be more pressing than those which concern us in particular, and this detachment even allows us to hope that our attitude will be objective. Still, we know the feminine world more intimately than do the men because we have our roots in it, we grasp more immediately than do men what it means to a human being to be fem-

inine; and we are more concerned with such knowledge. I have said
that there are more pressing problems, but this does not prevent us
from seeing some importance in asking how the fact of being women
will affect our lives. What opportunities precisely have been given us
and what withheld? What fate awaits our younger sisters, and what
directions should they take? It is significant that books by women on
women are in general animated in our day less by a wish to demand
our rights than by an effort toward clarity and understanding. As we
emerge from an era of excessive controversy, this book is offered as
one attempt among others to confirm that statement.

But it is doubtless impossible to approach any human problem with
a mind free from bias. The way in which questions are put, the points
of view assumed, presuppose a relativity of interest; all characteristics
imply values, and every objective description, so called, implies an
ethical background. Rather than attempt to conceal principles more
or less definitely implied, it is better to state them openly at the
beginning. This will make it unnecessary to specify on every page in
just what sense one uses such words as *superior, inferior, better, worse,
progress, reaction,* and the like. If we survey some of the works on
woman, we note that one of the points of view most frequently
adopted is that of the public good, the general interest; and one always means by this the benefit of society as one wishes it to be maintained or established. For our part, we hold that the only public good
is that which assures the private good of the citizens; we shall pass
judgment on institutions according to their effectiveness in giving
concrete opportunities to individuals. But we do not confuse the idea
of private interest with that of happiness, although that is another
common point of view. Are not women of the harem more happy than
women voters? Is not the housekeeper happier than the workingwoman? It is not too clear just what the word *happy* really means and
still less what true values it may mask. There is no possibility of measuring the happiness of others, and it is always easy to describe as
happy the situation in which one wishes to place them.

In particular those who are condemned to stagnation are often
pronounced happy on the pretext that happiness consists in being at
rest. This notion we reject, for our perspective is that of existentialist
ethics. Every subject plays his part as such specifically through exploits or projects that serve as a mode of transcendence; he achieves
liberty only through a continual reaching out toward other liberties.

There is no justification for present existence other than its expansion into an indefinitely open future. Every time transcendence falls back into immanence, stagnation, there is a degradation of existence into the *"en-soi"*—the brutish life of subjection to given conditions—and of liberty into constraint and contingence. This downfall represents a moral fault if the subject consents to it; if it is inflicted upon him, it spells frustration and oppression. In both cases it is an absolute evil. Every individual concerned to justify his existence feels that his existence involves an undefined need to transcend himself, to engage in freely chosen projects.

Now, what peculiarly signalizes the situation of woman is that she —a free and autonomous being like all human creatures—nevertheless finds herself living in a world where men compel her to assume the status of the Other. They propose to stabilize her as object and to doom her to immanence since her transcendence is to be overshadowed and forever transcended by another ego (*conscience*) which is essential and sovereign. The drama of woman lies in this conflict between the fundamental aspirations of every subject (ego)—who always regards the self as the essential—and the compulsions of a situation in which she is the inessential. How can a human being in woman's situation attain fulfillment? What roads are open to her? Which are blocked? How can independence be recovered in a state of dependency? What circumstances limit woman's liberty and how can they be overcome? These are the fundamental questions on which I would fain throw some light. This means that I am interested in the fortunes of the individual as defined not in terms of happiness but in terms of liberty.

Quite evidently this problem would be without significance if we were to believe that woman's destiny is inevitably determined by physiological, psychological, or economic forces. Hence I shall discuss first of all the light in which woman is viewed by biology, psychoanalysis, and historical materialism. Next I shall try to show exactly how the concept of the "truly feminine" has been fashioned—why woman has been defined as the Other—and what have been the consequences from man's point of view. Then from woman's point of view I shall describe the world in which women must live; and thus we shall be able to envisage the difficulties in their way as, endeavoring to make their escape from the sphere hitherto assigned them, they aspire to full membership in the human race.

Introduction to Book II

The women of today are in a fair way to dethrone the myth of femininity; they are beginning to affirm their independence in concrete ways; but they do not easily succeed in living completely the life of a human being. Reared by women within a feminine world, their normal destiny is marriage, which still means practically subordination to man; for masculine prestige is far from extinction, resting still upon solid economic and social foundations. We must therefore study the traditional destiny of woman with some care. In Book II I shall seek to describe how woman undergoes her apprenticeship, how she experiences her situation, in what kind of universe she is confined, what modes of escape are vouchsafed her. Then only—with so much understood—shall we be able to comprehend the problems of women, the heirs of a burdensome past, who are striving to build a new future. When I use the words *woman* or *feminine* I evidently refer to no archetype, no changeless essence whatever; the reader must understand the phrase "in the present state of education and custom" after most of my statements. It is not our concern here to proclaim eternal verities, but rather to describe the common basis that underlies every individual feminine existence.

BOOK I

Facts and Myths

PART I

DESTINY

CHAPTER I

The Data of Biology

Woman? Very simple, say the fanciers of simple formulas: she is a womb, an ovary; she is a female—this word is sufficient to define her. In the mouth of a man the epithet *female* has the sound of an insult, yet he is not ashamed of his animal nature; on the contrary, he is proud if someone says of him: "He is a male!" The term "female" is derogatory not because it emphasizes woman's animality, but because it imprisons her in her sex; and if this sex seems to man to be contemptible and inimical even in harmless dumb animals, it is evidently because of the uneasy hostility stirred up in him by woman. Nevertheless he wishes to find in biology a justification for this sentiment. The word *female* brings up in his mind a saraband of imagery—a vast, round ovum engulfs and castrates the agile spermatozoon; the monstrous and swollen termite queen rules over the enslaved males; the female praying mantis and the spider, satiated with love, crush and devour their partners; the bitch in heat runs through the alleys, trailing behind her a wake of depraved odors; the she-monkey presents her posterior immodestly and then steals away with hypocritical coquetry; and the most superb wild beasts—the tigress, the lioness, the panther—bed down slavishly under the imperial embrace of the male. Females sluggish, eager, artful, stupid, callous, lustful, ferocious, abased—man projects them all at once upon woman. And the fact is that she is a female. But if we are willing to stop thinking in platitudes, two questions are immediately posed: what does the female denote in the animal kingdom? And what particular kind of female is manifest in woman?

Males and females are two types of individuals which are differentiated within a species for the function of reproduction; they can be defined only correlatively. But first it must be noted that even the *division* of a species into two sexes is not always clear-cut.

In nature it is not universally manifested. To speak only of animals, it is well known that among the microscopic one-celled forms—infusoria, amœbæ, sporozoans, and the like—multiplication is fundamentally distinct from sexuality. Each cell divides and subdivides by itself. In many-celled animals or metazoans reproduction may take place asexually, either by schizogenesis—that is, by fission or cutting into two or more parts which become new individuals—or by blastogenesis—that is, by buds that separate and form new individuals. The phenomena of budding observed in the fresh-water hydra and other cœlenterates, in sponges, worms, and tunicates, are well-known examples. In cases of parthenogenesis the egg of the virgin female develops into an embryo without fertilization by the male, which thus may play no role at all. In the honeybee copulation takes place, but the eggs may or may not be fertilized at the time of laying. The unfertilized eggs undergo development and produce the drones (males); in the aphids males are absent during a series of generations in which the eggs are unfertilized and produce females. Parthenogenesis has been induced artificially in the sea urchin, the starfish, the frog, and other species. Among the one-celled animals (Protozoa), however, two cells may fuse, forming what is called a zygote; and in the honeybee fertilization is necessary if the eggs are to produce females. In the aphids both males and females appear in the autumn, and the fertilized eggs then produced are adapted for overwintering.

Certain biologists in the past concluded from these facts that even in species capable of asexual propagation occasional fertilization is necessary to renew the vigor of the race—to accomplish "rejuvenation"—through the mixing of hereditary material from two individuals. On this hypothesis sexuality might well appear to be an indispensable function in the most complex forms of life; only the lower organisms could multiply without sexuality, and even here vitality would after a time become exhausted. But today this hypothesis is largely abandoned; research has proved that under suitable conditions asexual multiplication can go on indefinitely without noticeable degeneration, a fact that is especially striking in the bacteria and Protozoa. More and more numerous and daring experiments in parthenogenesis are being performed, and in many species the male appears to be fundamentally unnecessary. Besides, if the value of intercellular exchange were demonstrated, that value would seem to stand as a sheer, unexplained fact. Biology certainly demonstrates the existence of sexual differentiation, but from the point of view of any end to be attained the science could not infer such differentiation from the structure of the cell, nor from the laws of cellular multiplication, nor from any basic phenomenon.[1]

The production of two types of gametes, the sperm and the egg, does not necessarily imply the existence of two distinct sexes; as a matter of fact, egg and sperm—two highly differentiated types of reproductive cells—may both be produced by the same individual. This occurs in normally hermaphroditic species, which are common among plants and are also to be found among the lower animals, such as annelid worms and mollusks. In them reproduction may be accomplished through self-fertilization or, more commonly, cross-fertilization. Here again certain biologists have attempted to account for the existing state of affairs. Some hold that the separation of the gonads (ovaries and testes) in two distinct individuals represents an evolutionary advance over hermaphroditism; others on the contrary regard the separate condition as primitive, and believe that hermaphroditism represents a degenerate state. These notions regarding the superiority of one system or the other imply the most debatable evolutionary theorizing. All that we can say for sure is that these two modes of reproduction coexist in nature, that they both succeed in accomplishing the survival of the species concerned, and that the differentiation of the gametes, like that of the organisms producing them, appears to

---

[1] In modern evolutionary theory, however, the mixing of hereditary factors (genes) brought about by sexual reproduction is considered highly important since it affords a constant supply of new combinations for natural selection to act upon. And sexual differentiation often plays an important part in sexual reproduction.—TR.

be accidental. It would seem, then, that the division of a species into male and female individuals is simply an irreducible fact of observation.

In most philosophies this fact has been taken for granted without pretense of explanation. According to the Platonic myth, there were at the beginning men, women, and hermaphrodites. Each individual had two faces, four arms, four legs, and two conjoined bodies. At a certain time they were split in two, and ever since each half seeks to rejoin its corresponding half. Later the gods decreed that new human beings should be created through the coupling of dissimilar halves. But it is only love that this story is intended to explain; division into sexes is given at the outset. Nor does Aristotle explain this division, for if matter and form must co-operate in all action, there is no necessity for the active and passive principles to be separated in two different categories of individuals. Thus St. Thomas proclaims woman an "incidental" being, which is a way of suggesting—from the male point of view—the accidental or contingent nature of sexuality. Hegel, however, would have been untrue to his passion for rationalism had he failed to attempt a logical explanation. Sexuality in his view represents the medium through which the subject attains a concrete sense of belonging to a particular kind (*genre*). "The sense of kind is produced in the subject as an effect which offsets this disproportionate sense of his individual reality, as a desire to find the sense of himself in another individual of his species through union with this other, to complete himself and thus to incorporate the kind (*genre*) within his own nature and bring it into existence. This is copulation" (*Philosophy of Nature*, Part 3, Section 369). And a little farther on: "The process consists in this, namely: that which they are in themselves, that is to say a single kind, one and the same subjective life, they also establish it as such." And Hegel states later that for the uniting process to be accomplished, there must first be sexual differentiation. But his exposition is not convincing: one feels in it all too distinctly the predetermination to find in every operation the three terms of the syllogism.

The projection or transcendence of the individual toward the species, in which both individual and species are fulfilled, could be accomplished without the intervention of a third element in the simple relation of progenitor to offspring; that is to say, reproduction could be asexual. Or, if there were to be two progenitors, they could be similar (as happens in hermaphroditic species) and differentiated only as particular individuals of a single type. Hegel's discussion reveals a most important significance of sexuality, but his mistake is always to argue from significance to necessity, to equate significance with necessity. Man gives significance to the sexes and their relations through sexual activity, just as he gives sense and value to all the functions that he exercises; but sexual activity is not necessarily implied in the nature of the human being. Merleau-Ponty notes in the *Phénoménologie de la perception* that human existence requires us to revise our ideas of necessity and contingence. "Existence," he says, "has no casual, fortuitous qualities, no content that does not contribute to the formation of its aspect; it does not admit the notion of sheer fact, for it is only through existence that the facts are manifested." True enough. But it is also true that there are conditions without which the very fact of existence itself would seem to be impossible. To be present in the world implies strictly that there exists a body which is at once a material thing in the world and a point of view toward this world; but nothing requires that this body have this or that particular structure. Sartre discusses in *L'Être et le néant* Heidegger's dictum to the effect that the real nature of man is bound up with death because of man's finite state. He shows that an existence which is finite and yet unlimited in time is conceivable; but none the less if death were not resident in human life, the relation of man to the world and to himself would be profoundly disarranged—so much so that the statement "Man is mortal" would be seen to have significance quite other than that of a mere fact of observation. Were he immortal, an existent would no longer be what we call a man. One of the essential features of his career is that the progress of his life through time creates behind him and before him the infinite past and future, and it would seem, then, that the perpetuation of the species is the correlative of his individual limitation. Thus we can regard the phenomenon of reproduction as founded in the very nature of being. But we must stop there. The perpetuation of the species does not necessitate sexual differentiation. True enough, this differentiation is characteristic of existents to such an extent that it belongs in any realistic definition of existence. But it nevertheless remains true that both a mind without a body and an immortal man are strictly inconceivable, whereas we can imagine a parthenogenetic or hermaphroditic society.

On the respective functions of the two sexes man has entertained a great variety of beliefs. At first they had no scientific basis, simply reflecting social myths. It was long thought—and it still is believed in certain primitive matriarchal societies—that the father plays no part in conception. Ancestral spirits in the form of living germs are supposed to find their way into the maternal body. With the advent of patriarchal institutions, the male laid eager claim to his posterity. It was still necessary to grant the mother a part in procreation, but it was conceded only that she carried and nourished the living seed, created by the father alone. Aristotle fancied that the fetus arose from the union of sperm and menstrual blood, woman furnishing only passive matter while the male principle contributed force, activity, movement, life. Hippocrates held to a similar doctrine, recognizing two kinds of seed, the weak or female and the strong or male. The theory of Aristotle survived through the Middle Ages and into modern times.

At the end of the seventeenth century Harvey killed female dogs shortly after copulation and found in the horns of the uterus small sacs that he thought were eggs but that were really embryos. The Danish anatomist Steno gave the name of ovaries to the female genital glands, previously called "feminine testicles," and noted on their surface the small swellings that von Graaf in 1677 erroneously identified with the eggs and that are now called Graafian follicles. The ovary was still regarded as homologous to the male gland. In the same year, however, the "spermatic animalcules" were discovered and it was proved that they penetrated into the uterus of the female; but it was supposed that they were simply nourished therein and that the coming individual was preformed in them. In 1694 a Dutchman, Hartsaker, drew a picture of the "homunculus" hidden in the spermatozoon, and in 1699 another scientist said that he had seen the spermatozoon cast off a kind of molt under which appeared a little man, which he also drew. Under these imaginative hypotheses, woman was restricted to the nourishment of an active, living principle already preformed in perfection. These notions were not universally accepted, and they were argued into the nineteenth century. The use of the microscope enabled von Baer in 1827 to discover the mammalian egg, contained inside the Graafian follicle. Before long it was possible to study the cleavage of the egg—that is, the early stage of development through cell division—and in 1835 sarcode, later called protoplasm, was discovered and the true nature of the cell began to be realized. In 1879 the penetration of the spermatozoon into the starfish egg was observed, and thereupon the equivalence of the nuclei of the two gametes, egg and sperm, was established. The details of their union within the fertilized egg were first worked out in 1883 by a Belgian zoologist, van Beneden.

Aristotle's ideas were not wholly discredited, however. Hegel held that the two sexes were of necessity different, the one active and the other passive, and of course the female would be the passive one. "Thus man, in consequence of that differentiation, is the active principle while woman is the passive principle because she remains undeveloped in her unity." [2] And even after the egg had been recognized as an active principle, men still tried to make a point of its quiescence as contrasted with the lively movements of the sperm. Today one notes an opposite tendency on the part of some scientists. The discoveries made in the course of experiments on parthenogenesis have led them to reduce the function of the sperm to that of a simple physicochemical reagent. It has been shown that in certain species the stimulus of an acid or even of a needle-prick is enough to initiate the cleavage of the egg and the development of the embryo. On this basis it has been boldly suggested that the male gamete (sperm) is not necessary for reproduction, that it acts at most as a ferment; further, that perhaps in time the co-operation of the male will become unnecessary in procreation—the answer, it would seem, to many a woman's prayer. But there is no warrant for so bold an expectation, for nothing warrants us in universalizing specific life processes. The phenomena of asexual propagation and of parthenogenesis appear to be neither more nor less fundamental than those of sexual reproduction. I have said that the latter has no claim *a priori* to be considered basic; but neither does any fact indicate that it is reducible to any more fundamental mechanism.

Thus, admitting no *a priori* doctrine, no dubious theory, we are confronted by a fact for which we can offer no basis in the nature of things nor any explanation through observed data, and the significance of which we cannot comprehend *a priori*. We can hope to grasp the significance of sexuality only by studying it in its concrete manifestations; and then perhaps the meaning of the word *female* will stand revealed.

I do not intend to offer here a philosophy of life; and I do not care

---

[2] Hegel: *Philosophy of Nature.*

to take sides prematurely in the dispute between the mechanistic and the purposive or teleological philosophies. It is to be noted, however, that all physiologists and biologists use more or less finalistic language, if only because they ascribe meaning to vital phenomena. I shall adopt their terminology. Without taking any stand on the relation between life and consciousness, we can assert that every biological fact implies transcendence, that every function involves a project, something to be done. Let my words be taken to imply no more than that.

In the vast majority of species male and female individuals co-operate in reproduction. They are defined primarily as male and female by the gametes which they produce—sperms and eggs respectively. In some lower plants and animals the cells that fuse to form the zygote are identical; and these cases of isogamy are significant because they illustrate the basic equivalence of the gametes.[3] In general the gametes are differentiated, and yet their equivalence remains a striking fact. Sperms and eggs develop from similar primordial germ cells in the two sexes. The development of oocytes from the primordial cells in the female differs from that of spermatocytes in the male chiefly in regard to the protoplasm, but the nuclear phenomena are clearly the same. The biologist Ancel suggested in 1903 that the primordial germ cell is indifferent and undergoes development into sperm or egg depending upon which type of gonad, testis or ovary, contains it. However this may be, the primordial germ cells of each sex contain the same number of chromosomes (that characteristic of the species concerned), which number is reduced to one half by closely analogous processes in male and female. At the end of these developmental processes (called spermatogenesis in the male and oogenesis in the female) the gametes appear fully matured as sperms and eggs, differing enormously in some respects, as noted below, but being alike in that each contains a single set of equivalent chromosomes.

Today it is well known that the sex of offspring is determined by

---

[3] Isogamous gametes are identical in appearance, but in some cases (certain fungi and protozoans) experiment has shown conclusively that invisible physiological differences exist, for two gametes will not fuse unless they come from different strains of the species. Here may be traced a sexual differentiation more fundamental than that of egg and sperm or male and female organism. As the author says, the gametes are equivalent; but it may well be that they are never absolutely identical, as the term *isogamy* implies.—TR.

the chromosome constitution established at the time of fertilization. According to the species concerned, it is either the male gamete or the female gamete that accomplishes this result. In the mammals it is the sperm, of which two kinds are produced in equal numbers, one kind containing an X-chromosome (as do all the eggs), the other kind containing a Y-chromosome (not found in the eggs). Aside from the X- and Y-chromosomes, egg and sperm contain an equivalent set of these bodies. It is obvious that when sperm and egg unite in fertilization, the fertilized egg will contain two full sets of chromosomes, making up the number characteristic of the species—48 in man, for example. If fertilization is accomplished by an X-bearing sperm, the fertilized egg will contain two X-chromosomes and will develop into a female (XX). If the Y-bearing sperm fertilizes the egg, only one X-chromosome will be present and the sex will be male (XY). In birds and butterflies the situation is reversed, though the principle remains the same; it is the eggs that contain either X or Y and hence determine the sex of the offspring. In the matter of heredity, the laws of Mendel show that the father and the mother play equal parts. The chromosomes contain the factors of heredity (genes), and they are conveyed equally in egg and sperm.

What we should note in particular at this point is that neither gamete can be regarded as superior to the other; when they unite, both lose their individuality in the fertilized egg. There are two common suppositions which—at least on this basic biological level—are clearly false. The first—that of the passivity of the female—is disproved by the fact that new life springs from the union of the two gametes; the living spark is not the exclusive property of either. The nucleus of the egg is a center of vital activity exactly symmetrical with the nucleus of the sperm. The second false supposition contradicts the first—which does not seem to prevent their coexistence. It is to the effect that the permanence of the species is assured by the female, the male principle being of an explosive and transitory nature. As a matter of fact, the embryo carries on the germ plasm of the father as well as that of the mother and transmits them together to its descendants under now male, now female form. It is, so to speak, an androgynous germ plasm, which outlives the male or female individuals that are its incarnations, whenever they produce offspring.

This said, we can turn our attention to secondary differences between egg and sperm, which are of the greatest interest. The essential peculiarity of the egg is that it is provided with means for nourishing and protecting the embryo; it stores up reserve material from which the fetus will build its tissues, material that is not living substance but inert yolk. In consequence the egg is of massive, commonly spherical form and relatively large. The size of birds' eggs is well known; in woman the egg is almost microscopic, about equal in size to a printed period (diameter .132–.135 mm.), but the human sperm is far smaller (.04–.06 mm. in length), so small that a cubic millimeter would hold 60,000. The sperm has a threadlike tail and a small, flattened oval head, which contains the chromosomes. No inert substance weighs it down; it is wholly alive. In its whole structure it is adapted for mobility. Whereas the egg, big with the future of the embryo, is stationary; enclosed within the female body or floating externally in water, it passively awaits fertilization. It is the male gamete that seeks it out. The sperm is always a naked cell; the egg may or may not be protected with shell and membranes according to the species; but in any case, when the sperm makes contact with the egg, it presses against it, sometimes shakes it, and bores into it. The tail is dropped and the head enlarges, forming the male nucleus, which now moves toward the egg nucleus. Meanwhile the egg quickly forms a membrane, which prevents the entrance of other sperms. In the starfish and other echinoderms, where fertilization takes place externally, it is easy to observe the onslaught of the sperms, which surround the egg like an aureole. The competition involved is an important phenomenon, and it occurs in most species. Being much smaller than the egg, the sperm is generally produced in far greater numbers (more than 200,000,000 to 1 in the human species), and so each egg has numerous suitors.

Thus the egg—active in its essential feature, the nucleus—is superficially passive; its compact mass, sealed up within itself, evokes nocturnal darkness and inward repose. It was the form of the sphere that to the ancients represented the circumscribed world, the impenetrable atom. Motionless, the egg waits; in contrast the sperm—free, slender, agile—typifies the impatience and the restlessness of existence. But allegory should not be pushed too far. The ovule has sometimes been likened to immanence, the sperm to transcendence, and it has been said that the sperm penetrates the female element only in losing its transcendence, its motility; it is seized and castrated by the inert mass that engulfs it after depriving it of its tail. This is magical action—disquieting, as is all passive action—whereas the activity of the male gamete is rational; it is movement measurable in terms of time and space. The truth is that these notions are hardly more than vagaries of the mind. Male and female gametes fuse in the fertilized egg; they are both suppressed in becoming a new whole. It is false to say that the egg greedily swallows the sperm, and equally so to say that the sperm victoriously commandeers the female cell's reserves, since in the act of fusion the individuality of both is lost. No doubt movement seems to the mechanistic mind to be an eminently rational phenomenon, but it is an idea no clearer for modern physics than action at a distance. Besides, we do not know in detail the physicochemical reactions that lead up to gametic union. We can derive a valid suggestion, however, from this comparison of the gametes. There are two interrelated dynamic aspects of life: it can be maintained only through transcending itself, and it can transcend itself only on condition that it is maintained. These two factors always operate together and it is unrealistic to try to separate them, yet now it is one and now the other that dominates. The two gametes at once transcend and perpetuate themselves when they unite; but in its structure the egg anticipates future needs, it is so constituted as to nourish the life that will wake within it. The sperm, on the contrary, is in no way equipped to provide for the development of the embryo it awakens. On the other hand, the egg cannot provide the change of environment that will stimulate a new outburst of life, whereas the sperm can and does travel. Without the foresight of the egg, the sperm's arrival would be in vain; but without the initiative of the latter, the egg would not fulfill its living potentialities.

We may conclude, then, that the two gametes play a fundamentally identical role; together they create a living being in which both of them are at once lost and transcended. But in the secondary and superficial phenomena upon which fertilization depends, it is the male element which provides the stimuli needed for evoking new life and it is the female element that enables this new life to be lodged in a stable organism.

It would be foolhardy indeed to deduce from such evidence that woman's place is in the home—but there are foolhardy men. In his book *Le Tempérament et le charactère*, Alfred Fouillée undertakes to found his definition of woman *in toto* upon the egg and that of man upon the spermatozoon; and a number of supposedly profound theories rest upon this play of doubtful analogies. It is a question to what philosophy of nature these dubious ideas pertain; not to the laws of heredity, certainly, for, according to these laws, men and women alike develop from an egg and a sperm. I can only suppose that in such misty minds there still float shreds of the old philosophy of the Middle Ages which taught that the cosmos is an exact reflection of a microcosm—the egg is imagined to be a little female, the woman a giant egg. These musings, generally abandoned since the days of alchemy, make a bizarre contrast with the scientific precision of the data upon which they are now based, for modern biology conforms with difficulty to medieval symbolism. But our theorizers do not look too closely into the matter. In all honesty it must be admitted that in any case it is a long way from the egg to woman. In the unfertilized egg not even the concept of femaleness is as yet established. As Hegel justly remarks, the sexual relation cannot be referred back to the relation of the gametes. It is our duty, then, to study the female organism as a whole.

It has already been pointed out that in many plants and in some animals (such as snails) the presence of two kinds of gametes does not require two kinds of individuals, since every individual produces both eggs and sperms. Even when the sexes are separate, they are not distinguished in any such fashion as are different species. Males and females appear rather to be variations on a common groundwork, much as the two gametes are differentiated from similar original tissue. In certain animals (for example, the marine worm *Bonellia*) the larva is asexual, the adult becoming male or female according to the circumstances under which it has developed. But as noted above (page 11), sex is determined in most species by the genotypic constitution of the fertilized egg. In bees the unfertilized eggs laid by the queen produce males exclusively; in aphids parthenogenetic eggs usually produce females. But in most animals all eggs that develop have been fertilized, and it is notable that the sexes are produced in approximately equal numbers through the mechanism of chromosomal sex-determination, already explained.

In the embryonic development of both sexes the tissue from which the gonads will be formed is at first indifferent; at a certain stage either testes or ovaries become established; and similarly in the development of the other sex organs there is an early indifferent period when the sex of the embryo cannot be told from an examination of these parts, from which, later on, the definitive male or female structures arise. All this helps to explain the existence of conditions intermediate between hermaphroditism and gonochorism (sexes separate). Very often one sex possesses certain organs characteristic of the other; a case in point is the toad, in which there is in the male a rudimentary ovary called Bidder's organ, capable of producing eggs under experimental conditions. Among the mammals there are indications of this sexual bipotentiality, such as the *uterus masculinus* and the rudimentary mammary glands in the male, and in the female Gärtner's canal and the clitoris. Even in those species exhibiting a high degree of sexual differentiation individuals combining both male and female characteristics may occur. Many cases of intersexuality are known in both animals and man; and among insects and crustaceans one occasionally finds examples of gynandromorphism, in which male and female areas of the body are mingled in a kind of mosaic.

The fact is that the individual, though its genotypic sex is fixed at fertilization, can be profoundly affected by the environment in which it develops. In the ants, bees, and termites the larval nutrition determines whether the genotypic female individual will become a fully developed female ("queen") or a sexually retarded worker. In these cases the whole organism is affected; but the gonads do not play a part in establishing the sexual differences of the body, or *soma*. In the vertebrates, however, the hormones secreted by the gonads are the essential regulators. Numerous experiments show that by varying the hormonal (endocrine) situation, sex can be profoundly affected. Grafting and castration experiments on adult animals and man have contributed to the modern theory of sexuality, according to which the soma is in a way identical in male and female vertebrates. It may be regarded as a kind of neutral element upon which the influence of the gonad imposes the sexual characteristics.[4] Some of the hormones secreted by the gonad act as stimulators, others as inhibitors. Even the genital tract itself is somatic, and embryological investigations show that it develops in the male or female direction from an indifferent and in some respects hermaphroditic condition under the hormonal influence. Intersexuality may result when the hormones are abnormal

---

[4] In connection with this view, it must be remembered that in man and many animals the soma is not strictly neutral, since all its cells are genotypically either male (XY) or female (XX). This is why the young individual normally produces either the male or the female hormonal environment, leading normally to the development of either male or female characteristics.—TR.

and hence neither one of the two sexual potentialities is exclusively realized.

Numerically equal in the species and developed similarly from like beginnings, the fully formed male and female are basically equivalent. Both have reproductive glands—ovaries or testes—in which the gametes are produced by strictly corresponding processes, as we have seen. These glands discharge their products through ducts that are more or less complex according to sex; in the female the egg may pass directly to the outside through the oviduct, or it may be retained for a time in the cloaca or the uterus before expulsion; in the male the semen may be deposited outside, or there may be a copulatory organ through which it is introduced into the body of the female. In these respects, then, male and female appear to stand in a symmetrical relation to each other. To reveal their peculiar, specific qualities it will be necessary to study them from the functional point of view.

It is extremely difficult to give a generally valid definition of the female. To define her as the bearer of the eggs and the male as bearer of the sperms is far from sufficient, since the relation of the organism to the gonads is, as we have seen, quite variable. On the other hand, the differences between the gametes have no direct effect upon the organism as a whole; it has sometimes been argued that the eggs, being large, consume more vital energy than do the sperms, but the latter are produced in such infinitely greater numbers that the expenditure of energy must be about equal in the two sexes. Some have wished to see in spermatogenesis an example of prodigality and in oogenesis a model of economy, but there is an absurd liberality in the latter, too, for the vast majority of eggs are never fertilized.[5] In no way do gametes and gonads represent in microcosm the organism as a whole. It is to this—the whole organism—that we must now direct our attention.

One of the most remarkable features to be noted as we survey the scale of animal life is that as we go up, individuality is seen to be more and more fully developed. At the bottom, life is concerned only in the survival of the species as a whole; at the top, life seeks expression through particular individuals, while accomplishing also the survival of the group. In some lower species the organism may be almost entirely reduced to the reproductive apparatus; in this case the egg,

---

[5] For example, a woman produces about 400 eggs and at most 25 or 30 children; in animals the disproportion is often much greater.—TR.

and hence the female, is supreme, since the egg is especially dedicated to the mere propagation of life; but here the female is hardly more than an abdomen, and her existence is entirely used up in a monstrous travail of ovulation. In comparison with the male, she reaches giant proportions; but her appendages are often tiny, her body a shapeless sac, her organs degenerated in favor of the eggs. Indeed, such males and females, although they are distinct organisms, can hardly be regarded as individuals, for they form a kind of unity made up of inseparable elements. In a way they are intermediate between hermaphroditism and gonochorism.

Thus in certain Crustacea, parasitic on the crab, the female is a mere sac enclosing millions of eggs, among which are found the minute males, both larval and adult. In *Edriolydnus* the dwarf male is still more degenerate; it lives under the shell of the female and has no digestive tract of its own, being purely reproductive in function. But in all such cases the female is no less restricted than the male; it is enslaved to the species. If the male is bound to the female, the latter is no less bound down, either to a living organism on which it exists as a parasite or to some substratum; and its substance is consumed in producing the eggs which the tiny male fertilizes.

Among somewhat higher animals an individual autonomy begins to be manifested and the bond that joins the sexes weakens; but in the insects they both remain strictly subordinated to the eggs. Frequently, as in the mayflies, male and female die immediately after copulation and egg-laying. In some rotifers the male lacks a digestive tract and dies after fecundation; the female is able to eat and survives long enough at least to develop and lay the eggs. The mother dies after the appearance of the next generation is assured. The privileged position held by the females in many insects comes from the fact that the production and sometimes the care of the eggs demand a long effort, whereas fecundation is for the most part quickly accomplished.

In the termites the enormous queen, crammed with nourishment and laying as many as 4,000 eggs per day until she becomes sterile and is pitilessly killed, is no less a slave than the comparatively tiny male who attends her and provides frequent fecundations. In the matriarchal ants' nests and beehives the males are economically useless and are killed off at times. At the season of the nuptial flight in ants, all the males emerge with females from the nest; those that succeed in mating with females die at once, exhausted; the rest are not permitted by the workers to re-enter the nest, and die of hunger or are killed. The fertilized female has a gloomy fate; she buries herself alone in the ground and often dies while laying her first eggs, or if she succeeds in founding a colony she remains shut in and may live for ten or twelve years constantly producing more eggs. The workers, females with atrophied sexuality, may live for several years, but their life is largely devoted to raising the larvæ. It is much the same with bees; the drone that succeeds in mating with the queen during the nuptial flight falls to earth disemboweled; the other drones return to the hive, where they live a lazy life and are in the way until at the approach of winter they are killed off by the workers. But the workers purchase their right to live by incessant toil; as in the ants they are undeveloped females. The queen is in truth enslaved to the hive, laying eggs continually. If she dies, the workers give several larvæ special food so as to provide for the succession; the first to emerge kills the rest in their cells.

In certain spiders the female carries the eggs about with her in a silken case until they hatch. She is much larger and stronger than the male and may kill and devour him after copulation, as does an insect, the praying mantis, around which has crystallized the myth of devouring femininity—the egg castrates the sperm, the mantis murders her spouse, these acts foreshadowing a feminine dream of castration. The mantis, however, shows her cruelty especially in captivity; and under natural conditions, when she is free in the midst of abundant food, she rarely dines on the male. If she does eat him, it is to enable her to produce her eggs and thus perpetuate the race, just as the solitary fertilized ant often eats some of her own eggs under the same necessity. It is going far afield to see in these facts a proclamation of the "battle of the sexes" which sets individuals, as such, one against another. It cannot simply be said that in ants, bees, termites, spiders, or mantises the female enslaves and sometimes devours the male, for it is the species that in different ways consumes them both. The female lives longer and seems to be more important than the male; but she has no independence—egg-laying and the care of eggs and larvæ are her destiny, other functions being atrophied wholly or in part.

In the male, on the contrary, an individual existence begins to be manifested. In impregnation he very often shows more initiative than the female, seeking her out, making the approach, palpating, seizing and forcing connection upon her. Sometimes he has to battle for her with other males. Accordingly the organs of locomotion, touch, and prehension are frequently more highly evolved in the male. Many female moths are wingless, while the males have wings; and often the males of insects have more highly developed colors, wing-covers, legs, and pincers. And sometimes to this endowment is added a seeming luxury of brilliant coloration. Beyond the brief moment of copulation the life of the male is useless and irresponsible; compared with the industriousness of the workers, the idleness of the drones seems a remarkable privilege. But this privilege is a social disgrace, and often the male pays with his life for his futility and partial independence. The species, which holds the female in slavery, punishes the male for his gesture toward escape; it liquidates him with brutal force.

In higher forms of life, reproduction becomes the creation of discrete organisms; it takes on a double role: maintenance of the species and creation of new individuals. This innovating aspect becomes the more unmistakable as the singularity of the individual becomes pronounced. It is striking then that these two essential elements—perpetuation and creation—are separately apportioned to the two sexes. This separation, already indicated at the moment when the egg is fertilized, is to be discerned in the whole generative process. It is not the essential nature of the egg that requires this separation, for in higher forms of life the female has, like the male, attained a certain autonomy and her bondage to the egg has been relaxed. The female fish, batrachian, or bird is far from being a mere abdomen. The less strictly the mother is bound to the egg, the less does the labor of reproduction represent an absorbing task and the more uncertainty there is in the relations of the two parents with their offspring. It can even happen that the father will take charge of the newly hatched young, as in various fishes.

Water is an element in which the eggs and sperms can float about and unite, and fecundation in the aquatic environment is almost always external. Most fish do not copulate, at most stimulating one another by contact. The mother discharges the eggs, the father the sperm—their role is identical. There is no reason why the mother, any more than the father, should feel responsibility for the eggs. In some species the eggs are abandoned by the parents and develop without assistance; sometimes a nest is prepared by the mother and sometimes she watches over the eggs after they have been fertilized. But very often it is the father who takes charge of them. As soon as he has fertilized them, he drives away the female to prevent her from eating them, and he protects them savagely against any intruder. Certain males have been described as making a kind of protective nest by blowing bubbles of air enclosed in an insulating substance; and in many cases they protect the developing eggs in their mouths or, as in the seahorse, in abdominal folds.

In the batrachians (frogs and toads) similar phenomena are to be seen. True copulation is unknown to them; they practice amplexus, the male embracing the female and thus stimulating her to lay her eggs. As the eggs are discharged, the sperm are deposited upon them. In the obstetrical toad the male wraps the strings of eggs about his hind legs and protects them, taking them into the water when the young are about to hatch as tadpoles.

In birds the egg is formed rather slowly inside the female; it is relatively large and is laid with some difficulty. It is much more closely associated with the mother than with the father, who has simply fertilized it in a brief copulation. Usually the mother sits on the eggs and takes care of the newly hatched young; but often the father helps in nest-building and in the protection and feeding of the young birds. In rare cases—for example, among the sparrows—the male does the incubating and rearing. Male and female pigeons secrete in the crop a milky fluid with which they both feed the fledglings. It is remarkable that in these cases where the male takes part in nourishing the young, there is no production of sperms during the time devoted to them— while occupied in maintaining life, the male has no urge to beget new living beings.

In the mammals life assumes the most complex forms, and individualization is most advanced and specific. There the division of the two vital components—maintenance and creation—is realized definitively in the separation of the sexes. It is in this group that the mother sustains the closest relations—among vertebrates—with her offspring, and the father shows less interest in them. The female organism is wholly adapted for and subservient to maternity, while sexual initiative is the prerogative of the male.

The female is the victim of the species. During certain periods in the year, fixed in each species, her whole life is under the regulation of a sexual cycle (the œstrus cycle), of which the duration, as well as the rhythmic sequence of events, varies from one species to another. This cycle consists of two phases: during the first phase the eggs (variable in number according to the species) become mature and the lining of the uterus becomes thickened and vascular; during the second phase (if fertilization has not occurred) the egg disappears, the uterine edifice breaks down, and the material is eliminated in a more or less noticeable temporary flow, known as menstruation in woman and related higher mammals. If fertilization does occur, the second phase is replaced by pregnancy. The time of ovulation (at the end of the first phase) is known as *oestrus* and it corresponds to the period of rut, heat, or sexual activity.

In the female mammal, rut is largely passive; she is ready and waiting to receive the male. It may happen in mammals—as in certain birds—that she solicits the male, but she does no more than appeal to him by means of cries, displays, and suggestive attitudinizing. She is quite unable to force copulation upon him. In the end it is he who makes the decision. We have seen that even in the insects, where the female is highly privileged in return for her total sacrifice to the species, it is usually the male who takes the initiative in fecundation; among the fishes he often stimulates the female to lay her eggs through his presence and contact; and in the frogs and toads he acts as a stimulator in amplexus. But it is in birds and mammals especially that he forces himself upon her, while very often she submits indifferently or even resists him.

Even when she is willing, or provocative, it is unquestionably the male who *takes* the female—she is *taken*. Often the word applies literally, for whether by means of special organs or through superior strength, the male seizes her and holds her in place; he performs the copulatory movements; and, among insects, birds, and mammals, he penetrates her. In this penetration her inwardness is violated, she is like an enclosure that is broken into. The male is not doing violence to the species, for the species survives only in being constantly renewed and would come to an end if eggs and sperms did not come together; but the female, entrusted with the protection of the egg, locks it away inside herself, and her body, in sheltering the egg, shields it also from the fecundating action of the male. Her body becomes, therefore, a resistance to be broken through, whereas in penetrating it the male finds self-fulfillment in activity.

His domination is expressed in the very posture of copulation—in almost all animals the male is *on* the female. And certainly the organ he uses is a material object, but it appears here in its animated state

—it is a tool—whereas in this performance the female organ is more in the nature of an inert receptacle. The male deposits his semen, the female receives it. Thus, though the female plays a fundamentally active role in procreation, she *submits to* the coition, which invades her individuality and introduces an alien element through penetration and internal fertilization. Although she may feel the sexual urge as a personal need, since she seeks out the male when in heat, yet the sexual adventure is immediately experienced by her as an interior event and not as an outward relation to the world and to others.

But the fundamental difference between male and female mammals lies in this: the sperm, through which the life of the male is transcended in another, at the same instant becomes a stranger to him and separates from his body; so that the male recovers his individuality intact at the moment when he transcends it. The egg, on the contrary, begins to separate from the female body when, fully matured, it emerges from the follicle and falls into the oviduct; but if fertilized by a gamete from outside, it becomes attached again through implantation in the uterus. First violated, the female is then alienated—she becomes, in part, another than herself. She carries the fetus inside her abdomen until it reaches a stage of development that varies according to the species—the guinea-pig is born almost adult, the kangaroo still almost an embryo. Tenanted by another, who battens upon her substance throughout the period of pregnancy, the female is at once herself and other than herself; and after the birth she feeds the newborn upon the milk of her breasts. Thus it is not too clear when the new individual is to be regarded as autonomous: at the moment of fertilization, of birth, or of weaning? It is note-worthy that the more clearly the female appears as a separate individual, the more imperiously the continuity of life asserts itself against her separateness. The fish and the bird, which expel the egg from the body before the embryo develops, are less enslaved to their offspring than is the female mammal. She regains some autonomy after the birth of her offspring—a certain distance is established between her and them; and it is following upon a separation that she devotes herself to them. She displays initiative and inventiveness in their behalf; she battles to defend them against other animals and may even become aggressive. But normally she does not seek to affirm her individuality; she is not hostile to males or to other females and shows little combative instinct.[6] In spite of Darwin's theory of sexual selection, now much disputed, she accepts without discrimination whatever male happens to be at hand. It is not that the female lacks individual abilities—quite the contrary. At times when she is free from maternal servitude she can now and then equal the male; the mare is as fleet as the stallion, the hunting bitch has as keen a nose as the dog, she-monkeys in tests show as much intelligence as males. It is only that this individuality is not laid claim to; the female renounces it for the benefit of the species, which demands this abdication.

The lot of the male is quite different. As we have just seen, even in his transcendence toward the next generation he keeps himself apart and maintains his individuality within himself. This characteristic is constant, from the insect to the highest animals. Even in the fishes and whales, which live peaceably in mixed schools, the males separate from the rest at the time of rut, isolate themselves, and become aggressive toward other males. Immediate, direct in the female, sexuality is indirect, it is experienced through intermediate circumstances, in the male. There is a distance between desire and satisfaction which he actively surmounts; he pushes, seeks out, touches the female, caresses and quiets her before he penetrates her. The organs used in such activities are, as I have remarked, often better developed in the male than in the female. It is notable that the living impulse that brings about the vast production of sperms is expressed also in the male by the appearance of bright plumage, brilliant scales, horns, antlers, a mane, by his voice, his exuberance. We no longer believe that the "wedding finery" put on by the male during rut, nor his seductive posturings, have selective significance; but they do manifest the power of life, bursting forth in him with useless and magnificent splendor. This vital superabundance, the activities directed toward mating, and the dominating affirmation of his power over the female in coitus itself—all this contributes to the assertion of the male individual as such at the moment of his living transcendence. In this respect Hegel is right in seeing the subjective element in the male, while the female remains wrapped up in the species. Subjectivity and separateness immediately signify conflict. Aggressiveness is one of the

---

[6] Certain fowls wrangle over the best places in the poultry-yard and establish a hierarchy of dominance (the "peck-order"); and sometimes among cattle there are cows that will fight for the leadership of the herd in the absence of males.

traits of the rutting male; and it is not explained by competition for mates, since the number of females is about equal to the number of males; it is rather the competition that is explained by this will to combat. It might be said that before procreating, the male claims as his own the act that perpetuates the species, and in doing battle with his peers confirms the truth of his individuality. The species takes residence in the female and absorbs most of her individual life; the male on the contrary integrates the specific vital forces into his individual life. No doubt he also submits to powers beyond his control: the sperms are formed within him and periodically he feels the rutting urge; but these processes involve the sum total of the organism in much less degree than does the œstrus cycle. The production of sperms is not exhausting, nor is the actual production of eggs; it is the development of the fertilized egg inside an adult animal that constitutes for the female an engrossing task. Coition is a rapid operation and one that robs the male of little vitality. He displays almost no paternal instinct. Very often he abandons the female after copulation. When he remains near her as head of a family group—monogamic family, harem, or herd—he nurtures and protects the community as a whole; only rarely does he take a direct interest in the young. In the species capable of high individual development, the urge of the male toward autonomy—which in lower animals is his ruin—is crowned with success. He is in general larger than the female, stronger, swifter, more adventurous; he leads a more independent life, his activities are more spontaneous; he is more masterful, more imperious. In mammalian societies it is always he who commands.

In nature nothing is ever perfectly clear. The two types, male and female, are not always sharply distinguished; while they sometimes exhibit a dimorphism—in coat color or in arrangement of spotting or mottling—that seems absolutely distinctive, yet it may happen, on the contrary, that they are indistinguishable and that even their functions are hardly differentiated, as in many fishes. All in all, however, and especially at the top of the animal scale, the two sexes represent two diverse aspects of the life of the species. The difference between them is not, as has been claimed, that between activity and passivity; for the nucleus of the egg is active and moreover the development of the embryo is an active, living process, not a mechanical unfolding. It would be too simple to define the difference as that between change and permanence: for the sperm can create only because its vitality is maintained in the fertilized egg, and the egg can persist only through developmental change, without which it deteriorates and disappears.

It is true, however, that in these two processes, *maintaining* and *creating* (both of which are active), the synthesis of becoming is not accomplished in the same manner. To *maintain* is to deny the scattering of instants, it is to establish continuity in their flow; to *create* is to strike out from temporal unity in general an irreducible, separate present. And it is true also that in the female it is the continuity of life that seeks accomplishment in spite of separation; while separation into new and individualized forces is incited by male initiative. The male is thus permitted to express himself freely; the energy of the species is well integrated into his own living activity. On the contrary, the individuality of the female is opposed by the interest of the species; it is as if she were possessed by foreign forces—alienated. And this explains why the contrast between the sexes is not reduced when—as in higher forms—the individuality of the organisms concerned is more pronounced. On the contrary, the contrast is increased. The male finds more and more varied ways in which to employ the forces he is master of; the female feels her enslavement more and more keenly, the conflict between her own interests and the reproductive forces is heightened. Parturition in cows and mares is much more painful and dangerous than it is in mice and rabbits. Woman—the most individualized of females—seems to be the most fragile, most subject to this pain and danger: she who most dramatically fulfills the call of destiny and most profoundly differs from her male.

In man as in most animals the sexes are born in approximately equal numbers, the sex ratio for Western man being about 105.5 males to 100 females. Embryological development is analogous in the two sexes; however, in the female embryo the primitive germinal epithelium (from which ovary or testis develops) remains neutral longer and is therefore under the hormonal influence for a longer time, with the result that its development may be more often reversed. Thus it may be that the majority of pseudo-hermaphrodites [7]

---

[7] This difficult subject is magnificently treated from every point of view in H. H. Young's *Genital Abnormalities, Hermaphroditism, and Related Adrenal Diseases* (Baltimore, 1937). According to Dr. Young, only twenty cases of true hermaphroditism in man have been medically attested; but pseudo-hermaphrodites —having gonads of one sex with genitalia and sometimes secondary sex characters of the opposite sex—are numerous.—TR.

are genotypically female subjects that have later become masculinized. One might suppose that the male organization is defined as such at the beginning, whereas the female embryo is slower in taking on its femininity; but these early phenomena of fetal life are still too little known to permit of any certainty in interpretation.

Once established, the genital systems correspond in the two sexes, and the sex hormones of both belong to the same chemical group, that of the sterols; all are derived in the last analysis from cholesterol. They regulate the secondary sexual differences of the soma. Neither the chemical formulæ of the hormones nor the anatomical peculiarities are sufficient to define the human female as such. It is her functional development that distinguishes her especially from the male.

The development of the male is comparatively simple. From birth to puberty his growth is almost regular; at the age of fifteen or sixteen spermatogenesis begins, and it continues into old age; with its appearance hormones are produced that establish the masculine bodily traits. From this point on, the male sex life is normally integrated with his individual existence: in desire and in coition his transcendence toward the species is at one with his subjectivity—he *is* his body.

Woman's story is much more complex. In embryonic life the supply of oocytes is already built up, the ovary containing about 40,000 immature eggs, each in a follicle, of which perhaps 400 will ultimately reach maturation. From birth, the species has taken possession of woman and tends to tighten its grasp. In coming into the world woman experiences a kind of first puberty, as the oocytes enlarge suddenly; then the ovary is reduced to about a fifth of its former size—one might say that the child is granted a respite. While her body develops, her genital system remains almost stationary; some of the follicles enlarge, but they fail to mature. The growth of the little girl is similar to that of the boy; at the same age she is sometimes even taller and heavier than he is. But at puberty the species reasserts its claim. Under the influence of the ovarian secretions the number of developing follicles increases, the ovary receives more blood and grows larger, one of the follicles matures, ovulation occurs, and the menstrual cycle is initiated; the genital system assumes its definitive size and form, the body takes on feminine contours, and the endocrine balance is established.

It is to be noted that this whole occurrence has the aspect of a *crisis*. Not without resistance does the body of woman permit the species to take over; and this struggle is weakening and dangerous. Before puberty almost as many boys die as girls; from age fourteen to eighteen, 128 girls die to 100 boys, and from eighteen to twenty-two, 105 girls to 100 boys.[8] At this period frequently appear such diseases as chlorosis, tuberculosis, scoliosis (curvature of the spine), and osteomyelitis (inflammation of the bone marrow). In some cases puberty is abnormally precocious, appearing as early as age four or five. In others, on the contrary, puberty fails to become established, the subject remaining infantile and suffering from disorders of menstruation (amenorrhea or dysmenorrhea). Certain women show signs of virilism, taking on masculine traits as a result of excessive adrenal secretion.

Such abnormalities in no way represent victories of the individual over the species; there is no way of escape, for as it enslaves the individual life, the species simultaneously supports and nourishes it. This duality is expressed at the level of the ovarian functions, since the vitality of woman has its roots in the ovaries as that of man in the testicles. In both sexes a castrated individual is not merely sterile; he or she suffers regression, degenerates. Not properly constituted, the whole organism is impoverished and thrown out of balance; it can expand and flourish only as its genital system expands and flourishes. And furthermore many reproductive phenomena are unconcerned with the individual life of the subject and may even be sources of danger. The mammary glands, developing at puberty, play no role in woman's individual economy: they can be excised at any time of life. Many of the ovarian secretions function for the benefit of the egg, promoting its maturation and adapting the uterus to its requirements; in respect to the organism as a whole they make for disequilibration rather than for regulation—the woman is adapted to the needs of the egg rather than to her own requirements.

From puberty to menopause woman is the theater of a play that unfolds within her and in which she is not personally concerned. Anglo-Saxons call menstruation "the curse"; in truth the menstrual cycle is a burden, and a useless one from the point of view of the individual. In Aristotle's time it was believed that each month blood

---

[8] Recent statistics show that in the United States among the white population there is no age level at which the death rate for women is higher than that of men. Among Negroes, where conditions are doubtless less favorable on the average, the female death rate is higher only between the ages of fifteen and nineteen. (Scheinfeld: *Women and Men*, Ch. xvi: Harcourt, Brace & Co., 1943.)—TR.

flowed away that was intended, if fertilization had occurred, to build up the blood and flesh of the infant, and the truth of that old notion lies in the fact that over and over again woman does sketch in outline the groundwork of gestation. In lower mammals this œstrus cycle is confined to a particular season, and it is not accompanied by a flow of blood; only in the primates (monkeys, apes, and the human species) is it marked each month by blood and more or less pain.[9] During about fourteen days one of the Graafian follicles that enclose the eggs enlarges and matures, secreting the hormone folliculin (estrin). Ovulation occurs on about the fourteenth day: the follicle protrudes through the surface of the ovary and breaks open (sometimes with slight bleeding), the egg passes into the oviduct, and the wound develops into the corpus luteum. The latter secretes the hormone progesterone, which acts on the uterus during the second phase of the cycle. The lining of the uterus becomes thickened and glandular and full of blood vessels, forming in the womb a cradle to receive the fertilized egg. These cellular proliferations being irreversible, the edifice is not resorbed if fertilization has not occurred. In the lower mammals the debris may escape gradually or may be carried away by the lymphatic vessels; but in woman and the other primates, the thickened lining membrane (endometrium) breaks down suddenly, the blood vessels and blood spaces are opened, and the bloody mass trickles out as the menstrual flow. Then, while the corpus luteum regresses, the membrane that lines the uterus is reconstituted and a new follicular phase of the cycle begins.

This complex process, still mysterious in many of its details, involves the whole female organism, since there are hormonal reactions between the ovaries and other endocrine organs, such as the pituitary, the thyroid, and the adrenals, which affect the central nervous system, the sympathetic nervous system, and in consequence all the viscera. Almost all women—more than eighty-five per cent—show more

---

[9] "Analysis of these phenomena in recent years has shown that they are similar in woman and the higher monkeys and apes, especially in the genus Rhesus. *It is evidently easier to experiment with these animals*," writes Louis Gallien (*La Sexualité*).

[In the United States extensive research has been done on the sex physiology of the larger apes by Yerkes and others, especially at the Laboratories of Primate Biology at Yale University and in Florida (Robert M. Yerkes: *Chimpanzees*; Yale University Press, 1943).—TR.]

or less distressing symptoms during the menstrual period. Blood pressure rises before the beginning of the flow and falls afterward; the pulse rate and often the temperature are increased, so that fever is frequent; pains in the abdomen are felt; often a tendency to constipation followed by diarrhea is observed; frequently there are also swelling of the liver, retention of urea, and albuminuria; many subjects have sore throat and difficulties with hearing and sight; perspiration is increased and accompanied at the beginning of the menses by an odor *sui generis*, which may be very strong and may persist throughout the period. The rate of basal metabolism is raised. The red blood count drops. The blood carries substances usually put on reserve in the tissues, especially calcium salts; the presence of these substances reacts on the ovaries, on the thyroid—which enlarges—and on the pituitary (regulator of the changes in the uterine lining described above)—which becomes more active. This glandular instability brings on a pronounced nervous instability. The central nervous system is affected, with frequent headache, and the sympathetic system is overactive; unconscious control through the central system is reduced, freeing convulsive reflexes and complexes and leading to a marked capriciousness of disposition. The woman is more emotional, more nervous, more irritable than usual, and may manifest serious psychic disturbance. It is during her periods that she feels her body most painfully as an obscure, alien thing; it is, indeed, the prey of a stubborn and foreign life that each month constructs and then tears down a cradle within it; each month all things are made ready for a child and then aborted in the crimson flow. Woman, like man, *is* her body;[1] but her body is something other than herself.

Woman experiences a more profound alienation when fertilization has occurred and the dividing egg passes down into the uterus and proceeds to develop there. True enough, pregnancy is a normal process, which, if it takes place under normal conditions of health and nutrition, is not harmful to the mother; certain interactions between her and the fetus become established which are even beneficial to her. In spite of an optimistic view having all too obvious social utility, however, gestation is a fatiguing task of no individual benefit

---

[1] "So I am my body, in so far, at least, as my experience goes, and conversely my body is like a life-model, or like a preliminary sketch, for my total being." (Merleau-Ponty: *Phénoménologie de la perception.*)

to the woman [2] but on the contrary demanding heavy sacrifices. It is often associated in the first months with loss of appetite and vomiting, which are not observed in any female domesticated animal and which signalize the revolt of the organism against the invading species.[3] There is a loss of phosphorus, calcium, and iron—the last difficult to make good later; metabolic overactivity excites the endocrine system; the sympathetic nervous system is in a state of increased excitement; and the blood shows a lowered specific gravity, it is lacking in iron, and in general it is similar "to that of persons fasting, of victims of famine, of those who have been bled frequently, of convalescents." [4] All that a healthy and well-nourished woman can hope for is to recoup these losses without too much difficulty after childbirth; but frequently serious accidents or at least dangerous disorders mark the course of pregnancy; and if the woman is not strong, if hygienic precautions are not taken, repeated childbearing will make her prematurely old and misshapen, as often among the rural poor. Childbirth itself is painful and dangerous. In this crisis it is most clearly evident that the body does not always work to the advantage of both species and individual at once; the infant may die, and, again, in being born it may kill its mother or leave her with a chronic ailment. Nursing is also a tiring service. A number of factors—especially the hormone prolactin—bring about the secretion of milk in the mammary glands; some soreness and often fever may accompany the process and in any case the nursing mother feeds the newborn from the resources of her own vitality. The conflict between species and individual, which sometimes assumes dramatic force at childbirth, endows the feminine body with a disturbing frailty. It has been well said that women "have infirmity in the abdomen"; and it is true that they have within them a hostile element—it is the species gnawing at their vitals. Their maladies are often caused not by some infection from without but by some internal maladjustment; for example, a false inflammation of the endometrium is set up through the reaction of the uterine lining to an abnormal excitation of the

---

[2] I am taking here an exclusively physiological point of view. It is evident that maternity can be very advantageous psychologically for a woman, just as it can also be a disaster.

[3] It may be said that these symptoms also signalize a faulty diet, according to some modern gynecologists.—Tr.

[4] Cf. H. Vignes in the *Traité de physiologie*, Vol. XI, edited by Roger and Binet.

ovaries; if the corpus luteum persists instead of declining after menstruation, it causes inflammation of the oviducts and uterine lining,
and so on.

In the end woman escapes the iron grasp of the species by way of
still another serious crisis; the phenomena of the menopause, the
inverse of puberty, appear between the ages of forty-five and fifty.
Ovarian activity diminishes and disappears, with resulting impoverish-
ment of the individual's vital forces. It may be supposed that the
metabolic glands, the thyroid and pituitary, are compelled to make
up in some fashion for the functioning of the ovaries; and thus, along
with the depression natural to the change of life, are to be noted signs
of excitation, such as high blood pressure, hot flashes, nervousness,
and sometimes increased sexuality. Some women develop fat deposits
at this time; others become masculinized. In many, a new endocrine
balance becomes established. Woman is now delivered from the servitude imposed by her female nature, but she is not to be likened to
a eunuch, for her vitality is unimpaired. And what is more, she is no
longer the prey of overwhelming forces; she is herself, she and her
body are one. It is sometimes said that women of a certain age constitute "a third sex"; and, in truth, while they are not males, they are
no longer females. Often, indeed, this release from female physiology
is expressed in a health, a balance, a vigor that they lacked before.

In addition to the primary sexual characteristics, woman has various secondary sexual peculiarities that are more or less directly produced in consequence of the first, through hormonal action. On the
average she is shorter than the male and lighter, her skeleton is more
delicate, and the pelvis is larger in adaptation to the functions of
pregnancy and childbirth; her connective tissues accumulate fat and
her contours are thus more rounded than those of the male. Appearance in general—structure, skin, hair—is distinctly different in the two
sexes. Muscular strength is much less in woman, about two thirds
that of man; she has less respiratory capacity, the lungs and trachea
being smaller. The larynx is relatively smaller, and in consequence the
female voice is higher. The specific gravity of the blood is lower in
woman and there is less hemoglobin; women are therefore less robust and more disposed to anemia than are males. Their pulse is more
rapid, the vascular system less stable, with ready blushing. Instability
is strikingly characteristic of woman's organization in general; among
other things, man shows greater stability in the metabolism of cal-

cium, woman fixing much less of this material and losing a good deal during menstruation and pregnancy. It would seem that in regard to calcium the ovaries exert a catabolic action, with resulting instability that brings on difficulties in the ovaries and in the thyroid, which is more developed in woman than in man. Irregularities in the endocrine secretions react on the sympathetic nervous system, and nervous and muscular control is uncertain. This lack in stability and control underlies woman's emotionalism, which is bound up with circulatory fluctuations—palpitation of the heart, blushing, and so forth—and on this account women are subject to such displays of agitation as tears, hysterical laughter, and nervous crises.

It is obvious once more that many of these traits originate in woman's subordination to the species, and here we find the most striking conclusion of this survey: namely, that woman is of all mammalian females at once the one who is most profoundly alienated (her individuality the prey of outside forces), and the one who most violently resists this alienation; in no other is enslavement of the organism to reproduction more imperious or more unwillingly accepted. Crises of puberty and the menopause, monthly "curse," long and often difficult pregnancy, painful and sometimes dangerous childbirth, illnesses, unexpected symptoms and complications—these are characteristic of the human female. It would seem that her lot is heavier than that of other females in just about the same degree that she goes beyond other females in the assertion of her individuality. In comparison with her the male seems infinitely favored: his sexual life is not in opposition to his existence as a person, and biologically it runs an even course, without crises and generally without mishap. On the average, women live as long as men, or longer; but they are much more often ailing, and there are many times when they are not in command of themselves.

These biological considerations are extremely important. In the history of woman they play a part of the first rank and constitute an essential element in her situation. Throughout our further discussion we shall always bear them in mind. For, the body being the instrument of our grasp upon the world, the world is bound to seem a very different thing when apprehended in one manner or another. This accounts for our lengthy study of the biological facts; they are one of the keys to the understanding of woman. But I deny that they establish for her a fixed and inevitable destiny. They are insufficient for setting up a hierarchy of the sexes; they fail to explain why woman is the Other; they do not condemn her to remain in this subordinate role forever.

It has been frequently maintained that in physiology alone must be sought the answers to these questions: Are the chances for individual success the same in the two sexes? Which plays the more important role in the species? But it must be noted that the first of these problems is quite different in the case of woman, as compared with other females; for animal species are fixed and it is possible to define them in static terms—by merely collecting observations it can be decided whether the mare is as fast as the stallion, or whether male chimpanzees excel their mates in intelligence tests—whereas the human species is forever in a state of change, forever becoming.

Certain materialist savants have approached the problem in a purely static fashion; influenced by the theory of psychophysiological parallelism, they sought to work out mathematical comparisons between the male and female organism—and they imagined that these measurements registered directly the functional capacities of the two sexes. For example, these students have engaged in elaborately trifling discussions regarding the absolute and relative weight of the brain in man and woman—with inconclusive results, after all corrections have been made. But what destroys much of the interest of these careful researches is the fact that it has not been possible to establish any relation whatever between the weight of the brain and the level of intelligence. And one would similarly be at a loss to present a psychic interpretation of the chemical formulæ designating the male and female hormones.

As for the present study, I categorically reject the notion of psychophysiological parallelism, for it is a doctrine whose foundations have long since been thoroughly undermined. If I mention it at all, it is because it still haunts many minds in spite of its philosophical and scientific bankruptcy. I reject also any comparative system that assumes the existence of a *natural* hierarchy or scale of values—for example, an evolutionary hierarchy. It is vain to ask if the female body is or is not more infantile than that of the male, if it is more or less similar to that of the apes, and so on. All these dissertations which mingle a vague naturalism with a still more vague ethics or æsthetics are pure verbiage. It is only in a human perspective that we can compare the female and the male of the human species. But man is defined as a being who is not fixed, who makes himself what he is. As Merleau-Ponty very justly puts it, man is not a natural species: he is a historical idea. Woman is not a completed reality, but rather a becoming, and it is in her becoming that she should be compared with man; that is to say, her *possibilities* should be defined. What gives rise to much of the debate is the tendency to reduce her to what she has been, to what she is today, in raising the question of her capabilities; for the fact is that capabilities are clearly manifested only when they have been realized—but the fact is also that when we have to do with a being whose nature is transcendent action, we can never close the books.

Nevertheless it will be said that if the body is not a *thing*, it is a situation, as viewed in the perspective I am adopting—that of Heidegger, Sartre, and Merleau-Ponty; it is the instrument of our grasp upon the world, a limiting factor for our projects. Woman is weaker than man; she has less muscular strength, fewer red blood corpuscles, less lung capacity; she runs more slowly, can lift less heavy weights, can compete with man in hardly any sport; she cannot stand up to him in a fight. To all this weakness must be added the instability, the lack of control, and the fragility already discussed: these are facts. Her grasp on the world is thus more restricted; she has less firmness and less steadiness available for projects that in general she is less capable of carrying out. In other words, her individual life is less rich than man's.

Certainly these facts cannot be denied—but in themselves they have no significance. Once we adopt the human perspective, interpreting the body on a basis of existence, biology becomes an abstract science; whenever the physiological fact (for instance, muscular inferiority) takes on meaning, this meaning is at once seen as dependent on a whole context; the "weakness" is revealed as such only in the light of the ends man proposes, the instruments he has available, and the laws he establishes. If he does not wish to seize the world, then the idea of a *grasp* on things has no sense; when in this seizure the full employment of bodily power is not required, above the available minimum, then differences in strength are annulled; wherever violence is contrary to custom, muscular force cannot be a basis for domination. In brief, the concept of *weakness* can be defined only with reference to existentialist, economic, and moral considerations. It has been said that the human species is antinatural, a statement that is hardly exact, since man cannot deny facts; but he establishes their truth by the way in which he deals with them; nature has reality for him only to the extent that it is involved in his activity—his own nature not excepted. As with her grasp on the world, it is again impossible to measure in the abstract the burden imposed on woman by her reproductive function. The bearing of maternity upon the individual life, regulated naturally in animals by the œstrus cycle and the seasons, is not definitely prescribed in woman—society alone is the arbiter. The bondage of woman to the species is more or less rigorous according to the number of births demanded by society and the degree of hygienic care provided for pregnancy and childbirth. Thus, while it is true that in the higher animals the individual existence is asserted more imperiously by the male than by the female, in the human species individual "possibilities" depend upon the economic and social situation.

But in any case it does not always happen that the male's individual privileges give him a position of superiority within the species, for in maternity the female acquires a kind of autonomy of her own. Sometimes, as in the baboons studied by Zuckermann,[5] the male does dominate; but in many species the two members of the pair lead a separate life, and in the lion the two sexes share equally in the duties of the den. Here again the human situation cannot be reduced to any other; it is not as single individuals that human beings are to be defined in the first place; men and women have never stood opposed to each other in single combat; the couple is an original *Mitsein*, a basic combination; and as such it always appears as a permanent or temporary element in a larger collectivity.

Within such a society, which is more necessary to the species, male or female? At the level of the gametes, at the level of the biological functions of coition and pregnancy, the male principle creates to maintain, the female principle maintains to create, as we have seen; but what are the various aspects of this division of labor in different forms of social life? In sessile species, attached to other organisms or to substrata, in those furnished by nature with abundant sustenance obtainable without effort, the role of the male is limited to fecundation; where it is necessary to seek, to hunt, to fight in order to provide the food needed by the young, the male in many cases co-operates

[5] *The Social Life of Monkeys and Apes* (1932).

in their support. This co-operation becomes absolutely indispensable in a species where the offspring remain unable to take care of themselves for a long time after weaning; here the male's assistance becomes extremely important, for the lives he has begotten cannot be maintained without him. A single male can fecundate a number of females each year; but it requires a male for every female to assure the survival of the offspring after they are born, to defend them against enemies, to wrest from nature the wherewithal to satisfy their needs. In human history the equilibrium between the forces of production and of reproduction is brought about by different means under different economic conditions, and these conditions govern the relations of male and female to offspring and in consequence to each other. But here we are leaving the realm of biology; by its light alone we could never decide the primacy of one sex or the other in regard to the perpetuation of the species.

But in truth a society is not a species, for it is in a society that the species attains the status of existence—transcending itself toward the world and toward the future. Its ways and customs cannot be deduced from biology, for the individuals that compose the society are never abandoned to the dictates of their nature; they are subject rather to that second nature which is custom and in which are reflected the desires and the fears that express their essential nature. It is not merely as a body, but rather as a body subject to taboos, to laws, that the subject is conscious of himself and attains fulfillment—it is with reference to certain values that he evaluates himself. And, once again, it is not upon physiology that values can be based; rather, the facts of biology take on the values that the existent bestows upon them. If the respect or the fear inspired by woman prevents the use of violence toward her, then the muscular superiority of the male is no source of power. If custom decrees—as in certain Indian tribes—that the young girls are to choose their husbands, or if the father dictates the marriage choice, then the sexual aggressiveness of the male gives him no power of initiative, no advantage. The close bond between mother and child will be for her a source of dignity or indignity according to the value placed upon the child—which is highly variable—and this very bond, as we have seen, will be recognized or not according to the presumptions of the society concerned.

Thus we must view the facts of biology in the light of an ontological, economic, social, and psychological context. The enslavement of the female to the species and the limitations of her various powers are extremely important facts; the body of woman is one of the essential elements in her situation in the world. But that body is not enough to define her as woman; there is no true living reality except as manifested by the concious individual through activities and in the bosom of a society. Biology is not enough to give an answer to the question that is before us: why is woman the *Other?* Our task is to discover how the nature of woman has been affected throughout the course of history; we are concerned to find out what humanity has made of the human female.

CHAPTER II

The Psychoanalytic Point of View

THE TREMENDOUS advance accomplished by psychoanalysis over psychophysiology lies in the view that no factor becomes involved in the psychic life without having taken on human significance; it is not the body-object described by biologists that actually exists, but the body as lived in by the subject. Woman is a female to the extent that she feels herself as such. There are biologically essential features that are not a part of her real, experienced situation: thus the structure of the egg is not reflected in it, but on the contrary an organ of no great biological importance, like the clitoris, plays in it a part of the first rank. It is not nature that defines woman; it is she who defines herself by dealing with nature on her own account in her emotional life.

An entire system has been built up in this perspective, which I do not intend to criticize as a whole, merely examining its contribution to the study of woman. It is not an easy matter to discuss psychoanalysis *per se*. Like all religions—Christianity and Marxism, for example— it displays an embarrassing flexibility on a basis of rigid concepts. Words are sometimes used in their most literal sense, the term *phallus*, for example, designating quite exactly that fleshy projection which marks the male; again, they are indefinitely expanded and take on symbolic meaning, the phallus now expressing the virile character and situation *in toto*. If you attack the letter of his doctrine, the psychoanalyst protests that you misunderstand its spirit; if you applaud its spirit, he at once wishes to confine you to the letter. The doctrine is of no importance, says one, psychoanalysis is a method; but the success of the method strengthens the doctrinaire in his faith. After all, where is one to find the true lineaments of psychoanalysis if not among the psychoanalysts? But there are heretics among these, just as there are among Christians and Marxists; and more than one psychoanalyst has declared that "the worst enemies of psychoanalysis are the psychoanalysts." In spite of a scholastic precision that often becomes pedantic, many obscurities remain to be dissipated. As Sartre and Merleau-Ponty have observed, the proposition "Sexuality is coextensive with existence" can be understood in two very different ways; it can mean that every experience of the existent has a sexual significance, or that every sexual phenomenon has an existential import. It is possible to reconcile these statements, but too often one merely slips from one to the other. Furthermore, as soon as the "sexual" is distinguished from the "genital," the idea of sexuality becomes none too clear. According to Dalbiez, "the sexual with Freud is the intrinsic aptitude for releasing the genital." But nothing is more obscure than the idea of "aptitude"—that is, of possibility—for only realization gives indubitable proof of what is possible. Not being a philosopher, Freud has refused to justify his system philosophically; and his disciples maintain that on this account he is exempt from all metaphysical attack. There are metaphysical assumptions behind all his dicta, however, and to use his language is to adopt a philosophy. It is just such confusions that call for criticism, while making criticism difficult.

Freud never showed much concern with the destiny of woman; it is clear that he simply adapted his account from that of the destiny of man, with slight modifications. Earlier the sexologist Marañon had stated that "As specific energy, we may say that the libido is a force of virile character. We will say as much of the orgasm." According to him, women who attain orgasm are "viriloid" women; the sexual impulse is "in one direction" and woman is only halfway along the road.[1] Freud never goes to such an extreme; he admits that woman's sexuality is evolved as fully as man's; but he hardly studies it in particular. He writes: "The libido is constantly and regularly male in essence, whether it appears in man or in woman." He declines to regard the feminine libido as having its own original nature, and therefore it will necessarily seem to him like a complex deviation from the human libido in general. This develops at first, he thinks, identically in the two sexes—each infant passes first through an oral phase that fixates it upon the maternal breast, and then through an anal phase; finally it reaches the genital phase, at which point the sexes become differentiated.

Freud further brought to light a fact the importance of which had not been fully appreciated: namely, that masculine erotism is defi-

---

[1] It is odd to find this theory again in D. H. Lawrence. In *The Plumed Serpent* Don Cipriano is careful never to let his mistress reach the orgasm; she must vibrate in tune with the man, not become individualized in her own pleasure. (Cf. footnote, p. 223.)

nitely located in the penis, whereas in woman there are two distinct
erotic systems: one the clitoral, which develops in childhood, the
other vaginal, which develops only after puberty. When the boy
reaches the genital phase, his evolution is completed, though he must
pass from the autoerotic inclination, in which pleasure is subjective,
to the heteroerotic inclination, in which pleasure is bound up with
an object, normally woman. This transition is made at the time of
puberty through a narcissistic phase. But the penis will remain, as in
childhood, the specific organ of erotism. Woman's libido, also passing through a narcissistic phase, will become objective, normally toward
man; but the process will be much more complex, because woman
must pass from clitoral pleasure to vaginal. There is only one genital
stage for man, but there are two for woman; she runs a much greater
risk of not reaching the end of her sexual evolution, of remaining at
the infantile stage and thus of developing neuroses.

While still in the autoerotic stage, the child becomes more or less
strongly attached to an object. The boy becomes fixed on his mother
and desires to identify himself with his father; this presumption terrifies him and he dreads mutilation at the hands of his father in punishment for it. Thus the castration complex springs from the Œdipus
complex. Then aggressiveness toward the father develops, but at the
same time the child interiorizes the father's authority; thus the superego is built up in the child and censures his incestuous tendencies.
These are repressed, the complex is liquidated, and the son is freed
from his fear of his father, whom he has now installed in his own
psyche under the guise of moral precepts.[2] The superego is more powerful in proportion as the Œdipus complex has been more marked
and more rigorously resisted.

Freud at first described the little girl's history in a completely corresponding fashion, later calling the feminine form of the process the
Electra complex; but it is clear that he defined it less in itself than
upon the basis of his masculine pattern. He recognized a very important difference between the two, however: the little girl at first has a
mother fixation, but the boy is at no time sexually attracted to the
father. This fixation of the girl represents a survival of the oral phase.

---

[2] "The superego or conscience is a precipitate of all the prohibitions and inhibitions that were originally inculcated into us by our parents, especially by the
father." (Brill: *Freud's Contribution to Psychiatry* [W. W. Norton & Co., 1944],
p. 153.)—Tr.

Then the child identifies herself with the father; but toward the age of five she discovers the anatomical difference between the sexes, and she reacts to the absence of the penis by acquiring a castration complex —she imagines that she has been mutilated and is pained at the thought. Having then to renounce her virile pretensions, she identifies herself with her mother and seeks to seduce the father. The castration complex and the Electra complex thus reinforce each other. Her feeling of frustration is the keener since, loving her father, she wishes in vain to be like him; and, inversely, her regret strengthens her love, for she is able to compensate for her inferiority through the affection she inspires in her father. The little girl entertains a feeling of rivalry and hostility toward her mother. Then the superego is built up also in her, and the incestuous tendencies are repressed; but her superego is not so strong, for the Electra complex is less sharply defined than the Œdipus because the first fixation was upon the mother, and since the father is himself the object of the love that he condemns, his prohibitions are weaker than in the case of his son-rival. It can be seen that like her genital development the whole sexual drama is more complex for the girl than for her brothers. In consequence she may be led to react to the castration complex by denying her femininity, by continuing obstinately to covet a penis and to identify herself with her father. This attitude will cause her to remain in the clitoral phase, to become frigid, or to turn toward homosexuality.

The two essential objections that may be raised against this view derive from the fact that Freud based it upon a masculine model. He assumes that woman feels that she is a mutilated man. But the idea of mutilation implies comparison and evaluation. Many psychoanalysts today admit that the young girl may regret not having a penis without believing, however, that it has been removed from her body; and even this regret is not general. It could not arise from a simple anatomical comparison; many little girls, in fact, are late in discovering the masculine construction, and if they do, it is only by sight. The little boy obtains from his penis a living experience that makes it an object of pride to him, but this pride does not necessarily imply a corresponding humiliation for his sisters, since they know the masculine organ in its outward aspect only—this outgrowth, this weak little rod of flesh can in itself inspire them only with indifference, or even disgust. The little girl's covetousness, when its exists, results from a previous evaluation of virility. Freud takes this for granted, when it should be accounted for.[3] On the other hand, the concept of the Electra complex is very vague, because it is not supported by a basic description of the feminine libido. Even in boys the occurrence of a definitely genital Œdipus complex is by no means general; but, apart from very few exceptions, it cannot be admitted that the father is a source of genital excitation for his young daughter. One of the great problems of feminine eroticism is that clitoral pleasure is localized; and it is only toward puberty that a number of erogenous zones develop in various parts of the body, along with the growth of vaginal sensation. To say, then, that in a child of ten the kisses and caresses of her father have an "intrinsic aptitude" for arousing clitoral pleasure is to assert something that in most cases is nonsense. If it is admitted that the Electra complex has only a very diffuse emotional character, then the whole question of emotion is raised, and Freudianism does not help us in defining emotion as distinguished from sexuality. What deifies the father is by no means the feminine libido (nor is the mother deified by the desire she arouses in the son); on the contrary, the fact that the feminine desire (in the daughter) is directed toward a sovereign being gives it a special character. It does not determine the nature of its object; rather it is affected by the latter. The sovereignty of the father is a fact of social origin, which Freud fails to account for; in fact, he states that it is impossible to say what authority decided, at a certain moment in history, that the father should take precedence over the mother—a decision that, according to Freud, was progressive, but due to causes unknown. "It could not have been the patriarchal authority, since it is just this authority which progress conferred upon the father," as he puts it in his last work.[4]

Adler took issue with Freud because he saw the deficiency of a system that undertook to explain human life upon the basis of sexuality alone; he holds that sexuality should be integrated with the total personality. With Freud all human behavior seems to be the outcome of desire—that is, of the search for pleasure—but for Adler man appears to be aiming at certain goals; for the sexual urge he substitutes motives, purposes, projects. He gives so large a place to the intelligence that often the sexual has in his eyes only a symbolic value.

---

[3] This discussion will be resumed at much greater length in Book II, Ch. i.

[4] Freud: *Moses and Monotheism*, translated by Katherine Jones (Alfred A. Knopf, 1939).

According to his system, the human drama can be reduced to three elemental factors: in every individual there is a *will to power*, which, however, is accompanied by an *inferiority complex;* the resulting conflict leads the individual to employ a thousand ruses in a *flight from reality*—a reality with which he fears he may not be able to cope; the subject thus withdraws to some degree from the society of which he is apprehensive and hence becomes afflicted with the neuroses that involve disturbance of the social attitude. In woman the inferiority complex takes the form of a shamed rejection of her femininity. It is not the lack of the penis that causes this complex, but rather woman's total situation; if the little girl feels penis envy it is only as the symbol of privileges enjoyed by boys. The place the father holds in the family, the universal predominance of males, her own education—everything confirms her in her belief in masculine superiority. Later on, when she takes part in sexual relations, she finds a new humiliation in the coital posture that places the woman underneath the man. She reacts through the "masculine protest": either she endeavors to masculinize herself, or she makes use of her feminine weapons to wage war upon the male. Through maternity she may be able to find an equivalent of the penis in her child. But this supposes that she begins by wholly accepting her role as woman and that she assumes her inferiority. She is divided against herself much more profoundly than is the male.

I shall not enlarge here upon the theoretical differences that separate Adler and Freud nor upon the possibilities of a reconciliation; but this may be said: neither the explanation based upon the sexual urge nor that based upon motive is sufficient, for every urge poses a motive, but the motive is apprehended only through the urge—a synthesis of Adlerianism and Freudianism would therefore seem possible of realization. In fact, Adler retains the idea of psychic causation as an integral part of his system when he introduces the concepts of goal and of finality, and he is somewhat in accord with Freud in regard to the relation between drives and mechanism: the physicist always recognizes determinism when he is concerned with conflict or a force of attraction. The axiomatic proposition held in common by all psychoanalysts is this: the human story is to be explained by the interplay of determinate elements. And all the psychoanalysts allot the same destiny to woman. Her drama is epitomized in the conflict between her "viriloid" and her "feminine" tendencies, the first expressed through the clitoral system, the second in vaginal erotism. As a child she identifies herself with her father; then she becomes possessed with a feeling of inferiority with reference to the male and is faced with a dilemma: either to assert her independence and become virilized—which, with the underlying complex of inferiority, induces a state of tension that threatens neurosis—or to find happy fulfillment in amorous submission, a solution that is facilitated by her love for the sovereign father. He it is whom she really seeks in lover or husband, and thus her sexual love is mingled with the desire to be dominated. She will find her recompense in maternity, since that will afford her a new kind of independence. This drama would seem to be endowed with an energy, a dynamism, of its own; it steadily pursues its course through any and all distorting incidents, and every woman is passively swept along in it.

The psychoanalysts have had no trouble in finding empirical confirmation for their theories. As we know, it was possible for a long time to explain the position of the planets on the Ptolemaic system by adding to it sufficiently subtle complications; and by superposing an inverse Œdipus complex upon the Œdipus complex, by disclosing desire in all anxiety, success has been achieved in integrating with the Freudian system the very facts that appear to contradict its validity. It is possible to make out a form only against a background, and the way in which the form is apprehended brings out the background behind it in positive detail; thus, if one is determined to describe a special case in a Freudian perspective, one will encounter the Freudian schema behind it. But when a doctrine demands the indefinite and arbitrary multiplication of secondary explanations, when observation brings to light as many exceptions as instances conformable to rule, it is better to give up the old rigid framework. Indeed, every psychoanalyst today is busily engaged after his fashion in making the Freudian concepts less rigid and in attempting compromises. For example, a contemporary psychoanalyst [5] writes as follows: "Wherever there is a complex, there are by definition a number of components. . . . The complex consists in the association of these disparate elements and not in the representation of one among them by the others." But the concept of a simple association of elements is unacceptable, for the psychic life is not a mosaic, it is a single whole in every one of its aspects and we must respect that unity. This is possible only by our

---

[5] Baudouin: *L'Âme enfantine et la psychanalyse.*

recovering through the disparate facts the original purposiveness of existence. If we do not go back to this source, man appears to be the battleground of compulsions and prohibitions that alike are devoid of meaning and incidental.

All psychoanalysts systematically reject the idea of *choice* and the correlated concept of value, and therein lies the intrinsic weakness of the system. Having dissociated compulsions and prohibitions from the free choice of the existent, Freud fails to give us an explanation of their origin—he takes them for granted. He endeavored to replace the idea of value with that of authority; but he admits in *Moses and Monotheism* that he has no way of accounting for this authority. Incest, for example, is forbidden because the father has forbidden it—but why did he forbid it? It is a mystery. The superego interiorizes, introjects commands and prohibitions emanating from an arbitrary tyranny, and the instinctive drives are there, we know not why: these two realities are unrelated because morality is envisaged as foreign to sexuality. The human unity appears to be disrupted, there is no thoroughfare from the individual to society; to reunite them Freud was forced to invent strange fictions, as in *Totem and Taboo*. Adler saw clearly that the castration complex could be explained only in a social context; he grappled with the problem of valuation, but he did not reach the source in the individual of the values recognized by society, and he did not grasp the fact that values are involved in sexuality itself, which led him to misjudge its importance.

Sexuality most certainly plays a considerable role in human life; it can be said to pervade life throughout. We have already learned from physiology that the living activity of the testes and the ovaries is integrated with that of the body in general. The existent is a sexual, a sexuate body, and in his relations with other existents who are also sexuate bodies, sexuality is in consequence always involved. But if body and sexuality are concrete expressions of existence, it is with reference to this that their significance can be discovered. Lacking this perspective, psychoanalysis takes for granted unexplained facts. For instance, we are told that the little girl is *ashamed* of urinating in a squatting position with her bottom uncovered—but whence comes this shame? And likewise, before asking whether the male is proud of having a penis or whether his pride is expressed in his penis, it is necessary to know what pride is and how the aspirations of the subject can be incarnated in an object. There is no need of taking sexuality as an irreducible datum, for there is in the existent a more original "quest of being," of which sexuality is only one of the aspects. Sartre demonstrates this truth in *L'Être et le néant,* as does Bachelard in his works on Earth, Air, and Water. The psychoanalysts hold that the primary truth regarding man is his relation with his own body and with the bodies of his fellows in the group; but man has a primordial interest in the substance of the natural world which surrounds him and which he tries to discover in work, in play, and in all the experiences of the "dynamic imagination." Man aspires to be at one concretely with the whole world, apprehended in all possible ways. To work the earth, to dig a hole, are activities as original as the embrace, as coition, and they deceive themselves who see here no more than sexual symbols. The hole, the ooze, the gash, hardness, integrity are primary realities; and the interest they have for man is not dictated by the libido, but rather the libido will be colored by the manner in which he becomes aware of them. It is not because it symbolizes feminine virginity that integrity fascinates man; but it is his admiration for integrity that renders virginity precious. Work, war, play, art signify ways of being concerned with the world which cannot be reduced to any others; they disclose qualities that interfere with those which sexuality reveals. It is at once in their light and in the light of these erotic experiences that the individual exercises his power of choice. But only an ontological point of view, a comprehension of being in general, permits us to restore the unity of this choice.

It is this concept of choice, indeed, that psycholanalysis most vehemently rejects in the name of determinism and the "collective unconscious"; and it is this unconscious that is supposed to supply man with prefabricated imagery and a universal symbolism. Thus it would explain the observed analogies of dreams, of purposeless actions, of visions of delirium, of allegories, and of human destinies. To speak of liberty would be to deny oneself the possibility of explaining these disturbing conformities. But the idea of liberty is not incompatible with the existence of certain constants. If the psychoanalytic method is frequently rewarding in spite of the errors in its theory, that is because there are in every individual case certain factors of undeniable generality: situations and behavior patterns constantly recur, and the moment of decision flashes from a cloud of generality and repetition. "Anatomy is destiny," said Freud; and this phrase is echoed by that of Merleau-Ponty: "The body is generality." Existence is all one, bridging the gaps between individual existents; it makes itself manifest in analogous organisms, and therefore constant factors will be found in the bonds between the ontological and the sexual. At a given epoch of history the techniques, the economic and social structure of a society, will reveal to all its members an identical world, and there a constant relation of sexuality to social patterns will exist; analogous individuals, placed in analogous conditions, will see analogous points of significance in the given circumstances. This analogy does not establish a rigorous universality, but it accounts for the fact that general types may be recognized in individual case histories.

The symbol does not seem to me to be an allegory elaborated by a mysterious unconscious; it is rather the perception of a certain significance through the analogue of the significant object. Symbolic significance is manifested in the same way to numerous individuals, because of the identical existential situation connecting all the individual existents and the identical set of artificial conditions that all must confront. Symbolism did not come down from heaven nor rise up from subterranean depths—it has been elaborated, like language, by that human reality which is at once *Mitsein* and separation; and this explains why individual invention also has its place, as in practice psychoanalysis has to admit, regardless of doctrine. Our perspective allows us, for example, to understand the value widely accorded to the penis.[6] It is impossible to account for it without taking our departure from an existential fact: the tendency of the subject toward *alienation*. The anxiety that his liberty induces in the subject leads him to search for himself in things, which is a kind of flight from himself. This tendency is so fundamental that immediately after weaning, when he is separated from the Whole, the infant is compelled to lay hold upon his alienated existence in mirrors and in the gaze of his parents. Primitive people are alienated in mana, in the totem; civilized people in their individual souls, in their egos, their names, their property, their work. Here is to be found the primary temptation to inauthenticity, to failure to be genuinely oneself. The penis is singularly adapted for playing this role of "double" for the little boy—it is for him at once a foreign object and himself; it is a plaything, a doll, and yet his own flesh; relatives and nurse-girls behave toward it as if it were a little person. It is easy to see, then, how it becomes for the child "an *alter ego* ordinarily more artful, more intelligent, and more

---

[6] We shall return to this subject at greater length in Book II. Ch. i.

clever than the individual." [7] The penis is regarded by the subject as at once himself and other than himself, because the functions of urination and later of erection are processes midway between the voluntary and the involuntary, and because it is a capricious and as it were a foreign source of pleasure that is felt subjectively. The individual's specific transcendence takes concrete form in the penis and it is a source of pride. Because the phallus is thus set apart, man can bring into integration with his subjective individuality the life that overflows from it. It is easy to see, then, that the length of the penis, the force of the urinary jet, the strength of erection and ejaculation become for him the measure of his own worth.[8]

Thus the incarnation of transcendence in the phallus is a constant; and since it is also a constant for the child to feel himself transcended —that is to say, frustrated in his own transcendence by the father—we therefore continually come upon the Freudian idea of the "castration complex." Not having that *alter ego*, the little girl is not alienated in a material thing and cannot retrieve her integrity. On this account she is led to make an object of her whole self, to set up herself as the Other. Whether she knows that she is or is not comparable with boys is secondary; the important point is that, even if she is unaware of it, the absence of the penis prevents her from being conscious of herself as a sexual being. From this flow many consequences. But the constants I have referred to do not for all that establish a fixed destiny —the phallus assumes such worth as it does because it symbolizes a dominance that is exercised in other domains. If woman should succeed in establishing herself as subject, she would invent equivalents of the phallus; in fact, the doll, incarnating the promise of the baby that is to come in the future, can become a possession more precious than the penis.[9] There are matrilineal societies in which the women keep in their possession the *masks* in which the group finds alienation; in

---

[7] Alice Balint: *La Vie intime de l'enfant*, p. 101.

[8] I have been told of peasant children amusing themselves in excremental competition; the one who produced the most copious and solid feces enjoyed a prestige unmatched by any other form of success, whether in games or even in fighting. The fecal mass here plays the same part as the penis—there is alienation in both cases.

[Pride in this peculiar type of eminence is by no means confined to European peasant children; it has been observed in young Americans and is doubtless well-nigh universal.—Tr.]

[9] We shall return to these ideas in the second part; I note them here only as a matter of method.

such societies the penis loses much of its glory. The fact is that a true human privilege is based upon the anatomical privilege only in virtue of the total situation. Psychoanalysis can establish its truths only in the historical context.

Woman can be defined by her consciousness of her own femininity no more satisfactorily than by saying that she is a female, for she acquires this consciousness under circumstances dependent upon the society of which she is a member. Interiorizing the unconscious and the whole psychic life, the very language of psychoanalysis suggests that the drama of the individual unfolds within him—such words as *complex, tendency,* and so on make that implication. But a life is a relation to the world, and the individual defines himself by making his own choices through the world about him. We must therefore turn toward the world to find answers for the questions we are concerned with. In particular psychoanalysis fails to explain why woman is the *Other.* For Freud himself admits that the prestige of the penis is explained by the sovereignty of the father, and, as we have seen, he confesses that he is ignorant regarding the origin of male supremacy.

We therefore decline to accept the method of psychoanalysis, without rejecting *en bloc* the contributions of the science or denying the fertility of some of its insights. In the first place, we do not limit ourselves to regarding sexuality as something given. The insufficiency of this view is shown by the poverty of the resulting descriptions of the feminine libido; as I have already said, the psychoanalysts have never studied it directly, but only in taking the male libido as their point of departure. They seem to ignore the fundamental ambivalence of the attraction exerted on the female by the male. Freudians and Adlerians explain the anxiety felt by the female confronted by the masculine sex as being the inversion of a frustrated desire. Stekel saw more clearly that an original reaction was concerned, but he accounts for it in a superficial manner. Woman, he says, would fear defloration, penetration, pregnancy, and pain, and such fear would restrain her desire— but this explanation is too rational. Instead of holding that her desire is disguised in anxiety or is contested by fear, we should regard as an original fact this blending of urgency and apprehension which is female desire: it is the indissoluble synthesis of attraction and repulsion that characterizes it. We may note that many female animals avoid copulation even as they are soliciting it, and we are tempted to accuse them of coquetry or hypocrisy; but it is absurd to pretend to explain primitive behavior patterns by asserting their similarity to complex modes of conduct. On the contrary, the former are in truth at the source of the attitudes that in woman are called coquetry and hypocrisy. The notion of a "passive libido" is baffling, since the libido has been defined, on the basis of the male, as a drive, an energy; but one would do no better to hold the opinion that a light could be at once yellow and blue—what is needed is the intuition of green. We would more fully encompass reality if instead of defining the libido in vague terms of "energy" we brought the significance of sexuality into relation with that of other human attitudes—taking, capturing, eating, making, submitting, and so forth; for it is one of the various modes of apprehending an object. We should study also the qualities of the erotic object as it presents itself not only in the sexual act but also to observation in general. Such an investigation extends beyond the frame of psychoanalysis, which assumes eroticism as irreducible.

Furthermore, I shall pose the problem of feminine destiny quite otherwise: I shall place woman in a world of values and give her behavior a dimension of liberty. I believe that she has the power to choose between the assertion of her transcendence and her alienation as object; she is not the plaything of contradictory drives; she devises solutions of diverse ranking in the ethical scale. Replacing value with authority, choice with drive, psychoanalysis offers an *Ersatz*, a substitute, for morality—the concept of normality. This concept is certainly most useful in therapeutics, but it has spread through psychoanalysis in general to a disquieting extent. The descriptive schema is proposed as a law; and most assuredly a mechanistic psychology cannot accept the notion of moral invention; it can in strictness render an account of the *less* and never of the more; in strictness it can admit of checks, never of creations. If a subject does not show in his totality the development considered as normal, it will be said that his development has been arrested, and this arrest will be interpreted as a lack, a negation, but never as a positive decision. This it is, among other things, that makes the psychoanalysis of great men so shocking: we are told that such and such a transference, this or that sublimation, has not taken place in them; it is not suggested that perhaps they have refused to undergo the process, perhaps for good reasons of their own; it is not thought desirable to regard their behavior as possibly motivated by purposes freely envisaged; the individual is always explained through ties with his past and not in respect to a future toward which he projects his aims. Thus the psychoanalysts never give us more than an inauthentic picture, and for the inauthentic there can hardly be found any other criterion than normality. Their statement of the feminine destiny is absolutely to the point in this connection. In the sense in which the psychoanalysts understand the term, "to identify oneself" with the mother or with the father is to *alienate oneself* in a model, it is to prefer a foreign image to the spontaneous manifestation of one's own existence, it is to play at being. Woman is shown to us as enticed by two modes of alienation. Evidently to play at being a man will be for her a source of frustration; but to play at being a woman is also a delusion: to be a woman would mean to be the object, the *Other*—and the Other nevertheless remains subject in the midst of her resignation.

The true problem for woman is to reject these flights from reality and seek self-fulfillment in transcendence. The thing to do, then, is to see what possibilities are opened up for her through what are called the virile and the feminine attitudes. When a child takes the road indicated by one or the other of its parents, it may be because the child freely takes up their projects; its behavior may be the result of a choice motivated by ends and aims. Even with Adler the will to power is only an absurd kind of energy; he denominates as "masculine protest" every project involving transcendence. When a little girl climbs trees it is, according to Adler, just to show her equality with boys; it does not occur to him that she likes to climb trees. For the mother her child is something quite other than an "equivalent of the penis." To paint, to write, to engage in politics—these are not merely "sublimations"; here we have aims that are willed for their own sakes. To deny it is to falsify all human history.

The reader will note a certain parallelism between this account and that of the psychoanalysts. The fact is that from the male point of view—which is adopted by both male and female psychoanalysts—behavior involving alienation is regarded as feminine, that in which the subject asserts his transcendence as virile. Donaldson, a historian of woman, remarked that the definitions: "man is a male human being, woman is a female human being," have been asymmetrically distorted; and it is among the psychoanalysts in particular that man is defined as a human being and woman as a female—whenever she behaves as a human being she is said to imitate the male. The psychoanalyst describes the female child, the young girl, as incited to identification with the mother and the father, torn between "viriloid" and "feminine" tendencies; whereas I conceive her as hesitating between the role of *object, Other* which is offered her, and the assertion of her liberty. Thus it is that we shall agree on a certain number of facts, especially when we take up the avenues of inauthentic flight open to women. But we accord them by no means the same significance as does the Freudian or the Adlerian. For us woman is defined as a human being in quest of values in a world of values, a world of which it is indispensable to know the economic and social structure. We shall study woman in an existential perspective with due regard to her total situation.

CHAPTER III

The Point of View
of Historical Materialism

THE THEORY of historical materialism has brought to light some most important truths. Humanity is not an animal species, it is a historical reality. Human society is an antiphysis—in a sense it is against nature; it does not passively submit to the presence of nature but rather takes over the control of nature on its own behalf. This arrogation is not an inward, subjective operation; it is accomplished objectively in practical action.

Thus woman could not be considered simply as a sexual organism, for among the biological traits, only those have importance that take on concrete value in action. Woman's awareness of herself is not defined exclusively by her sexuality: it reflects a situation that depends upon the economic organization of society, which in turn indicates what stage of technical evolution mankind has attained. As we have seen, the two essential traits that characterize woman, biologically speaking, are the following: her grasp upon the world is less extended than man's, and she is more closely enslaved to the species.

But these facts take on quite different values according to the economic and social context. In human history grasp upon the world has never been defined by the naked body: the hand, with its opposable thumb, already anticipates the instrument that multiplies its power; from the most ancient records of prehistory, we see man always as armed. In times when heavy clubs were brandished and wild beasts held at bay, woman's physical weakness did constitute a glaring inferiority: if the instrument required strength slightly beyond that at woman's disposal, it was enough to make her appear utterly powerless. But, on the contrary, technique may annul the muscular inequality of man and woman: abundance makes for superiority only in the perspective of a need, and to have too much is no better than to have enough. Thus the control of many modern machines requires only a part of the masculine resources, and if the minimum demanded is not above the female's capacity, she becomes, as far as this work is concerned, man's equal. Today, of course, vast displays of energy can be controlled by pressing a button. As for the burdens of maternity, they assume widely varying importance according to the customs of the country: they are crushing if the woman is obliged to undergo frequent pregnancies and if she is compelled to nurse and raise the children without assistance; but if she procreates voluntarily and if society comes to her aid during pregnancy and is concerned with child welfare, the burdens of maternity are light and can be easily offset by suitable adjustments in working conditions.

Engels retraces the history of woman according to this perspective in *The Origin of the Family, Private Property, and the State*, showing that this history depended essentially on that of techniques. In the Stone Age, when the land belonged in common to all members of the clan, the rudimentary character of the primitive spade and hoe limited the possibilities of agriculture, so that woman's strength was adequate for gardening. In this primitive division of labor, the two sexes constituted in a way two classes, and there was equality between these classes. While man hunts and fishes, woman remains in the home; but the tasks of domesticity include productive labor—making pottery, weaving, gardening—and in consequence woman plays a large part in economic life. Through the discovery of copper, tin, bronze, and iron, and with the appearance of the plow, agriculture enlarges its scope, and intensive labor is called for in clearing woodland and cultivating the fields. Then man has recourse to the labor of other men, whom he reduces to slavery. Private property appears: master of slaves and of the earth, man becomes the proprietor also of woman. This was "the great historical defeat of the feminine sex." It is to be explained by the upsetting of the old division of labor which occurred in consequence of the invention of new tools. "The same cause which had assured to woman the prime authority in the house— namely, her restriction to domestic duties—this same cause now assured the domination there of the man; for woman's housework henceforth sank into insignificance in comparison with man's productive labor—the latter was everything, the former a trifling auxiliary." Then maternal authority gave place to paternal authority, property being inherited from father to son and no longer from woman to her clan. Here we see the emergence of the patriarchal family founded upon private property. In this type of family woman is subjugated.

Man in his sovereignty indulges himself in sexual caprices, among others—he fornicates with slaves or courtesans or he practices polygamy. Wherever the local customs make reciprocity at all possible, the wife takes revenge through infidelity—marriage finds its natural fulfillment in adultery. This is woman's sole defense against the domestic slavery in which she is bound; and it is this economic oppression that gives rise to the social oppression to which she is subjected. Equality cannot be re-established until the two sexes enjoy equal rights in law; but this enfranchisement requires participation in general industry by the whole female sex. "Woman can be emancipated only when she can take part on a large social scale in production and is engaged in domestic work only to an insignificant degree. And this has become possible only in the big industry of modern times, which not only admits of female labor on a grand scale but even formally demands it. . . ."

Thus the fate of woman and that of socialism are intimately bound up together, as is shown also in Bebel's great work on woman. "Woman and the proletariat," he says, "are both downtrodden." Both are to be set free through the economic development consequent upon the social upheaval brought about by machinery. The problem of woman is reduced to the problem of her capacity for labor. Puissant at the time when techniques were suited to her capabilities, dethroned when she was no longer in a position to exploit them, woman regains in the modern world her equality with man. It is the resistance of the ancient capitalistic paternalism that in most countries prevents the concrete realization of this equality; it will be realized on the day when this resistance is broken, as is the fact already in the Soviet Union, according to Soviet propaganda. And when the socialist society is established throughout the world, there will no longer be men and women, but only workers on a footing of equality.

Although this chain of thought as outlined by Engels marks an advance upon those we have been examining, we find it disappointing—the most important problems are slurred over. The turning-point of all history is the passage from the regime of community ownership to that of private property, and it is in no wise indicated how this could have come about. Engels himself declares in *The Origin of the Family* that "at present we know nothing about it"; not only is he ignorant of the historical details: he does not even suggest any interpretation. Similarly, it is not clear that the institution of private property must necessarily have involved the enslavement of women. Historical materialism takes for granted facts that call for explanation: Engels assumes without discussion the bond of *interest* which ties man to property; but where does this interest, the source of social institutions, have its own source? Thus Engels's account remains superficial, and the truths that he does reveal are seemingly contingent, incidental. The fact is that we cannot plumb their meaning without going beyond the limits of historical materialism. It cannot provide solutions for the problems we have raised, because these concern the whole man and not that abstraction: *Homo œconomicus.*

It would seem clear, for example, that the very concept of personal possession can be comprehensible only with reference to the original condition of the existent. For it to appear, there must have been at first an inclination in the subject to think of himself as basically individual, to assert the autonomy and separateness of his existence. We can see that this affirmation would have remained subjective, inward, without validity as long as the individual lacked the practical means for carrying it out objectively. Without adequate tools, he did not sense at first any power over the world, he felt lost in nature and in the group, passive, threatened, the plaything of obscure forces; he dared think of himself only as identified with the clan: the totem, mana, the earth were group realities. The discovery of bronze enabled man, in the experience of hard and productive labor, to discover himself as creator; dominating nature, he was no longer afraid of it, and in the fact of obstacles overcome he found courage to see himself as an autonomous active force, to achieve self-fulfillment as an individual.[1] But this accomplishment would never have been attained had not man originally willed it so; the lesson of work is not inscribed upon a passive subject: the subject shapes and masters himself in shaping and mastering the land.

On the other hand, the affirmation of the subject's individuality is not enough to explain property: each conscious individual through challenge, struggle, and single combat can endeavor to raise himself

---

[1] Gaston Bachelard in *La Terre et les rêveries de la volonté* makes among others a suggestive study of the blacksmith. He shows how man, through the hammer and the anvil, asserts himself and his individuality. "The blacksmith's instant is an instant at once well marked off and magnified. It promotes the worker to the mastery of time, through the forcefulness of an instant" (p. 142); and farther on: "The man at the forge accepts the challenge of the universe arrayed against him."

to sovereignty. For the challenge to have taken the form of *potlatch* or ceremonial exchange of gifts—that is, of an economic rivalry—and from this point on for first the chief and then the members of the clan to have laid claim to private property, required that there should be in man another original tendency. As we have seen in the preceding chapter, the existent succeeds in finding himself only in estrangement, in alienation; he seeks through the world to find himself in some shape, other than himself, which he makes his own. The clan encounters its own alienated existence in the totem, the mana, the terrain it occupies; and when the individual becomes distinguished from the community, he requires a personal incarnation. The mana becomes individualized in the chief, then in each individual; and at the same time each person tries to appropriate a piece of land, implements, crops. Man finds himself in these goods which are his because he has previously lost himself in them; and it is therefore understandable that he places upon them a value no less fundamental than upon his very life. Thus it is that man's *interest* in his property becomes an intelligible relation. But we see that this cannot be explained through the tool alone: we must grasp in its entirety the attitude of man wielding the tool, an attitude that implies an ontological substructure, a foundation in the nature of his being.

On the same grounds it is impossible to *deduce* the oppression of woman from the institution of private property. Here again the inadequacy of Engels's point of view is obvious. He saw clearly that woman's muscular weakness became a real point of inferiority only in its relation to the bronze and iron tool; but he did not see that the limitations of her capacity for labor constituted in themselves a concrete disadvantage only in a certain perspective. It is because man is a being of transcendence and ambition that he projects new urgencies through every new tool: when he had invented bronze implements, he was no longer content with gardens—he wanted to clear and cultivate vast fields. And it was not from the bronze itself that this desire welled up. Woman's incapacity brought about her ruin because man regarded her in the perspective of his project for enrichment and expansion. And this project is still not enough to explain why she was oppressed; for the division of labor between the sexes could have meant a friendly association. If the original relation between a man and his fellows was exclusively a relation of friendship, we could not account for any type of enslavement; but no, this phenomenon is a result of the imperialism of the human consciousness, seeking always to exercise its sovereignty in objective fashion. If the human consciousness had not included the original category of the Other and an original aspiration to dominate the Other, the invention of the bronze tool could not have caused the oppression of woman.

No more does Engels account for the peculiar nature of this oppression. He tried to reduce the antagonism of the sexes to class conflict, but he was halfhearted in the attempt; the thesis is simply untenable. It is true that division of labor according to sex and the consequent oppression bring to mind in some ways the division of society by classes, but it is impossible to confuse the two. For one thing, there is no biological basis for the separation of classes. Again, the slave in his toil is conscious of himself as opposed to his master; and the proletariat has always put its condition to the test in revolt, thereby going back to essentials and constituting a threat to its exploiters. And what it has aimed at is its own disappearance as a class. I have pointed out in the Introduction how different woman's situation is, particularly on account of the community of life and interests which entails her solidarity with man, and also because he finds in her an accomplice; no desire for revolution dwells within her, nor any thought of her own disappearance as a sex—all she asks is that certain sequels of sexual differentiation be abolished.

What is still more serious, woman cannot in good faith be regarded simply as a worker; for her reproductive function is as important as her productive capacity, no less in the social economy than in the individual life. In some periods, indeed, it is more useful to produce offspring than to plow the soil. Engels slighted the problem, simply remarking that the socialist community would abolish the family— certainly an abstract solution. We know how often and how radically Soviet Russia has had to change its policy on the family according to the varying relation between the immediate needs of production and those of repopulation. But for that matter, to do away with the family is not necessarily to emancipate woman. Such examples as Sparta and the Nazi regime prove that she can be none the less oppressed by the males, for all her direct attachment to the State.

A truly socialist ethics, concerned to uphold justice without suppressing liberty and to impose duties upon individuals without abolishing individuality, will find most embarrassing the problems posed by the condition of woman. It is impossible simply to equate gestation with a *task*, a piece of work, or with a *service*, such as military service. Woman's life is more seriously broken in upon by a demand for children than by regulation of the citizen's employment—no state has ever ventured to establish obligatory copulation. In the sexual act and in maternity not only time and strength but also essential values are involved for woman. Rationalist materialism tries in vain to disregard this dramatic aspect of sexuality; for it is impossible to bring the sexual instinct under a code of regulations. Indeed, as Freud said, it is not sure that it does not bear within itself a denial of its own satisfaction. What is certain is that it does not permit of integration with the social, because there is in eroticism a revolt of the instant against time, of the individual against the universal. In proposing to direct and exploit it, there is risk of killing it, for it is impossible to deal at will with living spontaneity as one deals at will with inert matter; and no more can it be obtained by force, as a privilege may be.

There is no way of directly compelling woman to bring forth: all that can be done is to put her in a situation where maternity is for her the sole outcome—the law or the mores enjoin marriage, birth control and abortion are prohibited, divorce is forbidden. These ancient patriarchal restraints are just what Soviet Russia has brought back today; Russia has revived the paternalistic concepts of marriage. And in doing so, she has been induced to ask woman once more to make of herself an erotic object: in a recent pronouncement female Soviet citizens were requested to pay careful attention to their garb, to use make-up, to employ the arts of coquetry in holding their husbands and fanning the flame of desire. As this case shows clearly, it is impossible to regard woman simply as a productive force: she is for man a sexual partner, a reproducer, an erotic object—an Other through whom he seeks himself. In vain have the totalitarian or authoritative regimes with one accord prohibited psychoanalysis and declared that individual, personal drama is out of order for citizens loyally integrated with the community; the erotic experience remains one in which generality is always regained by an individuality. And for a democratic socialism in which classes are abolished but not individuals, the question of individual destiny would keep all its importance—and hence sexual differentiation would keep all its importance. The sexual relation that joins woman to man is not the same as that which he bears to her; and the bond that unites her to the child is *sui generis*, unique. She was not created by the bronze tool alone; and the machine alone will not abolish her. To claim for her every right, every chance to be an all-round human being does not mean that we should be blind to her peculiar situation. And in order to comprehend that situation we must look beyond the historical materialism that perceives in man and woman no more than economic units.

So it is that we reject for the same reasons both the sexual monism of Freud and the economic monism of Engels. A psychoanalyst will interpret all social claims of woman as phenomena of the "masculine protest"; for the Marxist, on the contrary, her sexuality only expresses her economic situation in more or less complex, roundabout fashion. But the categories of "clitorid" and "vaginal," like the categories of "bourgeois" or "proletarian," are equally inadequate to encompass a concrete woman. Underlying all individual drama, as it underlies the economic history of mankind, there is an existentialist foundation that alone enables us to understand in its unity that particular form of being which we call a human life. The virtue of Freudianism derives from the fact that the existent is a body: what he experiences as a body confronted by other bodies expresses his existential situation concretely. Similarly, what is true in the Marxian thesis is that the ontological aspirations—the projects for becoming— of the existent take concrete form according to the material possibilities offered, especially those opened up by technological advances. But unless they are integrated into the totality of human reality, sexuality and technology alone can explain nothing. That is why in Freud the prohibitions of the superego and the drives of the ego appear to be contingent, and why in Engels's account of the history of the family the most important developments seem to arise according to the caprices of mysterious fortune. In our attempt to discover woman we shall not reject certain contributions of biology, of psychoanalysis, and of historical materialism; but we shall hold that the body, the sexual life, and the resources of technology exist concretely for man only in so far as he grasps them in the total perspective of his existence. The value of muscular strength, of the phallus, of the tool can be defined only in a world of values; it is determined by the basic project through which the existent seeks transcendence.

PART II

HISTORY

CHAPTER IV

The Nomads

THIS has always been a man's world; and none of the reasons hitherto brought forward in explanation of this fact has seemed adequate. But we shall be able to understand how the hierarchy of the sexes was established by reviewing the data of prehistoric research and ethnography in the light of existentialist philosophy. I have already stated that when two human categories are together, each aspires to impose its sovereignty upon the other. If both are able to resist this imposition, there is created between them a reciprocal relation, sometimes in enmity, sometimes in amity, always in a state of tension. If one of the two is in some way privileged, has some advantage, this one prevails over the other and undertakes to keep it in subjection. It is therefore understandable that man would wish to dominate woman; but what advantage has enabled him to carry out his will?

The accounts of the primitive forms of human society provided by ethnographers are extremely contradictory, the more so as they are better informed and less systematized. It is peculiarly difficult to form an idea of woman's situation in the pre-agricultural period. We do not even know whether woman's musculature or her respiratory apparatus, under conditions different from those of today, were not as well developed as in man. She had hard work to do, and in particular it was she who carried the burdens. This last fact is of doubtful significance; it is likely that if she was assigned this function, it was because a man kept his hands free on the trail in order to defend himself against possible aggressors, animal or human; his role was the more dangerous and the one that demanded more vigor. It would appear, nevertheless, that in many cases the women were strong and tough enough to take part in the warriors' expeditions. We need recall only the tales of Herodotus and the more recent accounts of the amazons of Dahomey to realize that woman has shared in warfare—and with no less ferocity and cruelty than man; but even so, man's superior strength must have been of tremendous importance in the age of the club and the wild beast. In any case, however strong the women were, the bondage of reproduction was a terrible handicap in the struggle against a hostile world. Pregnancy, childbirth, and menstruation reduced their capacity for work and made them at times wholly dependent upon the men for protection and food. As there was obviously no birth control, and as nature failed to provide women with sterile periods like other mammalian females, closely spaced maternities must have absorbed most of their strength and their time, so that they were incapable of providing for the children they brought into the world. Here we have a first fact heavily freighted with consequences: the early days of the human species were difficult; the gathering, hunting, and fishing peoples got only meager products from the soil and those with great effort; too many children were born for the group's resources; the extravagant fertility of woman prevented her from active participation in the increase of these resources while she created new needs to an indefinite extent. Necessary as she was for the perpetuation of the species, she perpetuated it too generously, and so it was man who had to assure equilibrium between reproduction and production. Even in times when humanity most needed births, when maternity was most venerated, manual labor was the primary necessity, and woman was never permitted to take first place. The primitive hordes had no permanence in property or territory, and hence set no store by posterity; children were for them a burden, not a prized possession. Infanticide was common among the nomads, and many of the newborn that escaped massacre died from lack of care in the general state of indifference.

The woman who gave birth, therefore, did not know the pride of creation; she felt herself the plaything of obscure forces, and the painful ordeal of childbirth seemed a useless or even troublesome accident. But in any case giving birth and suckling are not *activities*, they are natural functions; no project is involved; and that is why woman found in them no reason for a lofty affirmation of her existence—she submitted passively to her biologic fate. The domestic labors that fell to her lot because they were reconcilable with the cares of maternity imprisoned her in repetition and immanence;[1] they were repeated from day to day in an identical form, which was perpetuated almost without change from century to century; they produced nothing new.

Man's case was radically different; he furnished support for the group, not in the manner of worker bees by a simple vital process, through biological behavior, but by means of acts that transcended his animal nature. *Homo faber* has from the beginning of time been an inventor: the stick and the club with which he armed himself to knock down fruits and to slaughter animals became forthwith instruments for enlarging his grasp upon the world. He did not limit himself to bringing home the fish he caught in the sea: first he had to conquer the watery realm by means of the dugout canoe fashioned from a tree-trunk; to get at the riches of the world he annexed the world itself. In this activity he put his power to the test; he set up goals and opened up roads toward them; in brief, he found self-realization as an existent. To maintain, he created; he burst out of the present, he opened the future. This is the reason why fishing and hunting expeditions had a sacred character. Their successes were celebrated with festivals and triumphs, and therein man gave recognition to his human estate. Today he still manifests this pride when he has built a dam or a skyscraper or an atomic pile. He has worked not merely to conserve the world as given; he has broken through its frontiers, he has laid down the foundations of a new future.

Early man's activity had another dimension that gave it supreme dignity: it was often dangerous. If blood were but a nourishing fluid, it would be valued no higher than milk; but the hunter was no

---

[1] This word, frequently used by the author, always signifies, as here, the opposite or negation of transcendence, such as confinement or restriction to a narrow round of uncreative and repetitious duties; it is in contrast to the freedom to engage in projects of ever widening scope that marks the untrammeled existent.—TR.

butcher, for in the struggle against wild animals he ran grave risks. The warrior put his life in jeopardy to elevate the prestige of the horde, the clan to which he belonged. And in this he proved dramatically that life is not the supreme value for man, but on the contrary that it should be made to serve ends more important than itself. The worst curse that was laid upon woman was that she should be excluded from these warlike forays. For it is not in giving life but in risking life that man is raised above the animal; that is why superiority has been accorded in humanity not to the sex that brings forth but to that which kills.

Here we have the key to the whole mystery. On the biological level a species is maintained only by creating itself anew; but this creation results only in repeating the same Life in more individuals. But man assures the repetition of Life while transcending Life through Existence; by this transcendence he creates values that deprive pure repetition of all value. In the animal, the freedom and variety of male activities are vain because no project is involved. Except for his service to the species, what he does is immaterial. Whereas in serving the species, the human male also remodels the face of the earth, he creates new instruments, he invents, he shapes the future. In setting himself up as sovereign, he is supported by the complicity of woman herself. For she, too, is an existent, she feels the urge to surpass, and her project is not mere repetition but transcendence toward a different future—in her heart of hearts she finds confirmation of the masculine pretensions. She joins the men in the festivals that celebrate the successes and the victories of the males. Her misfortune is to have been biologically destined for the repetition of Life, when even in her own view Life does not carry within itself its reasons for being, reasons that are more important than the life itself.

Certain passages in the argument employed by Hegel in defining the relation of master to slave apply much better to the relation of man to woman. The advantage of the master, he says, comes from his affirmation of Spirit as against Life through the fact that he risks his own life; but in fact the conquered slave has known this same risk. Whereas woman is basically an existent who gives Life and does not risk *her* life; between her and the male there has been no combat. Hegel's definition would seem to apply especially well to her. He says: "The other consciousness is the dependent consciousness for whom the essential reality is the animal type of life; that is to say, a mode of living bestowed by another entity." But this relation is to be distinguished from the relation of subjugation because woman also aspires to and recognizes the values that are concretely attained by the male. He it is who opens up the future to which she also reaches out. In truth women have never set up female values in opposition to male values; it is man who, desirous of maintaining masculine prerogatives, has invented that divergence. Men have presumed to create a feminine domain—the kingdom of life, of immanence—only in order to lock up women therein. But it is regardless of sex that the existent seeks self-justification through transcendence—the very submission of women is proof of that statement. What they demand today is to be recognized as existents by the same right as men and not to subordinate existence to life, the human being to its animality.

An existentialist perspective has enabled us, then, to understand how the biological and economic condition of the primitive horde must have led to male supremacy. The female, to a greater extent than the male, is the prey of the species; and the human race has always sought to escape its specific destiny. The support of life became for man an activity and a project through the invention of the tool; but in maternity woman remained closely bound to her body, like an animal. It is because humanity calls itself in question in the matter of living—that is to say, values the reasons for living above mere life—that, confronting woman, man assumes mastery. Man's design is not to repeat himself in time: it is to take control of the instant and mold the future. It is male activity that in creating values has made of existence itself a value; this activity has prevailed over the confused forces of life; it has subdued Nature and Woman. We must now see how this situation has been perpetuated and how it has evolved through the ages. What place has humanity made for this portion of itself which, while included within it, is defined as the Other? What rights have been conceded to it? How have men defined it?

CHAPTER V

Early Tillers of the Soil

WE have just seen that woman's lot was a very hard one in the primitive horde, and doubtless there was no great effort made to compensate for the cruel disadvantages that handicapped woman. But neither was woman put upon and bullied as happened later under paternalistic auspices. No institution ratified the inequality of the sexes; indeed, there were no institutions—no property, no inheritance, no jurisprudence. Religion was neuter: worship was offered to some asexual totem.

Institutions and the law appeared when the nomads settled down on the land and became agriculturists. Man no longer limited himself to harsh combat against hostile forces; he began to express himself through the shape he imposed upon the world, to think of the world and of himself. At this point the sexual differentiation was reflected in the structure of the human group, and it took on a special form. In agricultural communities woman was often clothed in an extraordinary prestige. This prestige is to be explained essentially by the quite new importance that the child acquired in a civilization based on working the soil. In settling down on a certain territory, men established ownership of it, and property appeared in a collectivized form. This property required that its possessors provide a posterity, and maternity became a sacred function.

Many tribes lived under a communal regime, but this does not mean that the women belonged to all the men in common—it is hardly held today that promiscuity was ever the general practice—but men and women experienced religious, social, and economic existence only as a group: their individuality remained a purely biological fact. Marriage, whatever its form—monogamy, polygamy, or polyandry—was only a secular accident, creating no mystical tie. It involved no servitude for the wife, for she was still integrated with her clan. The whole body of a clan, unified under a single totem, possessed in a mystical sense a single mana, materially the common enjoyment of a single territory. According to the process of alienation I have already discussed, the clan found self-awareness in this territory under an objective and concrete form; through the permanence of the land, therefore, the clan became a real unity, whose identity persisted through the passage of time.

This existentialist position alone enables us to understand the identification that has existed up to the present time between the clan, the tribe, or the family, and property. In place of the outlook of the nomadic tribes, living only for the moment, the agricultural community substituted the concept of a life rooted in the past and connected with the future. Veneration was accorded to the totemic ancestor who gave his name to the members of the clan; and the clan took a profound interest in its own descendants, for it would achieve survival through the land that it would bequeath to them and that they would exploit. The community sensed its unity and desired a continued existence beyond the present; it recognized itself in its children, recognized them as its own; and in them it found fulfillment and transcendence.

Now, many primitive peoples were ignorant of the part taken by the father in the procreation of children (and in a few cases this seems to be true even today); they regarded children as the reincarnation of ancestral spirits that hover about certain trees or rocks, in certain sacred places, and come down and enter the bodies of women. Sometimes it was held that the woman ought not to be a virgin, so as to permit this infiltration; but other peoples believed that it could occur as well through the nostrils or the mouth. In any case, defloration was secondary in the matter, and for reasons of a mystical nature it was rarely the prerogative of the husband.

But the mother was obviously necessary for the birth of the child; she it was who protected and nourished the germ within her body, and therefore it was through her that the life of the clan in the visible world was propagated. Thus she came to play a role of the first importance. Very often the children belonged to their mother's clan, carried its name, and shared its rights and privileges, particularly in the use of the land held by the clan. Communal property was handed down by the women: through them ownership in the fields and harvests was assured to members of the clan, and conversely these members were destined through their mothers for this or that domain. We may suppose, then, that in a mystical sense the earth belonged to the women: they had a hold, at once religious and legal, upon the

land and its fruits. The tie between woman and land was still closer
than that of ownership, for the matrilineal regime was characterized
by a veritable assimilation of woman to the earth; in both the permanence of life—which is essentially generation—was accomplished
through the reproduction of its individual embodiments, its avatars.

Among the nomads procreation seemed hardly more than accidental, and the wealth of the soil remained unknown; but the husbandman marveled at the mystery of the fecundity that burgeoned in his
furrows and in the maternal body; he realized that he had been engendered like the cattle and the crops, he wanted his clan to engender
other men who would perpetuate it while perpetuating the fertility
of the fields; all nature seemed to him like a mother: the land is
woman and in woman abide the same dark powers as in the earth.[1]
It was for this reason in part that agricultural labor was entrusted to
woman; able to summon ancestral spirits into her body, she would
also have power to cause fruits and grain to spring up from the
planted fields. In both cases there was no question of a creative act,
but of a magic conjuration. At this stage man no longer limited himself to gathering the products of the soil, but he did not as yet know
his power. He stood hesitant between technique and magic, feeling
himself passive, dependent upon Nature, which dealt out life and
death at random. To be sure, he realized more or less clearly the
effectiveness of the sexual act and of the techniques by which he
brought the land under cultivation. Yet children and crops seemed
none the less to be gifts of the gods, and the mysterious emanations
from the female body were believed to bring into this world the riches
latent in the mysterious sources of life.

Such beliefs are still deep-rooted and are alive today in many Indian, Australian, and Polynesian tribes. In some a sterile woman is
considered dangerous for the garden, in others it is thought that the
harvest will be more abundant if it is gathered by a pregnant woman;
in India naked women formerly pushed the plow around the field at
night, and so on. These beliefs and customs have always taken on all
the more importance because they harmonized with the practical interests of the community. Maternity dooms woman to a sedentary
existence, and so it is natural that she remain at the hearth while man
hunts, goes fishing, and makes war. But among primitive peoples the

---

[1] "Hail, Earth, mother of men, may you be fertile in the embrace of God and
may you be filled with fruits for man's use," says an old Anglo-Saxon incantation.

gardens were small and located within the village limits, and their cultivation was a domestic task; the use of Stone Age tools demanded no great strength. Economics and religion were at one in leaving agricultural labor to the women. As domestic industry developed, it also was their lot: they wove mattings and blankets and they made pottery. Frequently they took charge of barter; commerce was in their hands. Through them, therefore, the life of the clan was maintained and extended; children, flocks, crops, utensils, all the prosperity of the group, depended on their labor and their magic powers—they were the soul of the community. Such powers inspired in men a respect mingled with fear, which was reflected in their worship. In woman was to be summed up the whole of alien Nature.

As I have already said, man never thinks of himself without thinking of the Other; he views the world under the sign of duality, which is not in the first place sexual in character. But being different from man, who sets himself up as the same, it is naturally to the category of the Other that woman is consigned; the Other includes woman. At first she is not of sufficient importance to incarnate the Other all by herself, and so a subdivision is apparent at the heart of the Other: in the ancient cosmogonies a single element often has an incarnation that is at once male and female; thus the Ocean (male) and the Sea (feminine) are for the ancient Babylonians the double incarnation of cosmic chaos. When woman's role enlarges, she comes to represent almost in its entirety the region of the Other. Then appear those feminine divinities through whom the idea of fecundity is worshipped. At Susa was found the oldest figure of the Great Goddess, the Great Mother with long robe and high coiffure whom in other statues we see crowned with towers. The excavations in Crete have yielded several such images. She is at times steatopygous and crouching, at times slender and standing erect, sometimes dressed and often naked, her arms pressed beneath her swelling breasts. She is the queen of heaven, a dove her symbol; she is also the empress of hell, whence she crawls forth, symbolized in a serpent. She is made manifest in the mountains and the woods, on the sea, and in springs of water. Everywhere she creates life; if she kills, she also revives the dead. Capricious, luxurious, cruel as Nature, at once propitious and fearsome, she reigns over all the Ægean Archipelago, over Phrygia, Syria, Anatolia, over all western Asia. She is called Ishtar in Babylonia, Astarte among Semitic peoples, and Gæa, Rhea, or Cybele by the Greeks. In Egypt we come upon her under the form of Isis. Male divinities are subordinated to her.

Supreme idol in the far realms of heaven and hell, woman is on earth surrounded with taboos like all sacred beings, she is herself taboo; because of the powers she holds, she is looked upon as a magician, a sorceress. She is invoked in prayers, sometimes she becomes a priestess as with the Druids among the ancient Celts. In certain instances she takes part in tribal government, and may even become sole ruler. These remote ages have bequeathed to us no literature. But the great patriarchal epochs preserved in their mythology, their monuments, and their traditions the memory of the times when woman occupied a very lofty situation. From the feminine point of view, the Brahmanic epoch shows regression from that of the *Rig-Veda*, and the latter from that of the preceding primitive stage. Bedouin women of the pre-Islamic period enjoyed a status quite superior to that assigned them by the Koran. The great figures of Niobe, of Medea, evoke an era in which mothers took pride in their children, regarding them as treasures peculiarly their own. And in Homer's poems Andromache and Hecuba had an importance that classic Greece no longer attributed to women hidden in the shadow of the gynæceum.

These facts have led to the supposition that in primitive times a veritable reign of women existed: the matriarchy. It was this hypothesis, proposed by Bachofen, that Engels adopted, regarding the passage from the matriarchate to the patriarchate as "the great historical defeat of the feminine sex." But in truth that Golden Age of Woman is only a myth. To say that woman was the *Other* is to say that there did not exist between the sexes a reciprocal relation: Earth, Mother, Goddess—she was no fellow creature in man's eyes; it was *beyond* the human realm that her power was affirmed, and she was therefore *outside of* that realm. Society has always been male; political power has always been in the hands of men. "Public or simply social authority always belongs to men," declares Lévi-Strauss at the end of his study of primitive societies.

For the male it is always another male who is the fellow being, the other who is also the same, with whom reciprocal relations are established. The duality that appears within societies under one form or another opposes a group of men to a group of men; women constitute a part of the property which each of these groups possesses and which is a medium of exchange between them. The mistake has come from a confusion of two forms of alterity or otherness, which are mutually exclusive in point of fact. To the precise degree in which woman is regarded as the absolute Other—that is to say, whatever her magic powers, as the inessential—it is to that degree impossible to consider her as another subject.[2] Women, therefore, have never composed a separate group set up *on its own account* over against the male grouping. They have never entered into a direct and autonomous relation with the men. "The reciprocal bond basic to marriage is not set up between men and women, but between men and men by means of women, who are only the principal occasion for it," says Lévi-Strauss.[3] The actual condition of woman has not been affected by the type of filiation (mode of tracing descent) that prevails in the society to which she belongs; whether the system be patrilineal, matrilineal, bilateral, or nondifferentiated (the nondifferentiation never being strictly adhered to), she is always under the guardianship of the males. The only question is whether the woman after marriage will remain subject to the authority of her father or of her older brother—an authority that will extend also to her children—or whether she will become subject to that of her husband. "Woman, in herself, is never more than the symbol of her line . . . matrilineal filiation is but the authority of the woman's father or brother, which extends back to the brother's village," to quote Lévi-Strauss again. She is only the intermediary of authority, not the one who holds it. The fact is that the relations of two groups of men are defined by the system of filiation, and not the relation between the two sexes.

In practice the actual condition of woman is not bound up with this or that type of authority. It may happen that in the matrilineal system she has a very high position; still, we must be careful to note that the presence of a woman chief or queen at the head of a tribe by no means signifies that women are sovereign therein: the accession to the throne of Catherine the Great in no way modified the

---

[2] This discrimination, as we shall see, has been perpetuated. The epochs that have regarded woman as the Other are those which refuse most harshly to integrate her with society by right of being human. Today she can become an *other* who is also an equal only in losing her mystic aura. The antifeminists have always played upon this equivocation. They are glad to exalt woman as the *Other* in such a manner as to make her alterity absolute, irreducible, and to deny her access to the human *Mitsein.*

[3] *Les Structures élémentaires de la parenté.*

lot of the Russian peasant women; and it is no less frequent for her to live in an abject condition. Furthermore, the cases are very rare in which the wife remains living with her clan, her husband being permitted only hasty, even clandestine visits. Almost always she goes away to live under her husband's roof, a fact that is enough to show the primacy of the male. "Behind the shifting modes of filiation," writes Lévi-Strauss, "the persistence of the patrilocal residence bears witness to the fundamentally asymmetrical relation between the sexes that marks human society." Since woman keeps her children with her, the result is that the territorial organization of the tribe does not correspond with its totemic organization—the former is dependent on circumstances, contingent; the latter is rigorously established. But practically the first has the more importance, for the place where people live and work counts more than their mystical connection.

In the more widespread transitional regimes there are two kinds of authority, the one religious, the other based on the occupation and working of the land, which interlock. For being only a secular institution, marriage has no less a great social importance, and the conjugal family, although stripped of religious significance, has a vigorous life on the human plane. Even in groups where great sexual freedom exists, it is proper for the woman who brings a child into the world to be married; she is unable to form an autonomous group, alone with her progeny. And the religious protection of her brother is insufficient: the presence of a spouse is required. He often has heavy responsibilities in regard to his children. They do not belong to his clan, but nevertheless it is he who must provide for them and bring them up. Between husband and wife, father and son, are formed bonds of cohabitation, of work, of common interests, of affection. The relations between this secular family and the totemic clan are highly complex, as is attested by the diversity of marriage rites. Originally the husband bought a wife from a strange clan, or at least there was an exchange of valuables between one clan and the other, the first handing over one of its members, the second furnishing cattle, fruits, or labor in return. But since the husband assumed responsibility for his wife and her children, he might also receive remuneration from the bride's brothers.

The balance between mystical and economic realities is an unstable one. A man is frequently much more strongly attached to his son than to his nephews; he will prefer to assert himself as father when he is in a position to do so. And this is why every society tends to assume a patriarchal form when man's evolution brings him to the point of self-awareness and the imposition of his will. But it is important to underline the statement that even when he was still perplexed before the mysteries of Life, of Nature, and of Woman, he was never without his power; when, terrified by the dangerous magic of woman, he sets her up as the essential, it is he who poses her as such and thus he really acts as the essential in this voluntary alienation. In spite of the fecund powers that pervade her, man remains woman's master as he is the master of the fertile earth; she is fated to be subjected, owned, exploited like the Nature whose magical fertility she embodies. The prestige she enjoys in men's eyes is bestowed by them; they kneel before the Other, they worship the Goddess Mother. But however puissant she may thus appear, it is only through the conceptions of the male mind that she is apprehended as such.

All the idols made by man, however terrifying they may be, are in point of fact subordinate to him, and that is why he will always have it in his power to destroy them. In primitive societies that subordination is not recognized and openly asserted, but it has immediate existence, in the nature of the case; and it will readily be made use of once man acquires clearer self-consciousness, once he dares to assert himself and offer resistance. And as a matter of fact, even when man felt himself as something given and passive, subject to the accidents of sun and rain, he was also finding fulfillment through transcendence, through project; spirit and will were already asserting themselves against the confusedness and the fortuity of life.

The totemic ancestor, whose multiple incarnations woman assumed, was more or less distinctly a male principle under its animal or arboreal name; woman perpetuated its existence in the flesh, but her role was only nourishing, never creative. In no domain whatever did she create; she maintained the life of the tribe by giving it children and bread, nothing more. She remained doomed to immanence, incarnating only the static aspect of society, closed in upon itself. Whereas man went on monopolizing the functions which threw open that society toward nature and toward the rest of humanity. The only employments worthy of him were war, hunting, fishing; he made conquest of foreign booty and bestowed it on the tribe; war, hunting, and fishing represented an expansion of existence, its projection toward the world. The male remained alone the incarnation of transcendence. He did not as yet have the practical means for wholly dominating Woman-Earth; as yet he did not dare to stand up against her—but already he desired to break away from her.

In my view we must seek in this desire the deep-seated reason for the celebrated custom of exogamy, which is widespread among matrilineal societies. Even if man is ignorant of his part in procreation, marriage is for him a matter of vast importance: through marriage he arrives at the dignity of man's estate, and a plot of land becomes his. He is bound to the clan through his mother, through her to his ancestors and to all that makes up his very substance; but in all his secular functions, in work, in marriage, he aspires to escape from this circle, to assert transcendence over immanence, to open up a future different from the past in which his roots are sunk. The prohibition of incest takes different forms according to the types of relationship recognized in different societies, but from primitive times to our day it keeps the same meaning: what man desires to possess is that which he *is not*, he seeks union with what appears to be *Other* than himself. The wife, therefore, should not share in the mana of the husband, she should be a stranger to him and hence a stranger to his clan. Primitive marriage is sometimes based on an abduction, real or symbolic, and surely violence done upon another is the most obvious affirmation of that one's alterity. In taking his wife by force the warrior demonstrates that he is capable of annexing the wealth of strangers and of bursting the bounds of the destiny assigned to him by birth. Wife-purchase under its various forms—payment of tribute, giving of service—if less dramatic, is of the same import.[4]

---

[4] We find in the thesis of Lévi-Strauss, already cited, confirmation of this idea, in somewhat different form. It appears from his study that the prohibition of incest is not at all the primal fact underlying exogamy, but rather that it reflects in negative form a positive desire for exogamy. There is no immediate reason why a woman should be unfit for intercourse with the men of her own clan; but it is socially useful for her to be a part of the exchanges through which each clan establishes reciprocal relations with another, instead of keeping to itself. "Exogamy has a value that is less negative than positive . . . it forbids endogamy . . . not certainly because of any biological danger inherent in consanguineous marriage but because social benefit results from exogamous marriage." The group should not squander for private purposes the women who constitute one of its possessions, but should use them as a means of communication; if marriage with a woman of the clan is forbidden, "the only reason is that she is *the same* when she should (and therefore can) become *the other*. . . . Women sold into slavery may be the same as those originally offered for exchange in primitive times. All that is required in

Little by little man has acted upon his experience, and in his symbolic representations, as in his practical life, it is the male principle that has triumphed. Spirit has prevailed over Life, transcendence over immanence, technique over magic, and reason over superstition. The devaluation of woman represents a necessary stage in the history of humanity, for it is not upon her positive value but upon man's weakness that her prestige is founded. In woman are incarnated the disturbing mysteries of nature, and man escapes her hold when he frees himself from nature. It is the advance from stone to bronze that enables him through his labor to gain mastery of the soil and to master himself. The husbandman is subject to the hazards of the soil, of the germination of seeds, of the seasons; he is passive, he prays, he waits; that is why totemic spirits once thronged the world of man; the peasant is subject to the caprices of these powers round about him. The workman, on the contrary, shapes his tool after his own design; with his hands he forms it according to his project; confronting passive nature, he overcomes her resistance and asserts his sovereign will. If he quickens his strokes on the anvil, he finishes his tool sooner, whereas nothing can hasten the ripening of grain. He comes to realize his responsibility for what he is making: his skill or clumsiness will make or break it; careful, clever, he develops his skill to a point of perfection in which he takes pride: his success depends not upon the favor of the gods but upon himself. He challenges his fellows, he is elated with success. And if he still gives some place to rituals, he feels that exact techniques are much more important; mystical values take second rank and practical interests the first. He is not fully liberated from the gods. But he sets them apart from himself as he separates himself from them; he relegates them to their Olympian heaven and keeps the terrestrial domain to himself. The great god Pan begins to fade when the first hammer blow resounds and the reign of man begins.

Man learns his power. In the relation of his creative arm to the fabricated object he experiences causation: planted grain may or may not germinate, but metal always reacts in the same way to fire, to tempering, to mechanical treatment. This world of tools could be embraced within clear concepts: rational thought, logic, and mathematics could now appear. The whole concept of the universe is over-

---

either case is the *mark of otherness*, which is the result of a certain position in the social structure and not an innate characteristic."

thrown. The religion of woman was bound to the reign of agriculture, the reign of irreducible duration, of contingency, of chance, of waiting, of mystery; the reign of *Homo faber* is the reign of time manageable as space, of necessary consequences, of the project, of action, of reason. Even when he has to do with the land, he will henceforth have to do with it as workman; he discovers that the soil can be fertilized, that it is good to let it lie fallow, that such and such seeds must be treated in such and such a fashion. It is he who makes the crops grow; he digs canals, he irrigates or drains the land, he lays out roads, he builds temples: he creates a new world.

The peoples who have remained under the thumb of the goddess mother, those who have retained the matrilineal regime, are also those who are arrested at a primitive stage of civilization. Woman was venerated only to the degree that man made himself the slave of his own fears, a party to his own powerlessness: it was in terror and not in love that he worshipped her. He could achieve his destiny only as he began by dethroning her.[5] From then on, it was to be the male principle of creative force, of light, of intelligence, of order, that he would recognize as sovereign. By the side of the goddess mother arises a god, son or lover, who is still subordinate to her but who resembles her trait for trait and is associated with her. He also incarnates a principle of fecundity, appearing as a bull, the Minotaur, the Nile fertilizing the Egyptian lowlands. He dies in autumn and is reborn in the spring, after the wife mother, invulnerable but disconsolate, has devoted her powers to finding his body and bringing it back to life. We see this couple first appearing in Crete, and we find it again on every Mediterranean shore: in Egypt it is Isis and Horus, Astarte and Adonis in Phœnicia, Cybele and Attis in Asia Minor, and in Hellenic Greece it is Rhea and Zeus.

And then the Great Mother was dethroned. In Egypt, where the situation of woman continues to be exceptionally favorable, Nut, who incarnates the sky, and Isis, the fertile soil, spouse of the Nile, and Osiris remain goddesses of extreme importance; but nevertheless it is Ra, god of the sun, of light, and of virile force, who is supreme. In Babylon Ishtar is no more than wife of Bel-Marduk. He it is who

---

[5] Certainly this condition is necessary, but it is not the whole story: there are patrilineal cultures that have congealed at a primitive stage; others, like that of the Mayas, that have crumbled. There is no absolute superiority or inferiority between societies of maternal or paternal authority, but only the latter have evolved technically and ideologically.

creates all things and assures their harmony. The god of the Semites is male. When Zeus comes to power on high, Gæa, Rhea, and Cybele must abdicate. In Demeter there remains only a divinity of secondary rank, but still imposing. The Vedic gods have spouses, but the latter have no such claim to worship as the former. The Roman Jupiter knows no equal.[6]

Thus the triumph of the patriarchate was neither a matter of chance nor the result of violent revolution. From humanity's beginnings, their biological advantage has enabled the males to affirm their status as sole and sovereign subjects; they have never abdicated this position; they once relinquished a part of their independent existence to Nature and to Woman; but afterward they won it back. Condemned to play the part of the Other, woman was also condemned to hold only uncertain power: slave or idol, it was never she who chose her lot. "Men make the gods; women worship them," as Frazer has said; men indeed decide whether their supreme divinities shall be females or males; woman's place in society is always that which men assign to her; at no time has she ever imposed her own law.

Perhaps, however, if productive work had remained within her strength, woman would have accomplished *with* man the conquest of nature; the human species would have made its stand against the gods through both males and females; but woman was unable to avail herself of the promised benefits of the tool. Engels gave only an incomplete explanation for her degradation: it is not enough to say that the invention of bronze and iron profoundly disturbed the equilibrium of the forces of production and that thus the inferior position of woman was brought about; this inferiority is not sufficient in itself to explain the oppression that woman has suffered. What was unfortunate for her was that while not becoming a fellow workman with the laborer, she was also excluded from the human *Mitsein*. The fact that woman is weak and of inferior productive capacity does not explain this exclusion; it is because she did not share his way of

---

[6] It is of interest to note (according to Begouen, *Journal de Psychologie*, 1934) that in the Aurignacian period one comes across numerous statuettes of women with sexual features emphasized by exaggeration: they are notable for their plump contours and for the importance given to the vulva. Moreover, one finds in the caves also isolated vulvas, coarsely carved. In the Solutrean and Magdalenian these figures disappear. In the Aurignacian, masculine statuettes are very rare and there are no representations of the male organ. In the Magdalenian one still finds a few vulvas represented and, in contrast, a large number of phalli.

working and thinking, because she remained in bondage to life's mysterious processes, that the male did not recognize in her a being like himself. Since he did not accept her, since she seemed in his eyes to have the aspect of the *other*, man could not be otherwise than her oppressor. The male will to power and expansion made of woman's incapacity a curse.

Man wished to exhaust the new possibilities opened up by the new techniques: he resorted to a servile labor force, he reduced his fellow man to slavery. The work of the slaves being much more effective than what woman could do, she lost the economic role she had played in the tribe. And in his relation to the slave the master found a much more radical confirmation of his sovereignty than in the limited authority he held over woman. Being venerated and feared because of her fecundity, being *other* than man and sharing the disturbing character of the *other*, woman in a way held man in dependence upon her, while being at the same time dependent upon him; the reciprocity of the master-slave relation was what she *actually* enjoyed, and through that fact she escaped slavery. But the slave was protected by no taboo, he was nothing but a man in servitude, not different but inferior: the dialectical expression of his relation to his master was to take centuries to come into existence. In organized patriarchal society the slave was only a beast of burden with a human face; the master exercised tyrannical authority, which exalted his pride—and he turned against woman. Everything he gained he gained against her; the more powerful he became, the more she declined.

In particular, when he became owner of the land,[7] he claimed also ownership of woman. Formerly he was *possessed* by the mana, by the land; now he *has* a soul, *owns* certain lands; freed from Woman, he now demands for himself a woman and a posterity. He wants the work of the family, which he uses to improve his fields, to be totally *his*, and this means that the workers must belong to him: so he enslaves his wife and children. He needs heirs, in whom his earthly life will be prolonged because he hands down his property to them, and who will perform for him after his death the rites and observances needed for the repose of his soul. The cult of domestic gods is superposed upon the organization of private property, and the inheritor fulfills a function at once economic and mystic. Thus from the day when agriculture ceased to be an essentially magic operation and first

[7] See Part I, Ch. iii.

became creative labor, man realized that he was a generative force; he laid claim to his children and to his crops simultaneously.[8]

In primitive times there was no more important ideological revolution than that which replaced matrilineal with patrilineal descent; thereafter the mother fell to the rank of nurse and servant, while authority and rights belonged to the father, who handed them on to his descendants. Man's necessary part in procreation was realized, but beyond this it was affirmed that only the father engenders, the mother merely nourishes the germ received into her body, as Æschylus says in the *Eumenides*. Aristotle states that woman is only matter, whereas movement, the male principle, is "better and more divine." In making posterity wholly his, man achieved domination of the world and subjugation of woman. Although represented in ancient myths and in Greek drama [9] as the result of violent struggle, in truth the transition to paternal authority was, as we have seen, a matter of gradual change. Man reconquered only what he already possessed, he put the legal system into harmony with reality. There was no struggle, no victory, no defeat.

But the old legends have profound meaning. At the moment when man asserts himself as subject and free being, the idea of the Other arises. From that day the relation with the Other is dramatic: the existence of the Other is a threat, a danger. Ancient Greek philosophy showed that alterity, otherness, is the same thing as negation, therefore Evil. To pose the Other is to define a Manichæism. That is why religions and codes of law treat woman with such hostility as they do. By the time humankind reached the stage of written mythology and law, the patriarchate was definitively established: the males were to write the codes. It was natural for them to give woman a subordinate position, yet one could suppose that they would look upon her with the same benevolence as upon children and cattle—but not at all. While setting up the machinery of woman's oppression, the legisla-

---

[8] Just as woman was likened to the furrow, so the phallus was to the plow, and vice versa. On a picture of the Kassite epoch representing a plow are traced symbols of the generative act; later the phallus-plow identification was frequently represented in plastic art. The word *Iak* in certain Australasian languages designates both phallus and spade. There is known an Assyrian prayer addressed to a god whose "plow has fertilized the earth."

[9] The *Eumenides* represents the triumph of the patriarchate over the matriarchate. The tribunal of the gods declared Orestes to be the son of Agamemnon before he is the son of Clytemnestra—the ancient maternal authority and rights were dead, killed by the audacious revolt of the male!

tors are afraid of her. Of the ambivalent powers with which she was formerly invested, the evil aspects are now retained: once sacred, she becomes impure. Eve, given to Adam to be his companion, worked the ruin of mankind; when they wish to wreak vengeance upon man, the pagan gods invent woman; and it is the first-born of these female creatures, Pandora, who lets loose all the ills of suffering humanity. The Other—she is passivity confronting activity, diversity that destroys unity, matter as opposed to form, disorder against order. Woman is thus dedicated to Evil. "There is a good principle, which has created order, light, and man; and a bad principle, which has created chaos, darkness, and woman," so said Pythagoras. The Laws of Manu define woman as a vile being who should be held in slavery. Leviticus likens her to the beasts of burden owned by the patriarch. The laws of Solon give her no rights. The Roman code puts her under guardianship and asserts her "imbecility." Canon law regards her as "the devil's doorway." The Koran treats woman with utter scorn.

And yet Evil is necessary to Good, matter to idea, and darkness to light. Man knows that to satisfy his desires, to perpetuate his race, woman is indispensable; he must give her an integral place in society: to the degree in which she accepts the order established by the males, she is freed from her original taint. The idea is very clearly stated in the Laws of Manu: "a woman assumes through legitimate marriage the very qualities of her husband, like a river that loses itself in the ocean, and she is admitted after death to the same celestial paradise." And similarly the Bible paints a commendatory portrait of the "virtuous woman" (Proverbs xxi, 10–31). Christianity respects the consecrated virgin, and the chaste and obedient wife, in spite of its hatred for the flesh. As an associate in the cult, woman can even play an important religious role: the Brahmani in India, the flaminica in Rome, each is as holy as her husband. In the couple the man dominates, but the union of male and female principles remains necessary to the reproductive mechanism, to the maintenance of life, and to the order of society.

It is this ambivalence of the Other, of Woman, that will be reflected in the rest of her history; she will be subjected to man's will up to our own times. But this will is ambiguous: by complete possession and control woman would be abased to the rank of a thing; but man aspires to clothe in his own dignity whatever he conquers and possesses; the Other retains, it seems to him, a little of her primitive magic. How to make of the wife at once a servant and a companion is one of the problems he will seek to solve; his attitude will evolve through the centuries, and that will entail an evolution also in the destiny of woman.[1]

---

[1] We shall study that evolution in the West. The history of woman in the East, in India, in China, has been in effect that of a long and unchanging slavery. From the Middle Ages to our times, we shall center this study on France, where the situation is typical.

CHAPTER VI

Patriarchal Times and Classical Antiquity

Woman was dethroned by the advent of private property, and her lot through the centuries has been bound up with private property: her history in large part is involved with that of the patrimony. It is easy to grasp the fundamental importance of this institution if one keeps in mind the fact that the owner transfers, alienates, his existence into his property; he cares more for it than for his very life; it overflows the narrow limits of this mortal lifetime, and continues to exist beyond the body's dissolution—the earthly and material incorporation of the immortal soul. But this survival can only come about if the property remains in the hands of its owner: it can be his beyond death only if it belongs to individuals in whom he sees himself projected, who are *his*. To cultivate the paternal domain, to render worship to the manes of the father—these together constitute one and the same obligation for the heir: he assures ancestral survival on earth and in the underworld. Man will not agree, therefore, to share with woman either his gods or his children. He will not succeed in making good his claims wholly and forever. But at the time of patriarchal power, man wrested from woman all her rights to possess and bequeath property.

For that matter, it seemed logical to do so. When it is admitted that a woman's children are no longer hers, by the same token they have no tie with the group from whence the woman has come. Through marriage woman is now no longer lent from one clan to another: she is torn up by the roots from the group into which she was born, and annexed by her husband's group; he buys her as one buys a farm animal or a slave; he imposes his domestic divinities upon her; and the children born to her belong to the husband's family. If she were an inheritor, she would to an excessive degree transmit the wealth of her father's family to that of her husband; so she is carefully excluded from the succession. But inversely, because she owns nothing, woman does not enjoy the dignity of being a person; she herself forms a part of the patrimony of a man: first of her father, then of her husband. Under the strictly patriarchal regime, the father can, from their birth on, condemn to death both male and female children; but in the case of the former, society usually limits his power: every normal newborn male is allowed to live, whereas the custom of exposing girl infants is widespread. Among the Arabs there was much infanticide: girls were thrown into ditches as soon as born. It is an act of free generosity on the part of the father to accept the female child; woman gains entrance into such societies only through a kind of grace bestowed upon her, not legitimately like the male. In any case the defilement of childbirth appears to be much worse for the mother when the baby is a girl: among the Hebrews, Leviticus requires in this case a purification two months longer than when a boy is brought into the world. In societies having the custom of the "blood price," only a small sum is demanded when the victim is of female sex: her value compared to the male's is like the slave's compared with the free man's.

When she becomes a young girl, the father has all power over her; when she marries he transfers it *in toto* to the husband. Since a wife is his property like a slave, a beast of burden, or a chattel, a man can naturally have as many wives as he pleases; polygamy is limited only by economic considerations. The husband can put away his wives at his caprice, society according them almost no security. On the other hand, woman is subjected to a rigorously strict chastity. In spite of taboos, matrilineal societies permit great freedom of behavior; prenuptial chastity is rarely required, and adultery is viewed without much severity. On the contrary, when woman becomes man's property, he wants her to be virgin and he requires complete fidelity under threats of extreme penalties. It would be the worst of crimes to risk giving inheritance rights to offspring begotten by some stranger; hence it is that the paterfamilias has the right to put the guilty spouse to death. As long as private property lasts, so long will marital infidelity on the part of the wife be regarded like the crime of high treason. All codes of law, which to this day have upheld inequality in the matter of adultery, base their argument upon the gravity of the fault of the wife who brings a bastard into the family. And if the right to take the law into his own hands has been abolished since Augustus, the Napoleonic Code still promises the indulgence of the jury to the husband who has himself executed justice.

When the wife belonged at once to the paternal clan and to the conjugal family, she managed to retain a considerable freedom between the two series of bonds, which were confused and even in opposition, each serving to support her against the other: for example, she could often choose her husband according to her fancy, because marriage was only a secular event, not affecting the fundamental structure of society. But in the patriarchal regime she is the property of her father, who marries her off to suit himself. Attached thereafter to her husband's hearth, she is no more than his chattel and the chattel of the clan into which she has been put.

When the family and the private patrimony remain beyond question the bases of society, then woman remains totally submerged. This occurs in the Moslem world. Its structure is feudal; that is, no state has appeared strong enough to unify and rule the different tribes: there is no power to check that of the patriarchal chief. The religion created when the Arab people were warlike and triumphant professed for woman the utmost scorn. The Koran proclaims: "Men are superior to women on account of the qualities in which God has given them pre-eminence and also because they furnish dowry for women"; woman never had either real power nor mystic prestige. The Bedouin woman works hard, she plows and carries burdens: thus she sets up with her spouse a bond of reciprocal dependence; she walks abroad freely with uncovered face. The veiled and sequestered Moslem woman is still today in most social strata a kind of slave.

I recall seeing in a primitive village of Tunisia a subterranean cavern in which four women were squatting: the old one-eyed and toothless wife, her face horribly devastated, was cooking dough on a small brazier in the midst of an acrid smoke; two wives somewhat younger, but almost as disfigured, were lulling children in their arms—one was giving suck; seated before a loom, a young idol magnificently decked out in silk, gold, and silver was knotting threads of wool. As I left this gloomy cave—kingdom of immanence, womb, and tomb—in the corridor leading upward toward the light of day I passed the male, dressed in white, well groomed, smiling, sunny. He was returning from the marketplace, where he had discussed world affairs with other men; he would pass some hours in this retreat of his at the heart of the vast universe to which he belonged, from which he was not separated. For the withered old women, for the young wife doomed to the same rapid decay, there was no universe other than the smoky cave, whence they emerged only at night, silent and veiled.

The Jews of Biblical times had much the same customs as the Arabs. The patriarchs were polygamous, and they could put away their wives almost at will; it was required under severe penalties that the young wife be turned over to her husband a virgin; in case of adultery, the wife was stoned; she was kept in the confinement of domestic duties, as the Biblical portrait of the virtuous woman proves: "She seeketh wool, and flax . . . she riseth also while it is yet night . . . her candle goeth not out by night . . . she eateth not the bread of idleness." Though chaste and industrious, she is ceremonially unclean, surrounded with taboos; her testimony is not acceptable in court. Ecclesiastes speaks of her with the most profound disgust: "And I find more bitter than death the woman, whose heart is snares and nets, and her hands as bands . . . one man among a thousand have I found; but a woman among all those have I not found." Custom, if not the law, required that at the death of her husband the widow should marry a brother of the departed.

This custom, called the *levirate*, is found among many Oriental peoples. In all regimes where woman is under guardianship, one of the problems that must be faced is what to do with widows. The most extreme solution is to sacrifice them on the tomb of the husband. But it is not true that even in India the law has ever required such holocausts; the Laws of Manu permit wife to survive husband. The spectacular suicides were never more than an aristocratic fashion. Much more frequently the widow is handed over to the heirs of the husband. The levirate sometimes takes the form of polyandry; to forestall the uncertainties of widowhood, all the brothers in a family are given as husbands to one woman, a custom that serves also to protect the tribe against the possible infertility of the husband. According to a passage in Cæsar, it appears that in Brittany all the men of a family had thus in common a certain number of women.

The patriarchate was not established everywhere in this radical form. In Babylon the laws of Hammurabi acknowledged certain rights of woman; she receives a part of the paternal estate, and when she marries, her father provides a dowry. In Persia polygamy was customary; the wife was required to be absolutely obedient to her husband, chosen for her by her father when she was of marriageable age; but she was held in honor more than among most Oriental peoples. Incest was not forbidden, and marriage was frequent between brother and sister. The wife was responsible for the education of children—

boys up to the age of seven and girls up to marriage. She could receive a part of her husband's estate if the son showed himself unworthy; if she was a "privileged spouse" she was entrusted with the
guardianship of minor children and the management of business matters if the husband died without having an adult son. The marriage
regulations show clearly the importance that the existence of a posterity had for the head of a family. It appears that there were five
forms of marriage: [1] (1) When the woman married with her parents'
consent, she was called a "privileged spouse"; her children belonged
to her husband. (2) When a woman was an only child, the first of
her children was sent back to her parents to take the place of their
daughter; after this the wife became a "privileged spouse." (3) If a
man died unmarried, his family dowered and received in marriage
some woman from outside, called an adopted wife; half of her children belonged to the deceased, the other half to her living husband.
(4) A widow without children when remarried was called a servant
wife; she was bound to assign half of the children of her second marriage to the dead husband. (5) The woman who married without the
consent of her parents could not inherit from them before her oldest
son, become of age, had given her as "privileged spouse" to his own
father; if her husband died before this, she was regarded as a minor
and put under guardianship. The institution of the adopted wife and
the servant wife enabled every man to be survived by descendants,
to whom he was not necessarily connected by a blood relationship.
This confirms what I was saying above; for this relationship was in a
way invented by man in the wish to·acquire beyond his own death an
immortality on earth and in the underworld.

It was in Egypt that woman enjoyed most favorable conditions.
The goddess mothers retained their prestige in becoming wives; the
couple was the religious and social unit; woman seemed to be allied
with and complementary to man. Her magic was so slightly hostile
that even the fear of incest was overcome and sister and wife were
combined without hesitation.[2] Woman had the same rights as man,
the same powers in court; she inherited, she owned property. This
remarkably fortunate situation was by no means due to chance: it
came from the fact that in ancient Egypt the land belonged to the

---

[1] This outline follows C. Huart: *Perse antique et la civilisation iranienne,*
pp. 195–6.
[2] In certain cases, at least, the brother was bound to marry his sister.

king and to the higher castes of priests and soldiers; private individuals could have only the use and produce of landed property—the usufruct—the land itself remained inalienable. Inherited property had little value, and apportioning it caused no difficulty. Because of the absence of private patrimony, woman retained the dignity of a person. She married without compulsion and if widowed she could remarry at her pleasure. The male practiced polygamy; but though all the children were legitimate, there was only one real wife, the one who alone was associated in religion and bound to him legally; the others were only slaves without any rights at all. The main wife did not change status in marrying: she remained mistress of her property and free to do business. When Pharaoh Bochoris established private property, woman occupied so strong a position that she could not be dislodged; Bochoris opened the era of contracts, and marriage itself became contractual.

There were three types of marriage contracts: one concerned servile marriage; the woman became the man's property, but there was sometimes the specification that he would have no other concubine; at the same time the legitimate spouse was regarded as the man's equal, and all their goods were held in common; often the husband agreed to pay her a sum of money in case of divorce. This custom led later to a type of contract particularly favorable to the wife: the husband granted to her an artificial trust. There were severe penalties against adultery, but divorce was almost free for both parties. The putting into effect of these contracts tended strongly to reduce polygamy; the women monopolized the fortunes and bequeathed them to their children, leading to the advent of a plutocratic class. Ptolemy Philopater decreed that women could no longer dispose of their property without authorization by their husbands, which made them permanent minors. But even at the time when they had a privileged status, unique in the ancient world, women were not socially the equals of men. Sharing in religion and in government, they could act as regent, but the pharaoh was male; the priests and soldiers were men; women took only a secondary part in public life; and in private life there was demanded of them a fidelity without reciprocity.

The customs of the Greeks remained very similar to the Oriental; but they did not include polygamy. Just why is unknown. It is true that maintenance of a harem has always been a heavy expense: it was Solomon in all his glory, the sultans of *The Arabian Nights*,

kings, chieftains, the rich, who could indulge themselves in the luxury
of a vast seraglio; the average man was content with three or four
wives; the peasant rarely had more than two. Besides—except in
Egypt, where there was no special private property—regard for preserving the patrimony intact led to the bestowal on the eldest son of
special rights in the paternal estate. On this account there was established a hierarchy among the wives, the mother of the chief heir being clothed in a dignity far above that of the others. If the wife had
property of her own, if she had a dowry, she was for her husband a
person: he was joined to her by a bond at once religious and exclusive.

On the basis of this situation, no doubt, was established the custom
of recognizing only a single wife. But in point of fact the Greek citizen remained agreeably polygamous in practice, since he could satisfy
his desires with the prostitutes of the city and the handmaidens of
his gynæceum. "We have hetairas for the pleasures of the spirit,"
said Demosthenes, "*pallages* (concubines) for sensual pleasure, and
wives to give us sons." The concubine replaced the wife in the master's bed when she was ill, indisposed, pregnant, or recovering from
childbirth; thus there is no great difference between gynæceum and
harem. In Athens the wife was shut up in her quarters, held under
severe constraint by law, and watched over by special magistrates.
She remained all her life a perpetual minor, under the control of her
guardian, who might be her father, her husband, the latter's heir, or,
in default of these, the State, represented by public officials. These
were her masters, and she was at their disposal like a commodity, the
control of the guardian extending over both her person and her property. The guardian could transfer his rights at will: the father gave
his daughter in marriage or into adoption; the husband could put
away his wife and hand her over to a new husband. Greek law, however, assured to the wife a dowry, which was used for her maintenance and was to be restored in full if the marriage was dissolved;
the law also authorized the wife in certain rare cases to ask for divorce; but these were the only guarantees granted her by society.
The whole estate was, of course, bequeathed to male children, the
dowry representing, not property acquired through relationship, but
a kind of contribution required of the guardian. Yet, thanks to the
custom of the dowry, the widow no longer passed like a hereditary
possession into the hands of her husband's heirs: she was restored to
the guardianship of her parents.

One of the problems arising in societies based on inheritance through the male line is what happens to the estate if there are no male descendants. The Greeks established the custom of the *epiclerate:* the female heir must marry her eldest relative in her father's family (genos); thus the property left to her by her father would be passed on to children belonging to the same group, the domain would remain the property of the family (genos). The *epiclere* was not a female heir—merely a means for producing a male heir. This custom put her wholly at man's mercy, since she was turned over automatically to the first-born of the males of her family, who most often turned out to be an old man.

Since the oppression of woman has its cause in the will to perpetuate the family and to keep the patrimony intact, woman escapes complete dependency to the degree in which she escapes from the family; if a society that forbids private property also rejects the family, the lot of woman in it is found to be considerably ameliorated. In Sparta the communal regime was in force, and it was the only Greek city in which woman was treated almost on an equality with man. The girls were raised like the boys; the wife was not confined in her husband's domicile: indeed, he was allowed to visit her only furtively, by night; and his wife was so little his property that on eugenic grounds another man could demand union with her. The very idea of adultery disappeared when the patrimony disappeared; all children belonged in common to the city as a whole, and women were no longer jealously enslaved to one master; or, inversely, one may say that the citizen, possessing neither private wealth nor specific ancestry, was no longer in possession of woman. Women underwent the servitude of maternity as did men the servitude of war; but beyond the fulfilling of this civic duty, no restraint was put upon their liberty.

Along with the free women just commented on and the slaves living within the genos, there were also prostitutes in Greece. Primitive peoples practiced the prostitution of hospitality—a yielding up of woman to the transient guest, which doubtless had its mystic justification—and also sacred prostitution, intended to release for the common good the mysterious powers of fecundation. These customs existed in classical antiquity. Herodotus relates that in the fifth century B.C. each Babylonian woman was in duty bound once in her lifetime to yield herself to a stranger in the temple of Mylitta for money, which she contributed to the wealth of the temple; thereafter she went home to lead a chaste life. Religious prostitution has persisted to the present time among the dancing girls of Egypt and the baya-deres .of India, who constitute respected castes of musicians and dancers. But usually, in Egypt, in India, in western Asia, sacred prosti-tution passed over into legal, mercenary prostitution, the sacerdotal class finding this traffic profitable. Even among the Hebrews there were mercenary prostitutes.

In Greece, especially along the seacoast, in the islands, and in the cities thronged with visitors, were the temples in which were to be found the "young girls hospitable to strangers," as Pindar called them. The money they earned was destined for the religious establishment —that is, for the priests and indirectly for their maintenance. In reality, there was hypocritical exploitation—at Corinth and elsewhere —of the sexual needs of sailors and travelers, and it was already venal or mercenary prostitution in essence. It remained for Solon to make an institution of the traffic. He bought Asiatic slaves and shut them up in the "dicterions" located near the temple of Venus at Athens, not far from the port. The management was in the hands of *porno-tropoi*, who were responsible for the financial administration of the establishment. Each girl received wages, and the net profit went to the State. Afterward private establishments, *kapaileia*, were opened, with a red priapus serving as business sign. Before long, in addition to the slaves, Greek women of low degree were taken in as boarders. The "dicterions" were regarded as so essential that they received rec-ognition as inviolable places of refuge. The prostitutes were persons of low repute, however; they had no social rights, their children were excused from supporting them, they had to wear a special costume of many-colored cloth, ornamented with bouquets, and they had to dye their hair with saffron.

In addition to the women of the "dicterions," there were also free courtesans, who can be placed in three categories: the dicteriads, much like the licensed prostitutes of today; the auletrids, dancers and flute-players; and the hetairas, women of the demimonde, mostly from Corinth, who carried on recognized liaisons with the most nota-ble men of Greece and who played the social role of the modern "woman of the world." The first were recruited among freed women and Greek girls of the lower classes; they were exploited by the pro-curers and led a life of misery. The second were often able to get rich because of their talent as musicians; most celebrated was Lamia, mistress of an Egyptian Ptolemy, and then of his conqueror, Demetrius Poliorcetes, King of Macedonia. As for the third and last category, it is well known that several shared the glory of their lovers. Free to make disposal of themselves and of their fortunes, intelligent, cultivated, artistic, they were treated as persons by the men who found enchantment in their company. By virtue of the fact that they escaped from the family and lived on the fringes of society, they escaped also from man; they could therefore seem to him to be fellow beings, almost equals. In Aspasia, in Phryne, in Lais was made manifest the superiority of the free woman over the respectable mother of a family.

These brilliant exceptions apart, woman in Greece was reduced to semislavery, without even the liberty to complain. In the great classical period woman was firmly shut away in the gynæceum; Pericles said that "the best woman is she of whom men speak the least." Plato aroused the raillery of Aristophanes when he advocated the admission of matrons to the administration of the Republic and proposed giving girls a liberal education. But according to Xenophon, wife and husband were strangers, and in general the wife was required to be a watchful mistress of the house, prudent, economical, industrious as a bee, a model stewardess. In spite of this modest status of woman, the Greeks were profoundly misogynous. From ancient epigrammatists to the classical writers, woman was constantly under attack, not for loose conduct—she was too severely controlled for that —and not because she represented the flesh; it was especially the burdens and discomforts of marriage that weighed on the men. We must suppose that in spite of woman's low condition she none the less held a place of importance in the house; she might sometimes disobey, and she could overwhelm her husband with scenes, tears, and nagging, so that marriage, intended to enslave woman, was also a ball and chain for man. In the figure of Xantippe are summed up all the grievances of the Greek citizen against the shrewish wife and against the adversities of married life.

In Rome it was the conflict between family and State that determined the history of woman. Etruscan society was matrilineal, and it is probable that in the time of the monarchy Rome still practiced exogamy under a matrilineal regime: the Latin kings did not hand on power from one to another in the hereditary fashion. It is certainly true that after the death of Tarquin patriarchal authority was established: agricultural property, the private estate—therefore the family —became the unitary basis of society. Woman was to be closely bound to the patrimony and hence to the family group. The laws even deprived her of the protection extended to Greek women; she lived a life of legal incapacity and of servitude. She was, of course, excluded from public affairs, all "masculine" positions being severely forbidden her; and in her civil life she was a permanent minor. She was not directly deprived of her share in the paternal heritage, but by indirect means she was prevented from exercising control of it— she was put under the authority of a guardian. "Guardianship," says Gaius, "was established in the interest of the guardians themselves, so that the woman, whose presumptive heirs they are, could not rob them of the heritage by willing it to others, nor reduce it by expenditures and debts."

The first guardian of a woman was her father; in his absence his male relatives performed this function. When a woman married, she passed into the hands of her husband; there were three types of marriage: the *conferatio*, in which the couple offered to the capitoline Jupiter a cake of wheat in the presence of the *flamen dialis*; the *coemptio*, a fictitious sale in which the plebeian father "mancipated" his daughter to the husband; and the *usus*, the result of a year's cohabitation. All these were with *"manu,"* meaning that the husband replaced the father or other guardian; his wife became like one of his daughters, and he had complete control henceforth over her person and her property. But from the time of the law of the Twelve Tables, because the Roman woman belonged at once to the paternal and the conjugal clans, conflicts arose, which were at the source of her legal emancipation. In fact, marriage with *manu* despoiled the agnate guardians. To protect these paternal relatives, a form of marriage *sine manu* came in; here the woman's property remained under the guardian's control, the husband acquired rights over her person only. Even this power was shared with her paterfamilias, who retained an absolute authority over his daughter. The domestic tribunal was empowered to settle the disputes that could bring father and husband into conflict; such a court permitted the wife an appeal from father to husband or from husband to father; she was not the chattel of any one individual. Moreover, although the family was very powerful (as is proved by the very existence of this tribunal, independent of the public tribunals), the father and head of a family was before all a citizen. His authority was unlimited, he was absolute ruler of wife and children; but these were not his property; rather, he controlled their existence for the public good: the wife who brought children into the world and whose domestic labor often included farm work was most useful to the country and was profoundly respected.

We observe here a very important fact that we shall come upon throughout the course of history: abstract rights are not enough to define the acutal concrete situation of woman; this depends in large part on her economic role; and frequently abstract liberty and concrete powers vary in inverse ratio. Legally more enslaved than the Greek, the woman of Rome was in practice much more deeply integrated in society. At home she sat in the atrium, the center of the dwelling, instead of being hidden away in the gynæceum; she directed the work of the slaves; she guided the education of the children, and frequently she influenced them up to a considerable age. She shared the labors and cares of her husband, she was regarded as co-owner of his property. The matron was called *domina;* she was mistress of the home, associate in religion—not the slave, but the companion of man. The tie that bound her to him was so sacred that in five centuries there was not a single divorce. Women were not restricted to their quarters, being present at meals and celebrations and going to the theater. On the street men gave them right of way, consuls and lictors made room for them to pass. Woman played a prominent role in history, according to such legends as those of the Sabine women, Lucretia, and Virginia; Coriolanus yielded to the supplications of his mother and his wife; the law of Lucinius, sanctioning the triumph of Roman democracy, was inspired by his wife; Cornelia forged the souls of the Gracchi. "Everywhere men rule over women," said Cato, "and we who govern all men are ourselves governed by our women."

Little by little the legal status of the Roman woman was brought into agreement with her actual condition. At the time of the patrician oligarchy each head of a family was an independent sovereign within the Republic; but when the power of the State became firmly established, it opposed the concentration of wealth and the arrogance of the powerful families. The domestic tribunal disappeared before the public courts. And woman gained increasingly important rights. Four authorities had at first limited her freedom: the father and the husband had control of her person, the guardian and the *manus* of her property. The State took advantage of the opposition of the father and husband in order to limit their rights: cases of adultery, divorce, and so on were to be judged in the State courts. Similarly, *manus* and guardianship were destroyed, the one by the other. For the guardian's benefit the *manus* had already been separated from marriage; later the *manus* became an expedient used by women in escaping their guardians, whether by contracting fictitious marriages or by securing complaisant guardians from the father or the State. Under the legislation of the Empire, guardianship was to be entirely abolished.

Woman also gained a positive guarantee of independence: her father was required to provide her with a dowry. This did not go back to her male relatives after dissolution of the marriage, and it never belonged to her husband; the wife could at any time demand its restitution through immediate divorce, which put the man at her mercy. According to Plautus, "In accepting the dowry, he sold his power." From the end of the Republic on, the mother was entitled to the respect of her children on an equality with the father; she was entrusted with the care of her offspring in case of guardianship or of bad conduct on the part of her husband. Under Hadrian, an act of the Senate conferred upon her—when she had three children and when any of them died without issue—the right to inherit from each of them intestate. And under Marcus Aurelius the evolution of the Roman family was completed: from the year 178 on, children were the heirs of their mother, triumphing over the male relatives; henceforth the family was based upon *conjunctio sanguinis* and the mother took a place of equality with the father; the daughter inherited like her brothers.

We observe in the history of Roman law, however, a tendency contradicting that which I have just described; the power of the State, while making woman independent of the family, took her back under its own guardianship; it made her legally incompetent in various ways.

Indeed, she would take on a disturbing importance if she could be at once wealthy and independent; so it was going to be necessary to take away from her with one hand what had been yielded to her with the other. The Oppian law, forbidding luxury to Roman women, was passed at the moment when Hannibal was threatening Rome; once the danger was past, the women demanded that it be repealed. In an oration, Cato demanded its retention; but the appearance of the matrons assembled in the public square carried the day against him. Various laws, increasing in severity as the mores became more loose, were later proposed, but without much success: they hardly did more than give rise to fraud. Only the Velleian act of the Senate triumphed, forbidding women to "intercede" for others—that is, to enter into contracts with others—which deprived her of almost every legal capacity. Thus it was just when woman was most fully emancipated that the inferiority of her sex was asserted, affording a remarkable example of the process of male justification of which I have spoken: when women's rights as daughter, wife, or sister are no longer limited, it is her equality with man, as a sex, that is denied her; "the imbecility, the weakness of the sex" is alleged, in domineering fashion.

The fact is that the matrons made no very good use of their new liberty; but it is also true that they were not allowed to turn it to positive account. The result of these two contrary tendencies—an individualist tendency that freed woman from the family and a statist tendency that infringed upon her autonomy as an individual—was to make her situation unbalanced. She could inherit, she had equal rights with the father in regard to the children, she could testify. Thanks to the institution of the dowry, she escaped conjugal oppression, she could divorce and remarry at will; but she was emancipated only in a negative way, since she was offered no concrete employment of her powers. Economic freedom remained abstract, since it produced no political power. Thus it was that, lacking equal capacity to *act*, the Roman women *demonstrated*: they swarmed tumultuously through the city, they besieged the courts, they fomented plots, they raised objections, stirred up civil strife; in procession they sought out the statue of the Mother of Gods and bore it along the Tiber, thus introducing Oriental divinities into Rome; in the year 114 the scandal of the Vestal Virgins burst forth and their organization was suppressed.

When the collapse of the family made the ancient virtues of private life useless and outdated, there was no longer any established morality for woman, since public life and its virtues remained inaccessible to her. Women could choose between two solutions: either continue obstinately to respect the values of their grandmothers, or no longer recognize any values. At the end of the first century and the beginning of the second we see many women continuing to be the companions and associates of their husbands as they were during the Republic: Plotina shared the glory and the responsibilities of Trajan; Sabina made herself so famous through her benefactions that in her lifetime she was deified in statuary; under Tiberius, Sextia refused to survive Æmilius Scaurrus, and Pascea to survive Pomponius Labeus; Pauline opened her veins with Seneca; Pliny the Younger had made famous Arria's "*non dolet, Pæte*"; [3] Martial praised Claudia Rufina, Virginia, and Sulpicia as wives beyond reproach and devoted mothers. But there were many women who refused maternity and who helped to raise the divorce rate. The laws still forbade adultery, so some matrons went so far as to have themselves registered as prostitutes in order to facilitate their debauchery. [4]

Up to that time Latin literature had always treated women respectfully, but then the satirists were let loose against them. They attacked not woman in general but specifically women of that particular time. Juvenal reproached them for their lewdness and gluttony; he found fault with them for aspiring to men's occupations—they meddled in politics, plunged into the files of legal papers, disputed with grammarians and rhetoricians, went in passionately for hunting, chariot racing, fencing, and wrestling. They were rivals of the men, especially in their taste for amusement and in their vices; they lacked sufficient education to envisage higher aims; and besides, no goal was set up for them; action was still forbidden for them. The Roman woman of the old Republic had a place on earth, but she was chained to it for lack of abstract rights and economic independence; the Roman woman of the decline was the typical product of false emancipation, having only an empty liberty in a world of which man remained in fact the sole master: she was free—but for nothing.

---

[3] When her husband, Pætus, was in serious trouble with the authorities, Arria stabbed herself, saying: "It does not hurt, Pætus," which encouraged him to do likewise.—TR.

[4] Rome, like Greece, officially tolerated prostitution. There were two classes of courtesans: those who were confined in brothels, and the "good prostitutes," those who practiced their profession in freedom but were not allowed to wear the usual married woman's costume. They had some influence on fashion, dress, and the arts, but they never occupied any such lofty position as the Athenian hetairas.

CHAPTER VII

Through the Middle Ages to Eighteenth-century France

THE EVOLUTION of woman's condition was not a continuous process. When the great invasions came, all civilization was again called in question. Roman law itself came under the influence of a new ideology, Christianity; and in the following centuries the barbarians succeeded in imposing their laws. The economic, social, and political situation was turned upside down: that of woman felt the repercussion.

Christian ideology has contributed no little to the oppression of woman. Doubtless there is in the Gospel a breath of charity that extends to women as to lepers; and it was, to be sure, humble folk, slaves, and women who clung most passionately to the new law. In early Christian times women were treated with relative honor when they submitted themselves to the yoke of the Church; they bore witness as martyrs side by side with men. But they could take only a secondary place as participants in worship, the "deaconesses" were authorized to carry out only such lay tasks as caring for the sick and aiding the poor. And if marriage was held to be an institution demanding mutual fidelity, it seemed obvious that the wife should be totally subordinated to her husband: through St. Paul the Jewish tradition, savagely antifeminist, was affirmed.

St. Paul enjoined self-effacement and discretion upon women; he based the subordination of woman to man upon both the Old and the New Testaments. "For the man is not of the woman; but the woman of the man. Neither was the man created for the woman; but the woman for the man." And in another place: "For the husband is the head of the wife, even as Christ is the head of the church. . . . Therefore as the church is subject unto Christ, so let the wives be to their own husbands in everything." In a religion that holds the flesh accursed, woman becomes the devil's most fearsome temptation.

Tertullian writes: "Woman, you are the devil's doorway. You have led astray one whom the devil would not dare attack directly. It is your fault that the Son of God had to die; you should always go in mourning and in rags." St. Ambrose: "Adam was led to sin by Eve and not Eve by Adam. It is just and right that woman accept as lord and master him whom she led to sin." And St. John Chrysostom: "Among all savage beasts none is found so harmful as woman." When the canon law was set up in the fourth century, marriage was viewed as a concession to human frailty, something incompatible with Christian perfection. "Let us take ax in hand and cut off at its roots the fruitless tree of marriage," wrote St. Jerome. From the time of Gregory VI, when celibacy was imposed on the priesthood, the dangerous character of woman was more severely emphasized: all the Fathers of the Church proclaimed her abjectly evil nature. St. Thomas was true to this tradition when he declared that woman is only an "occasional" and incomplete being, a kind of imperfect man. "Man is above woman, as Christ is above man," he writes. "It is unchangeable that woman is destined to live under man's influence, and has no authority from her lord." Moreover, the canon law admitted no other matrimonial regime than the dowry scheme, which made woman legally incompetent and powerless. Not only did the masculine occupations remain closed to her, but she was forbidden to make depositions in court, and her testimony was not recognized as having weight. The emperors were affected to some extent by the influence of the Church Fathers. Justinian's legislation honored woman as wife and mother, but held her subservient to these functions; it was not to her sex but to her situation within the family that she owed her legal incompetence. Divorce was forbidden and marriage was required to be performed in public. The mother's authority over her children was equal to the father's, and she had the same rights in their inheritances; if her husband died she became their legal guardian. The Velleian act of the Senate was modified so that in future a woman could make contracts for the benefit of a third party; but she could not contract for her husband; her dowry became inalienable—it was the patrimony of the children and she was forbidden to dispose of it.

These laws came into contact with Germanic traditions in the territories occupied by the barbarians. In peacetime the Germans had no chieftain, the family being an independent society in which woman was completely under male domination, though she was respected and had some rights. Marriage was monogamous, and adultery was severely punished. In wartime the wife followed her husband into battle, sharing his lot in life and death, as Tacitus reports. Woman's inferiority was due to physical weakness and was not moral, and since women could act as priestesses and prophetesses, they may have been better educated than the men.

These traditions were continued into the Middle Ages, woman being in a state of absolute dependence on father and husband. The Franks did not maintain the Germanic chastity: polygamy was practiced; woman was married without her consent, and put away at her husband's caprice; and she was treated as a servant. The laws gave her strong protection from injury and insult, but only as man's property and mother of his children. As the State became powerful, the same changes occurred as in Rome: guardianship became a public charge, protecting woman, but also continuing her enslavement.

When feudalism emerged from the convulsions of the early Middle Ages, woman's position seems to have been most uncertain. Feudalism involved confusion of authority between sovereignty and property, between public and private rights and powers. This explains why woman was alternately elevated and abased under this regime. At first she had no private rights because she had no political power, and this was because the social order up to the eleventh century was founded on might alone, and the fief was property held by military force, a power not wielded by woman. Later, woman could inherit in the absence of male heirs; but her husband was guardian and exercised control over the fief and its income; she was a part of the fief, by no means emancipated.

The domain was no longer a family affair, as in the time of the Roman gens: it belonged to the suzerain; and woman also. He chose her husband, and her children belonged to him rather than to her husband, being destined to become vassals who would protect his wealth. Thus she was slave of the domain and of the master of this domain through the "protection" of a husband imposed upon her: there have been few periods in which her lot was harder. An heiress —that meant land and a castle. At twelve or less she might be given in marriage to some baron. But more marriages meant more property, so annulments were frequent, hypocritically authorized by the Church. Pretexts were easily found in the rules against marriage between persons related in even remote degree and not necessarily by

blood. Many women of the eleventh century had been thus repudiated four or five times.

If widowed, woman was expected to accept at once a new master.
In the *chansons de geste* we see Charlemagne marrying in a group all
the widows of his barons killed in Spain; and many epic poems tell
of king or baron disposing tyrannically of girls and widows. Wives
were beaten, chastised, dragged by the hair. The knight was not interested in women; his horse seemed much more valuable to him.
In the *chansons de geste* young women always made the advances,
but once they were married, a one-sided fidelity was demanded of
them. Girls were brought up rudely, with rough physical exercises and
without modesty or much education. When grown up, they hunted
wild beasts, made difficult pilgrimages, defended the fief when the
master was abroad. Some of these chatelaines were avaricious, perfidious, cruel, tyrannical, like the men; grim tales of their violence have
come down to us. But all such were exceptions; ordinarily the chate-
laine passed her days in spinning, saying her prayers, waiting on her
husband, and dying of boredom.

The "knightly love" appearing in the Midi in the twelfth century
may have softened woman's lot a little, whether it arose from the
relations between the lady and her young vassals or from the cult of
the Virgin or from the love of God in general. There is doubt that
the courts of love ever really existed, but it is sure that the Church
exalted the cult of the mother of the Redeemer to such a degree
that we can say that in the thirteenth century God had been made
woman. And the life of ease of noble dames permitted conversation,
polite manners, and poetry to flourish. Learned women, such as
Eleanor of Aquitaine and Blanche of Navarre, supported poets, and
a widespread cultural flowering lent to woman a new prestige.
Knightly love has often been regarded as platonic; but the truth is
that the feudal husband was guardian and tyrant, and the wife sought
an extramarital lover; knightly love was a compensation for the bar-
barism of the official mores. As Engels remarks: "Love, in the modern
sense of the word, appeared in antiquity only outside the bounds of
official society. The point where antiquity stopped in its search for
sexual love is just where the Middle Ages started: adultery." And that
is indeed the form that love will assume as long as the institution of
marriage lasts.

But it was not knightly love nor was it religion or poetry but quite other causes that enabled woman to gain some ground as feudalism came to an end. As royal power increased, the feudal lord gradually lost much of his authority, including that of deciding vassal marriages, and the right to use the wealth of his wards. When the fief contributed money instead of military service to the crown, it became a mere patrimony and there was no longer any reason why the two sexes should not be treated on a footing of equality. In France the unmarried or widowed woman had all the rights of man; as proprietor of a fief, she administered justice, signed treaties, decreed laws. She even played a military role, commanding troops and joining combat: there were female soldiers before Joan of Arc, and if the Maid caused astonishment, she did not scandalize.

So many factors combine against woman's independence, however, that they never seem to have been all abolished at once. Physical weakness no longer counted, but in the case of married women subordination remained useful to society. Hence marital authority survived the passing of feudalism. We see the same paradox that exists today: the woman who is most fully integrated in society has the fewest privileges. Under civil feudalism marriage remained as it was under military feudalism: the husband was still his wife's guardian. When the bourgeoisie arose, it followed the same laws; the girl and the widow have the rights of man; but in marriage woman was a ward, to be beaten, her conduct watched over in detail, and her fortune used at will. The interests of property require among nobility and bourgeoisie that a single administrator take charge. This could be a single woman; her abilities were admitted; but from feudal times to our days the married woman has been deliberately sacrificed to private property. The richer the husband, the greater the dependence of the wife; the more powerful he feels socially and economically, the more authoritatively he plays the paterfamilias. On the contrary, a common poverty makes the conjugal tie a reciprocal tie. Neither feudalism nor the Church freed woman. It was rather in emerging from serfdom that the passage from the patriarchal to the truly conjugal family was accomplished. The serf and his wife owned nothing; they had the use of house and furnishings, but that was no reason for the man to try to be master of a wife without wealth. On the contrary, common interests brought them together and raised the wife to the rank of companion. When serfdom was abolished, poverty remained; husband and wife lived on a footing of equality in small rural communities and among the workers; in free labor woman found real autonomy because she played an economic and social part of real importance. In the comedies and fables of the Middle Ages is reflected a society of workers, small merchants, and peasants in which the husband had no advantages over his wife except the strength to beat her; but she opposed guile to force, and the pair thus lived in equality. Meanwhile the rich woman paid with her subjection for her idleness.

Woman still retained a few privileges in the Middle Ages, but in the sixteenth century were codified the laws that lasted all through the Old Regime; the feudal mores were gone and nothing protected woman from man's wish to chain her to the hearth. The code denied woman access to "masculine" positions, deprived her of all civil capacities, kept her, while unmarried, under the guardianship of her father, who sent her into a convent if she failed to marry later, and if she did marry put her and her property and children completely under her husband's authority. He was held responsible for her debts and conduct, and she had little direct relation with public authorities or persons who were strangers to her family. She seemed in work and in motherhood more a servant than an associate: the objects, the values, the beings she created were not her own wealth but belonged to the family, therefore to the man who was its head. In other countries woman was no better off: her political rights were none and the mores were severe. All the European legal codes were erected on a basis of canon law, Roman law, and Germanic law—all unfavorable to woman. Every country had private property and the family and was regulated according to the demands of these institutions.

In all these countries one of the results of the "honest woman's" enslavement to the family was the existence of prostitution. Maintained hypocritically on the fringes of society, the prostitutes played a most important part in it. Christianity poured out its scorn upon them, but accepted them as a necessary evil. Both St. Augustine and St. Thomas asserted that the suppression of prostitution would mean the disruption of society by debauch: "Prostitutes are to a city what sewers are to a palace." In the early Middle Ages the mores were so licentious that whores were hardly needed; but when the bourgeois family was established and rigorous monogamy became the rule, a man had to look for pleasure outside the home.

Against prostitution the efforts of Charlemagne, and later those of Charles IX in France, and those of Maria Theresa in Austria in the eighteenth century [1] were all alike failures. The organization of society made prostitution necessary. As Schopenhauer was to put it pompously: "Prostitutes are human sacrifices on the altar of monogamy." Lecky, historian of European morals, formulated the same idea somewhat differently: "Supreme type of vice, they are the greatest guardians of virtue." The usury of the Jews and the extraconjugal sexuality of the prostitutes were alike denounced by Church and State; but society could not get along without financial speculation and extramarital love; these functions were therefore assigned to wretched castes, segregated in ghettos or in restricted quarters. The prostitutes like the Jews were obliged to wear distinctive signs on their clothing; they were helpless against the police; for most, life was difficult. But many prostitutes were free; some made a good living. As in the time of the Greek hetairas, the high life of gallantry offered more opportunities to feminine individualism than did the life of the "honest woman."

In France the single woman occupied a peculiar position; her independence was in startling contrast to the bondage of the wife; she was a remarkable personage. But then the mores deprived her of all that the law had bestowed; she possessed all civil rights—but these were abstract and empty; she enjoyed neither economic autonomy nor social dignity; generally the old maid spent her life in the shadow of her father's family or joined others like her within the convents, where she scarcely knew any other form of liberty than disobedience and sin—just as the Roman women of the decadence found freedom only through vice. Negation was still the lot of women, since their emancipation remained negative.

In such conditions it was obviously rare for a woman to be able to act or simply to make her presence felt. In the working classes economic oppression nullified the inequality of the sexes, but it deprived the individual of all opportunity; among the nobility and the bourgeoisie the female sex as such was browbeaten: woman had only a parasitic existence; she had little education; only under exceptional circumstances could she envisage and carry out any concrete project.

---

[1] Casanova writes with amusing asperity about the efforts of the Empress Maria Theresa to advance morality by legislation and cites the thieving activities of "a legion of vile spies . . . the Commissaries of Chastity." (*Memoirs*, Vol. III.)—TR.

Queens and regents had this rare pleasure: their sovereignty lifted them above their sex. In France the Salic law forbade women to succeed to the throne; but beside their husbands, or after their death, they sometimes played a great role, as did, for example, St. Clotilda, St. Radegonde, and Blanche of Castile. Living in a convent made woman independent of man: certain abbesses wielded great power; Héloïse gained fame as an abbess as much as for her love. From the mystical relation that bound them to God, feminine souls drew all the inspiration and the strength of a male soul; and the respect paid them by society enabled them to accomplish difficult enterprises. Joan of Arc's adventure had in it something of the miraculous, and besides it was only a brief escapade. But the story of St. Catherine of Siena is significant; in the midst of a quite normal existence she created in Siena a great reputation by her active benevolence and by the visions that testified to her intense inner life; thus she acquired the authority necessary for success, which women usually lack. Appeal was made to her influence in exhorting those condemned to death, in bringing back wanderers, and in allaying quarrels between families and cities. She had the support of a society that recognized itself in her, and thus it was that she could fulfill her mission of pacification, preaching from city to city submission to the Pope, keeping up extensive correspondence with bishops and rulers, and in the end being chosen by Florence as ambassadress to go to seek out the Pope in Avignon. Queens by divine right, and saints by their dazzling virtues were assured a social support that enabled them to act on an equality with men. From other women, in contrast, only a modest silence was called for.

On the whole, men in the Middle Ages held a rather unfavorable opinion of women. The court poets, to be sure, exalted love; in the *Roman de la Rose* young men were urged to devote themselves to the service of the ladies. But opposed to this literature (inspired by that of the troubadours) were the writings of bourgeois inspiration, which attacked women with malignancy: fables, comedies, and lays charged them with laziness, coquetry, and lewdness. Their worst enemies were the clerics, who laid the blame on marriage. The Church had made it a sacrament and yet had forbidden it to the Christian elite: there lay a contradiction which was at the source of the "quarrel of women." Various clerics wrote "lamentations" and diatribes about woman's failings, the martyrdom of man in marriage, and so on; and their opponents tried to prove woman's superiority. This quarrel went on through the fifteenth century, until for the first time we see a woman take up her pen in defense of her sex when Christine de Pisan made a lively attack on the clerics in her *Épître au Dieu d'Amour*. Later she maintained that if little girls were as well taught, they would "understand the subtleties of all the arts and sciences" as well as boys. The truth of the matter was that this dispute concerned women only indirectly. No one dreamed of demanding for them a social role different from the one they had. It was rather a matter of contrasting the life of the cleric with the married state; that is to say, it was a male problem raised by the Church's ambiguous attitude in regard to marriage. This conflict Luther solved by refusing to accept the celibacy of priests. The situation of woman was not affected by that literary war; the "quarrel" was a secondary phenomenon reflecting social attitudes but not changing them.

Woman's legal status remained almost unchanged from the beginning of the fifteenth century to the nineteenth, but in the privileged classes her actual situation did improve. The Italian Renaissance was an individualistic epoch favorable for the emergence of strong personalities, regardless of sex. Women were powerful sovereigns, military fighters and leaders, artists, writers, and musicians. Most of these women of distinction were courtesans, free in spirit, manners, and finances, and their crimes and orgies are legendary. In later centuries the same license marked those women of rank or fortune who could escape the harsh common morality of the times. Apart from queens—Catherine de Medici, Elizabeth, Isabella—and such saints as Theresa and Catherine, who showed what women could achieve under favorable circumstances, the positive accomplishments of women were few, for education and other advantages were largely denied them through the sixteenth century.

In the seventeenth century women of leisure applied themselves to arts and letters, playing an important part in the salons as culture spread in higher social levels. In France Mme de Rambouillet, Mme de Sévigné, and others enjoyed vast renown, and elsewhere Queen Christine, Mlle de Schurman, and others were similarly celebrated. Through such qualities and prestige, women of rank or reputation began to penetrate into the world of men, finally showing in the person of Mme de Maintenon how great an influence can be exerted in affairs of state by an adroit woman, working behind the scenes. And a few personalities escaped from the bourgeois repression to make their mark in the world; a hitherto unknown species appeared: the actress. The first woman was seen on the stage in 1545. Even at the beginning of the seventeenth century most actresses were actors' wives, but later they became independent in career as in private life. The courtesan attained her most accomplished incarnation in Ninon de Lenclos, who carried her independence and liberty to the highest extreme then permitted to a woman.

In the eighteenth century woman's freedom continued to increase. The mores were still strict: the young girl got only a sketchy education; and she was married off or sent into a convent without being consulted. The rising middle class imposed a strict morality upon wives. But women of the world led extremely licentious lives, and the upper middle class was contaminated by such examples; neither the convent nor the home could contain woman. Once again, for the majority this liberty remained abstract and negative: there was little more than the search for pleasure. But the intelligent and ambitious created opportunities. The salon took on new splendor; women protected and inspired the writer and made up his public; they studied philosophy and science and set up laboratories of physics and chemistry. In politics the names of Mme de Pompadour and Mme du Barry indicate woman's power; they really controlled the State. Actresses and women of gallantry enjoyed vast renown. Thus throughout the Old Regime the cultural sphere was the one most accessible to women who attempted to do something. Yet none ever reached the heights of a Dante or a Shakespeare, a fact that is explained by the general mediocrity of their situation. Culture was never an attribute of any but the feminine elite, never of the mass; and it is often from the mass that masculine genius has arisen. Even the privileged were surrounded with obstacles, and while nothing hindered the flights of a St. Theresa or a Catherine the Great, a thousand circumstances conspired against the woman writer. In *A Room of One's Own* Virginia Woolf contrasts the meager and restricted life of an imaginary sister of Shakespeare with his life of learning and adventure. It was only in the eighteenth century that a middle-class woman, Mrs. Aphra Behn, a widow, earned her living by her pen like a man. Others followed her example, but even in the nineteenth century they were often obliged to hide. They did not have even "a room of their own"; that is to say, they did not enjoy that material independence which is one of the necessary conditions for inner liberty. In England, Virginia Woolf remarks, women writers have always aroused hostility.

In France things were somewhat more favorable, because of the alliance between the social and the intellectual life, but, in general, opinion was hostile to "bluestockings." From the Renaissance on, women of rank and of wit, with Erasmus and other men, wrote in defense of women. Marguerite of Navarre did most for the cause, proposing, in opposition to licentious mores, an ideal of sentimental mysticism and of chastity without prudery that would reconcile marriage with love for the honor and happiness of women. The enemies of woman were not silent, of course. They revived the old arguments of the Middle Ages, and published *Alphabets* with a fault of woman for every letter. A libertine literature—*Cabinet Satyrique* and the like —arose to attack feminine follies, while the religious cited St. Paul, the Church Fathers, and Ecclesiastes for woman's disparagement.

The very successes of women aroused new attacks against them: the affected women called *précieuses* alienated public opinion; the *Précieuses ridicules* and *Femmes savantes* were applauded, though Molière was no enemy of women: he sharply attacked enforced marriage, demanding freedom of sentiment for the young girl and respect and independence for the wife. Bossuet preached against woman, and Boileau wrote satires, arousing fiery defenders of the sex. Poulain de la Barre, the leading feminist of the time, published in 1673 *De l'égalité des deux sexes*. Men, he thought, used their superior strength to favor their own sex, and women acquiesced by habit in their dependence. They had never had a fair chance—neither liberty nor education. Thus they could not be judged by past performance, he argued, and nothing indicated that they were inferior to men. He demanded real education for women.

The eighteenth century was also divided in the matter. Some writers tried to prove that woman had no immortal soul. Rousseau dedicated woman to husband and to maternity, thus speaking for the middle class. "Women's entire education should be relative to men," he said; ". . . woman was made to yield to man and to put up with his injustice." The democratic and individualist ideal of the eighteenth century, however, was favorable to women; to most philosophers they seemed to be human beings equal to those belonging to the stronger sex. Voltaire denounced the injustice of woman's lot. Diderot felt that her inferiority had been largely *made* by society. Montesquieu believed paradoxically that "it is against reason and nature that women be in control of the home . . . not at all that they govern an empire." Helvétius showed that the absurdity of woman's education is what creates the inferiority of woman. But it was Mercier who almost alone, in his *Tableau de Paris,* waxed indignant at the misery of workingwomen and thus opened the fundamental question of feminine labor. Condorcet wanted women to enter political life, considering them equal to man if equally educated. "The more women have been enslaved by the laws," he said, "the more dangerous has been their empire. . . . It would decline if it were less to women's interest to maintain it, if it ceased to be their sole means of defending themselves and escaping from oppression."

CHAPTER VIII

Since the French Revolution: the Job and the Vote

IT might well have been expected that the Revolution would change the lot of woman. It did nothing of the sort. That middle-class Revolution was respectful of middle-class institutions and values and it was accomplished almost exclusively by men. It is important to emphasize the fact that throughout the Old Regime it was the women of the working classes who as a sex enjoyed most independence. Woman had the right to manage a business and she had all the legal powers necessary for the independent pursuit of her calling. She shared in production as seamstress, laundress, burnisher, shopkeeper, and so on; she worked either at home or in small places of business; her material independence permitted her a great freedom of behavior: a woman of the people could go out, frequent taverns, and dispose of her body as she saw fit almost like a man; she was her husband's associate and equal. It was on the economic, not on the sexual plane that she suffered oppression. In the country the peasant woman took a considerable part in farm labor; she was treated as a servant; frequently she did not eat at the table with her husband and sons, she slaved harder than they did, and the burdens of maternity added to her fatigue. But as in ancient agricultural societies, being necessary to man she was respected by him; their goods, their interests, their cares were all in common; she exercised great authority in the home. These are the women who, out of the midst of their hard life, might have been able to assert themselves and demand their rights; but a tradition of timidity and of submissiveness weighed on them. The *cahiers* of the States-General contained but few feminine claims, and these were restricted to keeping men out of women's occupations. And certainly women were to be seen beside their men in demonstrations and riots; these women went to seek at Versailles "the baker, his wife, and his little journeyman." But it was not the common people who led the Revolution and enjoyed its fruits.

As for the middle-class women, some ardently took up the cause of liberty, such as Mme Roland and Lucile Desmoulins. One of them who had a profound influence on the course of events was Charlotte Corday when she assassinated Marat. There was some feminist agitation. Olympe de Gouges proposed in 1789 a "Declaration of the Rights of Woman," equivalent to the "Declaration of the Rights of Man," in which she asked that all masculine privilege be abolished; but she perished before long on the scaffold. Short-lived journals appeared, and fruitless efforts were made by a few women to undertake political activities.

In 1790 the right of the eldest and the masculine prerogative in inheritance were abolished; girls and boys became equals in this respect. In 1792 a law was passed establishing divorce and thus relaxing matrimonial bonds. But these were only insignificant victories. Middle-class women were too well integrated in the family to feel any definite solidarity as a sex; they did not constitute a separate caste capable of imposing claims: economically they led a parasitic existence. Thus it was that while women who, in spite of their sex, could have taken part in events were prevented from doing so on account of their class, those belonging to the active class were condemned to stand aside as being women. When economic power falls into the hands of the workers, then it will become possible for the workingwoman to win rights and privileges that the parasitic woman, noble or middle-class, has never obtained.

During the liquidation of the Revolution woman enjoyed a liberty that was anarchic. But when society underwent reorganization, she was firmly enslaved anew. From the feminist point of view, France was ahead of other countries; but unfortunately for the modern Frenchwoman, her status was decided during a military dictatorship; the Code Napoléon, fixing her lot for a century, greatly retarded her emancipation. Like all military men, Napoleon preferred to see in woman only a mother; but as heir to a bourgeois revolution, he was not one to disrupt the structure of society and give the mother preeminence over the wife. He forbade the investigation of paternity; he set stern conditions for the unwed mother and the natural child. The married woman herself, however, did not find refuge in her dignity as mother; the feudal paradox was perpetuated. Girl and wife were deprived of the attribute of citizenship, which prevented them from practicing law and acting as guardian. But the celibate woman, the spinster, enjoyed full civil powers, while marriage preserved the old dependency. The wife owed *obedience* to her husband; he could have her condemned to solitary confinement for adultery and get a divorce from her; if he killed her, caught in the act, he was excusable in the eyes of the law; whereas the husband was liable to penalty only if he brought a concubine into the home, and it was in this case only that the wife could obtain a divorce from him. The man decided where to live and had much more authority over the children than did the wife; and, except where the wife managed a commercial enterprise, his authorization was necessary for her to incur obligations. Her person and property were both under rigorous marital control.

During the nineteenth century jurisprudence only reinforced the rigors of the Code. Divorce was abolished in 1826, and was not restored until 1884, when it was still very difficult to obtain. The middle class was never more powerful, but it was uneasy in its authority, mindful of the menaces implied in the industrial revolution. Woman was declared made for the family, not for politics; for domestic cares and not for public functions. Auguste Comte declared that there were radical differences, physical and moral, between male and female which separated them profoundly, especially in the human race. Femininity was a kind of "prolonged infancy" that set woman aside from "the ideal of the race" and enfeebled her mind. He foresaw the total abolition of female labor outside the home. In morality and love woman might be set up as superior; but man acted, while she remained in the home without economic or political rights.

Balzac expressed the same ideal in more cynical terms. In the *Physiologie du mariage* he wrote: "The destiny of woman and her sole glory are to make beat the hearts of men . . . she is a chattel and properly speaking only a subsidiary to man." Here he speaks for the antifeminist middle class, in reaction against both eighteenth-century license and the threatening progressive ideas of the time. Balzac showed that bourgeois marriage where love is excluded naturally leads to adultery, and he exhorted husbands to keep a firm rein, deny their wives all education and culture, and keep them as unattractive as possible. The middle class followed this program, confining women to the kitchen and the home, closely watching their behavior, keeping them wholly dependent. In compensation they were held in honor and treated with the most exquisite politeness. "The married woman is a slave whom one must be able to set on a throne," said Balzac. She must be yielded to in trifles, given first place; instead of making her carry burdens as among primitives one must rush forward to relieve her of any painful task and of all care—and at the same time of all responsibility. Most bourgeois women accepted this gilded confinement, and the few who complained were unheard. Bernard Shaw remarks that it is easier to put chains on men than to remove them, if the chains confer benefits. The middle-class woman clung to her chains because she clung to the privileges of her class. Freed from the male, she would have to work for a living, she felt no solidarity with workingwomen, and she believed that the emancipation of bourgeois women would mean the ruin of her class.

The march of history, however, was not stopped by such obstinate resistance; the coming of the machine destroyed landed property and furthered the emancipation of the working class along with that of women. All forms of socialism, wresting woman away from the family, favor her liberation: Plato envisioned a communal regime and promised women an autonomy in it such as they enjoyed in Sparta. With the utopian socialisms of Saint-Simon, Fourier, and Cabet was born the utopia of the "free woman"; the slavery of worker and of woman was to be abolished, for women like men were human beings. Unfortunately this reasonable idea did not prevail in the school of Saint-Simonism. Fourier, for example, confused the emancipation of women with the rehabilitation of the flesh, demanding for every individual the right to yield to the call of passion and wishing to replace marriage with love; he considered woman not as a person but only in her amorous function. Cabet promised the complete equality of the sexes, but he restricted woman's share in politics. Others demanded better education for women rather than emancipation. The lofty notion of woman the regenerating influence persisted through the nineteenth century and appears in Victor Hugo. But woman's cause was rather discredited by the ineptitude of woman's partisans. Clubs, magazines, delegations, movements like "Bloomerism"—all went down in ridicule. The most intelligent women of the time, like Mme de Staël and George Sand, remained apart from these movements while fighting their own battles for freedom. But feminism was favored in general by the reform movement of the nineteenth century because it sought justice in equality. Proudhon was a remarkable exception. He broke the alliance between feminism and socialism, relegating the honest woman to the home and to dependence on the male, and attempting to demonstrate her inferiority. "Housewife or harlot" was the choice he offered. But like all antifeminists he addressed ardent litanies to "the true woman," slave and mirror of the male. In spite of this devotion, he was unable to make his own wife happy: the letters of Mme Proudhon are no more than a long lament.

These theoretical debates did not affect the course of events: rather they were a hesitant reflection of things taking place. Woman regained an economic importance that had been lost since prehistoric times, because she escaped from the hearth and assumed in the factory a new part in production. It was the machine that made possible this upheaval, for the difference in physical strength between male and female workers was to a large extent annulled. As the swift growth of industry demanded a larger working force than the males alone could furnish, the collaboration of women became necessary. That was the grand revolution of the nineteenth century, which transformed the lot of woman and opened for her a new era. Marx and Engels gauged its whole range, and they promised women a liberation implied in that of the proletariat. In fact, "woman and the worker have this in common: that they are both oppressed," said Bebel. And both would escape together from oppression, thanks to the importance their work would take on through technological evolution. Engels showed that the lot of woman has been closely tied to the history of private property; a calamity put the patriarchate in place of the matrilineal regime and enslaved woman to the patrimony. But the industrial revolution was the counterpart of that loss of rights and would lead to feminine emancipation. His conclusion has already been quoted (page 55).

At the beginning of the nineteenth century woman was more shamefully exploited than were male workers. Labor at home constituted what the English called the "sweating system"; in spite of constant toil, the workingwoman did not earn enough to satisfy her needs. Jules Simon in *L'Ouvrière* and even the conservative Leroy-Beaulieu in *Le Travail des femmes au XIXe*, published in 1873, denounced odious abuses; the latter says that more than two hundred thousand women workers in France earned less than fifty centimes a day. It is understandable that they made haste to get out into the factories; besides, it was not long before nothing was left to do outside the workshops except needlework, laundering, and housework—all slave's work, earning famine wages. Even lacemaking, millinery, and the like were monopolized by the factories. By way of compensation, there were large opportunities for employment in the cotton, wool, and silk industries; women were used especially in spinning-and weaving-mills. The employers often preferred them to men. "They do better work for less pay." This cynical formula lights up the drama of feminine labor. For it is through labor that woman has conquered her dignity as a human being; but it was a remarkably hard-won and protracted conquest.

Spinning and weaving were done under lamentably unhygienic conditions. "In Lyon," wrote Blanqui, "in the lace workshops some of the women are compelled to work almost hanging on straps while they use both hands and feet." In 1831 the silk workers labored in summer from three o'clock in the morning until dark, and in winter from five to eleven at night, seventeen hours a day, "in workshops that were often unwholesome and where the sunlight never penetrated," as Norbert Truquin said. "Half of these young girls became consumptive before finishing their apprenticeship. When they complained, they were accused of putting on airs."[1]

Moreover, the male employees took advantage of the young working girls. "To attain their ends, they made use of the most shocking means: want and hunger," said the anonymous author of the *Vérité sur les événements de Lyon*. Sometimes women did farm work in addition to their labor at the factory. They were cynically exploited. In a note in *Das Kapital* Marx relates the following: "The manufacturer, Mr. E., informed me that he employed women only at his power looms, that he gave preference to married women and among them to those who had families at home to support, because these were more attentive and docile than the unmarried and had to work to the very end of their strength in order to obtain the necessaries of life for their families." And Marx adds: "Thus it is that woman's true qualities are warped to her disadvantage, and all the moral and delicate elements in her nature become the means for enslaving her and making her suffer." Summing up Marx and commenting on Bebel, G. Derville wrote: "Pet or beast of burden: such is woman almost exclusively today. Supported by man when she does not work, she is still supported by him when she works herself to death." The situation of the work-

---

[1] N. Truquin: *Mémoires et aventures d'un prolétaire*. Quoted from E. Dolléans: *Histoire du mouvement ouvrier*, Vol. I.

ingwoman was so deplorable that Sismondi and Blanqui demanded that women be denied access to the workrooms. The reason for their condition was in part because women at first did not know how to defend themselves and organize themselves in unions. Women's "associations" dated from 1848, and at the beginning these were associations of industrial workers. The movement advanced very slowly, as these figures show:

In 1905, there were 69,405 women out of 781,392 unionized workers; in 1908, 88,906 out of 957,120; in 1912, 92,336 out of 1,064,413.

In 1920, there were 239,016 workingwomen and female employees unionized out of 1,580,967 workers; and among women farm laborers only 36,193 unionized out of a total of 1,083,957. In all, there were 292,000 women unionized out of a total of 3,076,585 union workers. It was a tradition of resignation and submission, a lack of solidarity and collective consciousness, that left them thus disarmed before the new opportunities that were opening up for them.

The result of this attitude was that female labor was slowly and tardily regulated. Only in 1874 did the law intervene; and yet, in spite of the campaigns waged under the Empire, there were only two provisions concerning women: one forbade night work for female minors and required that they be allowed to rest on Sundays and holidays, and their workday was limited to twelve hours; as for women over twenty-one, no more was done than to forbid underground labor in mines and quarries. The first charter for feminine labor was dated November 2, 1892; it forbade night work and limited the factory day; but it left the door open for all kinds of fraud. In 1900 the day was limited to ten hours; in 1905 the weekly day of rest was made obligatory; in 1907 the workingwoman was granted free handling of her income; in 1909 leave with pay was guaranteed to women for childbirth; in 1911 the provisions of 1892 were strongly reasserted; in 1913 the periods of rest before and after childbirth were regulated in detail, and dangerous and excessive forms of labor were forbidden. Little by little social legislation was set up and feminine labor was surrounded with hygienic precautions: chairs were required for saleswomen, long sessions at outside displays were forbidden, and so on. The International Labor Office led to international conventions on the sanitary conditions of women's labor, leave to be granted for pregnancy, and so forth.

A second consequence of the resigned inertia of female workers appeared in the wages they had to be satisfied with. The phenomenon of low wages for women has been variously explained, and it is due to a complex of factors. It is not enough to say that women's needs are less than those of men: that is only justification by afterthought. The truth is, rather, that women, as we have seen, were unable to defend themselves against their exploiters; they had to meet the competition of the prisons, which threw on the market products fabricated without expense for labor; and they competed with one another. It must be remarked in addition that woman was seeking emancipation through labor in a society in which the family continued to exist: tied to her father's or her husband's hearth, she was most often satisfied to bring extra money into the family exchequer; she worked outside the family, but for it; and since the workingwoman did not have to provide for the whole of her needs, she was led to accept remuneration far below what a man required. Since a significant number of women were thus content with depreciated wages, the pay of women in general was of course set at a level most advantageous to the employer.

The woman worker in France, according to a study made in the years 1889–93, received only half the pay of a man for a day's work equal to that of a man. According to the investigation of 1908, the highest hourly wages of workers at home did not exceed twenty centimes per hour and went as low as five centimes; it was impossible for a woman thus exploited to live without charity or a protector. In America in 1918 a woman got only half a man's wage. At about this time in the German mines a woman got approximately twenty-five per cent less than a man for digging the same amount of coal. Between 1911 and 1943 women's wages in France were raised a little more rapidly than the men's, but they remained definitely lower.

If employers warmly welcomed women because of the low wages they would accept, this same fact gave rise to opposition from the male workers. Between the cause of the proletariat and that of women there was no such immediate solidarity as Bebel and Engels claimed. The problem was presented in somewhat the same way as that of the Negro laborer in the United States. The most oppressed minorities of a society are readily used by the oppressors as a weapon against the whole class to which they belong; thus these minorities seem to their class at first to be enemies, and a more profound comprehension of the situation is needed in order that the interests of blacks and whites, of women workers and men workers, may achieve unity instead of being opposed to each other. It is understandable that male workers at first saw a formidable danger in this cut-rate competition and that they exhibited hostility to it. Only when women have been integrated into the life of trade-unionism have they been able to defend their own interests and cease endangering those of the working class as a whole.

For all these difficulties, progress continued in the field of female labor. In 1900 there were still 900,000 home workers in France making clothes, leather goods, funeral wreaths, bags, beadwork, and novelties; but the number has subsequently diminished considerably. In 1906, 42 per cent of women of working age (between eighteen and sixty) were employed in farming, industry, business, banking, insurance, office work, and the learned professions. According to a census taken just before the last war, we find that of all women from eighteen to sixty, about 42 per cent in France are workers, 37 per cent in Finland, 34.2 in Germany, 27.7 in India, 26.9 in England, 19.2 in Holland, and 17.7 per cent in the United States. But in France and India the figures are high because of the importance of rural labor. Outside the peasantry, there were in France in 1940 about 500,000 female heads of businesses, 1,000,000 women employees, 2,000,000 women workers, and 1,500,000 self-employed or unemployed women. Among the workers there were 650,000 domestics; 1,200,000 worked in the finishing industries (440,-000 in textiles, 315,000 in clothing, 380,000 in home dressmaking). Regarding women in commerce, the learned professions, and the public services, France, England, and the United States are of about the same rank.

One of the most basic problems of woman, as we have seen, is the reconciliation of her reproductive role and her part in productive labor. The fundamental fact that from the beginning of history doomed woman to domestic work and prevented her taking part in the shaping of the world was her enslavement to the generative function. In female animals there is a physiological and seasonal rhythm that assures the economizing of their strength; in women, on the contrary, between puberty and the menopause nature sets no limits to the number of her pregnancies. Certain civilizations forbid early marriage, and it is said that in certain Indian tribes a rest of at least two years between childbirths is assured to women; but in general, woman's fecundity has been unregulated for many centuries. Contraceptives have been in existence since antiquity,[2] usually to be used by the woman: potions, suppositories, vaginal tampons; but they remained the secret of prostitutes and doctors. Perhaps this secret was known to those Roman women of the decline whose sterility was attacked by the satirists. But contraceptives were practically unknown to the Middle Ages in Europe; scarcely a trace of them is to be found up to the eighteenth century. For many women life in those times was an uninterrupted succession of pregnancies; even women of easy virtue paid for their licentious lovemaking by frequent childbearing.

At certain epochs man has strongly felt the need to reduce the size of the population; but at the same time nations have feared becoming weak. In times of crisis and misery the birth rate may have been reduced by late marriage, but it remained the general rule to marry young and have as many children as the woman could produce; infant mortality alone reduced the number of living children. As early as the seventeenth century the Abbé de Pure [3] protested against the "love dropsy" to which women were condemned; and Mme de Sévigné advised her daughter to avoid too frequent pregnancies. But it was in the eighteenth century that Malthusianism developed in France. First the wealthy classes, then the whole of the population found it reasonable to limit the number of children according to the means of the parents, and contraceptive measures began to be customary. In 1778 the demographer Moreau wrote: "Rich women are not the only ones who regard the propagation of the species as an old-fashioned imposition; already these disastrous secrets, unknown to all animals but man, have reached the country; nature is deceived even in the

---

[2] "The earliest known reference to birth-control methods appears to be an Egyptian papyrus of about 2000 B.C., which recommends application in the vagina of a bizarre mixture of crocodile excrement, honey, soda, and a gummy substance," according to P. Ariès: *Histoire des populations françaises.* [In Norman Himes's *Medical History of Contraception* (1936), the date of this papyrus, found at Kahun in 1889, is given as about 1850 B.C. Himes presents photographs of this historic document and discusses the chemical nature of the substances mentioned.—TR.] Persian physicians at the time of the Middle Ages knew thirty-one recipes, of which only nine were to be used by the male. Soranos, at the time of Hadrian, prescribed that the woman who did not wish to conceive should, at the time of ejaculation, "hold her breath, draw her body back a little so that the sperm could not penetrate into the *os uteri*, rise immediately, squat down, and bring on sneezing."

[3] In the *Précieuse* (1656).

villages." The practice of *coitus interruptus* spread first among the middle classes, then among country people and the workers; the already existing antivenereal protection became a contraceptive that found widespread use especially after the discovery of vulcanization, toward 1840.[4] In Anglo-Saxon countries "birth control" is officially sanctioned [5] and numerous methods have been developed for dissociating those two formerly inseparable functions: the sexual and the reproductive. Medical research in Vienna and elsewhere, in setting forth precisely the mechanism of conception and the conditions favorable to it, has indicated also the ways of avoiding it. In France contraceptive propaganda and the sale of pessaries and other supplies are forbidden; but "birth control" is none the less widely practiced.

As for abortion, it is nowhere officially sanctioned by the laws. Roman law accorded no especial protection to embryonic life; it regarded the *nasciturus* (to be born) as a part of the maternal body, not as a human being. In the period of the decline abortion seemed to be a normal practice, and even the legislator who wished to encourage childbearing did not venture to forbid it. If a wife rejected her infant against her husband's will, he could have her punished, but it was her disobedience that constituted the offense. Throughout the whole of Oriental and Greco-Roman civilization abortion was permitted by law.

It was Christianity which revolutionized moral ideas in this matter by endowing the embryo with a soul; for then abortion became a crime against the fetus itself. According to St. Augustine, "Any woman who acts in such a way that she cannot give birth to as many children as she is capable of makes herself guilty of that many murders, just as with the woman who tries to injure herself after conception." Ecclesiastical law developed gradually, with interminable discussions on such questions as when the soul actually enters the body of the fetus. St. Thomas and others set the time of animation at about the fortieth day for males and the eightieth day for females. Different degrees of guilt were attached to abortion in the Middle Ages according to when it was performed and why: "There is a great

---

[4] "About 1930 an American firm sold twenty million protective items in one year. Fifteen American factories produced a million and a half of them per day." (P. Ariès.)

[5] Connecticut and Massachusetts still stand out as exceptions in the United States, where "states' rights" apply to such matters.—TR.

difference between the poor woman who destroys her infant on account of the difficulty of supporting it, and her who has no aim other than hiding the crime of fornication," said the book of penitence. An edict of Henri II in 1556 was the basis for regarding abortion as murder and punishable with death. The Code of 1791 excused the woman but punished her accomplices. In the nineteenth century the idea that abortion is murder disappeared; it was regarded rather as a crime against the State. The French law of 1810 forbade it absolutely, with heavy penalties; but physicians always practiced it whenever it was a question of saving the mother's life. The law was too strict and at the end of the century few arrests were made and still fewer convictions reached. New laws were passed in 1923 and 1939, with some variations in the penalties; and in 1941 abortion was decreed a crime against the safety of the State. In other countries the crime and its punishment have been variously regarded, but in general laws and courts have been much more lenient with the woman having the abortion than with her accomplices. The Church, however, has in no way softened its rigor, and in 1917 the code of canon law called for the excommunication of all concerned in an abortion. The Pope has again quite recently declared that as between the life of the mother and that of the infant, the former must be sacrificed: of course the mother, being baptized, can gain entrance to heaven—oddly enough, hell never enters these calculations—whereas the fetus is doomed to limbo for eternity.[6] Abortion has been officially recognized during a brief period only: in Germany before Nazism, and in Russia before 1936. But in spite of religion and the law, it holds a place of considerable importance in all countries. In France abortions number each year from 800,000 to 1,000,000—about as many as there are births

---

[6] We will return in Book II to the discussion of this view, noting here only that the Catholics are far from keeping to the letter of St. Augustine's doctrine. The confessor whispers to the young fiancée the day before the wedding that she can behave in no matter what fashion with her husband from the moment that intercourse is properly completed; positive methods of birth control, including *coitus interruptus*, are forbidden, but one has the right to make use of the calendar established by the Viennese sexologists (the "rhythm") and commit the act of which the sole recognized end is reproduction on days when conception is supposed to be impossible for the woman. There are spiritual advisers who even give this calendar to their flock. As a matter of fact, there are plenty of Christian mothers who have only two or three children though they did not completely sever marital relations after the last accouchement.

—two thirds of those aborted being married women, many already having one or two children.

Thus it is, then, that in spite of prejudices, opposition, and the survival of an outdated morality, we have witnessed the passage from free fecundity to a fecundity controlled by the State or by individuals. Progress in obstetrical science has considerably reduced the dangers of confinement; and the pain of childbirth is on the way out. At this time—March 1949—legislation has been passed in England requiring the use of certain anesthetic methods; they are already in general application in the United States and are beginning to spread in France. Artificial insemination completes the evolutionary advance that will enable humanity to master the reproductive function. These changes are of tremendous importance for woman in particular; she can reduce the number of her pregnancies and make them a rationally integral part of her life, instead of being their slave. During the nineteenth century woman in her turn emancipated herself from nature; she gained mastery of her own body. Now protected in large part from the slavery of reproduction, she is in a position to assume the economic role that is offered her and will assure her of complete independence.

The evolution of woman's condition is to be explained by the concurrent action of these two factors: sharing in productive labor and being freed from slavery to reproduction. As Engels had foreseen, woman's social and political status was necessarily to be transformed. The feminist movement, sketched out in France by Condorcet, in England by Mary Wollstonecraft in her *Vindication of the Rights of Woman*, and taken up again at the beginning of the nineteenth century by the Saint-Simonists, had been unable to accomplish definite results, as it lacked concrete bases. But now, with woman in industry and out of the home, her demands began to take on full weight. They were to make themselves heard to the very center of the bourgeoisie. In consequence of the rapid development of industrial civilization, landed property lost importance in relation to personal property, and the principle of the unity of the family group lost force. The liquidity of capital allowed its holder, instead of being possessed by it, to possess it without reciprocal cares of ownership, and to dispose of it at will. It was through the patrimony that woman had been most strongly attached to her spouse; with the patrimony a thing of the past, they were simply in juxtaposition, and not even their children united them with a firmness comparable to that of property interest. Thus the individual was to gain independence against the group.

This process was especially striking in America, where modern capitalism triumphed: divorce was to flourish and husband and wife to seem no more than provisional associates. In France, where the rural population was a factor of importance and the Code Napoléon placed the married woman under guardianship, the process of evolution was bound to be slow. In 1884 divorce was restored, and the wife could obtain it if the husband committed adultery. In the matter of penology, however, the sex difference was retained: adultery was a legal offense only when committed by the wife. The power of trusteeship, granted with reservations in 1907, was fully obtained only in 1917. In 1912 the determination of natural paternity was authorized. It was necessary to wait until 1938 and 1942 to see the status of the married woman modified: the duty of obedience was then abrogated, though the father remained the head of the family. He determined the place of residence, though the wife could oppose his choice if she had good arguments. Her legal powers were increased; but in the confused statement: "the married woman has full legal powers. These powers are limited only by the marriage contract and the law," the last part of the article contradicts the first. The equality of husband and wife was not yet an accomplished fact.

As for political rights, we can say that they were not easily achieved in France, England, and the United States. In 1867 John Stuart Mill made before the English Parliament the first speech ever officially presented in favor of votes for women. In his writings he imperiously demanded equality for woman and man within the family and in society at large. "I am convinced that social arrangements which subordinate one sex to the other by law are bad in themselves and form one of the principal obstacles which oppose human progress; I am convinced that they should give place to a perfect equality." Following him, Englishwomen organized politically under Mrs. Fawcett's leadership; the Frenchwomen rallied behind Maria Deraismes, who between 1868 and 1871 examined the lot of woman in a series of public conferences; she kept up a lively controversy with Alexandre Dumas *fils*, who gave the advice: "Kill her" to the husband deceived by an unfaithful wife. Léon Richier, who was the true founder of feminism, produced in 1869 "The Rights of Woman" and organized the international congress on the subject, held in 1878. The question of the right to vote was not yet raised, the women limiting themselves to claiming civil rights. For thirty years the movement remained very timid, in France as in England. Numerous groups were formed, but little was accomplished, because, as we have noted, women lacked solidarity as a sex.

The Socialist Congress of 1879 proclaimed the equality of the sexes, but feminism was a secondary interest since woman's emancipation was seen as depending on the liberation of the workers in general. In contrast, the bourgeois women were demanding new rights within the frame of existing social institutions and were far from being revolutionaries. They favored such virtuous reforms as the suppression of alcoholism, pornographic literature, and prostitution. A Feminist Congress was held in 1892, which gave its name to the movement but accomplished little else. A few advances were made, but in 1901 the question of votes for women was brought up for the first time before the Chamber of Deputies, by Viviani. The movement gained in importance, and in 1909 the French Union for Woman Suffrage was founded, with meetings and demonstrations organized by Mme Brunschwig. A woman-suffrage bill passed the Chamber in 1919, but failed in the Senate in 1922. The situation was complicated: to revolutionary feminism and the "independent" feminism of Mme Brunschwig was added a Christian feminism, when Pope Benedict XV in 1919 pronounced in favor of votes for women. The Catholics felt that women in France represented a conservative and religious element; but the radicals feared precisely this. As late as 1932, extended debates took place in the Chamber and in the Senate, and all the antifeminist arguments of a half century were brought forward: the gallant thought that woman was on a pedestal and should stay there; the notion that the "true woman" would remain at home and not lose her charm in voting, since she governs men without need of the ballot. And more seriously it was urged that politics would disrupt families; that women are different anyway—they do not perform military service. And it was asked: should prostitutes have the vote? Men were better educated; women would vote as told to by their husbands; if they wished to be free, let them first get free from their dressmakers; and anyway there were more women than men in France! Poor as these arguments were, it was necessary to wait until 1945 for the Frenchwoman to gain her political enfranchisement.

New Zealand gave woman full rights in 1893, and Australia followed in 1908. But in England and America the victory was difficult. Victorian England isolated woman in the home; Jane Austen hid herself in order to write; scientists proclaimed that woman was "a subspecies destined only for reproduction." Feminism was very timid until about 1903, when the Pankhurst family founded in London the Women's Social and Political Union, and feminist agitation took on a singular and militant character. For the first time in history women were to be seen taking action as women, which gives a special interest to the "suffragette" adventure. For fifteen years they exerted pressure, at first without violence, marching with banners, invading meetings, getting arrested, putting on hunger strikes, marching on Parliament with shawled workers and great ladies in line together, holding meetings, inciting further arrests, parading in columns miles long when votes on suffrage were being taken in Parliament. In 1912 more violent tactics were adopted: they burned houses, slashed pictures, trampled flowerbeds, threw stones at the police, overwhelmed Lloyd George and Sir Edward Grey with repeated delegations, interrupted public speeches. The war intervened. English women got the vote with restrictions in 1918, and the unrestricted vote in 1928. Their success was in large part due to the services they rendered during the war.

The American woman has from the first been more emancipated than her European sister. At the beginning of the nineteenth century women had to share with men the hard work of pioneering; they fought at their side; they were far fewer than the men, and this put a high value on them. But gradually their condition approached that of the women of the Old World; they were highly regarded and dominant within the family, but social control remained entirely in male hands. Toward 1830 certain women began to lay claim to political rights; and they undertook a campaign in favor of the Negroes. Lucretia Mott, the Quakeress, founded an American feminist association, and at a convention in 1840 there was issued a manifesto of Quaker inspiration which set the tone for all American feminism. "Man and woman were created equals, provided by the Creator with inalienable rights. . . . The government is set up only to safeguard these rights. . . . Man has made a civic corpse of the married woman. . . . He is usurping the prerogatives of Jehovah who alone can assign human beings to their sphere of action." Three years later Harriet Beecher

Stowe wrote *Uncle Tom's Cabin*, which aroused public opinion in favor of the Negroes. Emerson and Lincoln supported the feminist movement. After the Civil War the feminists demanded in vain that the amendment giving the vote to the Negroes should give it also to women; taking advantage of an ambiguity, Susan B. Anthony and fourteen comrades voted in Rochester; she was fined one hundred dollars. In 1869 she founded the National Association for Woman Suffrage, and in the same year Wyoming gave women the vote. In 1893 Colorado followed, then in 1896 Idaho and Utah.

Progress was very slow thereafter; but economically women succeeded better than in Europe. In 1900, 5,000,000 women worked in the United States, including a large number in business and the learned professions. There were lawyers, doctors, professors, and as many as 3,373 woman pastors. Mary Baker Eddy founded the Christian Science Church. Women's clubs flourished, with about 2,000,000 members in 1900. But only nine states had given the vote to women. In 1913 the suffrage movement was organized on the militant English model. It was directed by two women: Doris Stevens and a Quakeress, Alice Paul, who arranged for meetings, parades, and other such manifestations. In Chicago for the first time a Woman's Party was founded. In 1917 the suffragettes stood at the doors of the White House, banners in hand, sometimes chained to ironwork so as not to be dislodged. They were arrested after six months but put on a hunger strike in prison and were soon released. After new disorders, a committee of the House met with one from the Woman's Party, and on January 10, 1918 a constitutional amendment was passed. The Senate failed to pass it by two votes at that time, but did pass it a year later, and woman suffrage became the law of the land in 1920. Inter-American conferences led up to the signing in 1933 by nineteen American republics of a convention giving to women equality in all rights.

In Sweden also there existed a very important feminist movement. Invoking old Swedish tradition, the feminists demanded the right "to education, to work, to liberty." Women writers especially took the lead in this struggle, and it was the moral aspect of the problem that interested them at first. Grouped in powerful associations, they won over the liberals, but ran up against the hostility of the conservatives. The Norwegian women won the suffrage in 1907, the Finnish women in 1906, but the Swedish women were to wait for years.

Latin countries, like Oriental countries, keep woman in subjection less by the rigor of the laws than by the severity of custom. In Italy, Fascism systematically hindered the progress of feminism. Seeking alliance with the Church, leaving the family untouched, and continuing a tradition of feminine slavery, Fascist Italy put woman in double bondage: to the public authorities and to her husband. The course of events was very different in Germany. A student named Hippel hurled the first manifesto of German feminism in 1790, and at the beginning of the nineteenth century a sentimental feminism was flourishing, akin to that of George Sand. In 1848 the first German woman feminist, Louise Otto, demanded for women the right to share in reforms of nationalist character and founded in 1865 a woman's association. German Socialists favored feminism, and Clara Zetkin in 1892 was among the party leaders. Female workers and Socialists formed a federation. Women took active part in the war, in 1914; and after the German defeat women got the vote and were active in political life. Rosa Luxemburg battled in the Spartacus group beside Liebknecht and was assassinated in 1919. The majority of German women came out for the party of order; several sat in the Reichstag. Thus it was upon emancipated women that Hitler imposed anew the Napoleonic ideal: "*Küche, Kirche, Kinder.*" And he declared that "the presence of a woman would dishonor the Reichstag." As Nazism was anti-Catholic and antibourgeois, it gave a privileged place to motherhood, freeing women very largely from marriage through the protection it gave to unmarried mothers and to natural children. As in Sparta, woman depended upon the State much more than upon any individual man, and this gave her at once more and less independence than a middle-class woman would have living under a capitalist regime.

It is in Soviet Russia that the feminist movement has made the most sweeping advances. It began among female student intellectuals at the end of the nineteenth century, and was even then connected with violent and revolutionary activity. During the Russo-Japanese War women replaced men in many kinds of work and made organized demands for equality. After 1905 they took part in political strikes and mounted the barricades; and in 1917, a few days before the Revolution, they held a mass demonstration in St. Petersburg, demanding bread, peace, and the return of their men. They played a great part in the October rising and, later, in the battle against invasion. Faithful to Marxist tradition, Lenin bound the emancipation of women to that of the workers; he gave them political and economic equality.

Article 122 of the Constitution of 1936 states: "In Soviet Russia woman enjoys the same rights as man in all aspects of economic, official, cultural, public, and political life." And this has been more precisely stated by the Communist International, which makes the following demands: "Social equality of man and woman before the law and in practical life. Radical transformation in conjugal rights and the family code. Recognition of maternity as a social function. Making a social charge of the care and education of children and adolescents. The organization of a civilizing struggle against the ideology and the traditions that make woman a slave." In the economic field woman's conquests have been brilliant. She gets equal wages and participates on a large scale in production; and on account of this she has assumed a considerable social and political importance. There were in 1939 a great many women deputies to the various regional and local soviets, and more than two hundred sat in the Supreme Soviet of the U.S.S.R. Almost ten million are members of unions. Women constitute forty per cent of the workers and employees of the U.S.S.R.; and many women workers have become Stakhanovites. It is well known that Russian women took a great part in the last war, penetrating even into masculine aspects of production such as metallurgy and mining, rafting of timber, and railroading. Women also distinguished themselves as aviators and parachute jumpers, and they formed partisan armies.

This activity of women in public life raised a difficult problem: what should be woman's role in family life? During a whole period means had been sought to free her from domestic bonds. On the 16th of November 1924 the Comintern in plenary session proclaimed: "The Revolution is impotent as long as the notion of family and of family relations continues to exist." The respect thereupon accorded to free unions, the facility of divorce, and the legalizing of abortions assured woman's liberty with relation to the male; laws concerning maternity leave, day nurseries, kindergartens, and the like alleviated the cares of maternity. It is difficult to make out through the haze of passionate and contradictory testimony just what woman's concrete situation really was; but what is sure is that today the requirements of repeopling the country have led to a different political view of the family:

the family now appears as the elementary cell of society, and woman is both worker and housekeeper.[7] Sexual morality is of the strictest; the laws of 1936 and 1941 forbid abortion and almost suppress divorce; adultery is condemned by custom. Strictly subordinated to the State like all workers, strictly bound to the home, but having access to political life and to the dignity conferred by productive labor, the Russian woman is in a singular condition which would repay the close study that circumstances unfortunately prevent me from undertaking.

The United Nations Commission on the Status of Women at a recent session demanded that equality in rights of the two sexes be recognized in all countries, and it passed several motions tending to make this legal statute a concrete reality. It would seem, then, that the game is won. The future can only lead to a more and more profound assimilation of woman into our once masculine society.

If we cast a general glance over this history, we see several conclusions that stand out from it. And this one first of all: the whole of feminine history has been man-made. Just as in America there is no Negro problem, but rather a white problem;[8] just as "anti-semitism is not a Jewish problem: it is our problem";[9] so the woman problem has always been a man's problem. We have seen why men had moral prestige along with physical strength from the start; they created values, mores, religions; never have women disputed this empire with them. Some isolated individuals—Sappho, Christine de Pisan, Mary Wollstonecraft, Olympe de Gouges—have protested against the harshness of their destiny, and occasionally mass demonstrations have been made; but neither the Roman matrons uniting against the Oppian law nor the Anglo-Saxon suffragettes could have succeeded with their pressure unless the men had been quite disposed to submit to it. Men have always held the lot of woman in their hands; and they have determined what it should be, not according to her interest, but rather with regard to their own projects, their fears, and their needs.

---

[7] Olga Michakova, secretary of the central committee of the Communist Youth Organization, declared in 1944 in an interview: "Soviet women should try to make themselves as attractive as nature and good taste permit. After the war they should dress like women and have a feminine gait. . . . Girls are to be told to behave properly and walk like girls, and for this reason they will probably wear very narrow skirts which will compel a graceful carriage."

[8] Cf. Myrdal: *The American Dilemma.*

[9] Cf. J.-P. Sartre: *Réflexions sur la question juive.*

When they revered the Goddess Mother, it was because they feared Nature; when the bronze tool allowed them to face Nature boldly, they instituted the patriarchate; then it became the conflict between family and State that defined woman's status; the Christian's attitude toward God, the world, and his own flesh was reflected in the situation to which he consigned her; what was called in the Middle Ages "the quarrel of women" was a quarrel between clerics and laymen over marriage and celibacy; it was the social regime founded on private property that entailed the guardianship of the married woman, and it is the technological evolution accomplished by men that has emancipated the women of today. It was a transformation in masculine ethics that brought about a reduction in family size through birth control and partially freed woman from bondage to maternity. Feminism itself was never an autonomous movement: it was in part an instrument in the hands of politicians, in part an epiphenomenon reflecting a deeper social drama. Never have women constituted a separate caste, nor in truth have they ever as a sex sought to play a historic role. The doctrines that object to the advent of woman considered as flesh, life, immanence, the Other, are masculine ideologies in no way expressing feminine aspirations. The majority of women resign themselves to their lot without attempting to take any action; those who have tried to change it have intended not to be confined within the limits of their peculiarity and cause it to triumph, but to rise above it. When they have intervened in the course of world affairs, it has been in accord with men, in masculine perspectives.

This intervention, in general, has been secondary and episodic. The classes in which women enjoyed some economic independence and took part in production were the oppressed classes, and as women workers they were enslaved even more than the male workers. In the ruling classes woman was a parasite and as such was subjected to masculine laws. In both cases it was practically impossible for woman to take action. The law and the mores did not always coincide, and between them the equilibrium was established in such a manner that woman was never concretely free. In the ancient Roman Republic economic conditions gave the matron concrete powers, but she had no legal independence. Conditions were often similar for woman in peasant civilizations and among the lower commercial middle class: mistress-servant in the house, but socially a minor. Inversely, in epochs of social disintegration woman is set free; but in ceasing to be man's vassal, she loses her fief; she has only a negative liberty, which is expressed in license and dissipation. So it was with woman during the decline of Rome, the Renaissance, the eighteenth century, the Directory (1795–9). Sometimes she succeeded in keeping busy, but found herself enslaved; or she was set free and no longer knew what to do with herself. One remarkable fact among others is that the married woman had her place in society but enjoyed no rights therein; whereas the unmarried female, honest woman or prostitute, had all the legal capacities of a man, but up to this century was more or less excluded from social life.

From this opposition of legal rights and social custom has resulted, among other things, this curious paradox: free love is not forbidden by law, whereas adultery is an offense; but very often the young girl who "goes wrong" is dishonored, whereas the misconduct of the wife is viewed indulgently; and in consequence many young women from the seventeenth century to our own day have married in order to be able to take lovers freely. By means of this ingenious system the great mass of women is held closely in leading strings: exceptional circumstances are required if a feminine personality is to succeed in asserting itself between these two series of restraints, theoretical or concrete. The women who have accomplished works comparable to those of men are those exalted by the power of social institutions above all sexual differentiation. Queen Isabella, Queen Elizabeth, Catherine the Great were neither male nor female—they were sovereigns. It is remarkable that their femininity, when socially abolished, should have no longer meant inferiority: the proportion of queens who had great reigns is infinitely above that of great kings. Religion works the same transformation: Catherine of Siena, St. Theresa, quite beyond any physiological consideration, were sainted souls; the life they led, secular and mystic, their acts, and their writings rose to heights that few men have ever reached.

It is quite conceivable that if other women fail to make a deep impression upon the world, it is because they are tied down in their situation. They can hardly take a hand in affairs in other than a negative and oblique manner. Judith, Charlotte Corday, Vera Zasulich were assassins; the *Frondeuses* were conspirators; during the Revolution, during the Commune, women battled beside the men against the established order. Against a liberty without rights, without powers, woman has been permitted to rise in refusal and revolt, while being forbidden to participate in positively constructive effort; at the most she may succeed in joining men's enterprises through an indirect road. Aspasia, Mme de Maintenon, the Princess des Ursins were counselors who were listened to seriously—yet somebody had to be willing to listen to them. Men are glad to exaggerate the extent of these influences when they wish to convince woman that she has chosen the better part; but as a matter of fact, feminine voices are silent when it comes to concrete action. They have been able to stir up wars, not to propose battle tactics; they have directed politics hardly more than in the degree that politics is reduced to intrigue; the true control of the world has never been in the hands of women; they have not brought their influence to bear upon technique or economy, they have not made and unmade states, they have not discovered new worlds. Through them certain events have been set off, but the women have been pretexts rather than agents. The suicide of Lucretia has had value only as a symbol. Martyrdom remains open to the oppressed; during the Christian persecutions, on the morrow of social or national defeats, women have played this part of witness; but never has a martyr changed the face of the world. Even when women have started things and made demonstrations, these moves have taken on weight only when a masculine decision has effectively extended them. The American women grouped around Harriet Beecher Stowe aroused public opinion violently against slavery; but the true reasons for the War of Secession were not of a sentimental order. The "woman's day" of March 8, 1917 may perhaps have precipitated the Russian Revolution—but it was only a signal.

Most female heroines are oddities: adventuresses and originals notable less for the importance of their acts than for the singularity of their fates. Thus if we compare Joan of Arc, Mme Roland, Flora Tristan, with Richelieu, Danton, Lenin, we see that their greatness is primarily subjective: they are exemplary figures rather than historical agents. The great man springs from the masses and he is propelled onward by circumstances; the masses of women are on the margin of history, and circumstances are an obstacle for each individual, not a springboard. In order to change the face of the world, it is first necessary to be firmly anchored in it; but the women who are firmly rooted in society are those who are in subjection to it; unless designated for action by divine authority—and then they have shown themselves to be as capable as men—the ambitious woman and the heroine are

strange monsters. It is only since women have begun to feel themselves at home on the earth that we have seen a Rosa Luxemburg, a
Mme Curie appear. They brilliantly demonstrate that it is not the
inferiority of women that has caused their historical insignificance:
it is rather their historical insignificance that has doomed them to
inferiority.[1]

This fact is glaringly clear in the domain in which women have
best succeeded in asserting themselves—that is, the domain of culture. Their lot has been deeply bound up with that of arts and letters; among the ancient Germans the functions of prophetess and
priestess were already appropriate to women. Because of woman's
marginal position in the world, men will turn to her when they strive
through culture to go beyond the boundaries of their universe and
gain access to something other than what they have known. Courtly
mysticism, humanist curiosity, the taste for beauty which flourished
in the Italian Renaissance, the preciosity of the seventeenth century,
the progressive idealism of the eighteenth—all brought about under
different forms an exaltation of femininity. Woman was thus the guiding star of poetry, the subject matter of the work of art; her leisure
allowed her to consecrate herself to the pleasures of the spirit: inspiration, critic, and public of the writer, she became his rival; she it
was who often made prevail a mode of sensibility, an ethic that fed
masculine hearts, and thus she intervened in her own destiny—the
education of women was in large part a feminine conquest. And yet,
however important this collective role of the intellectual woman may
have been, the individual contributions have been in general of less
value. It is because she has not been engaged in action that woman
has had a privileged place in the domains of thought and of art;
but art and thought have their living springs in action. To be situated
at the margin of the world is not a position favorable for one who
aims at creating anew: here again, to emerge beyond the given, it is
necessary first to be deeply rooted in it. Personal accomplishment is
almost impossible in the human categories that are maintained collectively in an inferior situation. "Where would you have one go,
with skirts on?" Marie Bashkirtsev wanted to know. And Stendhal

---

[1] It is remarkable that out of a thousand statues in Paris (excepting the queens
that for a purely architectural reason form the corbel of the Luxembourg) there
should be only ten raised to women. Three are consecrated to Joan of Arc. The
others are statues of Mme de Ségur, George Sand, Sarah Bernhardt, Mme Bou-
cicaut and the Baroness de Hirsch, Maria Deraismes, and Rosa Bonheur.

said: "All the geniuses who are born *women* are lost to the public good." To tell the truth, one is not born a genius: one becomes a genius; and the feminine situation has up to the present rendered this becoming practically impossible.

The antifeminists obtain from the study of history two contradictory arguments: (1) women have never created anything great; and (2) the situation of woman has never prevented the flowering of great feminine personalities. There is bad faith in these two statements; the successes of a privileged few do not counterbalance or excuse the systematic lowering of the collective level; and that these successes are rare and limited proves precisely that circumstances are unfavorable for them. As has been maintained by Christine de Pisan, Poulain de la Barre, Condorcet, John Stuart Mill, and Stendhal, in no domain has woman ever really had her chance. That is why a great many women today demand a new status; and once again their demand is not that they be exalted in their femininity: they wish that in themselves, as in humanity in general, transcendence may prevail over immanence; they wish to be accorded at last the abstract rights and concrete possibilities without the concurrence of which liberty is only a mockery.[2]

This wish is on the way to fulfillment. But the period in which we live is a period of transition; this world, which has always belonged to the men, is still in their hands; the institutions and the values of the patriarchal civilization still survive in large part. Abstract rights are far from being completely granted everywhere to women: in Switzerland they do not yet vote; in France the law of 1942 maintains in attenuated form the privileges of the husband. And abstract rights, as I have just been saying, have never sufficed to assure to woman a definite hold on the world: true equality between the two sexes does not exist even today.

In the first place, the burdens of marriage weigh much more heavily upon woman than upon man. We have noted that servitude to maternity has been reduced by the use—admitted or clandestine—of birth control; but the practice has not spread everywhere nor is it

---

[2] Here again the antifeminists take an equivocal line. Now, regarding abstract liberty as nothing, they expatiate on the great concrete role that the enslaved woman can play in the world—what then, is she asking for? Again, they disregard the fact that negative license opens no concrete possibilities, and they reproach women who are abstractly emancipated for not having produced evidence of their abilities.

invariably used. Abortion being officially forbidden, many women either risk their health in unsupervised efforts to abort or find themselves overwhelmed by their numerous pregnancies. The care of children like the upkeep of the home is still undertaken almost exclusively by woman. Especially in France the antifeminist tradition is so tenacious that a man would feel that he was lowering himself by helping with tasks hitherto assigned to women. The result is that it is more difficult for woman than for man to reconcile her family life with her role as worker. Whenever society demands this effort, her life is much harder than her husband's.

Consider for example the lot of peasant women. In France they make up the majority of women engaged in productive labor; and they are generally married. Customs vary in different regions: the Norman peasant woman presides at meals, whereas the Corsican woman does not sit at table with the men; but everywhere, playing a most important part in the domestic economy, she shares the man's responsibilities, interests, and property; she is respected and often is in effective control—her situation recalls that of woman in the old agricultural communities. She often has more moral prestige than her husband, but she lives in fact a much harder life. She has exclusive care of garden, sheepfold, pigpen, and so on, and shares in the hard labor of stablework, planting, plowing, weeding, and haying; she spades, reaps, picks grapes, and sometimes helps load and unload wagons with hay, wood, and so forth. She cooks, keeps house, does washing, mending, and the like. She takes on the heavy duties of maternity and child care. She gets up at dawn, feeds the poultry and other small livestock, serves breakfast to the men, goes to work in field, wood, or garden; she draws water, serves a second meal, washes the dishes, works in the fields until time for dinner, and afterward spends the evening mending, cleaning, shelling corn, and what not. Having no time to care for her own health, even when pregnant, she soon gets misshapen; she is prematurely withered and worn out, gnawed by sickness. The compensations man finds in occasional social life are denied to her: he goes in town on Sundays and market days, meets other men, drinks and plays cards in cafés, goes hunting and fishing. She stays at home on the farm and knows no leisure. Only the well-off peasant women, who have servants or can avoid field labor, lead a well-balanced life: they are socially honored and at home exert a great deal of authority without being crushed by work. But for the most part rural labor reduces woman to the condition of a beast of burden.

The businesswoman and the female employer who runs a small enterprise have always been among the privileged; they are the only women recognized since the Middle Ages by the Code as having civil rights and powers. Female grocers, dairy dealers, landladies, tobacconists have a position equivalent to man's; as spinsters or widows, they can in themselves constitute a legal firm; married, they have the same independence as their husbands. Fortunately their work can be carried on in the place where they live, and usually it is not too absorbing.

Things are quite otherwise for the woman worker or employee, the secretary, the saleswoman, all of whom go to work outside the home. It is much more difficult for them to combine their employment with household duties, which would seem to require at least three and a half hours a day, with six hours on Sunday—a good deal to add to the hours in factory or office. As for the learned professions, even if lawyers, doctors, and professors obtain some housekeeping help, the home and children are for them also a burden that is a heavy handicap. In America domestic work is simplified by ingenious gadgets; but the elegant appearance required of the workingwoman imposes upon her another obligation, and she remains responsible for house and children.

Furthermore, the woman who seeks independence through work has less favorable possibilities than her masculine competitors. Her wages in most jobs are lower than those of men; her tasks are less specialized and therefore not so well paid as those of skilled laborers; and for equal work she does not get equal pay. Because of the fact that she is a newcomer in the universe of males, she has fewer chances for success than they have. Men and women alike hate to be under the orders of a woman; they always show more confidence in a man; to be a woman is, if not a defect, at least a peculiarity. In order to "arrive," it is well for a woman to make sure of masculine backing. Men unquestionably occupy the most advantageous places, hold the most important posts. It is essential to emphasize the fact that men and women, economically speaking, constitute two castes.[3]

---

[3] In America the great fortunes often fall finally into women's hands: younger than their husbands, they survive them and inherit from them; but by that time they are aged and rarely have the initiative to make new investments; they are en-

The fact that governs woman's actual condition is the obstinate survival of extremely antique traditions into the new civilization that is just appearing in vague outline. That is what is misunderstood by hasty observers who regard woman as not up to the possibilities now offered to her or again who see in these possibilities only dangerous temptations. The truth is that her situation is out of equilibrium, and for that reason it is very difficult for her to adapt herself to it. We open the factories, the offices, the faculties to woman, but we continue to hold that marriage is for her a most honorable career, freeing her from the need of any other participation in the collective life. As in primitive civilizations, the act of love is on her part a service for which she has the right to be more or less directly paid. Except in the Soviet Union,[4] modern woman is everywhere permitted to regard her body as capital for exploitation. Prostitution is tolerated,[5] gallantry encouraged. And the married woman is empowered to see to it that her husband supports her; in addition she is clothed in a social dignity far superior to that of the spinster. The mores are far from conceding to the latter sexual possibilities equivalent to those of the bachelor male; in particular maternity is practically forbidden her, the unmarried mother remaining an object of scandal. How, indeed, could the myth of Cinderella [6] not keep all its validity? Everything still encourages the young girl to expect fortune and happiness from some Prince Charming rather than to attempt by herself their difficult and uncertain conquest. In particular she can hope to rise, thanks to him, into a caste superior to her own, a miracle that could

---

joyers of income rather than proprietors. It is really men who handle the capital funds. At any rate, these privileged rich women make up only a tiny minority. In America, much more than in Europe, it is almost impossible for a woman to reach a high position as lawyer, doctor, etc.

[4] At least according to official doctrine.

[5] In Anglo-Saxon countries prostitution has never been regulated. Up to 1900 English and American common law did not regard it as an offense except when it made public scandal and created disorder. Since that date repression has been more or less rigorously imposed, more or less successfully, in England and in the various states of the United States, where legislation in the matter is very diverse. In France, after a long campaign for abolition, the law of April 13, 1946 ordered the closing of licensed brothels and the intensifying of the struggle against procuring: "Holding that the existence of these houses is incompatible with the essential principles of human dignity and the role awarded to woman in modern society." But prostitution continues none the less to carry on. It is evident that the situation cannot be modified by negative and hypocritical measures.

[6] Cf. Philip Wylie: *Generation of Vipers* (Farrar, Straus & Co., 1942).

not be bought by the labor of her lifetime. But such a hope is a thing of evil because it divides her strength and her interests; [7] this division is perhaps woman's greatest handicap. Parents still raise their daughter with a view to marriage rather than to furthering her personal development; she sees so many advantages in it that she herself wishes for it; the result is that she is often less specially trained, less solidly grounded than her brothers, she is less deeply involved in her profession. In this way she dooms herself to remain in its lower levels, to be inferior; and the vicious circle is formed: this professional inferiority reinforces her desire to find a husband.

Every benefit always has as its bad side some burden; but if the burden is too heavy, the benefit seems no longer to be anything more than a servitude. For the majority of laborers, labor is today a thankless drudgery, but in the case of woman this is not compensated for by a definite conquest of her social dignity, her freedom of behavior, or her economic independence; it is natural enough for many woman workers and employees to see in the right to work only an obligation from which marriage will deliver them. Because of the fact that she has taken on awareness of self, however, and because she can also free herself from marriage through a job, woman no longer accepts domestic subjection with docility. What she would hope is that the reconciliation of family life with a job should not require of her an exhausting, difficult performance. Even then, as long as the temptations of convenience exist—in the economic inequality that favors certain individuals and the recognized right of woman to sell herself to one of these privileged men—she will need to make a greater moral effort than would a man in choosing the road of independence. It has not been sufficiently realized that the temptation is also an obstacle, and even one of the most dangerous. Here it is accompanied by a hoax, since in fact there will be only one winner out of thousands in the lottery of marriage. The present epoch invites, even compels women to work; but it flashes before their eyes paradises of idleness and delight: it exalts the winners far above those who remain tied down to earth.

The privileged place held by men in economic life, their social usefulness, the prestige of marriage, the value of masculine backing, all this makes women wish ardently to please men. Women are still, for the most part, in a state of subjection. It follows that woman sees

---

[7] We will return to this point at some length in Book II.

herself and makes her choices not in accordance with her true nature
in itself, but as man defines her. So we must first go on to describe
woman such as men have fancied her in their dreams, for what-in-
men's-eyes-she-seems-to-be is one of the necessary factors in her real
situation.

PART III

M Y T H S

CHAPTER IX

Dreams, Fears, Idols

Hɪsᴛᴏʀʏ has shown us that men have always kept in their hands
all concrete powers; since the earliest days of the patriarchate they
have thought best to keep woman in a state of dependence; their
codes of law have been set up against her; and thus she has been definitely established as the Other. This arrangement suited the economic interests of the males; but it conformed also to their ontological
and moral pretensions. Once the subject seeks to assert himself, the
Other, who limits and denies him, is none the less a necessity to him:
he attains himself only through that reality which he is not, which is
something other than himself. That is why man's life is never abundance and quietude; it is dearth and activity, it is struggle. Before him,
man encounters Nature; he has some hold upon her, he endeavors to
mold her to his desire. But she cannot fill his needs. Either she appears simply as a purely impersonal opposition, she is an obstacle and
remains a stranger; or she submits passively to man's will and permits assimilation, so that he takes possession of her only through consuming her—that is, through destroying her. In both cases he remains
alone; he is alone when he touches a stone, alone when he devours a

fruit. There can be no presence of an other unless the other is also present in and for himself: which is to say that true alterity—otherness—is that of a consciousness separate from mine and substantially identical with mine.

It is the existence of other men that tears each man out of his immanence and enables him to fulfill the truth of his being, to complete himself through transcendence, through escape toward some objective, through enterprise. But this liberty not my own, while assuring mine, also conflicts with it: there is the tragedy of the unfortunate human consciousness; each separate conscious being aspires to set himself up alone as sovereign subject. Each tries to fulfill himself by reducing the other to slavery. But the slave, though he works and fears, senses himself somehow as the essential; and, by a dialectical inversion, it is the master who seems to be the inessential. It is possible to rise above this conflict if each individual freely recognizes the other, each regarding himself and the other simultaneously as object and as subject in a reciprocal manner. But friendship and generosity, which alone permit in actuality this recognition of free beings, are not facile virtues; they are assuredly man's highest achievement, and through that achievement he is to be found in his true nature. But this true nature is that of a struggle unceasingly begun, unceasingly abolished; it requires man to outdo himself at every moment. We might put it in other words and say that man attains an authentically moral attitude when he renounces *mere being* to assume his position as an existent; through this transformation also he renounces all possession, for possession is one way of seeking mere being; but the transformation through which he attains true wisdom is never done, it is necessary to make it without ceasing, it demands a constant tension. And so, quite unable to fulfill himself in solitude, man is incessantly in danger in his relations with his fellows: his life is a difficult enterprise with success never assured.

But he does not like difficulty; he is afraid of danger. He aspires in contradictory fashion both to life and to repose, to existence and to merely being; he knows full well that "trouble of spirit" is the price of development, that his distance from the object is the price of his nearness to himself; but he dreams of quiet in disquiet and of an opaque plenitude that nevertheless would be endowed with consciousness. This dream incarnated is precisely woman; she is the wished-for intermediary between nature, the stranger to man, and the fellow being who is too closely identical.[1] She opposes him with neither the hostile silence of nature nor the hard requirement of a reciprocal relation; through a unique privilege she is a conscious being and yet it seems possible to possess her in the flesh. Thanks to her, there is a means for escaping that implacable dialectic of master and slave which has its source in the reciprocity that exists between free beings.

We have seen that there were not at first free women whom the males had enslaved nor were there even castes based on sex. To regard woman simply as a slave is a mistake; there were women among the slaves, to be sure, but there have always been free women—that is, women of religious and social dignity. They accepted man's sovereignty and he did not feel menaced by a revolt that could make of him in turn the object. Woman thus seems to be the inessential who never goes back to being the essential, to be the absolute Other, without reciprocity. This conviction is dear to the male, and every creation myth has expressed it, among others the legend of Genesis, which, through Christianity, has been kept alive in Western civilization. Eve was not fashioned at the same time as the man; she was not fabricated from a different substance, nor of the same clay as was used to model Adam: she was taken from the flank of the first male. Not even her birth was independent; God did not spontaneously choose to create her as an end in herself and in order to be worshipped directly by her in return for it. She was destined by Him for man; it was to rescue Adam from loneliness that He gave her to him, in her mate was her origin and her purpose; she was his complement on the order of the inessential. Thus she appeared in the guise of privileged prey. She was nature elevated to transparency of consciousness; she was a conscious being, but naturally submissive. And therein lies the wondrous hope that man has often put in woman: he hopes to fulfill himself as a being by carnally possessing a being, but at the same time confirming his sense of freedom through the docility of a free person. No man would consent to be a woman, but every man wants women to exist. "Thank God for having created woman." "Nature is good since she has given women to men." In such expressions man once more asserts

---

[1] ". . . Woman is not the useless replica of man, but rather the enchanted place where the living alliance between man and nature is brought about. If she should disappear, men would be alone, strangers lacking passports in an icy world. She is the earth itself raised to life's summit, the earth become sensitive and joyous; and without her, for man the earth is mute and dead," writes Michel Carrouges ("*Les Pouvoirs de la femme,*" *Cahiers du Sud,* No. 292).

with naïve arrogance that his presence in this world is an ineluctable fact and a right, that of woman a mere accident—but a very happy accident. Appearing as the Other, woman appears at the same time as an abundance of being in contrast to that existence the nothingness of which man senses in himself; the Other, being regarded as the object in the eyes of the subject, is regarded as *en soi*; therefore as a being. In woman is incarnated in positive form the lack that the existent carries in his heart, and it is in seeking to be made whole through her that man hopes to attain self-realization.

She has not represented for him, however, the only incarnation of the Other, and she has not always kept the same importance throughout the course of history. There have been moments when she has been eclipsed by other idols. When the City or the State devours the citizen, it is no longer possible for him to be occupied with his personal destiny. Being dedicated to the State, the Spartan woman's condition was above that of other Greek women. But it is also true that she was transfigured by no masculine dream. The cult of the leader, whether he be Napoleon, Mussolini, or Hitler, excludes all other cults. In military dictatorships, in totalitarian regimes, woman is no longer a privileged object. It is understandable that woman should be deified in a rich country where the citizens are none too certain of the meaning of life: thus it is in America. On the other hand, socialist ideologies, which assert the equality of all human beings, refuse now and for the future to permit any human category to be object or idol: in the authentically democratic society proclaimed by Marx there is no place for the Other. Few men, however, conform exactly to the militant, disciplined figure they have chosen to be; to the degree in which they remain individuals, woman keeps in their eyes a special value. I have seen letters written by German soldiers to French prostitutes in which, in spite of Nazism, the ingrained tradition of virgin purity was naïvely confirmed. Communist writers, like Aragon in France and Vittorini in Italy, give a place of the first rank in their works to woman, whether mistress or mother. Perhaps the myth of woman will some day be extinguished; the more women assert themselves as human beings, the more the marvelous quality of the Other will die out in them. But today it still exists in the heart of every man.

A myth always implies a subject who projects his hopes and his fears toward a sky of transcendence. Women do not set themselves up as Subject and hence have erected no virile myth in which their projects are reflected; they have no religion or poetry of their own: they still dream through the dreams of men. Gods made by males are the gods they worship. Men have shaped for their own exaltation great virile figures: Hercules, Prometheus, Parsifal; woman has only a secondary part to play in the destiny of these heroes. No doubt there are conventional figures of man caught in his relations to woman: the father, the seducer, the husband, the jealous lover, the good son, the wayward son; but they have all been established by men, and they lack the dignity of myth, being hardly more than clichés. Whereas woman is defined exclusively in her relation to man. The asymmetry of the categories—male and female—is made manifest in the unilateral form of sexual myths. We sometimes say "the sex" to designate woman; she is the flesh, its delights and dangers. The truth that for woman man is sex and carnality has never been proclaimed because there is no one to proclaim it. Representation of the world, like the world itself, is the work of men; they describe it from their own point of view, which they confuse with absolute truth.

It is always difficult to describe a myth; it cannot be grasped or encompassed; it haunts the human consciousness without ever appearing before it in fixed form. The myth is so various, so contradictory, that at first its unity is not discerned: Delilah and Judith, Aspasia and Lucretia, Pandora and Athena—woman is at once Eve and the Virgin Mary. She is an idol, a servant, the source of life, a power of darkness; she is the elemental silence of truth, she is artifice, gossip, and falsehood; she is healing presence and sorceress; she is man's prey, his downfall, she is everything that he is not and that he longs for, his negation and his *raison d'être*.

"To be a woman," says Kierkegaard in *Stages on the Road of Life*, "is something so strange, so confused, so complicated, that no one predicate comes near expressing it and that the multiple predicates that one would like to use are so contradictory that only a woman could put up with it." This comes from not regarding woman positively, such as she seems to herself to be, but negatively, such as she appears to man. For if woman is not the only *Other*, it remains none the less true that she is always defined as the Other. And her ambiguity is just that of the concept of the Other: it is that of the human situation in so far as it is defined in its relation with the Other. As I have already said, the Other is Evil; but being necessary to the Good, it turns into the Good; through it I attain to the Whole, but it also separates me therefrom; it is the gateway to the infinite and the measure of my finite nature. And here lies the reason why woman incarnates no stable concept; through her is made unceasingly the passage from hope to frustration, from hate to love, from good to evil, from evil to good. Under whatever aspect we may consider her, it is this ambivalence that strikes us first.

Man seeks in woman the Other as Nature and as his fellow being. But we know what ambivalent feelings Nature inspires in man. He exploits her, but she crushes him, he is born of her and dies in her; she is the source of his being and the realm that he subjugates to his will; Nature is a vein of gross material in which the soul is imprisoned, and she is the supreme reality; she is contingence and Idea, the finite and the whole; she is what opposes the Spirit, and the Spirit itself. Now ally, now enemy, she appears as the dark chaos from whence life wells up, as this life itself, and as the over-yonder toward which life tends. Woman sums up nature as Mother, Wife, and Idea; these forms now mingle and now conflict, and each of them wears a double visage.

Man has his roots deep in Nature; he has been engendered like the animals and plants; he well knows that he exists only in so far as he lives. But since the coming of the patriarchate, Life has worn in his eyes a double aspect: it is consciousness, will, transcendence, it is the spirit; and it is matter, passivity, immanence, it is the flesh. Æschylus, Aristotle, Hippocrates proclaimed that on earth as on Olympus it is the male principle that is truly creative: from it came form, number, movement; grain grows and multiplies through Demeter's care, but the origin of the grain and its verity lie in Zeus; woman's fecundity is regarded as only a passive quality. She is the earth, and man the seed; she is Water and he is Fire. Creation has often been imagined as the marriage of fire and water; it is warmth and moisture that give rise to living things; the Sun is the husband of the Sea; the Sun, fire, are male divinities; and the Sea is one of the most nearly universal of maternal symbols. Passively the waters accept the fertilizing action of the flaming radiations. So also the sod, broken by the plowman's labor, passively receives the seeds within its furrows. But it plays a necessary part: it supports the living germ, protects it and furnishes the substance for its growth. And that is why man continued to worship the goddesses of fecundity, even after the Great Mother was dethroned; [2] he is indebted to Cybele for his crops, his herds, his whole prosperity. He even owes his own life to her. He sings the praises of water no less than fire. "Glory to the sea! Glory to its waves surrounded with sacred fire! Glory to the wave! Glory to the fire! Glory to the strange adventure," cries Goethe in the Second Part of *Faust*. Man venerates the Earth: "The matron Clay," as Blake calls her. A prophet of India advises his disciples not to spade the earth, for "it is a sin to wound or to cut, to tear the mother of us all in the labors of cultivation. . . . Shall I go take a knife and plunge it into my mother's breast? . . . Shall I hack at her flesh to reach her bones? . . . How dare I cut off my mother's hair?" In central India the Baidya also consider it a sin to "tear their earth mother's breast with the plow." Inversely, Æschylus says of Œdipus that he "dared to seed the sacred furrow wherein he was formed." Sophocles speaks of "paternal furrows" and of the "plowman, master of a distant field that he visits only once, at the time of sowing." The loved one of an Egyptian song declares: "I am the earth!" In Islamic texts woman is called "field . . . vineyard." St. Francis of Assisi speaks in one of his hymns of "our sister, the earth, our mother, keeping and caring for us, producing all kinds of fruits, with many-colored flowers and with grass." Michelet, taking the mud baths at Acqui, exclaimed: "Dear mother of all! We are one. I came from you, to you I return! . . ." And so it is in periods when there flourishes a vitalist romanticism that desires the triumph of Life over Spirit; then the magical fertility of the land, of woman, seems to be more wonderful than the contrived operations of the male; then man dreams of losing himself anew in the maternal shadows that he may find there again the true sources of his being. The mother is the root which, sunk in the depths of the cosmos, can draw up its juices; she is the fountain whence springs forth the living water, water that is also a nourishing milk, a warm spring, a mud made of earth and water, rich in restorative virtues.[3]

---

[2] "I sing the earth, firmly founded mother of all, venerable grandmother, supporting on her soil all that lives," says a Homeric hymn. And Æschylus also glorifies the land which "brings forth all beings, supports them, and then receives in turn their fertile seed."

[3] "Literally, woman is Isis, fecund nature. She is the river and the riverbed, the root and the rose, the earth and the cherry tree, the vine-stock and the grape." (Carrouges, loc. cit.)

But more often man is in revolt against his carnal state; he sees himself as a fallen god: his curse is to be fallen from a bright and ordered heaven into the chaotic shadows of his mother's womb. This fire, this pure and active exhalation in which he likes to recognize himself, is imprisoned by woman in the mud of the earth. He would be inevitable, like a pure Idea, like the One, the All, the absolute Spirit; and he finds himself shut up in a body of limited powers, in a place and time he never chose, where he was not called for, useless, cumbersome, absurd. The contingency of all flesh is his own to suffer in his abandonment, in his unjustifiable needlessness. She also dooms him to death. This quivering jelly which is elaborated in the womb (the womb, secret and sealed like the tomb) evokes too clearly the soft viscosity of carrion for him not to turn shuddering away. Wherever life is in the making—germination, fermentation—it arouses disgust because it is made only in being destroyed; the slimy embryo begins the cycle that is completed in the putrefaction of death. Because he is horrified by needlessness and death, man feels horror at having been engendered; he would fain deny his animal ties; through the fact of his birth murderous Nature has a hold upon him.

Among primitive peoples childbirth is surrounded by the most severe taboos; in particular, the placenta must be carefully burned or thrown into the sea, for whoever should get possession of it would hold the fate of the newborn in his hands. That membranous mass by which the fetus grows is the sign of its dependency; when it is destroyed, the individual is enabled to tear himself from the living magma and become an autonomous being. The uncleanness of birth is reflected upon the mother. Leviticus and all the ancient codes impose rites of purification upon one who has given birth; and in many rural districts the ceremony of churching (blessing after childbirth) continues this tradition. We know the spontaneous embarrassment, often disguised under mocking laughter, felt by children, young girls, and men at sight of the pregnant abdomen, the swollen bosom of the woman with child. In museums the curious gaze at waxen embryos and preserved fetuses with the same morbid interest they show in a ravaged tomb. With all the respect thrown around it by society, the function of gestation still inspires a spontaneous feeling of revulsion. And if the little boy remains in early childhood sensually attached to the maternal flesh, when he grows older, becomes socialized, and takes note of his individual existence, this same flesh frightens him;

he would ignore it and see in his mother only a moral personage. If he is anxious to believe her pure and chaste, it is less because of amorous jealousy than because of his refusal to see her as a body. The adolescent is discountenanced, he blushes, if while roaming with his companions he happens to meet his mother, his sisters, any of his female relatives: it is because their presence calls him back to those realms of immanence whence he would fly, exposes roots from which he would tear himself loose. The little boy's irritation when his mother kisses and cajoles him has the same significance; he disowns family, mother, maternal bosom. He would like to have sprung into the world, like Athena fully grown, fully armed, invulnerable.[4] To have been conceived and then born an infant is the curse that hangs over his destiny, the impurity that contaminates his being. And, too, it is the announcement of his death. The cult of germination has always been associated with the cult of the dead. The Earth Mother engulfs the bones of her children. They are women—the Parcæ, the Moirai—who weave the destiny of mankind; but it is they, also, who cut the threads. In most popular representations Death is a woman, and it is for women to bewail the dead because death is their work.[5]

Thus the Woman-Mother has a face of shadows: she is the chaos whence all have come and whither all must one day return; she is Nothingness. In the Night are confused together the multiple aspects of the world which daylight reveals: night of spirit confined in the generality and opacity of matter, night of sleep and of nothingness. In the deeps of the sea it is night: woman is the *Mare tenebrarum*, dreaded by navigators of old; it is night in the entrails of the earth. Man is frightened of this night, the reverse of fecundity, which threatens to swallow him up. He aspires to the sky, to the light, to the sunny summits, to the pure and crystalline frigidity of the blue sky; and under his feet there is a moist, warm, and darkling gulf ready to draw him down; in many a legend do we see the hero lost forever as he falls back into the maternal shadows—cave, abyss, hell.

But here again is the play of ambivalence: if germination is always associated with death, so is death with fecundity. Hated death ap-

---

[4] See below (p. 199) the study of Montherlant, who embodies this attitude in exemplary fashion.

[5] Demeter typifies the *mater dolorosa*. But other goddesses—Ishtar, Artemis—are cruel. Kali holds in her hand a cranium filled with blood. A Hindu poet addresses her: "The heads of thy newly killed sons hang like a necklace about thy neck. . . . Thy form is beautiful like rain clouds, thy feet are soiled with blood."

pears as a new birth, and then it becomes blessed. The dead hero is resurrected, like Osiris, each spring, and he is regenerated by a new birth. Man's highest hope, says Jung, in *Metamorphoses of the Libido*, "is that the dark waters of death become the waters of life, that death and its cold embrace be the motherly bosom, which like the ocean, although engulfing the sun, gives birth to it again within its depths." A theme common to numerous mythologies is the burial of the sun-god in the bosom of the ocean and his dazzling reappearance. And man at once wants to live but longs for repose and sleep and nothingness. He does not wish he were immortal, and so he can learn to love death. Nietzsche writes: "Inorganic matter is the maternal bosom. To be freed of life is to become true again, it is to achieve perfection. Whoever should understand that would consider it a joy to return to the unfeeling dust." Chaucer put this prayer into the mouth of an old man unable to die:

> With my staff, night and day
> I strike on the ground, my mother's doorway,
> And I say: Ah, mother dear, let me in.

Man would fain affirm his individual existence and rest with pride on his "essential difference," but he wishes also to break through the barriers of the ego, to mingle with the water, the night, with Nothingness, with the Whole. Woman condemns man to finitude, but she also enables him to exceed his own limits; and hence comes the equivocal magic with which she is endued.

In all civilizations and still in our day woman inspires man with horror: it is the horror of his own carnal contingence, which he projects upon her. The little girl, not yet in puberty, carries no menace, she is under no taboo and has no sacred character. In many primitive societies her very sex seems innocent: erotic games are allowed from infancy between boys and girls. But on the day she can reproduce, woman becomes impure; and rigorous taboos surround the menstruating female. Leviticus gives elaborate regulations, and many primitive societies have similar rules regarding isolation and purification. In matriarchal societies the powers attributed to menstruation were ambivalent: the flow could upset social activities and ruin crops; but it was also used in love potions and medicines. Even today certain Indians put in the bow of the boat a mass of fiber soaked in menstrual blood, to combat river demons. But since patriarchal times only evil powers have been attributed to the feminine flow. Pliny said that a menstruating woman ruins crops, destroys gardens, kills bees, and so on; and that if she touches wine, it becomes vinegar; milk is soured, and the like. An ancient English poet put the same notion into rhyme:

> Oh! Menstruating woman, thou'st a fiend
> From whom all nature should be screened!

Such beliefs have survived with considerable power into recent times. In 1878 it was declared in the *British Medical Journal* that "it is an undoubted fact that meat spoils when touched by menstruating women," and cases were cited from personal observation. And at the beginning of this century a rule forbade women having "the curse" to enter the refineries of northern France, for that would cause the sugar to blacken. These ideas still persist in rural districts, where every cook knows that a mayonnaise will not be successful if a menstruating woman is about; some rustics believe cider will not ferment, others that bacon cannot be salted and will spoil under these circumstances. A few vaguely factual reports may offer some slight support for such beliefs; but it is obvious from their importance and universality that they must have had a superstitious or mystical origin. Certainly there is more here than reaction to blood in general, sacred as it is. But menstrual blood is peculiar, it represents the essence of femininity. Hence it can supposedly bring harm to the woman herself if misused by others. According to C. Lévi-Strauss, among the Chago the girls are warned not to let anyone see any signs of the flow; clothes must be buried, and so on, to avoid danger. Leviticus likens menstruation to gonorrhea, and Vigny associates the notion of uncleanness with that of illness when he writes: "Woman, sick child and twelve times impure."

The periodic hemorrhage of woman is strangely timed with the lunar cycle; and the moon also is thought to have her dangerous caprices.[6] Woman is a part of that fearsome machinery which turns

---

[6] The moon is a source of fertility; it appears as "master of women"; it is often believed that in the form of man or serpent it couples with women. The serpent is an epiphany of the moon; it sheds its skin and renews itself, it is immortal, it is an influence promoting fecundity and knowledge. It is the serpent that guards the

the planets and the sun in their courses, she is the prey of cosmic energies that rule the destiny of the stars and the tides, and of which men must undergo the disturbing radiations. But menstrual blood is supposed to act especially on organic substances, halfway between matter and life: souring cream, spoiling meat, causing fermentation, decomposition; and this less because it is blood than because it issues from the genital organs. Without comprehending its exact function, people have realized that it is bound to the reproduction of life: ignorant of the ovary, the ancients even saw in the menses the complement of the sperm. The blood, indeed, does not make woman impure; it is rather a sign of her impurity. It concerns generation, it flows from the parts where the fetus develops. Through menstrual blood is expressed the horror inspired in man by woman's fecundity.

One of the most rigorous taboos forbids all sexual relations with a woman in a state of menstrual impurity. In various cultures offenders have themselves been considered impure for certain periods, or they have been required to undergo severe penance; it has been supposed that masculine energy and vitality would be destroyed because the feminine principle is then at its maximum of force. More vaguely, man finds it repugnant to come upon the dreaded essence of the mother in the woman he possesses; he is determined to dissociate these two aspects of femininity. Hence the universal law prohibiting incest,[7] expressed in the rule of exogamy or in more modern forms; this is why man tends to keep away from woman at the times when she is especially taken up with her reproductive role: during her menses, when she is pregnant, in lactation. The Œdipus complex— which should be redescribed—does not deny this attitude, but on the contrary implies it. Man is on the defensive against woman in so far as she represents the vague source of the world and obscure organic development.

It is in this guise also, however, that woman enables her group, sep-

---

sacred springs, the tree of life, the fountain of youth. But it is also the serpent that took from man his immortality. Persian and rabbinical traditions maintain that menstruation is to be attributed to the relations of the woman with the serpent.

[7] According to the view of a sociologist, G. P. Murdock, in *Social Structure* (Macmillan, 1949), incest prohibition can be fully accounted for only by a complex theory involving factors contributed by psychoanalysis, sociology, cultural anthropology, and behavioristic psychology. No simple explanation, like "instinct," or "familiar association," or "fear of inbreeding," is at all satisfactory.—TR.

arated from the cosmos and the gods, to remain in communication
with them. Today she still assures the fertility of the fields among
the Bedouins and the Iroquois; in ancient Greece she heard the subterranean voices; she caught the language of winds and trees: she was
Pythia, sibyl, prophetess; the dead and the gods spoke through her
mouth. She keeps today these powers of divination: she is medium,
reader of palms and cards, clairvoyant, inspired; she hears voices, sees
apparitions. When men feel the need to plunge again into the midst
of plant and animal life—as Antæus touched the earth to renew his
strength—they make appeal to woman. All through the rationalist
civilizations of Greece and Rome the underworld cults continued to
exist. They were ordinarily marginal to the official religious life; they
even took on in the end, as at Eleusis, the form of mysteries: their
meaning was opposite to that of the solar cults in which man asserted his will to independence and spirituality; but they were complementary to them; man sought to escape from his solitude through
ecstasy: that was the end and aim of the mysteries, the orgies, the
bacchanals. In a world reconquered by the males, it was a male god,
Dionysus, who usurped the wild and magical power of Ishtar, of
Astarte; but still they were women who reveled madly around his
image: mænads, thyiads, bacchantes summoned the men to holy
drunkenness, to sacred frenzy. Religious prostitution played a similar
part: it was a matter at once of unloosing and channeling the powers
of fecundity. Popular festivals today are still marked by outbursts of
eroticism; woman appears here not simply as an object of pleasure,
but as a means for attaining to that state of *hybris*, riotousness, in
which the individual exceeds the bounds of self. "What a human being possesses deep within him of the lost, of the tragic, of the 'blinding wonder' can be found again nowhere but in bed," writes G. Bataille.

In the erotic release, man embraces the loved one and seeks to lose
himself in the infinite mystery of the flesh. But we have seen that, on
the contrary, his normal sexuality tends to dissociate Mother from
Wife. He feels repugnance for the mysterious alchemies of life,
whereas his own life is nourished and delighted with the savory fruits
of earth; he wishes to take them for his own; he covets Venus newly
risen from the wave. Woman is disclosed first as wife in the patriarchate, since the supreme creator is male. Before being the mother of the
human race, Eve was Adam's companion; she was given to man so

that he might possess her and fertilize her as he owns and fertilizes the soil; and through her he makes all nature his realm. It is not only a subjective and fleeting pleasure that man seeks in the sexual act. He wishes to conquer, to take, to possess; to have woman is to conquer her; he penetrates into her as the plowshare into the furrow; he makes her his even as he makes his the land he works; he labors, he plants, he sows: these images are old as writing; from antiquity to our own day a thousand examples could be cited: "Woman is like the field, and man is like the seed," says the law of Manu. In a drawing by André Masson there is a man with spade in hand, spading the garden of a woman's vulva.[8] Woman is her husband's prey, his possession.

The male's hesitation between fear and desire, between the fear of being in the power of uncontrollable forces and the wish to win them over, is strikingly reflected in the myth of Virginity. Now feared by the male, now desired or even demanded, the virgin would seem to represent the most consummate form of the feminine mystery; she is therefore its most disturbing and at the same time its most fascinating aspect. According to whether man feels himself overwhelmed by the encircling forces or proudly believes himself capable of taking control of them, he declines or demands to have his wife delivered to him a virgin. In the most primitive societies where woman's power is great, it is fear that rules him; it is proper for the woman to be deflorated before the wedding night. Marco Polo states of the Tibetans that "none of them would want to take to wife a girl that was a virgin." This refusal has sometimes been explained in a rational way: man would not want a wife who had not already aroused masculine desires. The Arab geographer El Bekri, speaking of the Slavs, reports that "if a man marries and finds his wife a virgin, he says to her: 'If you were any good, men would have made love to you and one would have taken your virginity.' Then he drives her out and repudiates her." It is claimed, even, that some primitives will take in marriage only a woman who has already been a mother, thus giving proof of her fecundity.

But the true motives underlying these widespread customs of defloration are mystical. Certain peoples imagine that there is a serpent

---

[8] Rabelais calls the male sex organ "nature's plowman." We have noted the religious and historical origin of the associations: phallus-plowshare and woman-furrow.

in the vagina which would bite the husband just as the hymen is broken; some ascribe frightful powers to virginal blood, related to menstrual blood and likewise capable of ruining the man's vigor. Through such imagery is expressed the idea that the feminine principle has the more strength, is more menacing, when it is intact.[9]

There are cases where the question of defloration is not raised; for example, among the Trobriand Islanders described by Malinowski, the girls are never virgins because sexual play is permitted from infancy. In certain cultures the mother, the older sister, or some matron systematically deflowers the young girl and throughout her childhood enlarges the vaginal orifice. Again, the defloration may be performed at puberty, the women making use of a stick, a bone, or a stone and regarding it merely as a surgical operation. In other tribes the girl is subjected at puberty to a savage initiation: men drag her outside the village and deflower her by violation or by means of objects. A common rite consists in offering the virgins to strangers passing through —whether it is thought that they are not allergic to a mana dangerous only to males of the tribe, or whether it is a matter of indifference what evils are let loose on strangers. Still more often it is the priest, or the medicine man, or the cacique, the tribal chieftain, who deflowers the bride during the night before the wedding. On the Malabar Coast the Brahmans are charged with this duty, which they are said to perform without pleasure and for which they lay claim to good pay. It is well known that all sacred objects are dangerous for the profane, but that consecrated individuals can handle them without risk; it is understandable, then, that priests and chiefs can conquer the maleficent forces against which the husband must be protected. In Rome only a symbolic ceremony remained as a vestige of such customs: the fiancée was seated on the phallus of a stone Priapus, which served the double purpose supposedly of increasing her fecundity and absorbing the too powerful—and for that reason evil—fluids with which she was charged. The husband may protect himself in still another way: he deflowers the virgin himself, but in the midst of ceremonies that at the critical moment make him invulnerable; for instance, he may operate with a stick or a bone in the presence of the whole village. In Samoa he uses his finger wrapped in a white cloth, which is torn into bloody bits and these distributed to the persons present. Or the hus-

---

[9] Thence comes the strength in combat attributed to virgins: for example, the Valkyries and the Maid of Orléans.

band may be allowed to deflower his wife in normal fashion, but is not to ejaculate inside her for three days, so that the generative germ may not be contaminated by the hymeneal blood.

Through a transvaluation that is classical in the realm of the sacred, virginal blood becomes in less primitive societies a propitious symbol. There still are villages in France where, on the morning after the wedding, the bloodstained sheets are displayed before relatives and friends. What happened is that in the patriarchal regime man became master of woman; and the very powers that are frightening in wild beasts or in unconquered elements became qualities valuable to the owner able to domesticate them. From the fire of the wild horse, the violence of lightning and cataracts, man has made means to prosperity. And so he wishes to take possession of the woman intact in all her richness. Rational motives play a part, no doubt, in the demand for virtue imposed on the young girl: like the chastity of the wife, the innocence of the fiancée is necessary so that the father may run no risk, later, of leaving his property to a child of another. But virginity is demanded for more immediate reasons when a man regards his wife as his personal property. In the first place, it is always impossible to realize positively the idea of possession; in truth, one never has any thing or any person; one tries then to establish ownership in negative fashion. The surest way of asserting that something is mine is to prevent others from using it. And nothing seems to a man to be more desirable than what has never belonged to any human being: then the conquest seems like a unique and absolute event. Virgin lands have always fascinated explorers; mountain-climbers are killed each year because they wish to violate an untouched peak or even because they have merely tried to open a new trail up its side; and the curious risk their lives to descend underground in the depths of unplumbed caverns. An object that men have already used has become an instrument; cut from its natural ties, it loses its most profound properties: there is more promise in the untamed flow of torrents than in the water of public fountains.

A virgin body has the freshness of secret springs, the morning sheen of an unopened flower, the orient luster of a pearl on which the sun has never shone. Grotto, temple, sanctuary, secret garden—man, like the child, is fascinated by enclosed and shadowy places not yet animated by any consciousness, which wait to be given a soul: what he alone is to take and to penetrate seems to be in truth created by him.

And more, one of the ends sought by all desire is the using up of the desired object, which implies its destruction. In breaking the hymen man takes possession of the feminine body more intimately than by a penetration that leaves it intact; in the irreversible act of defloration he makes of that body unequivocally a passive object, he affirms his capture of it. This idea is expressed precisely in the legend of the knight who pushed his way with difficulty through thorny bushes to pick a rose of hitherto unbreathed fragrance; he not only found it, but broke the stem, and it was then that he made it his own. The image is so clear that in popular language to "take her flower" from a woman means to destroy her virginity; and this expression, of course, has given origin to the word "defloration."

But virginity has this erotic attraction only if it is in alliance with youth; otherwise its mystery again becomes disturbing. Many men of today feel a sexual repugnance in the presence of maidenhood too prolonged; and it is not only psychological causes that are supposed to make "old maids" mean and embittered females. The curse is in their flesh itself, that flesh which is object for no subject, which no man's desire has made desirable, which has bloomed and faded without finding a place in the world of men; turned from its proper destination, it becomes an oddity, as disturbing as the incommunicable thought of a madman. Speaking of a woman of forty, still beautiful, but presumably virgin, I have heard a man say coarsely: "It must be full of spiderwebs inside." And, in truth, cellars and attics, no longer entered, of no use, become full of unseemly mystery; phantoms will likely haunt them; abandoned by people, houses become the abode of spirits. Unless feminine virginity has been dedicated to a god, one easily believes that it implies some kind of marriage with the demon. Virgins unsubdued by man, old women who have escaped his power, are more easily than others regarded as sorceresses; for the lot of woman being bondage to another, if she escapes the yoke of man she is ready to accept that of the devil.

Freed from evil spirits by defloration rites or purified through her virginity, as the case may be, the new wife may well seem a most desirable prey. Embracing her, it is all the riches of life that the lover would possess. She is the whole fauna, the whole flora of the earth; gazelle and doe, lilies and roses, downy peach, perfumed berry, she is precious stones, nacre, agate, pearl, silk, the blue of the sky, the cool water of springs, air, flame, land and sea. Poets of East and West have metamorphosed woman's body into flowers, fruits, birds. Here again, from the writings of antiquity, the Middle Ages, and modern times, what might well be cited would make an abundant anthology. Who does not know the Song of Songs? The lover says to his love:

> *Thou hast doves' eyes . . .*
> *Thy hair is as a flock of goats . . .*
> *Thy teeth are like a flock of sheep that are even shorn . . .*
> *Thy temples are like a piece of a pomegranate . . .*
> *Thy two breasts are like two young roes . . .*
> *Honey and milk are under thy tongue. . . .*

In *Arcane 17*, André Breton resumes the eternal canticle: "Mélusine at the moment of the second cry: she has sprung up from her slender haunches, her belly is all the wheat of August, her torso flares up like fireworks from her curved waist, molded after the two wings of the swallow; her breasts are ermines taken at the very moment of their natural cry, blinding the beholder with the brightness of the ardent coals of their burning mouths. And her arms are the twin souls of streams that sing and perfume. . . ."

Man finds again in woman bright stars and dreamy moon, the light of the sun, the shade of grottoes; and, conversely, the wild flowers of thickets, the proud garden rose are women. Nymphs, dryads, sirens, undines, fairies haunt the fields and woods, the lakes, oceans, moorland. Nothing lies deeper in the hearts of men than this animism. For the sailor, the sea is a woman, dangerous, treacherous, hard to conquer, but cherished the more for his effort to subdue her. The proud mountain, rebellious, virginal, and wicked, is a woman for the alpinist who wills, at the peril of his life, to violate her. It is sometimes asserted that these comparisons reveal sexual sublimation; but rather they express an affinity between woman and the elements that is as basic as sexuality itself. Man expects something other than the assuagement of instinctive cravings from the possession of a woman: she is the privileged object through which he subdues Nature. But other objects can play this part. Sometimes man seeks to find again upon the body of young boys the sandy shore, the velvet night, the scent of honeysuckle. But sexual penetration is not the only manner of accomplishing carnal possession of the earth. In his novel *To a God Unknown*, Steinbeck presents a man who has chosen a mossy rock as mediator between himself and nature; in *Chatte*, Colette describes a young husband who has centered his love on his favorite cat, because, through this wild and gentle animal, he has a grasp on the sensual universe which the too human body of his wife fails to give him. The Other can be incarnated in the sea, the mountain, as perfectly as in woman; they oppose to man the same passive and unforeseen resistance that enables him to fulfill himself; they are an unwillingness to overcome, a prey to take possession of. If sea and mountain are women, then woman is also sea and mountain for her lover.[1]

But it is not casually given to any woman whatever to serve in this way as intermediary between man and the world; man is not satisfied merely to find in his partner sex organs complementary to his own. She must incarnate the marvelous flowering of life and at the same time conceal its obscure mysteries. Before all things, then, she will be called upon for youth and health, for as man presses a living creature in his embrace, he can find enchantment in her only if he forgets that death ever dwells in life. And he asks for still more: that his loved one be beautiful. The ideal of feminine beauty is variable, but certain demands remain constant; for one thing, since woman is destined to be possessed, her body must present the inert and passive qualities of an object. Virile beauty lies in the fitness of the body for action, in strength, agility, flexibility; it is the manifestation of transcendence animating a flesh that must never sink back upon itself. The feminine ideal is symmetrical only in such societies as Sparta, Fascist Italy, and Nazi Germany, which destine woman for the State and not for the individual, which regard her exclusively as mother and make no place for eroticism.

But when woman is given over to man as his property, he demands that she represent the flesh purely for its own sake. Her body is not perceived as the radiation of a subjective personality, but as a thing sunk deeply in its own immanence; it is not for such a body to have reference to the rest of the world, it must not be the promise of things other than itself: it must end the desire it arouses. The most naïve

---

[1] A significant phrase of Samivel is cited by Bachelard (*La Terre et les rêveries de la volonté*): "These mountains lying around me in a circle I have ceased little by little to regard as enemies to fight, as females to trample upon, or as trophies to conquer so as to provide for myself and for others true witness of my own worth." The ambivalence woman–mountain is established through the common idea of "enemy to fight," "trophy," and "witness" of power.

form of this requirement is the Hottentot ideal of the steatopygous Venus, for the buttocks are the part of the body with fewest nerves, where the flesh seems an aimless fact. The taste of Orientals for fat women is of similar nature; they love the absurd richness of this adipose proliferation, enlivened as it is by no project, with no meaning other than simply to be there.[2] Even in civilizations where sensuality is more subtle and ideas of form and harmony are entertained, the breasts and the buttocks remain favored objects, because of their unnecessary, gratuitous blooming.

Costumes and styles are often devoted to cutting off the feminine body from any possible transcendence: Chinese women with bound feet could scarcely walk, the polished fingernails of the Hollywood star deprive her of her hands; high heels, corsets, panniers, farthingales, crinolines were intended less to accentuate the curves of the feminine body than to augment its incapacity. Weighted down with fat, or on the contrary so thin as to forbid all effort, paralyzed by inconvenient clothing and by the rules of propriety—then woman's body seems to man to be his property, his thing. Make-up and jewelry also further this petrification of face and body. The function of ornamental attire is very complex; with certain primitives it has a religious significance; but more often its purpose is to accomplish the metamorphosis of woman into idol. Ambiguous idol! Man wishes her to be carnal, her beauty like that of fruits and flowers; but he would also have her smooth, hard, changeless as a pebble. The function of ornament is to make her share more intimately in nature and at the same time to remove her from the natural, it is to lend to palpitating life the gelid urgency of artifice.

Woman becomes plant, panther, diamond, mother-of-pearl, by blending flowers, furs, jewels, shells, feathers with her body; she perfumes herself to spread an aroma of the lily and the rose. But feathers, silk, pearls, and perfumes serve also to hide the animal crudity of her flesh, her odor. She paints her mouth and her cheeks to give

---

[2] "The Hottentots, among whom steatopygy is neither as developed nor as usual as with the female Bushman, regard this conformation as of æsthetic value, and they knead the buttocks of their girls from infancy to develop them. Similarly the artificial fattening of woman—a veritable stuffing, the two essential features of which are immobility and abundant ingestion of appropriate foods, particularly milk—is met with in various parts of Africa. It is still practiced by the well-off Arab and Israelite citizen of Algeria, Tunis, and Morocco." (Luquet: *"Les Vénus des cavernes," Journal de Psychologie,* 1934.)

them the solid fixity of a mask; her glance she imprisons deep in kohl and mascara, it is no more than the iridescent ornament of her eyes; her hair, braided, curled, shaped, loses its disquieting plantlike mystery.

In woman dressed and adorned, nature is present but under restraint, by human will remolded nearer to man's desire. A woman is rendered more desirable to the extent that nature is more highly developed in her and more rigorously confined: it is the "sophisticated" woman who has always been the ideal erotic object. And the taste for a more natural beauty is often only a specious form of sophistication. Remy de Gourmont wanted woman to wear her hair down, rippling free as brooks and prairie grasses; but it would be on Veronica Lake's hair-do and not on an unkempt mop really left to nature that one could caress the undulations of water and grain fields. The younger and healthier a woman and the more her new and shining body seems endowed with everlasting freshness, the less useful artifice is to her; but it is always needful to conceal from the man the carnal weakness of the prey he clasps and the deterioration that threatens it. Because he fears her contingent destiny, because he fancies her changeless, necessary, man seeks to find on the face of woman, on her body and limbs, the exact expression of an ideal. Among primitive peoples this ideal is only that of the perfection of the popular type: a race with thick lips and a flat nose constructs a Venus with thick lips and flat nose; in later periods the canons of a more complex æsthetics are applied to women. But, in any case, the more the features and proportions of a woman seem contrived, the more she rejoices the heart of man because she seems to escape the vicissitudes of natural things. We come, then, to this strange paradox: man, wishing to find nature in woman, but nature transfigured, dooms woman to artifice. She is not only *physis* but quite as much *antiphysis*; and this not only in the civilization of electrical "permanents," of superfluous-hair removal by means of wax, of latex girdles, but also in the land of Negresses with lip disks, in China and everywhere on earth.

Swift denounced this mystification in his famous *Ode to Celia*; he describes with disgust the paraphernalia of the coquette and recalls with disgust the animal necessities of her body. He is twice wrong in his indignation; for man wishes simultaneously that woman be animal and plant and that she be hidden behind an artificial front;

he loves her rising from the sea and emerging from a fashionable dressmaker's establishment, naked and dressed, naked under her clothes—such, precisely, as he finds her in the universe of humanity. The city man seeks animality in woman; but for the young peasant, doing his army service, the whorehouse embodies all the magic of the city. Woman is field and pasture, but she is also Babylon.

However, this is woman's first lie, her first treason: namely, that of life itself—life which, though clothed in the most attractive forms, is always infested by the ferments of age and death. The very use man makes of woman destroys her most precious powers: weighed down by maternities, she loses her erotic attraction; even when she is sterile, it takes only the passage of time to alter her charms—infirm, homely, old, woman is horrifying. She is said to be withered, faded, as might be said of a plant. To be sure, in man, too, decrepitude is terrifying; but normally man does not experience older men as flesh; he has only an abstract unity with these separate and strange bodies. It is upon woman's body—this body which is destined for him—that man really encounters the deterioration of the flesh. It is through man's hostile eyes that Villon's *belle heaulmière* contemplates the degradation of her body. The old woman, the homely woman, are not merely objects without allure—they arouse hatred mingled with fear. In them reappears the disquieting figure of the Mother, when once the charms of the Wife have vanished.

But even the Wife is dangerous prey. In Venus risen from the wave—fresh foam, blond harvest—Demeter survives; when man takes possession of woman through the pleasure he gets from her, he also awakens in her the dubious power of fecundity: the organ he penetrates is the same as that which gives birth to the child. This is why in all societies man is protected by many taboos against the dangers of the female sex. The opposite is not true, woman has nothing to fear from the male; his sex is regarded as secular, profane. The phallus can be raised to the dignity of a god; but in his worship there is no element of terror, and in the course of daily life woman has no need of being mystically defended against him; he is always propitious. It is remarkable, too, that in many matrilineal societies a very free sexuality exists; but this is true only during woman's childhood, in her first youth, when coition is not connected with the idea of reproduction. Malinowski relates with some astonishment that young people who sleep together freely in the "bachelors' house" readily proclaim their amours; the fact is that the unmarried girl is regarded as unable to bear offspring, and the sexual act is therefore considered to be simply a calm secular pleasure. Once a woman is married, on the contrary, her husband must give her no signs of affection in public, he must not touch her; and any allusion to their intimate relations is sacrilege: she has then come to share in the fearful essence of the mother, and coition has become a sacred act. Thenceforth it is surrounded with prohibitions and precautions. Coition is forbidden at the time of cultivation of the land, the sowing of seeds, the setting of plants; in this case, it is to avoid wasting in relations between individuals the fecundating forces necessary for thriving crops and therefore for community welfare; it is out of respect for the powers concerned with fecundity that economy is here enjoined. But for the most part continence protects the manly strength of the husband; it is required when the man is to depart for fishing or hunting, and especially when he prepares for war. In uniting with woman the male principle is enfeebled, and the man must therefore avoid union whenever he needs to maintain his strength entire.

It is a question whether the horror inspired in man by woman comes from that inspired by sexuality in general, or vice versa. It is noteworthy that, in Leviticus particularly, nocturnal emission is regarded as a defilement, though woman is not concerned in it. And in our modern societies masturbation is popularly regarded as a danger and a sin: many children and young people who are addicts practice it only with horrible fear and anguish. It is the interference of society and particularly of parents that makes a vice of solitary pleasure; but more than one young boy has been spontaneously frightened by his ejaculations: blood or semen, any flowing away of his own substance seems to him disquieting; it is his life, his mana that is escaping. However, even if a man can subjectively go through erotic experiences without woman being present, she is objectively implied in his sexuality: as Plato says in the myth of the Androgynes, the organism of the male supposes that of the female. Man discovers woman in discovering his own sex, even if she is present neither in flesh and blood nor in imagery; and inversely it is in so far as she incarnates sexuality that woman is redoubtable. We can never separate the immanent and the transcendent aspects of living experience: what I fear or desire is always an embodiment of my own existence, but nothing happens to me except it comes through what is not me. The non-ego is implied in nocturnal emissions, in erections, if not definitely under the form of woman, at least as Nature and Life: the individual feels himself to be possessed by a magic not of himself.

Indeed, the ambivalence of his feelings toward woman reappears in his attitude toward his own sex organ: he is proud of it, he laughs at it, he is ashamed of it. The little boy challenges comparison of his penis with those of his comrades: his first erection fills him with pride and fright at once. The grown man regards his organ as a symbol of transcendence and power; it pleases his vanity like a voluntary muscle and at the same time like a magical gift: it is a liberty rich in all the contingency of the fact given yet freely wished; it is under this contradictory aspect that he is enchanted with it, but he is suspicious of deception. That organ by which he thought to assert himself does not obey him; heavy with unsatisfied desires, unexpectedly becoming erect, sometimes relieving itself during sleep, it manifests a suspect and capricious vitality. Man aspires to make Spirit triumph over Life, action over passivity; his consciousness keeps nature at a distance, his will shapes her, but in his sex organ he finds himself again beset with life, nature, and passivity.

"The sexual organs," writes Schopenhauer, "are the true seat of the will, of which the opposite pole is the brain." What he calls "will" is attachment to life, which is suffering and death, while "the brain" is thought, which is detached from life in imagining it. Sexual shame, according to him, is the shame we feel before our stupid infatuation with the carnal. Even if we take exception to the pessimism of his theories, he is right in seeing in the opposition: sex *vs.* brain, the expression of man's duality. As subject, he poses the world, and remaining outside this posed universe, he makes himself ruler of it; if he views himself as flesh, as sex, he is no longer an independent consciousness, a clear, free being: he is involved with the world, he is a limited and perishable object. And no doubt the generative act passes beyond the frontiers of the body; but at the same moment it establishes them. The penis, father of generations, corresponds to the maternal womb; arising from a germ that grew in woman's body, man is himself a carrier of germs, and through the sowing which gives life, it is his own life that is renounced. "The birth of children," says Hegel, "is the death of parents." The ejaculation is a promise of death, it is an assertion of the species against the individual; the existence of the sex organ and its activity deny the proud

singularity of the subject. It is this contesting of life against spirit
that makes the organ scandalous. Man glories in the phallus when he
thinks of it as transcendence and activity, as a means for taking possession of the other; but he is ashamed of it when he sees it as merely
passive flesh through which he is the plaything of the dark forces
of Life. This shame is readily concealed in irony. The sex organ of
another easily arouses laughter; erection often seems ridiculous, because it seems like an intended action but is really involuntary, and
the mere presence of the genital organs, when it is referred to, evokes
mirth. Malinowski relates that for the savages among whom he was
living it was sufficient to mention the name of the "shameful parts"
to arouse inextinguishable laughter; many jokes called Rabelaisian or
"smutty" go hardly beyond this rudimentary word play. Among certain primitives the women are given the right, during the days consecrated to weeding the gardens, to violate brutally any stranger who
ventures near; they attack him all together and frequently leave him
half-dead. The men of the tribe laugh at this exploit; by this violation
the victim has been made passive and dependent flesh; he has been
possessed by the women, and through them by their husbands; whereas
in normal coition man wishes to establish himself as the possessor.

But just here he will learn—with the best of evidence—the ambiguity of his carnal situation. He takes great pride in his sexuality only
in so far as it is a means of appropriating the Other—and this dream
of possession ends only in frustration. In authentic possession the
other is abolished as such, it is consumed and destroyed: only the Sultan in *The Arabian Nights* has the power to cut off each mistress's
head when dawn has come to take her from his couch. Woman survives man's embraces, and in that very fact she escapes him; as soon
as he loosens his arms, his prey becomes again a stranger to him;
there she lies, new, intact, ready to be possessed by a new lover in as
ephemeral a manner. One of the male's dreams is to "brand" the
woman in such a way that she will remain forever his; but the most
arrogant well knows that he will never leave with her anything more
than memories and that the most ardent recollections are cold in
comparison with an actual, present sensation. A whole literature has
expatiated upon this frustration. It is made objective in woman, and
she is called inconstant and traitress because her body is such as to
dedicate her to man in general and not to one man in particular.

But her treason is more perfidious still: she makes her lover in truth her prey. Only a body can touch another body; the male masters the flesh he longs for only in becoming flesh himself; Eve is given to Adam so that through her he may accomplish his transcendence, and she draws him into the night of immanence. His mistress, in the vertigoes of pleasure, encloses him again in the opaque clay of that dark matrix which the mother fabricated for her son and from which he desires to escape. He wishes to possess her: behold him the possessed himself! Odor, moisture, fatigue, ennui—a library of books has described this gloomy passion of a consciousness made flesh. Desire, which frequently shrouds disgust, reveals disgust again when it is satisfied. It has been said: "*Post coitum homo animal triste.*" And again: "*La chair est triste.*" And yet man has not even found final satisfaction in his loved one's arms. Soon desire is reborn in him; and frequently this is not merely desire for woman in general, but for this particular one. Now she wields a power that is peculiary disquieting. For, in his own body, man feels the sexual need only as a general need analogous to hunger and thirst, a need without particular object: the bond that holds him to this especial feminine body has, then, been forged by the Other. It is a bond as mysterious as the impure and fertile abdomen where it has its roots, a kind of passive force: it is magic.

The threadbare vocabulary of the serial novels describing woman as a sorceress, an enchantress, fascinating and casting a spell over man, reflects the most ancient and universal of myths. Woman is dedicated to magic. Alain said that magic is spirit drooping down among things; an action is magical when, instead of being produced by an agent, it emanates from something passive. Just so men have always regarded woman as the immanence of what is given; if she produces harvests and children, it is not by an act of her will; she is not subject, transcendence, creative power, but an object charged with fluids. In the societies where man worships these mysteries, woman, on account of these powers, is associated with religion and venerated as priestess; but when man struggles to make society triumph over nature, reason over life, and the will over the inert, given nature of things, then woman is regarded as a sorceress. The difference between a priest and a magician is well known: the first controls and directs forces he has mastered in accord with the gods and the laws, for the common good, in the name of all members of the group; the magician operates apart from society, against the gods and the laws, according to his own deep interests. Now, woman is not fully integrated into the world of men; as the other, she is opposed to them. It is natural for her to use the power she has, not to spread through the community of men and into the future the bold emprise of transcendence, but, being apart, opposed, to drag the males into the solitude of separation, into the shades of immanence. Woman is the siren whose song lures sailors upon the rocks; she is Circe, who changes her lovers into beasts, the undine who draws fishermen into the depths of pools. The man captivated by her charms no longer has will-power, enterprise, future; he is no longer a citizen, but mere flesh enslaved to its desires, cut off from the community, bound to the moment, tossed passively back and forth between torture and pleasure. The perverse sorceress arrays passion against duty, the present moment against all time to come; she detains the traveler far from home, she pours him the drink of forgetfulness.

Seeking to appropriate the Other, man must remain himself; but in the frustration of impossible possession he tries to become that other with whom he fails to be united; then he is alienated, he is lost, he drinks the philter that makes him a stranger to himself, he plunges into the depths of fleeting and deadly waters. The Mother dooms her son to death in giving him life; the loved one lures her lover on to renounce life and abandon himself to the last sleep. The bond that unites Love and Death is poignantly illuminated in the legend of Tristan, but it has a deeper truth. Born of the flesh, the man in love finds fulfillment as flesh, and the flesh is destined to the tomb. Here the alliance between Woman and Death is confirmed; the great harvestress is the inverse aspect of the fecundity that makes the grain thrive. But she appears, too, as the dreadful bride whose skeleton is revealed under her sweet, mendacious flesh.[3]

Thus what man cherishes and detests first of all in woman—loved one or mother—is the fixed image of his animal destiny; it is the life that is necessary to his existence but that condemns him to the finite and to death. From the day of his birth man begins to die: this is the truth incarnated in the Mother. In procreation he speaks for the species against himself: he learns this in his wife's embrace; in excitement and pleasure, even before he has engendered, he forgets

---

[3] For example, in Prévert's ballet *Le Rendez-vous* [seen in New York during the winter of 1949–50—Tr.] and Cocteau's *Le Jeune Homme et la Mort*, Death is represented in the form of a beloved young girl.

his unique ego. Although he endeavors to distinguish mother and wife, he gets from both a witness to one thing only: his mortal state. He wishes to venerate his mother and love his mistress; at the same time he rebels against them in disgust and fear.

Many attitudes are possible for the man, as he puts emphasis on one or another aspect of the fleshly drama. If a man does not feel that life is unique, if he is not much concerned with his peculiar destiny, if he does not fear death, he will joyfully accept his animality. Among the Moslems woman is reduced to an abject condition because of the feudal structure of society, which does not permit appeal to the State against the family, and because of the religion, which, expressing the warlike ideals of that civilization, has dedicated man directly to Death and has deprived woman of her magic. What should he fear on earth, he who is prepared at any moment to be plunged into the voluptuous orgies of the Mohammedan paradise? Man can in such case tranquilly enjoy woman without needing to be defended either from himself or from her. The tales of *The Arabian Nights* represent woman as a source of soothing delights, in the same way as are fruits, preserves, rich cakes, and perfumed oils. We find today that same sensual benevolence among many Mediterranean peoples: preoccupied with the moment, not aspiring to immortality, the man of the Midi, who through the brightness of sky and sea sees Nature under her favoring aspect, will love women with the gourmand's relish. By tradition he scorns them enough to prevent his regarding them as persons: he hardly differentiates between the pleasantness of their bodies and that of sand and wave; he feels no horror of the flesh either in them or in himself. Vittorini says in *In Sicily* that at the age of seven he discovered the naked body of woman with tranquil astonishment. The rationalist thought of Greece and Rome supports this easy attitude. The optimistic philosophy of the Greeks went beyond the Pythagorean Manichæism; the inferior is subordinated to the superior and thus is useful to him. These harmonious ideologies manifest no hostility to the flesh whatever. Oriented toward the heaven of Ideas, or toward the City or the State, the individual regarding himself as Spirit (Noῦs) or as citizen considered that he had risen above his animal nature; whether he abandoned himself to pleasure or practiced asceticism, woman, solidly integrated in male society, had only a secondary importance. To be sure, rationalism never triumphed completely and the erotic experience kept in

these civilizations its ambivalent character: rites, mythology, literature attest this. But the attractions and the dangers of femininity
were manifested in weakened form only.

It is Christianity which invests woman anew with frightening
prestige: fear of the other sex is one of the forms assumed by the
anguish of man's uneasy conscience. The Christian is divided within
himself; the separation of body and soul, of life and spirit, is complete; original sin makes of the body the enemy of the soul; all ties of
the flesh seem evil.[4] Only as redeemed by Christ and directed toward
the kingdom of heaven can man be saved; but originally he is only
corruption; his birth dooms him not only to death but to damnation;
it is by divine Grace that heaven can be opened to him, but in all the
forms of his natural existence there is a curse. Evil is an absolute
reality; and the flesh is sin. And of course, since woman remains always the Other, it is not held that reciprocally male and female are
both flesh: the flesh that is for the Christian the hostile *Other* is precisely woman. In her the Christian finds incarnated the temptations
of the world, the flesh, and the devil. All the Fathers of the Church
insist on the idea that she led Adam into sin. We must quote Tertullian again: "Woman! You are the gateway of the devil. You persuaded him whom the devil dared not attack directly. Because of
you the Son of God had to die. You should always go dressed in
mourning and in rags." All Christian literature strives to enhance the
disgust that man can feel for woman. Tertullian defines her as
"*templum œdificatum super cloacam*" ["a temple built over a sewer"].
St. Augustine called attention with horror to the obscene commingling of the sexual and excretory organs: "*Inter fœces et urinam
nascimur*" ["We are born between feces and urine"]. The aversion
of Christianity in the matter of the feminine body is such that while
it is willing to doom its God to an ignominious death, it spares Him
the defilement of being born: the Council of Ephesus in the Eastern
Church and the Lateran Council in the West declare the virgin birth
of Christ. The first Fathers of the Church—Origen, Tertullian, and
Jerome—thought that Mary had been brought to bed in blood and

---

4 Up to the end of the twelfth century the theologians, except St. Anselme,
considered that according to the doctrine of St. Augustine original sin is involved
in the very law of generation: "Concupiscence is a vice . . . human flesh born
through it is a sinful flesh," writes St. Augustine. And St. Thomas: "The union
of the sexes transmits original sin to the child, being accompanied, since the Fall,
by concupiscence."

filth like other women; but the opinion of St. Ambrose and St. Augustine was the one that prevailed. The body of the Virgin remained closed. Since the Middles Ages the fact of having a body has been considered, in woman, an ignominy. Even science was long paralyzed by this disgust. Linnæus in his treatise on nature avoided as "abominable" the study of woman's sexual organs. The French physician des Laurens asked himself the scandalized question: "How can this divine animal, full of reason and judgment, which we call man, be attracted by these obscene parts of woman, defiled with juices and located shamefully at the lowest part of the trunk?"

Today many other influences interfere with that of Christian thought; and this has itself a number of aspects. But, in the Puritan world among others, hate of the flesh continues to exist; it is expressed, for example, in Faulkner's *Light in August*; the initial sexual adventures of the hero are terribly traumatic. Throughout literature it is common to show a young man upset to the point of nausea after his first coition; and if in actuality such a reaction is very rare, it is not by chance that it is so often described. Especially in Anglo-Saxon countries, which are steeped in Puritanism, woman arouses in most adolescents and in many men a terror more or less openly admitted. The feeling exists rather strongly in France. Michel Leiris writes in his *Âge d'homme:* "At present I tend to regard the feminine organ as something unclean or as a wound, not less attractive on that account, but dangerous in itself, like everything bloody, mucous, infected." The idea of venereal disease expresses these fears. Woman causes fright not because she gives diseases; the truth is that the diseases seem abominable because they come from woman: I have been told of young people who imagine that too frequent intercourse is enough to give gonorrhea. It is a common belief also that on account of coition a man loses his muscular strength and his clearheadedness, and that his phosphorus is used up and his sensitivity is dulled. True enough, masturbation implies these same dangers; and society even considers it, for moral reasons, as more injurious than the normal sexual function. Legitimate marriage and the wish to have children are protective against the bad effects of eroticism. But I have already said that in every sexual act the Other is implicated; and the Other most often wears the visage of woman. With her, man senses most definitely the passivity of his own flesh. Woman is vampire, she eats and drinks him; her organ feeds gluttonously upon his. Certain psychoanalysts have attempted to provide scientific support for these fancies, suggesting that all the pleasure woman gets from intercourse might come from the fact that she symbolically castrates him and takes possession of his penis. But it would seem that these theories should themselves be submitted to psychoanalysis, and it is likely that the physicians who invent them are engaged in projecting their own ancestral terrors.

The source of these terrors lies in the fact that in the Other, quite beyond reach, alterity, otherness, abides. In patriarchal societies woman retains many of the disquieting powers she possessed in primitive societies. That is why she is never left to Nature, but is surrounded with taboos, purified by rites, placed in charge of priests; man is adjured never to approach her in her primitive nakedness, but through ceremonials and sacraments, which draw her away from the earth and the flesh and change her into a human creature; whereupon the magic she exercises is canalized, like the lightning since the invention of lightning rods and electrical power plants. It even becomes possible to use her powers in the general interest; and here we see another phase in that oscillation which marks the relation of man to his female. He loves her to the extent that she is his, he fears her in so far as she remains the other; but it is as the fearsome other that he seeks to make her more profoundly his—and this is what will bring him to elevate her to the dignity of being a person and lead him to recognize in her a fellow creature.

Feminine magic was deeply domesticated in the patriarchal family. Woman gives society the opportunity of integrating the cosmic forces in her. In his work *Mitra-Varouna*, Dumézil points out that in India as in Rome there are two ways of displaying virile power: first, in Varuna and Romulus, in the Gandharvas and the Luperci, this power is aggression, rape, disorder, wanton violence; in this case woman appears as a being to be ravished, violated; the ravished Sabine women, apparently sterile, were lashed with whips of bullhide, to compensate for too much violence by more violence. But, second and on the contrary, Mithra, Numa, the Brahmans, and the flamens (priests) stand for law and order in the city: in this case woman is bound to her husband in a marriage marked by elaborate rites, and, working with him, she gives him assurance of dominating all the female forces of nature; in Rome the priest of Jupiter resigned his position if his wife died. And likewise in Egypt, after Isis lost her supreme power as goddess mother, she remained nevertheless generous, smiling, kind, and good, the magnificent wife of Osiris. But when woman is thus the associate of man, complementary, his "better half," she is of necessity endowed with a conscious ego, a soul. He could not depend so intimately upon a creature who did not share in the essence of humanity. As we have already noted, the Laws of Manu promised to the legitimate wife the same paradise as to her husband. The more the male becomes individualized and lays claim to his individuality, the more certainly he will recognize also in his companion an individual and a free being. The Oriental, careless of his own fate, is content with a female who is for him a means of enjoyment; but the dream of the Occidental, once he rises to consciousness of his own uniqueness, is to be taken cognizance of by another free being, at once strange and docile. The Greek never found the female imprisoned in the gynæceum to be the fellow being he required, so he bestowed his love upon male companions whose flesh was informed like his with consciousness and freedom; or he gave his love to the hetairas, made almost his equals by their intelligence, culture, and wit. But when circumstances permit, it is the wife who can best satisfy man's demands. The Roman citizen recognized in the matron a person: in Cornelia, in Arria, he had his counterpart.

It was Christianity, paradoxically, that was to proclaim, on a certain plane, the equality of man and woman. In her, Christianity hates the flesh; if she renounces the flesh, she is God's creature, redeemed by the Saviour, no less than is man: she takes her place beside the men, among the souls assured of the joys of heaven. Men and women are both servants of God, almost as asexual as the angels and together, through grace, resistant to earthly temptations. If she agrees to deny her animality, woman—from the very fact that she is the incarnation of sin—will be also the most radiant incarnation of the triumph of the elect who have conquered sin.[5] Of course, the divine Saviour who effects the redemption of men is male; but mankind must co-operate in its own salvation, and it will be called upon to manifest its submissive good will in its most humiliated and perverse aspect. Christ is God; but it is a woman, the Virgin Mary, who reigns over all humankind. Yet only the marginal sects revive in woman the ancient

---

[5] This explains the privileged place she occupies, for example, in Claudel's work.

privileges and powers of the great goddesses—the Church expresses and serves a patriarchal civilization in which it is meet and proper for woman to remain appended to man. It is through being his docile servant that she will be also a blessed saint. And thus at the heart of the Middle Ages arises the most highly perfected image of woman propitious to man: the countenance of the Mother of Christ is framed in glory. She is the inverse aspect of Eve the sinner; she crushes the serpent underfoot; she is the mediatrix of salvation, as Eve was of damnation.

It was as Mother that woman was fearsome; it is in maternity that she must be transfigured and enslaved. The virginity of Mary has above all a negative value: that through which the flesh has been redeemed is not carnal; it has not been touched or possessed. Similarly the Asiatic Great Mother was not supposed to have a husband: she had engendered the world and reigned over it in solitary state; she could be wanton at her caprice, but her grandeur as Mother was not diminished by any wifely servitude. In the same way Mary knew not the stain of sexuality. Like the warlike Minerva, she is ivory tower, citadel, impregnable donjon. The priestesses of antiquity, like most Christian saints, were also virgin: woman consecrated to the good should be dedicated in the splendor of her intact strength; she should conserve in its unconquered integrity the essence of her femininity. If Mary's status as spouse be denied her, it is for the purpose of exalting the Woman Mother more purely in her. But she will be glorified only in accepting the subordinate role assigned to her. "I am the servant of the Lord." For the first time in human history the mother kneels before her son; she freely accepts her inferiority. This is the supreme masculine victory, consummated in the cult of the Virgin— it is the rehabilitation of woman through the accomplishment of her defeat. Ishtar, Astarte, Cybele were cruel, capricious, lustful; they were powerful. As much the source of death as of life, in giving birth to men they made men their slaves. Under Christianity life and death depend only upon God, and man, once out of the maternal body, has escaped that body forever; the earth now awaits his bones only. For the destiny of his soul is played out in regions where the mother's powers are abolished; the sacrament of baptism makes ridiculous those ceremonies in which the placenta was burned or drowned. There is no longer any place on earth for magic: God alone is king. Nature, originally inimical, is through grace rendered powerless to harm. Maternity as a natural phenomenon confers no power. So there remains for woman, if she wishes to rise above her original fault, only to bow to the will of God, which subordinates her to man. And through this submission she can assume a new role in masculine mythology. Beaten down, trampled upon when she wished to dominate and as long as she had not definitely abdicated, she could be honored as vassal. She loses none of her primitive attributes, but these are reversed in sign; from being of evil omen they become of good omen; black magic turns to white. As servant, woman is entitled to the most splendid deification.

And since woman has been subjected as Mother, she will be cherished and respected first of all as Mother. Of the two ancient aspects of maternity, man today wishes to know only the smiling, attractive face. Limited in time and space, having but one body and one finite life, man is but a lone individual in the midst of a Nature and a History that are both foreign to him. Woman is similarly limited, and like man she is endowed with mind and spirit, but she belongs to Nature, the infinite current of Life flows through her; she appears, therefore, as the mediatrix between the individual and the cosmos. When the mother has become a figure of reassurance and holiness, man naturally turns to her in love. Lost in nature, he seeks to escape; but separated from her he wishes to go back. Established firmly in the family, in society, conforming to the laws and customs, the mother is the very incarnation of the Good: nature, to which she belongs in part, becomes good, no longer an enemy of the spirit; and if she remains mysterious, hers is a smiling mystery, like that of Leonardo da Vinci's madonnas. Man does not wish to be woman, but he dreams of enfolding within him all that exists, including therefore this woman, whom he is not; in his worship of his mother he endeavors to take possession of her strange wealth. To recognize that he is son of his mother is to recognize his mother in himself, it is to become one with femininity in so far as femininity is connection with the earth, with life, and with the past.

In Vittorini's *In Sicily*, what the hero seeks in visiting his mother is his native land, its fragrance and its fruits, his childhood, the memory of his ancestors, the traditions, the roots from which his personal life has cut him off. It is this very enrooting that in man exalts his pride in his transcendence; it pleases him to observe with admiration how he tears himself from his mother's arms to go forth for adventure, the future, war. This departure would be less moving if there had been no one to try to detain him: it would appear like an accident, not a hard-won victory. And, too, he is pleased to know that those arms remain ready to welcome him back. After the strain of battle the hero likes to enjoy again the repose of immanence with his mother: she is refuge, sleep; at the caress of her hands he sinks again into nature's bosom, he lets himself be carried onward in life's vast flow as quietly as in the womb or in the grave. And if tradition would have him die calling upon his mother, it is because even death itself, under the maternal eye, is domesticated, in correspondence with birth, indissolubly linked with all life of the flesh.

The mother remains associated with death as in the antique myth of the Parcæ; it is for her to lay out the dead, to mourn their passing. But her role is precisely to integrate death with life, with society, with the general welfare. And so the cult of "heroic mothers" is systematically encouraged: if society can persuade mothers to yield up their sons to death, then it feels it has the right to kill them off. On account of the influence the mother has over her sons, it is advantageous for society to have her in hand: that is why the mother is surrounded with so many marks of respect, she is endowed with all the virtues, a religion is created with special reference to her, from which it is forbidden to depart at the risk of committing sacrilege and blasphemy. She is made guardian of morals; servant of man, servant of the powers that be, she will tenderly guide her children along appointed ways. The more resolutely optimistic a society is, the more docilely will it submit to this gentle authority, the more the mother will be transfigured. The American "mom" has become the idol described by Philip Wylie in *Generation of Vipers*, because the official ideology of America is the most obstinate optimism. To glorify the mother is to accept birth, life, and death under their animal and humanly social forms at once, it is to proclaim the harmony of nature and society. Because he dreamed of achieving this synthesis, Auguste Comte made woman the divinity of the Humanity of the future. But the same considerations incite all revolutionaries against the figure of the mother; in flouting her, they reject the *status quo* it is intended to impose upon them through the motherly guardian of laws and customs.[6]

---

[6] The poem by Michel Leiris entitled *La Mère* should be given here complete; but a few characteristic lines will have to suffice:

The respect that haloes the Mother, the prohibitions that surround her, suppress the hostile disgust that is mingled spontaneously with the carnal tenderness she inspires. A certain masked horror of maternity survives, however. It is of especial interest to note that since the Middle Ages a secondary myth has been in existence, permitting free expression of this repugnance: it is the myth of the Mother-in-Law. From fable to vaudeville, man flouts maternity in general through his wife's mother, whom no taboo protects. He loathes the thought that the woman he loves should have been engendered: his mother-in-law is the visible image of the decrepitude to which she has doomed her daughter in bringing her forth. Her fat and her wrinkles give notice of the fat and the wrinkles coming to the young bride whose future is thus mournfully prefigured; at her mother's side she seems no longer like an individual, but like a phase of a species; she is no longer the wished-for prey, the cherished companion, because her individual and separate existence merges into universal life. Her individuality is derisively contested by generality, the autonomy of her spirit by her being rooted in the past and in the flesh: it is this derision to which man gives objective existence in a grotesque personage. But if his laugh is full of rancor, it is because he knows well enough that his wife's lot is the lot of all: it is his. In every country tales and legends have similarly incarnated the cruel aspect of maternity in the stepmother. It is her stepmother who would have Snow White perish. In the figure of the wicked stepmother—like Mme Fichini, whipping Sophie through Mme de Ségur's books—survives the antique Kali with her necklace of severed heads.

Yet close behind the sainted Mother presses the throng of female white magicians who offer for man's use the juices of herbs and the radiations of the stars: grandmothers, old women with kindly eyes, goodhearted servants, Sisters of Mercy, nurses with wonderfully gentle hands, the loved one of Verlaine's dream:

The mother in black, mauve, violet,/ thief of time,/ she is the sorceress whose hidden diligence brings you into the world, who rocks your cradle, who lays you on the bier, when she does not abandon her shriveled body—the ultimate plaything —to your hands which place it gently in the coffin. . . .

The mother / sightless statue, calamity, totality set up in the center of the inviolate sanctuary / she is nature which caresses you, the wind which perfumes you with incense, the world which pervades you in its entirety, mounts you up to heaven . . . and spoils you. . . .

The mother, her hip round or bony, her breast quivering or firm / she is the decline promised, from the beginning, to every woman. . . .

Sweet, pensive and dark and surprised at nothing,
And who at times will kiss you on the forehead like a child.

To them is ascribed the pure mystery of gnarled vine and fresh water; they dress and heal wounds; their wisdom is the silent wisdom of life, they understand without words. In their presence man forgets his pride; he knows the sweetness of yielding and becoming once more a child, for with such women he need not struggle for prestige: he could not begrudge nature her nonhuman powers; and in their devotedness the wise initiates who take care of him recognize the fact that they are his servants; he submits to their kindly power because he knows that in this submission he remains their master. Sisters, childhood friends, pure young girls, all the mothers of the future belong to this beneficent band. And his wife herself, her erotic magic once dissipated, is regarded by many men less as a sweetheart than as the mother of their children.[7] When once the mother has been sanctified and enslaved, one need not be affrighted to find her again in the companion, who is also sanctified and submissive. To redeem the mother is to redeem the flesh, and hence carnal union and the wife.

Deprived of her magic weapons by the marriage rites and subordinated economically and socially to her husband, the "good wife" is man's most precious treasure. She belongs to him so profoundly that she partakes of the same essence as he; she has his name, his gods, and he is responsible for her. He calls her his "better half." He takes pride in his wife as he does in his house, his lands, his flocks, his wealth, and sometimes even more; through her he displays his power before the world: she is his measure and his earthly portion. In the Oriental view, a woman should be fat: people can see that she is well nourished and she does honor to her lord and master.[8] A Moslem is better thought of the more wives he has and the more flourishing their appearance. In bourgeois society one of the roles assigned to woman is *to make a good showing*: her beauty, charm, intelligence, elegance are the outward and visible signs of her husband's wealth, as is the custom-built body of his car. If he is rich he covers her with fur and jewels; if not so rich, he will boast of her morality and her

---

[7] In America, at least, it is very common for the husband and father not yet middle-aged to call his wife "mother" or "mummie" in familiar discourse.—TR.

[8] See note on page 158.

housekeeping. The most destitute, if he has obtained a woman to serve him, believes he owns something in the world: the hero of *The Taming of the Shrew* calls all his neighbors in to see how authoritatively he can subdue his wife. Every man in a way recalls King Candaules: he exhibits his wife because he believes that in this way he is advertising his own merits.

But woman flatters not only man's social vanity; she is the source of a more intimate pride. He is delighted with his domination of her; upon those realistic symbols of the plowshare opening the furrow are superposed—when woman is a person—more spiritual symbols: the husband "forms" his wife not erotically alone, but also morally and intellectually; he educates her, marks her, sets his imprint upon her. One of the daydreams in which man takes delight is that of imbuing things with his will—modeling their form, penetrating their substance. And woman is *par excellence* the "clay in his hands," which can be passively worked and shaped; in yielding she resists, thus allowing masculine activity to go on indefinitely. A too plastic substance is soon finished and done with, because it is easy to work; but what is precious in woman is that something in her somehow eludes every embrace; thus man is master of a reality all the more worthy of being mastered in that it is constantly escaping control.

Woman awakens in man an unknown being whom he recognizes with pride as himself; in the blameless orgies of marriage he discovers the splendors of his own animal nature: he is the Male. And in like manner woman is female, but this word now acquires the most complimentary implications: the female animal, brooding over her young, giving them suck, licking them, defending them, saving them at the risk of her life—this female is an example for mankind; man with emotion demands this patience, this devotion from his companion; it is Nature again, but penetrated with all the virtues that are useful to society, to the family, to the head of the family, which he understands how to lock up in the home. One of the wishes common to man and child is to unveil the secret hidden inside of things; from this point of view matter is deceptive. When a doll is ripped open, there is its belly outside, it has no more inwardness. The inner nature of living things is more impenetrable; the feminine belly is the symbol of immanence, of depth; it gives up its secrets in part, as when pleasure is revealed in the expression of a woman's face; but it also holds them back; man inveigles the obscure palpitations of life into his house without this mystery being destroyed by possession. Woman transposes the functions of the female animal into the world of humanity; she maintains life, reigning over the realms of immanence; she brings the warmth and the intimacy of the womb into the home; she it is who cares for and animates the dwelling where the past is preserved, the future prefigured; she brings forth the next generation and she feeds the children already born. Thanks to her, the existence that man disperses through the outside world in work and activity is concentrated again within her immanence: when he comes home at night, he is once more at anchor on the earth; through his wife the continuity of his days is assured; whatever may be the hazards he confronts in the outer world, she guarantees the recurrence of meals, of sleep; she restores whatever has been destroyed or worn out by activity, preparing food for the weary worker, caring for him when he is sick, mending, washing. And into the conjugal universe that she sets up and keeps going, she brings the whole vast world: she lights fires, puts flowers around the house, domesticates the emanations of sun, water, and earth. A bourgeois writer cited by Bebel seriously sums up this ideal as follows: "Man longs not only for one whose heart beats for him alone, but whose hand laves his brow, who radiates peace, order, tranquillity, and who exercises a quiet control over him and over the things he finds when he gets home each day; he wants someone to exhale over everything the indefinable perfume of woman, the vivifying warmth of life at home."

Since the appearance of Christianity the figure of woman has obviously been spiritualized to a considerable extent; the beauty, the warmth, the intimacy that man wishes to enjoy through woman, are no longer tangible qualities; instead of summing up the immediate and savory quality of things, she becomes their soul; deeper than the carnal mystery, a secret and pure presence in her heart reflects the truth of the world. She is the soul of the house, of the family, of the home. And she is the soul of such larger groups, also, as the city, state, and nation. Jung remarks that cities have always been likened to the Mother, because they contain the citizens in their bosom: hence Cybele is represented as crowned with towers. And likewise one speaks of the "mother country"; but it is not only the nourishing soil, it is a more subtle reality that finds its symbol in woman. In the Old Testament and in the Apocalypse, Jerusalem and Babylon are not merely mothers: they are also wives. There are virgin cities,

and whorish cities like Babel and Tyre. And so France has been called
the "eldest daughter of the Church"; France and Italy are Latin sisters. Woman's femininity and not her function is brought out in the
statues that represent France, Rome, and Germania and in those of
the Place de la Concorde which personify Strasbourg and Lyon. This
likening of places to women is not purely symbolical: it is emotionally
felt by many men.[9] Very often the traveler seeks in woman the key
to the countries he visits: when he embraces an Italian or Spanish
woman, it seems to him that he possesses the fragrant essence of Italy
or Spain. "When I arrive in a new city, I always begin by visiting a
brothel," a journalist remarked. If a cinnamon chocolate can disclose
all Spain for Gide, so much the more will the kisses of exotic lips
give over to the lover a whole country with its flora and its fauna,
its traditions and its culture. Woman does not sum up political institutions, or economic resources; but she incarnates at once their
material core and their mystic mana. From Lamartine's *Graziella* to
the novels of Pierre Loti and the tales of Morand, we see the stranger
endeavoring to grasp the soul of a region through women. Mignon,
Sylvia, Mireille, Colomba, Carmen reveal the innermost reality of
Italy, Valais, Provence, Corsica, Andalusia. That Goethe gained the
love of the Alsatian Frederika seemed to the Germans a symbol of
the annexation of Alsace by Germany; on the other hand, when
Colette Baudoche refused to marry a German, in Barrès's eyes it was
Alsace repulsing Germany. He symbolizes Aigues-Mortes and a whole
subtle and sensitive civilization in the small figure of Bernice; she
represents also the sensitiveness of the writer himself. For in her
who is the soul of nature, of cities, of the universe, man also perceives his mysterious double; man's soul is Psyche, a woman. Psyche
has feminine traits in Poe's *Ulalume*:

> Here once, through an alley Titanic,
>   Of cypress, I roamed with my Soul—
>   Of cypress, with Psyche, my Soul. . . .

---

[9] It is allegorical in the shameful poem Claudel recently perpetrated in which
he calls Indochina "That yellow woman"; it is emotional, on the contrary, in these
verses by a Negro poet:
> The soul of the dark country where the elders sleep
> lives and speaks
> tonight
> in the restless energy along your incurved reins.

> *Thus I pacified Psyche and kissed her . . .*
> *And I said: "What is written, sweet sister,*
> *On the door of this legended tomb?" . . .*

And Mallarmé, in dialogue at the theater with "a soul or rather our idea of it" (to wit, the divinity in the human spirit), calls the soul "a most exquisite abnormal lady" (*sic*). The Christian world has substituted less carnal presences for nymphs and fairies; but homes, landscapes, cities, and individuals themselves are still haunted by an impalpable femininity.

This truth, enshrouded in the night of things, also shines forth in the sky; perfectly immanent, the Soul is at the same time transcendence, the Idea. Not only are cities and nations clothed in feminine attributes, but also abstract entities, such as institutions: the Church, the Synagogue, the Republic, Humanity are women; so also are Peace, War, Liberty, the Revolution, Victory. Man feminizes the ideal he sets up before him as the essential Other, because woman is the material representation of alterity; that is why almost all allegories, in language as in pictorial representation, are women.[1] Woman is Soul and Idea, but she also is a mediatrix between them: she is the divine Grace, leading the Christian toward God, she is Beatrice guiding Dante in the beyond, Laura summoning Petrarch to the lofty summits of poetry. In all the doctrines that unify Nature and Spirit she appears as Harmony, Reason, Truth. The gnostic sects made Wisdom a woman, Sophia, crediting her with the redemption of the world and even its creation. Here we see woman no longer as flesh, but as glorified substance; she is no longer to be possessed, but venerated in her intact splendor; the pale dead of Poe are fluid as water, wind, memory; for chivalric love, for *les précieux*, and through all the tradition of gallantry, woman is no longer an animal creature but is rather an ethereal being, a breath, a glow. Thus is the opacity of the female Night transformed into transparency, and wickedness to purity.[2]

---

[1] Philology is rather mystifying on this question; all linguists agree in recognizing that the assignment of genders to concrete words is purely accidental. In French, however, most abstract entities are feminine; e.g., *beauté, loyauté,* etc., and in German most imported, foreign, *other* words are feminine; e.g., *die Bar.*

[2] The idea is in these passages of Novalis:

"Nocturnal ecstasy, celestial slumber, you descend upon me; the landscape mounts up gently, above the landscape floats my spirit, released, regenerated. The

The downward influence of woman is reversed; she summons man no longer earthward but toward the sky. Goethe proclaims it at the end of *Faust*:

> *The Eternal Feminine*
> *Beckons us upward.*

The Virgin Mary being the most fully realized and generally venerated image of woman regenerated and consecrated to the Good, it is of interest to see how she is represented in literature and pictures. These are extracts from the litanies addressed to her in the Middle Ages by the fervent Christian:

. . . Most high Virgin, thou art the fertile Dew, the Fountain of Joy, the Channel of pity, the Well of living waters which cool our fervors.

Thou art the Breast from which God gives orphans to suck. . . .

Thou art the Marrow, the tiny Bit, the Kernel of all good things, Thou art the guileless Woman whose love never changes. . . .

Thou art the subtle Physician whose like is not to be found in Salerno or Montpellier. . . .

Thou art the Lady with healing hands. . . . Thou makest the paralyzed to walk, thou reformest the base, thou revivest the dead.

We find again in these invocations most of the feminine traits we have noted. The Virgin is fecundity, dew, wellspring of life; many statuettes show her at the well, the spring, the fountain; the phrase "Fountain of life" is one of the most widely used; she is not creative, but she fructifies, she makes what was hidden in the earth spring forth into the light of day. She is the deep reality hidden under the appearance of things: the Kernel, the Marrow. Through her is desire appeased: she is what is given to man for his satisfaction. She heals and strengthens; she is intermediary between man and life; life comes

---

words become a cloud through which I glimpse the transfigured lineaments of my well-beloved."

"Are we then pleasing to you, also, somber Night? . . . A precious balm flows from your hands, a ray falls from your bright sheaf. . . . We are seized with an emotion, obscure and inexpressible: I see a serious face, joyfully startled, bending over me gently and in quiet reflection, and I discern beneath the entwining ringlets the Mother's beloved youthfulness. . . . More heavenly than the shining stars appear the eyes of infinity which the Night has opened within us."

from God, therefore she is intermediary between humanity and God. Tertullian called her "the devil's doorway"; but, transfigured, she is the doorway to heaven. In paintings we see her opening a door or a window upon paradise, or placing a ladder between the earth and the firmament. She is shown more directly as advocate, pleading for man before her Son, and on the Day of Judgment, her bosom bared, making supplication to Christ in the name of her glorious maternity. She protects children, and her pitying love follows men on the sea, the field of battle, through every hazard. She sways divine Justice, smilingly weighting on the side of charity the scales that tell the worth of souls.

This role of pity and tenderness is one of the most important of all those which have been assigned to woman. Even when fully integrated in a society, woman subtly extends its frontiers because she has the insidious generosity of Life. To be sure, this gap between the planned works of man and the contingence of nature seems disquieting in some cases; but it becomes beneficial when woman, too docile to threaten man's works, limits herself to enriching them and softening their too rugged lines. Male gods represent Destiny; in goddesses one finds arbitrary benevolence, capricious favor. The Christian God is full of the rigors of Justice, the Virgin is full of the gentleness of charity. Here on earth men are defenders of the law, of reason, of necessity; woman is aware of the original contingency of man himself and of this necessity in which he believes; hence come both the mysterious irony that flits across her lips and her pliant generosity. She heals the wounds of the males, she nurses the newborn, and she lays out the dead; she knows everything about man that attacks his pride and humiliates his self-will. While she inclines before him and humbles the flesh to the spirit, she stays on the fleshly frontiers of the spirit, softening, as I have said, the hard angles of man's constructions and bestowing upon them unforeseen luxury and grace. Woman's power over men comes from the fact that she gently recalls them to a modest realization of their true condition; it is the secret of her disillusioned, sorrowful, ironical, and loving wisdom. In women even frivolity, capriciousness, and ignorance are charming virtues because they flourish this side of and beyond the world where man chooses to live but where he does not like to feel himself confined. Over against set meanings and tools made for useful purposes, she upholds the mystery of intact things; she wafts the breath of poetry through city streets, over cultivated fields. Poetry is supposed to catch what exists beyond the prose of every day; and woman is an eminently poetic reality since man projects into her all that he does not resolve to be. She incarnates the Dream, which is for man most intimate and most strange: what he does not wish and does not do, toward which he aspires and which cannot be attained; the mysterious Other who is deep immanence and far-off transcendence will lend the dream her traits. Thus it is that Aurélia visits Nerval in a dream and gives him the whole world in the image of the dream: "She began to enlarge in a bright ray of light in such a way that little by little the garden took on her shape, and the flowerbeds and the trees became the roses and the festoons of her vestments; while her face and her arms impressed their shape upon the reddened clouds in the sky. I lost sight of her as she was transfigured, for she seemed to vanish as she took on grandeur. 'Oh, flee not from me!' I cried; 'for nature dies with you.' "

Woman being the very substance of man's poetic work, it is understandable that she should appear as his inspiration: the Muses are women. A Muse mediates between the creator and the natural springs whence he must draw. Woman's spirit is profoundly sunk in nature, and it is through her that man will sound the depths of silence and of the fecund night. A Muse creates nothing by herself; she is a calm, wise Sibyl, putting herself with docility at the service of a master. Even in concrete and practical realms her counsel will be useful. Man would fain attain his ends without the often embarrassing aid of other men; but he fancies that woman speaks from a sense of different values, with an instinctive wisdom of her own, in close accord with the real. Man seeks her "intuitions" as he might interrogate the stars. Such "intuition" is injected even into business and politics: Aspasia and Mme de Maintenon still have successful careers today.[3]

Another function that man readily entrusts to woman is the weighing of values; she is a privileged judge. Man dreams of an Other not only to possess her but also to be ratified by her; to be ratified by other men, his peers, demands a constant tension; hence he wishes consideration from outside to confer an absolute value upon his life, his enterprises, and himself. The consideration of God is hidden, alien, disquieting; even in times of faith only a few mystics longed for it.

---

[3] But the truth is, of course, that women display intellectual qualities perfectly identical with those of men.

This divine role has most often devolved upon woman. Being the Other, she remains exterior to man's world and can view it objectively; and being close to man and dominated by him, she does not establish values foreign to his nature. She it is who in each particular case will report the presence or absence of courage, strength, beauty, while giving outside confirmation of their universal value. Men are too much involved in their co-operative and competitive relations to act as a public for one another. Woman is outside the fray: her whole situation destines her to play this role of concerned spectator. The knight jousts for his lady in the tourney; poets seek the approbation of women. Setting out to conquer Paris, Rastignac plans first to *have* women, not so much to possess them physically as to enjoy the reputation that only they can give a man. Balzac projected in such young heroes the story of his own youth: he began to educate and shape himself in the company of older mistresses; and woman plays this educational role not only in his *Lys dans la vallée*. It is assigned to her in Flaubert's *Éducation sentimentale*, in Stendahl's novels, and in many other stories of apprenticeship. We have noted before that woman is *physis* and *antiphysis*: that is, she incarnates Nature no more than she does Society; in her is summed up the civilization and culture of an epoch, as we see in the poems of chivalry, in the *Decameron*, in *Astrée*. She launches new fashions, presides in the salons, influences and reflects opinion. Renown and glory are women; and Mallarmé said: "The crowd is a woman." In the company of women the young man is initiated into "society," and into that complex reality called "life." Woman is a special prize which the hero, the adventurer, and the rugged individualist are destined to win. In antiquity we see Perseus delivering Andromeda, Orpheus seeking Eurydice in the underworld, and Troy fighting to protect fair Helen. The novels of chivalry are concerned chiefly with such prowess as the deliverance of captive princesses. What would Prince Charming have for occupation if he had not to awaken the Sleeping Beauty? The myth of the king marrying a shepherdess gratifies man as much as woman. The rich man needs to give or his useless wealth remains an abstraction: he must have someone at hand to give to. The Cinderella myth, which Philip Wylie treats kindly in *Generation of Vipers*, flourishes especially in prosperous countries like America. How should the men there spend their surplus money if not upon a woman? Orson Welles, among others, has embodied in *Citizen Kane* that imperial and false generosity: it is to glorify his own power that Kane chooses to shower his gifts upon an obscure singer and to impose her upon the public as a great queen of song; and we could mention many a small-time Citizen Kane in France. When the hero of another film, *The Razor's Edge*, returns from India equipped with absolute wisdom, the only thing he finds to do with it is to redeem a prostitute.

It is clear that in dreaming of himself as donor, liberator, redeemer, man still desires the subjection of woman; for in order to awaken the Sleeping Beauty, she must have been put to sleep; ogres and dragons must be about if there are to be captive princesses. The more man acquires a taste for difficult enterprises, however, the more it will please him to give woman independence. To conquer is still more fascinating than to give gifts or to release.

Thus the ideal of the average Western man is a woman who freely accepts his domination, who does not accept his ideas without discussion, but who yields to his arguments, who resists him intelligently and ends by being convinced. The greater his pride, the more dangerous he likes his adventures to be: it is much more splendid to conquer Penthesilea than it is to marry a yielding Cinderella. "The warrior loves danger and sport," said Nietzsche; "that is why he loves woman, the most dangerous sport of all." The man who likes danger and sport is not displeased to see woman turn into an amazon if he retains the hope of subjugating her.[4] What he requires in his heart of hearts is that this struggle remain a game for him, while for woman it involves her very destiny. Man's true victory, whether he is liberator or conquerer, lies just in this: that woman freely recognizes him as her destiny.

Thus the expression "to have a woman" hides a double significance: her functions as object and as arbiter are not distinguished. From the moment when woman is regarded as a person, she cannot be conquered except with her consent; she must be won. It is the Sleeping Beauty's smile that crowns the efforts of Prince Charming; the captive princess's tears of joy and gratitude make the knight's prowess valid. On the other hand, her measuring gaze does not have the aloof

---

4 American detective stories—and others written in the American manner—offer a striking example. The heroes of Peter Cheyney, among others, are always at grips with an extremely dangerous woman, untamable by all others; after a running battle through the length of the story, she is finally conquered by Campion or Callaghan and falls into his arms.

severity of a masculine gaze, it is susceptible to charm. Thus heroism and poetry are modes of seduction; but in letting herself be charmed, woman glorifies heroism and poetry. In the view of the individualist, she holds a prerogative yet more essential: she seems to him to be not the measure of values recognized by all, but the revelation of his special merits and of his very being. A man is judged by his fellows according to what he does both objectively and with regard to generally accepted standards. But some of his qualities, and among others his vital qualities, can interest woman only; he is virile, charming, seductive, tender, cruel only in reference to her. If he sets a high value on these more secret virtues, he has an absolute need of her; through her he will experience the miracle of seeming to himself to be another, another who is also his profoundest ego. There is a passage from Malraux which expresses admirably what the individualist expects from his loved woman. Kyo is questioning himself: " 'We hear the voices of others with our ears, our own voices with our throats.' Yes. One hears his own life, also, with his throat—and those of others? . .˙. In the eyes of others, I am what I have done. . . . But to May alone he was not what he had done; and to him alone she was something quite other than her biography. The embrace in which love unites two beings against solitude did not provide its relief for man; it was for the madman, for the incomparable monster, dearest of all things, that everyone is to himself and that he cherishes in his heart. Since the death of his mother, May was the only person for whom he was not Kyo Gisors but a most intimate companion. . . . Men are not my fellows, they are persons who look upon me and judge me; my fellows are those who love me and do not look upon me, who love me regardless of everything, degradation, baseness, treason, who love me and not what I have done or shall do, who will love me as long as I shall love myself, even to the point of suicide." [5]

What makes the attitude of Kyo human and moving is that it implies reciprocity and that he asks May to love him as he is, not to send back a fawning reflection. With many men this demand is degraded: instead of an exact revelation, they seek to find in two living eyes their image haloed with admiration and gratitude, deified. Woman has often been compared to water because, among other reasons, she is the mirror in which the male, Narcissus-like, contemplates himself: he bends over her in good or bad faith. But in any

---

[5] *La Condition humaine (Man's Fate)*.

case what he really asks of her is to be, outside of him, all that which he cannot grasp inside himself, because the inwardness of the existent is only nothingness and because he must project himself into an object in order to reach himself. Woman is the supreme recompense for him since, under a shape foreign to him which he can possess in her flesh, she is his own apotheosis. He embraces this "incomparable monster," himself, when he presses in his arms the being who sums up the World for him and upon whom he has imposed his values and his laws. Then, in uniting with this other whom he has made his own, he hopes to reach himself. Treasure, prey, sport and danger, nurse, guide, judge, mediatrix, mirror, woman is the Other in whom the subject transcends himself without being limited, who opposes him without denying him; she is the Other who lets herself be taken without ceasing to be the Other, and therein she is so necessary to man's happiness and to his triumph that it can be said that if she did not exist, men would have invented her.

They did invent her.[6] But she exists also apart from their inventiveness. And hence she is not only the incarnation of their dream, but also its frustration. There is no figurative image of woman which does not call up at once its opposite: she is Life and Death, Nature and Artifice, Daylight and Night. Under whatever aspect we consider her, we always find the same shifting back and forth, for the nonessential returns necessarily to the essential. In the figures of the Virgin Mary and Beatrice, Eve and Circe still exist.

"Through woman," writes Kierkegaard in *In Vino Veritas*, "ideality enters into life, and what would man be without her? Many a man has become a genius thanks to some young girl . . . but none has ever become a genius thanks to the young girl who gave him her hand in marriage. . . ."

"Woman makes a man productive in ideality through a negative relation. . . . Negative relations with woman can make us infinite . . . positive relations with woman make a man finite for the most part." Which is to say that woman is necessary in so far as she remains an Idea into which man projects his own transcendence; but that she is inauspicious as an objective reality, existing in and for herself. Kierkegaard holds that by refusing to marry his fiancée he established the only valid relation to woman. And he is right in a sense:

---

[6] "Man created woman, and with what? With a rib of his god, of his ideal," says Nietzsche in *The Twilight of the Idols*.

namely, that the myth of woman set up as the infinite Other entails
also its opposite.

Because she is a false Infinite, an Ideal without truth, she stands
exposed as finiteness and mediocrity and, on the same ground, as
falsehood. In Laforgue she appears in this light; throughout his works
he gives voice to his rancor against a mystification for which he
blamed man as much as woman. Ophelia, Salome, are in fact only
"petites femmes." Hamlet seems to think: "Thus would Ophelia have
loved me, as her boon and because I was socially and morally superior
to what her girlish friends had. And those small, common remarks
that she would make, at lamp-lighting time, on ease and comfort!"
Woman makes man dream; yet she thinks of comfort, of stew for
supper; one speaks to her of her soul when she is only a body. And
while her lover fondly believes he is pursuing the Ideal, he is actually
the plaything of nature, who employs all this mystification for the ends
of reproduction. Woman in truth represents the everyday aspects of
life; she is silliness, prudence, shabbiness, boredom.

Man has succeeded in enslaving woman; but in the same degree he
has deprived her of what made her possession desirable. With woman
integrated in the family and in society, her magic is dissipated rather
than transformed; reduced to the condition of servant, she is no longer
that unconquered prey incarnating all the treasures of nature. Since
the rise of chivalric love it is a commonplace that marriage kills love.
Scorned too much, respected too much, too much an everyday matter,
the wife ceases to have erotic attraction. The marriage rites were
originally intended to protect man against woman; she becomes his
property. But all that we possess possesses us in turn, and marriage is
a form of servitude for man also. He is taken in the snare set by nature:
because he desired a fresh young girl, he has to support a heavy matron
or a desiccated hag for life. The dainty jewel intended to decorate his
existence becomes a hateful burden: Xantippe has always been a type
of woman most horrifying to man; in ancient Greece and in the Middle Ages she was, as we have seen, the theme of many lamentations.
But even when the woman is young there is a hoax in marriage, since,
while being supposed to socialize eroticism, it succeeds only in killing it.

The fact is that eroticism implies a claim of the instant against
time, of the individual against the group; it affirms separation against
communication; it is rebellion against all regulation; it contains a

principle hostile to society. Customs are never bent quite to the rigor of institutions and laws; against these love has ever hurled defiance. In its sensual form love in Greece and Rome was turned toward young men or courtesans; chivalric love, at once carnal and platonic, was always destined for another's wife. *Tristan* is the epic of adultery. The period which, around 1900, created anew the myth of woman is that in which adultery became the theme of all literature. Certain writers, like Henry Bernstein, in a supreme effort to defend bourgeois institutions, struggled to reintegrate eroticism and love into marriage; but there was more truth in Porto-Riche's *Amoureuse*, in which the incompatibility of these two orders of values was shown. Adultery can disappear only with marriage itself. For the aim of marriage is in a way to immunize man against *his own* wife: but other women keep—for him—their heady attraction; and to them he will turn. Women make themselves a party to this. For they rebel against an order of things which undertakes to deprive them of all their weapons. In order to separate woman from Nature, to subject her to man through ceremonies and contracts, she has been elevated to the dignity of being a human person, she has been given liberty. But liberty is precisely that which escapes all subjugation; and if it be granted to a being originally possessed of maleficent powers, she becomes dangerous. She becomes the more so in that man stops at half-measures; he accepts woman in the masculine world only in making a servant of her and frustrating her transcendence; the liberty given to her can have none but a negative use; she chooses to reject this liberty. Woman has been free only in becoming a captive; she renounces this human privilege in order to regain her power as a natural object. By day she perfidiously plays her role of docile servant, but at night she changes into cat, or hind; she slips again into her siren's skin or, riding on a broomstick, she takes off for the devil's dances. Sometimes, to be sure, she works her nocturnal magic upon her own husband; but it is wiser to hide her metamorphoses from her master; she chooses strangers as prey; they have no rights over her, and for them she is still vegetation, wellspring, star, sorceress. She is thus fated for infidelity: it is the sole concrete form her liberty can assume. She is unfaithful beyond even her desires, thoughts, awareness; by virtue of the fact that she is regarded as an object, she is offered to any subjectivity who chooses to take possession of her. Locked away in a harem, hidden behind veils, it is still by no means sure that she will not arouse desire in someone;

and to inspire desire in a stranger is already to fail her husband and society. But, further, she is often a willing accomplice in the deed; only through deceit and adultery can she prove that she is nobody's chattel and give the lie to the pretensions of the male. This is the reason why the husband's jealousy is so quick to awaken; we see in legends how a woman can be suspected without reason, condemned on the least suspicion, like Genevieve of Brabant and Desdemona. Even before any suspicion arose, Griselda [7] was subjected to the most severe tests; this tale would be absurd if woman was not suspect in advance; there is no question of demonstrating her misbehavior: it is for her to prove her innocence.

This is, indeed, why jealousy can be insatiable. We have seen that possession can never be positively realized; even if all others are forbidden to dip therein, one never possesses the spring in which one's thirst is quenched: he who is jealous knows this full well. In essence woman is fickle, as water is fluid; and no human power can contradict a natural truth. Throughout literature, in *The Arabian Nights* as in the *Decameron*, we see the clever ruses of woman triumph over the prudence of man. Moreover, it is not alone through individualistic will that he is the jailer: it is society that makes him—as father, brother, husband—responsible for his woman's conduct. Chastity is enforced upon her for economic and religious reasons, since each citizen ought to be authenticated as the son of his proper father.

But it is also very important to compel woman to adapt herself exactly to the role society has forced upon her. There is a double demand of man which dooms woman to duplicity: he wants the woman to be his and to remain foreign to him; he fancies her as at once servant and enchantress. But in public he admits to only the first of these desires; the other is a sly demand that he hides in the secrecy of his heart and flesh. It is against morality and society; it is wicked like the Other, like rebellious Nature, like the "bad woman." Man does not devote himself wholly to the Good which he sets up and claims to put in force; he retains shameful lines of communication with the Bad. But wherever the Bad dares indiscreetly to show its face uncovered, man goes to war against it. In the shadows of night man invites woman to sin. But in full daylight he disowns the sin and the fair sinner. And the women, themselves sinners in the secrecy of the bed, are only the more passionate in the public worship of virtue. Just

---

[7] Eleventh-century type of wifely virtue.—Tr.

as among primitive people the male sex is secular while that of the female is charged with religious and magical powers, so the misbehavior of a man in more modern societies is only a minor folly, often regarded indulgently; even if he disobeys the laws of the community, man continues to belong to it; he is only an *enfant terrible*, offering no profound menace to the order of society.

If, on the other hand, woman evades the rules of society, she returns to Nature and to the demon, she looses uncontrollable and evil forces in the collective midst. Fear is always mixed with the blame attached to woman's licentious conduct. If the husband does not succeed in keeping his wife in the path of virtue, he shares in her fault; in the eyes of society his misfortune is a blot on his honor; there are civilizations severe enough to require him to kill the wrongdoer in order to dissociate himself from her crime. In others the complaisant husband is punished by such mockeries as parading him naked astride a jackass. And the community undertakes to chastise the guilty one in his place: she has offended not him alone, but the whole collectivity. These customs have existed in a particularly harsh form in superstitious and mystical Spain, a sensual land terrorized by the flesh. Calderón, Lorca, Valle Inclán have used this theme in many dramas. In Lorca's *House of Bernarda* the village gossips would punish the seduced girl by burning her with a live coal "in the place where she sinned." In Valle Inclán's *Divine Words* the adulterous woman appears as a sorceress dancing with the demon; her fault once discovered, the village assembles to tear off her clothes and then drown her. According to many traditions, the woman sinner was thus disrobed; then she was stoned, as reported in the Bible, or she was buried alive, drowned, or burned. The meaning of these tortures is that she was in this way given back to Nature after being deprived of her social dignity; by her sin she had let loose natural emanations of evil: the expiation was carried out in a kind of sacred orgy in which the women—demanding, striking, massacring the guilty one—released in their turn fluids of mysterious but beneficial nature, since the avengers were acting in accordance with society's rules.

This savage severity disappears as superstition diminishes and fear is dissipated. But in rural districts godless gypsies are still viewed with suspicion as homeless vagabonds. The woman who makes free use of her attractiveness—adventuress, vamp, *femme fatale*—remains a disquieting type. The image of Circe survives in the bad woman of the

Hollywood films. Women have been burnt as witches simply because they were beautiful. And in the prudish umbrage of provincial virtue before women of dissolute life, an ancient fear is kept alive.

It is in truth these very dangers that, for the adventurous man, make woman an enticing game. Disdaining marital rights and refusing the support of the laws of society, he will try to conquer her in single combat. He tries to get possession of the woman even in her resistance; he pursues her in the very liberty through which she escapes him. In vain. One does not play a part when free: the free woman will often act as such against man. Even the Sleeping Beauty may awaken with displeasure, she may not regard her awakener as a Prince Charming at all, she may not smile. Just this happens in the case of Citizen Kane, whose protégée is seen to be under oppression and whose generosity is revealed as a will to power and tyranny. The hero's wife listens indifferently to the tale of his exploits; the Muse of whom the poet dreams may yawn when she listens to his stanzas. The amazon can with ennui decline combat; and she may also emerge victorious. The Roman women of the decadence, many American women of today, impose their caprices or their rule upon men. Where is Cinderella?

Man wants to give, and here is woman taking for herself. It is becoming a matter of self-defense, no longer a game. From the moment when woman is free, she has no other destiny than what she freely creates for herself. The relation of the two sexes is then a relation of struggle. Now become a fellow being, woman seems as formidable as when she faced man as a part of alien Nature. In place of the myth of the laborious honeybee or the mother hen is substituted the myth of the devouring female insect: the praying mantis, the spider. No longer is the female she who nurses the little ones, but rather she who eats the male; the egg is no longer a storehouse of abundance, but rather a trap of inert matter in which the spermatozoon is castrated and drowned. The womb, that warm, peaceful, and safe retreat, becomes a pulp of humors, a carnivorous plant, a dark, contractile gulf, where dwells a serpent that insatiably swallows up the strength of the male. The same dialectic makes the erotic object into a wielder of black magic, the servant into a traitress, Cinderella into an ogress, and changes all women into enemies: it is the payment man makes for having in bad faith set himself up as the sole essential.

This hostile visage, however, is the definitive face of woman no

more than the others. Rather, a Manichæism is introduced in the
heart of womankind. Pythagoras likened the good principle to man
and the bad principle to woman. Men have tried to overcome the
bad by taking possession of woman; they have succeeded in part. But
just as Christianity, by bringing in the idea of redemption and salvation, has given the word *damnation* its full meaning, just so it is in
contrast to the sanctified woman that the bad woman stands out in
full relief. In the course of that "quarrel of women" which has lasted
from the Middle Ages until now, certain men have wished to recognize only the blessed woman of their dreams, others only the cursed
woman who belies their dreams. But in truth, if man can find *everything* in woman, it is because she has both these faces. She represents
in a living, carnal way all the values and anti-values that give sense
to life. Here, quite clear-cut, are Good and Evil in opposition to each
other under the form of the devoted Mother and the perfidious Mistress; in the old English ballad *Lord Randal, My Son*, a young knight,
poisoned by his mistress, comes home to die in his mother's arms.
Richepin's *La Glu* takes up the same theme with more bathos and
bad taste in general. Angelic Micaëla stands in contrast to dark
Carmen. Mother, faithful fiancée, patient wife—all stand ready to
bind up the wounds dealt to man's heart by "vamps" and witches.
Between these clearly fixed poles can be discerned a multitude of ambiguous figures, pitiable, hateful, sinful, victimized, coquettish, weak,
angelic, devilish. Woman thus provides a great variety of behavior
and sentiment to stimulate man and enrich his life.

Man is delighted by this very complexity of woman: a wonderful
servant who is capable of dazzling him—and not too expensive. Is she
angel or demon? The uncertainty makes her a Sphinx. We may note
here that one of the most celebrated brothels of Paris operated under
this ægis, the sign of the sphinx. In the grand epoch of femininity, at
the time of corsets, Paul Bourget, Henri Bataille, and the French
cancan, the theme of the Sphinx was all the rage in plays, poetry,
and songs: "Who are you, whence come you, strange Sphinx?" And
there is still no end to dreaming and debating on the feminine mystery. It is indeed to preserve this mystery that men have long begged
women not to give up long skirts, petticoats, veils, long gloves, high-
heeled shoes: everything that accentuates difference in the Other
makes her more desirable, since what man wants to take possession
of is the Other as such. We find Alan Fournier chiding English-

women for their frank manlike way of shaking hands: what excites him is the modest reserve of Frenchwomen. Woman must remain secret, unknown, if she is to be adored as a faraway princess. There is no reason to suppose that Fournier was especially deferential to the women in his life; but he put all the wonder of childhood, of youth, all the nostalgia for lost paradises into a woman of his own creation, a woman whose first virtue was to appear inaccessible. His picture of Yvonne de Galais is traced in white and gold.

But men cherish even woman's defects if they create mystery. "A woman should have her caprices," a man said authoritatively to an intelligent woman. The caprice is unpredictable, it lends woman the grace of waves in water; falsehood adorns her with fascinating reflections; coquetry, even perversity, gives her a heady perfume. Deceitful, elusive, unintelligible, double-dealing—thus it is that she best lends herself to the contradictory desires of man; she is Maya in innumerable disguises. It is a commonplace to represent the Sphinx as a young woman: virginity is one of the secrets that men find most exciting— the more so as they are greater libertines; the young girl's purity allows hope for every kind of license, and no one knows what perversities are concealed in her innocence. Still close to animal and plant, already amenable to social forms, she is neither child nor adult; her timid femininity inspires no fear, but a mild disquiet. We feel that she is one of the privileged exponents of feminine mystery. As "the true young girl" disappears, however, her cult has become somewhat out of date. On the other hand, the figure of the prostitute, whom Gantillon triumphantly presented on the French stage in *Maya*,[8] has kept much of its prestige. It is one of the most plastic feminine types, giving full scope to the grand play of vices and virtues. For the timorous puritan, the prostitute incarnates evil, shame, disease, damnation; she inspires fear and disgust; she belongs to no man, but yields herself to one and all and lives off such commerce. In this way she regains that formidable independence of the luxurious goddess mothers of old, and she incarnates the Femininity that masculine society has not sanctified and that remains charged with harmful powers. In the sexual act the male cannot possibly imagine that he owns her; he has simply delivered himself over to the demon of the flesh. This is a humiliation, a defile-

---

[8] *Maya* was presented in New York in 1928. It was closed by the district attorney after a run of fifteen performances, a triumph of official morality if not of realism in the American theater.—TR.

ment peculiarly resented by the Anglo-Saxons, who regard the flesh as
more or less abominable. On the other hand, a man who is not afraid
of the flesh will enjoy its generous and straightforward affirmation by
the prostitute; he will sense in her the exaltation of a femininity that
no morality has made wishy-washy. He will find again upon her body
those magic virtues which formerly made woman sister to the stars
and sea; a Henry Miller,[9] going to bed with a prostitute, feels that he
sounds the very depths of life, death, and the cosmos; he meets God
in the deep, moist shadows of a receptive vagina. Since she is a kind
of pariah, living at the margin of a hypocritically moral world, we can
also regard the *"fille perdue"* as the invalidator of all the official virtues; her low estate relates her to the authentic saints; for that which
has been downtrodden shall be exalted. Mary Magdalene was a favorite of Christ; sin opens heaven's gate more readily than does a hypocritical virtue. Dostoyevsky's Raskolnikov sacrifices at Sonia's feet the
arrogant masculine pride that led him to crime; he has aggravated by
the murder that will to separation which is in every man: a humble
prostitute, resigned, abandoned by all, can best receive the avowal of
his abdication.[1] The phrase *fille perdue* awakens disturbing echoes. For
many men dream of losing themselves, but it is not so simple, one does
not easily succeed in attaining Evil in positive form; and even the
demoniac is frightened by excessive crimes. Woman enables one to
celebrate without great risk Black Masses where Satan is evoked without being exactly invited; she exists at the margin of the masculine
world; acts concerned with her are truly of no consequence; but she is
a human being and it is possible therefore to carry out dark revolts
through her against human law. From Musset to Georges Bataille,
real, hideously fascinating debauch is that carried on in company with
whores. The Marquis de Sade and Sacher-Masoch satisfy upon women
the desires that haunt them; their disciples, and most men who have

---

[9] *Tropic of Cancer* (1934).—TR.

[1] Marcel Schwob states this myth poetically in his *Livre de Monelle:* "I will
tell you about the little whores and you will know how it begins. . . . See, they
cry out with pity for you and caress your hand with their emaciated hands. They
understand you only if you are most unhappy; they weep with you and console
you . . . not one of them, you see, can remain with you. They would be too sad
and are ashamed to stay when you weep no more, they dare not look at you. They
teach you the lesson they have to teach you and then they go away. They come
through cold and rain to kiss you on the forehead and dry your eyes, and the
frightful shadows receive them again. . . . It is not well to think of what they
have doubtless done in the shadows."

"vices" to satisfy, commonly turn to prostitutes. Of all women they are the most submissive to the male, and yet more able to escape him; this it is that makes them take on so many varied meanings. There is no feminine type, however—virgin, mother, wife, sister, servant, loved one, fiercely virtuous one, smiling odalisque—who is not capable of summing up thus the vagrant yearnings of men.

It is for psychology—especially psychoanalysis—to discover why an individual is drawn more particularly to one or another aspect of the many-faced Myth, and why he incarnates it in some one special female. But this myth is implied in all the complexes, the obsessions, the psychoses. Many neuroses in particular have their source in a madness for the forbidden that can appear only if taboos have been previously established; a social pressure from outside is not sufficient to explain its presence; in fact, social prohibitions are not simply conventions; they have—among other meanings—a developmental significance that each person experiences for himself.

By way of example, it will be of interest to examine the "Œdipus complex," considered too often as being produced by a struggle between instinctual tendencies and social regulations, whereas it is first of all an inner conflict within the subject himself. The attachment of the infant for the mother's breast is at first an attachment to Life in its immediate form, in its generality and its immanence; the rejection by weaning is the beginning of the rejection by abandonment, to which the individual is condemned once he emerges as a separate being from the Whole. It is from that point, and as he becomes more individualized and separate, that the term *sexual* can be applied to the inclination he retains for the maternal flesh henceforth detached from his. His sensuality is then directed through another person, it has become transcendence toward an object foreign to him. But the quicker and the more decidedly the child realizes himself as subject, the more the fleshly bond, opposing his autonomy, is going to become harassing to him. Then he shuns his mother's caresses; and her authority, the rights she has over him, sometimes her very presence, all inspire in him a kind of shame. In particular it seems embarrassing and obscene to be aware of her as flesh, and he avoids thinking of her body; in the horrified feeling aroused by his father or stepfather or a lover, there is not so much a pang of jealousy as a sense of scandal.[2]

---

[2] This situation is sensitively depicted in A. Moravia's *Two Adolescents* (*Agostino*) (Farrar, Straus & Young, 1950).—TR.

To remind him thus that his mother is a carnal being is to remind him of his own birth, an event that he repudiates with all his strength or at least wants to give the dignity of a grand cosmic phenomenon. He feels that his mother should sum up Nature, which invests all individuals without belonging to any; he hates to have her become some man's prey, not, as is often maintained, because he wants to have her himself, but because he wishes her to be beyond all possession: she should not have the paltry dimensions of wife or mistress. When his sexuality becomes manly at adolescence, however, it may well happen that his mother's body arouses him erotically; but this is because she reminds him of femininity in general; and very often the desire aroused by the sight of a thigh or a breast disappears at the young man's realization that this flesh is his mother's flesh. There are numerous cases of perversion, since, adolescence being a disordered period, it is a time of perversion, when disgust leads to sacrilege, and temptation is born of the forbidden. But it is not to be believed that at first the son quite simply wishes to have intercourse with his mother and that exterior prohibitions interfere and tyrannically prevent him; on the contrary, desire is born just because of that prohibition which is set up in the heart of the individual himself. This prohibition is the most normal general reaction. But here again the interdiction does not come from a social regulation repressing instinctive desires. Rather, respect is the sublimation of an original disgust; the young man refuses to regard his mother as carnal; he transfigures her and assimilates her to one of the pure images of sacred womanhood which society holds up for his admiration. Thus he helps to strengthen the ideal figure of the Mother who will be concerned with the welfare of the next generation. But this figure has so much force only because it is called forth by an inner, individual dialectic. And since every woman is endowed with the general essence of Woman, therefore of the Mother, it is certain that the attitude held toward the Mother will have repercussions in a man's relations with wife and mistresses—but less simply than is often supposed. The adolescent who has felt definite, sensual sex desire for his mother may well have been simply desiring woman in general. In this case the ardor of his temperament will be appeased with no matter what woman, for he is no victim of incestuous nostalgia.[3] Inversely, a young

---

[3] Stendahl is a striking example.

man who has felt a tender but platonic reverence for his mother may wish in every instance for woman to share in the maternal purity.

The importance of sexuality, and therefore ordinarily of woman, in both normal and abnormal behavior is surely well known. It may happen that other objects are feminized. Since woman is indeed in large part man's invention, he can invent her in the male body: in pederasty some pretense of sexual distinction is kept up. But as a rule it is unquestionably in feminine persons that Woman is sought for. It is through her, through what is in her of the best and the worst, that man, as a young apprentice, learns of felicity and suffering, of vice, virtue, lust, renunciation, devotion, and tyranny—that as an apprentice he learns to know himself. Woman is sport and adventure, but also a test. She is the triumph of victory and the more bitter triumph of frustration survived; she is the vertigo of ruin, the fascination of damnation, of death. There is a whole world of significance which exists only through woman; she is the substance of men's acts and sentiments, the incarnation of all the values that call out their free activity. It is understandable that, were he condemned to the most cruel disappointments, man would not be willing to relinquish a dream within which all his dreams are enfolded.

This, then, is the reason why woman has a double and deceptive visage: she is all that man desires and all that he does not attain. She is the good mediatrix between propitious Nature and man; and she is the temptation of unconquered Nature, counter to all goodness. She incarnates all moral values, from good to evil, and their opposites; she is the substance of action and whatever is an obstacle to it, she is man's grasp on the world and his frustration; as such she is the source and origin of all man's reflection on his existence and of whatever expression he is able to give to it; and yet she works to divert him from himself, to make him sink down in silence and in death. She is servant and companion, but he expects her also to be his audience and critic and to confirm him in his sense of being; but she opposes him with her indifference, even with her mockery and laughter. He projects upon her what he desires and what he fears, what he loves and what he hates. And if it is so difficult to say anything specific about her, that is because man seeks the whole of himself in her and because she is All. She is All, that is, on the plane of the inessential;

she is all the Other. And, as the other, she is other than herself, other than what is expected of her. Being all, she is never quite *this* which she should be; she is everlasting deception, the very deception of that existence which is never successfully attained nor fully reconciled with the totality of existents.

CHAPTER X

The Myth of Woman in Five Authors

To confirm this analysis of the feminine myth as it appears in a general view, we shall now consider the special and variously combined forms that it has assumed in certain writers. The attitudes toward women of Montherlant, D. H. Lawrence, Claudel, Breton, and Stendhal, for example, have seemed to me to be typical.

1

MONTHERLANT OR THE BREAD OF DISGUST

Montherlant belongs to the long tradition of males who have adopted as their own the proud Manichæism of Pythagoras. Following Nietzsche, he holds that only epochs marked by weakness have exalted the Eternal Feminine and that the hero should rise in revolt against the Magna Mater. A specialist in heroism, he undertakes to dethrone her. Woman—she is night, disorder, immanence. "These convulsive shadows are nothing more than the feminine in its pure state," he cries apropos of Mme Tolstoy in *Sur les femmes*. According to him, it is the stupidity and the baseness of the men of today that have lent an air of positive worth to feminine deficiencies: we hear about women's instinct, their intuition, their divination, when it is in order to denounce their lack of logic, their obstinate ignorance, their inability to grasp reality. They are in fact neither observers nor psychologists; they can neither see things nor understand living beings; their mystery is a snare and a delusion, their unfathomable treasures have the depth of nothingness; they have nothing to give to man and can only do him injury. For Montherlant it is first of all the mother who is the great enemy; in a youthful publication, *L'Exil*, he shows us a mother who prevents her son from getting engaged; in *Les Olympiques* the adolescent who would give himself to sport is "barred" through his mother's timid egotism; in *Les Célibataires* as in *Les Jeunes Filles* the mother is given hateful characteristics. Her crime is to wish to keep her son forever enclosed within the darkness of her body; she mutilates him so she can keep him all to herself and thus fill the sterile void in her being; she is the most deplorable of teachers; she clips the child's wings, she holds him back, far from the summits to which he aspires; she makes him stupid and degrades him.

These complaints are not without foundation. But through the explicit reproaches Montherlant heaps upon the woman mother it is clearly seen that what he detests, in her, is the fact of his own birth. He believes he is God, he wants to be God; and this because he is male, because he is a "superior man," because he is Montherlant. A god is no engendered being; his body, if he has one, is a will cast in firm and disciplined muscles, not a mass of flesh vulgarly subject to life and death; he holds the mother responsible for this perishable flesh, contingent, vulnerable, and disowned by himself. "The only place on his body where Achilles was vulnerable was where his mother had held him," says Montherlant in *Sur les femmes*. He has never been willing to accept the conditions implied in being human; what he calls his pride is from first to last a terrified flight from the risks that confront a free being involved with the world in a body of flesh and blood; he claims to assert his liberty while rejecting the involvement; without ties, rootless, he fancies himself a supremely self-sufficient subjective being; but the memory of his carnal origin upsets this dream, and he takes refuge in a procedure that is habitual with him: instead of rising above his origin, he repudiates it.

For Montherlant the mistress is as ill-omened as the mother; she prevents man from reviving the god within him. Woman's lot, he declares, is life in its immediacy; she lives on sensations, she wallows in immanence, she has a rage to live—and wishes to confine man in such poor estate. She does not feel the *élan* of his transcendence, she has no sense of grandeur; she loves her lover in his weakness and not in his strength, in his misery and not in his joy; she wants him disarmed and unhappy to the point of wishing to convince him of his misery against all the evidence. He surpasses her and thus escapes her; but she knows how to reduce him to size so as to get him under control. For she needs him, she is not self-sufficient, she is a parasite. Through the eyes of Dominique, in *Le Songe*, Montherlant shows the strolling women of Ranelagh "hanging on their lovers' arms like invertebrate creatures similar to large snails in disguise." Except for women athletes, according to him, women are incomplete beings, doomed to slavery; soft and lacking in muscle, they have no grasp on the world;

so they work hard to annex a lover or, better, a husband. Montherlant may not use the myth of the praying mantis, but he expresses its content: to love is, for woman, to devour; pretending to give, she takes. He quotes Mme Tolstoy's cry: "I live in him, for him; I require him to do the same for me," and he depicts the dangers of such loving fury; he finds a terrible truth in the saying of Ecclesiastes: "A man who wishes you ill is better than a woman who wishes you well." He cites Marshal Lyautey's experience: "A man of mine who marries is reduced to half a man." He regards marriage as particularly ill-omened for the "superior man"; it is ridiculously bourgeois—can you imagine saying: "Mrs. Æschylus," or "I am going to dine with the Dantes"? It weakens the prestige of a great man; and, above all, marriage destroys the magnificent solitude of the hero; he "needs to be undisturbed in his own thoughts." [1] I have already said that Montherlant has chosen a liberty *without object*; that is to say, he prefers an illusion of autonomy to the authentic liberty that takes action in the world; it is this detachment and freedom from responsibility that he means to defend against woman; she is heavy, she weighs one down. "It was a harsh symbol, indeed, a man unable to walk upright because the woman he loved was on his arm." [2] "I was aflame, she extinguishes me. I was walking on the water, she takes my arm and I sink." [3] How is it she has so much power, since she is only lack, poverty, negation, and since her magic is an illusion? Montherlant does not explain. He simply says with arrogance that "the lion with good reason fears the mosquito." But the answer is obvious: it is easy to imagine yourself sovereign when you are alone, to think yourself strong when you carefully avoid taking up any burden. Montherlant has chosen the easy way; he claims to practice the cult of arduous values, but he seeks to gain them easily. "The wreaths we ourselves bestow upon ourselves are the only ones worth wearing," says the King in *Pasiphaé*. A convenient principle! Montherlant overloads his brow, he drapes himself in the purple; but a glance from any stranger would suffice to reveal that his diadems are of painted paper, and that, like Hans Christian Andersen's king, he is quite naked. To walk on the water in fancy is much less wearying than to go forward in earnest

---

[1] *Sur les femmes.*
[2] *Les Jeunes Filles.*
[3] Ibid.

on the roads of the earth. And that is why the lion, Montherlant, avoids in terror woman, the mosquito: he dreads the test of reality.[4]

If Montherlant had really deflated the myth of the eternal feminine, it would be in order to congratulate him on the achievement: it is by denying Woman that we can help women to assume the status of human beings. But, as we have seen, he does not smash the idol: he changes it into a monster. He, too, believes in that vague and basic essence, femininity; he holds with Aristotle and St. Thomas that woman is to be defined negatively; woman is woman through the lack of virility; that is the fate to which every female individual must submit without being able to modify it. Whoever presumes to escape from it puts herself at the bottom of the scale of humanity: she fails to become a man, she gives up being a woman; she is only a ludicrous caricature, a false show. It gives her no reality to be a body and a conscious mind: a Platonist when it suits him, Montherlant seems to hold that only the Ideas of femininity and of virility have actuality; the individual who partakes of neither the one nor the other only appears to exist. He condemns without appeal those "vampires of the night" who have the audacity to pose as autonomous subjects, to think, to act. And in tracing the portrait of Andrée Hacquebaut he means to prove that any woman who strives to become a personage transforms herself into a grimacing puppet. Of course Andrée is homely, ill-favored, badly dressed, and even dirty, her nails and wrists dubious: the small amount of culture attributed to her has been enough to kill her femininity completely. Costals tells us she is intelligent, but Montherlant convinces us of her stupidity on every page devoted to her. Costals asserts he is sympathetic toward her; Montherlant makes her odious to us. By such clever double-dealing the stupidity of the feminine intelligence is proved, and it is established that an original defectiveness perverts in woman any virile qualities she may aim at.

Montherlant is quite willing to make an exception for female athletes; by the independent exercising of the body they can win a spirit, a soul. Yet it would be easy to bring them down from these heights;

---

4 This process is considered by Adler as the classical root of the psychoses. The individual, torn between a "will to power" and an "inferiority complex," puts as much distance as possible between society and himself so as not to have to face the test of reality. He knows that this would undermine the pretenses that he can maintain only under the cover of bad faith.

Montherlant delicately moves away from the lady winner of the thousand-meter race, to whom he offers an enthusiastic hymn, because he has no doubt of seducing her easily, and he wishes to spare her that fall. Dominique has not kept her lofty place on the summits where she was called by Alban; she has fallen in love with him: "She who had been all spirit and all soul now perspired, spread her odors, and, getting out of breath, gave little coughs." [5] Revolted, Alban drove her away. One can esteem a woman who through the discipline of sport has killed her carnal nature, but it is an odious scandal that an autonomous existence should reside in woman's flesh; feminine flesh is hateful from the moment a conscious mind inhabits it. What is fitting and proper for a woman is to be purely flesh. Montherlant approves the Oriental attitude: as an object to be enjoyed, the weaker sex has a place in the world, humble no doubt, but worthy; it finds justification in the pleasure the male derives from it and in this pleasure alone. The ideal woman is perfectly stupid and perfectly submissive; she is always ready to accept the male and never makes any demands upon him. Such a one is Douce, whom Alban appreciates at his convenience, "Douce, admirably silly and always the more lusted after the more silly she was . . . useless apart from love and to be evaded then with gentle firmness." [6] Such a one is Radidja, the little Arab, calm beast of love docilely accepting pleasure and money. Such, one can imagine, was that "feminine beast" met with on a Spanish train: "She had so besotted an air that I began to desire her." [7] The author explains: "What is irritating in women is their claim to reason; let them exaggerate their animality and they suggest the superhuman."

And yet Montherlant is by no means an Oriental sultan; first of all, he is lacking in sensuality. He is far from taking his pleasure in the "feminine beasts" without some reservation; they are sick, unwholesome, never quite clean. [8] Costals confides to us that young boys' hair smells better and more strongly than women's; sometimes he experiences disgust in Solange's presence, in the presence of "that sweetish, almost sickening odor and that muscleless, nerveless body, like a white slug." He dreams of embraces more worthy of him, be-

---

[5] *Le Songe.*
[6] *Ibid.*
[7] *La Petite Infante de Castille.*
[8] *Les Jeunes Filles.*

tween equals, where the sweetness would derive from strength overcome. The Oriental delights voluptuously in woman and thus establishes a carnal reciprocity between lovers: this is made manifest in
the ardent invocations of the Song of Songs, the tales of *The Arabian
Nights*, and countless Arab poems in praise of the loved one. To be
sure, there are bad women; but there are also delightful ones, and
the sensual man abandons himself in their arms with confidence,
without feeling humiliated. Whereas Montherlant's hero is always
on the defensive: "To take without being taken, sole acceptable formula for relations between the superior man and woman." [9] He speaks
readily of the moment of desire, which seems to him an aggressive,
virile moment; he evades that of enjoyment, for perhaps he would be
in danger of discovering that he, too, perspires, pants, "gives off his
odors"; but no, who would venture to breathe his odor, to feel his
damp sweat? His disarmed flesh exists for no one, because no one is
there before him: he is the lone consciousness, a pure presence, transparent and supreme; and if for his own consciousness pleasure exists,
he takes no note of it: that would be to give someone an advantage
over him. He speaks with complacency of the pleasure he gives, never
of that which he receives, for to receive is a form of dependence.
"What I ask of a woman is to give her pleasure"; [1] the living heat of
sex enjoyment would mean complicity: he admits of none; he prefers
the supercilious solitude of domination. He seeks cerebral not sensual
satisfactions with women.

And first of all he seeks the satisfactions of a pride that calls for
expression, but without running risks. Before woman "one has the
same feeling as before a horse or a bull one is about to come to grips
with: the same uncertainty and the same inclination to try one's
ability." [2] To try it against other men would be foolhardy; they would
interfere in the test; they would impose unexpected technicalities, they
would render an alien verdict. But with a horse or a bull one remains
one's own judge, which is much more sure. It is the same with a
woman: if she be well chosen, one remains alone though confronting
her: "I do not love in equality, because I seek in woman the child."
This truism explains nothing. Why does he seek a child, not an
equal? Montherlant would be more sincere if he would declare that

---

[9] *Les Jeunes Filles.*
[1] Ibid.
[2] *La Petite Infante de Castille.*

he, Montherlant, has no equal; and more precisely that he does not wish to have, for his equal would frighten him. At the Olympic games he admires in sports the rigor of the competition and the relative standings determined without the possibility of cheating; but he has not himself learned the lesson. Later on, in his works and in his life, his heroes, like himself, avoid all real competition: they have to do with animals, landscapes, children, woman-children—and never with equals. Though lately enthusiastic over the severe purity of sport, Montherlant accepts as mistresses only women from whom his timid pride has nothing to fear in the way of judgment; he selects such as are "passive and vegetal," infantile, stupid, venal. He will systematically avoid attributing mature human mentality to them, and if he discovers any trace of it, he takes fright and leaves; there is no question of establishing any intersubjective relation with the woman: in man's realm she is to be only a simple animated object, never is she to be envisaged as subject; never is her point of view to be taken seriously into consideration. Montherlant's hero professes an ethics that is supposed to be arrogant and that is only convenient: he has regard only for its relations to himself. He becomes attached to woman—or rather he attaches himself to woman—not to enjoy her, but to enjoy himself: being absolutely inferior, woman's existence brings out in relief the substantial, essential, and indestructible superiority of the male—without risk.

Thus Douce's stupidity allows Alban "to reconstruct in some measure the sensations of the antique demigod marrying a fabulous Goose." [3] When he touches Solange, behold Costals changed into a superb lion: "As soon as they were seated close together, he put his hand on the young girl's thigh (outside her clothes), then he held it against the center of her body *as a lion* holds his paw spread out on the meat he has captured." [4] This act, which, in darkened movie houses, many men perform every day without fanfare, Costals announces as being "the primitive gesture of the Overlord, the *Seigneur.*" If, like him, they had a sense of grandeur, lovers and husbands who practice endearments before intercourse would experience these mighty metamorphoses at a bargain. "He sniffed vaguely at this woman's face, *like a lion* that, tearing to pieces the meat held between his paws, stops now and then to lick it."

---

[3] *Le Songe.*
[4] *Les Jeunes Filles.* The four following quotations are also from this work.

This carnivorous arrogance is not the only pleasure derived by the male from his female; she is the pretext for him to experiment with his own feelings freely and always without risk, firing blanks, so to speak. Costals, one night, will amuse himself even by suffering until, having had enough of his pain, he cheerfully attacks a chicken leg. Only rarely can one permit oneself such a caprice. But there are other joys, lordly or subtle. For instance, condescension; Costals condescends to reply to certain letters from women, and sometimes even takes some pains about it. To an ambitious little country girl he wrote at the end of a pedantic dissertation: "I doubt whether you can understand me, but that is much better than for me to have *come down* to your level." It pleases him at times to model a woman in his image: "I want you to be like my scarf . . . I have not *raised* you to my level for you to be anything different from myself." He amuses himself in creating some pleasant memories for Solange. But it is above all when he sleeps with a woman that he rapturously senses his own prodigality. Giver as he is of joy, giver of peace, of warmth, of strength, of pleasure, he comes laden with the riches he dispenses. He owes nothing to his mistresses; often he pays them so as to make sure; but even when the intercourse is without payment, the woman is unilaterally his debtor: she gives nothing, he takes. Thus he finds it absolutely normal, the day he deflowers Solange, to send her to the dressing-room; even if a woman is tenderly beloved, it would be strange to see the man put himself out for her; he is male by divine right, she is by divine right doomed to injection vessel and bidet. Costals's pride imitates boorishness so faithfully that it becomes hard to see what distinguishes him from an ill-bred traveling salesman.

The first duty of a woman is to submit to the demands of his generosity; when he fancies that Solange does not appreciate his caresses, Costals becomes white with rage. If he cares for Radidja, it is because her face lights up with joy when he enters her. Then he enjoys feeling himself at once the beast of prey and the magnificent prince. One asks with some perplexity, however, what can be the origin of the frenzy to take and overwhelm if the woman taken and overwhelmed is only a poor thing, insipid flesh in which stirs a substitute consciousness. How can Costals waste so much time with these empty creatures? These contradictions indicate the worth of a pride that is only vanity.

A more subtle pleasure for the strong, the generous, the masterful, is pity for the wretched. Now and then Costals is moved to feel in his heart such brotherly concern, such sympathy for the humble, such "pity for women." [5] What can be more touching than the unexpected gentleness of hard men? He fancies himself like that noble statue in Épinal when he bends over these sick animals—that is, women. He even likes to see sportswomen defeated, wounded, tired out, bruised; as for the rest, he wants them to be as defenseless as possible. Their monthly sickness disgusts him and yet Costals lets us know that "with women he had always preferred those days when he knew they were menstruating." [6] He may happen to yield to this pity, to go as far as making promises, if not to the point of keeping them: he promises to help Andrée, to marry Solange. When pity departs from his soul, these promises die: has he not the right to contradict himself? He is the one who makes the rules of the game he plays, with himself as sole partner.

Inferior, pitiful—this is not enough. Montherlant wishes woman to be contemptible. He asserts sometimes that the conflict between desire and contempt is a drama of pathos: "Ah, to desire what one disdains, what a tragedy! . . . To have to attract and repulse in almost a single movement, to light and throw away quickly as we do with a match—such is the tragedy of our relations with women!" [7] In truth there is no tragedy except from the point of view of the match, a negligible point of view. As for the match-lighter, careful not to burn his fingers, it is only too clear that this action enchants him. If it did not please him to "desire what he disdains," he would not systematically refuse to desire what he esteems: Alban would not repulse Dominique, he would choose to "love in equality"; and he could avoid so much disdaining of what he desires: after all, it is hard to see *a priori* what is so contemptible in a little Spanish dancer who is young, pretty, ardent, and sincere. Is it because she is poor, of low class, uncultured? One fears that in Montherlant's eyes these are indeed defects. But, above all, he scorns her as being a woman, on principle. He says truly enough that it is not the feminine mystery that causes male dreams, but rather these dreams that create the mystery. But he, too, projects into the object what he subjectively calls for: it is not because they are contemptible that he disdains

---

[5] One of his works is actually entitled *Pitié pour les femmes!*—Tr.

[6] *Les Jeunes Filles.*

[7] *La Petite Infante de Castille.*

women, it is because he would disdain them that they seem to him so abject. He feels that he tarries on heights that are the more lofty the greater the distance is between the women and himself.

This explains why he selects for his heroes ladyloves wanting in wealth and refinement. For the great writer Costals he provides a provincial old maid tormented by sex and ennui, and a lower-middle-class woman of the extreme Right, unsophisticated and full of self-interest. It is gauging a superior person with very humble units of measurement, and the result of this maladroit if prudent procedure is that he seems to us quite small. But no matter, Costals believes himself great. The most minor weaknesses of woman are enough to feed his vanity. A passage from *Les Jeunes Filles* is peculiarly significant. Before going to bed with Costals, Solange is getting ready for the night. "She had to go to the W.C. and Costals recalled that mare he once had, so proud, so exquisite that she never urinated or broke wind when he was in the saddle." Here comes to light the hatred of the flesh (one thinks of Swift: Celia defecates), the willingness to liken a woman to a domesticated animal, the refusal to permit her any autonomy, were it only in the matter of urination. But above all, while Costals waxes indignant, he forgets that he too has a bladder and a colon. In like manner when he is disgusted with a sweaty and odorous woman, he abolishes all his own bodily secretions: he is a pure spirit served by muscles and a sex of steel. "Disdain is more noble than desire," declares Montherlant in *Aux fontaines du désire*; and Alvaro cries in *Le Maître de Santiago*: [8] "Disgust is bread to me." What an alibi scorn is when one is feeling well pleased with oneself! From the fact that one ponders and judges, one feels oneself radically different from the other whom one condemns, one clears oneself without cost from the faults of which one accuses the other. With what frenzy has Montherlant all his life given vent to his contempt for people! To denounce their stupidity is enough to make him consider himself intelligent, their cowardice to feel courageous. At the beginning of the Nazi occupation of France he threw himself into an orgy of scorn for his defeated compatriots: *he* is neither French nor defeated, he soars above it all. In an indirect phrase he agrees that on the whole he, Montherlant, who is doing the accusing, did no more than the others to prevent the defeat; he was not even

---

[8] Published in translation in *The Master of Santiago* with four other plays (Alfred A. Knopf, 1951).—TR.

willing to serve as an officer. But forthwith he takes up his accusations with a fury that carries him far away from his own case.[9] If he pretends to be very sorry for his feelings of disgust, it is to feel them more sincerely and enjoy them the more. In fact, he finds so many conveniences in this sort of thing that he seeks systematically to drag woman down into abjectness. He amuses himself tempting poor girls with money or jewels: if they accept his malevolent presents, he feels jubilation. He plays a sadistic game with Andrée for amusement, not to make her suffer but to see her abase herself. He incites Solange to infanticide; she accepts the prospect, and Costals's senses take fire: he possesses this potential murderess in a ravishment of scorn.

The key to this attitude is given us by his fable of the caterpillars: whatever may have been its hidden intent, it is sufficiently significant as it stands.[1] Urinating on some caterpillars, Montherlant amuses himself by sparing certain ones, by exterminating others; he bestows a laughing pity upon such as struggle for life and generously lets them have their chance; this game enchants him. Without the caterpillars the urinary stream would have been only an excretion; it becomes an instrument of life or death; before the crawling insects, the man relieving his bladder knows the despotic solitude of God—not to be threatened in return. Thus in dealing with woman-beasts the male, from the height of his pedestal, now cruel, now kind, just and capricious in turn, gives, takes away, gratifies, shows pity, gets irritated; he acts only in accordance with his good pleasure; he is supreme, free, unique. But these beasts must remain nothing but beasts; they will be selected on purpose, their weaknesses will be humored, they will be treated as beasts with such mad obstinacy that they will in the end accept their status. In the same way the whites of Louisiana and Georgia are delighted with the little pilferings and fibs of the blacks: they feel reassured of the superiority conferred by their skin color; and if one of these Negroes persists in being honest, he will be maltreated the more for it. And similarly in the concentration camps the abasement of men was systematically carried out: the Master Race found in this abjection proof that it was indeed of superhuman essence.

To judge the validity of Montherlant's attitude toward women, it will be well to examine his ethics more closely. For in the end we

[9] *Le Solstice de juin*, p. 301.
[1] Ibid., p. 286.

must know *in the name of what* women are, in his view, to be condemned. His attitude has no positive counterpart that might serve as
its explanation; it expresses only his own existential choice. In truth,
this hero has chosen fear. There is in every consciousness an aspiration
toward sovereignty; but it can take affirmative action only in risking itself. No superiority is ever given, since man is nothing when reduced to his subjectivity; hierarchies can be set up only in accordance
with men's acts and works; merit must be continually redemonstrated.
Montherlant says so himself. "One has rights over only that which
one is ready to risk." But he has never been ready to risk *himself*
among his equals. And it is because he does not dare to confront
humanity that he does away with it. "An enraging obstacle, these
human beings," says the King in *La Reine morte*. The trouble is that
they give the lie to the agreeable fairyland that the man of vanity
creates around himself. They must be repudiated. It is noteworthy
that *not one* of Montherlant's works paints for us a man-to-man conflict; coexistence is the great living drama, but it eludes him. His hero
always stands alone before animals, children, women, landscapes; he
is the prey of his own desires (like the Queen in *Pasiphaé*) or of his
own demands (like the Master of Santiago), but there is never *anyone* at his side. Even Alban in *Le Songe* has no comrade: he disdains
Prinet alive, and becomes excited about him only over his corpse.
Montherlant's works, like his life, admit of only *one* consciousness.

Herewith all sentiment disappears from this universe. There can
be no intersubjective relation if there is only one subject. Love is a
joke; but it is contemptible not in the name of friendship, for "friendship lacks guts." [2] And all human solidarity is haughtily rejected. The
hero was not engendered, he is not limited by space and time: "I see
no sensible reason for interesting myself more in outer affairs that
are contemporaneous with me than in those of no matter what year
of the past." [3] Nothing happening to another is of any account to
him: "To tell the truth, events have never been of moment to me.
I liked them only for the rays they made in me in passing through
me. . . . Let them be, then, what they will." [4] Action is impossible:
"To have had ardor, energy, audacity and not to have been able to
put them at the disposition of anyone whatever because of lack

---

[2] *Aux fontaines du désir.*
[3] *La Possession de soi-même*, p. 13.
[4] *Le Solstice de juin*, p. 316.

of confidence in anything human at all!" [5] That is to say, all *transcendence* is prohibited. Montherlant recognizes this. Love and friendship are trifles, scorn prevents action. He does not believe in art for art's sake, and he does not believe in God. There remains only the immanence of pleasure: "My sole ambition has been to make better use of my senses than others do," he cries in 1925.[6] And again: "In sum, what do I want? The possession in peace and poetry of persons who please me." [7] And in 1941: "But as for me, I who accuse others, what have I done with these twenty years? They have been as a dream of pleasure for me. I have lived both in length and in breadth, getting drunk on what I like: what a mouth-to-mouth with life!" [8] Well and good. But is it not precisely because she wallows in immanence that woman was trampled upon? What more lofty ends, what grand designs does Montherlant hold up in opposition to the possessive love of the mother and the mistress? He also seeks "possession"; and when it comes to "mouth-to-mouth with life," many a woman could give him points. Does he not know that women's sensuality is no less tempestuous than men's? If one is to rank the sexes by this criterion, perhaps women would stand higher than men. To tell the truth, in this field Montherlant's incoherencies are monstrous. In the name of "alternation" he declares that from the very fact that nothing is worth anything, everything is of equal value; he accepts all, he would embrace one and all, and he is pleased when his largeness of spirit terrifies mothers of families. Yet he it was who during the occupation demanded an "inquisition" [9] to censor films and newspapers. The thighs of American girls nauseate him; the shiny sex of a bull excites him: every man to his taste. Each one builds "fairyland" anew after his own fashion; in the name of what values does this great orgiast spit with disgust upon the orgies of others? Because they are not his? But does all morality then consist in being Montherlant?

He would evidently reply that to enjoy is not everything: it must be done with style. Pleasure should be the other aspect of a renuncia-

----

[5] *Aux fontaines du désir.*

[6] Ibid.

[7] Ibid.

[8] *Le Solstice de juin*, p. 301.

[9] "We demand an organization having discretionary power to arrest all who might, in its judgment, injure the human quality of the French. A kind of inquisition in the name of the human quality of the French." (*Le Solstice de juin*, p. 270.)

tion, that the voluptuary may feel himself to be also of the stuff of hero and saint. But many women are expert in reconciling their pleasures with the lofty image they have formed of themselves. Why should we believe that Montherlant's narcissistic dreams have more worth than theirs?

For, truly, it is with dreams that we are dealing. The words with which Montherlant juggles—grandeur, sanctity, heroism—are but futilities because he denies them any objective meaning. Montherlant has been afraid to risk his superiority among men; to make himself drunk on that heady wine, he retired into the clouds: the Unique is surely supreme. He shuts himself up in a chamber of illusion: the mirrors send back his reflection repeated to infinity and he believes that he suffices to populate the world; but he is only a recluse, the prisoner of himself. He thinks he is free, but he sells his liberty for the profit of his ego; he models the statue of Montherlant according to norms borrowed from the statue factory in Épinal. Alban repulsing Dominique because, seeing himself in a mirror, he finds his visage moronic illustrates that slavery. One is in fact a moron only in the eyes of others. The proud Alban subordinates his feelings to that collective consciousness which he scorns. Montherlant's liberty is an attitude, not a reality. Action being impossible for him, since he has no aim, he consoles himself with gestures: he is a mime. Women make convenient partners, they give him his cue, he takes for himself the leading role, he wreaths his own brow with the laurel of victory and assumes the purple robe. But it all takes place on his private stage; thrown before the public, in real daylight, under a real sky, our comedian no longer sees clearly, no longer stands erect, he reels, he falls. Costals cries in a moment of lucidity: "At bottom what buffoonery are these 'victories' over women!" [1] Yes. The values, the accomplishments offered us by Montherlant are a sad buffoonery. The lofty deeds that intoxicate him are but gestures, never real undertakings: he is touched by the suicide of Peregrinus, by the audacity of Pasiphaë, by the elegance of the Japanese gentleman who sheltered his opponent under his umbrella before finishing him off in a duel. But he declares that "the person of the opponent and the ideas he is supposed to represent are not, then, of so very great importance." [2] This declaration had a peculiar ring in 1941. All war is beautiful, he says

---

[1] *Les Jeunes Filles.*
[2] *Le Solstice de juin*, p. 211.

again, whatever the outcome; strength is always to be admired, whatever cause it serves. "Combat without faith is the formula to which we are forced in the end, if we wish to maintain the only acceptable concept of man: that in which he is at once hero and sage." [3] Montherlant's lofty indifference to all causes and his preference for the pseudo-sublime are illustrated in *La Reine morte* and *Le Maître de Santiago*.

In these dramas, both significant in their pretentiousness, we see two imperial males who sacrifice to their empty pride women guilty of nothing more than being human: for punishment one loses her life, the other her soul. Once again, if we ask in the name of what, the author haughtily answers: in the name of nothing. He did not want the King to have too clear motives of state for killing Ines; for then this murder would be only a commonplace political crime. "Why am I killing her? There is doubtless a reason, but I cannot pick it out," he says. The reason is that the solar principle must triumph over terrestrial banality; but this principle, as we realize, illuminates no goal: it requires destruction, nothing more. As for Alvaro, Montherlant tells us in a preface that, regarding certain men of that time, he takes an interest in "their clear-cut faith, their scorn of outer reality, their relish for ruin, their craze for nothingness." It is to this craze, indeed, that the master of Santiago sacrifices his daughter. Perhaps it might be embellished with the iridescent word *mystical*. Is it not stupid to prefer happiness to mysticism? The truth is that sacrifices and renunciations make sense only in the perspective of an aim, a human purpose; and aims that transcend individual love and personal happiness can take shape only in a world that recognizes the value both of love and of happiness; "shopgirl morality" is more authentic than fairy tales of emptiness because it has its roots in life and reality, whence the higher aspirations can arise. It is easy to imagine Ines de Castro at Buchenwald, and the King officiously bustling about the German Embassy for reasons of state. Many a little shopgirl during the occupation earned a respect we do not accord to Montherlant. He is full of superficial words that are dangerous by reason of their very emptiness: his superhuman mysticism sanctions any amount of temporal devastation. What happens is that in the dramas we are discussing this mysticism finds expression through two murders, one physical, the other moral; Alvaro—grim, alone, ignored

---

[3] Ibid., p. 211.

—has not far to go to become a Grand Inquisitor; nor the King—misunderstood, denied—a Himmler. One kills women, kills Jews, kills effeminate men and Christians under Jewish influence, one kills all one has interest or pleasure in killing, in the name of these lofty ideas. Mystical negatives can be expressed only through negations. True transcendence is a positive movement toward the future, man's future. The false hero, to persuade himself that he has traveled far, that he soars high aloft, looks constantly backwards and downwards; he scorns, he accuses, he oppresses, he persecutes, he tortures, he murders. He regards himself as superior to his neighbor by virtue of the wrong he does him. Such are the summits that Montherlant points out to us with a haughty gesture, when he pauses momentarily from his "mouth-to-mouth with life."

"Like the donkey working the Arab water-wheel, I turn, I turn, blindly, endlessly retracing my steps. But I never bring up fresh water." There is little to be added to this avowal signed by Montherlant in 1927. The fresh water has never gushed forth. Perhaps Montherlant should have lighted the pyre of Peregrinus: it was the most logical solution. He has preferred to take refuge in self-worship. Instead of giving himself to this world, which he knew not how to fertilize, he was content to see himself reflected in it; and he ordered his life in accordance with this mirage, a mirage visible to no eyes but his. "Princes are at ease under all circumstances, even in defeat," he writes; [4] and because he enjoys the defeat, he thinks he is king. He has learned from Nietzsche that "woman is the diversion of the hero," and he thinks that to divert himself with women is all that is needed to make a hero of him. And so on after the same fashion. As Costals says, "At bottom, what dreadful buffoonery!"

2
D. H. LAWRENCE OR PHALLIC PRIDE

Lawrence is poles apart from a Montherlant. Not for him to define the special relations of woman and of man, but to restore both of them to the verity of Life. This verity lies neither in display nor in the will: it involves animality, in which the human being has his roots. Lawrence passionately rejects the antithesis: sex—brain; he has a cosmic optimism that is radically opposed to the pessimism of

---

[4] *Le Solstice de juin*, p. 312.

Schopenhauer; the will-to-live expressed in the phallus is joy, and herein should be the source of thought and action unless these are to be respectively empty concept and sterile mechanism. The sex cycle pure and simple is not enough because it falls back into immanence: it is a synonym of death; but still this mutilated reality, sex and death, is better than an existence cut off from the humus of the flesh. Man needs more than, like Antæus, to renew contact now and then with the earth; his life as a man should be wholly an expression of his virility, which immediately presupposes and demands woman. She is therefore neither diversion nor prey; she is not an object confronting a subject, but a pole necessary for the existence of the pole of opposite sign. Men who have misunderstood this truth, a Napoleon for example, have failed of their destiny as men: they are defectives. It is not by asserting his singularity, but by fulfilling his generality as intensely as possible that the individual can be saved: male or female, one should never seek in erotic relations the triumph of one's pride or the exaltation of one's ego; to use one's sex as tool of the will, that is the fatal mistake; one must break the barriers of the ego, transcend even the limits of consciousness, renounce all personal sovereignty. Nothing could be more beautiful than that little statue of a woman in labor: "A terrible face void, peaked, *abstracted almost into meaninglessness* by the weight of sensation beneath." [5]

This ecstasy is one neither of sacrifice nor abandon; there is no question of either of the two sexes permitting the other to swallow it up; neither man nor woman should seem like a "broken-off fragment" of a couple; the sex part is not a still aching scar; each member of the couple is a complete being, perfectly polarized; when one feels assured in his virility, the other in her femininity, "each acknowledges the perfection of the polarized sex circuit"; [6] the sexual act is, without annexing, without surrender of either partner, a marvelous fulfillment of each one by the other. When Ursula and Birkin finally found each other, they gave each other reciprocally that stellar equilibrium which alone can be called liberty. "She was for him what he was for her, the immemorial magnificence of the *other reality*, mystic and palpable." [7] Having access to each other in the generous extortion of pas-

---

[5] *Women in Love* (Modern Library), p. 88. (Italics mine.)
[6] Ibid., p. 228.
[7] Ibid., p. 366.

sion, two lovers together have access to the Other, the All. Thus with
Paul and Clara in the moment of love: [8] "What was she? A strong,
strange wild life, that breathed with his in the darkness through this
hour. It was all so much bigger than themselves that he was hushed.
They had met, and included in their meeting the thrust of the mani-
fold grass-stems, the cry of the peewit, the wheel of the stars." Lady
Chatterley and Mellors attained to the same cosmic joys: blending
one with the other, they blend with the trees, the light, the rain.
Lawrence develops his doctrine broadly in *The Defense of Lady
Chatterley*: [9] "Marriage is only an illusion if it is not lastingly and
radically phallic, if it is not bound to the sun and the earth, to the
moon, to the stars and planets, to the rhythm of the seasons, the
years, the lustra, and the centuries. Marriage is nothing if it is not
based on a correspondence of blood. For blood is the substance of
the soul." "The blood of man and the blood of woman are two eternally different streams which cannot mix." That is why these two
streams embrace the totality of life in their meanderings. "The phallus is a quantity of blood that fills the valley of blood in the female.
The powerful stream of masculine blood overwhelms in its ultimate
depths the grand stream of feminine blood . . . however, neither
breaks through its barriers. It is the most perfect form of communion . . . and it is one of the greatest of mysteries." This communion
is a miraculous enrichment of life; but it demands that the claims of
the "personality" be abolished. When personalities seek to reach each
other without renouncing themselves, as is common in modern civilization, their attempt is doomed to frustration. There is in such cases
a sexuality "personal, blank, cold, nervous, poetic," which tends to
disintegrate the vital stream of each. The lovers treat each other as
instruments, engendering hate: so it is with Lady Chatterley and
Michaelis; they remain shut up in their subjectivity; they can experience a fever such as alcohol or opium gives, but it is without object:
they fail each to discover the reality of the other; they gain access to
nothing. Lawrence would have condemned Costals without appeal.
He has painted in the figure of Gerard, in *Women in Love*, one of
these proud and egoistic males; and Gerard is in large part responsible
for the hell into which he hurls himself with Gudrun. Cerebral, willful, he delights in the empty assertion of his ego and hardens him-

---

[8] *Sons and Lovers*, p. 415.
[9] These passages are translated from the French version.—TR.

self against life: for the pleasure of mastering a fiery mare, he keeps her head at a gate behind which a train passes with thunderous commotion; he draws blood from her rebellious flanks and intoxicates himself with his own power. This will to domination abases the woman against whom it is exercised; lacking strength, she is transformed into a slave. Gerard leans over Pussum: "Her inchoate look of a violated slave, whose fulfillment lies in her further and further violation, made his nerves quiver . . . his was the only will, she was the passive substance of his will." That is a miserable kind of domination; if the woman is only a passive substance, what the male dominates is nothing. He thinks he is taking something, enriching himself: it is a delusion. Gerard takes Gudrun in his arms: "she was the rich, lovely substance of his being. . . . So she was passed away and gone in him, and he was perfected." But as soon as he quits her, he finds himself alone and empty; and the next day she fails to come to the rendezvous. If the woman is strong, the male demand arouses a similar, symmetrical demand in her; fascinated and rebellious, she becomes masochistic and sadistic in turn. Gudrun is overwhelmed with agitation when she sees Gerard press the flanks of the raging mare between his thighs; but she is agitated also when Gerard's nurse tells her "many's the time I've pinched his little bottom for him." Masculine arrogance provokes feminine resistance. While Ursula is conquered and saved by the sexual purity of Birkin, as Lady Chatterley was by that of the gamekeeper, Gerard drags Gudrun into a struggle without end. One night, unhappy, broken down by mourning for his father, he let himself go in her arms. "She was the great bath of life, he worshipped her. Mother and substance of all life she was. . . . But the miraculous, soft effluence of her breast suffused over him, over his seared, damaged brain, like a healing lymph, like a soft, soothing flow of life itself, perfect as if he were bathed in the womb again." That night they feel something of what a communion with woman could be; but it is too late; his happiness is vitiated, for Gudrun is not really present; she lets Gerard sleep on her shoulder, but she stays awake, impatient, separate. It is the punishment meted out to the individual who is a victim of himself: he cannot, being solitary, invade her solitude; in raising the barriers of his ego, he has raised those of the Other: he will never be reunited with her. At the end Gerard dies, killed by Gudrun and by himself.

Thus it would at first appear that neither of the two sexes has an advantage. Neither is subject. Woman is no more a mere pretext than she is man's prey. Malraux[1] notes that for Lawrence it is not enough, as it is for the Hindu, that woman be the occasion for contact with the infinite, like, for example, a landscape: that would be making an object of her, in another fashion. She is just as real as the man, and a real communion is what he should achieve. This is why the heroes who have Lawrence's approval demand from their mistresses much more than the gift of their bodies: Paul does not permit Miriam to give herself to him as a tender sacrifice; Birkin does not want Ursula to limit herself to seeking pleasure in his arms; cold or burning, the woman who remains closed up within herself leaves man to his solitude: he should repulse her. Both ought to give themselves body and soul. If this gift were made, they would remain forever faithful. Lawrence is a partisan of monogamous marriage. There is the quest for variety only if one is interested in the peculiarities of individuals; but phallic marriage is founded on generality. When the virility-femininity circuit is established, desire for change is inconceivable: it is a complete circuit, closed and definitive.

Reciprocal gift, reciprocal fidelity: have we here in truth the reign of mutuality? Far from it. Lawrence believes passionately in the supremacy of the male. The very expression "phallic marriage," the equivalence he sets up between "sexual" and "phallic," constitute sufficient proof. Of the two blood streams that are mysteriously married, the phallic current is favored. "The phallus serves as a means of union between two rivers; it conjoins the two different rhythms into a single flow." Thus the man is not only one of the two elements in the couple, but also their connecting factor; he provides their transcendence: "The bridge to the future is the phallus." For the cult of the Goddess Mother, Lawrence means to substitute a phallic cult; when he wishes to illuminate the sexual nature of the cosmos, it is not woman's abdomen but man's virility that he calls to mind. He almost never shows a man agitated by a woman; but time and again he shows woman secretly overwhelmed by the ardent, subtle, and insinuating appeal of the male. His heroines are beautiful and healthy, but not heady; whereas his heroes are disquieting fauns. It is male animals that incarnate the agitation and the powerful mystery of Life; women feel the spell: this one is affected by a fox, that one is taken

---

[1] Preface to *L'Amant ae Lady Chatterley*.

with a stallion, Gudrun feverishly challenges a herd of young oxen; she is overwhelmed by the rebellious vigor of a rabbit.

A social advantage for man is grafted upon this cosmic advantage. No doubt because the phallic stream is impetuous, aggressive, because it spreads into the future—Lawrence explains himself but imperfectly —it is for man to "carry forward the banner of life"; [2] he is intent upon aims and ends, he incarnates transcendence; woman is absorbed in her sentiment, she is all inwardness; she is dedicated to immanence. Not only does man play the active role in the sexual life, but he is active also in going beyond it; he is rooted in the sexual world, but he makes his escape from it; woman remains shut up in it. Thought and action have their roots in the phallus; lacking the phallus, woman has no rights in either the one or the other: she can play a man's role, and even brilliantly, but it is just a game, lacking serious verity. "Woman is really polarized downwards towards the center of the earth. Her deep positivity is in the downward flow, the moon-pull. And man is polarized upwards, toward the sun and the day's activity." [3] For woman "the deepest consciousness is in the loins and the belly." [4] If this is perverted and her flow of energy is upward, to the breast and head, woman may become clever, noble, efficient, brilliant, competent in the manly world; but, according to Lawrence, she soon has enough of it, everything goes pop, and she returns to sex, "which is her business at the present moment." [5] In the domain of action man should be the initiator, the positive; woman is the positive on the emotional level.

Thus Lawrence rediscovers the traditional bourgeois conception of Bonald, of Auguste Comte, of Clément Vautel. Woman should subordinate her existence to that of man. "She ought to believe in you, and in the deep purpose you stand for." [6] Then man will pay her an infinite tenderness and gratitude. "Ah, how good it is to come home to your wife when she *believes* in you and submits to your purpose that is beyond her. . . . You feel unfathomable gratitude to the woman who loves you." [7] Lawrence adds that to merit such devotion,

---

[2] *Fantasia of the Unconscious* (Thomas Seltzer, 1922), p. 138.
[3] Ibid., p. 279.
[4] Ibid., p. 279.
[5] Ibid., p. 280.
[6] Ibid., p. 285.
[7] Ibid., pp. 287–8.

the man must be genuinely occupied with a great design; if his project is but a false goal, the couple breaks down in low deceptiveness. Better to shut oneself up again in the feminine cycle of love and death, like Anna Karenina and Vronsky, Carmen and Don José, than to lie to each other like Pierre and Natasha.

But there is always this reservation: what Lawrence is extolling—after the fashion of Proudhon and Rousseau—is monogamous marriage in which the wife derives the justification of her existence from the husband. Lawrence writes as hatefully as Montherlant against the wife who wishes to reverse the roles. Let her cease playing the Magna Mater, claiming to have in her keeping the verity of life; monopolizing, devouring, she mutilates the male, causing him to fall back into immanence and turning him away from his purposes. Lawrence is far from execrating maternity: quite the contrary. He is glad to be flesh, he willingly accepts his birth, he is fond of his mother; mothers appear in his works as splendid examples of true femininity; they are pure renunciation, absolute generosity, all their living warmth is devoted to their children: they gladly accept their becoming men, they are proud of it. But one should fear the egoistic *amante* who would take a man back to his childhood; she hampers the *élan*, the flight of the male. "The moon, the planet of women, sways us back." [8] She talks unceasingly of love; but for her love is to take, it is to fill this void she feels within her; such love is close to hate. Thus Hermione, suffering from a terrible sense of deficiency because she has never been able to give herself, wants to annex Birkin. She fails. She tries to kill him, and the voluptuous ecstasy she feels in striking him is identical with the egoistic spasm of sex pleasure. [9]

Lawrence detests modern women, creatures of celluloid and rubber laying claim to a consciousness. When woman has become sexually conscious of herself, "there she is functioning away from her own head and her own consciousness of herself and her own automatic self-will." [1] He forbids her to have an independent sensuality; she is made to give herself, not to take. Through Mellors's mouth, Lawrence cries aloud his horror of lesbians. But he finds fault also with the woman who in the presence of the male takes a detached or aggressive attitude; Paul feels wounded and irritated when Miriam caresses his loins

---

[8] *Fantasia of the Unconscious*, p. 286.

[9] *Women in Love.*

[1] *Fantasia of the Unconscious,* p. 114.

and says to him: "you are beautiful." Gudrun, like Miriam, is at fault when she feels enchanted with the good looks of her lover: this contemplation separates them, as much as would the irony of frozen intellectual females who find the penis comic or male gymnastics ridiculous. The eager quest for pleasure is not less to be condemned: there is an intense, solitary enjoyment that also causes separation, and woman should not strain for it. Lawrence has drawn numerous portraits of these independent, dominating women, who miss their feminine vocation. Ursula and Gudrun are of this type. At first Ursula is a monopolizer. "Man must render himself up to her. He must be quaffed to the dregs by her." [2] She will learn to conquer her desire. But Gudrun is obstinate; cerebral, artistic, she mildly envies men their independence and their chances for activity; she perseveres in keeping her individuality intact; she wants to live for herself; she is ironic and possessive, and she will always remain shut up in her subjectivity.

Miriam, in *Sons and Lovers*, is the most significant figure because she is the least sophisticated. Gerard is in part responsible for Gudrun's failure; but Miriam, as far as Paul is concerned, carries her weight of unhappiness alone. She too would rather be a man, and she hates men; she is not satisfied with herself as woman, she wants to "distinguish herself"; so the grand stream of life does not flow through her. She can be like a sorceress or a priestess, never like a bacchante; she is stirred by things only when she has re-created them in her soul, giving them a religious value: this very fervor separates her from life; she is poetical, mystical, maladjusted. "Her exaggerated effort locked itself . . . she was not awkward and yet she never made the right movement." She seeks inward joys, and reality frightens her; sexuality scares her; when she sleeps with Paul, her heart stands apart in a kind of horror; she is always consciousness, never life. She is not a companion; she refuses to melt and blend with her lover; she wishes to absorb him into herself. He is irritated by this desire of hers, he flies into a violent rage when he sees her caressing flowers: one would say that she wanted to tear out their hearts. He insults her: "You are a beggar of love; you have no need of loving, but of being loved. You wish to *fill yourself full of love* because you lack something, I don't know what." Sexuality was not made for filling voids; it should be the expression of a whole being. What women

---

call love is their avidity before the virile force of which they want to take possession. Paul's mother thinks clearly regarding Miriam: "she wants all of him, she wants to extract him from himself and devour him." The young girl is glad when her friend is sick, because she can take care of him: she pretends to serve him, but it is really a method of imposing her will upon him. Because she remains apart from Paul, she raises in him "an ardor comparable to fever, such as opium induces"; but she is quite incapable of bringing him joy and peace; from the depth of her love, within her secret self "she detested Paul because he loved her and dominated her." And Paul edges away from her. He seeks his equilibrium with Clara; beautiful, lively, animal, she gives herself unreservedly; and they attain moments of ecstasy which transcend them both; but Clara does not understand this revelation. She thinks she owes this joy to Paul himself, to his special nature, and she wishes to take him for herself. She fails to keep him because she, too, wants him all for herself. As soon as love is individualized, it is changed into avid egotism, and the miracle of eroticism vanishes.

Woman must give up personal love; neither Mellors nor Don Cipriano is willing to say words of love to his mistress. Terese, the model wife, is indignant when Kate asks her if she loves Don Ramón.[3] "He is my life," she replies; the gift she has yielded to him is something quite other than love. Woman should, like man, abdicate from all pride and self-will; if she incarnates life for the man, so does he for her; Lady Chatterley finds peace and joy only because she recognizes this truth: "she would give up her hard and brilliant feminine power, which fatigued and hardened her, she would plunge into the new bath of life, into the depths of its entrails where sang the voiceless song of adoration"; then is she summoned to the rapture of bacchantes; blindly obeying her lover, seeking not herself in his arms, she composes with him a harmonious couple, in tune with the rain, the trees, and the flowers of springtime. Just so Ursula in Birkin's arms renounces her individuality, and they attain to a "stellar equilibrium." But *The Plumed Serpent* best reflects Lawrence's ideal in its integrity. For Don Cipriano is one of those men who "carry forward the banners of life"; he has a mission to which he is so completely devoted that in him virility is transcended and exalted to the point of divinity: if he has himself anointed god, it is not a mystification; it is simply that every man who is fully man is a god; he merits therefore the

---

[3] *The Plumed Serpent* (Alfred A. Knopf, 1926, 1951), p. 408.

absolute devotion of a woman. Full of Occidental prejudices, Kate at first refuses to accept this dependence, she clings to her personality and to her limited existence; but little by little she lets herself be penetrated by the great stream of life; she gives Cipriano her body and her soul. This is not a surrender to slavery; for before deciding to live with him she demands that he acknowledge his need for her; he does acknowledge it since in fact woman is necessary to man; then she agrees never to be anything other than his mate; she adopts his aims, his values, his universe. This submission is expressed even in their erotic relation; Lawrence does not want the woman to be tensed in the effort toward her acme of pleasure, separated from the male by the spasm that shakes her; he deliberately denies her the orgasm; Don Cipriano moves away from Kate when he feels her approaching that nervous enjoyment: "the white ecstasy of frictional satisfaction, the throes of Aphrodite of the foam"; she renounces even this sexual autonomy. "Her strange seething feminine will and desire subsided in her and swept away, leaving her soft and powerfully potent, like the hot springs of water that gushed up so noiseless, so soft, yet so powerful, with a sort of secret potency." [4]

We can see why Lawrence's novels are, above all, "guidebooks for women." It is much more difficult for woman than for man to "accept the universe," for man submits to the cosmic order autonomously, whereas woman needs the mediation of the male. There is really a surrender when for woman the Other takes the shape of an alien consciousness and will; on the contrary, an autonomous submission, as by man, remarkably resembles a sovereign decision. Either the heroes of Lawrence are condemned at the start, or from the start they hold the secret of wisdom; [5] their submission to the cosmos has been accomplished so long since, and they derive from it so much inner certainty, that they seem as arrogant as any proud individualist; there is a god who speaks through them: Lawrence himself. As for woman, it is for her to bow down before their divinity. In so far

---

[4] *The Plumed Serpent*, p. 422. Lawrence presents Kate's approach to "orgiastic satisfaction" as "repulsive" to Cipriano; and he says of her that after "the first moment of disappointment . . . came the knowledge that she did not really want it, that it was really nauseous to her." All this dreadful nonsense seems hardly worth the dignity of citation, except as it pitilessly exposes Lawrence's basic view of woman.—TR.

[5] Excepting Paul of *Sons and Lovers*, the most alive of all of them. But this is the only one of the novels which shows us a masculine apprenticeship.

as man is a phallus and not a brain, the individual who has his share
of virility keeps his advantages; woman is not evil, she is even good—
but subordinated. It is once more the ideal of the "true woman" that
Lawrence has to offer us—that is, the woman who unreservedly accepts being defined as the Other.

3
CLAUDEL AND THE HANDMAID OF THE LORD

The originality of Claudel's Catholicism lies in an optimism so stubborn that evil itself is turned into good.

> "*Evil itself*
> "*Involves its good which we must not permit to be lost.*" [6]

Claudel approves of all creation, adopting the point of view which
cannot fail to be that of the Creator—since the latter is supposed to
be all-powerful, omniscient, and benevolent. Without hell and sin,
there would be neither free will nor salvation; when He caused this
world to rise out of nothing, God foresaw the Fall and the Redemption. In the eyes of both Jews and Christians, Eve's disobedience put
her daughters in a very bad position; everyone knows how severely
the Fathers of the Church berated woman. But on the contrary we
shall see her justified if we admit that she has served to forward the
divine purposes. "Woman! that service she once upon a time rendered to God through her disobedience in the Garden of Eden; that
deep understanding established between her and Him; that flesh
which through the Fall she gave over to the Redemption!" [7] And
certainly she is the source of sin, and through her man lost Eden.
But the sins of men have been redeemed, and this world is blessed
anew: "We have by no means departed from that delightful paradise
where God first placed us!" [8] "All the earth is the Promised Land." [9]

Nothing that has come from the hand of God, nothing that He
has given can be bad in itself: "Nothing that He has made is fruitless." [1] And there is even nothing that is not necessary. "All the things
He has created . . . are simultaneously necessary to each other." [2]

---

[6] *Partage de Midi.*
[7] *Les Aventures de Sophie.*
[8] *La Cantate à trois voix.*
[9] *Conversations dans le Loir-et-Cher.*
[1] *Le Soulier de satin.*
[2] *L'Annonce faite à Marie.*

Thus woman has her place in the harmony of the universe; but this is not an ordinary place; there is "a strange passion and, in Lucifer's eyes, a scandalous one, which binds the Eternal to that momentary flowering of Nothingness." [3]

Most assuredly woman can be a destroyer: Claudel has incarnated in Lechy [4] the bad woman leading man to perdition; in *Partage de Midi*, Ysé ruins the life of men snared in her love. But if there were not this danger of ruin, no more would salvation exist. Woman is the "element of hazard which He has deliberately introduced into His colossal construction." [5] It is good that man should know the temptations of the flesh. "It is this enemy within us that gives our life its dramatic element, this poignant salt. If the soul were not thus brutally attacked, it would be asleep, and behold, it leaps up. . . . Through battle is the way to victory." [6] Not only by the way of the spirit, but by the way of the flesh is man called upon to become aware of his soul. "And what flesh more powerful for speaking to man than woman?" [7] All that tears him from slumber, from security, is useful; love in whatever form it comes has this virtue of appearing as a profoundly disturbing element "in our little personal world, set in order by our mediocre reason." [8] Very often woman is but a deceptive bearer of illusion: "I am the promise which cannot be kept and my charm lies in just that. I am the sweetness of what is, with the regret for what is not." [9] But there is usefulness also in illusion; this is what the Guardian Angel proclaims to Donna Prouhèze:

"*Even sin! Sin also serves!*"
"*So it was good that he loved me?*"
"*It was good that you taught him desire.*"
"*Desire for an illusion? For a shadow that forever escapes him?*"
"*The desire is for what is, the illusion is of what is not. Desire through illusion*
Is for what is, through what is not." [1]

---

[3] *Les Aventures de Sophie.*
[4] *L'Échange.*
[5] *Ibid.*
[6] *L'Oiseau noir dans le soleil levant.*
[7] *Le Soulier de satin.*
[8] *Positions et propositions.*
[9] *La Ville.*
[1] *Le Soulier de satin.*

Prouhèze by the will of God has been for Rodrigue: "A sword through his heart." [2]

But woman is not only this blade in God's hand; the good things of this world are not always to be declined: they are also sustenance; man is to take them and make them his own. The well-beloved will embody for him all the appreciable beauty of the universe; she will be a canticle of adoration upon his lips. "How beautiful you are, Violaine, and how beautiful is this world, where you are!" [3]

"Let me breathe your fragrance, which is as the fragrance of the earth, when, bright, washed with water like an altar, it produces blue and yellow flowers."

"And as the fragrance of summer, which is scented with straw and grass, and as the fragrance of autumn." [4]

She sums up all nature: rose and lily, star, fruit, bud, wind, moon, sun, fountain, "the placid commotion of a great seaport in the noon-day sun." [5] And she is still much more—a fellow being: "Someone human, like myself. . . ." [6]

"Someone to listen to what I say and to have confidence in me."

"A companion with gentle voice who takes us in her arms and assures us she is a woman." [7]

Body and soul, it is by taking her to his heart that man finds his roots in the earth and thereby finds fulfillment. He takes her, and she is not easy to carry, but man is not made to be unattached. He is astonished at this heavy encumbrance, but he will not rid himself of it, for this charge is also precious: "I am a great treasure," says Violaine.

Woman fulfills her earthly destiny, reciprocally, by giving herself to man.

"For what use being woman if not to be taken?" . . .

"But you, dear heart, say: I was not created in vain, and he who is chosen to take me surely exists!"

"Ah, what joy for me to fill that heart which awaits me." [8]

Of course this union of man and woman is to be consummated in

---

[2] *Le Soulier de satin.*
[3] *L'Annonce faite à Marie.*
[4] *La Ville.*
[5] *Le Soulier de satin.*
[6] Ibid.
[7] *Le Pain dur.*
[8] *La Cantate à trois voix.*

the presence of God; it is holy and pertains to the eternal; it should be agreed to through a deep act of the will and cannot be broken according to individual caprice. "Love, the assent given by two free persons one to the other, has seemed to God so great a thing that He has made a sacrament of it. Here as everywhere the sacrament gives reality to what was only a supreme desire of the heart." [9] It is not joy alone that the man and the woman give each other through this union. It is sacrifice and the schooling of two souls which will have to be forever content with one another, says Claudel. Each will gain possession of the other, they will discover each other's souls. Each has come into the world by and for the other. And each appears justified, necessary, through the other, who is thus completed.

"When could she ever get along without me? When shall I ever cease to be that without which she could not be herself?"

"For what is it we call death if not the ceasing to be necessary?" [1]

In the wonderful necessity of this union, paradise is regained, death conquered:

"Here finally reconstituted from one man and one woman, is that being who was in Paradise." [2]

"Never otherwise than the one by the other shall we succeed in getting rid of death." [3]

Finally, under the form of another, each attains to the Other in all completeness—that is, to God. Claudel says that what we give one to the other is God under different aspects, and he suggests that the love of God appeals in the same way as that of fellow creatures to the feeling that by ourselves we are incomplete. The Supreme Good is something outside and beyond us.

Thus each finds in the other the meaning of his terrestrial existence and also irrefutable proof of the insufficiency of this life:

"What I ask of you and what I would give to you is not appropriate to time but to eternity." [4]

The roles of man and of woman are not exactly symmetrical, however. On the social level man's primacy is evident. Claudel believes in hierarchies and, among others, in that of the family: it is the hus-

---

[9] *Positions et propositions.*
[1] *Le Soulier de satin.*
[2] *Feuilles de saints.*
[3] *Le Soulier de satin.*
[4] *Le Père humilié.*

band who is the head. Anne Vercors rules over her house. Don Pélage thinks of himself as the gardener who has been entrusted with the care of that delicate plant, Donna Prouhèze; it gives him a mission that she does not dream of refusing him. The mere fact of being a male confers an advantage. "Who am I, poor girl, to compare myself with the male of my race?" asks Sygne.[5] It is man who plows the fields, who builds the cathedrals, who fights with the sword, explores the world, conquers territory—who acts, who undertakes. Through him are accomplished the plans of God upon this earth. Woman appears to be only an auxiliary. She is the one who stays in place, who waits, and who keeps things up: "I am she who remains, and am always there," says Sygne.

She protects Coûfontaine's inheritance, she keeps his accounts in order while he is away fighting for the Cause. Woman brings to the warrior the succor of hope: "I bring irresistible hope."[6] And that of pity: "I have had pity upon him. For where would he turn, seeking his mother, if not to the woman who humbles herself, in a spirit of intimacy and shame."[7]

Claudel does not hold it against man that woman thus knows him in his feebleness; on the contrary, he would regard as sacrilege the male pride displayed in Montherlant and Lawrence. It is good for man to realize that he is carnal and pitiable, for him not to forget his origin and the death that corresponds to it.

But in marriage the wife gives herself to the husband, who becomes responsible for her: Lâla lies on the ground before Cœuvre and he sets his foot upon her. The relation of wife to husband, of daughter to father, of sister to brother, is a relation of vassalage. Sygne in George's hands takes an oath like a knight's to his sovereign, or a nun's when she makes profession of faith.

Fidelity and loyalty are the greatest human virtues of the female vassal. Mild, humble, resigned as woman, she is proud and indomitable in the name of her race, her lineage; such are the proud Sygne of Coûfontaine and Tête d'Or's princess who carries away the body of her slain father on her shoulders, who bears the misery of a rude and solitary life, the agonies of a crucifixion, and who attends Tête d'Or in his anguish before dying at his side. Conciliating, mediating, thus

---

[5] *L'Otage.*
[6] *La Ville.*
[7] *L'Échange.*

woman often appears to us: she is Esther pliant to the commands of Mordecai, Judith obedient to the priests; her weakness, her timidity, her modesty she can conquer through loyalty to the Cause, which is hers since it is her master's; in her devotion she acquires a strength that makes of her the most valuable of instruments.

On the human plane she thus appears to draw her grandeur from her very subordination. But in the eyes of God she is a perfectly autonomous person. The fact that for man existence is transcended while for woman it simply continues establishes a difference between them only on earth: in any case it is not upon earth that transcendence is fully accomplished, but in God. And woman has with Him a tie as direct as has her companion—more intimate even, and more secret. It is through a man's voice, a priest's, that God speaks to Sygne; but Violaine hears His voice in the solitude of her heart, and Prouhèze has dealings only with the Guardian Angel. Claudel's most sublime figures are women—Sygne, Violaine, Prouhèze. This is in part because sanctity lies, according to him, in renunciation. And woman is less involved with human projects, she has less personal will: being made for giving herself, not for taking, she is closer to perfect devotedness. She will be the one to transcend those earthly joys which are legitimate and good, but the sacrifice of which is better yet. Sygne does it for a definite reason: to save the Pope. Prouhèze is resigned to it first of all because she loves Rodrigue with a forbidden love:

"Would you then have wished me to put an adulteress into your arms? . . . I would have been only a woman soon to die upon your breast and not that eternal star for which you thirst." [8]

But when that love could become legitimate, she makes no attempt to achieve it in this world, for she knows that her true marriage with Rodrigue in some mystical realm can be accomplished only through her denial:

"Then shall I give him to God naked and lacerated, that He may restore him in a thunderclap, then shall I have a spouse and hold a god in my embrace." [9]

Violaine's resolve is still more mysterious and gratuitous; for she chose leprosy and blindness when she could have been legitimately joined to a man whom she loved and who loved her.

---

[8] *Le Soulier de satin.*
[9] Ibid.

"Perhaps we loved each other too much for it to be just, to be good, for us to have each other." [1]

But if his women are thus remarkably devoted to the heroism of sanctity, it is above all because Claudel still views them in a masculine perspective. To be sure, each sex incarnates the Other in the eyes of the opposite sex; but in man's eyes woman often appears in spite of everything as an *absolute other*. There is a mystical excellence of which "we know that we are by ourselves incapable and thence comes this power of woman over us which is like that of divine Grace." [2] The *we* here means males only and not the human species, and as opposed to their imperfection woman is the challenge of the infinite. In a sense we have here a new principle of subordination. Through the communion of saints each individual is an instrument for all the others; but woman is more particularly an instrument of salvation for man, and not vice versa. *Le Soulier de satin* is the epic of Rodrigue's salvation. The drama begins with the prayer that his brother addresses to God in his favor; it ends with the death of Rodrigue, whom Prouhèze has led into sanctity. But, in a different sense, woman thus gains fullest autonomy. For her mission is within her, and, accomplishing the salvation of man or serving as an example for him, she accomplishes in solitude her own salvation. Pierre de Craon foretells her destiny to Violaine, and in his heart he receives the wonderful fruits of her sacrifice; he will exalt her in the eyes of man through the stones of cathedrals. But actually Violaine achieved her salvation without assistance. There is in Claudel a woman-mysticism related to that of Dante before Beatrice, to that of the Gnostics, to that, even, of the Saint-Simonian tradition which calls woman regeneratrix. But from the fact that men and women are equally God's creatures, he attributes an autonomous destiny to her also. So that with him woman fulfills herself as subject by making herself *other*—"I am the Servant of the Lord"; and it is in her *pour-soi*, her own free consciousness of self, that she appears as the Other.

There is a passage in the *Aventures de Sophie* that comes close to summing up the whole Claudelian conception. God, we read, has entrusted to woman "this visage, which, however remote and deformed it may be, is a sure image of His perfection. He has made her desirable. He has conjoined the end and the beginning. He has made

---

[1] *La Jeune Fille Violaine.*
[2] Ibid.

her capable of restoring to man that creative slumber in which she was herself conceived. She is the pillar of destiny. She is the gift. She is the possibility of possession. . . . She is the point of attachment of the kindly tie that unceasingly unites the Creator with His work. She understands Him. She is the soul which sees and acts. She shares with Him in some way the patience and power of creation."

In one sense it would seem that woman could not be more highly exalted. But at bottom Claudel does no more than express poetically the Catholic tradition in a slightly modernized form. It has been said that the earthly calling of woman is in no way destructive of her supernatural autonomy; but, inversely, in recognizing this, the Catholic feels authorized to maintain in this world the prerogatives of the male. Venerating woman *in God*, men treat her in this world as a servant, even holding that the more one demands complete submission of her, the more surely one will advance her along the road of her salvation. To devote herself to children, husband, home, estate, Country, Church—this is her lot, the lot which the bourgeoisie has always assigned to her. Man gives his activity, woman her person. To sanctify this ranking in the name of the divine will is not at all to modify it, but on the contrary to intend its eternal fixation.

4
BRETON OR POETRY

In spite of the great gulf that separates the religious world of Claudel from the poetic universe of Breton, there is between them an analogy in the role they assign to woman: she is a disturbing factor; she tears man from the sleep of immanence; mouth, key, door, bridge, she is Beatrice leading Dante into the beyond. "The love of man for woman, if we apply ourselves for a moment to the observation of the world of the senses, continues to crowd the sky with gigantic and tawny flowers. It remains the most terrible stumbling-block for the spirit that always feels the need of believing itself in a place of safety." Love of another leads to the love of the Other. "It is at the highest point of elective love for a certain being that the floodgates of love for humanity open wide." But for Breton the beyond is not a far heaven: it is right here, it is disclosed to such as can push aside the veils of daily banality; eroticism, for one thing, dissipates the allurement of false knowledge. "In our day the sexual world . . . has not, as far as I know, ceased to oppose its unbreakable core of night to our

will to penetrate the universe." To throw oneself into the mystery is
the only way to find out about it. Woman is an enigma and she poses
enigmas; her many aspects together form "the unique being in whom
it is vouchsafed us to see the last incarnation of the Sphinx"; and that
is why she is revelation. "You were the very likeness of the secret,"
says Breton to a woman he loves. And a little farther on: "The revelation you brought to me I knew to be a revelation before I even knew
in what it might consist."

This is to say that woman is poetry. And she plays this same role
with Gérard de Nerval; but in his Sylvia and Aurelia she has the
quality of a memory or of a phantom, because the dream, more true
than the real, does not coincide exactly with it. For Breton the coin-
cidence is perfect: there is only one world; poetry is objectively present in things, and woman is unequivocally a being of flesh and blood.
One comes across her, not in a half-dream, but wide awake, on a commonplace day that has its date like all the other days in the calendar
—April 12, October 4, or whatever—in a commonplace setting: a
café, some street corner. But she is always distinguished by some unusual trait. Nadja "walked along with her head held high, quite unlike
the other passers-by . . . with curious make-up. . . . I had never
seen such eyes." Breton accosts her. "She smiled, but most mysteriously, and, I would say, as if she knew all about the situation." In
his *L'Amour fou:* "This young woman who had just entered was as if
enclosed in a vapor—dressed in fire? . . . and I can declare that in
this place, on May 29, 1934, this woman was *scandalously* beautiful"
(Breton's italics). At once the poet realizes that she has a part to
play in his destiny. Sometimes this is only a fleeting, secondary role,
such as that of the child with Delilah eyes in *Vases communicants;*
even here little miracles spring up around her: Breton has a rendezvous with this Delilah and the same day reads a favorable article
signed by a friend long lost sight of and named Samson. Sometimes
the prodigies multiply; the unknown of May 29, an undine who was
doing a swimming act in a music hall, had been foretold in a pun on
the theme "*Ondine, on dîne,*" heard in a restaurant; and her first
long evening out with the poet had been minutely described in a
poem written by him eleven years before. The most remarkable of
these sorceresses is Nadja: she predicts the future, she gives utterance
to words and images that her friend has in mind at the same instant;
her dreams and her sketches are oracular: "I am the wandering soul,"

she says; she guides her life "in a peculiar manner, which relies upon pure intuition only and never ceases to partake of the marvelous"; around her what seems objectively to be chance sows a profusion of strange events. She is so wonderfully liberated from regard for appearances that she scorns reason and the laws: she winds up in an asylum. She was "a free spirit, somewhat like those spirits of the air with whom certain magical arts permit the formation of a momentary attachment but to whom there could be no question of submission." So she failed to play fully her feminine role. Clairvoyant, Pythic, inspired, she remains too near the unreal creatures who visited Nerval; she opens the doors of the supernatural world; but she is incapable of giving it because she is unable to give herself.

It is in love that woman is fulfilled and is really attained to; special, accepting a special destiny—and not floating rootless through the universe—then she sums up All. The moment when her beauty reaches its highest expression is at that hour of the night when "she is the perfect mirror in which all that has been, all that has been called upon to be, is bathed adorably in what is going to be *this time*." For Breton "to find the place and the formula" is confused with "to get possession of the truth in a soul and body." And this possession is possible only in reciprocal love—carnal love, of course. "The picture of the woman one loves ought to be not only an image at which one smiles, but, more, an oracle one questions"; but it will be an oracle only if the woman herself is something other than an idea or an image; she should be "the cornerstone of the material world." For the seer it is this very world that is Poetry, and in this world it is necessary for him to possess Beatrice in actuality. "Reciprocal love alone conditions the magnetization on which nothing can take hold, which makes the flesh sunlight and imprints in splendor on the flesh that the spirit is an ever flowing spring, changeless and always alive, the water of which is guided once for all to flow amongst the wild thyme and the marsh marigold."

This indestructible love could not be other than unique. It is the paradox of Breton's attitude that in his works, from V*ases communicants* to *Arcane* 17, he obstinately avows a unique and eternal love for various women. But he explains that there are social conditions that by denying him free choice lead a man to mistaken choices; besides, through these errors he is in reality seeking *one* woman. And if he recalls the beloved faces, he "will likewise discern in all these women's faces only one face: the *last* face he has loved" (Breton's italics). "How many times, besides, have I been able to realize that under quite dissimilar appearances a most exceptional trait in common sought to define itself from one to another of these faces!" He enquires of the undine in *L'Amour fou*: "Are you at last that woman, is it only today that you were to come?" But in *Arcane 17*: "Well do you know that in seeing you for the first time, I recognized you without a moment's hesitation." In a perfected, renovated world the couple would be indissoluble, in consequence of a reciprocal and absolute giving: since the well-beloved is everything, how could there be room for another? She is this other, also; and the more fully so, the more she is herself. "The unusual is inseparable from love. Because you are unique, you can never fail to be for me always another, another you. Through all the diversity of those innumerable flowers yonder, it is you the mutable I love, in chemise of red, naked, in chemise of gray." And referring to a different but equally unique woman, Breton writes: "Reciprocal love, as I see it, is an arrangement of mirrors which, from the thousand angles that the unknown can take for me, reflects the true image of her whom I love, ever more astonishing in divination of my own desire and more endued with life."

This unique woman, at once carnal and artificial, natural and human, casts the same spell as the equivocal objects dear to the surrealists: she is like the spoon-shoe, the table-wolf, the marble-sugar that the poet finds at the flea market or invents in a dream; she shares in the secret of familiar objects suddenly revealed in their true nature, and in the secret of plants and stones. She is all things.[3]

But more especially she is Beauty above and beyond all other things. Beauty for Breton is not a contemplated idea but a reality that is revealed—hence exists—only through passion; there is no beauty in the world except through woman.

"There, deep within the human crucible in that paradoxical region where the fusion of two beings who have really chosen each other restores to all things the values lost from the time of ancient suns, where, however, solitude also rages, through one of those fantasies

---

[3]   *Ma femme à la chevelure de feu de bois*
        Aux pensées d'éclair de chaleur
        A la taille de sablier
  . . . *Ma femme au sexe d'algue et de bonbons anciens*
  . . . *Ma femme aux yeux de savane.*

of nature which around Alaskan craters causes snow to lie under the ashes—that is where years ago I called for search to be made for a new beauty, the beauty envisaged exclusively in passional ends."

"Convulsive beauty will be erotic, veiled, exploding-fixed, magic-circumstantial, or will not be at all."

From woman all that exists derives its meaning: "It is precisely through love and love alone that the fusion of essence and existence is realized in the highest degree." It is realized for the lovers and at the same time through the whole world. "The perpetual re-creation and recoloring of the world in a single being, as they are achieved by love, send forward a thousand rays to light up the earthly world." For all poets, almost, woman incarnates nature; but for Breton she not only expresses nature: she releases it. For nature does not speak a plain language, it is necessary to penetrate nature's secrets to get at her truth, which is the same thing as her beauty: poetry is thus not simply a reflection, but rather a key; and here woman is not distinguished from poetry. This is why she is the indispensable mediatress without whom all the earth is voiceless: "She is wont, is nature, to be lighted up and to be darkened, to render me service or disservice, only in accordance with the rising and the sinking for me of the flames in a hearth which is love, the only love, that of *one* being. In the absence of such love I have known truly vacant skies. It needed only a great rainbow of fire arching from me to lend worth to what exists. . . . I contemplate unto dizziness your hands open above the fire of twigs we have just lighted, now burning brightly—your enchanting hands, your transparent hands that hover above the fire of my life." Each woman he loves is a wonder of nature: "A small unforgettable fern clinging to the inner wall of a most ancient well." ". . . Something dazzling and so momentous that she could not but recall to mind . . . the grand physical necessity of nature, while making one more tenderly dream of the nonchalance of certain tall flowers that are just opening." But inversely: every natural wonder is confounded with the well-beloved; he is exalting her when with emotion he views a grotto, a flower, a mountain.

But beauty is still something more than beauty. It merges with "the deep night of consciousness"; it is truth and eternity, the absolute. Thus the aspect of nature made manifest by woman is not temporal and secondary; it is rather the necessary essence of nature, an essence not set once for all as Plato imagined, but "exploding-fixed."

"I find within myself no other treasure than the key which, since I have known you, opens this limitless meadow for me, through which I shall be led onward until the day of my death. . . . For a woman and a man, forever you and I, shall in their turn glide ever onward to where the path is lost in the oblique light, at the boundaries of life and its forgetting. . . ."

Thus woman, through the love she inspires and shares, is the only possible salvation for each man. In *Arcane 17* her mission is broadened and made precise: she must save humanity. Breton has always been in the Fourier tradition, which demands the rehabilitation of the flesh and exalts woman as erotic object; it is quite in line for him to reach the Saint-Simonian idea of regeneration through woman. But as society now stands, it is the male who dominates—so much so that it is an insult for a Gourmont to say of Rimbaud: "A girlish temperament!" However, "it is high time for woman's ideas to prevail over man's, whose bankruptcy is clear enough in the tumult of today. . . . Yes, it is always the lost woman who sings in man's imagination but who—after what trials for them both!—should be also the woman regained. And first she must regain herself, learn to know herself, through those hells which, without his more than doubtful aid, man's attitude in general sets up around her."

The role she should fill is before all one of pacification. Breton is astonished that she does not take advantage of her priceless power of appealing to man and extend her arms between those who are struggling together, crying: "You are brothers." If today woman appears maladjusted, ill-balanced, it is in consequence of the treatment man's tyranny has inflicted upon her; but she retains a miraculous power because her roots are sunk deep into the living sources of life, the secrets of which the males have lost. "It is Mélusine whom I invoke, I see no other who can subjugate this savage epoch. I invoke the whole woman, and yet woman such as she is today, woman deprived of her human position, prisoner of her shifting roots, to be sure, but also kept by them in providential communication with the elemental forces of nature. . . . Woman deprived of her human position, the myth has it thus, through the impatience and the jealousy of man."

Today, then, we may well espouse the cause of woman; while we await the restoration to her of her true value in life, the time has come "to declare oneself in art unequivocally against man and for woman." "The woman-child. Art should be systematically preparing for her accession to the whole empire of perceptible things." Why the woman-child? Breton explains it for us: "I choose the woman-child not to oppose her to the other woman but because it seems to me that in her and only in her is to be found in a state of absolute transparency the *other* prism of vision . . ." (Breton's italics).

To the extent that woman is simply identified as a human being, she will be as unable as male human beings to save this world in distress; it is femininity as such that introduces into civilization that *other* element which is the truth of life and of poetry and which alone can deliver humanity.

Breton's perspective being exclusively poetic, it is exclusively as poetry, hence as the *other*, that woman is viewed therein. If the question of her own private destiny were raised, the reply would be involved with the ideal of reciprocal love: woman has no vocation other than love; this does not make her inferior, since man's vocation is also love. But one would like to know if for her also love is key to the world and revelation of beauty. Will she find that beauty in her lover, or in her own image? Will she be capable of that poetic action which realizes poetry through a sentient being, or will she limit herself to approving the work of her male? She is poetry in essence, directly— that is to say, for man; we are not told whether she is poetry for herself also. Breton does not speak of woman as subject. No more does he ever evoke the image of the bad woman. In his work in general— in spite of some manifestoes and pamphlets in which he reviles the human herd—he strives not to catalogue the superficial rebellings of the world but to reveal its secret truth: woman interests him only because she is a privileged voice. Deeply anchored in nature, very close to earth, she appears also to be the key to the beyond. There is in Breton the same esoteric naturalism as was in the Gnostics who saw in Sophia the principle of the Redemption and even of the creation, as was in Dante choosing Beatrice for his guide and in Petrarch enkindled by the love of Laura. And that is why the being who is most firmly anchored in nature, who is closest to the ground, is also the key to the beyond. Truth, Beauty, Poetry—she is All: once more all under the form of the Other, All except herself.

5
STENDHAL OR THE ROMANTIC OF REALITY

If I leave the present epoch and go back now to Stendhal, it is because, in emerging from this carnival atmosphere where Woman is disguised variously as fury, nymph, morning star, siren, I find it a relief to come upon a man who lives among women of flesh and blood.

Stendhal loved women sensually from childhood; he projected upon them his adolescent aspirations: he liked to fancy himself saving a fair unknown from danger and winning her love. Arriving in Paris, what he wants most ardently is "a charming woman; we shall adore each other, she will know my soul." Grown old, he writes in the dust the initials of the women he has loved best. "I think that reverie has been what I have most enjoyed," he confides. And images of women are what feed his dreams; their memory gives lively interest to landscapes. "The line of the cliffs as seen when approaching Arbois, I think, and coming from Dôle by the highway, was for me a tangible and evident image of Métilde's soul." Music, painting, architecture—everything he prized—he cherished with the feeling of an unhappy lover. If he is strolling in Rome, as each page turns, a woman arises; in the regrets, the desires, the sorrows, the joys they stirred up in him he understood the inclination of his own heart; he would have them as his judges: he frequents their salons, he tries to appear brilliant in their eyes; to them he has owed his greatest joys, his greatest pains, they have been his main occupation; he prefers their love to any friendship, their friendship to that of men. Women inspire his books, feminine figures people them; the fact is that he writes for them in large part. "I take my chance of being read in 1900 by the souls I love, the Mme Rolands, the Mélanie Guilberts. . . ." They were the very substance of his life. How did they come to have that preferment?

This tender friend of women does not believe in the feminine mystery, precisely because he loves them as they really are; no essence defines woman once for all; to him the idea of "the eternal feminine" seems pedantic and ridiculous. "Pedants have for two thousand years reiterated the notion that women have a more lively spirit, men more solidity; that women have more delicacy in their ideas and men greater power of attention. A Paris idler who once took a walk in the Versailles Gardens concluded that, judging from all he saw, the trees grow ready trimmed." The differences to be noted between men and women reflect the difference in their situations. Why, for instance, should women not be more romantic than their lovers? "A woman occupied in embroidering, dull work that uses only the hands, dreams of her lover; whereas this lover, riding in the open with his squadron, is put under arrest if he makes a wrong move." Similarly, women are accused of lacking judgment. "Women prefer the emotions to reason, and it is quite simple: since according to our stupid customs they are not charged with any family responsibility, *reason is never useful to them.* . . . Let your wife run your business affairs with the farmers on two of your pieces of property, and I wager that the accounts will be kept better than if you did it yourself." If but few feminine geniuses are found in history, it is because society deprives them of all means for expressing themselves. "All geniuses who are born *women* are lost to the public welfare; once fate gives them means to make themselves known, you will see them achieve the most difficult attainments."

The worst handicap they have is the besotting education imposed upon them; the oppressor always strives to dwarf the oppressed; man intentionally deprives women of their opportunities. "We leave idle in women qualities of great brilliance that could be rich in benefit for themselves and for us." At ten the little girl is quicker and more clever than her brother; at twenty the young fellow is a man of wit and the young girl "a great awkward idiot, shy and afraid of a spider"; the blame is to be laid on her training. Women should be given just as much instruction as boys. Antifeminists raise the objection that cultivated and intelligent women are monsters, but the whole trouble is that they are still exceptional; if all of them could have access to culture as naturally as men, they would profit by it as naturally. After they have been thus injured, they are subjected to laws contrary to nature: married against their feelings, they are expected to be faithful, and divorce, if resorted to, is itself held a matter of reproach, like misconduct. A great many women are doomed to idleness, when there is no happiness apart from work. This state of affairs makes Stendhal indignant, and he sees in it the source of all the faults for which women are reproached. They are not angels, nor demons, nor sphinxes: merely human beings reduced to semislavery by the imbecile ways of society.

It is precisely because they are oppressed that the best of them avoid the defects that disfigure their oppressors; they are in themselves neither inferior nor superior to man; but by a curious reversal their unhappy situation favors them. It is well known how Stendhal hated serious-mindedness: money, honors, rank, power seemed to him the most melancholy of idols; the vast majority of men sell themselves for profit; the pedant, the man of consequence, the bourgeois, the husband—all smother within them every spark of life and truth; larded with ready-made ideas and acquired sentiments and conformable to social routines, their personalities contain nothing but emptiness; a world peopled by these soulless creatures is a desert of ennui. There are many women, unfortunately, who wallow in the same dismal swamps; these are dolls with "narrow and Parisian ideas," or often hypocritical devotees. Stendhal experiences "a mortal disgust for respectable women and their indispensable hypocrisy"; they bring to their frivolous occupations the same seriousness that makes their husbands stiff with affectation; stupid from bad education, envious, vain, gossipy, worthless through idleness, cold, dry, pretentious, malicious, they populate Paris and the provinces; we see them swarming behind the noble figure of a Mme de Rênal, a Mme de Chasteller. The one Stendhal has painted with the most malevolent care is without doubt Mme Grandet, in whom he has set forth the exact negative of a Mme Roland, a Métilde. Beautiful but expressionless, scornful and without charm, she is formidable in her "celebrated virtue" but knows not the true modesty that comes from the soul; filled with admiration for herself, puffed up with her own importance, she can only copy the outer semblance of grandeur; fundamentally she is vulgar and base; "she has no character . . . she bores me," thinks M. Leuwen. "Perfectly reasonable, careful for the success of her plans," her whole ambition is to make her husband a cabinet minister; "her spirit is arid"; prudent, a conformist, she has always kept away from love, she is incapable of a generous act; when passion breaks out in that dry soul, there is burning but no illumination.

This picture need only be reversed to show clearly what Stendhal asks of women: it is first of all not to permit themselves to be caught in the snares of seriousness; and because of the fact that the things supposed to be of importance are out of their range, women run less risk than men of getting lost in them; they have better chances of preserving that naturalness, that naïveté, that generosity which Stendhal puts above all other merit. What he likes in them is what today we call their authenticity: that is the common trait in all the women he loved or lovingly invented; all are free and true beings. Some of them flaunt their freedom most conspicuously: Angela Pietragrua, "strumpet sublime, in the Italian manner, *à la* Lucretia Borgia," and Mme Azur, "strumpet *à la* Du Barry . . . one of the least vain and frivolous Frenchwomen I have met," scoff openly at social conventions. Lamiel laughs at customs, mores, laws; the Sanseverina joins ardently in intrigue and does not hesitate at crime. Others are raised above the vulgar by their vigor of spirit: such is Menta, and another is Mathilde de la Môle, who criticizes, disparages, and scorns the society around her and wants to be distinguished from it. With others, again, liberty assumes a quite negative aspect; the remarkable thing in Mme de Chasteller is her attitude of detachment from everything secondary; submissive to the will of her father and even to his opinions, she none the less disputes bourgeois values by the indifference which she is reproached for as childishness and which is the source of her insouciant gaiety. Clélia Conti also is distinguished for her reserve; balls and other usual amusements of young girls leave her cold; she always seems distant "whether through scorn for what is around her, or through regret for some absent chimera"; she passes judgment on the world, she is indignant at its baseness.

But it is in Mme de Rênal that independence of soul is most deeply hidden; she is herself unaware that she is not fully resigned to her lot; it is her extreme delicacy, her lively sensitivity, that show her repugnance for the vulgarity of the people around her; she is without hypocrisy; she has preserved a generous heart, capable of violent emotions, and she has a flair for happiness. The heat of this fire which is smoldering within her can hardly be felt from outside, but a breath would be enough to set her all ablaze.

These women are, quite simply, *alive;* they know that the source of true values is not in external things but in human hearts. This gives its charm to the world they live in: they banish ennui by the simple fact of their presence, with their dreams, their desires, their pleasures, their emotions, their ingenuities. The Sanseverina, that "active soul," dreads ennui more than death. To stagnate in ennui "is to keep from dying, she said, not to live"; she is "always impassioned over something, always in action, and gay, too." Thoughtless, childish or profound, gay or grave, daring or secretive, they all reject the heavy sleep in which humanity is mired. And these women who have been able to maintain their liberty—empty as it has been—will rise through passion to heroism once they find an objective worthy of them; their spiritual power, their energy, suggest the fierce purity of total dedication.

But liberty alone could hardly give them so many romantic attributes: pure liberty gives rise rather to esteem than to emotion; what touches the feelings is the effort to reach liberty through the obstructive forces that beat it down. It is the more moving in women in that the struggle is more difficult. Victory over mere external coercion is enough to delight Stendhal; in his *Chroniques italiennes* he immures his heroines deep within convents, he shuts them up in the palaces of jealous husbands. Thus they have to invent a thousand ruses to rejoin their lovers; secret doors, rope ladders, bloodstained chests, abductions, seclusions, assassinations, outbursts of passion and of disobedience are treated with the most intelligent ingenuity; death and impending tortures add excitement to the audacities of the mad souls he depicts for us. Even in his maturer work Stendhal remains sensitive to this obvious romanticism: it is the outward manifestation of what springs from the heart; they can no more be distinguished from each other than a mouth can be separated from its smile. Clélia invents love anew when she invents the alphabet that enables her to correspond with Fabrice. The Sanseverina is described for us as "an always sincere soul who never acted with prudence, who abandoned herself wholly to the impression of the moment"; it is when she plots, when she poisons the prince, and when she floods Parma that this soul is revealed to us: she is herself no more than the sublime and mad escapade she has chosen to live. The ladder that Mathilde de la Môle sets against her windowsill is no mere theatrical prop: it is, in tangible form, her proud imprudence, her taste for the extraordinary, her provocative courage. The qualities of these souls would not be displayed were they not surrounded by such inimical powers as prison walls, a ruler's will, a family's severity.

But the most difficult constraints to overcome are those which each person encounters within himself: here the adventure of liberty is most dubious, most poignant, most pungent. Clearly Stendhal's sympathy for his heroines is the greater the more closely they are confined. To be sure, he likes the strumpets, sublime or not, who have trampled upon the conventions once for all; but he cherishes Métilde more tenderly, held back as she is by her scruples and her modesty. Lucien Leuwen enjoys being with that free spirit Mme de Hocquincourt; but he passionately loves the chaste, reserved, and hesitant Mme de Chasteller; he admires the headstrong soul of the Sanseverina, who flinches at nothing; but he prefers Clélia to her, and it is the young girl who wins Fabrice's heart. And Mme de Rênal, fettered by her pride, her prejudices, and her ignorance, is of all the women created by Stendhal perhaps the one who most astounds him. He frequently locates his heroines in a provincial, limited environment, under the control of a husband or an imbecile father; he is pleased to make them uncultured and even full of false notions. Mme de Rênal and Mme de Chasteller are both obstinately legitimist; the former is timid and without experience; the latter has a brilliant intelligence but does not appreciate its value; thus they are not responsible for their mistakes, but rather they are as much the victims of them as of institutions and the mores; and it is from error that the romantic blossoms forth, as poetry from frustration.

A clear-headed person who decides upon his acts in full knowledge of the situation is to be curtly approved or blamed; whereas one admires with fear, pity, irony, love, the courage and the stratagems of a generous heart trying to make its way in the shadows. It is because women are baffled that we see flourishing in them such useless and charming virtues as their modesty, their pride, their extreme delicacy; in a sense these are faults, for they give rise to deception, oversensitiveness, fits of anger; but they are sufficiently accounted for by the situation in which women are placed. Women are led to take pride in little things or at least in "things of merely sentimental value" because all the things "regarded as important" are out of their reach. Their modesty results from their dependent condition: because they are forbidden to show their capabilities in action, they call in question their very being. It seems to them that the perception of others, especially that of their lover, reveals them truly as they are: they fear this and try to escape from it. A real regard for value is expressed in their flights, their hesitations, their revolts, and even in their lies; and this is what makes them worthy of respect; but it is expressed awkwardly, even in bad faith; and this is what makes them touching and even mildly comic. It is when liberty is taken in its own snares and cheats against itself that it is most deeply human and therefore to Stendhal most engaging.

Stendhal's women are touching when their hearts set them unforeseen problems: no law, no recipe, no reasoning, no example from without can any longer guide them; they have to decide for themselves, alone. This forlornness is the high point of freedom. Clélia was brought up in an atmosphere of liberal ideas, she is lucid and reasonable; but opinions acquired from others, true or false, are of no avail in a moral conflict. Mme de Rênal loves Julien in spite of her morality, and Clélia saves Fabrice against her better judgment: there is in the two cases the same going beyond all recognized values. This hardihood is what arouses Stendhal's enthusiasm; but it is the more moving in that it scarcely dares to avow itself, and on this account it is more natural, more spontaneous, more authentic. In Mme de Rênal audacity is hidden under innocence: not knowing about love, she is unable to recognize it and so yields to it without resistance; it would seem that because of having lived in the dark she is defenseless against the flashing light of passion; she receives it, dazzled, whether it is against heaven and hell or not. When this flame dies down, she falls back into the shadows where husbands and priests are in control. She has no confidence in her own judgment, but whatever is clearly present overwhelms her; as soon as she finds Julien again, she gives him her soul once more. Her remorse and the letter that her confessor wrests from her show to what lengths this ardent and sincere soul had to go in order to escape from the prison where society shut her away and attain to the heaven of happiness.

In Clélia the conflict is more clearly conscious; she hesitates between her loyalty to her father and her amorous pity; she tries to think of arguments. The triumph of the values Stendhal believes in seems to him the more magnificent in that it is regarded as a defeat by the victims of a hypocritical civilization; and he is delighted to see them using trickery and bad faith to make the truth of passion and happiness prevail over the lies they believe in. Thus Clélia is at once laughable and deeply affecting when she promises the Madonna not to *see* Julien any more and then for two years accepts his kisses and embraces on condition that she keep her eyes shut!

With the same tender irony Stendhal considers Mme de Chasteller's hesitancies and Mathilde de la Môle's incoherencies; so many detours, reversals, scruples, hidden victories and defeats in order to arrive at certain simple and legitimate ends! All this is for him the most ravishing of comedies. There is drollery in these dramas because the actress is at once judge and culprit, because she is her own dupe, because she imposes roundabout ways upon herself when she need only decree that the Gordian knot be cut. But nevertheless these inner struggles reveal all the most worthy solicitude that could torture a noble soul: the actress wants to retain her self-respect; she puts her approbation of herself above that of others and thus becomes herself an absolute. These echoless, solitary debates are graver than a cabinet crisis; when Mme de Chasteller asks herself whether she is or is not going to respond to Lucien Leuwen's love, she is making a decision concerning herself and also the world. Can one, she asks, have confidence in others? Can one rely on one's own heart? What is the worth of love and human pledges? Is it foolish or generous to believe and to love?

Such interrogations put in question the very meaning of life, the life of each and of all. The so-called serious man is really futile, because he accepts ready-made justifications for his life; whereas a passionate and profound woman revises established values from moment to moment. She knows the constant tension of unsupported freedom; it puts her in constant danger: she can win or lose all in an instant. It is the anxious assumption of this risk that gives her story the colors of a heroic adventure. And the stakes are the highest there are: the very meaning of existence, this existence which is each one's portion, his only portion. Mina de Vanghel's escapade can in a sense seem absurd; but it involves a whole scheme of ethics. "Was her life a miscalculation? Her happiness had lasted eight months. Hers was a soul too ardent to be contented with the reality of life." Mathilde de la Môle is less sincere than Clélia or Mme de Chasteller; she regulates her actions according to the idea of herself which she has built up, not according to the clear actuality of love, of happiness: would it be more haughty and grand to save oneself than to be lost, to humiliate oneself before one's beloved than to resist him? She also is alone in the midst of her doubts, and she is risking that self-respect which means more to her than life. It is the ardent quest for valid reasons for living, the search through the darkness of ignorance, of prejudices, of frauds, in the shifting and feverish light of passion, it is the infinite risk of happiness or death, of grandeur or shame, that gives glory to these women's lives.

Woman is of course unaware of the seductiveness she spreads around her; to contemplate herself, to act the personage, is always an inauthentic attitude; Mme Grandet, comparing herself with Mme Roland, proves by the act that she is not like her. If Mathilde de la

Môle remains engaging, it is because she gets herself involved in her comedies and because she is frequently the prey of her heart just when she thinks she is in control of it; she touches our feelings to the degree that she escapes her own will. But the purest heroines are quite unselfconscious. Mme de Rênal is unaware of her elegance, as Mme de Chasteller is of her intelligence. In this lies one of the deep joys of the lover, with whom both reader and author identify themselves; he is the witness through whom these secret riches come to light; he is alone in admiring that vivacity which Mme de Rênal's glances spread abroad, that "lively, mercurial, profound spirit" which Mme de Chasteller's entourage fails to appreciate; and even if others appreciate the Sanseverina's mind, he is the one who penetrates farthest into her soul.

Before woman, man tastes the pleasure of contemplation; he is enraptured with her as with a landscape or a painting; she sings in his heart and tints the sky. This revelation reveals him to himself: it is impossible to comprehend the delicacy of women, their sensitiveness, their ardor, without becoming a delicate, sensitive, and ardent soul; feminine sentiments create a world of nuances, of requirements the discovery of which enriches the lover: in the company of Mme de Rênal, Julien becomes a different person from that ambitious man he had resolved to be, he makes a new choice. If a man has only a superficial desire for a woman, he will find it amusing to seduce her. But true love really transfigures his life. "Love such as Werther's opens the soul . . . to sentiment and to the enjoyment of the *beautiful* under whatever form it presents itself, however ill-clothed. It brings happiness even without wealth. . . ." "It is a new aim in life to which everything is related and which changes the face of everything. Love-passion flings all nature with its sublimities before a man's eyes like a novelty just invented yesterday." Love breaks the everyday routine, drives ennui away, the ennui in which Stendhal sees such deep evil because it is the lack of any reason for living or dying; the lover has an aim and that is enough to turn each day into an adventure: what a pleasure for Stendhal to spend three days hidden in Menta's cave! Rope ladders, bloodstained caskets, and the like express in his novels this taste for the extraordinary. Love—that is to say, woman—makes apparent the true ends of existence: beauty, happiness, fresh sensations, and a new world. It tears out a man's soul and thereby gives him possession of it; the lover feels the same tension, knows the same risks as his mistress, and proves himself more authentically than in his professional career. When Julien hesitates at the foot of a ladder placed by Mathilde, he puts in question his entire destiny: in that moment his true measure is taken. It is through women, under their influence, in reaction to their behavior, that Julien, Fabrice, Lucien work out their apprenticeship in dealing with the world and themselves. Test, reward, judge, friend—woman truly is in Stendhal what Hegel was for a moment tempted to make of her: that other consciousness which in reciprocal recognition gives to the other subject the same truth that she receives from him. Two who know each other in love make a happy couple, defying time and the universe; such a couple is sufficient unto itself, it realizes the absolute.

But all this presupposes that woman is not pure alterity: she is subject in her own right. Stendhal never limits himself to describing his heroines as functions of his heroes: he gives them a destiny of their own. He has attempted a still rarer enterprise, one that I believe no novelist has before undertaken: he has projected himself into a female character. He does not hover over Lamiel like Marivaux over Marianne or Richardson over Clarissa Harlowe; he assumes her destiny just as he had assumed Julien's. On this account Lamiel's outline remains somewhat speculative, but it is singularly significant. Stendhal has raised all imaginable obstacles about the young girl: she is a poor peasant, ignorant, coarsely raised by people imbued with all the prejudices; but she clears from her path all moral barriers once she understands the full meaning of the little words: "that's silly." Her new freedom of mind allows her in her own fashion to act upon all the impulses of her curiosity, her ambition, her gaiety. Before so stout a heart, material obstacles could not but be smoothed away, and her only problem will be to shape a destiny worthy of her in a mediocre world. She must find fulfillment in crime and death; but this is also Julien's lot. There is no place for great souls in society as it exists. And men and women are in the same boat.

It is noteworthy that Stendhal should be at once so deeply romantic and so decidedly feministic; usually feminists are rational minds who in all matters take a universal point of view; but Stendhal demands woman's emancipation not only in the name of liberty in general but also in the name of individual happiness. Love, he believes, will have nothing to lose; on the contrary, it will be the more true as woman, being man's equal, is able to understand him the more completely. No doubt certain qualities admired in women will disappear; but their worth comes from the freedom they express. This will be manifested under other forms, and the romantic will not vanish from the world. Two separate beings, in different circumstances, face to face in freedom and seeking justification of their existence through one another, will always live an adventure full of risk and promise. Stendhal puts his trust in truth. To depart from it means a living death; but where it shines forth, there shine forth also beauty, happiness, love, and a joy that carries its own justification. That is why he rejects the mystifications of the serious, as he rejects the false poetry of the myths. Human reality suffices him. Woman according to him is simply a human being: nor could any shape of dreams be more enrapturing.

6
SUMMARY

It is to be seen from these examples that each separate writer reflects the great collective myths: we have seen woman as *flesh*; the flesh of the male is produced in the mother's body and re-created in the embraces of the woman in love. Thus woman is related to *nature*, she incarnates it: vale of blood, open rose, siren, the curve of a hill, she represents to man the fertile soil, the sap, the material beauty and the soul of the world. She can hold the keys to *poetry*; she can be *mediatrix* between this world and the beyond: grace or oracle, star or sorceress, she opens the door to the supernatural, the surreal. She is doomed to *immanence*; and through her passivity she bestows peace and harmony—but if she declines this role, she is seen forthwith as a praying mantis, an ogress. In any case she appears as the *privileged Other*, through whom the subject fulfills himself: one of the measures of man, his counterbalance, his salvation, his adventure, his happiness.

But these myths are very differently orchestrated by our authors. The *Other* is particularly defined according to the particular manner in which the *One* chooses to set himself up. Every man asserts his freedom and transcendence—but they do not all give these words the same sense. For Montherlant transcendence is a situation: he is the transcendent, he soars in the sky of heroes; woman crouches on earth, beneath his feet; it amuses him to measure the distance that separates him from her; from time to time he raises her up to him, takes her, and then throws her back; never does he lower himself down to her realm of slimy shadows. Lawrence places transcendence in the phallus; the phallus is life and power only by grace of woman; immanence is therefore good and necessary; the false hero who pretends to be above setting foot on earth, far from being a demigod, fails to attain man's estate. Woman is not to be scorned, she is deep richness, a warm spring; but she should give up all personal transcendence and confine herself to furthering that of her male. Claudel asks her for the same devotion: for him, too, woman should maintain life while man extends its range through his activities; but for the Catholic all earthly affairs are immersed in vain immanence: the only transcendent is God; in the eyes of God the man in action and the woman who serves him are exactly equal; it is for each to surpass his or her earthly state: salvation is in all cases an autonomous enterprise. For Breton the rank of the sexes is reversed; action and conscious thought, in which the male finds his transcendence, seem to Breton to constitute a silly mystification that gives rise to war, stupidity, bureaucracy, the negation of anything human; it is immanence, the pure, dark presence of the real, which is truth; true transcendence would be accomplished by a return to immanence. His attitude is the exact opposite of Montherlant's: the latter likes war because in war one gets rid of women, Breton venerates woman because she brings peace. Montherlant confuses mind and subjectivity—he refuses to accept the given universe; Breton thinks that mind is objectively present at the heart of the world; woman endangers Montherlant because she breaks his solitude; she is revelation for Breton because she tears him out of his subjectivity. As for Stendhal, we have seen that for him woman hardly has a mystical value: he regards her as being, like man, a transcendent; for this humanist, free beings of both sexes fulfill themselves in their reciprocal relations; and for him it is enough if the *Other* be simply an other so that life may have what he calls "a pungent saltiness." He is not seeking a "stellar equilibrium," he is not fed on the bread of disgust; he is not looking for a miracle; he does not wish to be concerned with the cosmos or with poetry, but with free human beings.

More, Stendhal feels that he is himself a clear, free being. The others—and this is a most important point—pose as transcendents but feel themselves prisoners of a dark presence in their own hearts: they project this "unbreakable core of night" upon woman. Montherlant has an Adlerian complex, giving rise to his thick-witted bad faith: it is this tangle of pretensions and fears that he incarnates in woman; his disgust for her is what he dreads feeling for himself. He would trample underfoot, in woman, the always possible proof of his own insufficiency; he appeals to scorn to save him; and woman is the trench into which he throws all the monsters that haunt him.[4] The life of Lawrence shows us that he suffered from an analogous though more purely sexual complex: in his works woman serves as a compensation myth, exalting a virility that the writer was none too sure of; when he describes Kate at Don Cipriano's feet, he feels as if he had won a male triumph over his wife, Frieda; nor does he permit his companion to raise any questions: if she were to oppose his aims he would doubtless lose confidence in them; her role is to reassure him. He asks of her peace, repose, faith, as Montherlant asks for certainty regarding his superiority: they demand what is missing in them. Claudel's lack is not that of self-confidence: if he is timid it is only in secret with God. Nor is there any trace of the battle of the sexes in his work. Man boldly assumes woman's weight; she is a possibility for temptation or for salvation. It would seem that for Breton man is true only through the mystery that is within him; it pleases him for Nadja to see that star toward which he moves and which is like "the heart of a heartless flower." In his dreams, his presentiments, the spontaneous flow of his stream of consciousness—in such activities, which escape the control of the will and the reason, he recognizes his true self; woman is the visible image of that veiled presence which is infinitely more essential than his conscious personality.

Stendhal is in tranquil agreement with himself; but he needs woman as she needs him in order to gather his diffuse existence into the unity of a single design and destiny: it is as though man reaches manhood for another; but still he needs to have the lending of the other's consciousness. Other males are too indifferent toward their fellows; only the loving woman opens her heart to her lover and shelters him there, wholly. Except for Claudel, who finds in God his preferred witness, all the writers we have considered expect that woman will cherish in them what Malraux calls "this incomparable monster"

---

[4] Stendhal has passed judgment in advance upon the cruelties with which Montherlant amuses himself: "What to do when indifferent? Love lightly, but without the horrors. The horrors always come from a small soul who needs reassurance regarding his own merits."

known to themselves only. In co-operation or contest men face each other as generalized types. Montherlant is for his fellows a writer, Lawrence a doctrinaire, Breton a school principal, Stendhal a diplomat or man of wit; it is woman who reveals in one a magnificent and cruel prince, in another a disquieting faun, in this one a god or a sun or a being "black and cold as a man struck by lightning at the feet of the Sphinx," [5] in the last a seducer, a charmer, a lover.

For each of them the ideal woman will be she who incarnates most exactly the *Other* capable of revealing him to himself. Montherlant, the solar spirit, seeks pure animality in her; Lawrence, the phallicist, asks her to sum up the feminine sex in general; Claudel defines her as a soul-sister; Breton cherishes Mélusine, rooted in nature, pinning his hope on the woman-child; Stendhal wants his mistress intelligent, cultivated, free in spirit and behavior: an equal. But the sole earthly destiny reserved for the equal, the woman-child, the soul-sister, the woman-sex, the woman-animal is always man! Whatever ego may seek himself through her, he can find himself only if she is willing to act as his crucible. She is required in every case to forget self and to love. Montherlant consents to have pity upon the woman who allows him to measure his virile potency; Lawrence addresses a burning hymn to the woman who gives up being herself for his sake; Claudel exalts the handmaid, the female servant, the devotee who submits to God in submitting to the male; Breton is in hopes of human salvation from woman because she is capable of total love for her child or her lover; and even in Stendhal the heroines are more moving than the masculine heroes because they give themselves to their passion with a more distraught violence; they help man fulfill his destiny, as Prouhèze contributes to the salvation of Rodrigue; in Stendhal's novels it often happens that they save their lovers from ruin, prison, or death. Feminine devotion is demanded as a duty by Montherlant and Lawrence; less arrogant, Claudel, Breton, and Stendhal admire it as a generous free choice; they wish for it without claiming to deserve it; but—except for the astounding Lamiel—all their works show that they expect from woman that altruism which Comte admired in her and imposed upon her, and which according to him constituted a mark at once of flagrant inferiority and of an equivocal superiority.

We could multiply examples, but they would invariably lead us to the same conclusions. When he describes woman, each writer dis-

---

[5] Breton's *Nadja*.

closes his general ethics and the special idea he has of himself; and in her he often betrays also the gap between his world view and his egotistical dreams. The absence or insignificance of the feminine element throughout the work of an author is in its own way symptomatic; but that element is extremely important when it sums up in its totality all the aspects of the Other, as happens with Lawrence. It remains important when woman is viewed simply as an other but the writer is interested in the individual adventure of her life, as with Stendhal; it loses importance in an epoch such as ours when personal problems of the individual are of secondary interest. Woman, however, as the other still plays a role to the extent that, if only to transcend himself, each man still needs to learn more fully what he is.

CHAPTER XI

Myth and Reality

THE MYTH of woman plays a considerable part in literature; but what is its importance in daily life? To what extent does it affect the customs and conduct of individuals? In replying to this question it will be necessary to state precisely the relations this myth bears to reality.

There are different kinds of myths. This one, the myth of woman, sublimating an immutable aspect of the human condition—namely, the "division" of humanity into two classes of individuals—is a static myth. It projects into the realm of Platonic ideas a reality that is directly experienced or is conceptualized on a basis of experience; in place of fact, value, significance, knowledge, empirical law, it substitutes a transcendental Idea, timeless, unchangeable, necessary. This idea is indisputable because it is beyond the given: it is endowed with absolute truth. Thus, as against the dispersed, contingent, and multiple existences of actual women, mythical thought opposes the Eternal Feminine, unique and changeless. If the definition provided for this concept is contradicted by the behavior of flesh-and-blood women, it is the latter who are wrong: we are told not that Femininity is a false entity, but that the women concerned are not feminine. The contrary facts of experience are impotent against the myth. In a way, however, its source is in experience. Thus it is quite true that woman is other than man, and this alterity is directly felt in desire, the embrace, love; but the real relation is one of reciprocity; as such it gives rise to authentic drama. Through eroticism, love, friendship, and their alternatives, deception, hate, rivalry, the relation is a struggle between concious beings each of whom wishes to be essential, it is the mutual recognition of free beings who confirm one another's freedom, it is the vague transition from aversion to participation. To pose Woman is to pose the absolute Other, without reciprocity, denying against all experience that she is a subject, a fellow human being.

In actuality, of course, women appear under various aspects; but

each of the myths built up around the subject of woman is intended
to sum her up *in toto*; each aspires to be unique. In consequence, a
number of incompatible myths exist, and men tarry musing before
the strange incoherencies manifested by the idea of Femininity. As
every woman has a share in a majority of these archetypes—each of
which lays claim to containing the sole Truth of woman—men of
today also are moved again in the presence of their female companions to an astonishment like that of the old sophists who failed to
understand how man could be blond and dark at the same time!
Transition toward the absolute was indicated long ago in social
phenomena: relations are easily congealed in classes, functions in
types, just as relations, to the childish mentality, are fixed in things.
Patriarchal society, for example, being centered upon the conservation of the patrimony, implies necessarily, along with those who own
and transmit wealth, the existence of men and women who take property away from its owners and put it into circulation. The men—ad-
venturers, swindlers, thieves, speculators—are generally repudiated by
the group; the women, employing their erotic attraction, can induce
young men and even fathers of families to scatter their patrimonies,
without ceasing to be within the law. Some of these women appropriate their victims' fortunes or obtain legacies by using undue influence;
this role being regarded as evil, those who play it are called "bad
women." But the fact is that quite to the contrary they are able to
appear in some other setting—at home with their fathers, brothers,
husbands, or lovers—as guardian angels; and the courtesan who
"plucks" rich financiers is, for painters and writers, a generous patron-
ess. It is easy to understand in actual experience the ambiguous personality of Aspasia or Mme de Pompadour. But if woman is depicted
as the Praying Mantis, the Mandrake, the Demon, then it is most
confusing to find in woman also the Muse, the Goddess Mother,
Beatrice.

As group symbols and social types are generally defined by means
of antonyms in pairs, ambivalence will seem to be an intrinsic quality
of the Eternal Feminine. The saintly mother has for correlative the
cruel stepmother, the angelic young girl has the perverse virgin: thus
it will be said sometimes that Mother equals Life, sometimes that
Mother equals Death, that every virgin is pure spirit or flesh dedicated
to the devil.

Evidently it is not reality that dictates to society or to individuals their choice between the two opposed basic categories; in every period, in each case, society and the individual decide in accordance with their needs. Very often they project into the myth adopted the institutions and values to which they adhere. Thus the paternalism that claims woman for hearth and home defines her as sentiment, inwardness, immanence. In fact every existent is at once immanence and transcendence; when one offers the existent no aim, or prevents him from attaining any, or robs him of his victory, then his transcendence falls vainly into the past—that is to say, falls back into immanence. This is the lot assigned to woman in the patriarchate; but it is in no way a vocation, any more than slavery is the vocation of the slave. The development of this mythology is to be clearly seen in Auguste Comte. To identify Woman with Altruism is to guarantee to man absolute rights in her devotion, it is to impose on women a categorical imperative.

The myth must not be confused with the recognition of significance; significance is immanent in the object; it is revealed to the mind through a living experience; whereas the myth is a transcendent Idea that escapes the mental grasp entirely. When in *L'Age d'homme* Michel Leiris describes his vision of the feminine organs, he tells us things of significance and elaborates no myth. Wonder at the feminine body, dislike for menstrual blood, come from perceptions of a concrete reality. There is nothing mythical in the experience that reveals the voluptuous qualities of feminine flesh, and it is not an excursion into myth if one attempts to describe them through comparisons with flowers or pebbles. But to say that Woman is Flesh, to say that the Flesh is Night and Death, or that it is the splendor of the Cosmos, is to abandon terrestrial truth and soar into an empty sky. For man also is flesh for woman; and woman is not merely a carnal object; and the flesh is clothed in special significance for each person and in each experience. And likewise it is quite true that woman—like man—is a being rooted in nature; she is more enslaved to the species than is the male, her animality is more manifest; but in her as in him the given traits are taken on through the fact of existence, she belongs also to the human realm. To assimilate her to Nature is simply to act from prejudice.

Few myths have been more advantageous to the ruling caste than the myth of woman: it justifies all privileges and even authorizes their abuse. Men need not bother themselves with alleviating the pains and the burdens that physiologically are women's lot, since these are "intended by Nature"; men use them as a pretext for increasing the misery of the feminine lot still further, for instance by refusing to grant to woman any right to sexual pleasure, by making her work like a beast of burden.[1]

Of all these myths, none is more firmly anchored in masculine hearts than that of the feminine "mystery." It has numerous advantages. And first of all it permits an easy explanation of all that appears inexplicable; the man who "does not understand" a woman is happy to substitute an objective resistance for a subjective deficiency of mind; instead of admitting his ignorance, he perceives the presence of a "mystery" outside himself: an alibi, indeed, that flatters laziness and vanity at once. A heart smitten with love thus avoids many disappointments: if the loved one's behavior is capricious, her remarks stupid, then the mystery serves to excuse it all. And finally, thanks again to the mystery, that negative relation is perpetuated which seemed to Kierkegaard infinitely preferable to positive possession; in the company of a living enigma man remains alone—alone with his dreams, his hopes, his fears, his love, his vanity. This subjective game, which can go all the way from vice to mystical ecstasy, is for many a more attractive experience than an authentic relation with a human being. What foundations exist for such a profitable illusion?

Surely woman is, in a sense, mysterious, "mysterious as is all the world," according to Maeterlinck. Each is *subject* only for himself; each can grasp in immanence only himself, alone: from this point of view the *other* is always a mystery. To men's eyes the opacity of the self-knowing self, of the *pour-soi,* is denser in the *other* who is feminine; men are unable to penetrate her special experience through any working of sympathy: they are condemned to ignorance of the quality of woman's erotic pleasure, the discomfort of menstruation, and the pains of childbirth. The truth is that there is mystery on both sides: as the *other* who is of masculine sex, every man, also, has within him a presence, an inner self impenetrable to woman; she in turn is in ignorance of the male's erotic feeling. But in accordance with the

---

[1] Cf. Balzac: *Physiology of Marriage:* "Pay no attention to her murmurs, her cries, her pains; *nature has made her for our use* and for bearing everything: children, sorrows, blows and pains inflicted by man. Do not accuse yourself of hardness. In all the codes of so-called civilized nations, man has written the laws that ranged woman's destiny under this bloody epigraph: "*Væ victis!* Woe to the weak!"

universal rule I have stated, the categories in which men think of the world are established *from their point of view, as absolute:* they misconceive reciprocity, here as everywhere. A mystery for man, woman is considered to be mysterious in essence.

To tell the truth, her situation makes woman very liable to such a view. Her physiological nature is very complex; she herself submits to it as to some rigmarole from outside; her body does not seem to her to be a clear expression of herself; within it she feels herself a stranger. Indeed, the bond that in every individual connects the physiological life and the psychic life—or better the relation existing between the contingence of an individual and the free spirit that assumes it—is the deepest enigma implied in the condition of being human, and this enigma is presented in its most disturbing form in woman.

But what is commonly referred to as the mystery is not the subjective solitude of the conscious self, nor the secret organic life. It is on the level of communication that the word has its true meaning: it is not a reduction to pure silence, to darkness, to absence; it implies a stammering presence that fails to make itself manifest and clear. To say that woman is mystery is to say, not that she is silent, but that her language is not understood; she is there, but hidden behind veils; she exists beyond these uncertain appearances. What is she? Angel, demon, one inspired, an actress? It may be supposed either that there are answers to these questions which are impossible to discover, or, rather, that no answer is adequate because a fundamental ambiguity marks the feminine being; and perhaps in her heart she is even for herself quite indefinable: a sphinx.

The fact is that she would be quite embarrassed to decide *what* she *is;* but this not because the hidden truth is too vague to be discerned: it is because in this domain there is no truth. An existent *is* nothing other than what he does; the possible does not extend beyond the real, essence does not precede existence: in pure subjectivity, the human being *is not anything.* He is to be measured by his acts. Of a peasant woman one can say that she is a good or a bad worker, of an actress that she has or does not have talent; but if one considers a woman in her immanent presence, her inward self, one can say absolutely nothing about her, she falls short of having any qualifications. Now, in amorous or conjugal relations, in all relations where the woman is the vassal, the other, she is being dealt with in her immanence. It is noteworthy that the feminine comrade, colleague, and associate are without mystery; on the other hand, if the vassal is male, if, in the eyes of a man or a woman who is older, or richer, a young fellow, for example, plays the role of the inessential object, then he too becomes shrouded in mystery. And this uncovers for us a substructure under the feminine mystery which is economic in nature.

A sentiment cannot be supposed to *be* anything. "In the domain of sentiments," writes Gide, "the real is not distinguished from the imaginary. And if to imagine one loves is enough to be in love, then also to tell oneself that one imagines oneself to be in love when one is in love is enough to make one forthwith love a little less." Discrimination between the imaginary and the real can be made only through behavior. Since man occupies a privileged situation in this world, he is in a position to show his love actively; very often he supports the woman or at least helps her; in marrying her he gives her social standing; he makes her presents; his independent economic and social position allows him to take the initiative and think up contrivances: it was M. de Norpois who, when separated from Mme de Villeparisis, made twenty-four-hour trips to visit her. Very often the man is busy, the woman idle: he *gives* her the time he passes with her; she takes it: is it with pleasure, passionately, or only for amusement? Does she accept these benefits through love or through self-interest? Does she love her husband or her marriage? Of course, even the man's evidence is ambiguous: is such and such a gift granted through love or out of pity? But while normally a woman finds numerous advantages in her relations with a man, his relations with a woman are profitable to a man only in so far as he loves her. And so one can almost judge the degree of his affection by the total picture of his attitude.

But a woman hardly has means for sounding her own heart; according to her moods she will view her own sentiments in different lights, and as she submits to them passively, one interpretation will be no truer than another. In those rare instances in which she holds the position of economic and social privilege, the mystery is reversed, showing that it does not pertain to *one* sex rather than the other, but to the situation. For a great many women the roads to transcendence are blocked: because they *do* nothing, they fail to *make themselves* anything. They wonder indefinitely what they *could have* become, which sets them to asking about what they *are*. It is a vain question. If man fails to discover that secret essence of femininity, it is simply because it does not exist. Kept on the fringe of the world, woman cannot be objectively defined through this world, and her mystery conceals nothing but emptiness.

Furthermore, like all the oppressed, woman deliberately dissembles her objective actuality; the slave, the servant, the indigent, all who depend upon the caprices of a master, have learned to turn toward him a changeless smile or an enigmatic impassivity; their real sentiments, their actual behavior, are carefully hidden. And moreover woman is taught from adolescence to lie to men, to scheme, to be wily. In speaking to them she wears an artificial expression on her face; she is cautious, hypocritical, play-acting.

But the Feminine Mystery as recognized in mythical thought is a more profound matter. In fact, it is immediately implied in the mythology of the absolute Other. If it be admitted that the inessential conscious being, too, is a clear subjectivity, capable of performing the *Cogito*, then it is also admitted that this being is in truth sovereign and returns to being essential; in order that all reciprocity may appear quite impossible, it is necessary for the Other to be for itself an other, for its very subjectivity to be affected by its otherness; this consciousness which would be alienated as a consciousness, in its pure immanent presence, would evidently be Mystery. It would be Mystery in itself from the fact that it would be Mystery for itself; it would be absolute Mystery.

In the same way it is true that, beyond the secrecy created by their dissembling, there is mystery in the Black, the Yellow, in so far as they are considered absolutely as the inessential Other. It should be noted that the American citizen, who profoundly baffles the average European, is not, however, considered as being "mysterious": one states more modestly that one does not understand him. And similarly woman does not always "understand" man; but there is no such thing as a masculine mystery. The point is that rich America, and the male, are on the Master side and that Mystery belongs to the slave.

To be sure, we can only muse in the twilight byways of bad faith upon the positive reality of the Mystery; like certain marginal hallucinations, it dissolves under the attempt to view it fixedly. Literature always fails in attempting to portray "mysterious" women; they can appear only at the beginning of a novel as strange, enigmatic figures;

but unless the story remains unfinished they give up their secret in the end and they are then simply consistent and transparent persons. The heroes in Peter Cheyney's books, for example, never cease to be astonished at the unpredictable caprices of women: no one can ever guess how they will act, they upset all calculations. The fact is that once the springs of their action are revealed to the reader, they are seen to be very simple mechanisms: this woman was a spy, that one a thief; however clever the plot, there is always a key; and it could not be otherwise, had the author all the talent and imagination in the world. Mystery is never more than a mirage that vanishes as we draw near to look at it.

We can see now that the myth is in large part explained by its usefulness to man. The myth of woman is a luxury. It can appear only if man escapes from the urgent demands of his needs; the more relationships are concretely lived, the less they are idealized. The fellah of ancient Egypt, the Bedouin peasant, the artisan of the Middle Ages, the worker of today has in the requirements of work and poverty relations with his particular woman companion which are too definite for her to be embellished with an aura either auspicious or inauspicious. The epochs and the social classes that have been marked by the leisure to dream have been the ones to set up the images, black and white, of femininity. But along with luxury there was utility; these dreams were irresistibly guided by interests. Surely most of the myths had roots in the spontaneous attitude of man toward his own existence and toward the world around him. But going beyond experience toward the transcendent Idea was deliberately used by patriarchal society for purposes of self-justification; through the myths this society imposed its laws and customs upon individuals in a picturesque, effective manner; it is under a mythical form that the group-imperative is indoctrinated into each conscience. Through such intermediaries as religions, traditions, language, tales, songs, movies, the myths penetrate even into such existences as are most harshly enslaved to material realities. Here everyone can find sublimation of his drab experiences: deceived by the woman he loves, one declares that she is a Crazy Womb; another, obsessed by his impotence, calls her a Praying Mantis; still another enjoys his wife's company: behold, she is Harmony, Rest, the Good Earth! The taste for eternity at a bargain, for a pocket-sized absolute, which is shared by a majority of men, is satisfied by myths. The smallest emotion, a slight annoyance, becomes the reflection of a timeless Idea—an illusion agreeably flattering to the vanity.

The myth is one of those snares of false objectivity into which the man who depends on ready-made valuations rushes headlong. Here again we have to do with the substitution of a set idol for actual experience and the free judgments it requires. For an authentic relation with an autonomous existent, the myth of Woman substitutes the fixed contemplation of a mirage. "Mirage! Mirage!" cries Laforgue. "We should kill them since we cannot comprehend them; or better tranquilize them, instruct them, make them give up their taste for jewels, make them our genuinely equal comrades, our intimate friends, real associates here below, dress them differently, cut their hair short, say anything and everything to them." Man would have nothing to lose, quite the contrary, if he gave up disguising woman as a symbol. When dreams are official community affairs, clichés, they are poor and monotonous indeed beside the living reality; for the true dreamer, for the poet, woman is a more generous fount than is any down-at-heel marvel. The times that have most sincerely treasured women are not the period of feudal chivalry nor yet the gallant nineteenth century. They are the times—like the eighteenth century—when men have regarded women as fellow creatures; then it is that women seem truly romantic, as the reading of *Liaisons dangereuses*, *Le Rouge et le noir*, *Farewell to Arms*, is sufficient to show. The heroines of Laclos, Stendhal, Hemingway are without mystery, and they are not the less engaging for that. To recognize in woman a human being is not to impoverish man's experience: this would lose none of its diversity, its richness, or its intensity if it were to occur between two subjectivities. To discard the myths is not to destroy all dramatic relation between the sexes, it is not to deny the significance authentically revealed to man through feminine reality; it is not to do away with poetry, love, adventure, happiness, dreaming. It is simply to ask that behavior, sentiment, passion be founded upon the truth.[2]

"Woman is lost. Where are the women? The women of today are not women at all!" We have seen what these mysterious slogans

[2] Laforgue goes on to say regarding woman: "Since she has been left in slavery, idleness, without occupation or weapon other than her sex, she has over-developed this aspect and has become the Feminine. . . . We have permitted this hypertrophy; she is here in the world for our benefit. . . . Well! that is all wrong. . . . Up to now we have played with woman as if she were a doll. This has lasted altogether too long! . . ."

mean. In men's eyes—and for the legion of women who see through men's eyes—it is not enough to have a woman's body nor to assume the female function as mistress or mother in order to be a "true woman." In sexuality and maternity woman as subject can claim autonomy; but to be a "true woman" she must accept herself as the Other. The men of today show a certain duplicity of attitude which is painfully lacerating to women; they are willing on the whole to accept woman as a fellow being, an equal; but they still require her to remain the inessential. For her these two destinies are incompatible; she hesitates between one and the other without being exactly adapted to either, and from this comes her lack of equilibrium. With man there is no break between public and private life: the more he confirms his grasp on the world in action and in work, the more virile he seems to be; human and vital values are combined in him. Whereas woman's independent successes are in contradiction with her femininity, since the "true woman" is required to make herself object, to be the Other.

It is quite possible that in this matter man's sensibility and sexuality are being modified. A new æsthetics has already been born. If the fashion of flat chests and narrow hips—the boyish form—has had its brief season, at least the overopulent ideal of past centuries has not returned. The feminine body is asked to be flesh, but with discretion; it is to be slender and not loaded with fat; muscular, supple, strong, it is bound to suggest transcendence; it must not be pale like a too shaded hothouse plant, but preferably tanned like a workman's torso from being bared to the open sun. Woman's dress in becoming practical need not make her appear sexless: on the contrary, short skirts made the most of legs and thighs as never before. There is no reason why working should take away woman's sex appeal.[3] It may be disturbing to contemplate woman as at once a social personage and carnal prey: in a recent series of drawings by Peynet (1948), we see a young man break his engagement because he was seduced by the pretty mayoress who was getting ready to officiate at his marriage. For a woman to hold some "man's position" and be desirable at the same time has long been a subject for more or less ribald joking; but gradually the impropriety and the irony have become blunted, and it

---

[3] A point that hardly needs to be made in America, where even cursory acquaintance with any well-staffed business office will afford confirmatory evidence.—TR.

would seem that a new form of eroticism is coming into being—perhaps it will give rise to new myths.

What is certain is that today it is very difficult for women to accept at the same time their status as autonomous individuals and their womanly destiny; this is the source of the blundering and restlessness which sometimes cause them to be considered a "lost sex." And no doubt it is more comfortable to submit to a blind enslavement than to work for liberation: the dead, for that matter, are better adapted to the earth than are the living. In all respects a return to the past is no more possible than it is desirable. What must be hoped for is that the men for their part will unreservedly accept the situation that is coming into existence; only then will women be able to live in that situation without anguish. Then Laforgue's prayer will be answered: "Ah, young women, when will you be our brothers, our brothers in intimacy without ulterior thought of exploitation? When shall we clasp hands truly?" Then Breton's "Mélusine, no longer under the weight of the calamity let loose upon her by man alone, Mélusine set free . . ." will regain "her place in humanity." Then she will be a full human being, "when," to quote a letter of Rimbaud, "the infinite bondage of woman is broken, when she will live in and for herself, man—hitherto detestable—having let her go free."

BOOK II

Woman's Life Today

PART IV

THE FORMATIVE YEARS

CHAPTER XII

Childhood

O NE is not born, but rather becomes, a woman. No biological, psychological, or economic fate determines the figure that the human female presents in society; it is civilization as a whole that produces this creature, intermediate between male and eunuch, which is described as feminine. Only the intervention of someone else can establish an individual as an *Other*. In so far as he exists in and for himself, the child would hardly be able to think of himself as sexually differentiated. In girls as in boys the body is first of all the radiation of a subjectivity, the instrument that makes possible the comprehension of the world: it is through the eyes, the hands, that children apprehend the universe, and not through the sexual parts. The dramas of birth and of weaning unfold after the same fashion for nurslings of both sexes; these have the same interests and the same pleasures; sucking is at first the source of their most agreeable sensations; then they go through an anal phase in which they get their greatest satisfactions from the excretory functions, which they have in common. Their genital development is analogous; they explore their bodies with the same curiosity and the same indifference; from clitoris and penis they derive the same vague pleasure. As their sensibility comes to require an object, it is turned toward the mother: the soft, smooth, resilient feminine flesh is what arouses sexual desires, and these desires are prehensile; the girl, like the boy, kisses, handles, and caresses her mother in an aggressive way; they feel the same jealousy if a new child is born, and they show it in similar behavior patterns: rage, sulkiness, urinary difficulties; and they resort to the same coquettish tricks to gain the love of adults. Up to the age of twelve the little girl is as strong as her brothers, and she shows the same mental powers; there is no field where she is debarred from engaging in rivalry with them. If, well before puberty and sometimes even from early infancy, she seems to us to be already sexually determined, this is not because mysterious instincts directly doom her to passivity, coquetry, maternity; it is because the influence of others upon the child is a factor almost from the start, and thus she is indoctrinated with her vocation from her earliest years.

The world is at first represented in the newborn infant only by immanent sensations; he is still immersed in the bosom of the Whole as he was when he lived in a dark womb; when he is put to the breast or the nursing bottle he is still surrounded by the warmth of maternal flesh. Little by little he learns to perceive objects as distinct and separate from himself, and to distinguish himself from them. Meanwhile he is separated more or less brutally from the nourishing body. Sometimes the infant reacts to this separation by a violent crisis; [1] in any case, it is about when the separation is accomplished, toward the age of six months, perhaps, that the child begins to show the desire to attract others through acts of mimicry that in time become real showing off. Certainly this attitude is not established through a considered choice; but it is not necessary to *conceive* a situation for it to *exist*. The nursling lives directly the basic drama of every existent: that of his relation to the Other. Man experiences with anguish his being turned loose, his forlornness. In flight from his freedom, his subjectivity, he would fain lose himself in the bosom of the Whole.

---

[1] Judith Gautier relates in her memoirs that she wept and pined so pitifully when taken from her nurse that they had to bring her back, and she was not weaned until much later.

Here, indeed, is the origin of his cosmic and pantheistic dreams, of his longing for oblivion, for sleep, for ecstasy, for death. He never succeeds in abolishing his separate ego, but at least he wants to attain the solidity of the in-himself, the *en-soi*, to be petrified into a thing. It is especially when he is fixed by the gaze of other persons that he appears to himself as being one.

It is in this perspective that the behavior of the child must be interpreted: in carnal form he discovers finiteness, solitude, forlorn desertion in a strange world. He endeavors to compensate for this catastrophe by projecting his existence into an image, the reality and value of which others will establish. It appears that he may begin to affirm his identity at the time when he recognizes his reflection in a mirror— a time that coincides with that of weaning: [2] his ego becomes so fully identified with this reflected image that it is formed only in being projected. Whether or not the mirror actually plays a more or less considerable part, it is certain that the child commences toward the age of six months to mimic his parents, and under their gaze to regard himself as an object. He is already an autonomous subject, in transcendence toward the outer world; but he encounters himself only in a projected form.

When the child develops further, he fights in two ways against his original abandonment. He attempts to deny the separation: rushing into his mother's arms, he seeks her living warmth and demands her caresses. And he attempts to find self-justification through the approbation of others. Adults seem to him like gods, for they have the power to confer existence upon him. He feels the magic of the gaze that makes of him now a delightful little angel, now a monster. His two modes of defense are not mutually exclusive: on the contrary, they complement each other and interpenetrate. When the attempt at enticement succeeds, the sense of justification finds carnal confirmation in the kisses and caresses obtained: it all amounts to a single state of happy passivity that the child experiences in his mother's lap and under her benevolent gaze. There is no difference in the attitudes of girls and boys during the first three or four years; both try to perpetuate the happy condition that preceded weaning; in

---

[2] This theory was proposed by Dr. Lacan in *Les Complexes familiaux dans la formation de l'individu*. This observation, one of primary importance, would explain how it is that in the course of its development "the ego retains the ambiguous aspect of a spectacle."

both sexes enticement and showing-off behavior occur: boys are as desirous as their sisters of pleasing adults, causing smiles, making themselves admired.

It is more satisfying to deny the anguish than to rise above it, more radical to be lost in the bosom of the Whole than to be petrified by the conscious egos of others: carnal union creates a deeper alienation than any resignation under the gaze of others. Enticement and showing off represent a more complex, a less easy stage than simple abandon in the maternal arms. The magic of the adult gaze is capricious. The child pretends to be invisible; his parents enter into the game, trying blindly to find him and laughing; but all at once they say: "You're getting tiresome, you are not invisible at all." The child has amused them with a bright saying; he repeats it, and this time they shrug their shoulders. In this world, uncertain and unpredictable as the universe of Kafka, one stumbles at every step.[3] That is why many children are afraid of growing up; they are in despair if their parents cease taking them on their knees or letting them get into the grown-ups' bed. Through the physical frustration they feel more and more cruelly the forlornness, the abandonment, which the human being can never be conscious of without anguish.

This is just where the little girls first appear as privileged beings. A second weaning, less brutal and more gradual than the first, withdraws the mother's body from the child's embraces; but the boys especially are little by little denied the kisses and caresses they have been used to. As for the little girl, she continues to be cajoled, she is allowed to cling to her mother's skirts, her father takes her on his knee and strokes her hair. She wears sweet little dresses, her tears and caprices are viewed indulgently, her hair is done up carefully, older people are amused at her expressions and coquetries—bodily contacts and agreeable glances protect her against the anguish of solitude. The little boy, in contrast, will be denied even coquetry; his efforts at enticement, his play-acting, are irritating. He is told that "a man doesn't ask to be kissed. . . . A man doesn't look at himself in mirrors. . . . A man doesn't cry." He is urged to be "a little man"; he will obtain adult approval by becoming independent of adults. He will please them by not appearing to seek to please them.

---

[3] In her *Orange bleue*, Yassu Gauclère relates anecdotes of childhood illustrating the inconsistent behavior of both her father and her mother; her childish conclusion was that "the conduct of grown-ups is decidedly incomprehensible."

Many boys, frightened by the hard independence they are condemned to, wish they were girls; formerly, when boys were dressed in early years like girls, they often shed tears when they had to change from dresses to trousers and saw their curls cut. Certain of them held obstinately to the choice of femininity—one form of orientation toward homosexuality. Maurice Sachs (in *Le Sabbat*) says: "I wished passionately to be a girl and I pushed my unawareness of the grandeur of being male to the point of meaning to urinate in a sitting position."

But if the boy seems at first to be less favored than his sisters, it is because great things are in store for him. The demands placed upon him at once imply a high evaluation. Maurras relates in his memoirs that he was jealous of a younger brother whom his mother and grandmother were cajoling. His father took his hand and drew him from the room, saying to him: "We are men, let us leave those women." The child is persuaded that more is demanded of boys because they are superior; to give him courage for the difficult path he must follow, pride in his manhood is instilled into him; this abstract notion takes on for him a concrete aspect: it is incarnated in his penis. He does not spontaneously experience a sense of pride in his little lazy sex, but rather through the attitude of the group around him. Mothers and nurses keep alive the tradition that identifies the phallus and the male idea; whether they recognize its prestige in amorous gratitude or in submission, or whether they get a sense of revenge in coming upon it in the nursling in a very humble form, they treat the infantile penis with remarkable complacency. Rabelais tells us about the tricks and comments of Gargantua's nurses, and history has preserved those of the nurses of Louis XIII. More modest women still give a nickname to the little boy's sex, speaking to him of it as of a small person who is at once himself and other than himself: they make of it, according to the expression already cited, an "*alter* ego usually more sly, more intelligent, and more clever than the individual." [4]

Anatomically the penis is well suited for this role; projecting free of the body, it seems like a little natural plaything, a kind of puppet. Elders will lend value to the child, then, in conferring it upon his double. A father told me about one of his sons who at the age of three still sat down to urinate; surrounded with sisters and girl cousins, he was a timid and sad child. One day his father took him to

---

[4] A. Balint: *La Vie intime de l'enfant.* Cf. Book I, pp. 47–8.

the toilet, saying: "I am going to show you how men do it." Thereafter the child, proud of urinating while standing, scorned girls "who urinate through a hole"; his disdain originally arose not because they lacked an organ but because they had not been singled out and initiated by the father, as he had. Thus, far from the penis representing a direct advantage from which the boy could draw a feeling of superiority, its high valuation appears on the contrary as a compensation—invented by adults and ardently accepted by the child—for the hardships of the second weaning. Thus he is protected against regret for his lost status as nursling and for his not being a girl. Later on he will incarnate his transcendence and his proud sovereignty in his sex.[5]

The lot of the little girl is very different. Mothers and nurses feel no reverence or tenderness toward her genitals; they do not direct her attention toward that secret organ, invisible except for its covering, and not to be grasped in the hand; in a sense she has no sex organ. She does not experience this absence as a lack; evidently her body is, for her, quite complete; but she finds herself situated in the world differently from the boy; and a constellation of factors can transform this difference, in her eyes, into an inferiority.

There are few questions more extensively discussed by psychoanalysts than the celebrated feminine "castration complex." Most would admit today that penis envy is manifested in very diverse ways in different cases.[6] To begin with, there are many little girls who remain ignorant of the male anatomy for some years. Such a child finds it quite natural that there should be men and women, just as there is a sun and a moon: she believes in essences contained in words and her curiosity is not analytic at first. For many others this tiny bit of flesh hanging between boys' legs is insignificant or even laughable; it is a peculiarity that merges with that of clothes or haircut. Often it is first seen on a small newborn brother and, as Helene Deutsch puts it, "when the little girl is very young she is not impressed by the penis of her little brother." She cites the case of a

---

[5] See Book I, p. 48.

[6] In addition to the works of Freud and Adler, an abundant literature on the subject is in existence. Abraham was first to voice the idea that the little girl might consider her sex as a wound resulting from a mutilation. Karen Horney, Jones, Jeanne Lampt de Groot, Helene Deutsch, and A. Balint have studied the question from the psychoanalytic point of view. Saussure essays to reconcile psychoanalysis with the ideas of Piaget and Luquet. See also Pollack: *Les Idées des enfants sur la différence des sexes.*

girl of eighteen months who remained quite indifferent to the discovery of the penis and attached no importance to it until much later, in accordance with her personal interests. It may even happen that the penis is considered to be an anomaly: an outgrowth, something vague that hangs, like wens, breasts, or warts; it can inspire disgust. Finally, the fact is that there are numerous cases where the little girl does take an interest in the penis of a brother or playmate; but that does not mean that she experiences jealousy of it in a really sexual way, still less that she feels deeply affected by the absence of that organ; she wants to get it for herself as she wants to get any and every object, but this desire can remain superficial.

There is no doubt that the excretory functions, and in particular the urinary functions, are of passionate interest to children; indeed, to wet the bed is often a form of protest against a marked preference of the parents for another child. There are countries where the men urinate while seated, and there are cases of women who urinate standing, as is customary with many peasants, among others; but in contemporary Western society, custom generally demands that women sit or crouch, while the erect position is reserved for males. This difference constitutes for the little girl the most striking sexual differentiation. To urinate, she is required to crouch, uncover herself, and therefore hide: a shameful and inconvenient procedure. The shame is intensified in the frequent cases in which the girl suffers from involuntary discharge of urine, as for instance when laughing immoderately; in general her control is not so good as that of the boys.

To boys the urinary function seems like a free game, with the charm of all games that offer liberty of action; the penis can be manipulated, it gives opportunity for action, which is one of the deep interests of the child. A little girl on seeing a boy urinating exclaimed admiringly: "How convenient!" [7] The stream can be directed at will and to a considerable distance, which gives the boy a feeling of omnipotence. Freud spoke of "the burning ambition of early diuretics"; Stekel has discussed this formula sensibly, but it is true, as Karen Horney says,[8] that the "fantasies of omnipotence, especially those of sadistic character, are frequently associated with the male urinary

---

[7] Cited by A. Balint.

[8] "The Genesis of the Castration Complex in Woman," *International Journal of Psychoanalysis*, 1923–4.

stream"; these fantasies, which are lasting in certain men,[9] are important in the child. Abraham speaks of the "great pleasure women derive from watering the garden with a hose"; I believe, in agreement with the theories of Sartre and of Bachelard,[1] that identifying the hose with the penis is not necessarily the source of this pleasure—though it is clearly so in certain cases. Every stream of water in the air seems like a miracle, a defiance of gravity: to direct, to govern it, is to win a small victory over the laws of nature; and in any case the small boy finds here a daily amusement that is denied his sisters. It permits the establishment through the urinary stream of many relations with things such as water, earth, moss, snow, and the like. There are little girls who in their wish to share these experiences lie on their backs and try to make the urine spurt upward or practice urinating while standing. According to Karen Horney, they envy also the possibility of exhibiting which the boy has. She reports that "a patient, upon seeing a man urinating in the street, suddenly exclaimed: 'If I could ask one gift from Providence, it would be to have for once in my life the power of urinating like a man.'" To many little girls it seems that the boy, having the right to touch his penis, can make use of it as a plaything, whereas their organs are taboo.

That all the factors combine to make possession of a male sex organ seem desirable to many girls is a fact attested by numerous inquiries made and confidences received by psychiatrists. Havelock Ellis [2] cites these remarks made by a patient of Dr. S. E. Jelliffe, called Zenia: "The gushing of water in a jet or spray especially from a long garden hose, has always been highly suggestive to me, recalling the act of urination as witnessed in childhood in my brothers or even in other boys." A correspondent, Mrs. R. S., told Ellis that as a child she greatly desired to handle a boy's penis and imagined scenes involving such behavior with urination; one day she was allowed to hold a garden hose. "It seemed delightfully like holding a penis." She asserted that the penis had no sexual significance for her; she knew about the urinary function only. A most interesting case, that of Florrie, is reported by Havelock Ellis [3] (and later analyzed by Stekel); I give here a detailed summary:

---

[9] Cf. Montherlant, Book I, p. 209.

[1] See Book I, p. 46.

[2] *Studies in the Psychology of Sex*, "Undinism" (Random House ed., Vol. III, p. 429).

[3] H. Ellis, op. cit., Vol. III, p. 121.

The woman concerned is very intelligent, artistic, active, biologically normal, and not homosexual. She says that the urinary function played a great role in her childhood; she played urinary games with her brothers, and they wet their hands without feeling disgust. "My earliest ideas of the superiority of the male were connected with urination. I felt aggrieved with nature because I lacked so useful and ornamental an organ. No teapot without a spout felt so forlorn. It required no one to instil into me the theory of male predominance and superiority. Constant proof was before me." She took great pleasure in urinating in the country. "Nothing could come up to the entrancing sound as the stream descended on crackling leaves in the depth of a wood and she watched its absorption. Most of all she was fascinated by the idea of doing it into water" [as are many little boys]. Florrie complains that the style of her knickers prevented her from trying various desired experiments, but often during country walks she would hold back as long as she could and then suddenly relieve herself standing. "I can distinctly remember the strange and delicious sensation of this forbidden delight, and also my puzzled feeling that it came standing." In her opinion, the style of children's clothing has great importance for feminine psychology in general. "It was not only a source of annoyance to me that I had to unfasten my drawers and then squat down for fear of wetting them in front, but the flap at the back, which must be removed to uncover the posterior parts during the act, accounts for my early impression that in girls this function is connected with those parts. The first distinction in sex that impressed me—the one great difference in sex—was that boys urinated standing and that girls had to sit down. . . . The fact that my earliest feelings of shyness were more associated with the back than the front may have thus originated." All these impressions were of great importance in Florrie's case because her father often whipped her until the blood came and also a governess had once spanked her to make her urinate; she was obsessed by masochistic dreams and fancies in which she saw herself whipped by a school mistress under the eyes of all and having to urinate against her will, "an idea that gives one a curious sense of gratification." At the age of fifteen it happened that under urgent need she urinated standing in a deserted street. "In trying to analyze my sensations I think the most prominent lay in the shame that came from standing, and the consequently greater distance the stream had to descend. It seemed to make the affair important and conspicuous, even though clothing hid it. In the ordinary attitude there is a kind of privacy. As a small child, too, the stream had not far to go, but at the age of fifteen I was tall and it seemed to give one a glow of shame to think of this stream falling unchecked such a distance. (I am sure that the ladies who fled in horror from the urinette at Portsmouth ⁴ thought it most indecent for a woman to stride across an earthenware boat on the ground, a leg on each side, and standing there to pull up her clothes and do a stream which descended unabashed all that way.)" She renewed this experience at twenty and frequently thereafter. She felt a mixture of shame and pleasure at the idea that she might be surprised and that she would be incapable of stopping. "The stream seemed to be drawn from me without my consent, and *yet with even more pleasure than if I were doing it freely*. [The italics are Florrie's.] This curious feeling—that it is being drawn away by some unseen power which is determined that one shall do it—is an entirely feminine pleasure and a subtle charm. . . . There is a fierce charm in the torrent that binds one to its will by a mighty force." Later Florrie developed a flagellatory eroticism always combined with urinary obsessions.

This case is of great interest because it throws light on several elements in the child's experience. But there are evidently special circumstances that confer enormous importance upon them. For normally reared little girls, the urinary privilege of the boy is something too definitely secondary to call forth directly a feeling of inferiority. The psychoanalysts who, following Freud, suppose that the mere discovery of the penis by a little girl would be enough to cause a trauma profoundly misunderstand the mentality of the child; this mentality is much less rational than they seem to suppose, for it does not envisage clear-cut categories and it is not disturbed by contradiction. When the small girl sees the penis and declares: "I had one, too," or "I will have one, too," or even "I have one, too," it is not an insincere self-justification; presence and absence are not mutually exclusive; as his drawings show, the child believes much less in

----

⁴ In allusion to an episode previously related: at Portsmouth a modern retiring room for ladies was opened which called for the standing position; all the clients were seen to depart hastily as soon as they entered.

what he *sees* with his eyes than in significant *types* that he has set up once for all. He often draws without looking, and in any case his perceptions are strongly colored by what he puts into them. In emphasizing just this point, Saussure [5] cites this important observation of Luquet: "Once a sketch is seen to be erroneous, it is as if nonexistent; the child *literally no longer sees it*, being in a way hypnotized by the new sketch that replaces it, just as he pays no attention to accidental lines on his paper." The male anatomy constitutes a powerful formation that often impresses itself upon the little girl's attention; and she *literally no longer sees* her own body. Saussure mentions the case of a little girl of four who, while trying to urinate like a boy between the bars of a gate, said that she wished she had "a long little thing that streams." She was affirming at once that she had and did not have a penis, which is in harmony with the thinking by "participation" described in children by Piaget. The little girl readily believes that all children are born with a penis but that later the parents cut off some of them to make girls; this idea satisfies the artificialism of the child, who, deifying her parents, "conceives of them as the source of everything she has," as Piaget puts it; the child does not at first see castration as a punishment.

In order for her state to assume the character of a frustration, it is necessary for the little girl to be already, for some reason, dissatisfied with her situation; as Helene Deutsch justly remarks, an exterior event like the sight of a penis could not in itself bring about an internal development: "The sight of the male organ can have a traumatic effect," she says, "but only provided that a long chain of earlier experiences calculated to produce this effect has preceded it." If the little girl finds herself unable to satisfy her desire by masturbation or exhibition, if her parents repress her autoeroticism, if she feels she is less loved, less admired than her brothers, then she will project her dissatisfaction upon the male organ. "The discovery made by the little girl of her anatomical difference from the boy serves to confirm a need previously felt; it is her rationalization of it, so to speak." [6] And Adler has insisted precisely on the fact that it is the valuation established by the parents and associates that lends to the boy the

---

[5] "*Psychogenèse et psychanalyse*," *Revue française de psychanalyse*, 1933.

[6] See Helene Deutsch: *The Psychology of Women* (Grune & Stratton, 1944), Vol. I, pp. 319 ff. She cites also the authority of K. Abraham and J. H. W. van Ophuijsen.

prestige of which the penis becomes the explanation and symbol in the eyes of the little girl. People consider her brother superior; he is himself swollen with pride in his manhood; so she envies him and feels frustrated. Sometimes she holds it against her mother, more rarely against her father; or she may blame herself for the mutilation, or she may console herself in thinking that the penis is hidden in the body and will come out some day.

But even if the young girl has no serious penis envy, the absence of the organ will certainly play an important role in her destiny. The major benefit obtained from it by the boy is that, having an organ that can be seen and grasped, he can at least partially identify himself with it. He projects the mystery of his body, its threats, outside of himself, which enables him to keep them at a distance. True enough, he does scent danger in connection with his penis, he fears its being cut off; but this is a fright easier to overcome than the diffuse apprehension felt by the little girl in regard to her "insides," an apprehension that will often be retained for life. She is extremely concerned about everything that happens inside of her, she is from the start much more opaque to her own eyes, more profoundly immersed in the obscure mystery of life, than is the male. Because he has an *alter ego* in whom he sees himself, the little boy can boldly assume an attitude of subjectivity; the very object into which he projects himself becomes a symbol of autonomy, of transcendence, of power; he measures the length of his penis; he compares his urinary stream with that of his companions; later on, erection and ejaculation will become grounds for satisfaction and challenge. But the little girl cannot incarnate herself in any part of herself. To compensate for this and to serve her as *alter ego*, she is given a foreign object: a doll. It should be noted that the word *poupée* (doll) is also applied to the bandage around a wounded finger; a dressed-up finger, distinguished from the others, is regarded with amusement and a kind of pride, the child shows signs of the process of identification by his talk to it. But it is a statuette with a human face—or, that lacking, an ear of corn, even a piece of wood—which will most satisfyingly serve the girl as substitute for that double, that natural plaything: the penis.

The main difference is that, on the one hand, the doll represents the whole body, and, on the other, it is a passive object. On this account the little girl will be led to identify her whole person and to regard this as an inert given object. While the boy seeks himself in the penis as an autonomous subject, the little girl coddles her doll and dresses her up as she dreams of being coddled and dressed up herself; inversely, she thinks of herself as a marvelous doll.[7] By means of compliments and scoldings, through images and words, she learns the meaning of the terms *pretty* and *homely*; she soon learns that in order to be pleasing she must be "pretty as a picture"; she tries to make herself look like a picture, she puts on fancy clothes, she studies herself in a mirror, she compares herself with princesses and fairies. Marie Bashkirtsev gives us a striking example of this childish coquetry. It is not by chance that, being weaned late—at three and a half—she felt strongly, at the age of four to five, the need to make herself admired, to live for others. The shock of weaning must have been violent in a child so old, and she must have tried the more passionately to compensate for the separation inflicted upon her; in her journal she writes: "At five I dressed in my mother's laces, with flowers in my hair, and went to dance in the drawing-room. I was the great dancer Petipa, and the whole family were there *to look at me*."

This narcissism appears so precociously in the little girl, it will play so fundamental a part in her life as a woman, that it is easy to regard it as arising from a mysterious feminine instinct. But we have seen above that in reality it is not an anatomical fate that dictates her attitude. The difference that distinguishes boys is a fact that she can take in a number of ways. To have a penis is no doubt a privilege, but it is one whose value naturally decreases when the child loses interest in its excretory functions and becomes socialized. If its value is retained in the child's view beyond the age of eight or nine, it is because the penis has become the symbol of manhood, which is socially valued. The fact is that in this matter the effect of education and surroundings is immense. All children try to compensate for the separation inflicted through weaning by enticing and show-off behavior; the boy is compelled to go beyond this state; he is rid of narcissism by having his attention directed to his penis; while the little girl is confirmed in the tendency to make herself object, which all young children have in common. The doll is a help, but it no longer has a determining role;

---

[7] The analogy between woman and doll is maintained into adulthood; in French a woman is commonly called a doll, and similarly in English; also a dressed-up woman is said to be "dolled up."

the boy, too, can cherish a teddy bear, or a puppet into which he projects himself; it is within the totality of their lives that each factor—penis or doll—takes on its importance.

Thus the passivity that is the essential characteristic of the "feminine" woman is a trait that develops in her from the earliest years. But it is wrong to assert that a biological datum is concerned; it is in fact a destiny imposed upon her by her teachers and by society. The great advantage enjoyed by the boy is that his mode of existence in relation to others leads him to assert his subjective freedom. His apprenticeship for life consists in free movement toward the outside world; he contends in hardihood and independence with other boys, he scorns girls. Climbing trees, fighting with his companions, facing them in rough games, he feels his body as a means for dominating nature and as a weapon for fighting; he takes pride in his muscles as in his sex; in games, sports, fights, challenges, trials of strength, he finds a balanced exercise of his powers; at the same time he absorbs the severe lessons of violence; he learns from an early age to take blows, to scorn pain, to keep back the tears. He undertakes, he invents, he dares. Certainly he tests himself also as if he were another; he challenges his own manhood, and many problems result in relation to adults and to other children. But what is very important is that there is no fundamental opposition between his concern for that objective figure which is his, and his will to self-realization in concrete projects. It is by *doing* that he creates his existence, both in one and the same action.

In woman, on the contrary, there is from the beginning a conflict between her autonomous existence and her objective self, her "being-the-other"; she is taught that to please she must try to please, she must make herself object; she should therefore renounce her autonomy. She is treated like a live doll and is refused liberty. Thus a vicious circle is formed; for the less she exercises her freedom to understand, to grasp and discover the world about her, the less resources will she find within herself, the less will she dare to affirm herself as subject. If she were encouraged in it, she could display the same lively exuberance, the same curiosity, the same initiative, the same hardihood, as a boy. This does happen occasionally, when the girl is given a boyish bringing up; in this case she is spared many problems.[8] It is noteworthy that

---

[8] At least during early childhood. Under present social conditions, the conflicts of adolescence, on the contrary, may well be exaggerated.

this is the kind of education a father prefers to give his daughter; and women brought up under male guidance very largely escape the defects of femininity. But custom is opposed to treating girls like boys. I have known of little village girls of three or four being compelled by their fathers to wear trousers.[9] All the other children teased them: "Are they girls or boys?"—and they proposed to settle the matter by examination. The victims begged to wear dresses. Unless the little girl leads an unusually solitary existence, a boyish way of life, though approved by her parents, will shock her entourage, her friends, her teachers. There will always be aunts, grandmothers, cousins around to counteract the father's influence. Normally he is given a secondary role with respect to his daughters' training. One of the curses that weigh heavily upon women—as Michelet has justly pointed out—is to be left in women's hands during childhood. The boy, too, is brought up at first by his mother, but she respects his maleness and he escapes very soon;[1] whereas she fully intends to fit her daughter into the feminine world.

We shall see later how complex the relations of mother to daughter are: the daughter is for the mother at once her double and another person, the mother is at once overweeningly affectionate and hostile toward her daughter; she saddles her child with her own destiny: a way of proudly laying claim to her own femininity and also a way of revenging herself for it. The same process is to be found in pederasts, gamblers, drug addicts, in all who at once take pride in belonging to a certain confraternity and feel humiliated by the association: they endeavor with eager proselytism to gain new adherents. So, when a child comes under their care, women apply themselves to changing her into a woman like themselves, manifesting a zeal in which arrogance and resentment are mingled; and even a generous mother, who sincerely seeks her child's welfare, will as a rule think that it is wiser to make a "true woman" of her, since society will more readily accept her if this is done. She is therefore given little girls for playmates, she is entrusted to female teachers, she lives among the older women as in the days of the Greek gynæceum, books and games are chosen for her which initiate her into her destined sphere, the treasures of feminine wisdom are poured into her ears, feminine virtues are urged upon her,

---

[9] Quite in accordance with current American fashion!—Tr.

[1] There are of course many exceptions; but we cannot undertake here to study the part played by the mother in the boy's development.

she is taught cooking, sewing, housekeeping, along with care of her person, charm, and modesty; she is dressed in inconvenient and frilly clothes of which she has to be careful, her hair is done up in fancy style, she is given rules of deportment: "Stand up straight, don't walk like a duck"; to develop grace she must repress her spontaneous movements; she is told not to act like a would-be boy, she is forbidden violent exercises, she is not allowed to fight. In brief, she is pressed to become, like her elders, a servant and an idol. Today, thanks to the conquests of feminism, it is becoming more and more normal to encourage the young girl to get an education, to devote herself to sports; but lack of success in these fields is more readily pardoned in her than in a boy; and success is made harder by the demands made upon her for another kind of accomplishment: at any rate she must be *also* a woman, she must not *lose* her femininity.

When very young the girl child resigns herself to all this without too much trouble. The child moves on the play and dream level, playing at being, playing at doing; to do and to be are not clearly distinguished when one is concerned only with imaginary accomplishments. The little girl can compensate for the present superiority of the boys by the promises that are inherent in her womanly destiny and that she already fulfills in play. Because she knows as yet only her childhood universe, her mother at first seems to her to be endowed with more authority than her father; she imagines the world to be a kind of matriarchate; she imitates her mother and identifies herself with her; frequently she even reverses their respective roles: "When I am big and you are little . . ." she likes to say to her mother. The doll is not only her double; it is also her child. These two functions do not exclude each other, inasmuch as the real child is also an *alter ego* for the mother. When she scolds, punishes, and then consoles her doll, she is at once vindicating herself as against her mother and assuming, herself, the dignity of a mother: she combines in herself the two elements of the mother-daughter pair. She confides in her doll, she brings it up, exercises upon it her sovereign authority, sometimes even tears off its arms, beats it, tortures it. Which is to say she experiences subjective affirmation and identification through the doll. Frequently the mother is associated in this imaginary life: The child plays with her mother at being father and mother of the doll, making a couple that excludes the man. Here again there is no "maternal instinct," innate and mysterious. The little girl ascertains that the care of children falls upon the mother, she is so taught; stories heard, books read, all her little experiences confirm the idea. She is encouraged to feel the enchantment of these future riches, she is given dolls so that these values may henceforth have a tangible aspect. Her "vocation" is powerfully impressed upon her.

Because the little girl feels that children will be her lot, and also because she is more interested in her "insides" than is the boy, she is especially curious about the mystery of procreation. She soon ceases to believe that babies are born in cabbages, carried in the doctor's bag, or brought by storks; she soon learns, especially if brothers and sisters arrive, that babies develop in the mother's body. Besides, modern parents make less of a mystery about it than was formerly the custom. The little girl is generally more amazed than frightened, because the phenomenon seems magical to her; she does not as yet grasp all the physiological implications. At first she is unaware of the father's part and supposes that a woman becomes pregnant from eating certain foods. This is a legendary theme (in stories queens give birth to a little girl or a fine boy after having eaten a certain fruit, or a special kind of fish), and one that later leads certain women to associate the idea of gestation with that of the digestive system. These problems and discoveries together engage much of the interest of the young girl and help to nourish her imagination. I will bring forward as typical one of Jung's cases,[2] which has remarkable similarities with that of little Hans, analyzed by Freud at about the same time:

Toward three, Anna began to ask where babies came from, and for a time believed they were little angels. At four she had a new brother, without having appeared to notice her mother's pregnancy. On returning from a short visit to her grandmother's, she showed jealousy of the new baby, misbehaving in various ways and frequently accusing her mother of not telling the truth, because she suspected her of having lied about the birth. She asked whether she would become a woman like her mother. She called to her parents at night, saying she was frightened by what she had heard about an earthquake and asking questions about it. One day she asked point-blank where her brother was before he was born, why he did not come sooner, and the like. She seemed pleased to be told that he grew like a plant inside the mother; but she asked how he

---

[2] From *Les Conflits de l'âme enfantine.*

got out, since he couldn't walk, and if there was a hole in the chest, and so on. Then she declared she knew storks brought babies; but she ceased to worry about earthquakes. A little later, seeing her father in bed, she asked if he too had a plant growing inside him. She dreamed that the little animals fell out of her Noah's ark through a hole in the bottom. She put her doll under her skirt and then had it "come out." She was wondering about the father's role, and one day lay on his bed face-down and, kicking with her legs, asked if that wasn't what Papa did. Later she asked if eyes and hair are planted in the head, after she had planted some seeds in the garden. Her father explained that they were present as germs in the child before developing, and she asked how her little brother got inside Mamma, who had planted him there, how he got out. Her father asked what she thought, and she indicated her sex organ; he said that was right. But she still wanted to know how he got in, and so her father explained that it is the father who furnishes the seed. This seemed to satisfy her, and being almost fully informed by the time she was five, she had no further trouble with the subject.

This history is characteristic, though often the little girl asks less precisely about the role of the father, or the parents are evasive on this point. Many a little girl puts a pillow under her apron to play at being pregnant, or walks with a doll in the folds of her skirt and drops it in the cradle; she may give it the breast. Boys, like girls, wonder at the mystery of motherhood; all children have an imagination "of depth" which makes them conceive the idea of secret riches in the interior of things; they all feel the miracle of encasements, of dolls that contain other similar dolls, of boxes containing other boxes, of pictures that contain replicas of decreasing size; all are delighted to see a bud taken apart, to observe the chick in its shell, to watch as "Japanese flowers" expand when floated in a dish of water. It was a small boy who cried with delight: "Oh, it's a mother!" when he opened an Easter egg filled with small sugar eggs. To make a baby emerge from one's body: that is as fine as any feat of legerdemain. The mother seems to be endowed with marvelous fairy powers. Many boys regret the lack of such a privilege; if, later on, they steal birds' eggs and trample down young plants, if they destroy life about them in a kind of frenzy, it is in revenge for their inability to bring forth life; while the little girl takes pleasure in the thought that she will create life one day.

In addition to this hope which playing with dolls makes concrete, family life provides the little girl with other possibilities for self-expression. A large part of the housework is within the capability of a very young child; the boy is commonly excused, but his sister is allowed, even asked, to sweep, dust, peel vegetables, wash the baby, watch the soup kettle. In particular, the eldest sister is often concerned in this way with motherly tasks; whether for convenience or because of hostility and sadism, the mother thus rids herself of many of her functions; the girl is in this manner made to fit precociously into the universe of serious affairs; her sense of importance will help her in assuming her femininity. But she is deprived of happy freedom, the carefree aspect of childhood; having become precociously a woman, she learns all too soon the limitations this estate imposes upon a human being; she reaches adolescence as an adult, which gives her history a special character. A child overburdened with work may well become prematurely a slave, doomed to a joyless existence. But if no more than an effort suited to her powers is asked of her, she is proud to feel herself as capable as a grown-up, and she enjoys sharing responsibility with adults. This equal sharing is possible because it is not a far cry from child to housekeeper. A man expert in his trade is separated from the stage of childhood by his years of apprenticeship. Thus the little boy finds his father's activities quite mysterious, and the man he is to become is hardly sketched out in him at all. On the contrary, the mother's activities are quite accessible to the girl; "she is already a little woman," as her parents say; and it is sometimes held that she is more precocious than the boy. In truth, if she is nearer to the adult stage it is because this stage in most women remains traditionally more or less infantile. The fact is that the girl is conscious of her precocity, that she takes pride in playing the little mother toward the younger children; she is glad to become important, she talks sensibly, she gives orders, she assumes airs of superiority over her brothers of infantile rank, she converses on a footing of equality with her mother.

In spite of all these compensations, she does not accept without regret the fate assigned to her; as she grows, she envies the boys their vigor. Parents and grandparents may poorly conceal the fact that they would have preferred male offspring to female; or they may show more affection for the brother than the sister. Investigations make it clear that the majority of parents would rather have sons than daughters. Boys are spoken to with greater seriousness and esteem, they are granted more rights; they themselves treat girls scornfully; they play by themselves, not admitting girls to their group, they offer insults: for one thing, calling girls "prissy" or the like and thus recalling the little girl's secret humiliation. In France, in mixed schools, the boys' caste deliberately oppresses and persecutes the girls' caste.

If the girls want to struggle with the boys and fight for their rights, they are reprimanded. They are doubly envious of the activities peculiar to the boys: first, because they have a spontaneous desire to display their power over the world, and, second, because they are in protest against the inferior status to which they are condemned. For one thing, they suffer under the rule forbidding them to climb trees and ladders or on roofs. Adler remarks that the notions of high and low have great importance, the idea of elevation in space implying a spiritual superiority, as may be seen in various heroic myths; to attain a summit, a peak, is to stand out beyond the common world of fact as sovereign subject (ego); among boys, climbing is frequently a basis for challenge. The little girl, to whom such exploits are forbidden and who, seated at the foot of a tree or cliff, sees the triumphant boys high above her, must feel that she is, body and soul, their inferior. And it is the same if she is left *behind* in a race or jumping match, if she is thrown *down* in a scuffle or simply kept on the side lines.

As she becomes more mature, her universe enlarges, and masculine superiority is perceived still more clearly. Very often identification with the mother no longer seems to be a satisfying solution; if the little girl at first accepts her feminine vocation, it is not because she intends to abdicate; it is, on the contrary, in order to rule; she wants to be a matron because the matrons' group seems privileged; but when her company, her studies, her games, her reading, take her out of the maternal circle, she sees that it is not the women but the men who control the world. It is this revelation—much more than the discovery of the penis—that irresistibly alters her conception of herself.

The relative rank, the hierarchy, of the sexes is first brought to her attention in family life; little by little she realizes that if the father's authority is not that which is most often felt in daily affairs, it is actually supreme; it only takes on more dignity from not being degraded to daily use; and even if it is in fact the mother who rules as mistress of the household, she is commonly clever enough to see to it that the father's wishes come first; in important matters the mother demands, rewards, and punishes in his name and through his authority. The life of the father has a mysterious prestige: the hours he spends at home, the room where he works, the objects he has around him, his pursuits, his hobbies, have a sacred character. He supports the family, and he is the responsible head of the family. As a rule his work takes him outside, and so it is through him that the family communicates with the rest of the world: he incarnates that immense, difficult, and marvelous world of adventure; he personifies transcendence, he is God.[3] This is what the child feels physically in the powerful arms that lift her up, in the strength of his frame against which she nestles. Through him the mother is dethroned as once was Isis by Ra, and the Earth by the Sun.

But here the child's situation is profoundly altered: she was to become one day a woman like her all-powerful mother—she will never be the sovereign father; the bond attaching her to her mother was an active emulation—from her father she can but passively await an expression of approval. The boy thinks of his father's superiority with a feeling of rivalry; but the girl has to accept it with impotent admiration. I have already pointed out that what Freud calls the Electra complex is not, as he supposes, a sexual desire; it is a full abdication of the subject, consenting to become object in submission and adoration. If her father shows affection for his daughter, she feels that her existence is magnificently justified; she is endowed with all the merits that others have to acquire with difficulty; she is fulfilled and deified. All her life she may longingly seek that lost state of plenitude and peace. If the father's love is withheld, she may ever after feel herself guilty and condemned; or she may look elsewhere for a valuation of herself and become indifferent to her father or even hostile. Moreover, it is not alone the father who holds the keys to the world: men in general share normally in the prestige of manhood; there is no occasion for regarding them as "father substitutes." It is directly, as men, that grandfathers, older brothers, uncles, playmates' fathers,

---

[3] "His generous presence inspired great love and extreme fear in me," says Mme de Noailles in speaking of her father. "At first he astounded me. The first man astounds a little girl. I felt strongly that everything depended upon him."

family friends, teachers, priests, doctors, fascinate the little girl. The emotional concern shown by adult women toward Man would of itself suffice to perch him on a pedestal.[4]

Everything helps to confirm this hierarchy in the eyes of the little girl. The historical and literary culture to which she belongs, the songs and legends with which she is lulled to sleep, are one long exaltation of man. It was men who built up Greece, the Roman Empire, France, and all other nations, who have explored the world and invented the tools for its exploitation, who have governed it, who have filled it with sculptures, paintings, works of literature. Children's books, mythology, stories, tales, all reflect the myths born of the pride and the desires of men; thus it is that through the eyes of men the little girl discovers the world and reads therein her destiny.

The superiority of the male is, indeed, overwhelming: Perseus, Hercules, David, Achilles, Lancelot, the old French warriors Du Guesclin and Bayard, Napoleon—so many men for one Joan of Arc; and behind her one descries the great male figure of the archangel Michael! Nothing could be more tiresome than the biographies of famous women: they are but pallid figures compared with great men; and most of them bask in the glory of some masculine hero. Eve was not created for her own sake but as a companion for Adam, and she was made from his rib. There are few women in the Bible of really high renown: Ruth did no more than find herself a husband. Esther obtained favor for the Jews by kneeling before Ahasuerus, but she was only a docile tool in the hands of Mordecai; Judith was more audacious, but she was subservient to the priests, and her exploit, of dubious aftertaste, is by no means to be compared with the clean, brilliant triumph of young David. The goddesses of pagan mythology are frivolous or capricious, and they all tremble before Jupiter. While

---

[4] It is noteworthy that the worship of the father is to be met with especially in the eldest of the children, and indeed a man is more interested in his first paternity than in later ones; he often consoles his daughter, as he consoles his son, when their mother is monopolized by newcomers, and she is likely to become ardently attached to him. On the contrary, a younger sister never can have her father all to herself, without sharing him; she is commonly jealous at once of him and of her elder sister; she attaches herself to that same elder sister whom the father's favor invests with high prestige, or she turns to her mother, or she revolts against the family and looks for help outside. In many families the youngest daughter gains a privileged position in some other way. Many things, of course, can motivate special preferences in the father. But almost all the cases I know of confirm this observation on the different attitudes of the older and younger sisters.

Prometheus magnificently steals fire from the sun, Pandora opens her box of evils upon the world.

There are in legend and story, to be sure, witches and hags who wield fearful powers. Among others, the figure of the Mother of the Winds in Andersen's *Garden of Paradise* recalls the primitive Great Goddess: her four gigantic sons obey her in fear and trembling, she beats them and shuts them up in sacks when they misbehave. But these are not attractive personages. More pleasing are the fairies, sirens, and undines, and these are outside male domination; but their existence is dubious, hardly individualized; they intervene in human affairs but have no destiny of their own: from the day when Andersen's little siren becomes a woman, she knows the yoke of love, and suffering becomes her lot.

In modern tales as in ancient legends man is the privileged hero. Mme de Ségur's books are a curious exception: they describe a matriarchal society where the husband, when he is not absent, plays a ridiculous part; but commonly the figure of the father, as in the real world, is haloed with glory. The feminine dramas of *Little Women* unfold under the ægis of a father deified by absence. In novels of adventure it is the boys who take a trip around the world, who travel as sailors on ships, who live in the jungle on breadfruit. All important events take place through the agency of men. Reality confirms what these novels and legends say. If the young girl reads the papers, if she listens to the conversation of grown-ups, she learns that today, as always, men run the world. The political leaders, generals, explorers, musicians, and painters whom she admires are men; certainly it is men who arouse enthusiasm in her heart.

This prestige is reflected in the supernatural world. As a rule, in consequence of the large part played by religion in the life of women, the little girl, dominated by her mother more than is her brother, is also more subject to religious influences. Now, in Western religions God the Father is a man, an old gentleman having a specifically virile attribute: a luxuriant white beard.[5] For Christians, Christ is still more definitely a man of flesh and blood, with a long blond beard. Angels

---

[5] "I no longer suffered from my inability to *see* God, for I recently succeeded in imagining him in the image of my late grandfather, an image that to tell the truth was rather human; but I had soon made it more Godlike by separating my grandfather's head from the torso and mentally placing it against a background of blue sky where white clouds formed a collar for it," confides Yassu Gauclère in her *Orange bleue*.

have no sex, according to the theologians; but they have masculine names and appear as good-looking young men. God's representatives on earth: the Pope, the bishop (whose ring one kisses), the priest who says Mass, he who preaches, he before whom one kneels in the secrecy of the confessional—all these are men. For a pious little girl, her relations with the everlasting Father are analogous to those she has with the earthly father; as the former develop on the plane of imagination, she knows an even more nearly total resignation. The Catholic religion among others exerts a most confused influence upon the young girl.[6] The Virgin hears the words of the angel on her knees and replies: "Behold the *handmaid* of the Lord." Mary Magdalene lies at Christ's feet, washing them with her tears and drying them with the hairs of her head, her long woman's hair. The saints kneel and declare their love for the shining Christ. On her knees, breathing the odor of incense, the young girl abandons herself to the gaze of God and the angels: a masculine gaze. There has been frequent insistence on the similarities between erotic language and the mystical language spoken by women; for instance, St. Theresa writes of Jesus: "Oh, my Well-Beloved, through Thy love I am reconciled not to feel, here below, the inexpressible kiss of Thy mouth . . . but I pray Thee to fire me with Thy love. . . . Ah, let me in my burning frenzy hide within Thy heart. . . . I would become the prey of Thy love . . ." and so on.

But it is not to be concluded that these effusions are always sexual; the fact is rather that when feminine sexuality develops, it is pervaded with the religious sentiment that women ordinarily direct toward man from early childhood. True it is that the little girl experiences in the presence of her confessor, and even when alone at the foot of the altar, a thrill very similar to what she will feel later in her lover's embrace: this means that feminine love is one of the forms of experience in which a conscious ego makes of itself an object for a being who transcends it; and these passive delights, too, are the enjoyment of the young feminine devotee lingering in the shadowy church.

Head bowed, face buried in her hands, she knows the miracle of

---

[6] Beyond question the women are infinitely more passive, more subservient to man, servile, and abased in the Catholic countries, such as Italy, Spain, or France, than in such Protestant regions as the Scandinavian and Anglo-Saxon countries. And that flows in large part from the women's own attitude: the cult of the Virgin, confession, and the rest lead them toward masochism.

renunciation: on her knees she mounts toward heaven; her surrender to the arms of God assures her an Assumption fleecy with clouds and angels. It is from this marvelous experience that she copies her earthly future. The child can find it also through many other roads: everything invites her to abandon herself in daydreams to men's arms in order to be transported into a heaven of glory. She learns that to be happy she must be loved; to be loved she must await love's coming. Woman is the Sleeping Beauty, Cinderella, Snow-White, she who receives and submits. In song and story the young man is seen departing adventurously in search of woman; he slays the dragon, he battles giants; she is locked in a tower, a palace, a garden, a cave, she is chained to a rock, a captive, sound asleep: she waits.

Un jour mon prince viendra . . . *Some day he'll come along, the man I love*—the words of popular songs fill her with dreams of patience and of hope.

Thus the supreme necessity for woman is to charm a masculine heart; intrepid and adventurous though they may be, it is the recompense to which all heroines aspire; and most often no quality is asked of them other than their beauty. It is understandable that the care of her physical appearance should become for the young girl a real obsession; be they princesses or shepherdesses, they must always be pretty in order to obtain love and happiness; homeliness is cruelly associated with wickedness, and one is in doubt, when misfortunes shower the ugly, whether their crimes or their ill-favored looks are being punished. Frequently the beautiful young creatures, with a glorious future in store, are seen at first as victims; the stories of Genevieve of Brabant, of Griselda, are not so simple as they seem; love and suffering are disquietingly mingled in them; woman assures her most delicious triumphs by first falling into depths of abjection; whether God or a man is concerned, the little girl learns that she will become all-powerful through deepest resignation: she takes delight in a masochism that promises supreme conquests. St. Blandine, her white body blood-streaked under the lion's claws, Snow-White laid out as if dead in a glass coffin, the Beauty asleep, the fainting Atala, a whole flock of delicate heroines bruised, passive, wounded, kneeling, humiliated, demonstrate to their young sister the fascinating prestige of martyred, deserted, resigned beauty. It need not astonish us that while her brother plays the hero, the young girl quite willingly plays the martyr: pagans throw her to the lions, Bluebeard drags her by the hair, her husband, the King, exiles her to forest depths; she submits, she suffers, she dies, and her head wears the halo of glory. "While still a little girl," writes Mme de Noailles, "I wanted to attract the affection of men, to disquiet them, to be rescued by them, to die in their arms." We find a remarkable example of these masochistic day-dreamings in Marie Le Hardouin's *Voile noire:*

> At seven, from I know not what rib, I created my first man. He was tall, slender, very young, dressed in black satin with long sleeves trailing to the ground. He had blond hair in long, heavy curls. . . . I called him Edmond. . . . Then I gave him two brothers, Charles and Cedric, and the three, alike in dress and appearance, made me feel strange delights. . . . Their tiny feet and fine hands gave me all kinds of inner movements. . . . I became their sister Marguerite . . . and loved to feel myself wholly at their mercy, Edmond having the right of life and death over me. . . . He had me whipped on the slightest pretext. . . . When he spoke to me I was overcome with fear and could only stammer: "Yes, my lord," feeling the strange pleasure of being idiotic. . . . When my sufferings became too great, I begged for mercy and kissed his hand, while, my heart finally breaking, I reached that state in which one wants to die from excess of pleasure.

More or less precociously the little girl dreams that she is old enough for love; at nine or ten she amuses herself by making up her face, she pads her bodice, disguises herself as a grown-up lady. But she does not seek any actual erotic experience with little boys: if she happens to hide with them and play at "showing things to each other," it is only a matter of sexual curiosity. But the partner in her amorous reveries is an adult, either purely imaginary or based upon real individuals; in the latter case, the child is satisfied to love at a distance. A very good example of these childish daydreams will be found in the memoirs of Colette Audry, *Aux yeux du souvenir*; she relates that she discovered love at the age of five:

> That, of course, had nothing to do with the little sexual pleasures of childhood, the satisfaction I felt, for example, when I sat astride on a certain chair or caressed myself before going to sleep. . . . All they had in common was that I carefully hid both from

those about me. . . . My love for this young man consisted in
thinking of him before going to sleep and imagining wonderful
stories. . . . I was in love successively with all my father's head
clerks. . . . I was never deeply grieved when they left, for they
were hardly more than a pretext for my dreams. . . . When I
went to bed I took my revenge for being too young and timid. I
made careful preparations; I found no trouble making him seem
present, but I had to transform myself so that I could see myself,
ceasing to be "I" and becoming "she." First of all, I was eighteen
and beautiful. . . . I had an elegant box of candy. . . . I had
brown hair in short curls and was dressed in a long muslin gown.
An absence of ten years had separated us. He returned looking
scarcely older, and the sight of this marvelous creature overwhelmed him. She seemed hardly to remember him, she was full
of ease, indifference, and wit. I composed truly brilliant dialogue
for this first meeting. There followed misunderstandings, a whole
difficult conquest, cruel hours of discouragement and jealousy for
him. At last, driven to extremes, he avowed his love. She listened in
silence and just when he thought all was lost, she said she had never
ceased loving him, and they embraced a little . . . I saw the two
near together, on a bench in a park usually, heard their murmurs,
and at the same time I felt the warm contact of their bodies. But
from that point everything came apart. I never got as far as marriage.[7] . . . The next morning I thought about it a little, while
washing. I admired my soapy face (though at other times I did not
consider myself beautiful) and felt that somehow it hopefully beck-
oned me toward the distant future. But I had to hurry; once my
face was wiped, all was over, and in the glass I saw once more my
commonplace childish head, which no longer interested me.

Games and daydreams orient the little girl toward passivity; but
she is a human being before becoming a woman, and she knows already that to accept herself as a woman is to become resigned and to
mutilate herself; if the resignation is tempting, the mutilation is
hateful. Man, Love, are still far in the mists of the future; at present

[7] Counter to the masochistic imaginings of Marie Le Hardouin, those of Colette
Audry are of a sadistic type. She wants the beloved to be wounded, in danger,
and she saves him heroically, not without having humiliated him. This is a personal note, characteristic of a woman who will never accept passivity and will seek
to win her independence as a human being.

the little girl seeks activity and independence, like her brothers. The burden of liberty is not heavy upon children, because it does not imply responsibility; they know they are safe under adult protection: they are not tempted to run away. Her spontaneous surge toward life, her enjoyment of playing, laughing, adventure, lead the little girl to view the maternal sphere as narrow and stifling. She would like to escape from her mother's authority, an authority that is exercised in a much more intimate and everyday manner than is anything the boys have to accept. Rare indeed are the instances when the mother's authority is as comprehending and discreet as in the case of that "Sido" whom Colette has lovingly depicted. Apart from the quasi-pathological cases —and they are common [8]—where the mother is a kind of brute, satisfying on the child her will to domination and her sadism, her daughter is the privileged object before whom she claims to stand as sovereign subject; this claim leads the child to rise in revolt. Colette Audry has described this revolt of a normal child against a normal mother:

I could not have replied with the truth, however innocent it might have been, for I never felt innocent before Mamma. She was the great essential person, and I had such a grudge against her that I have not got over it yet. There was deep within me a kind of savage open sore that I was sure to find always inflamed. . . . Without regarding her as too severe or beyond her rights, I just thought: "No, no, no," with all my might. I did not reproach her for her arbitrary power, her orders and prohibitions, but for her *desire to humble me*, sometimes plainly stated, sometimes read in her eyes or voice. When she told lady visitors that children are much more amenable after a punishment, her words stuck in my gorge, unforgettable: I could not vomit them up, nor could I swallow them. This anger represented my guilt before her and also my shame before myself (for after all she scared me, and by way of reprisal I had to my credit only a few violent words and insolent attitudes), but it was also my glory, in spite of everything: as long as the sore was there, and while there lived the mute rage that seized me at the mere repetition of the words *to humble, amenable, punishment, humiliation*—for so long I would not be humbled.

---

[8] Cf. V. Leduc: *L'Asphyxie*; S. de Tervagnes: *La Haine maternelle*; H. Bazin: *Vipère au poing*.

The rebellion is the more violent when, as often happens, the mother has lost her prestige. She is the one who waits, submits, complains, weeps, makes scenes: an ungrateful role that in daily life leads to no apotheosis; as a victim she is looked down on; as a shrew, detested; her fate seems the prototype of rapid *recurrence*: life only repeats itself in her, without going anywhere; firmly set in her role as housekeeper, she puts a stop to the expansion of existence, she becomes obstacle and negation. Her daughter wishes *not* to be like her, worshipping women who have escaped from feminine servitude: actresses, writers, teachers; she engages avidly in sports and in study, she climbs trees, tears her clothes, tries to rival the boys.

Usually she has a best friend in whom she confides; it is an exclusive friendship like an amorous passion, which ordinarily involves the sharing of sexual secrets, the little girls exchanging and discussing such information as they have been able to obtain. Often enough a triangle is formed, one of the girls liking her friend's brother. So in *War and Peace* Sonia is Natasha's best friend and loves her brother Nicolas. In any case such friendship is shrouded in mystery, and it may be said in general that at this stage children love to have secrets; the girl makes a secret of the most insignificant things, in reaction against the mystery-making that is often the response to her curiosity. Having secrets is also one way of giving herself importance, something she seeks in every way to acquire: trying to interfere with grownups, inventing stories for their benefit in which she only half believes and in which she plays an important part, and the like. Among her companions she pretends to scorn the boys as much as they do her; she and her friends form a separate group, giggling and making fun of the boys.

But in fact she is pleased when they treat her on a footing of equality, and she tries to gain their approval. She would like to belong to the privileged caste. The same movement that in the primitive horde woman directed against male dominance is manifested in each new initiate through refusal of her lot: in her, transcendence condemns the absurdity of immanence. She does not like being intimidated by the rules of decency, bothered by her clothes, enslaved to household cares, stopped short in all her flights. Numerous inquiries have been made on this point, almost all [9] giving the same result: practically all

---

[9] An exception is a school in Switzerland where boys and girls, getting the same education under favorable conditions of comfort and freedom, all said they

the boys—like Plato in his time—declared that they would be horrified to be girls; almost all the girls regretted not being boys. According to Havelock Ellis's statistics, one boy in a hundred would like to be a girl; more than 75 per cent of the girls would prefer to change sex. According to Karl Pipal's research (quoted by Baudouin in *L'Âme enfantine*), out of 20 boys of twelve to fourteen, 18 said they would prefer anything in the world to being girls. Out of 22 girls, 19 wanted to be boys, giving the following reasons: "Boys are better off, they do not have to suffer as women do. . . . My mother would love me more. . . . A boy does more interesting work. . . . A boy has more aptitude for studies. . . . I would have fun scaring girls. . . . I would no longer be afraid of boys. . . . They are freer. . . . Boys' games are more fun. . . . They are not bothered by their clothes." This last point often recurs: most girls complain that their dresses bother them, that they do not have liberty of movement, that they are obliged to be careful not to spot their light-colored skirts and dresses.[1]

At ten or twelve years of age most little girls are truly "*garçons manqués*"—that is to say, children who lack something of being boys. Not only do they feel it as a deprivation and an injustice, but they find that the regime to which they are condemned is unwholesome. In girls the exuberance of life is restrained, their idle vigor turns into nervousness; their too prissy occupations do not use up their superabundant energy; they become bored, and, through boredom and to compensate for their position of inferiority, they give themselves up to gloomy and romantic daydreams; they get a taste for these easy escape mechanisms and lose their sense of reality; they yield to their emotions with uncontrolled excitement; instead of acting, they talk, often commingling serious phrases and senseless words in hodgepodge fashion. Neglected, "misunderstood," they seek consolation in narcissistic fancies: they view themselves as romantic heroines of fiction, with self-admiration and self-pity. Quite naturally they become

---

were satisfied; but such circumstances are exceptional. Assuredly girls *could* be quite as happy as boys; but in existing society the fact is that they commonly are not.

[1] In America this great problem has been solved, while the fashion lasts, by the girls' common adoption of what were formerly masculine work-clothes; i.e., blue denim overalls (called "blue jeans," or "dungarees") or some other form of trousers. This type of costume, while practical enough for children at play, becomes distasteful on young women who come no nearer to manual labor than wielding a pen or riding a bicycle.—Tr.

coquettish and stagy, these defects becoming more conspicuous at puberty. Their malaise shows itself in impatience, tantrums, tears; they enjoy crying—a taste that many women retain in later years—largely because they like to play the part of victims: at once a protest against their hard lot and a way to make themselves appealing. Little girls sometimes watch themselves cry in a mirror, to double the pleasure.

Most young girls' dramas concern their family relationships; they seek to break their ties with mother: now they show hostility toward her, now they retain a keen need for her protection; they would like to monopolize father's love; they are jealous, sensitive, demanding. They often make up stories, imagining that their parents are not really their parents, that they are adopted children. They attribute to their parents a secret life; they muse on their relationships; they often imagine that father is misunderstood, unhappy, that he does not find in his wife an ideal companion such as his daughter could be for him; or, on the contrary, that mother regards him rightly as coarse and brutal, that she is horrified at all physical relations with him. Fantasies, histrionics, childish tragedies, false enthusiasms, odd behavior—the reason for all these must be sought not in a mysterious feminine soul but in the child's environment, her situation.

It is a strange experience for an individual who feels himself to be an autonomous and transcendent subject, an absolute, to discover inferiority in himself as a fixed and preordained essence: it is a strange experience for whoever regards himself as the One to be revealed to himself as otherness, alterity. This is what happens to the little girl when, doing her apprenticeship for life in the world, she grasps what it means to be a woman therein. The sphere to which she belongs is everywhere enclosed, limited, dominated, by the male universe: high as she may raise herself, far as she may venture, there will always be a ceiling over her head, walls that will block her way. The gods of man are in a sky so distant that in truth, for him, there are no gods: the little girl lives among gods in human guise.

This situation is not unique. The American Negroes know it, being partially integrated in a civilization that nevertheless regards them as constituting an inferior caste; what Bigger Thomas, in Richard Wright's *Native Son*,[2] feels with bitterness at the dawn of his life is this definitive inferiority, this accursed alterity, which is written in the

---

[2] New York: Harper & Brothers; 1940.

color of his skin: he sees airplanes flying by and he knows that because he is black the sky is forbidden to him. Because she is a woman, the little girl knows that she is forbidden the sea and the polar regions, a thousand adventures, a thousand joys: she was born on the wrong side of the line. There is this great difference: the Negroes submit with a feeling of revolt, no privileges compensating for their hard lot, whereas woman is offered inducements to complicity. I have previously [3] called to mind the fact that along with the authentic demand of the subject who wants sovereign freedom, there is in the existent an inauthentic longing for resignation and escape; the delights of passivity are made to seem desirable to the young girl by parents and educators, books and myths, women and men; she is taught to enjoy them from earliest childhood; the temptation becomes more and more insidious; and she is the more fatally bound to yield to those delights as the flight of her transcendence is dashed against harsher obstacles.

But in thus accepting her passive role, the girl also agrees to submit unresistingly to a destiny that is going to be imposed upon her from without, and this calamity frightens her. The young boy, be he ambitious, thoughtless, or timid, looks toward an open future; he will be a seaman or an engineer, he will stay on the farm or go away to the city, he will see the world, he will get rich; he feels free, confronting a future in which the unexpected awaits him. The young girl will be wife, mother, grandmother; she will keep house just as her mother did, she will give her children the same care she herself received when young—she is twelve years old and already her story is written in the heavens. She will discover it day after day without ever making it; she is curious but frightened when she contemplates this life, every stage of which is foreseen and toward which each day moves irresistibly.

This explains why the little girl, more than her brothers, is preoccupied with the mysteries of sexuality. True enough, boys are also passionately interested in these matters; but they are not most concerned about their role as husband and father, in their futures. Whereas for the girl marriage and motherhood involve her entire destiny; and from the time when she begins to glimpse their secrets, her body seems to her to be odiously threatened. The magic of maternity has been dissipated: by more or less adequate means the girl has been informed, and whether early or late she knows that the baby

---

[3] Introduction, p. xxi.

does not arrive by chance in the maternal body and that it is not caused to emerge by the wave of a wand; she questions herself anxiously. Often it no longer seems marvelous but rather horrible that a parasitic body should proliferate within her body; the very idea of this monstrous swelling frightens her.

And how will the baby get out? Even if no one has told her about the screams and the pains of childbirth, she has overheard remarks or read the words of the Bible: "In sorrow thou shalt bring forth children"; she has a presentiment of tortures that she cannot even imagine in detail; she devises strange operations in the umbilical region. If she supposes that the fetus will be expelled through the anus, she gets no reassurance from that idea: little girls have been known to undergo attacks of psychosomatic constipation when they thought they had discovered the birth process. Precise explanations will not prove to be of great assistance: pictures of swelling, tearing, hemorrhage, will haunt her. The young girl will suffer the more from these visions the more imaginative she is; but none can face them without a shudder. Colette relates how her mother found her in a faint after reading the description of a birth by Zola, painted in crude and shocking colors and in minute detail.

The reassurances given by grown-ups leave the child uneasy; as she gets older, she learns not to take the word of adults any more, and it is often in just these matters concerning reproduction that she catches them lying. She knows also that they regard the most frightful things as normal; if she has experienced some violent physical shock—a tonsillectomy, a tooth pulled, a felon lanced—she will project the pain she remembers upon a future childbirth.

The physical nature of pregnancy and birth at once suggests that "something physical" takes place between husband and wife. The word *blood* frequently occurring in such expressions as "child of the same blood," "pure blood," "mixed blood," sometimes gives direction to the childish imagination; it may be supposed, for instance, that marriage involves some solemn rite of transfusion. But more often the "something physical" is connected with the urinary and excremental apparatus; in particular, children are inclined to believe that the man urinates into the woman. The sexual operation is thought of as *dirty*. This is extremely upsetting to the child for whom "dirty" things have been severely tabooed: how then can adults accept such things as an integral part of life? The child is kept from being scandalized at first by the absurdity of what he discovers: he sees no sense in what he hears, or reads, or writes; it all seems unreal to him. In Carson McCullers's delightful book *The Member of the Wedding*,[4] the young heroine comes upon two lodgers naked in bed, and the very anomaly of the situation prevents her from feeling it to be important:

> It was a summer Sunday and the hall door of the Marlowes' room was open. She could see only a portion of the room, part of the dresser and only the footpiece of the bed with Mrs. Marlowe's corset on it. But there was a sound in the quiet room she could not place, and when she stepped over the threshold she was startled by a sight that, after a single glance, sent her running to the kitchen, crying: Mr. Marlowe is having a fit! Berenice had hurried through the hall, but when she looked into the front room, she merely bunched her lips and banged the door. . . . Frankie had tried to question Berenice and find out what was the matter. But Berenice had only said that they were common people and added that with a certain party in the house they ought at least to know enough to shut a door. Though Frankie knew she was the certain party, still she did not understand. What kind of a fit was it? she asked. But Berenice would only answer: Baby, just a common fit. And Frankie knew from the voice's tones that there was more to it than she was told. Later she only remembered the Marlowes as common people. . . .

When children are warned against strangers or when a sexual incident is explained to them, it is likely that reference will be made to the diseased, to maniacs, to the insane; it is a convenient explanation. A child touched by her neighbor at the movies, or one who has seen a passer-by expose himself, believes that she has had to do with a madman. To be sure, it is unpleasant to encounter insanity: an epileptic attack, a hysterical outburst, or a violent quarrel, upsets the order of the adult world, and the child who sees it feels endangered; but after all, just as there are in a harmonious society a certain number of beggars, of the lame, and of the infirm with hideous sores, so there may be found in it also certain abnormals, without disturbance of its foundations. It is when parents, friends, teachers, are suspected

---

4 Houghton Mifflin Company, 1946. Dramatized and presented with success on the New York stage in the 1949–50 season.—TR.

of celebrating black Masses in secret that the child becomes really frightened. An incident in point is cited from Dr. Liepmann's *Jeunesse et sexualité.*

> When I was first told about the sexual relations between man and woman, I denied that such things were possible since my parents would have had to do likewise, and I thought too highly of them to believe it. I said that it was much too disgusting for me ever to do it. Unfortunately I was to be undeceived shortly after, when I heard what my parents were doing . . . that was a fearful moment; I hid my face under the bedclothes and stopped my ears, and wished I were a thousand miles from there.

How make the transition from the thought of clothed and dignified people who enjoin decency, reserve, the life of reason, to that of two naked animals confronting each other? Here, indeed, is a self-defamation of adults which shakes their pedestal, which darkens the sky. Frequently the child obstinately refuses to accept the revelation: "My parents don't do that," she insists. Or she tries to construct for herself a decent picture of coition: as one little girl put it, "When a child is wanted, the parents go to the doctor's office; they undress, they blindfold themselves because they mustn't look; then the doctor attaches them together and sees to it that all goes well"; she had transformed the act of love into a surgical operation, unpleasant, no doubt, but as correct as a session with the dentist. Yet in spite of denial and flight from reality, uneasiness and doubt creep into the childish heart, and an effect is produced as painful as that of weaning: it is no longer a matter of separating the girl from the mother's flesh, but of the crumbling around her of the protective universe; she finds herself without a roof over her head, abandoned, absolutely alone before a dark future.

And what increases the little girl's distress is that she fails to discern clearly the shape of the equivocal curse that weighs upon her. Her information is incoherent, the books are contradictory; even technical explanations fail to dissipate the thick darkness; a hundred questions arise: Is the sexual act painful? Or delightful? How long does it last —five minutes or all night? One reads here that a woman has become a mother after a single embrace, there that she remains sterile after hours of sexual pleasure. Do people "do it" every day? Or only occasionally? The child seeks to inform herself by reading the Bible, by consulting dictionaries, by asking her friends about it, and so she gropes in obscurity and disgust. Dr. Liepmann's research produced an interesting document on this matter. Here are some of the replies given him by young girls concerning their first knowledge of sexuality:

I continued to go astray among my odd and nebulous ideas. No one broached the subject, neither my mother nor my school-teachers; no book treated the subject fully. A kind of perilous and ugly mystery was woven about the act, which at first had seemed to me so natural. The big girls of twelve made use of crude jokes to bridge the chasm between themselves and my classmates. All that was still vague and disgusting; we argued as to where the baby was formed; if perhaps the thing took place only once in man, since marriage was the occasion for so much fuss. My menstruation at fifteen was a new surprise. . . .

Sexual initiation! Not to be mentioned in our house! . . . I hunted in books, but wore myself out without finding the road. . . . For my schoolteacher the question did not seem to exist. . . . A book finally showed me the truth, and my overexcitement disappeared; but I was most unhappy, and it took me a long time to understand that eroticism and sexuality alone constitute real love.

Stages of my initiation: (I) First questions and unsatisfactory notions, age three and a half to eleven. . . . No answers. . . . My pet rabbit had young when I was seven, and my mother told me that in animals and people the young grew inside the mother and emerged through the flank, which seemed to me unreasonable . . . a nursemaid told me about pregnancy, birth, and menstruation. . . . At length, to my last question on his function, my father replied with vague stories about pistil and pollen. (II) There were some attempts at personal initiation, age eleven to thirteen. I consulted an encyclopedia and a medical book. . . . Only theoretical information in strange, big words. (III) Some command of acquired knowledge, age thirteen to twenty: (a) through daily life; (b) through scientific books.

At eight I played with a boy of the same age. I repeated to him what my mother had told me: A woman has many eggs inside her

. . . a child is born from one of these eggs whenever the mother strongly desires it. . . . He called me stupid and said that when the butcher and his wife wanted a baby, they went to bed and acted indecently. I was shocked. . . . When I was twelve and a half we had a maid who told me scandalous tales of all kinds. . . . From shame I said nothing of this to Mamma; but when I asked her if sitting on a gentleman's knees could give one a baby, she explained everything to me as well as she could.

I learned at school where babies come from, and I felt it was something frightful. But how did they come into the world? Two of us formed a monstrous idea of it all; especially after meeting a man one dark winter morning, who showed his sexual parts and asked us if that were not something good to devour. We felt the deepest repugnance and were literally nauseated. Until I was twenty-one I thought babies were born through the navel.

A little girl asked me if I knew where babies come from. Finally she called me a goose and said they come from inside women and to make them it was necessary for women to do something quite disgusting with men. Then she went into details, but I was unable to believe that such things could be possible. Sleeping in my parents' room, I later heard take place what I had thought was impossible, and I was ashamed of my parents. All this made of me another being. I felt frightful moral suffering, regarding myself as a depraved creature because I was now aware of things.

It should be said that even clear instruction would not solve the problem; with the best will in the world on the part of parents and teachers, it is impossible to put the erotic experience into words and concepts; it is to be comprehended only in living it; any analysis, however serious, is bound to have a comic side and it will fail to express the truth. When, beginning with the poetic amours of the flowers and the nuptials of fishes, and proceeding by way of the chick, the kitten, and the kid, one has attained the level of the human species, one can very well elucidate in theory the mystery of generation—but the mystery of sexual pleasure and love remains complete.

How is one to explain the pleasure of a kiss or a caress to the passionless child? Family kisses are given and received, sometimes even on the lips; why should that contact of mucous membranes have, in certain cases, vertiginous effects? It is like describing colors to the blind. As long as there is no intuition of the excitement and the desire that give its meaning and its unity to the erotic function, the various elements that compose it will seem shocking and monstrous. In particular, the little girl is revolted when she realizes that she is virginal and closed, and that, to change her into a woman, it will be necessary for a man's sexual organ to penetrate her. Because exhibitionism is a widespread perversion, many young girls have seen the penis in a state of erection; in any case, they have seen the sex organs of male animals, and unfortunately that of the horse has often drawn their gaze; this may well be frightening. Fear of childbirth, fear of the male sex organ, fear of the "crises" that threaten married people, disgust for indecent behavior, mockery for actions that are without any significance—all this often leads the little girl to declare: "I will never get married." [5] That would be the surest defense against the pain, the foolishness, the obscenity. In vain the attempt to explain to her that one day neither defloration nor childbirth would seem so terrible to her, that millions of women have gone through with it all and have been none the worse for the experience. When a child has fear of some external occurrence, we rid her of it; but if we predict that later she will accept it quite naturally, then she feels dread of encountering herself—changed, astray—in the distant future. The metamorphosis of the caterpillar into chrysalis and then into butterfly makes the child uneasy: Is it still the same caterpillar after its long sleep? Will it recognize itself in this bright winged thing? I have known little girls whom the sight of a chrysalis plunged into a frightened reverie.

And yet the metamorphosis does take place. The little girl does not grasp its meaning, but she notices that something is changing subtly

---

[5] A passage from Yassu Gauclère's *Orange bleue* expresses this feeling: "Filled with repugnance, I prayed God to vouchsafe me a religious vocation in which I would escape the laws of maternity. And after having thought long upon the repugnant mysteries that in spite of myself I possessed within me, and fortified by such repulsion as by a sign from heaven, I decided that chastity was certainly my vocation." For one thing, the idea of perforation horrified her. "So that is what makes the wedding night terrible! This discovery overwhelmed me, adding to my earlier disgust the physical fear of this operation, which I fancied extremely painful. My terror would have been still greater if I had supposed that birth took place through the same channel, but having long known that children were born from the mother's belly, I believed that they separated off from it by a process of segmentation."

in her relations with the world and with her own body: she is aware
of contacts, tastes, odors, that were formerly indifferent to her;
strange pictures pass through her mind; she hardly recognizes herself
in mirrors; she feels "funny," things seem "funny." Such is little
Emily, whom Richard Hughes describes in *The Innocent Voyage:* [6]

> It was her own tenth birthday. . . . Emily, for coolness, sat up
> to her chin in water, and hundreds of infant fish were tickling with
> their inquisitive mouths every inch of her body, a sort of expres-
> sionless light kissing.
>
> Anyhow she had lately come to hate being touched—but this was
> abominable. At last, when she could stand it no longer, she clam-
> bered out and dressed.

Even the tranquil Tessa in Margaret Kennedy's *The Constant
Nymph* [7] felt this strange distraction:

> Suddenly she had become intensely miserable. She stared down
> into the darkness of the hall, cut in two by the moonlight which
> streamed in through the open door. She could not bear it. She
> jumped up with a little cry of exasperation. "Oh!" she exclaimed.
> "How I hate it all!" . . . She ran out to hide herself in the moun-
> tains, frightened and furious, pursued by a desolate foreboding
> which seemed to fill the quiet house. As she stumbled up toward
> the pass she kept murmuring to herself: "I wish I could die! I
> wish I was dead!"
>
> She knew that she did not mean this; she was not in the least
> anxious to die. But the violence of such a statement seemed to
> satisfy her. . . .

This disturbing moment is described at length in Carson McCullers's book *The Member of the Wedding:*

> This was the summer when Frankie was sick and tired of being
> Frankie. She hated herself, and had become a loafer and a big no-
> good who hung around the summer kitchen: dirty and greedy and
> mean and sad. Besides being too mean to live, she was a criminal.

---

[6] New York: Harper & Brothers; 1940.
[7] Garden City, N.Y.: Doubleday, Page & Co.; 1925.

. . . Then the spring of that year had been a long queer season. Things began to change and Frankie did not understand this change. . . . There was something about the green trees and the flowers of April that made Frankie sad. She did not know why she was sad, but because of this peculiar sadness, she began to realize that she ought to leave the town. . . . She ought to leave the town and go to some place far away. For the late spring, that year, was lazy and too sweet. The long afternoons flowered and lasted and the green sweetness sickened her. . . . Many things made Frankie suddenly wish to cry. Very early in the morning she would sometimes go out into the yard and stand for a long time looking at the sunrise sky. And it was as though a question came into her heart, and the sky did not answer. Things she had never noticed much before began to hurt her: home lights watched from the evening sidewalks, an unknown voice from an alley. She would stare at the lights and listen to the voice, and something inside her stiffened and waited. But the lights would darken, the voice fall silent, and though she waited, that was all. She was afraid of these things that made her suddenly wonder who she was, and what she was going to be in the world, and why she was standing at that minute, seeing a light, or listening, or staring up into the sky: alone. She was afraid, and there was a queer tightness in her chest.

. . . She went around town, and the things she saw and heard seemed to be left somehow unfinished, and there was the tightness in her that would not break. She would hurry to do something, but what she did was always wrong. . . . After the long twilights of this season, when Frankie had walked around the sidewalks of the town, a jazz sadness quivered her nerves and her heart stiffened and almost stopped.

What is happening in this time of unrest is that the child's body is becoming the body of a woman and is being made flesh. Except in cases of glandular insufficiency, where the subject remains fixed at an infantile stage, the crisis of puberty supervenes at about the age of twelve or thirteen.[8] This crisis begins much earlier in the girl than in the boy, and it brings much more important changes. The young girl meets it with uneasiness, with displeasure. When the breasts and the body hair are developing, a sentiment is born which sometimes be-

---

[8] The physiological processes concerned have been described in Book I, Ch. i.

comes pride but which is originally shame; all of a sudden the child becomes modest, she will not expose herself naked even to her sisters or her mother, she inspects herself with mingled astonishment and horror, and she views with anguish the enlargement of this firm and slightly painful core, appearing under each nipple, hitherto as inoffensive as the navel. She is disturbed to feel that she has a vulnerable spot; this sore spot is surely a slight matter in comparison with the pain of a burn or a toothache; but whether from injuries or sicknesses, pains were always something abnormal; whereas the young breast is normally the seat of one knows not what dull disaffection. Something is taking place—not an illness—which is implied in the very laws of existence, but still is of the nature of a struggle, a laceration. From infancy to puberty the girl has grown, of course, but she has never been conscious of her growth: day after day her body was always a present fact, definite, complete; but now she is "developing." The very word seems horrifying; vital phenomena are reassuring only when they have reached a state of equilibrium and have taken on the fully formed aspect of a fresh flower, a glossy animal; but in the development of her breasts the girl senses the ambiguity of the word *living*. She is neither gold nor diamond, but a strange form of matter, ever changing, indefinite, deep within which unclean alchemies are in course of elaboration. She is accustomed to a head of hair quietly rippling like a silken skein; but this new growth in her armpits and at her middle transforms her into a kind of animal or alga. Whether or not she is well forewarned, she feels in these changes the presentiment of a finality which sweeps her away from selfhood: she sees herself thrown into a vital cycle that overflows the course of her private existence, she divines a dependence that dooms her to man, to children, and to death. In themselves her breasts would seem to be a useless and obtrusive proliferation. Arms, legs, skin, muscles, even the rounded bottom on which she sits—up to now all these have had their obvious usefulness; only her sex, clearly a urinary organ, has seemed to be somewhat dubious, but secret and invisible to others. Under her sweater or blouse her breasts make their display, and this body which the girl has identified with herself she now apprehends as flesh. It becomes an object that others see and pay attention to. "For two years," a woman told me, "I wore a cape to hide my chest, I was so ashamed of it." And another: "I still recall the strange confusion I felt when a friend of the same age, but more developed than I was, bent down to pick up a ball and I saw through the opening of her bodice two breasts that were already full. I blushed on my own account at the sight of this body so near mine in age, on which mine would be modeled." Still another woman told me this: "At thirteen I was taking a walk, wearing a short dress and with my legs bare. A man, chuckling, made some comment on my large calves. Next day my mother had me wear stockings and lengthen my skirts, but I shall never forget the sudden shock I felt at being *seen naked.*" The young girl feels that her body is getting away from her, it is no longer the straightforward expression of her individuality; it becomes foreign to her; and at the same time she becomes for others a thing: on the street men follow her with their eyes and comment on her anatomy. She would like to be invisible; it frightens her to become flesh and to show her flesh.

This distaste is expressed by many young girls through the wish to be thin; they no longer want to eat, and if they are forced to, they have vomiting spells; they constantly watch their weight. Others become pathologically timid; for them it is torture to enter a drawing-room or even to go out in the street. From such beginnings psychoses may now and then develop. A typical case of this kind is described by Janet in *Les Obsessions et la psychasthénie,* under the name of Nadia:

Nadia, a young girl of wealthy and intelligent family, was stylish, artistic, and an excellent musician; but from infancy she was obstinate and irritable. "She demanded excessive affection from family and servants, but she was so exigent and dominating that she soon alienated people; when mockery was used as a means of reforming her, she acquired a sense of shame with reference to her body." Then, too, her need for affection made her wish to remain a spoiled child, made her fear growing up. . . . A precocious puberty added to her troubles: "since men like plump women, she would remain thin." Pubic hair and growing breasts added to her fears. From the age of eleven it seemed to her that everybody eyed her legs and feet. The appearance of menstruation drove her half mad, and believing that she was the only one in the world having the monstrosity of pubic hair, she labored up to the age of twenty to rid herself of this "savage decoration" by depilation. . . . She was so afraid of becoming plump—when she "would be ashamed to show herself"—that she tried all kinds of prayers and conjurations to prevent normal growth, for "no one would love her if she became fat." Finally she decided not to eat, so as "to remain a little girl"; and when she yielded to her mother's pleas to take some food, she knelt for hours, writing out vows and tearing them up. Her mother died when she was eighteen, and then she imposed on herself so severe a regime that she gnawed on her handkerchief and rolled on the floor from excess of hunger. She was pretty, but believed that her face was puffy and covered with pimples, asserting that her doctor, who could not see them, lacked understanding of her condition. She left her family and hid in a small apartment, never going out; there she lived most of the time in the dark, thinking that her appearance was so horrible that to be seen was intolerable.

Very often the parental attitude serves to inculcate in the girl a sense of shame regarding her appearance. One woman reported to Stekel [9] as follows:

> I suffered from a very keen sense of physical inferiority, which was accentuated by continual nagging at home. . . . Mother, in her excessive pride, wanted me to appear at my best, and she always found many faults which required "covering up" to point out to the dressmaker; for instance, drooping shoulders! Outstanding hips! Too flat in the back! Bust too prominent! And so on. I was particularly worried on account of the appearance of my limbs . . . and I was nagged on account of my gait. . . . There was some truth in every criticism . . . but sometimes I was so embarrassed, particularly during my "flapper" stage, that at times I was at a loss to know how to move about. If I met someone my first thought was: "If I could only hide my feet!"

This feeling of shame leads the girl to act awkwardly and to blush incessantly; this blushing increases her timidity and itself involves a phobia. Stekel speaks of one woman who "as a girl blushed so abnormally and violently that for a year she wore bandages over her face under pretense of having a toothache."

Sometimes the girl does not as yet feel ashamed of her body, in what may be called the stage of prepuberty, before the appearance

<hr />

[9] In *Frigidity in Woman* (New York: Liveright Publishing Corporation; 1943), Vol. II, pp. 71–2.

of the menses; she is proud of becoming a woman and watches the maturing of her bosom with satisfaction, padding her dress with handkerchiefs and taking pride in it before her elders; she does not yet grasp the significance of what is taking place in her. Her first menstruation reveals this meaning, and her feelings of shame appear. If they were already present, they are strengthened and exaggerated from this time on. All the evidence agrees in showing that whether the child has been forewarned or not, the event always seems to her repugnant and humiliating. Frequently her mother has neglected to inform her; it has been noted [1] that mothers more readily explain to their daughters the mysteries of pregnancy, childbirth, and even sexual relations than the facts of menstruation. They themselves seem to abhor this feminine burden, with a horror that reflects the ancient mystical fears of males and that the mothers pass on to their off-spring. When the girl finds the suspicious spots on her clothing, she believes she is a victim of a diarrhea or a fatal hemorrhage or some shameful disease. According to a study reported in 1896 by Havelock Ellis, among 125 pupils in an American high school, 36 knew ab-solutely nothing on the subject at the time of their first menses, 39 had some vague knowledge; more than half, that is, were in igno-rance of the matter. According to Helene Deutsch, things were much the same in 1946. Instances of attempted suicide are not unknown, and indeed it is natural enough for the young girl to be frightened as her life blood seems to be flowing away, perhaps from some injury to the internal organs. Even if wise instruction spares her too vivid anxiety, the girl feels ashamed, soiled; and she hastens to the wash-stand, she tries to cleanse or conceal her dirty linen. In *Aux yeux du souvenir*, Colette Audry describes at length a typical experience, here given in abbreviated form.

One night, when undressing, I thought I must be ill, but said nothing in the hope that it would be gone in the morning. . . . Four weeks later it happened again, more excessively, and I put my underwear in the basket for soiled clothes. My mother came to my room to explain things. I cannot recall the effect her words had on me, but when my sister Kiki looked in curiously, I was upset and cried to her to go away. I wanted my mother to punish her

---

[1] Cf. the works of Daly and Chadwick, cited by Helene Deutsch in *The Psychology of Women*, p. 152.

for coming in without knocking. My mother's air of calm satisfaction maddened me, and when she went out I was plunged into a brutal night.

Two memories came back to me all of a sudden: An old physician meeting us on the street remarked: "Your daughter is growing up, madame," and all at once I detested him without knowing why. A little later Kiki saw my mother putting a package of small napkins in a drawer and in reply to Kiki's question she said, with the lofty air of grown-ups who reveal a quarter of the truth while withholding three quarters: "They are for Colette, before long." Speechless, incapable of framing a single question, I detested my mother.

All through that night I turned and twisted in bed. It couldn't be possible. I would wake up, Mamma was wrong, it would pass and not return. . . . Next day, secretly changed and soiled, I must confront the others. I hated my sister, suddenly though unknowingly given such superiority over me. Then I began to hate men, who would never experience that, who knew about it. And I detested women, who took it so easily and who, if they knew about me, would gleefully think: "Now it is your turn." . . . I walked uneasily and dared not run. . . . It was over, and I began again to hope foolishly that it would not happen again. A month later I had to yield to the evidence. . . . Thenceforth there was in my memory a "before." The rest of my life would be no more than an "after."

Things happen in analogous fashion for most young girls. Many of them are horrified at the thought of revealing their secret to family and associates. A friend of mine, who had no mother and lived with her father and governess, told me she passed three months in fear and shame, hiding her spotted underwear, before her condition was discovered. Even peasant women, who supposedly would be hardened by their acquaintance with the cruder aspects of animal life, regard this curse with horror because menstruation still carries a taboo in the country. I knew a young farmer's wife who during a whole winter washed her linen secretly in an icy brook and even put on her chemise still wet in order to conceal her unspeakable secret. I could mention a hundred similar facts. Even avowal of this surprising misfortune does not mean deliverance. No doubt the mother who brutally slapped her daughter, saying: "Idiot, you are too young," is exceptional. But more than one will show bad humor; most fail to give the child adequate information, and the latter remains filled with anxiety concerning the new status that the first menstruation inaugurates. She wonders whether the future may not have further painful surprises in store for her; or she fancies that henceforth she can become pregnant through the mere presence or touch of a man and thus feels real terror in regard to males. Even if she is spared these pangs through intelligent explanations, she is not so easily given peace of mind. Previously the little girl, with a bit of self-deception, could consider herself as still a sexless being, or she could think of herself not at all; she might even dream of awakening changed into a man; but now, mothers and aunts whisper flatteringly: "She's a big girl now"; the matrons' group has won: she belongs to it. And so she is placed without recourse on the women's side. It may be that she is proud of it; she thinks that she has become a grown-up and that this will revolutionize her existence. For instance, Thyde Monnier says in *Moi:*

> Several of us had become "big girls" during vacation; others reached that estate while at school, and then one after another we went "to see the blood" in the courtyard water-closets where they sat enthroned like queens receiving their subjects.

But the little girl is soon undeceived, for she sees that she has gained no new privileges at all, life following its usual course. The only novelty is the untidy event that is repeated each month; there are children who weep for hours when they realize that they are condemned to this fate. And what strengthens their revolt still further is the knowledge that this shameful blemish is known also to men; they would prefer at least that their humiliating feminine condition might remain shrouded in mystery for males. But no; father, brothers, cousins, all the men know, and even joke about it sometimes. Here disgust at her too fleshly body arises or is exacerbated in the girl. And though the first surprise is over, the monthly annoyance is not similarly effaced; at each recurrence the girl feels again the same disgust at this flat and stagnant odor emanating from her—an odor of the swamp, of wilted violets—disgust at this blood, less red, more dubious, than that which flowed from her childish abrasions. Day and night she must think of making her changes, must keep watch of her underwear, her sheets, must solve a thousand little practical and repugnant problems. In economical families the sanitary napkins are washed each month and put back with the clean handkerchiefs; she must put these excreta from herself in the hands of whoever does the washing—laundress, maid, mother, or older sister. The pads sold by druggists under fancy names like "Modess" or "Edelweiss" are thrown away after use; but on trips, visits, or excursions it is not so easy to get rid of them, especially when disposal in the toilet is expressly forbidden. The young girl, when at her period, may feel horrified at the sanitary napkin and refuse to undress except in the dark, even before her sister. This annoying and cumbersome object may be displaced during violent exercise, and it is a worse humiliation than losing her panties on the street. Such a dreadful prospect sometimes gives rise to psychopathological states. By a kind of natural malice, certain illnesses and pains often begin only after the flow, which may at first pass unnoticed; young girls are often not yet regulated: they run the risk of being surprised while out for a walk, on the street, visiting friends; they run the risk—like Mme de Chevreuse [2]—of spotting their clothes or whatever they are seated on; some girls are kept in constant apprehension by such a possibility. The more repellent this feminine blemish seems to the young girl, the more watchful she must be against exposing herself to the dread humiliation of an accident or a sharing of her secret.

Dr. W. Liepmann, in *Jeunesse et sexualité*, obtained, among others, the following statements on this matter during the course of his research on juvenile sexuality:

At sixteen, when I was indisposed for the first time, I was very much frightened when I discovered it one morning. Truth to tell, I knew it had to happen; but I was so ashamed of it that I stayed in bed all the forenoon and to all questions I replied that I could not get up.

I was astounded when at twelve I menstruated for the first time. I was scared, and as my mother simply remarked that it would happen every month, I considered it a great indecency and refused to admit that it did not happen also to men.

---

[2] Mme de Chevreuse was disguised as a man during the period of civil wars called the *Fronde*, and was unmasked, after a long ride on horseback, by the spots of blood that were noticed on her saddle.

My mother had told me about menstruation, and I was much disappointed when, being indisposed, I joyfully ran to wake my mother saying: "Mamma, I have it!" and she only said: "And you wake me up for that!" Nevertheless I considered the event a real revolution in my life.

I was greatly frightened when, at my first menstruation, I saw that the flow did not stop after a few minutes. Yet I said nothing to anybody. I was just fifteen; moreover, I suffered very little pain from it. Only once I had such pains that I fainted and lay on the floor in my room for three hours. Still I said nothing about it.

It happened first when I was almost thirteen. I had talked it over with schoolmates and felt quite proud of becoming a grown-up. I explained importantly to my gymnastics teacher that today it was impossible for me to join the class because I was indisposed.

My mother did not warn me. In her case it began at nineteen, and in fear of being scolded for dirtying her underwear, she went out and buried the clothes in a field.

At eighteen I had my period for the first time, without any fore-knowledge. That night I suffered from a great flow and severe cramps. In the morning I went sobbing to my mother for advice. She only reprimanded me severely for soiling the bed, without further explanation. I wondered in anguish what crime I had committed. [This case came from a poor Berlin family.]

I already knew about it. I awaited the event impatiently, because I hoped that then my mother would tell me how babies were made. The great day arrived: but my mother said nothing. None the less I thought joyfully: "Now you too can make children: you are a woman."

This crisis occurs at a still tender age; the boy reaches adolescence only toward fifteen or sixteen; the girl changes to a woman at thirteen or fourteen.[3] But it is not from this difference in ages that the

---

[3] Certain statistics indicate that for the United States puberty is reached in boys at an average age of 14 years and 9 months, and in girls at 13 years and 9 months.—Tr.

essential difference in their experience comes; no more does it reside in the physiological phenomena that give the girl's experience its shocking force: puberty takes on a radically different significance in the two sexes because it does not portend the same future to both of them.

It is true enough that at the moment of puberty boys also feel their bodies as an embarrassment, but being proud of their manhood from an early age, they proudly project toward manhood the moment of their development; with pride they show one another the hair growing on their legs, a manly attribute; their sex organ is more than ever an object of comparison and challenge. Becoming adult is an intimidating metamorphosis: many adolescent boys are anguished at the thought of the exigent liberty to come; but they joyfully assume the dignity of being male.

The little girl, on the contrary, in order to change into a grown-up person, must be confined within the limits imposed upon her by her femininity. The boy sees with wonder in his growing hairiness vague promises of things to come: the girl stands abashed before the "brutal and prescribed drama" that decides her destiny. Just as the penis derives its privileged evaluation from the social context, so it is the social context that makes menstruation a curse. The one symbolizes manhood, the other femininity; and it is because femininity signifies alterity and inferiority that its manifestation is met with shame. The girl's life has always seemed to her to be determined by that vague essence to which the lack of a penis has not been enough to give a positive shape: but she becomes aware of herself in the red flow from between her thighs. If she has already accepted her condition, she greets the event with joy—"Now you are a woman." If she has always refused to accept her condition, the bloody verdict stuns her; most often she falters: the monthly uncleanness makes her inclined to feel disgust and fear. "So that is what is meant by the words 'to be a woman'!" The set fate that up to now weighed upon her indistinctly and from without is crouching in her belly; there is no escape; she feels she is caught.

In a sexually equalitarian society, woman would regard menstruation simply as her special way of reaching adult life; the human body in both men and women has other and more disagreeable needs to be taken care of, but they are easily adjusted to because, being common to all, they do not represent blemishes for anyone; the menses inspire horror in the adolescent girl because they throw her into an inferior and defective category. This sense of being declassed will weigh heavily upon her. She would retain her pride in her bleeding body if she did not lose her pride in being human. And if she succeeds in keeping this last, she will feel much less keenly the humiliation of her flesh; the young girl who opens up for herself the avenues of transcendence in athletic, social, intellectual, and mystical activities will not regard her sexual specialization as a mutilation, and she will easily rise above it. If the young girl at about this stage frequently develops a neurotic condition, it is because she feels defenseless before a dull fatality that condemns her to unimaginable trials; her femininity means in her eyes sickness and suffering and death, and she is obsessed with this fate.

An example that strikingly illustrates these anxieties is one of a patient described by Helene Deutsch [4] under the name of Molly. An abbreviated synopsis follows:

Molly was fourteen when she began to suffer from psychic disorders; she was the fourth child in a family of five siblings. Her father is described as extremely strict and narrow-minded. He criticized the appearance and behavior of his children at every meal. The mother was worried and unhappy; and every so often the parents were not on speaking terms; one brother ran away from home. The patient was a gifted youngster, a good tap dancer; but she was timid, took the family troubles seriously, and was afraid of boys. She took the greatest interest in her older sister's pregnancy, knew the details, and heard that women often die in childbirth. She took care of the baby for two months; when the sister left the house, there was a terrible scene and the mother fainted. Molly's thoughts were much concerned with separation, fainting, and death.

The mother reported that the patient had begun to menstruate several months previously. She acted rather embarrassed about it and told her mother: "That thing is here." She went with her sister to buy some menstrual pads; on meeting a man in the street, she hung her head. In general she acted "disgusted with herself." She never had pain during her periods, but tried to hide them from her mother, even when the latter saw stains on the sheets. She told her

---

[4] *The Psychology of Women*, Vol. I, pp. 175–8.

sister: "Anything might happen to me now. I might have a baby."
When told: "You have to live with a man for that to happen,"
she replied: "Well, I am living with two men—my father and your
husband."

The father did not permit his daughters to go out after dark on
account of soldiers being in the town and because one heard stories
of rape. These fears helped to give Molly the idea of men being
redoubtable creatures. From her first menstruation her anxiety
about becoming pregnant and dying in childbirth became so severe
that after a time she refused to leave her room, and now she sometimes stays in bed all day; if she goes out to play, the thought of
leaving the immediate vicinity gives her an attack of "shaking."
She lies awake listening to noises, and fears that someone is trying
to enter the house; she has fits of weeping, she daydreams, and she
writes poetry. She has eating spells, to keep her from fainting; she
fears to go in cars, cannot go to school or otherwise lead a normal
life.

An analogous case history is that of Nancy, which is not concerned
with the onset of menstruation but with the anxiety of the little girl
in regard to her insides.[5]

Toward the age of thirteen the little girl was on intimate terms
with her older sister, and she had been proud to be in her confidence when the sister was secretly engaged and then married: to
share the secret of a grown-up was to be accepted among the adults.
She lived for a time with her sister; but when the latter told her
that she was going "to buy" a baby, Nancy got jealous of her
brother-in-law and of the coming child: to be treated again as a
child to whom one made little mysteries of things was unbearable.
She began to experience internal troubles and wanted to be operated on for appendicitis. The operation was a success, but during
her stay at the hospital Nancy lived in a state of severe agitation;
she made violent scenes with a nurse she disliked; she tried to seduce
the doctor, said she "knew everything," and tried to get him to
spend the night with her—probably sure he would not agree, but
wishing he would accept her as a grown-up. She accused herself of
being to blame for the death of a little brother some years before.

---

[5] Ibid., pp. 59–71. Much abbreviated here.

And in particular she felt sure that they had not removed her appendix or had left a part of it inside her; her claim that she had swallowed a penny was probably intended to make sure an X-ray would be taken.

This desire for an operation—especially the removal of the appendix—is often met with at that age; young girls express in this way their fantasies of rape, pregnancy, and childbirth. They feel vague threats inside them, and they hope that the surgeon will save them from this unknown danger that lies in wait for them.

And it is not the appearance of her menses alone that announces her womanly destiny to the girl. Other dubious phenomena are appearing in her. So far her erotic feeling has been clitorid. It is difficult to find out whether masturbation is less common in the girl than in the boy; she engages in the practice during her first two years, perhaps even from the first months of her life; it would seem that she gives it up at about two, to take it up again later. The anatomical conformation of that stalk planted in the male flesh makes it more tempting to touch than is a hidden mucous area; but chance contacts—the child climbing ropes or trees, or riding a bicycle—the friction of clothes, touching in games, or even initiation by playmates, older children, or adults, may often make the girl aware of sensations which she endeavors to revive manually.

In any case the pleasure, when it is obtained, is an independent sensation: it has the light and innocent character of all childish diversions.[6] The girl hardly connects these private enjoyments with her womanly destiny; her sexual relations with boys, if any existed, were based essentially on curiosity. And now she feels herself shot through with confused emotions in which she does not recognize herself. The sensitivity of the erogenous zones is developing, and these are so numerous in woman that her whole body may be regarded as erogenous. This fact is revealed to her by family caresses, innocent kisses, the indifferent touch of a dressmaker, a doctor, or a hairdresser, by a friendly hand upon her hair or the nape of her neck; she comes to know, and often deliberately to seek, a deeper thrill in play relations, in wrestling with boys or girls. So it was with Gilbertine grappling with Proust in the Champs-Élysées; she felt strange languors in the

---

[6] Except, of course, in the many cases where the direct or indirect intervention of parents, or religious scruples, make it a sin.

arms of her partners as she danced under the unsuspicious eye of her mother. Then, too, even a well-protected maidenhood is exposed to more specific experiences; in "well-bred" circles silence is maintained with one accord concerning these regrettable incidents. But very often some of the caresses of family friends, uncles and cousins, not to mention grandfathers and fathers, are much less inoffensive than the mother imagines; a teacher or a priest or a doctor may have been bold, indiscreet. Accounts of such experiences will be found in Violette Leduc's *Asphyxie*, in S. de Tervagnes's *Haine maternelle*, in Yassu Gauclère's *Orange bleue*, and in Casanova's *Memoirs*. Stekel regards grandfathers, among others, as often very dangerous.

I was fifteen. The day before the funeral my grandfather came to stay at our house. Next morning, after my mother got up, he came and asked to get in bed to play with me; I rose at once without answering him. . . . I began then to be afraid of men.

Another young girl remembered having had a severe shock at eight or ten when her grandfather, an old man of seventy, tampered with her genitals, inserting his finger. The child felt severe pain but was afraid to speak of the incident. From that time she had great fear of everything sexual.[7]

Such incidents are usually unmentioned by the little girl because of shame. Besides, if she tells her parents, their reaction is often to scold her: "Don't say such things." "You are naughty." She keeps silent also regarding certain peculiar actions of strangers. A girl related the following to Dr. Liepmann:[8]

We had rented a basement room from a cobbler. When our landlord was alone, he often came to find me, took me in his arms, and held me in a long embrace, moving backward and forward. Moreover, his kiss was not superficial, as he put his tongue in my mouth. I detested him on account of this way of acting. But I never said a word about it, being very much scared.

In addition to enterprising playmates and perverse friends, there is that knee pressed against the little girl's in the moving-picture theater, that hand which at night in the train glides along her leg,

[7] Stekel: *Frigidity in Woman*.
[8] *Jeunesse et sexualité*.

those young fellows who titter as she goes by, those men who follow her on the street, those embraces, those furtive touches. She has little idea of the meaning of these adventures. There is often a strange jumble in the head of the fifteen-year-old, because her theoretical knowledge and these actual experiences do not blend. She has already felt all the heat of roused senses and desire, but she fancies—like Francis Jammes's Clara d'Ellébeuse—that a man's kiss would be enough to make her a mother. Clara had exact information concerning genital anatomy, but when her dancing partner embraced her, she blamed a migraine for the emotion she felt.

No doubt young girls are better informed now than formerly, but some psychiatrists hold that not a few adolescent girls are still unaware that the genitals have other than a urinary function.[9] At any rate, they see little relation between their sexual emotions and the existence of their genital organs, because there is no sign as clear as the masculine erection to indicate this correlation. Between their romantic daydreams of men—that is, love—and the crudity of certain facts known to them, there exists such a hiatus that they arrive at no synthesis of the two. Thyde Monnier[1] relates that she and some friends swore to ascertain how a man is constructed and report on it to the others:

> Having entered my father's room purposely without knocking, I reported as follows: "It looks like a leg-of-mutton sleeve; that is, it is like a roller and then comes something round." It was difficult to explain. I made a drawing, three in fact, and each took one away, hidden down her neck, and from time to time looked at it and burst out laughing, and then became dreamy. . . . How could innocent girls like us make any connection between this object and the sentimental songs, the pretty little romantic stories in which love, wholly composed of respect, timidity, sighs, and hand-kissings, is sublimated to the point of castration?

Nevertheless, through reading, conversation, sights seen and words overheard, the young girl attaches meaning to the disturbances of her flesh; she becomes all appeal, desire. In and through her excitements, thrills, moistenings, vague discomforts, her body takes on a new and

---

[9] Helene Deutsch: *The Psychology of Women*, Vol. I, p. 175.
[1] In *Moi*.

disquieting dimension. The young man openly welcomes his erotic tendencies because he joyfully assumes his virile estate; with him sexual desire is aggressive and grasping in nature; in it he sees affirmation of his subjectivity, his transcendence; he boasts of it among his fellows; his sex organ continues to serve as a double in which he takes pride; the urge that drives him toward the female is of the same kind as that which throws him against the world, and he recognizes himself in both. The sexual life of the little girl, on the contrary, has always been secret; when her eroticism changes and invades all her flesh, its mystery becomes agonizing: she suffers from the disturbance as from a shameful illness; it is not active: it is a state from which, even in imagination, she cannot find relief by any decision of her own. She does not dream of taking, shaping, violating: her part is to await, to want; she feels dependent; she scents danger in her alienated flesh.

For her diffuse hopefulness, her dream of happy passivity, reveals her body to her clearly as an object destined for another; she would fain realize the sexual experience only in its immanence; it is the *contact* of the hand, of the mouth, of another flesh that she wants and not the hand, mouth, and flesh of the other. She leaves in shadow the image of her partner, or she loses it in ideal mists. Yet, she cannot prevent his presence from haunting her. Her juvenile terrors and revulsions in regard to man have taken on a more equivocal character than formerly, and at the same time one more agonizing. Those feelings arose before from a profound divorce between her childish organism and her adult future; now they have their source in the very complexity the young girl senses in her flesh. She realizes that she is destined for possession, since she wants it; and she revolts against her desires. She simultaneously longs for and dreads the shameful passivity of the willing prey. The thought of appearing nude before a man overwhelms her with excitement; but she feels also that she will then be helpless under his gaze. The hand that lays hold on her, that touches her, has a yet more imperious urgency than have the eyes: her fright is still greater. But the most obvious and the most detestable symbol of physical possession is penetration by the sex organ of the male. The young girl hates to think that someone can perforate this body which she identifies with herself as one perforates leather, or can tear it as one tears cloth. But what the young girl objects to more than the injury and its accompanying pain is that the injury and the pain should be *inflicted*. A young girl once said to me: "It is horrible to think of being *impaled* by a man." It is not fear of the virile member that gives rise to horror of the male, but the fear is the corroboration and symbol of the horror; the idea of penetration acquires its obscene and humiliating sense within a more general frame, of which it is, in turn, an essential element.

The young girl's anxiety is expressed in tormenting nightmares and haunting phantoms: the very time she feels within herself an insidious willingness is just when the idea of rape in many cases becomes obsessing. This idea is manifested in dreams and in behavior through numerous more or less definite symbols. Before going to sleep the girl looks under the bed in fear of finding some robber with dubious intentions; she thinks she hears burglars in the house; an attacker comes in through the window, armed with a knife, to stab her. Men frighten her more or less. She begins to feel a certain disgust for her father; the smell of his tobacco becomes unbearable, she hates to go to the bathroom after him; even if she is still affectionate, this physical repulsion is often felt; she assumes an exasperated air, as if the child were already hostile to her father, as often happens with younger sisters. Psychiatrists say they often meet with a certain dream in their young patients: they fancy they have been violated by a man in the presence of an older woman who permits the act. Clearly they are in symbolical fashion asking their mother's permission to yield to their desires.

For one of the constraints that bear upon them most odiously is that of hypocrisy. The young girl is·dedicated to "purity" and "innocence" just when she is discovering in herself and all around her the mysterious stirrings of life and sex. She is supposed to be white as snow, transparent as crystal, she is dressed in filmy organdy, her room is papered in dainty colors, voices are lowered at her approach, she is forbidden salacious books. Now, there is not a "good little girl" who does not indulge in "abominable" thoughts and desires. She strives to conceal them even from her closest friend, even from herself; she wants to live and to think only according to rules; her distrust of herself gives her a sly, unhappy, sickly air; and later on, nothing will be more difficult for her than to overcome these inhibitions. And, despite all her repressions, she feels crushed under the weight of unspeakable transgressions. She undergoes her metamorphosis into a woman not only in shame but in remorse.

It is understandable that the awkward age should be for the girl a period of painful disturbance. She does not want to remain a child. But the adult world seems frightening or boring. As Colette Audry says:

> So I wanted to grow up, but I never thought seriously of leading a life such as I saw adults leading . . . and thus the wish to grow up without ever assuming adult status was still kept alive within me, never would I make one with parents, housekeepers, home-makers, and heads of families.

The young girl would rid herself of her mother's yoke, but she feels also a keen need of her protection. What makes this refuge necessary is the series of transgressions that weighs on her conscience, such as solitary practices, dubious friendships, and improper reading. The following letter written by a girl of fifteen and cited by Helene Deutsch [2] is characteristic:

> Mother wants me to wear a long dress at the big dance party at the Ws'—my first long dress. She is surprised that I don't want to. I begged her to let me wear my short pink dress for the last time. I am so afraid. The long dress makes me feel as if Mummy were going on a long trip and I did not know when she would return. Isn't that silly? And sometimes she looks at me as though I were still a little girl. Ah, if she knew! She would tie my hands to the bed, and despise me.

In Stekel's *Frigidity in Woman* [3] will be found a remarkable account of a feminine childhood. In it a Viennese girl (*Backfisch*) presents a detailed confession at the age of twenty-one. It constitutes a concrete synthesis of all the phenomena we have studied separately. A condensed version follows:

> "At the age of five I chose for my playmate Richard, a boy of six or seven. . . . For a long time I had wanted to know how one can tell whether a child is a girl or a boy. I was told: by the earrings . . . or by the nose. This seemed to satisfy me, though I had a feeling that they were keeping something from me. Suddenly Rich-

---

[2] *The Psychology of Women*, Vol. I, p. 121.
[3] Vol. I, p. 176.

ard expressed a desire to urinate. . . . Then the thought came to me of lending him my chamber-pot. . . . When I saw his organ, which was something entirely new to me, I went into highest rap-tures: 'What have you there? My, isn't that nice! I'd like to have something like that, too.' Whereupon I took hold of the membrum and held it enthusiastically. . . . My great-aunt's cough awoke us . . . and from that day on our doings and games were carefully watched."

At nine she played "marriage" and "doctor" with two other boys of eight and ten; they touched her parts and one day one of the boys touched her with his organ, saying that her parents had done just the same thing when they got married. "This aroused my in-dignation: 'Oh, no! They never did such a nasty thing!' " She kept up these games for a long time in a strong sexual friendship with the two boys. One day her aunt caught her and there was a fright-ful scene with threats to put her in the reformatory. She was pre-vented from seeing Arthur, whom she preferred, and she suffered a good deal from it; her work went badly, her writing was de-formed, and she became cross-eyed. She started another intimacy with Walter and Franz. "Walter became the goal of all thoughts and feeling. I permitted him very submissively to reach under my dress while I sat or stood in front of him at the table, pretending to be busy with a writing exercise; whenever my mother . . . opened the door, he withdrew his hand on the instant; I, of course, was busy writing. . . . In the course of time we also behaved as hus-band and wife; but I never allowed him to stay long; whenever he thought he was inside me, I tore myself away saying that somebody was coming. . . . I did not reflect that this was 'sinful.' . . ."

"My childhood boy friendships were now over. All I had left were girl friends. I attached myself to Emmy, a highly refined, well-educated girl. One Christmas we exchanged gilded heart-shaped lockets with our initials engraved on them—we were, I believe, about twelve years of age at the time—and we looked upon this as a token of 'engagement'; we swore eternal faithfulness 'until death do us part.' I owe to Emmy a goodly part of my training. She taught me also a few things regarding sexual matters. As far back as during my fifth grade at school I began seriously to doubt the veracity of the stork story. I thought that children developed within the body and that the abdomen must be cut open before a child can be brought out. She filled me with particular horror of self-abuse. In school the Gospels contributed a share towards opening our eyes with regard to certain sexual matters. For instance, when Mary came to Elizabeth, the child is said to have 'leaped in her womb'; and we read other similarly remarkable Bible passages. We underscored these words; and when this was discovered the whole class barely escaped a 'black mark' in deportment. My girl friend told me also about the 'ninth month reminder' to which there is a reference in Schiller's *Die Räuber*. . . . Emmy's father moved from our locality and I was again alone. We corresponded, using for the purpose a cryptic alphabet which we had devised between ourselves; but I was lonesome and finally I attached myself to Hedl, a Jewish girl. Once Emmy caught me leaving school in Hedl's company; she created a scene on account of her jealousy. . . . I kept up my friendship with Hedl until I entered the commercial school. We became close friends. We both dreamed of becoming sisters-in-law sometime, because I was fond of one of her brothers. He was a student. Whenever he spoke to me I became so confused that I gave him an irrelevant answer. At dusk we sat in the music room, huddled together on the little divan, and often tears rolled down my cheek for no particular reason as he played the piano.

"Before I befriended Hedl, I went to school for a number of weeks with a certain girl, Ella, the daughter of poor people. Once she caught her parents in a 'tête-à-tête.' The creaking of the bed had awakened her. . . . She came and told me that her father had crawled on top of her mother, and that the mother had cried out terribly; and then the father said to her mother: 'Go quickly and wash so that nothing will happen!' After this I was angry at her father and avoided him on the street, while for her mother I felt the greatest sympathy. (He must have hurt her terribly if she cried out so!)

"Again with another girl I discussed the possible length of the male membrum; I had heard that it was 12 to 15 cm long. During the fancy-work period (at school) we took the tape-measure and indicated the stated length on our stomachs, naturally reaching to the navel. This horrified us; if we should ever marry we would be literally impaled."

She saw a male dog excited by the proximity of a female, and felt strange stirrings inside herself. "If I saw a horse urinate in the street, my eyes were always glued to the wet spot in the road; I believe the length of time (urinating) is what always impressed me." She watched flies in copulation and in the country domesticated animals doing the same.

"At twelve I suffered a severe attack of tonsillitis. A friendly physician was called in. He seated himself on my bed and presently he stuck his hand under the covers, almost touching me on the genitalia. I exclaimed: 'Don't be so rude!' My mother hurried in; the doctor was much embarrassed. He declared I was a horrid monkey, saying he merely wanted to pinch me on the calf. I was compelled to ask his forgiveness. . . . When I finally began to menstruate and my father came across the blood-stained cloths on one occasion, there was a terrible scene. How did it happen that he, so clean a man, had to live among such dirty females? . . . I felt the injustice of being put in the wrong on account of my menstruation."

At fifteen she communicated with another girl in shorthand "so that no one else could decipher our missives. There was much to report about conquests. She copied for me a vast number of verses from the walls of lavatories; I took particular notice of one. It seemed to me that love, which ranged so high in my fantasy, was being dragged in the mud by it. The verse read: 'What is love's highest aim? Four buttocks on a stem.' I decided I would never get into that situation; a man who loves a young girl would be unable to ask such a thing of her.

"At fifteen and a half I had a new brother. I was tremendously jealous, for I had always been the only child in the family. My friend reminded me to observe 'how the baby boy was constructed,' but with the best intentions I was unable to give her the desired information . . . I could not look there. At about this time another girl described to me a bridal night scene. . . . I think that then I made up my mind to marry after all, for I was very curious; only the 'panting like a horse,' as mentioned in the description, offended my æsthetic sense. . . . Which one of us girls would not have gladly married then, to undress before the beloved husband and be carried to bed in his arms? It seemed so thrilling!"

It may be objected—although the case is normal and not pathological—that this child was exceptionally "perverse"; but in truth she was only watched less closely than others. If the curiosities and the desires of "well-bred" girls are not expressed in acts, they none the less exist in the form of fantasies and games. I once knew a young girl who was very pious and disconcertingly innocent—since become a thorough woman, steeped in maternity and devotion—who, quivering with excitement, said one night to an older sister: "How marvelous it must be to undress before a man! Make believe you are my husband"; and she undressed herself, trembling with emotion. No education can prevent the little girl from becoming conscious of her body and from musing on her destiny; at most, strict repression can be imposed, which will later weigh heavily upon her sexual life. What is desirable is that she should be taught, on the contrary, to accept herself without being self-satisfied and without shame.

We are now acquainted with the dramatic conflict that harrows the adolescent girl at puberty: she cannot become "grown-up" without accepting her femininity; and she knows already that her sex condemns her to a mutilated and fixed existence, which she faces at this time under the form of an impure sickness and a vague guiltiness. Her inferiority was sensed at first merely as a deprivation; but the lack of a penis has now become defilement and transgression. So she goes onward toward the future, wounded, shameful, culpable.

CHAPTER XIII

The Young Girl

THROUGHOUT her childhood the little girl suffered bullying and curtailment of activity; but none the less she felt herself to be an autonomous individual. In her relations with family and friends, in her schoolwork and her games, she seemed at the time a transcendent being: her future passivity was only a dream. With puberty, the future not only approaches: it takes residence in her body; it assumes the most concrete reality. It retains the fateful quality it has always had. While the adolescent boy makes his way actively toward adulthood, the young girl awaits the opening of this new, unforeseeable period, the plot of which henceforth is woven and toward which time is bearing her. She is already free of her childish past, and the present seems but a time of transition; it contains no valid aims, only occupations. Her youth is consumed in waiting, more or less disguised. She is awaiting Man.

The adolescent boy, too, undoubtedly dreams of woman, he longs for her; but she will never be more than an element in his life: she does not sum up his destiny. But the girl, since childhood and whether she intends to stay within or go beyond the bounds of femininity, has looked to the male for fulfillment and escape; he wears the shining face of Perseus or St. George; he is the liberator; he is rich and powerful, he holds the keys to happiness, he is Prince Charming. She thinks that under his caresses she will feel herself borne along by the vast current of Life, as when she reposed in the maternal bosom; yielding herself to his gentle authority, she will find again the same security as in her father's arms: the magic of embraces and glances will petrify her once more into an idol. She has always been convinced of male superiority; this male prestige is not a childish mirage; it has economic and social foundations; men are surely masters of the world. Everything tells the young girl that it is for her best interests to become their vassal: her parents urge her to it; the father is proud of his daughter's success, the mother sees a prosperous future in it; friends envy and admire the one who gets the most masculine attention; in American colleges the social standing of a co-ed is measured by the number of "dates" she has.

Marriage is not only an honorable career and one less tiring than many others: it alone permits a woman to keep her social dignity intact and at the same time to find sexual fulfillment as loved one and mother. It is thus that her entourage envisages her future, as does she herself. There is unanimous agreement that getting a husband—or in some cases a "protector"—is for her the most important of undertakings. In her eyes man incarnates the Other, as she does for the man; but this *Other* seems to her to be on the plane of the essential, and with reference to him she sees herself as the inessential. She will free herself from the parental home, from her mother's hold, she will open up her future, not by active conquest but by delivering herself up, passive and docile, into the hands of a new master.

It has been often asserted that if she resigns herself to such submission, it means that she is inferior to boys materially and morally and is incapable of rivalry with them: abandoning a hopeless contest, she leaves to a member of the superior caste the task of assuring her happiness. But the fact is that her resignation comes not from any predetermined inferiority: on the contrary, it is that which gives rise to all her insufficiencies; that resignation has its source in the adolescent girl's past, in the society around her, and particularly in the future assigned to her.

True enough, puberty transforms the young girl's body. It is more fragile than formerly; the feminine organs are vulnerable, and delicate in their functioning; her strange and bothersome breasts are a burden, they remind her of their presence by quivering painfully during violent exercise. For the future, her muscular power, endurance, and agility will be inferior to those qualities in a man. The imbalance of her hormones creates nervous and vasomotor instability. Menstruation is painful: headaches, overfatigue, abdominal pains, make normal activities distressing or impossible; psychic difficulties often appear; nervous and irritable, a woman may be temporarily in a state of semi-lunacy; the control of the nerve centers over the peripheral and sympathetic systems is no longer assured; circulatory difficulties and certain autointoxications make the body seem a screen interposed between the woman and the world, a fiery mist that settles over her, stifling her and cutting her off. Apprehended through this complaining and passive flesh, the whole universe seems a burden too heavy to bear. Overburdened, submerged, she becomes a stranger to herself because she is a stranger to the rest of the world. Syntheses break down, moments of time are no longer connected, other people are recognized but absent-mindedly; and if reasoning and logic remain intact, as in melancholia, they are put to the service of emotional manifestations arising from a state of organic disorder. These facts are of great importance; but what gives them weight is woman's attitude toward them.

At about thirteen is the time when boys go through a real apprenticeship in violence, when their aggressiveness is developed, their will to power, their love for competition; and it is at just this time that the girl gives up rough games. Sports are still open to her; but sport, which means specialization and obedience to artificial rules, is by no means the equivalent of a free and habitual resort to force; it is a marginal feature of life; it does not provide information on the world and the self as intimately as does a free fight, an unpremeditated climb. The sportswoman never knows the conquering pride of a boy who pins his opponent's shoulders to the ground. Moreover, in many countries most girls have no urge toward sports; since scuffles and climbing are forbidden, their bodies have to suffer things only in a passive manner; much more definitely than when younger, they must give up *emerging* beyond what is given and asserting themselves *above* other people: they are forbidden to explore, to venture, to extend the limits of the possible. In particular, the *competitive* attitude, most important to young men, is almost unknown to them. To be sure, women make comparisons among themselves, but competition, challenge, is something quite different from these passive comparisons: two free beings confront each other as having on the world a hold that they propose to enlarge; to climb higher than a playmate, to force an arm to yield and bend, is to assert one's sovereignty over the world in general. Such masterful behavior is not for girls, especially when it involves violence.

In the adult world, no doubt, brute force plays no great part in normal times; but nevertheless it haunts that world; many kinds of masculine behavior spring from a root of possible violence: on every street corner squabbles threaten; usually they flicker out; but for a man to feel in his fists his will to self-affirmation is enough to reassure him of his sovereignty. Against any insult, any attempt to reduce him to the status of object, the male has recourse to his fists, to exposure of himself to blows: he does not let himself be transcended by others, he is himself at the heart of his subjectivity. Violence is the authentic proof of each one's loyalty to himself, to his passions, to his own will; radically to deny this will is to deny oneself any objective truth, it is to wall oneself up in an abstract subjectivity; anger or revolt that does not get into the muscles remains a figment of the imagination. It is a profound frustration not to be able to register one's feelings upon the face of the world.

In the United States it is quite impossible for a Negro, in the South, to use violence against the whites; this rule is the key to the mysterious "black soul"; the way the Negro feels in the white world, the behavior by which he adjusts himself to it, the compensations he seeks, his whole way of feeling and acting are to be explained on the basis of the passivity to which he is condemned. In France during the occupation those who had made up their minds not to resort to violence against the forces of occupation even under provocation (whether through selfish prudence or because they had imperative work to do) felt a profound alteration in their status in the world: the caprice of others determined whether they were to be changed into objects; their subjectivity no longer had means of concrete expression, being only a secondary phenomenon.

In the same way, the universe does not wear a similar aspect for the adolescent boy who is permitted to give imperious notice of his existence and for the adolescent girl whose sentiments have no immediate effectiveness. The one constantly questions the world; he can, at any moment, rise up against whatever is; and he therefore feels that when he accepts it, he actively ratifies it. The other simply submits; the world is defined without reference to her, and its aspect is immutable as far as she is concerned. This lack of physical power leads to a more general timidity: she has no faith in a force she has not experienced in her body; she does not dare to be enterprising, to revolt, to invent; doomed to docility, to resignation, she can take in society only a place already made for her. She regards the existing state of affairs as something fixed.

One woman told me that throughout her youth she had fiercely denied her physical weakness though she knew better; to have admitted it would have been to lose zest and courage for undertaking anything whatever in the intellectual and political fields. I knew a young girl, brought up in boyish fashion and exceptionally vigorous, who thought she was as strong as a man; though she was very pretty and though she was regularly afflicted with painful menstruation, she was quite unconscious of her femininity; she had the bluntness, the exuberant vitality, and the initiative of a boy; and she had a boy's hardihood, not hesitating to intervene with her fists in the street if she saw a child or a woman being molested. One or two unpleasant experiences, however, showed her that brute force is on the side of the males. When she had become aware of how weak she really was, she lost most of her assurance; this began her evolution toward femininity, in which she assumed her passivity and accepted dependency. Not to have confidence in one's body is to lose confidence in oneself. One needs only to see the importance young men place in their muscles to understand that every subject regards his body as his objective expression.

The young man's erotic impulses only go to confirm his pride in his body: therein he sees the sign of his transcendence and his power. The young girl may succeed in accepting the fact of her desires, but usually they retain a cast of shame. Her whole body is a source of embarrassment. The mistrust that as a small child she felt in regard to her "insides" helps to give to the menstrual crisis the dubious character that renders it odious to her. It is because of the psychic state induced by her menstrual slavery that it constitutes a heavy handicap. The threat which hangs over the young girl at certain periods may seem so intolerable that she will give up excursions and other pleasures for fear of her disgrace becoming known. The horror this inspires has repercussions throughout her organic structure and intensifies its disturbed and painful condition. We have noted that one of the characteristics of female psychology is the close relation between the endocrine secretions and nervous regulation: there is a reciprocal action. The body of a woman—particularly that of a young girl—is a "hysterical" body, in the sense that there is, so to speak, no distance between the psychic life and its physiological realization. The disorders of puberty are made worse by the upsetting effect their discovery has upon the young girl. Because her body seems suspect to her, and because she views it with alarm, it seems to her to be sick: it is sick. We have seen that in fact this body is delicate, and there are genuinely organic disorders arising in it; but gynecologists agree that nine tenths of their patients are imaginary invalids; that is, either

their illnesses have no physiological reality at all or the organic disorder is itself brought on by a psychic state: it is psychosomatic. It
is in great part the anxiety of being a woman that devastates the
feminine body.

It is clear that if the biological condition of woman does constitute
a handicap, it is because of her general situation. Nervous and vasomotor instability, unless pathological, keeps her from no profession:
among males, too, there is great variety of temperament.[1] A monthly
indisposition of a day or two, while painful, is no more of an obstacle; indeed, many women accommodate themselves to it, and in particular those to whom the monthly "curse" might well be most bothersome: athletes, travelers, dancers, women who do heavy work. Most
professions call for no greater energy than woman can offer. And in
sports the end in view is not success independent of physical equipment; it is rather the attainment of perfection within the limitations
of each physical type: the featherweight boxing champion is as much
a champion as is the heavyweight; the woman skiing champion is not
the inferior of the faster male champion: they belong to two different
classes. It is precisely the female athletes who, being positively interested in their own game, feel themselves least handicapped in comparison with the male. It remains true that her physical weakness does
not permit woman to learn the lessons of violence; but if she could
assert herself through her body and face the world in some other
fashion, this deficiency would be easily compensated for. Let her
swim, climb mountain peaks, pilot an airplane, battle against the
elements, take risks, go out for adventure, and she will not feel before the world that timidity which I have referred to. It is in a total
situation which leaves her few outlets that her peculiarities take on
their importance—not directly, but by confirming the inferiority complex set up in childhood.

This complex, further, will weigh heavily upon her intellectual accomplishments. It has often been remarked that after puberty the girl
loses ground in the intellectual and artistic domains. There are many
reasons for this. One of the commonest is that the adolescent girl is
not given the encouragement accorded to her brothers—quite the contrary. She is expected to be *also* a *woman*, and she has to add the

---

[1] Cf. W. H. Sheldon's *The Varieties of Temperament* (Harper & Brothers,
1942).—TR.

duties of her professional study to those implied in her femininity.
The woman director of a professional school offers the following remarks on this subject:

> The young girl becomes suddenly a person who earns her living
> by having a job. She has new desires which no longer have any-
> thing to do with her family. It happens often enough that she has
> to work rather hard. . . . She gets home at night tired to death,
> her head feeling as if stuffed with the events of the day. . . . How
> will she be greeted? Her mother sends her on an errand. There is
> housework left for her to finish, and she has still to take care of her
> own wardrobe. Impossible to escape all the private thoughts that
> continue to preoccupy her. She feels unhappy, compares her situa-
> tion with that of her brother who has no home duties, and she feels
> rebellious.[2]

The housekeeping chores and common drudgery, which mothers do
not hesitate to impose on schoolgirls or apprentices, overwork them
in the end. During the war I saw students in my classes at Sèvres
overburdened with family tasks superimposed upon their schoolwork:
one came down with Pott's disease, another with meningitis. The
mother, as we shall see, is secretly hostile to her daughter's liberation,
and she takes to bullying her more or less deliberately; but the boy's
effort to become a man is respected, and he is granted much liberty.
The girl is required to stay at home, her comings and goings are
watched: she is in no way encouraged to take charge of her own
amusements and pleasures. It is unusual to see women organize by
themselves a long hike or a trip on foot or by bicycle, or devote themselves to games such as billiards or bowling.

Beyond the lack of initiative that is due to women's education,
custom makes independence difficult for them. If they roam the
streets, they are stared at and accosted. I know young girls who, without being at all timid, find no enjoyment in taking walks alone in
Paris because, importuned incessantly, they must be always on the
alert, which spoils their pleasure. If girl students run in gay groups
through the streets, as boys do, they make a spectacle of themselves;
to walk with long strides, sing, talk, or laugh loudly, or eat an apple,
is to give provocation; those who do will be insulted or followed or

---

[2] Cited by Liepmann in *Jeunesse et sexualité*.

spoken to. Careless gaiety is in itself bad deportment; the self-control that is imposed on women and becomes second nature in "the well-bred young girl" kills spontaneity; her lively exuberance is beaten down. The result is tension and ennui.

This ennui is catching: young girls quickly tire of one another; they do not band together in their prison for mutual benefit; and this is one of the reasons why the company of boys is necessary to them. This incapacity to be self-sufficient engenders a timidity that extends over their entire lives and is marked even in their work. They believe that outstanding success is reserved for men; they are afraid to aim too high. We have seen that little girls of fourteen, comparing themselves with boys, declared that "the boys are better." This is a debilitating conviction. It leads to laziness and mediocrity. A young girl, who had no special deference for the stronger sex, was reproaching a man for his cowardice; it was remarked that she herself was a coward. "Oh, a woman, that's different!" declared she, complacently.

The fundamental reason for such defeatism is that the adolescent girl does not think herself responsible for her future; she sees no use in demanding much of herself since her lot in the end will not depend on her own efforts. Far from consigning herself to man because she recognizes her inferiority, it is because she is thus consigned to him that, accepting the idea of her inferiority, she establishes its truth.

And, actually, it is not by increasing her worth as a human being that she will gain value in men's eyes; it is rather by modeling herself upon their dreams. When still inexperienced, she is not always aware of this fact. She may be as aggressive as the boys; she may try to make their conquest with a rough authority, a proud frankness; but this attitude almost surely dooms her to failure. All girls, from the most servile to the haughtiest, learn in time that to please they must abdicate. Their mothers enjoin upon them to treat the boys no longer as comrades, not to make advances, to take a passive role. If they wish to start a friendship or a flirtation, they must carefully avoid seeming to take the initiative in it; men do not like *garçons manqués*, or bluestockings, or brainy women; too much daring, culture, or intelligence, too much character, will frighten them. In most novels, as George Eliot remarks, it is the blonde and silly heroine who is in the end victorious over the more mannish brunette; and in *The Mill on the Floss* Maggie tries in vain to reverse the roles; but she finally dies and the blonde Lucy marries Stephen. In *The Last of the Mo-*

hicans the vapid Alice gains the hero's heart, not the valiant Clara; in *Little Women* the likable Jo is only a childhood playmate for Laurie: his love is reserved for the insipid Amy and her curls.

To be feminine is to appear weak, futile, docile. The young girl is supposed not only to deck herself out, to make herself ready, but also to repress her spontaneity and replace it with the studied grace and charm taught her by her elders. Any self-assertion will diminish her femininity and her attractiveness. The young man's journey into existence is made relatively easy by the fact that there is no contradiction between his vocation as human being and as male; and this advantage is indicated even in childhood. Through self-assertion in independence and liberty, he acquires his social value and concurrently his prestige as male: the ambitious man, like Balzac's Rastignac, aims at wealth, celebrity, and women in one and the same enterprise; one of the stereotypes which stimulate his effort is that of the powerful and famous man whom women adore.

But for the young woman, on the contrary, there is a contradiction between her status as a real human being and her vocation as a female. And just here is to be found the reason why adolescence is for a woman so difficult and decisive a moment. Up to this time she has been an autonomous individual: now she must renounce her sovereignty. Not only is she torn, like her brothers, though more painfully, between the past and the future, but in addition a conflict breaks out between her original claim to be subject, active, free, and, on the other hand, her erotic urges and the social pressure to accept herself as passive object. Her spontaneous tendency is to regard herself as the essential: how can she make up her mind to become the inessential? But if I can accomplish my destiny only as the *Other*, how shall I give up my Ego? Such is the painful dilemma with which the woman-to-be must struggle. Oscillating between desire and disgust, between hope and fear, declining what she calls for, she lingers in suspense between the time of childish independence and that of womanly submission. It is this uncertainty that, as she emerges from the awkward age, gives her the sharp savor of a fruit still green.

The young girl reacts variably to this situation according to her earlier tendencies. The "little mother," the matron-to-be, can easily resign herself to her metamorphosis; but she may have taken on, as "little mother," a taste for authority which leads her to rebel against the masculine yoke: she is ready to found a matriarchate but not to become an erotic object and a servant. This will frequently be the case with older sisters who have taken on heavy responsibilities while still quite young. The *garçon manqué*, on discovering that she is a woman, sometimes has a burning sense of deception, which may lead straight to homosexuality; however, what she sought in independence and violence was possession of the world: she cannot as a rule wish to give up the power of her femininity, the experience of maternity, a whole area of her destiny. Usually, though with some resistance, the young girl accepts her femininity; she has already known the charm of passivity, at the stage of childish coquetry, with her father and in her erotic reveries; she sees its power; vanity is soon mingled with the shame her flesh inspires. That hand, that look which stirred her feelings, was an appeal, a prayer; her body seems endowed with magic virtues; it is a treasure, a weapon; she is proud of it. Her coquetry, often lost during the free years of childhood, is revived again. She tries different make-ups, ways of doing her hair; instead of hiding her breasts, she massages them to make them grow, she studies her smile in the mirror.

The connection between sex feeling and allurement is so close that in all cases where erotic sensitivity is not awakened, no desire to please is observed in the subject. Experiment has shown that patients suffering from thyroid deficiency—and hence apathetic and disagreeable—can be transformed by the injection of glandular extracts: they begin to smile, they become gay, full of airs and graces. Psychologists imbued with a materialistic philosophy have boldly declared coquetry to be an "instinct" secreted by the thyroid gland; but this doubtful explanation is no more valid here than for early childhood. The fact is that in all cases of organic deficiency, such as anemia, the body is borne like a burden; a hostile stranger, it neither hopes nor promises anything. When it recovers its balance and its vitality, the subject at once recognizes it as his and, through it, seeks transcendence toward others.

For the young girl, erotic transcendence consists in becoming prey in order to gain her ends. She becomes an object, and she sees herself as object; she discovers this new aspect of her being with surprise: it seems to her that she has been doubled; instead of coinciding exactly with herself, she now begins to exist *outside*. Thus in Rosamond Lehmann's *Invitation to the Waltz* [3] we see Olivia discover in the

---

[3] New York: Henry Holt & Co.; 1932.

mirror an unknown figure: it is she-as-object suddenly confronting herself. This gives rise to a transitory but bewildering emotion:

Nowadays a peculiar emotion accompanied the moment of looking into the mirror: fitfully, rarely a stranger might emerge: a new self.

It had happened two or three times already. . . . She looked in the glass and saw herself. . . . Well, what was it? . . . But this was something else. This was a mysterious face; both dark and glowing: hair tumbling down, pushed back and upwards, as if in currents of fierce energy. Was it the frock that did it? Her body seemed to assemble itself harmoniously within it, to become centralised, to expand, both static and fluid; alive. It was the portrait of a young girl in pink. All the room's reflected objects seemed to frame, to present her, whispering: Here are You. . . .

What astounds Olivia is the promise she thinks she reads in that image in which she recognizes her childhood dreams and which is herself. But the young girl loves also in its carnal actuality this body which enchants her like that of another. She gives herself caresses, she kisses her rounded shoulder, the bend of her arm, she gazes at her chest, her legs; solitary pleasure becomes the pretext for daydreaming, in it she seeks an affectionate possession of herself. In the adolescent there is opposition between love of herself and the erotic urge that sends her toward the object to be possessed: her narcissism, as a rule, disappears at the time of sexual maturity. Instead of woman's being a passive object for her lover as for herself, there is a basic confusion in her eroticism. In a complex impulse, she aspires to the glorification of her body through the homage of the males to whom this body is destined; and it would be oversimplification to say that she wants to be beautiful in order to charm, or that she seeks to charm in order to gain assurance of her beauty: in the solitude of her boudoir, in the drawing-rooms where she tries to attract attention, she does not distinguish the desire of the man from the love of her own ego. This confusion is manifest in Marie Bashkirtsev. We have seen already that a late weaning disposed her more than other children to wish to be considered and given value by others; from the age of five until the end of adolescence she devoted her love entirely to her image; she madly admired her hands, her face, her gracefulness. She writes:

"I am my own heroine." She wants to become a singer so as to be *gazed at* by a dazzled public and so as to *scan them in return* with a proud look; but this "autism" is expressed in romantic dreams; from the age of twelve she is in love: that is, she wants to be loved, and in the adoration she wishes to inspire she seeks only the confirmation of the love she gives herself. She dreams that the Duke of H., whom she loves without ever having spoken to him, throws himself at her feet: "You will be dazzled by my splendor and you will love me. . . . You are worthy of only such a woman as I hope to be." We find this same ambivalence again in the Natasha of *War and Peace*:

> That morning she had returned to her favorite mood—love of, and delight in, herself. "How charming that Natasha is!" she said again, speaking as some third, collective, male person. "Pretty, a good voice, young, and in nobody's way if only they leave her in peace."

Katherine Mansfield has also described, in *Prelude*,[4] a case in which narcissism and the romantic desire for a woman's destiny are closely mingled:

> In the dining-room, by the flicker of a wood fire, Beryl sat on a hassock playing the guitar. . . . She played and sang half to herself, for she was watching herself playing and singing. The firelight gleamed on her shoes, on the ruddy belly of the guitar, and on her white fingers. . . .
> "If I were outside the window and looked in and saw myself I really would be rather struck," thought she. Still more softly she played the accompaniment—not singing now but listening.
> . . . "The first time that I ever saw you, little girl—oh, you had no idea that you were not alone—you were sitting with your little feet upon a hassock, playing the guitar. God, I can never forget. . . ." Beryl flung up her head and began to sing again:
>
> *Even the moon is aweary* . . .
>
> But there came a loud bang at the door. The servant girl's crimson face popped through. . . . But no, she could not stand that fool

---

4 In *The Short Stories of Katherine Mansfield* (Alfred A. Knopf, 1937).

of a girl. She ran into the dark drawing-room and began walking up and down. . . . Oh, she was restless, restless. There was a mirror over the mantel. She leaned her arms along and looked at her pale shadow in it. How beautiful she looked, but there was nobody to see, nobody. . . .

Beryl smiled, and really her smile *was* so adorable that she smiled again. . . .

This cult of the self is not expressed in the young girl through adoration of her physical person only; she wishes to possess and pay homage to her whole self. Such is the purpose of those intimate diaries in which she can freely pour out her soul. The diary of Marie Bashkirtsev is famous and may stand as a model of the genre. The young girl talks to her little notebook as she formerly talked to her dolls; it is a friend and confidante; she questions it as if it were a person. In its pages is inscribed a truth hidden from relatives, comrades, teachers, a truth with which the author is enraptured in solitude. A little girl of twelve who kept her diary until she was twenty wrote the following prefatory inscription:

> *I am your little notebook*
> *Nice, pretty and discreet*
> *Tell me all your secrets*
> *I am your little notebook.*[5]

Others give notice: "To be read only after my death" or "To be burned after my death." The sense of secrecy developed in the girl at prepuberty is bound to become more intense. She wraps herself in a grim solitude; she will not expose to those about her the hidden ego that she regards as her true self and that is in fact an imaginary personage: she may play at being a dancer like Tolstoy's Natasha, or a saint as did Marie Lenéru, or merely that unmatched marvel who is herself. There is always an enormous difference between this heroine and the objective person with whom her relatives and friends are familiar. She is also convinced that she is not understood; her relations with herself are then only the more impassioned: she is intoxicated with her isolation, she feels herself different, superior, exceptional; she promises herself that the future will be a re-

---

[5] Cited by Debesse in *La Crise d'originalité juvénile.*

venge upon the mediocrity of her present life. From this narrow and paltry existence she makes her escape in dreams. She has always liked to dream, and now she gives herself up to this bent more than ever; she masks an intimidating universe under poetic clichés, she bestows upon the male sex a halo of moonlight, pink clouds, and velvet nights; she makes of her body a temple of marble, jasper, and mother-of-pearl; she tells herself silly fairy stories. She sinks so often into such foolishness because she has no hold upon the world; if she were supposed to *act* she would have to see clearly, but she can *wait* in a fog. The young man dreams too: particularly of adventures where he plays an active part. The young girl prefers the marvelous above adventuring; she sheds an uncertain magical light over things and persons. Magic involves the idea of a passive force; because she is doomed to passivity and yet wants power, the adolescent girl must believe in magic: in that of her body, which will bring men under her yoke; in that of fate in general, which will crown her desires without her having to *do* anything. As for the real world, she tries to forget it.

At school I would sometimes escape from the subject being explained and take wing into the land of dreams . . ." writes a young girl.[6] "I was so absorbed in my delightful chimeras that I lost the sense of reality completely. I was riveted to my seat, and when I woke up I was amazed to find myself within four walls."

"I liked to go woolgathering much better than to write poetry," admits another, "to outline mentally pretty stories without head or tail or to invent a legend while gazing at the mountains in starlight. It is much more pleasant because it is *more vague* and leaves a sense of repose, of refreshment."

Daydreaming may become morbid and envelop the whole existence, as in the following case: [7]

Marie B., an intelligent and dreamy child, entering puberty at fourteen, had a psychic crisis with delusions of grandeur. Announcing that she was Queen of Spain, she assumed haughty airs, sang,

---

[6] Quoted by Marguerite Evard in *L'Adolescente*.

[7] After Borel: *Les Rêveries morbides*. Cited by Minkowski in *La Schizophrénie*.

issued commands. For two years this was repeated at each menstruation; then for eight years she led a normal life but was dreamy
and bitter about her social status. Toward twenty-three she grew
worse and was hospitalized for a time. At home, for three years she
remained in bed, disagreeable, lazy, and a burden to her family.
In the asylum again for good, she took no interest in life, but at
certain periods (menstrual?) she got up, draped herself, struck attitudes of hauteur, and smiled at the doctors, often showing some
eroticism. She sank further into her dream-world, careless of appearance and often naked, but wearing bizarre ornaments, such as a
tinfoil diadem and bracelets of ribbon. At times she made lucid
comments on her condition, saying that she was like a child playing with dolls and dressing up, as if living in a dream, an actress in
an imaginary world. She seemed, she said, to be living several lives
and in all of them she was the *principal personage*. She had a big
house and gave parties. She lived at the time of the cave men. She
could not count the number of her bedfellows. She had friends
once; there were flowers and perfumes and ermine; they gave her
rich presents. "When I am naked in the bedclothes, it brings back
old times." She admired herself in mirrors, became whatever she
wished, was foolish, took drugs, had lovers. She said she was the
mistress of one of the doctors. She told of having young children;
one of them travels, she said, and its father was a very chic man.
She had many such stories to tell, each an invented life that she
lived in imagination.

We can see that this morbid daydreaming was of a kind to assuage
the narcissism of the young girl who feels her life inadequate and fears
to face the realities of existence. Marie B. simply carried to an extreme a process of compensation which is common to many adolescent girls.

This solitary cult of self is not enough, however, for the young girl.
To find fulfillment she needs to exist in the consciousness of another,
and she often turns to her companions for aid and comfort. When
she was younger, her best friend served her as support in escaping the
maternal circle, in exploring the world—especially the world of sex.
Now her friend is at once an object that draws out the adolescent girl
beyond the limits of the ego and a witness who restores that self to
her. Some girls exhibit their nudity to one another, they compare

breasts: we recall, perhaps, that scene from *Mädchen in Uniform* which depicts these daring amusements of boarding-school girls; they go so far as to exchange caresses of general or precise nature. As Colette indicates in *Claudine à l'école* and, with less frankness, Rosamond Lehmann in *Dusty Answer*, there are lesbian tendencies in almost all young girls, tendencies that are hardly distinguishable from narcissistic enjoyment: each one covets in the other the softness of her own skin, the modeling of her own curves; and, vice versa, in her self-adoration is implied the worship of femininity in general. Man is, sexually, *subject*, and therefore men are normally separated from each other by the desire that drives them toward an object different from themselves. But woman is the absolute *object* of desire, and that is the reason why so many "special friendships" flourish in schools, colleges, and studios; some of them are purely platonic and others grossly carnal. In the former it is especially a matter of friends opening their hearts to one another, exchanging confidences; and the proof of the most impassioned confidence is to show to the chosen friend one's intimate diary. Instead of sexual embraces, the girl friends exchange marks of extreme devotion and often offer to one another in a round-about way a physical token of their feeling. Thus Natasha burns her arm with a red-hot ruler to prove her love for Sonya. Above all, they have many endearing names for each other and they exchange ardent letters. Here, for example, is what Emily Dickinson, young New England puritan, wrote to one of her friends, a young married woman:

> I think of you all today, and dreamed of you last night. . . . I was walking with you in the most wonderful garden, and helping you pick—roses, and although we gathered with all our might, the basket was never full. And so all day I pray I may walk with you, and gather roses again, and as night draws on, it pleases me, and I count impatiently the hours 'tween me and the darkness, and the dream of you and the roses, and the basket never full.

In his *L'Âme de l'adolescente*, Mendousse quotes many similar letters:

> Dear Suzanne . . . I would have liked to copy here some verses from the Song of Songs: how beautiful you are, my loved one, how beautiful you are! Like the mystic bride, you have been to me as

the rose of Sharon and the lily of the valley, and like her, you have been more to me than any ordinary girl; you have been a symbol, the symbol of the goodness of beautiful and lofty things . . . and for that, unsullied Suzanne, I love you with a pure and unselfish love which is tinged with religion.

Another girl, cited also by Mendousse, avows in her diary some less elevated sentiments:

There I was, my waist pressed by that small white hand, my hand resting on her rounded shoulder, my arm on her bare warm arm, held against the softness of her breast, with before me her pretty mouth, the lips parted over tiny teeth. . . . I trembled and was conscious of my flushed face.

In her book *L'Adolescente*, Mme Evard also has collected many of these intimate effusions:

To my beloved fairy, my dearest darling. My pretty fairy. Ah! Say that you love me still, say that for you I am always the devoted friend. I am sad, I love you so much, oh my L— and I cannot speak and tell you enough about my love; there are no words to describe my love. To say I *idolize* you is too little in comparison with what I feel; sometimes it seems as if my heart would burst. To be loved by you is just too beautiful, I cannot believe it. Ah, *my precious*, tell me, will you love me long? . . .

The descent from these exalted affections to guilty juvenile amours is very easy; sometimes one of the two friends dominates the other and exerts her strength sadistically; but often the affairs are reciprocal, without humiliation or struggle; the pleasure given and received remains as innocent as it was when each loved herself in solitude, without the doubling that makes a couple. But this very purity is insipid; when the adolescent girl wants to take part in life, yield to the Other, she wants to revive for her own benefit the magic of the paternal gaze, she demands the love and the love-making of a god. She will turn to a woman, who is less strange and less frightening than the male, but who will have something of male prestige: a woman with a profession, who earns her own living, who makes a certain show in the world, will easily be as fascinating as a man. We know how many "crushes" arise in pupils' hearts for teachers and mistresses in schools. In *Regiment of Women* Clemence Dane describes in a chaste style the most ardent passions. Sometimes the young girl confides her grand passion to her best friend: it may even happen that they share it and each prides herself on feeling it most keenly. Thus one school-girl writes to her friend as cited in Marguerite Evard's *L'Adolescente*:

> I am in bed with a cold and can only think about Mlle X. Never have I loved a teacher so much. In my first year I loved her a lot; but now it is a real love affair. I think I am more passionate than you are. I fancy I am kissing her; I half faint and rejoice to think of going back to school to see her.

More often she ventures to declare her sentiments to her idol directly, as in another case cited in the same work:

> With regard to you, dear mademoiselle, I am in an indescribable state. . . . When you are out of my sight, I would give anything to be with you; I think of you constantly. When you are in view, I have tears in my eyes and wish to hide; I am so small and ignorant compared to you. When you talk to me, I am embarrassed and moved, I seem to hear a fairy voice and a humming of things in love, impossible to reproduce; I watch your littlest doings, I lose track of the conversation and mumble some stupidity; you will call it all a great muddle. But I see something in it very clearly: that I love you from the depths of my soul.

The woman director of a professional school, according to Liepmann in *Jeunesse et sexualité*, reports as follows:

> I remember that when I was young myself we used to quarrel over the paper in which one of our young teachers brought her lunch and would pay up to twenty pfennigs for pieces of it. Her subway tickets were also valued in our rage for collecting.

Since she must play a masculine part, it is preferable for the loved woman to be unmarried: marriage does not always discourage the young admirer, but it bothers her; she dislikes having the object of her adoration appear as subjected to the power of a husband or lover. Very often these passions unfold in secret, or at least on a platonic level; but passage to definite eroticism is much easier than when the loved one is masculine; even if the young girl had not had facile experiences with friends of her own age, the feminine body does not frighten her; with her sisters or her mother she has often known an intimacy in which affection was subtly imbued with sensual feeling; and with the loved one whom she admires, the transition from affection to voluptuous pleasure will be made as insensibly. When Dorothy Wieck, in *Mädchen in Uniform,* kissed Herta Thill on the lips, this kiss was maternal and sexual at once. Between women there is complicity that disarms modesty; the excitement that one arouses in the other is generally without violence; homosexual caresses imply neither defloration nor penetration: they satisfy the clitoral eroticism of childhood without demanding new and disquieting changes. The young girl can realize her vocation as passive object without feeling herself deeply alienated. This is what Renée Vivien expresses in certain poems where she sings the light touch and the delicate kiss of those who are at once lovers and sisters and whose love-making leaves no marks on lips or breasts.[8]

What she promises to her friend in the poetic impropriety of the words *lips* and *breasts* is clearly not to violate her. And it is in part because of the fear of violence, of violation, that the adolescent girl often gives her first love to an older woman rather than to a man. The virile woman incarnates in the girl's eyes both her father and her mother: she has the father's authority and transcendence, she is the source and the standard of values, she surpasses the world as given, she is divine; but she also remains·a woman. Whether as a child the girl was too sparingly accorded maternal caresses or, on the contrary, she was coddled too long by her mother, she dreams, like her brothers, of the warm bosom; in this flesh now close to hers she finds again that carefree, direct fusion with life once lost at weaning; and in this

---

[8] *Nos corps sont pour leurs corps un fraternel miroir,*
Nos lunaires baisers ont de pâles douceurs,
Nos doigts ne froissent point le duvet d'une joue
Et nous pouvons quand la ceinture se dénoue
Être tout à la fois des amants et des sœurs.

L'Heure des mains jointes.

Car nous aimons la grâce et la délicatesse
Et ma possession ne meurtrit pas tes seins . . .
Ma bouche ne saurait mordre âprement ta bouche.

Sillages.

enveloping gaze of another the separation that makes her a lone individual is overcome. To be sure, every human relationship implies conflict, all love brings jealousy. But many of the difficulties that loom between the virgin and her first male lover are here smoothed away. The homosexual experience can take the shape of a true amour; it can bring so happy a balance to the young girl that she will want to perpetuate or repeat it, that she will retain a nostalgic memory of it; it can, indeed, bring to light or bring into being a lesbian propensity.[9]

But more often such an experience will represent only a stage: its very facility is its death warrant. In the love she gives an older woman the young girl is in love with her own future: she would identify herself with her idol; unless the idol's superiority is exceptional, she soon loses her aura. When the younger woman begins to assert herself, she judges and compares: the other, who has been chosen just because she was akin and not intimidating, has not sufficient *otherness* to impose herself for long; the male gods are more firmly established because the heaven where they reside is more distant. Her curiosity, her sensuality, lead the young girl to long for stronger embraces. Very often she views the homosexual adventure from the outset as merely a transition, an initiation, something temporary. She has played at love, jealousy, rage, pride, enjoyment, and suffering, with the idea, more or less freely admitted, that she is imitating without much risk the adventures she dreams of but for which she has not as yet the courage or the opportunity for undertaking in real life. She is destined for man, and knows it; and she wants the normal and complete lot of woman.

Man dazzles her, and yet he scares her, too. In order to accommodate the contradictory feelings she bears toward him, she will dissociate the male in him that frightens her and the bright divinity whom she piously adores. Abrupt and shy with her male comrades, she idolizes some distant Prince Charming: a movie actor whose portrait she pins up over her bed, a hero, dead or still living, but always inaccessible, an unknown noticed by chance whom she knows she will never see again. Such amours raise no problems. Very often it is a man of social or intellectual prestige but without physical appeal that the young girl looks to: say an aged and rather ridiculous professor. These older men are beyond the world of the adolescent, and she can devote herself to them in secret, as one consecrates oneself to God;

---

[9] See Chapter xv.

it is not humiliating, since there is no carnal desire. The elect may even be humble or homely, since in that case she only feels the safer. By choosing someone who is not attainable she may make of love an abstract subjective experience with no threat to her integrity; she feels the emotions of longing, hope, bitterness, but without real entanglement. Amusingly enough, the more distant the idol, the more brilliant he can be; the everyday piano teacher may better be unattractive, but the hero beyond reach is preferably handsome and masculine. The important thing is that in one way or another the element of sex be kept out of it, thus prolonging the narcissistic attitude of immanent eroticism, without the real presence of the Other.

In this way the adolescent girl, avoiding real experiences, often develops an intense imaginative life, sometimes, indeed, confusing her phantasms with reality. Helene Deutsch describes the significant case of a young girl who imagined an elaborate relationship with an older boy to whom she had never even spoken. She kept a diary of affecting scenes, with tears and embraces, partings and reconciliations, and wrote him letters, never sent, which she herself answered. All this was evidently a defense against real experiences that she feared.

This is a pathological extreme, but the process is normal. Marie Bashkirtsev maintained imaginary sentimental relations with an inaccessible nobleman, wishing to exalt her ego in circumstances that prevented her, being a woman, from making an independent success. She wished to be someone, but how accomplish it in skirts? She needed a man, but he must be of the highest. "To humble oneself before man's superiority must be the superior woman's greatest pride," she writes. Thus narcissism leads to masochism, as we see in the child already dreaming of Bluebeard and the holy martyrs. The ego is formed as it were for others, by others: the more powerful the others are, the richer and more powerful the ego is. To annihilate oneself before others is to realize others at once in and for oneself. Loved by Nero, Marie Bashkirtsev *would be* Nero. In truth, this dream of nothingness is a proud will to be; as a matter of fact, she never met a man sufficiently superb for her to lose herself in him. It is one thing to kneel before one's personally constructed god who remains afar off, and quite another to yield oneself to a male of flesh and blood. Many young girls persist in following this dream in the world of reality; they seek a man superior to all others in all things, one with fortune and fame, the absolute Subject who through his love will endow them with his splendor and essentiality. It idealizes their love to give it not because he is a male but because he is *that* lofty being. "I would have giants, and I find but men," a friend said to me. Because of these lofty requirements, the young girl disdains mere everyday aspirants and avoids the problems of sexuality. And she cherishes without risk a dream-image of herself, enchanting as an image, but to which she wishes by no means to conform. Thus Marie Le Hardouin, in *La Voile noire*, tells how she delighted in imagining herself the devoted victim of a man when she was in reality a domineering personality:

> We lived in misery. I put my eyes out mending his clothes. Sickness threatened our only child with death. But a gentle, crucified smile was on my lips, and in my eyes was that expression of silent courage which I have never been able to bear the sight of in real life without disgust.

Beyond these narcissistic yieldings, some young girls feel more realistically the need for a guide, a teacher. Escaping from parental control, they find this unaccustomed independence embarrassing; they can hardly do more than make a negative use of it, falling into caprice and extravagance; they wish to relinquish their liberty after all. The story of the capricious, haughty, rebellious, and unbearable young lady who gets amorously tamed by a sensible man is a standard pattern for cheap literature and the movies: it is a cliché flattering at once to men and women. This is the story told, for example, by Mme de Ségur in *Quel amour d'enfant!* The child Gisèle, disappointed by a too indulgent father, becomes attached to a severe old aunt; when a young girl, she comes under the influence of a fault-finding young man, Julien, who tells her harsh truths, humiliates her, tries to reform her; she marries a rich duke of bad character with whom she is unhappy, and only when, as a widow, she accepts the urgent love of her mentor does she at last find joy and wisdom. In Louisa M. Alcott's *Good Wives*, the self-willed Jo begins to fall in love with her future husband when he reproaches her severely for some blunder. In spite of the stubborn pride of American women, the Hollywood films have time and again shown these wild youngsters tamed by the wholesome brutality of a husband or lover: a slap or two or, better, a good spanking would appear to be sure means of seduction.

But in reality the transition from ideal love to sexual love is not quite so simple. Many women carefully avoid any close approach to the object of their affection for fear, more or less openly admitted, of being deceived. If the hero, the giant, the demigod, responds to the love he inspires and transforms it into an actual experience, the young girl takes fright; her idol becomes a male from whom she turns away in loathing. There are coquettish young things who "shoot the works" in the effort to attract a man they consider "interesting" or "fascinating," but are paradoxically upset if he shows in return a too lively interest in them; he appeals to them because he seems inaccessible: as a lover he seems too commonplace—"he's just a man like the rest." The girl blames him for her own loss of dignity, using it as a pretext for avoiding the physical contacts that affright her virgin sensibility. If she yields to her "ideal," she remains cold in his arms, and, as Stekel says, "it sometimes happens that a lofty-minded girl will commit suicide after such an event, or the whole edifice of her amorous imagination collapses because the Ideal stands revealed as a 'brutish animal.'"

This bent for the impossible frequently leads the young girl to fall in love with a man who is interested in one of her friends, and very often it is a married man. She is readily fascinated by a Don Juan; she dreams of subjugating and holding this seducer whom no woman has ever retained for long; she nurses the hope of reforming him, though she knows she will fail, and this is one of the reasons for her choice. Some young girls become forever incapable of real and complete love. Throughout their lives they will seek an ideal impossible of realization.

There is evidently a conflict between the girl's narcissism and the experiences to which she is destined by her sexuality. Woman will not accept her status as the inessential unless she becomes again the essential in the very act of abdication. Being made object, lo, she becomes an idol in which she recognizes herself with pride; but she spurns the implacable logic which makes her still the inessential. She would like to be a fascinating treasure, not a thing to be taken. She loves to seem a marvelous fetish, charged with magical emanations, not to see herself as flesh subject to seeing, touching, bruising: just so man likes woman as prey, but flees the ogress Demeter.

Proud she is of catching male interest, of arousing admiration, but what revolts her is to be caught in return. With the coming of puberty she has become acquainted with shame; and the shame lingers on, mingled with her coquetry and her vanity. Men's stares flatter and hurt her simultaneously; she wants only what she shows to be seen: eyes are always too penetrating. Hence the inconsistency that men find disconcerting: she displays her *décolleté*, her legs, and when they are looked at she blushes, feels vexation.[1] She enjoys inflaming the male, but if she sees that she has aroused his desire, she recoils in disgust. Masculine desire is as much an offense as it is a compliment; in so far as she feels herself responsible for her charm, or feels she is exerting it of her own accord, she is much pleased with her conquests, but to the extent that her face, her figure, her flesh are facts she must bear with, she wants to hide them from this independent stranger who lusts after them.

Just here is the deeper meaning of this basic modesty, which disconcertingly interferes with the boldest coquetries. A little girl can be astonishingly audacious because she does not realize that in taking the initiative she reveals her passivity: once she sees this, she is frightened and vexed. Nothing is more equivocal than a look; it exists at a distance, and at that distance it seems respectful, but it insensibly takes possession of the perceived image. The immature woman struggles in these snares. She starts to let herself go, but at once she tightens up and suppresses her rising desire. In her still unsettled body a caress is felt now as a delicate pleasure, now as a disagreeable tickling; a kiss moves her at first, then suddenly makes her laugh; each yielding is followed by a revolt; she lets herself be kissed, but she makes a show of wiping her lips; she is smiling and affectionate, then of a sudden ironical and hostile; she makes promises and deliberately forgets them.

In thus displaying a childish and perverse character the "unripe fruit" defends herself against man. The young girl has often been described as this half-wild, half-tamed creature. Colette, for one, depicts her in *Claudine à l'école* and also in *Blé en herbe*, in the form of the bewitching Vinca. She maintains an ardent interest in the world she faces and rules over in sovereign fashion; but she is also curious about man and feels a sensual and romantic desire for him. Vinca gets scratched in brambles, she catches crayfish, climbs trees, and yet she thrills when her playmate Phil touches her hand; she knows the excitement in which the body becomes the flesh and woman is first re-

---

[1] Hence that prime gesture of the 1920's: the very short skirt and the constant tugging to make it cover a little more of the knees.—TR.

vealed as woman. Aroused, she begins to wish to be pretty: at times she does her hair, puts on make-up, dresses in filmy organdy, she amuses herself by being coquettish and seductive; but as if she wished to exist *for herself* and not *for others*, at times she bundles up in old ungraceful dresses or wears unbecoming trousers; an important part of her disapproves of coquetry and considers it a surrender of principle. So she deliberately has inky fingers, goes uncombed and slatternly. This rebellious behavior gives her an awkwardness that she feels with vexation; she is irritated by it, blushes, redoubles her clumsiness, and shudders at her abortive attempts to be seductive. In this stage the young girl wishes to be a child no longer, but she does not accept becoming an adult, and she reproaches herself in turn for her childishness and her female resignation. She is in a position of continual denial.

This is the trait that characterizes the young girl and gives us the key to most of her behavior; she does not accept the destiny assigned to her by nature and by society; and yet she does not repudiate it completely; she is too much divided against herself to join battle with the world; she limits herself to a flight from reality or a symbolic struggle against it. Each of her desires has its corresponding anxiety: she is eager to come into possession of her future, but she dreads to break with her past; she wants to "have" a man, but she does not want him to have her as his prey. And behind each fear lurks a desire: violation horrifies her, but she yearns toward passivity. She is thus doomed to insincerity and all its subterfuges; she is predisposed to all kinds of negative obsessions that express the ambivalence of anxiety and desire.

Scornful laughter is one of the commonest methods of combat used in the adolescent struggle. Schoolgirls and working girls "burst" with laughter while telling one another sentimental or coarse stories or speaking of their flirtations; they giggle when passing men or seeing lovers embracing. I have known of schoolgirls going through the "lovers' lane" in the Luxembourg Gardens expressly to have a laugh; and of others who frequented Turkish baths to make fun of the fat women with their heavy abdomens and hanging breasts. To make game of the feminine body, to ridicule men, to laugh at love, together constitute a way of disowning sexuality. There is in these laughs, along with defiance of adults, a method of overcoming one's own embarrassment and constraint; one plays with words and images to kill the dangerous magic: I have seen young pupils "burst" with laughter at finding the word *femur* in a Latin text.

If the young girl lets herself be pawed or kissed, she will with all the more reason take her revenge by laughing in her partner's face or with her companions. I recall two young girls, one night in a railroad compartment, being "petted" one after the other by a traveling salesman, who was evidently enjoying his good luck; between times they laughed hysterically, reverting in a mixture of sexuality and shame to the typical behavior of the awkward age.

At this age young girls make use of strong language, as well as wild laughter: some of them have a vocabulary crude enough to make their brothers blush; this language is no doubt less shocking to them because, in their semi-ignorance, the expressions they use evoke no very precise images in their minds; the intention is, besides, rather to prevent such images than to produce them, or at least to dull them. The coarse stories schoolgirls tell one another are intended less to satisfy sexual feelings than to deny sexuality: this they wish to regard in its humorous aspect, as a mechanical or quasi-surgical operation. But like laughter, the use of obscene language is not merely a method of combat: it is also a defiance of adults, a kind of sacrilege, a deliberately perverse form of behavior. Flouting nature and society, the young girl challenges and braves them in a number of peculiar ways. Often noted are whimsical food habits: she eats pencil leads, sealing wafers, bits of wood, live shrimp; she swallows aspirin tablets by the dozen; she even consumes flies and spiders. I have known one girl, no fool, who made up frightful mixtures of coffee and white wine and forced herself to drink them; she also ate sugar soaked in vinegar. I saw another find a white worm in her salad and resolutely devour it. All children persist in testing the world with eyes and hands and, more intimately, with mouth and stomach; but at the awkward age the girl is more prone to explore in the realm of the indigestible and repellent. Very often what is "disgusting" attracts her. One such who was pretty, coquettish, and well-groomed when she felt like it, appeared really fascinated by everything "dirty": she handled insects, peered at soiled menstrual cloths, sucked blood from her scratches. Playing with untidy things is evidently a method of getting the best of disgust, a feeling that has become very important at the beginning of puberty: the little girl, as we have seen, feels disgust for her too carnal body, for her menstrual blood, for adult sexual practices, for the male to whom she is destined; she denies the feeling by enjoying with familiarity precisely what is repugnant to her. It is as if she were saying: "Since I must bleed every month, I suck out the blood from my scratches to prove that I'm not afraid of my blood. Since I shall have to submit to a revolting experience, I might as well devour a white worm."

This attitude is displayed much more clearly in the self-mutilation common at this age. The young girl may gash her thigh with a razor-blade, burn herself with a cigarette, peel off skin; to avoid having to attend a tiresome garden-party, a friend of my youth cut her foot with a hatchet severely enough to have to stay in bed six weeks. These sado-masochistic performances are at once an anticipation of the sexual experience and a protest against it; in passing these tests, one becomes hardened for all possible ordeals and reduces their harshness, including the ordeal of the wedding night. When she puts a snail on her breast, swallows a bottle of aspirin tablets, wounds herself, the young girl is hurling defiance at her future lover—"you will never inflict on me anything more hateful than I inflict on myself." These are proud and sullen gestures of initiation to the sexual adventure.

Fated as she is to be the passive prey of man, the girl asserts her right to liberty even to the extent of undergoing pain and disgust. When she cuts or burns herself, she is protesting against the impalement of her defloration: she protests by annulling. Masochistic, in that her conduct gives her pain, she is above all sadistic: as independent subject, she lashes, flouts, tortures this dependent flesh, this flesh condemned to the submission she detests—without wishing, however, to dissociate herself from it. For she does not choose, in spite of everything, really to repudiate her destiny. Her sado-masochistic aberrations involve a basic insincerity: if the girl lets herself practice them, it means that she accepts, through her repudiation, the womanly future in store for her; she would not mutilate her flesh with hatred if she had not first recognized herself as flesh.

Even her outbursts of violence rise from depths of resignation. When a boy revolts against his father, against the world, his violence is effective; he picks a quarrel with a comrade, he fights, he affirms his standing as subject with his fists: in a word, he imposes himself upon the world, he transcends it. But it is not for the adolescent girl to affirm or impose herself, and this is what fills her heart with revolt: she may hope neither to change the world nor to transcend it; she knows, or at least believes, that she is fettered—and perhaps she even wants to be; she can only destroy. There is desperation in her rage; when provoked she breaks glasses, window-panes, vases—not indeed to conquer fate, but simply by way of symbolic protest. In her present powerlessness the girl rebels against her future enslavement; and her vain outbursts, far from loosing her bonds, often serve only to tighten them.

Violent actions against herself or against her surrounding universe always have a negative character: they are more spectacular than effective. The combative boy regards his minor injuries as insignificant consequences of his positive activities, neither sought nor avoided for their own sakes (unless an inferiority complex puts him in a situation like the girl's). The girl watches herself suffer: she is savoring in her heart the taste of violence and revolt rather than feeling any interest in their results. Her perverseness derives from the fact that she remains anchored in the childish universe whence she cannot or will not really escape; she is struggling in her cage rather than trying to get out of it; her frame of mind is negative, reflex, symbolical.

In some cases this perversity may become a serious matter. Not a few young virgins are kleptomaniacs; kleptomania is a "sexual sublimation" of very dubious nature; the will to break the law, to violate a taboo, the heady excitement of the forbidden and perilous act—such defiance is certainly essential in the female thief, but it has a double aspect. To take things without right is arrogantly to affirm her independence, it is to play the part of subject regarding the things stolen and the society that condemns the theft, it is to deny law and order. But this defiance has also a masochistic side; the thief is fascinated by the risk she runs, by the abyss that yawns for her if she is apprehended; the danger of being caught is what gives the act of theft its voluptuous charm; then under disapproving eyes, under the hand on the shoulder, in the shame of it all, she would sense herself as object, wholly and without recourse.

To take without being taken, in anguish lest one become prey, this is the dangerous game of adolescent feminine sexuality. All the perverse and guilty behavior patterns of young girls have this same significance. Some specialize in sending anonymous letters, others find amusement in playing hoaxes on their associates: one girl of fourteen convinced a whole village that a house was haunted. They enjoy at the same time the secret exercise of their power, their disobedience, their defiance of society—and the risk of being found out! This last is such an important element in their enjoyment that frequently they unmask themselves; and they even accuse themselves at times of faults and crimes they have not committed. It is not surprising to find that refusal to become an object leads to making oneself an object: the mechanism is common to all the negative obsessions. In a single reaction, the hysterical paralytic patient fears the paralysis, desires it, and brings it about: cure comes only in ceasing to think about it, just as with psychasthentic tics.

The depth of her insincerity is what relates the normal young girl to these neurotic types. Manias, tics, plots, perversities—we find many neurotic symptoms in her because of that ambivalence of desire and dread which I have carefully pointed out. It is common enough, for example, for her to run away; she may go off at random, wander far from home, and after two or three days return of her own accord. There is no question here of a genuine departure, a real break with her family; it is only a comedy of escape, and the girl is often quite upset if anyone suggests taking her definitely away from her entourage: she wants to leave while not wanting to. Running away is sometimes connected with fantasies of prostitution: she fancies she is a prostitute, she plays the part more or less timidly; she puts on garish make-up, leans on the window-sill, and ogles the passers-by. In certain cases she leaves home and pushes the comedy so far that it becomes confused with reality. Such behavior often expresses disgust with sexual desire, a feeling of culpability: "since I have these thoughts, these appetites, I am no better than a prostitute, I am one," she thinks. Sometimes she endeavors to free herself: "let us have done, let us go to the bitter end," she says to herself; she would prove to herself that sexuality is a matter of slight importance by giving herself to the first comer.

At the same time, such an attitude may often express hostility to the mother, whether the young girl is alienated by her parent's austere virtue or suspects that the mother herself is of easy virtue; or it expresses resentment toward a too indifferent father. In any case this obsession—like the often associated fantasies of pregnancy I have mentioned—contains that inextricable confusion of revolt and complicity which marks the psychasthenic aberrations.

It is remarkable that in all those forms of behavior the young girl does not seek to transcend the natural and social order, she does not aim to extend the limits of the possible nor to work a transvaluation of values; she is content to display her revolt within the bounds of a world the frontiers and laws of which are preserved. That is the attitude often defined as "demoniac," which implies a fundamental dissimulation: the good is recognized in order to be flouted, the rule is laid down in order to be broken, the sacred is respected to make possible further sacrilege. The attitude of the young girl is to be defined essentially by the fact that, in the anguished shadows of her insincerity, she denies while accepting the world and her destiny.

She does not confine herself, however, to contesting negatively the situation imposed upon her; she endeavors also to compensate for its inadequacies. If the future scares her, the present dissatisfies her; she hesitates to become a woman; she is vexed to be still only a child; she has already left her past behind, but she has not yet entered upon a new life. She is busy, but she *does* nothing; because she does nothing, she *has* nothing, she *is* nothing. She must fill this void with play-acting and falsification. She is often reproached for being sly, untruthful, a "storyteller." The fact is that she is doomed to secrecy and lies. At sixteen a woman has already been through painful ordeals: puberty, monthlies, awakening of sexuality, first desires, first fevers, fears, disgusts, equivocal experiences; she has stored all this up in her heart, and she has learned to guard her secrets carefully. The single fact of having to hide her menstrual cloths and conceal her condition has already accustomed her to prevarication. In her tale *Old Mortality*, Katherine Anne Porter relates how young American girls in the South, about 1900, made themselves sick eating mixtures of salt and lemon to halt menstruation when they were going to a ball; they were afraid that the young men might discover their condition from the appearance of their eyes, contact with their hands, or possibly an odor, and this idea horrified them. It is not easy to play the idol, the fairy, the faraway princess, when one feels a bloody cloth between one's legs; and, more generally, when one is conscious of the primitive misery of being a body. The modesty that is spontaneous refusal to admit one's carnal nature verges on hypocrisy.

But, above all, the lie to which the adolescent girl is condemned is that she must pretend to be an object, and a fascinating one, when she senses herself as an uncertain, dissociated being, well aware of her blemishes. Make-up, false hair, girdles, and "reinforced" brassieres are all lies.[2] The very face itself becomes a mask: spontaneous

---

[2] The "reinforced" bras are plainly labeled "falsies" in the truthful United States.—TR.

expressions are artfully induced, a wondering passivity is mimicked; nothing is more astonishing than to discover suddenly a young girl's physiognomy, well known in its ordinary aspect, when it assumes its feminine function; its transcendence is laid aside and imitates immanence; the eyes no longer penetrate, they reflect; the body is no longer alive, it waits; every gesture and smile becomes an appeal. Disarmed, disposable, the young girl is now only an offered flower, a fruit to be picked.

Man encourages these allurements by demanding to be lured: afterward he is annoyed and reproachful. But he feels only indifference and hostility for the artless, guileless young girl. He finds seductive only the girl who spreads these snares; though herself on offer, she is lying in wait for prey; her passivity serves an enterprise, and she makes her weakness the instrumentality of her power; since she is not allowed to attack openly, she has to depend on stratagem and calculation; and it is to her advantage to seem to be freely given: she is therefore accused of being perfidious and traitorous, and with truth. But it is true that she is obliged to offer man the myth of her submission, because he insists upon domination, and her compliance would only be perverted from the start. Besides, her tricking is not entirely due to deliberate calculation. As we have seen, she has gone through earlier phases of childish play-acting and then of being herself, and to ask what is the truth of her nature means little in her situation since she can only *be*, not *act*. Her adolescent romancing seems truer to her potentialities than the vapid facts of her daily existence, and her extravagances give her a sense of importance in the absence of real activities. Like the child, she makes herself *count* by means of scenes and tantrums, deceptions, slanders, fantasies. She has no real will, but only shifting desires. But she sees her inconsequences as definitive and absolute: unable to control her future, she would attain the eternal. "I shall always want everything," writes Marie Lenéru. "I must choose my life if I am to accept it." And to this Anouilh's Antigone makes echo: "I want everything, immediately." Such childish imperiousness is to be found only in one who dreams one's destiny: the dream abolishes time and obstacles, but whoever has real projects in view has a sense of the finite which gauges his concrete power. The young girl wants *everything* because there is *nothing* that depends on her. Hence her aspect as *enfant terrible*. Thus Hilda in Ibsen's *The Master Builder* expects Solness to give her a kingdom: it is not for her to conquer it. Let him build high and climb; she, on the ground, has no concern for human frailty, no regard for limitations in her dreams of grandeur. Adults always seem paltry and overcautious to one who has nothing to risk; but the girl, not being put to the test of reality, can boast of the most astounding virtues without fear of contradiction.

Her uncertainty, however, also stems from this lack of control; she dreams of her infinitude, but she is none the less present herself in the personage she offers for the admiration of others, and this personage depends upon the minds of strangers. There is danger for her in this double that she identifies with herself and yet whose presence she must passively accept. That is why she is sensitive and vain. The least criticism, a bit of raillery, makes her wholly dubious. She derives her worth not from her own efforts, but from a capricious approval. Such reputation, not based on specific activities, seems, then, to be quantitatively measurable; the worth of merchandise declines when it becomes too common, and therefore the young girl is rare, exceptional, remarkable, extraordinary, only if no one else is. Her companions are rivals, enemies; she tries to disparage and disown them; she is jealous and spiteful.

It is clear that all these faults flow simply from the adolescent girl's situation. It is a most unfortunate condition to be in, to feel oneself passive and dependent at the age of hope and ambition, at the age when the will to live and to make a place in the world is running strong. At just this conquering age, woman learns that for her there is to be no conquest, that she must disown herself, that her future depends upon man's good pleasure. On the social as well as the sexual level new aspirations awake in her, only to remain unsatisfied; all her eagerness for action, whether physical or spiritual, is instantly thwarted. It is understandable that she can hardly regain her equilibrium. Her unstable temperament, her tears, her nervous crises, are less the consequence of physiological frailty than the evidence of her profound maladjustment.

But it may happen that the young girl authentically accepts this situation which she is prone to flee from in a thousand inauthentic ways. She is vexatious in her faults, but sometimes she is astonishing in her special qualities. Both have one and the same source. Her denial of the world, her restless expectation, her nothingness, she can use as a springboard to gain the heights in solitude and freedom.

The young girl, as we have seen, is inward, disturbed, the victim of severe conflicts, but this complexity enriches her, and her inner life develops more deeply than that of her brothers; she is more attentive to her feelings and so they become more subtly diversified; she has more psychologic insight than boys have, with their outward interests. She can give weight to the revolts that set her against the world. She avoids the snares of overseriousness and conformism. The deliberate lies of her associates encounter her irony and clairvoyance. She feels daily the ambiguity of her position: beyond sterile protests, she can bravely put in question official optimism, ready-made values, hypocritical and cheerful morality. So with Maggie in *The Mill on the Floss*, in whom George Eliot embodied the doubts and brave rebellions of her youth against Victorian England. The heroes—particularly Tom, Maggie's brother—obstinately uphold accepted principles, congeal morality in formal rules; but Maggie tries to put the breath of life into them, she upsets them, she goes to the limit of her solitude and emerges as a genuine free being, beyond the sclerosed universe of the males.

Of this liberty the adolescent girl can hardly do more than make a negative use. Yet her inactivity can engender a precious receptivity; thus she can be devoted, attentive, understanding, affectionate. Rosamond Lehmann's heroines are notable for this docile generosity. In *Invitation to the Waltz* we see Olivia still timid and awkward, hardly coquettish, surveying with emotional curiosity this world she is soon to enter. She listens closely to her successive partners in the dance, she tries to answer them according to their wishes, she becomes an echo, she vibrates, she accepts what comes. The heroine of *Dusty Answer*, Judith, is similarly engaging. She has not renounced childish delights: she likes to bathe naked at night in the river that runs by her garden, she loves nature, books, beauty, life; she is not narcissistic; she is not deceitful or egoistic, nor does she seek through men the exaltation of her ego: her love is a bestowal. She gives it to whosoever wins her over, man or woman, Jennifer or Roddy. She gives but does not lose herself: leading the independent life of a student, she has her own world, her projects. But what distinguishes her from a boy is her expectant attitude, her gentle docility. Subtly she is destined, in spite of it all, to the Other: in her eyes the Other has an aspect so marvelous that she is in love at once with all the young men of the family next door, with their house, their sister, their uni-

verse; Jennifer fascinates her not as a friend, but in her Otherness.
And she charms Roddy and his cousins by her willingness to mold
herself to them, to model herself to their desires; she personifies patience, gentleness, acceptance, and silent submissiveness.

Quite different is Tessa in Margaret Kennedy's *The Constant
Nymph*, at once spontaneous, mild, and devoted, but also captivating
in her way of taking those she loves into her heart. She refuses to
abdicate in the least: feminine finery, make-up, falsities, hypocrisies,
studied graces, prudence, and submissiveness are all repugnant to her;
she wants to be loved, but not behind a mask. She bends to Lewis's
whims, but without servility; she understands him, vibrates in accord
with him; but if they ever quarrel, caresses will not win her over.
The vain and haughty Florence can be conquered with kisses, but
Tessa works the miracle of remaining free in her love, which permits
her to love without hostility or pride. Her native simplicity has all
the attraction of artifice; to please she never cripples herself, cheap-
ens herself, or becomes set as object. Surrounded by artists wholly
wrapped up in musical creation, she does not feel this devouring
demon within her; she is wholly concerned in loving, understanding,
and helping them. This she does effortlessly, with an affectionate and
spontaneous generosity, and for this reason she remains perfectly independent even when she is forgetting self in favor of others. Thanks
to this pure authenticity, she is spared the usual conflicts of adolescence; she can bear the world's harshness, not being divided within
herself; she has at once the harmony of the careless child and that
of the woman of wisdom. The sensitive and generous young girl, receptive and ardent, is quite ready to become a woman capable of a
great love.

When she does not find love, she may find poetry. Because she
does not act, she observes, she feels, she records; a color, a smile
awakens profound echoes within her; her destiny is outside her, scattered in cities already built, on the faces of men already marked by
life; she makes contact, she relishes with passion and yet in a manner
more detached, more free, than that of a young man. Being poorly
integrated in the universe of humanity and hardly able to adapt herself therein, she, like the child, is able to see it objectively; instead of
being interested solely in her grasp on things, she looks for their significance; she catches their special outlines, their unexpected metamorphoses. She rarely feels a bold creativeness, and usually she lacks

the techniques of self-expression; but in her conversation, her letters, her literary essays, her sketches, she manifests an original sensitivity. The young girl throws herself into things with ardor, because she is not yet deprived of her transcendence; and the fact that she accomplishes nothing, that she is nothing, will make her impulses only the more passionate. Empty and unlimited, she seeks from deep within her nothingness to attain All. That is why she will devote a special love to Nature: still more than the adolescent boy, she worships it. Unconquered, inhuman, Nature subsumes most clearly the totality of what exists. The adolescent girl has not as yet acquired for her use any portion of the universal: hence it is her kingdom as a whole; when she takes possession of it, she also proudly takes possession of herself. Colette has often depicted these juvenile orgies, as in *Sido*:

> I loved the early dawn and would go down the sandy road, with my empty baskets, toward the river, where there were strawberries and currants. At half past three all was deep blue and moist and dim, and I could walk down into the heavy mist until it was up to my ears and my sensitive nostrils. . . . Then I felt my worth, and a state of grace, and my union with the earliest breeze, the first bird, the rising sun. . . . I would return, but not before eating my fill and circling through the woods and drinking from two hidden springs.

Mary Webb [3] also tells us of the ardent joys the young girl knows in intimacy with a familiar countryside:

> When the atmosphere of the house became too thunderous and Amber's nerves were strained to the breaking-point, she crept away to the upper woods. . . . It seemed to her that while Dormer lived by law, the forest lived by impulse. Through a gradual awakening to natural beauty, she reached a perception of beauty peculiar to herself. She began to perceive analogies. Nature became for her, not a fortuitous assemblage of pretty things, but a harmony, a poem solemn and austere. . . . Beauty breathed there, light shone there that was not of the flower or the star. A tremor, mysterious and thrilling, seemed to run with the light through . . . the whispering

---

[3] In *The House in Dormer Forest* (London: Jonathan Cape; 1928), pp. 185–90.

forest. . . . So her going out into the green world had in it something of a religious rite. On a still morning of early June . . . she came at last to the upper wood, and was instantly at grips with beauty. There was for her literally something of wrestling, of the mood which says: "I will not let thee go except thou bless me," in her communings with nature. . . . Leaning against a wild pear tree, she was aware, by her inward hearing, of the tidal wave of sap that rose so full and strong that she could almost imagine it roaring like the sea. Then a tremor of wind shook the flowering tree-tops, and she awoke again to the senses, to the strangeness of these utterances of the leaves. . . . Every petal, every leaf, seemed to be conning some memory of profundities whence it had come. Every curving flower seemed full of echoes too majestic for its fragility. . . . A breath of scented air came from the hilltops and stole among the branches. That which had form, and knew the mortality which is in form, trembled before that which passed, formless and immortal. . . . Because of it the place became no mere congregation of trees, but a thing fierce as stellar space. . . . For it possesses itself forever in a vitality withheld, immutable. It was this that drew Amber with breathless curiosity into the secret haunts of nature. It was this that struck her now into a kind of ecstasy. . . . That was what drew Amber, breathless, into these haunted places of nature and held her immobile in a rare ecstasy.

Women as diverse as Emily Brontë and Anna de Noailles have known such fervors in their youth—and retained them throughout life.

The passages just cited show how splendid a refuge the adolescent girl finds in the fields and woods. At home, mother, law, customs, routine hold sway, and she would fain escape these aspects of her past; she would in her turn become a sovereign subject. But, as a member of society, she enters upon adult life only in becoming a woman; she pays for her liberation by an abdication. Whereas among plants and animals she is a human being; she is freed at once from her family and from the males—a subject, a free being. She finds in the secret places of the forest a reflection of the solitude of her soul and in the wide horizons of the plains a tangible image of her transcendence; she is herself this limitless territory, this summit flung up toward heaven; she can follow these roads that lead toward the unknown future, she will follow them; seated on the hilltop, she is mistress of all the world's riches, spread out at her feet, offered for the taking. In the rush of water, the shimmer of light, she feels a presentiment of the joys, the tears, the ecstasies she has not yet known; the ripples on the pool, the dappled sunlight, give vague promise of the adventurings of her own heart.

Scents and colors speak a mysterious language, but one word sounds out triumphantly clear: the word *life*. Existence is not merely an abstract destiny set down in city records; it is the rich fleshly future. To have a body no longer seems a blemish to be ashamed of; in the desires that under the maternal eye the girl repudiates, she can recognize the sap that rises in the trees; she is no longer accursed, she lays claim proudly to her kinship with the leaves and flowers; she crumples a corolla, and she knows that one day a living prey will fill her empty hands. The flesh is no longer a defilement: it means joy and beauty. At one with earth and sky, the young girl is that vague breath which animates and kindles the universe, and she is each sprig of heather; an organism rooted in the soil and in infinite consciousness, she is at once spirit and life; her being is imperious and triumphant like that of the earth itself.

Beyond nature she sometimes seeks a reality more distant and more dazzling still; she tends to lose herself in mystic ecstasies. In eras of faith many young feminine souls look to God to fill the void within them; the holy vocation of Catherine of Siena, of Theresa of Ávila,[4] was made manifest in early life. Joan of Arc was a young girl. In other times the supreme objective is humanity, and then the mystical impulse flows into definite social projects. But it is also a youthful yearning for the absolute which kindles in such as Mme Roland and Rosa Luxemburg the flame that fires their lives. In her subjection, in her undoing, the young girl can sometimes summon the greatest audacities from the depths of her opposition. She may attain to poetry; she can also reach heroism. One of the ways of meeting the fact that she is poorly integrated in society is for her to pass beyond her limited horizons.

The richness and strength of their natures, in favorable circumstances, have enabled some women to go on as adults with the passionate designs of adolescence. But these are exceptions. Not without

---

[4] We shall consider the special characteristics of feminine mysticism later.

reason did George Eliot and Margaret Kennedy have their heroines, Maggie and Tessa, die young. The Brontë sisters suffered a harsh fate. The young girl is touching because she makes a stand, alone and weak, against the world. But the world is too strong; if she persists in her opposition, it breaks her. Belle de Zuylen, who dazzled Europe with the caustic power and originality of her wit, scared away all her suitors: her refusal to make any concessions condemned her to long years of dreary celibacy, which led her to declare the expression "*vierge et martyre*" redundant. Such obstinacy is uncommon. The vast majority of young girls see that the struggle is much too unequal, and in the end they yield. "You all die at fifteen," wrote Diderot to Sophie Volland. When the combat is—as most often happens—only a symbolic revolt, then defeat is certain. Demanding much in her dreams, filled with hope, but passive, the young girl evokes a pitying smile from adults; they expect her to become resigned. And in fact two years later we find the once queer and rebellious child calmed down and quite prepared to accept the life of a woman. Colette predicts this lot for Vinca, and so it is with the heroines of Mauriac's early novels. The crisis of adolescence is a kind of "travail" comparable to what Dr. Lagache calls the "travail" of mourning. The young girl slowly buries her childhood, puts away the independent and imperious being that was she, and enters submissively upon adult existence.

Certainly we cannot establish well-marked categories according to age only. There are women who remain children all their lives; the behavior I have described is sometimes continued to an advanced age. None the less, there is on the whole a great difference between the tender bud of fifteen and a "big girl." The latter is ready for reality; she hardly moves any longer on the plane of the imaginary; she is less divided against herself than formerly. Marie Bashkirtsev writes at about eighteen: "The more I advance toward the old age of my youth, the more unconcerned I become. Few things now disturb me and everything used to disturb me."

Irène Reweliotty has this to say:

To be acceptable to men, one must think and act like them, otherwise they treat you as a freak, and solitude becomes your lot.

As for me, I am now fed up with solitude and I want a crowd not merely around me but with me. . . . To live now, and no longer to exist and wait and dream and talk to myself, mute and inert.

And farther on:

Through being flattered, courted, and so on, I become fearfully ambitious. It is no longer the trembling, wondering happiness of the fifteen-year-old. It is a kind of cold, hard rage to take my revenge on life, to climb. I flirt, I play at loving. I do not love. . . . I gain in intelligence, in *sang-froid*, in habitual clear-sightedness. I lose my warmth of heart. It was like a clean break. . . . In two months I have left my childhood behind me.

These confessions of a nineteen-year-old girl [5] have almost the same ring:

Formerly, ah, what a conflict between a mentality that seemed incompatible with the present century and the calls of this century itself! Now I seem conscious of a certain calmness. Each new and grandiose idea that occurs to me, instead of causing a painful turmoil, an incessant destruction and reconstruction, is marvelously adapted to what is already in my mind. . . Now I move insensibly from theoretical ideas to life as it is, without a break.

The young girl has in the end accepted her femininity—unless she is especially ill-favored; and frequently she is happy to enjoy without cost the pleasures and triumphs it provides, before becoming definitely settled down in life; not as yet bound to any duties, irresponsible, at liberty, she none the less views the present as neither empty nor delusive, since it is only a stage; dressing up and flirting still seem but a game, and her dreams of the future hide its futility. In *The Waves* [6] Virginia Woolf thus records the thoughts of the young coquette Jinny, expressed in a conversation at college:

I feel myself shining in the dark. Silk is on my knee. My silk legs rub smoothly together. The stones of a necklace lie cold on

---

[5] Cited by Debesse in *La Crise d'originalité de l'adolescence*.
[6] New York: Harcourt, Brace & Co.; 1931.

my throat. . . . I am arrayed, I am prepared. . . . My hair is swept in one curve. My lips are precisely red. I am ready now to join men and women on the stairs, my peers. I pass them, exposed to their gaze, as they are to mine. . . . I now begin to unfurl, in this scent, in this radiance, as a fern when its curled leaves unfurl. . . . I feel a thousand capacities spring up in me. I am arch, gay, languid, melancholy by turns. I am rooted, but I flow. All gold, flowing that way, I say to this one, "Come. . . ." He approaches. He makes towards me. This is the most exciting moment I have ever known. I flutter. I ripple. . . . Are we not lovely sitting together here, I in my satin; he in black and white? My peers may look at me now. I look straight back at you, men and women. I am one of you. This is my world. . . . The door opens. The door goes on opening. Now I think, next time it opens the whole of my life will be changed. . . . The door opens. Oh, come, I say to this one, rippling gold from head to heels. "Come," and he comes towards me.

But as the girl matures, her mother's authority weighs more heavily upon her. If she does housework at home, she hates to be only an assistant, for she would like to devote her effort to her own home and her own children. Frequently she finds rivalry with her mother disagreeable, and she is especially disturbed if younger brothers or sisters are born; she feels that her mother has had her day and it is now time for her to have children, to take charge. If she works outside, she dislikes coming home and still being treated like a mere member of the family and not like an independent individual.

Less romantic than formerly, she begins to think much more about marriage than love. She no longer adorns her future husband with an impressive halo: what she wants is to have a substantial position in the world, to enter upon her life as a woman. In the book already mentioned, Virginia Woolf presents a rich young country girl's musings as follows:

For soon in the hot midday when the bees hum round the hollyhocks my lover will come. He will stand under the cedar tree. To his one word I shall answer my one word. What has formed in me I shall give him. I shall have children; I shall have maids in aprons; men with pitchforks; a kitchen where they bring the ailing lambs to warm in baskets, where the hams hang and the onions glisten. I shall be like my mother, silent in a blue apron locking up the cupboards.

In Mary Webb's *Precious Bane* [7] poor Prue dreams in similar fashion:

It seemed such a terrible thing never to marry. All girls got married. . . . And when girls got married, they had a cottage, and a lamp, maybe, to light when their man came home, or if it was only candles it was all one, for they could put them in the window, and he'd think "There's my missus now, lit the candles!" And then one day Mrs. Beguildy would be making a cot of rushes for 'em, and one day there'd be a babe in it, grand and solemn, and bidding letters sent round for the christening, and the neighbours coming round the babe's mother like bees round the queen. Often, when things went wrong, I'd say to myself, "Ne'er mind, Prue Sarn! There'll come a day when you'll be queen in your own skep."

For most grown-up girls, whether they work hard or lead a frivolous existence, whether they are confined at home or enjoy some liberty, to get a husband—or, at least, a steady sweetheart—becomes a more and more urgent business. This concern is often destructive of feminine friendships. The "best friend" loses her place of honor. The young girl sees rivals rather than allies in her companions. I knew one such who, intelligent and gifted, described herself in poems and literary essays as a "faraway princess"; she declared sincerely that she retained no affection for her childhood companions: if they were homely and stupid, they annoyed her; if charming, she feared them. The impatient hope for a man, often involving maneuvers, stratagems, and humiliations, narrows the young girl's horizon; she becomes egoistical and callous. And if Prince Charming is slow in making his appearance, then weariness and bitterness of spirit develop.

The young girl's character and behavior are the outcome of her situation: if this is modified, then the adolescent girl also takes on a different aspect. Today it is becoming possible for her to take her future into her own hands instead of entrusting it to a man. If she is absorbed in studies, sport, professional training, or some social or

---

[7] New York: E. P. Dutton & Co.; 1926.

political activity, she is released from obsession with the male, she is much less concerned with her sentimental and sexual conflicts. Still, she has much more difficulty than the young man in finding self-realization as an independent individual. As I have shown, neither her family nor the mores are favorable to her efforts in this direction.

Moreover, even when she chooses independence, she none the less makes a place in her life for man, for love. She is likely to fear that if she devotes herself completely to some undertaking, she will miss her womanly destiny. This feeling often remains unavowed, but it is there; it weakens well-defined purposes, it sets limits. In any case, the woman who works wishes to reconcile her professional success with purely feminine accomplishments; not only does this mean that she must devote considerable time to her appearance, but, what is more serious, it means that her vital interests are divided. Along with his regular program of work, the male student amuses himself with free flights of thought, and thence come his best inspirations; but woman's reveries take a very different direction: she will think about her personal appearance, about men, about love; she will give only what is strictly necessary to her studies, her career, when in these domains nothing is so necessary as the superfluous. It is not a matter of mental weakness, of an inability to concentrate, but rather of division between interests difficult to reconcile. A vicious circle is established and it is often astounding to see how readily a woman can give up music, study, her profession, once she has found a husband. She has clearly involved too little of herself in her plans to find much profit in accomplishing them. Everything combines to restrain her personal ambition, and enormous social pressure still urges her on to find social position and justification in marriage. It is natural that she should not seek by her own efforts to create her place in the world or should do so but timidly. As long as complete economic equality is not realized in society and as long as the mores authorize woman to profit as wife or mistress from the privileges held by certain men, so long will her dream of unearned success remain and hamper her own accomplishment.

But in whatever way the young girl attains adulthood, her apprenticeship is not yet over. Whether by slow gradations or all of a sudden, she must undergo her sexual initiation. There are young girls who hold aloof. If sexually disagreeable incidents have marred their childhood, if faulty education has gradually rooted in them a horror of sexuality, they may retain their childish repugnance for the male. It may happen, also, that circumstances may enforce a prolonged virginity upon certain women against their will. But usually the young girl fulfills her sexual destiny sooner or later. How she meets it evidently depends closely upon the events of her past. In any case it is a new experience, which comes to her under unforeseen circumstances and to which she reacts independently. We must now consider this new stage.

CHAPTER XIV

Sexual Initiation

In a sense, woman's sexual initiation, like man's, begins in earliest childhood. There is a theoretical and practical apprenticeship that goes on continuously from the oral, anal, and genital phases to adulthood. But the erotic experiences of the young girl are not simply an extension of her former sexual activities; very often they are unexpected and disagreeable; and they are always in the nature of a new event that makes a break with the past. When she is actually undergoing these experiences, all the young girl's problems are epitomized in sharp and urgent form. In certain cases the crisis is easily passed, but there are tragic instances in which the situation is resolved only by death or dementia. In all cases a woman's future is strongly affected by the way in which she reacts at this time. Psychiatrists all agree on the extreme importance of a woman's first erotic experiences: their repercussions are felt throughout the rest of her life.

The situation under consideration is profoundly different—biologically, socially, and psychologically—for man and woman. For a man, the transition from childish sexuality to maturity is relatively simple: erotic pleasure is objectified, desire being directed toward another person instead of being realized within the bounds of self. Erection is the expression of this need; with penis, hands, mouth, with his whole body, a man reaches out toward his partner, but he himself remains at the center of this activity, being, on the whole, the *subject* as opposed to *objects* that he perceives and *instruments* that he manipulates; he projects himself toward the other without losing his independence; the feminine flesh is for him a prey, and through it he gains access to the qualities he desires, as with any object. To be sure, he does not succeed in taking actual possession of them for himself, but at least he embraces them. The caress, the kiss, imply a partial check; but this check itself is a stimulant and a pleasure. The act of love is completed in the orgasm, its natural outcome. Coition has a definite physiological end and aim; in ejaculation the male rids himself of certain discomforting secretions; he obtains a complete relief, following upon sex excitement, which is unfailingly accompanied with pleasure. To be sure, this pleasure was not the only thing aimed at; it is often followed by disappointment: the need has disappeared, although he is not in all ways satisfied. In any case, a definite act has been consummated, and the man's body retains its integrity: his service to the species is combined with his personal enjoyment.

Woman's eroticism is much more complex, and it reflects the complexity of the feminine situation. We have seen [1] that instead of integrating the powerful drives of the species into her individual life, the female is the prey of the species, the interests of which are dissociated from the female's interests as an individual. This antinomy reaches its height in the human female; it is manifested, for one thing, in the opposition of the two organs: the clitoris and the vagina. At the stage of childhood the former is the center of feminine sex feeling. Though certain psychiatrists hold that vaginal sensitivity exists in some little girls, it is a matter of controversy, and anyway it has only secondary importance. The clitorid system remains unmodified in the adult,[2] and woman retains this erotic independence all her life; the clitorid orgasm, like that of the male, is a kind of detumescence, which is accomplished in a quasi-mechanical manner; but it is only indirectly connected with normal coition, and it plays no part in procreation.

Woman is penetrated and fecundated by way of the vagina, which becomes an erotic center only through the intervention of the male, and this always constitutes a kind of violation. Formerly it was by a real or simulated rape that a woman was torn from her childhood universe and hurled into wifehood; it remains an act of violence that changes a girl into a woman: we still speak of "taking" a girl's virginity, her flower, or "breaking" her maidenhead. This defloration is not the gradually accomplished outcome of a continuous evolution, it is an abrupt rupture with the past, the beginning of a new cycle. Sex pleasure thereafter is obtained through the contractions of the vaginal wall; do these contractions bring about a precise and definite orgasm? It is a point still in dispute. The anatomical data are vague. The Kinsey Report states the case as follows:

---

[1] Book I, Ch. i.

[2] Unless excision is practiced, as is the custom in some primitive tribes.

"There is a great deal of anatomic and clinical evidence that most of the interior of the vagina is without nerves. A considerable amount of surgery may be performed inside the vagina without need for anesthetics. Nerves have been demonstrated inside the vagina only in an area in the anterior wall, proximate to the base of the clitoris." However, in addition to the stimulation of that innervated zone, "the female may be conscious of the intrusion of an object into the vagina, particularly if vaginal muscles are tightened; but the satisfaction so obtained is probably related more to muscle tonus than it is to erotic nerve stimulation." (Page 576.)

None the less it is beyond doubt that vaginal pleasure exists; and vaginal masturbation, for that matter—in adult women—seems more common than Kinsey indicates.[3] But what is certain is that the vaginal reaction is a very complex one, which may be referred to as psychophysiological, because it not only involves the whole nervous system but also depends upon the whole experience and situation of the individual: it demands a profound acceptation on the part of the woman in her entirety.

The new erotic cycle inaugurated by the first copulation requires for its establishment a kind of montage or rearrangement in the nervous system, the elaboration of a pattern not previously outlined, which should include also the clitorid apparatus; this takes some time to bring about, and in some cases it may never be successfully accomplished. It is striking that in woman there is a choice of two systems, one of which perpetuates juvenile independence while the other consigns woman to man and childbearing. The normal sexual act in effect puts woman into a state of dependency upon the male and the species. It is the male—as in most animals—who has the aggressive role, the female submitting to his embrace. Normally, she can be

---

[3] The use of an artificial penis in solitary sexual gratification may be traced down from classic times, and doubtless prevailed in the very earliest human civilization. . . . The use of ordinary objects has reached an extraordinary degree of extent and variety. . . . In recent years the following are a few of the objects found in the vagina or bladder whence they could be removed only by surgical interference: pencils, sticks of sealing-wax, spools, wire hairpins, bone hairpins, bodkins, knitting-needles . . . compasses, glass stoppers, candles, corks, tumblers, forks, toothpicks, toothbrushes, pomade-pots (in a case recorded by Schroeder with a cockchafer inside, a makeshift substitute for the Japanese *rin-no-tama*), hen's eggs, etc. (Havelock Ellis: *Studies in the Psychology of Sex*, Vol. I, pp. 169, 171 ff.)

taken by the man at any time, whereas he can take her only when he is in a state of erection. Apart from cases of vaginismus, when the woman is sealed more effectively than by the hymen, feminine disinclination can be overcome; and even in vaginismus there are ways in which the male can relieve himself upon a body that his muscular power puts at his mercy. Since she is object, any inertia on her part does not seriously affect her natural role: a statement supported by the fact that many men do not trouble themselves to find out whether the women who bed with them desire coition or merely submit to it. It is even possible to copulate with a dead body. Coition cannot take place without the male's consent, and male satisfaction is its natural termination. Fecundation can occur without any pleasure being felt by the woman. But fecundation by no means represents for her the completion of the sexual process; on the contrary, her service to the species only begins at this point: it is fulfilled slowly and painfully, in pregnancy, childbirth, and lactation.

"Anatomic destiny" is thus profoundly different in man and woman, and no less different is their moral and social situation. Patriarchal civilization dedicated woman to chastity; it recognized more or less openly the right of the male to sexual freedom, while woman was restricted to marriage. The sexual act, if not sanctified by the code, by a sacrament, is for her a fault, a fall, a defeat, a weakness; she should defend her virtue, her honor; if she "yields," if she "falls," she is scorned; whereas any blame visited upon her conqueror is mixed with admiration. From primitive times to our own, intercourse has always been considered a "service" for which the male thanks the woman by giving her presents or assuring her maintenance; but to serve is to give oneself a master; there is no reciprocity in this relation. The nature of marriage, as well as the existence of prostitutes, is the proof: woman *gives herself,* man pays her and takes her. Nothing forbids the male to act the master, to take inferior creatures. Affairs with servant girls have always been tolerated, whereas the middle-class woman who gives herself to a chauffeur or a gardener loses caste. The savagely racist American men of the South have always been permitted by the mores to sleep with black women, before the Civil War as today, and they make use of this right with lordly arrogance; but a white woman who had commerce with a black in slavery days would have been put to death, and today she would probably be lynched.

To express the fact that he has copulated with a woman, a man says he has "possessed" her, or has "had" her; the Greeks called a woman who had not known man an unsubdued virgin; the Romans called Messalina "unconquered" because none of her lovers gave her full pleasure. So for the lover the act of love is conquest, victory. If erection is often regarded in another man as a comic parody on voluntary action, each one none the less views it in himself with a touch of vanity. The erotic vocabulary of males is drawn from military terminology: the lover has the mettle of a soldier, his organ is tense like a bow, to ejaculate is to "go off"; he speaks of attack, assault, victory. In his sex excitement there is a certain flavor of heroism. "The generative act," writes Benda in *Le Rapport d'Uriel*, "consisting in the occupation of one being by another, imposes on the one hand the idea of a conqueror, on the other of something conquered. Indeed, when referring to their love relations, the most civilized speak of conquest, attack, assault, siege, and of defense, defeat, surrender, clearly shaping the idea of love upon that of war. The act, involving the pollution of one person by another, confers a certain pride upon the polluter, and some humiliation upon the polluted, even when she consents."

This phraseology introduces a new myth: namely, that the man inflicts a defilement upon the woman. As a matter of fact, the seminal fluid is not in the nature of excrement; one speaks of "nocturnal pollution" because natural ends are not served; but because coffee will stain a light-colored dress, one does not call it filth that will soil the stomach. It is sometimes held, on the contrary, that woman is impure because she has "dirty discharges" and that she pollutes the male. To be the one who does the polluting confers in any case a very dubious superiority. As a matter of fact, the privileged position of man comes from the integration of his biologically aggressive role with his social function as leader or master; it is on account of this social function that the physiological differences take on all their significance. Because man is ruler in the world, he holds that the violence of his desires is a sign of his sovereignty; a man of great erotic capacity is said to be strong, potent—epithets that imply activity and transcendence. But, on the other hand, woman being only an object, she will be described as *warm* or *frigid*, which is to say that she will never manifest other than passive qualities.

The environment, the climate, in which feminine sexuality awakens is thus quite different from that which surrounds the adolescent male. More, the erotic attitude of the female is very complex at the moment when she faces the male for the first time. It is not true, as is sometimes maintained, that the virgin is unacquainted with sexual desire and that the man must awaken her sex feeling. This legend once again betrays the male's flair for domination, expressing his wish that she should be in no way independent, even in her longing for him. The fact is that in the male as well it is often contact with the opposite sex that rouses first desire, and inversely the majority of young girls long heatedly for caresses before they have ever felt the caressing hand. Isadora Duncan in *My Life* writes as follows:

> My breasts, which until then had been hardly perceptible, began to swell softly and astonish me with charming but embarrassing sensations. My hips, which had been like a boy's, took on another undulation, and through my whole being I felt one great surging, longing, unmistakable urge, so that I could no longer sleep at night but tossed and turned in feverish, painful unrest.

Stekel reports the following in the life history of a young woman patient:

> I began vigorously to flirt. I had to have, what I myself then called, a "nerve tickler." . . . I was a passionate dancer and while dancing I always shut my eyes the better to enjoy it. . . . During the dancing I was somewhat exhibitionistic; my sensuality seemed to overcome my feeling of shame. . . . During the first year I danced with avidity and great enjoyment. . . . I slept many hours, masturbated daily, often keeping it up for an hour at a stretch . . . frequently until I was bathed in sweat and, too fatigued to continue, I fell asleep. . . . I was on fire. I would have accepted the first man who would have asked me to marry him. I did not seek the man, but a man.[4]

The truth is that virginal desire is not expressed as a precise need: the virgin does not know exactly what she wants. The aggressive eroticism of childhood still survives in her; her first impulses were

---

[4] W. Stekel: *Frigidity in Woman*, Vol. II, pp. 75 ff.

prehensile, and she still wants to embrace, possess. She wants her coveted prey to be endowed with the qualities which, through taste, odor, touch, have appeared to her as values. For sexuality is not an isolated domain, it continues the dreams and joys of early sensuality; children and adolescents of both sexes like the smooth, creamy, satiny, mellow, elastic: what yields to pressure without collapsing or altering and glides under the look or the fingers. Like man, woman delights in the soft warmth of sand dunes, often likened to breasts, in the light feeling of silk, in the soft delicacy of eiderdown, in the bloom of flower or fruit; and the young girl loves especially pale pastel colors, the mist of tulle and muslin. She has no liking for rough fabrics, gravel, rockwork, bitter flavors, acid odors; what she, like her brothers, first caressed and cherished was her mother's flesh. In her narcissism, in her homosexual experiences, whether diffuse or definite, she acts as subject and seeks possession of a feminine body. When she confronts the male, she feels in her hands and her lips the desire to caress a prey actively. But crude man, with his hard muscles, his rough and often hairy skin, his strong odor, his coarse features, does not appeal to her as desirable; he even seems repulsive.[5]

If the prehensile, possessive, tendency remains especially strong in a woman, she, like Renée Vivien, will be oriented in the homosexual direction. Or she will choose only males whom she can treat like women: so with the heroine of Rachilde's *Monsieur Vénus*, who buys herself a young man; she enjoys caressing him passionately but does not let him deflorate her. There are women who like to fondle boys of thirteen or fourteen or even children, and who avoid grown men. But we have seen that in a majority of women a passive sexuality has also developed since childhood: woman likes to be embraced, caressed, and especially after puberty she wants to be flesh in a man's arms; the role of subject is normally assigned to him; she knows that; she has been told repeatedly "a man has no need of being good-looking"; she is not supposed to look for the inert qualities of an object in him, but for strength and virile power.

Thus she is divided against herself; she longs for a strong embrace that will make of her a quivering thing, but roughness and force are

---

[5] This is expressed in Renée Vivien's poem, given here in translation:

I am a woman and so I have no right to your beauty
. . . I am condemned to the ugliness of man
I am denied your hair, your eyes
Because your hair is long and fragrant.

also disagreeable deterrents that offend her. Her feeling is located both in her skin and in her hand, and the requirements of one are in part opposed to those of the other. In so far as she can, she chooses a compromise; she gives herself to a virile man, but one young and attractive enough to be a desirable object; in a good-looking youth she can find all the attractions she covets. In the Song of Songs there is a symmetry in the delights of wife and husband; she finds in him what he seeks in her: the fauna and flora of the earth, precious stones, streams, the stars. But she lacks the means for taking these treasures; her anatomy compels her to remain clumsy and impotent like a eunuch: the wish for possession is fruitless for want of an organ in which it is incarnated. And man declines the passive role, anyway. Frequently circumstances lead the young girl to yield to a male whose caresses move her though she finds no pleasure in looking at him or caressing him in return. It has not been sufficiently noted that in the repugnance that is mixed with her desires, there is not only fear of masculine aggressiveness but also a deep feeling of frustration: woman's sex pleasure must be obtained in opposition to the spontaneous surge of her sensuality, whereas in man the joy of touching and seeing has a common basis with specifically sexual pleasure.

But the elements of even passive eroticism are ambiguous. Nothing is so equivocal as a *touch*. Many men who handle all sorts of material without disgust hate to come into contact with plants or animals. Women's flesh may shiver agreeably or shudder at the touch of silk or velvet: I recall a friend of my youth who got goose flesh merely at the sight of a peach; the transition is facile from uneasiness to pleasant tickling, from irritation to pleasure; arms about the body can be a refuge and protection, but they may also imprison, suffocate. This ambiguity is maintained in the virgin because of her paradoxical situation: the organ in which her metamorphosis is to occur is sealed. The vague and heated call of her flesh spreads throughout her whole body except for the very place where coition must take place. There is no organ that permits the virgin to satisfy her active eroticism; and she has no actual experience with the one that dooms her to passivity.

Still, that passivity is not mere inertia. For a woman to be aroused, certain positive phenomena must be present: excitement of the erogenous zones, tumescence of certain erectile tissues, production of secretions, rise in temperature, and acceleration of the pulse and of breathing. Desire and sex pleasure demand an expenditure of vital force in woman as in man; although receptive in nature, feminine sex-hunger is in a sense active, it is manifested in a nervous and muscular tension. Apathetic and listless women are always cold. There is some question as to the existence of constitutional frigidity, and certainly psychic factors play a leading part in determining woman's erotic capacities; but it is not to be doubted that physiological inadequacies and lowered vitality are manifested in part through sexual indifference.

On the other hand, if the vital energy is expended in voluntary activities, such as sports, it is not turned into sexual channels: Scandinavian women are healthy, strong, and cold. Ardent women are those who combine languor with *fire*, like those of Italy and Spain—that is, those whose ardent vitality has only a carnal release. To *make* oneself an object, to *make* oneself passive, is a very different thing from *being* a passive object: a woman in love is neither asleep nor dead; there is a surge in her which unceasingly ebbs and flows: the ebb creates the spell that keeps desire alive. But it is easy to destroy the equilibrium between ardor and abandon. Male desire is tension; it can spread through a body whose nerves and muscles are taut: positions and movements that bring the organism into voluntary participation do not run counter to it, and often further it. On the contrary, all voluntary effort prevents the feminine flesh from being "taken"; this is why woman spontaneously [6] declines the forms of coition which demand effort and tension on her part; too sudden or too many changes in position, any call for consciously directed activities—whether words or behavior—tend to break the spell. The stress of unbridled ardors can cause irritation, contraction, tenseness: some women scratch or bite, their bodies stiffened and indued with unaccustomed strength; but these phenomena appear only when a certain paroxysmal state is reached, and this is reached only when the absence of any inhibition—physical as well as moral—permits complete concentration of living energy in the sexual act. This means that it is not enough for the young girl to *let herself go*; docile, languid, her mind elsewhere, she satisfies neither her partner nor herself. An active participation is asked of her in an adventure that is positively desired neither by her virgin body nor by her mind, beset as it is by taboos, prohibitions, prejudices, and exactions.

• • •

[6] We shall see later that there are psychological factors that may alter this primary attitude.

It is understandable that under these conditions woman's erotic induction is not easy. As we have seen, incidents of childhood or youth have rather frequently set up deep resistances in her that are sometimes insurmountable; more often the young girl goes on regardless of them, but then serious conflicts result. Her strict upbringing, her fear of sin, her sense of guilt toward her mother create powerful blocks. Virginity is valued so highly in many circles that to lose it outside legitimate marriage seems a real disaster. The young girl who yields through impulse or surprise thinks she is dishonored. The wedding night, which delivers the virgin to the tender mercies of a man whom, commonly enough, she has not really chosen, and which is supposed to accomplish in a few hours—or minutes—her entire sexual initiation, is an experience no easier. In general, any transition is distressing because of its definite and irreversible character: to become a woman is to break with the past, once for all. But this particular transition is more dramatic than any other; not only does it create a hiatus between yesterday and tomorrow; it also tears the young girl from the world of imagination wherein much of her life has unfolded and throws her into the real world. By analogy with the training of a bull, Michel Leiris calls the nuptial bed "the real thing"; for the virgin, indeed, this expression assumes its fullest and most fearsome sense. During the period of engagement, of flirting, of paying court, introductory as it was, she continued living in her accustomed universe of ceremony and reverie; her suitor spoke in romantic or at least polite accents; it was still possible to play hide-and-seek. And all at once she finds herself gazed upon by real eyes, grasped by real hands: it is the implacable reality of this gaze and this grasp that appalls her.

The role of initiator belongs to the young man anatomically and conventionally. To be sure, the virgin young man's first mistress also gives him his initiation; but even so he has an erotic independence clearly shown by the erection; his mistress simply provides in its reality the object he already desires: a woman's body. The young girl needs a man to reveal her own body to her: she is much more deeply dependent. From his earliest experiences man is ordinarily active, decisive, whether he pays his partner or more or less briefly courts and solicits her. The young girl, on the contrary, *is* courted and solicited in most cases; even when she first incites the man, it is he who then takes control of their relations; he is often older and more expert, and admittedly he should take charge of this adventure, which is new to her; his desire is more aggressive and imperious. Lover or husband, it is for him to lead her to the couch, where she has only to give herself over and do his bidding. Even if she has mentally accepted this domination, she becomes panic-stricken at the moment when she must actually submit to it.

In the first place, she shuns the enveloping gaze. Her modesty is in part a superficial acquirement, but it also has deep roots. Men and women all feel the shame of their flesh; in its pure, inactive presence, its unjustified immanence, the flesh exists, under the gaze of others, in its absurd contingence, and yet it is *oneself*: oh, to prevent it from existing for others, oh, to deny it! There are men who say they cannot bear to show themselves naked before a woman unless in a state of erection; and indeed through erection the flesh becomes activity, potency, the sex organ is no longer an inert object, but, like the hand or face, the imperious expression of a subjectivity. This is one of the reasons why modesty paralyzes young men much less than women; because of their aggressive role they are less exposed to being gazed at; and if they are, then they have little fear of being judged, for it is not inert qualities that their mistress demands of them: their complexes will rather depend upon their amatory power and their skill in giving pleasure; at least they can defend themselves, try to win the encounter. It is not given to woman to alter her flesh at will: when she no longer hides it, she yields it up without defense; even if she longs for caresses, she revolts at the idea of being seen and touched; and all the more since her breasts and bottom are a peculiarly fleshly growth; many adult women hate to be looked at from behind even when dressed; and one can imagine what resistance the neophyte in love must overcome in consenting to let herself be gazed upon. Doubtless a Phryne need have no fear of man's gaze; she unveils herself, on the contrary, with arrogant pride—she is clothed in her beauty. But even if she is Phryne's equal, the young girl never feels certain of it; she cannot take arrogant pride in her body unless male approval has confirmed her youthful vanity. And just this fells her with fear; her lover is still more redoubtable than a look: he is a judge. He is to reveal her to herself in very truth; though passionately enchanted with her own reflection, every young girl feels uncertain of herself at the moment of the masculine verdict; and so she wants the light out, she hides under the bedclothes. When she admires herself in the mirror, she is still only dreaming of herself, dreaming of herself as seen through masculine eyes; now the eyes are really there; impossible to deceive, impossible to struggle: a mysterious free being will make the decision—and without appeal. In the actual trial of the erotic experience the obsessions of childhood and adolescence are at length to be dissipated or confirmed forever. Many young girls are distressed by these too thick ankles, these too meager or too ample breasts, these slender thighs, this wart; and often they dread some hidden malformation. According to Stekel, all young girls are full of ridiculous fears, secretly believing that they may be physically abnormal. One, for example, regarded the navel as the organ of copulation and was unhappy about its being closed. Another thought she was a hermaphrodite.

Girls without these obsessions are often alarmed at the idea that certain actually nonexistent parts of the body will suddenly become visible. Will her new aspect arouse disgust? Indifference? An ironical remark? It must undergo the test of masculine judgment: the chips are down. This is the reason why the man's attitude will have deep and lasting effects. His ardor and affection can be a source of confidence that will stand the woman in good stead: to the age of eighty she will believe herself to be that blossom, that delightful creature, who one night caused the burgeoning of a man's desire. On the other hand, a maladroit lover or husband may give rise to an inferiority complex, on which lasting neuroses will sometimes be grafted; and the woman may feel such resentment as will lead to obstinate frigidity. Stekel reports striking examples: one woman suffered for years from crippling backache and frigidity, because on her wedding night the defloration was painful and her husband accused her of deceiving him in regard to her virginity. Another husband made uncomplimentary remarks about how "stubby and thick" his bride's legs were. She responded by immediate and lasting frigidity and later nervous troubles. Another frigid woman told how her husband brutally deplored her too slender proportions. And so on in numerous cases.

To be gazed at is one danger; to be manhandled is another. Women as a rule are unfamiliar with violence, they have not been through the tussles of childhood and youth as have men; and now the girl is laid hold of, swept away in a bodily struggle in which the man is the stronger. She is no longer free to dream, to delay, to maneuver: she is in his power, at his disposal. These embraces, so much like a hand-to-hand tussle, frighten her, for she has never tussled. She is used to the caresses of a fiancé, a comrade, a colleague, a civilized and polite man; but now he takes on a peculiar aspect, egoistical and headstrong; she is without recourse against this stranger. It is not uncommon for the young girl's first experience to be a real rape and for the man to act in an odiously brutal manner; in the country and wherever manners are rough, it often happens that—half consenting, half revolted—the young peasant girl loses her virginity in some ditch, in shame and fear. In any case, what very often happens in all circles and classes is for the virgin to be abruptly taken by an egoistic lover who is primarily interested in his own pleasure, or by a husband, sure of his conjugal rights, who feels insulted by his wife's resistance and even becomes enraged if the defloration is difficult.

Furthermore, however deferential and polite the man may be, the first penetration is always a violation. Because she desires caresses on lips or breasts, or even longs for a known or imagined pleasure more specifically sexual, what happens is that a man's sex organ tears the young girl and penetrates into regions where it has not been desired. Many writers have described the painful surprise of a virgin, lying enchanted in the arms of lover or husband, who believes she is at last to fulfill her voluptuous dreams and who feels an unexpected pain in her secret sexual parts; her dreams vanish, her excitement fades, and love assumes the aspect of a surgical operation.

Among the confessions collected by Dr. Liepmann,[7] I find a typical example. The girl belongs to a family in moderate circumstances and is very ignorant of sexual matters.

"I used to imagine that one could have a child by no more than kissing. At eighteen I met a gentleman of whom I was really enamored." She often went out with him, and during their talks he told her that if a young girl loves a man she should give herself because men cannot live without sex relations and if they cannot afford to marry they must have young girls. She held back. Later he arranged for an expedition that enabled them to spend the night together. . . . She objected, but she loved him and, being morally dominated, she followed him to a hotel, asking him to spare her. . . . He calmed her after a long resistance, and, no longer mistress of herself, she let him proceed. She remembered only that she trembled violently. Afterward, in the street, she felt it was all a bad

---

[7] Published in French under the title *Jeunesse et sexualité*.

dream from which she would awaken. She broke off with the man and knew no other during nine years, after which she married.

Defloration was a kind of rape in this case. But it can be painful even when quite voluntary. We know how fevered the young Isadora Duncan was. When she met a handsome actor, she fell in love at first sight and was courted ardently.[8]

> I, too, was aroused and dizzy, while an irresistible longing to press him closer and closer surged in me, until one night, losing all control and falling into a fury, he carried me to the sofa. Frightened but ecstatic and crying out in pain, I was initiated into the act of love. I confess that my first impressions were a horrible fright and an atrocious pain, as if someone had torn out several of my teeth at once; but a great pity for what he seemed to be suffering prevented me from running away from what was at first sheer mutilation and torture. . . . Next day what was at that time no more than a painful experience for me continued amidst my martyred cries and tears. I felt as if I were being mangled.

Before long she came to enjoy, first with this lover, then with others, the rapture she lyrically describes.

But in actual experience, as formerly in virginal musings, it is not the pain that seems most significant: the fact of penetration counts much more heavily. In coition man uses only an external organ, while woman is struck deep within her vitals. Doubtless many young men adventure not without anxiety into the secret dark of woman, once more feeling childhood's terror at the threshold of a cave or tomb, its fright at jaws, scythes, traps: they fancy that the swollen penis may be caught in the mucous sheath. Woman, once penetrated, has no such sense of danger; but in return she feels trespassed upon in her flesh.

The proprietor asserts his rights over his land, the housekeeper over her dwelling—"no trespassing!" Woman especially, in view of her frustration in transcendence, is jealous in the defense of her intimate concerns: her room, her closet, her boxes, are sacred. Colette relates

---

[8] *My Life.* The passage quoted is here translated in part from the French as cited by the author, since comparison with the American version (Boni & Liveright, third printing, 1928) would seem to indicate that there are some omissions in the latter.—TR.

how an old prostitute once said to her: "No man, madame, has ever entered my room; Paris is quite large enough for what I have to do with men." If not her body, she possessed a small terrain forbidden to others.

But the young girl has hardly more than her body which she can call her own: it is her greatest treasure; the man who enters her *takes* it from her; the common expression is justified by the actual experience. The humiliation she anticipated is undergone in fact: she is overpowered, forced to compliance, conquered. Like the female of most species, she is *under* the male during copulation.[9] Adler makes a great point of the resulting feeling of inferiority. From childhood on, the notions of superiority and inferiority are among the most important; it is impressive to climb high in trees; heaven is above the earth, hell below; to fall, to go down, is to fail, and to go up is to succeed; in wrestling, to win is to force the opponent's shoulders down to the ground. Now, the woman lies in the posture of defeat; worse, the man rides her as he would an animal subject to bit and reins. She always feels passive: she *is* caressed, penetrated; she undergoes coition, whereas the man exerts himself actively. True enough, the male organ is not a striated, voluntary muscle; it is neither plowshare nor sword, but only flesh; however, man imparts to it a movement that is voluntary; it goes back and forth, stops, moves again, while the woman takes it submissively. It is the man who decides what position is to be used in love-making—especially when the woman is new at the game—and he determines the duration and frequency of the act. She feels that she is an instrument: liberty rests wholly with the other. This is what has been expressed poetically by saying that woman is the violin, man the bow that makes her vibrate. "In love-making," says Balzac,[1] "apart from any question of the soul, woman is like a lyre which gives up its secret only to him who knows how to play on it." He *takes* his pleasure with her; he *gives* pleasure to her; the very words imply lack of reciprocity.

Woman is thoroughly indoctrinated with common notions that

---

[9] The position may, of course, be reversed, but in early experiences it is most unusual for the man to adopt other than the so-called normal position.

[1] *Physiologie du mariage.* In his *Bréviaire de l'amour expérimental* Jules Guyot also has this to say of the husband: "He is the player who produces harmony or cacophony with his hand and his bow. Woman is from this point of view verily a stringed instrument that will produce harmonious or discordant sounds according to how well or ill it is tuned."

endow masculine passion with splendor and make a shameful abdication of feminine sex feeling: woman's intimate experience confirms the fact of this asymmetry. It must not be forgotten that male and female adolescents gain awareness of their bodies in quite dissimilar fashion: the male assumes his easily and with pride in its desires; for the female, in spite of her narcissism, it is a strange and disquieting burden. The sex organ of a man is simple and neat as a finger; it is readily visible and often exhibited to comrades with proud rivalry; but the feminine sex organ is mysterious even to the woman herself, concealed, mucous, and humid, as it is; it bleeds each month, it is often sullied with body fluids, it has a secret and perilous life of its own. Woman does not recognize herself in it, and this explains in large part why she does not recognize its desires as hers. These manifest themselves in an embarrassing manner. Man "gets stiff," but woman "gets wet"; in the very word there are childhood memories of bed-wetting, of guilty and involuntary yielding to the need to urinate. Man feels the same disgust at involuntary nocturnal emissions; to eject a fluid, urine or semen, does not humiliate: it is an active operation; but it is humiliating if the liquid flows out passively, for then the body is no longer an organism with muscles, nerves, sphincters, under control of the brain and expressive of a conscious subject, but is rather a vessel, a container, composed of inert matter and but the plaything of capricious mechanical forces. If the body leaks—as an ancient wall or a dead body may leak—it seems to liquefy rather than to eject fluid: a horrid decomposition.

Feminine sex desire is the soft throbbing of a mollusk. Whereas man is impetuous, woman is only impatient; her expectation can become ardent without ceasing to be passive; man dives upon his prey like the eagle and the hawk; woman lies in wait like the carnivorous plant, the bog, in which insects and children are swallowed up. She is absorption, suction, humus, pitch and glue, a passive influx, insinuating and viscous: thus, at least, she vaguely feels herself to be. Hence it is that there is in her not only resistance to the subjugating intentions of the male, but also conflict within herself. To the taboos and inhibitions contributed by her education and by society are added feelings of disgust and denial coming from the erotic experience itself: these influences are mutually reinforced to such an extent that after the first coition a woman is often more than ever in revolt against her sexual destiny.

Finally, there is another factor that often gives man a hostile aspect and makes the sexual act a serious menace: it is the risk of impregnation. An illegitimate child is such a social and economic handicap for the unmarried woman that girls may commit suicide when they realize they are pregnant, and some girl mothers kill their newborn infants. A danger of such magnitude constitutes a sexual restraint sufficiently powerful to make many young girls keep to the prenuptial chastity prescribed by the mores. When this restraint is insufficient, the young girl is none the less terrified by the awful danger that lurks in her lover's body. Stekel refers to cases in which the terror is quite consciously felt and is sometimes expressed during coitus, in such expressions as: "If only nothing happens! I wonder if it is safe!" And even in marriage a child may not be desired, for reasons of health or economy.

If the woman lacks absolute confidence in her partner, whether lover or husband, her erotic feeling will be paralyzed by her feeling of prudence. Either she will keep anxious watch upon the man's activities, or she will be obliged to get up after coitus and take measures to rid herself of the living sperm he has deposited in spite of her. This hygienic procedure contrasts rudely with the sensuous magic of caresses; it accomplishes a complete separation of the bodies recently conjoined in mutual delight. At such a moment the sperms of the male seem like injurious germs, like offensive matter; she cleanses herself as one washes out a dirty vessel, while the man reposes in superb integrity. A young divorcée told me of her disgust, after a wedding night of doubtful pleasure, when she had to seek the bathroom while her husband nonchalantly smoked a cigarette: it seemed that the ruin of her marriage was made certain from that instant. Repugnance for the apparatus of injection and cleansing is unquestionably a frequent cause of female frigidity.

The availability of more certain and less embarrassing methods of contraception is a great step in the sexual emancipation of women. In a country, like the United States, where these improved methods are widely known, the number of young girls who are virgins at marriage is much smaller than in France. These methods unquestionably do permit a more carefree state of mind in the sexual act. But here again the young woman must overcome a certain repugnance before she can treat her body as a thing: she does not readily accept the idea of being pierced by a man, and she resigns herself no more cheerfully to being stoppered for his pleasure. Whether she seals off her uterus or introduces a spermicidal tampon, a woman aware of the uncertain values of body and of sex will be discommoded by such cold premeditation—and there are many men, too, who dislike the use of these safeguards. It is the total sex situation that justifies the separate elements: behavior that would seem objectionable on analysis seems natural enough when the bodies concerned are transfigured by the erotic qualities they assume; but inversely, when body and behavior are analyzed into separate and meaningless elements, these elements become indecent, obscene. The penetration which, regarded as union, fusion with the beloved, delights the woman in love, regains the surgical, indecent character it has in the child's mind if it occurs in the absence of sex excitement, desire, and pleasure, as may happen in the planned use of preventives. In any case, these precautions are not available to all women; many young girls are quite ignorant of any means of defense against the menace of pregnancy, and they feel with keen anxiety that their fate depends on the good will of the man they give themselves to.

It is understandable that an ordeal hedged about with such obstacles and fraught with such weighty meaning will often inflict serious traumas. It happens sometimes that a latent dementia præcox is brought out by the first experience. Stekel gives examples in *Frigidity in Woman*, two of which are briefly summarized here.

A girl of nineteen, taken with acute delirium, cried out that she would not, she would not, and tore off her clothes. At the clinic she quieted down, but later became incurably demented. Investigation showed that while unhappily in love with one man, she had spent a few nights with another, permitting intimacies though perhaps barely saving her virginity; all this was contrary to her training and beliefs, and from the ensuing conflicts she took refuge in insanity. (Vol. I, p. 76.)

A young woman of twenty-three was sent to a sanatorium because of depression and hallucinations. When seen by Stekel, she failed to notice visitors, wore an expression of horror, and seemed to be resisting sexual attack. Suddenly her expression changed to one of pleasure, she murmured endearing words, and evidently imitated a scene of seduction. It was later shown that she had been through an amatory experience with a married man. She recovered after a time, but refused all association with men, even an offer of marriage. (Vol. I, p. 81.)

In other cases the illness thus induced may not be so severe. Remorse over a lost virginity may bring on various phobias, in which, for example, the patient may show irrational fear of accidental impregnation from toilet seats or of injury to the hymen from dancing or even from stray pins or the like. In one of Stekel's cases, the girl finally confessed to her fiancé, married him, and was cured. In another case remorse and excessive self-depreciation followed yielding without pleasure. The patient recovered after she found another lover who gave her satisfaction and married her.

The Viennese girl whose confessions of childhood are summarized above (pages 323 ff.) related to Stekel her first adult experiences.

In spite of her rather extensive early experience, her "initiation" was none the less a real novelty to her. In brief, after two or three rather stormy scenes with various men, in carriages, parks, and apartments, from which she escaped without losing her virginity in spite of her curiosity and her avidity for "thrills," she met a tourist while on an excursion and accepted his kisses. In the woods there was mutual exposure and sex play, and two days later a brutal defloration, carried out by force and in spite of pleas for mercy. She then believed herself engaged, but he let her return to Vienna alone, after some brutal remarks. Bleeding and weeping, she told her unsympathetic mother and also her friend in the office where she worked. He was kind, but he continued his attentions, and she felt a "frightful shame" in responding to his intimate caresses. She met another man and in coition with him she was quite cold, feeling only disgust. After several other unsatisfactory affairs, and a course of treatment in a sanatorium, she met and married still another man, and in marriage her frigidity disappeared.

In these cases, chosen from many, the brutality of the man, or at least the abruptness of the event, is the factor that causes the trauma or arouses disgust. It is most favorable for the sexual initiation if, without violence or surprise and without set procedure or calculated delay, the young girl slowly learns to overcome her modesty, to know her partner, and to enjoy his love-making. From this point of view, one can only applaud the freedom of behavior that is enjoyed by young American women and that French girls are now beginning to win for themselves: they go on almost imperceptibly from "necking" and "petting" to complete sexual relations. The initiation is facilitated as it loses its tabooed aspect, as the girl feels more free with respect to her partner, and as his attitude of male domination tends to disappear; if her lover, too, is young, a timid novice, an equal, the girl's inhibitions are weaker; but under these conditions her metamorphosis into a woman will not be so profound a change.

Thus Colette's Vinca, in *Blé en herbe*, on the day after a rather rough defloration, displays a calmness that surprises her friend Phil: the point is that she did not feel that she was being "taken"; on the contrary she felt pride in ridding herself of her virginity, she experienced no overwhelming bewilderment; truth to tell, Phil was wrong in being astonished, for his sweetheart had not really come to know the male. Claudine was farther from being unscathed after a mere dance in Renaud's arms. I know of a French schoolgirl, still immature, who, after spending a night with a boy, ran in the morning to a friend's house and announced: "I have slept with C., and it was quite amusing." A professor in an American college told me that his students cease to be virgins before they really become women; their partners have too much respect for them to alarm their modesty, being themselves too bashful to arouse any tumult of feeling in the girls.

There are young girls who plunge into erotic experiences, one after another, in order to relieve their sexual anxiety; they hope in this way to rid themselves of their curiosity and their obsessive interest in sex; but their actions retain a theoretical cast that makes them as unreal as the fantasies in which others anticipate the future. To give oneself through defiance, through fear, or through puritanical rationalism is not to experience genuine erotic reality: only a substitute without much risk or savor is thus obtained. The sexual act is free from anxiety or shame because in such cases emotion remains superficial, and the flesh is not transported with desire. These deflowered virgins continue to be young girls; and it is very likely that when they do come to grips with a sensual and masterful man they will offer virginal resistance. In the meantime they remain still in a kind of awkward age; caresses tickle them, kisses often make them laugh, they look on physical love as a game and, if they happen not to be in a mood for such diversion, a lover's demands soon seem coarse and importunate; they retain feelings of disgust, phobias, adolescent modesty. If they never get beyond this stage—as, according to American men, many American women never do—they will spend their lives in a state of semifrigidity. True sexual maturity is to be found only in the woman who fully accepts carnality in sex desire and pleasure.

It is not to be supposed, however, that all difficulties are mitigated for women of ardent temperament. It may be quite the opposite. Feminine sexual excitement can reach an intensity unknown to man. Male sex excitement is keen but localized, and—except perhaps at the moment of orgasm—it leaves the man quite in possession of himself; woman, on the contrary, really loses her mind; for many this effect marks the most definite and voluptuous moment of the love affair, but it has also a magical and fearsome quality. A man may sometimes feel afraid of the woman in his embrace, so beside herself she seems, a prey to her aberration; the turmoil that she experiences transforms her much more radically than his aggressive frenzy transforms the male. This fever rids her of shame for the moment, but afterward she is ashamed and horrified to think of it. If she is to accept it happily— or proudly, even—she must have expanded freely in the warmth of pleasure; she can acknowledge her desires only if they have been gloriously satisfied: otherwise she angrily repudiates them.

Here we come to the crucial problem of feminine eroticism: at the beginning of woman's erotic life her surrender is not compensated for by a keen and certain enjoyment. She would sacrifice her modesty and her pride much more readily if in doing so she opened the gates of paradise. But defloration, as we have seen, is not an agreeable feature of young love; for it to be so, on the contrary, is most unusual; vaginal pleasure is not attained immediately. According to Stekel's statistics —which have been confirmed by numerous sexologists and psychoanalysts—scarcely 4 per cent of women have orgasmic pleasure from the beginning; 50 per cent attain vaginal orgasm only after weeks, months, or even years.

In this matter psychic factors play an essential part. The feminine body is peculiarly psychosomatic; that is, there is often close connection between the mental and the organic. A woman's moral inhibitions prevent the appearance of sex feeling; not being offset by pleasure, they tend to be perpetuated and to form a barrier of increasing strength. In many cases a vicious circle is set up: an initial awkwardness on the part of the man, a word, a crude gesture, a superior smile, will have repercussions throughout the honeymoon or even throughout married life. Disappointed by the lack of immediate pleasure, the young woman feels a lasting resentment unfavorable for happier relations subsequently.

In the absence of normal satisfaction, true enough, the man can always resort to stimulation of the clitoris, affording a pleasure that, in spite of moralistic fables, can give the woman orgasm and relaxation. But many women reject this because it seems, more than vaginal pleasure, to be *imposed*; for if woman suffers from the egoism of men intent only upon their own relief, she is also offended by a too obvious effort to give her pleasure. "To make the other feel pleasure," says Stekel, "means to dominate the other; to give oneself to someone is to abdicate one's will." Woman accepts sex pleasure much more readily if it seems to flow naturally from that felt by the man, as happens in normal coitus when successful. As Stekel remarks again: "Women submit gladly when they feel that their partners do not *wish* to subjugate them"; on the other hand, when they do feel that wish, they rebel. Many find it repugnant to be excited manually, because the hand is an instrument that does not participate in the pleasure it gives, it represents activity rather than the flesh. And if the male organ, even, seems not to be desirous flesh but a tool skillfully used, woman will feel the same repulsion. Moreover, any such compensation will seem to her to confirm the existence of the block that prevents her from feeling the sensations of a normal woman. Stekel notes after much observation that the whole desire of women called frigid tends toward the normal: "They want to obtain the orgasm after the fashion of [what they regard as] the normal woman, other methods not satisfying their moral requirements."

The man's attitude is thus of great importance. If his desire is violent and brutal, his partner feels that in his embraces she becomes a mere thing; but if he is too self-controlled, too detached, he does not seem to be flesh; he asks the woman to make an object of herself, without her having in return any hold on him. In both cases her pride rebels; for her to be able to reconcile her metamorphosis into a carnal object with her claim to her subjectivity, she must make him her prey while she is making herself his. This is why woman so often remains obstinately frigid. If her lover lacks seductive power, if he is cool, neglectful, awkward, he fails to awaken her sexuality, or he leaves her unsatisfied; but when virile and skillful, he may still arouse reactions of refusal; the woman fears his domination: some can find enjoyment only with men who are timid, poorly endowed, or even half impotent and who are no cause for fright.

Further, it is quite easy for a man to stir up bitterness and resentment in his mistress. And resentment is the most common source of feminine frigidity; in bed the woman punishes the male for all the wrongs she feels she has endured, by offering him an insulting coldness. There is often an aggressive inferiority complex apparent in her attitude, as who should say: "Since you don't love me, since I have defects that are displeasing and am quite contemptible, I shall no longer abandon myself to love, desire, and pleasure." She is thus revenged at once upon him and upon herself if he has humiliated her by neglect, if he has made her jealous, if he was slow in declaring his intentions, if he took her as a mistress when she wanted marriage. The grievance can flare up suddenly and set off this reaction even in a liaison that began happily. It is rare for the man who has aroused this enmity to succeed in overcoming it, but strong evidence of love or esteem may help the situation. Women who were defiant and unbending with a lover have been transformed by a wedding ring—happy, flattered, with clear conscience, all their inhibitions gone. But a new lover who is respectful, amorous, and sensitive can best transform the despitefully used woman into a happy mistress or wife; if he frees her from her inferiority complex, she will give herself with ardor.

Stekel's work on feminine frigidity (frequently quoted above) is primarily devoted to demonstrating the role of psychic factors in causing the condition. Many of his cases show clearly that very often the main factor is resentment against husband or lover. For example, in one case a young woman yielded in expectation of marriage, though, regarding herself as a "liberated woman," she did not insist on it. In actuality she was a slave to conventional morality, and when the man took her at her word, she gradually lost her sex feeling and finally refused his belated offer of marriage. She even contemplated suicide as a means of making his punishment complete. Again, a married woman repressed her feelings and became frigid because she fancied her husband had deceived her during an illness. In another case, a girl of seventeen found intense pleasure in a liaison. Becoming pregnant, she demanded marriage, but her lover hesitated for three weeks before acceding. She could not forgive him the three weeks of anxiety and became frigid, until a later explanation restored her normality.

Even when a woman overcomes all inner resistance and sooner or later attains the vaginal orgasm, her troubles are not over; for her sexual rhythm and that of the male do not coincide, her approach to the orgasm being as a rule much slower than the male's. This situation is referred to in the Kinsey Report, in part as follows:

> For perhaps three-quarters of all males, orgasm is reached within two minutes after the initiation of the sexual relation. . . . Considering the many upper level females who are so adversely conditioned to sexual situations that they may require ten to fifteen minutes of the most careful stimulation to bring them to climax, and considering the fair number of females who never come to climax in their whole lives, it is, of course, demanding that the male be quite abnormal in his ability to prolong sexual activity without ejaculation if he is required to match the female partner. (Page 580.)

We are told that in India the husband is accustomed to smoke or read during intercourse, thus taking his mind off his own sensations so as to prolong the act for his wife's benefit. In the West a Casanova [2] boasts rather of his ability to repeat the act, and his greatest pride is to make his partner cry for mercy, in which he seldom succeeds, according to erotic tradition. Men are prone to complain of the excessive demands of their companions: a frenzied uterus, an ogress, a glutton; she is never satisfied! Montaigne expresses this point of view in his *Essays:*

> They are incomparably more capable and ardent than we in the act of love, and the priest of antiquity, who was first a man and then a woman, testified as much . . . and we have learned, moreover, from their own mouths the proof that was once given, in different centuries, by an Emperor and an Empress of Rome, famous master workmen in this craft (he indeed deflowered in one night ten Sarmatian virgins, his captives, but she actually gave herself in

---

[2] Though it should be remembered that Casanova himself, as related in his *Memoirs*, was often as careful as any Oriental to assure his partner's satisfaction. And, of course, all recent works dealing with "sex technique" emphasize the importance of prolonging the act.—TR.

one night to twenty-five encounters, changing her companions according to her need and her liking,

> . . . *adhuc ardens rigidæ tentigine vulvæ,*
> *Et lassata viris, nondum satiata, recessit*); [3]

and after the dispute which occurred in Catalonia when a woman complained of the too assiduous addresses of her husband, not so much, I think, because she was made uncomfortable by them (for I believe in miracles only in matters of faith) . . . came out that noble sentence of the Queen of Aragon, by which, after mature deliberation with her council, the good Queen . . . decreed the number of six a day as the legitimate and necessary limit, relinquishing and foregoing a great part of the need and desire of her sex that she might, she said, establish an easy and consequently a permanent and immutable procedure.

It is certainly true that woman's sex pleasure is quite different from man's. I have already noted that it is uncertain whether vaginal feeling ever rises to a definite orgasm: statements by women on the matter are rare, and they remain extremely vague even when precision is attempted; it would appear that the reactions are widely variable in different individuals. But there is no doubt that for man coition has a definite biological conclusion: ejaculation. And certainly many other quite complex intentions are involved in aiming at this goal; but once attained, it seems a definite result, and if not the full satisfaction of desire, at least its termination for the time being. In woman, on the contrary, the goal is uncertain from the start, and more psychological in nature than physiological; she desires sex excitement and pleasure in general, but her body promises no precise conclusion to the act of love; and that is why coition is never quite terminated for her: it admits of no end. Male sex feeling rises like an arrow; when it reaches a certain height or threshold, it is fulfilled and dies abruptly in the orgasm; the pattern of the sexual act is finite and discontinuous. Feminine sex enjoyment radiates throughout the whole body; it is not

---

[3] The lines of Juvenal may be translated as follows:
> *Still burning with the lust of her turgid parts,*
> *Exhausted, but unsatisfied by the men, she made an end.*

The rest of the passage is quoted from Zeitlin's translation (Alfred A. Knopt, 1936), Vol. III, pp. 62–3.—TR.

always centered in the genital organs; even when it is, the vaginal contractions constitute, rather than a true orgasm, a system of waves that rhythmically arise, disappear, and re-form, attain from time to time a paroxysmal condition, become vague, and sink down without ever quite dying out. Because no definite term is set, woman's sex feeling extends toward infinity; it is often nervous or cardiac fatigue or psychic satiety that limits woman's erotic possibilities, rather than a specific gratification; even when overwhelmed, exhausted, she may never find full deliverance: *lassata nondum satiata*, as Juvenal put it.

A man is very wrong in undertaking to impose his own rhythm or timing upon his partner and in working furiously to give her an orgasm: he would often succeed only in shattering the form of eroticism she was on the way to experiencing in her special manner.[4] It is a form sufficiently plastic to set its own term: certain spasms localized in the vagina or in the sexual system as a whole, or involving the entire body, can constitute a resolution; in some women they are strong enough and are produced with sufficient regularity to be regarded as orgasms; but a woman in love can also find in the man's orgasm a conclusion that brings appeasement and satisfaction. And it is also possible for the erotic state to be quietly resolved in a gradual manner, without abrupt climax. Success does not require a mathematical synchronization of feeling, as in the oversimplified belief of many meticulous men, but the establishment of a complex erotic pattern. Many suppose that to "make" a woman feel pleasure is a matter of time and technique, indeed of violent action; they do not realize to what a degree woman's sexuality is conditioned by the total situation.

Sex pleasure in woman, as I have said, is a kind of magic spell; it demands complete abandon; if words or movements oppose the magic of caresses, the spell is broken. This is one of the reasons why the woman closes her eyes; physiologically, this is a reflex compensating for the dilation of the pupils; but she lowers her eyelids even in the dark. She would abolish all surroundings, abolish the singularity of the moment, of herself, and of her lover, she would fain be lost in a carnal night as shadowy as the maternal womb. And more especially she

---

[4] Lawrence saw clearly the contrast between these two forms of sex feeling. But his statement that woman *should* not experience the orgasm is arbitrary. It is a mistake to try to induce it at any cost; it is also wrong to withhold it at all times as does Don Cipriano in *The Plumed Serpent* (see p. 223 above).

longs to do away with the separateness that exists between her and the male; she longs to melt with him into one. As we have seen, she wants to remain subject while she is made object. Being more profoundly beside herself than is man because her whole body is moved by desire and excitement, she retains her subjectivity only through union with her partner; giving and receiving must be combined for both. If the man confines himself to taking without giving or if he bestows pleasure without receiving, the woman feels that she is being maneuvered, used; once she realizes herself as the Other, she becomes the inessential other, and then she is bound to deny her alterity.

This accounts for the fact that the moment when the two bodies separate is almost always distressing for the woman. After coition the man always disowns the flesh, regardless of whether he feels happy or depressed, the dupe of nature or the conqueror of woman; he becomes once more an honest body, he wants to sleep, take a bath, smoke a cigarette, go out for a breath of fresh air. The woman wants to prolong the carnal contact until the spell that made her flesh is completely dissipated; to separate is for her a painful uprooting like being weaned all over again; she feels resentful toward a lover who moves away from her too abruptly. But she is hurt even more by words that run counter to the amalgamation in which for a moment she has firmly believed. Madeleine Bourdouxhe tells of a woman who recoiled when her husband asked if she had enjoyed herself, putting her hand over his mouth; the expression horrifies many women because it reduces erotic pleasure to an immanent and separately felt sensation. "Was it enough? You want more? Was it good?"—the very fact of asking such questions emphasizes the separation, changes the act of love into a mechanical operation directed by the male. And that is, indeed, why he asks them. He really seeks domination much more than fusion and reciprocity; when the unity of the pair is broken, he is once more sole subject: to renounce this privileged position requires a great deal of love or of generosity. He likes to have the woman feel humiliated, possessed, in spite of herself; he always wants to take her a little more than she gives herself. Woman would be spared many difficulties if man did not carry in his train the many complexes that make him regard the act of love as a battle; then she could cease to view the bed as an arena.

And yet one does observe in the young girl a desire to be dominated, along with her narcissism and her pride. Masochism, according to some psychoanalysts, is one of woman's characteristics, and it is this tendency that enables her to adapt herself to her erotic destiny. But the concept of masochism is most confused, and we must take a close look at it.

Following Freud, psychoanalysts distinguish three types of masochism: one consists in the alliance of pain and sex pleasure, another would be feminine acceptance of erotic dependency, the third would rest upon a mechanism of self-punishment. In this view woman would be masochistic because pleasure and pain, for her, are allied through defloration and childbirth, and because she accepts her passive role.

We must note first of all that attributing an erotic value to pain does not at all imply behavior marked by passive submission. Frequently pain serves to raise muscle tonus, to reawaken sensitivity blunted by the very violence of sex excitement and pleasure; it is a sharp beam of light flashing in the night of the flesh, it raises the lover from the limbo where he swoons so that he may be hurled down again. Pain is normally a part of the erotic frenzy; bodies that delight to be bodies for the joy they give each other, seek to find each other, to unite, to confront each other in every possible manner. There is in erotic love a tearing away from the self, transport, ecstasy; suffering also tears through the limits of the ego, it is transcendence, a paroxysm; pain has always played a great part in orgies; and it is well known that the exquisite and the painful intermesh: a caress can become torture, torment can give pleasure. The embrace leads easily to biting, pinching, scratching; such behavior is not ordinarily sadistic; it shows a desire to blend, not to destroy; and the individual who suffers it is not seeking rejection and humiliation, but union; besides, it is not specifically masculine behavior—far from it. Pain, in fact, is of masochistic significance only when it is accepted and wanted as proof of servitude. As for the pain of defloration, it is not closely correlated with pleasure; and as for the sufferings of childbirth, all women fear them and are glad that modern obstetrical methods are doing away with them. Pain has no greater and no less a place in woman's sexuality than in man's.

Feminine docility, furthermore, is a very equivocal concept. We have seen that usually the young girl accepts *in imagination* the domination of a demigod, a hero, a male; but this is still no more than a narcissistic game. It in no way disposes her to submit in reality to the carnal exercise of such authority. Often, on the contrary, she rejects the man she admires and respects and gives herself to a man of no distinction. It is a mistake to seek in fantasies the key to concrete behavior; for fantasies are created and cherished as fantasies. The little girl who dreams of violation with mingled horror and acquiescence does not really *wish* to be violated, and if such a thing should happen it would be a hateful calamity. We have already noted a typical example of this dissociation in Marie Le Hardouin's *La Voile noire*, and she confesses further that "there is not a stealthy infamy that I have not committed in my dreams." And we may quote Marie Bashkirtsev again: "All my life I have sought to subject myself to some *illusory domination*, but all the men I tried were so commonplace in comparison to myself that I only felt disgust."

Still, it is true that the sexual role of woman is largely passive; but the actual performance of that passive part is no more masochistic than the normal aggressive behavior of the male is sadistic; woman can transcend caresses, excitement, and penetration, toward the attainment of her own pleasure, thus upholding her subjectivity; she can also seek union with her lover and give herself to him, which represents transcendence of self and not abdication. Masochism exists when the individual chooses to be made purely a thing under the conscious will of others, to see herself as a thing, to play at being a thing. "Masochism is an attempt not to fascinate the other by my objectivity, but to be myself fascinated by my objectivity in the eyes of the other." [5] Sade's Juliette and the young virgin in his *Philosophie dans le boudoir*, who give themselves to the male in every possible way but always for their own pleasure, are in no way masochistic. Neither are Lady Chatterley and Kate, in spite of their abandon. Masochism exists only when the *ego* is set up as separate and when this estranged self, or double, is regarded as dependent upon the will of others.

In this sense, indeed, a true masochism is to be observed in certain women. The young girl is inclined toward it, since she is often narcissistic and since narcissism consists in the setting up of the ego as a double, a stranger. If she feels from the beginning of her erotic initiation a high degree of excitation and desire, she will genuinely *live* her experiences inwardly and will cease to project them upon this ideal pole she calls "myself"; but if she is frigid, this outer "myself" will continue to be asserted, and then to be a man's thing seems a transgression.

---

[5] J.-P. Sartre: *L'Être et le néant*.

Now, "masochism, like sadism, is the assumption of guilt. I am guilty, in fact, simply because I am object." This idea of Sartre's is in line with the Freudian conception of self-punishment. The young girl considers herself to blame for submitting her ego to others, and she punishes herself for it by voluntarily redoubling her humiliation and slavishness; as we have seen, virgins feel defiant toward their lovers-to-be and punish themselves for their coming submissiveness by various kinds of self-torment; when the lover is finally real and present, they persist in this attitude. Frigidity, indeed, as we have seen, would appear to be a punishment that woman imposes as much upon herself as upon her partner: wounded in her vanity, she feels resentment against him and against herself, and she denies herself pleasure. In her masochism she will desperately enslave herself to the male, she will utter words of adoration, she will want to be humiliated, beaten; she will alienate her ego more and more profoundly for rage at having permitted the alienation to start. Such is rather clearly the behavior of Mathilde de la Môle, for example; she is vexed at having yielded to Julien; this is why, at times, she falls at his feet, willingly bends to his every caprice, sacrifices her hair to him; but at the same time she is revolted as much against him as against herself; we readily divine her cold as ice in his arms.

The sham abandon of the masochistic woman creates new barriers between her and enjoyment; and at the same time she is taking vengeance upon herself by means of this inability to know enjoyment. The vicious circle involving frigidity and masochism can be set up permanently, and may then induce sadistic behavior by way of compensation. Her erotic maturation, in some cases, may deliver a woman from her frigidity, her narcissism, and, accepting her passive sexuality, she may experience it in actuality instead of continuing her play-acting. For it is the paradox of masochism that the subject constantly asserts herself in the very effort to abdicate; it is in the unpremeditated giving of oneself, the spontaneous reaching out toward the other, that one attains forgetfulness of self. It is true, then, that woman is more liable than man to the masochistic temptation; her erotic position as passive object leads her to play at passivity; this game is the self-punishment to which she is invited by her narcissistic revolts and her resulting frigidity. The fact is that many women and in particular many young girls are masochists. Colette, referring to her first amorous experiences in *Mes apprentissages*, confides in us as follows:

With the connivance of youth and ignorance, I had indeed begun in a state of exaltation, a culpable exaltation, a hideous and impure adolescent surge. Many are the young girls, hardly of marriageable age as yet, who dream of being the private spectacle, the plaything, the licentious masterpiece of a mature man. It is an ugly longing that they atone for by satisfying it, a longing of a piece with the neuroses of puberty, the habit of gnawing chalk and charcoal, drinking mouthwash, reading indecent books, and sticking pins in one's palm.

The fact could not be better expressed that masochism belongs among the juvenile perversions, that it is no true solution of the conflict created by woman's sexual destiny, but a mode of escaping from it by wallowing in it. Masochism by no means represents the normal and happy flowering of feminine eroticism.

Such full development requires that—in love, affection, sensuality—woman succeed in overcoming her passivity and in establishing a relation of reciprocity with her partner. The dissimilarity that exists between the eroticism of the male and that of the female creates insoluble problems as long as there is a "battle of the sexes"; they can easily be solved when woman finds in the male both desire and respect; if he lusts after her flesh while recognizing her freedom, she feels herself to be the essential, her integrity remains unimpaired the while she makes herself object; she remains free in the submission to which she consents. Under such conditions the lovers can enjoy a common pleasure, in the fashion suitable for each, the partners each feeling the pleasure as being his or her own but as having its source in the other. The verbs *to give* and *to receive* exchange meanings; joy is gratitude, pleasure is affection. Under a concrete and carnal form there is mutual recognition of the ego and of the other in the keenest awareness of the other and of the ego. Some women say that they feel the masculine sex organ in them as a part of their own bodies; some men feel that they *are* the women they penetrate. These are evidently inexact expressions, for the dimension, the relation of the *other* still exists; but the fact·is that alterity has no longer a hostile implication, and indeed this sense of the union of really separate bodies is what gives its emotional character to the sexual act; and it is the more overwhelming as the two beings, who together in passion deny and assert their boundaries, are similar and yet unlike. This unlikeness, which too often isolates them, becomes the source of their enchantment when they do unite. The woman sees in man's virile impetuosity the reverse aspect of the passive fever that burns within her; the man's potency reflects the power she exercises upon him; this life-engorged organ belongs to her as her smile belongs to the man who floods her with pleasure. All the treasures of virility, of femininity, reflect each other, and thus they form an ever shifting and ecstatic unity. What is required for such harmony is not refinement in technique, but rather, on the foundation of the moment's erotic charm, a mutual generosity of body and soul.

This generosity is often inhibited in man by his vanity, in woman by her timidity. So long as her inhibitions persist, this generosity cannot prevail, which explains why full sexual flowering in woman is generally more or less delayed: she attains her erotic zenith toward the age of thirty-five. Unfortunately, if she is married, her husband is by that time too accustomed to her relative frigidity; she is still able to charm new lovers, but she begins to lose the bloom of youth: her days are numbered. It is precisely at the moment when they cease to be desirable that many women finally make up their minds to become frankly desirous.

The conditions under which woman's sexual life unfolds depend not only upon these matters but also upon her social and economic situation as a whole. It would be unrealistic to undertake further study apart from this context. But several conclusions of general value already emerge from our investigation. The erotic experience is one that most poignantly discloses to human beings the ambiguity of their condition; in it they are aware of themselves as flesh and as spirit, as the other and as subject. This conflict has a more dramatic shape for woman because at first she feels herself to be object and does not at once realize a sure independence in sex enjoyment; she must regain her dignity as transcendent and free subject while assuming her carnal condition—an enterprise fraught with difficulty and danger, and one that often fails. But the very difficulty of her position protects her against the traps into which the male readily falls; he is an easy dupe of the deceptive privileges accorded him by his aggressive role and by the lonely satisfaction of the orgasm; he hesitates to see himself fully as flesh. Woman lives her love in more genuine fashion.

Whether she adjusts herself more or less exactly to her passive role, woman is always frustrated as an active individual. It is not the possessive organ she envies the male: it is his prey.

It is an old paradox that the male inhabits a sensual world of sweetness, affection, gentleness, a feminine world, whereas woman moves in the male universe, which is hard and rough; her hands still long for contact with soft, smooth flesh: the adolescent boy, a woman, flowers, fur, the child; a whole region within her remains unoccupied and longs to possess a treasure like that which she gives the male. This explains the fact that in many women there subsists a tendency toward homosexuality more or less marked. There is a type of woman in whom, for a variety of complex reasons, this tendency manifests itself with unusual strength. Not all women are able and willing to solve their sexual problems in the standard fashion, the only manner approved by society. We must now turn our attention to those who choose forbidden ways.

CHAPTER XV

The Lesbian

We commonly think of the lesbian as a woman wearing a plain felt hat, short hair, and a necktie; her mannish appearance would seem to indicate some abnormality of the hormones. Nothing could be more erroneous than this confounding of the invert with the "viriloid" woman. There are many homosexuals among harem inmates, prostitutes, among most intentionally "feminine" women; and conversely a great many "masculine" women are heterosexual. Sexologists and psychiatrists confirm the common observation that the majority of female "homos" are in constitution quite like other women. Their sexuality is in no way determined by any anatomical "fate."

There is no doubt, however, that physiological characteristics may create peculiar situations. There is no rigorous biological distinction between the two sexes; an identical soma is acted upon by certain hormones the direction of which—toward maleness or femaleness—is genotypically determined [1] but can be diverted more or less during the development of the fetus, with the resulting appearance of individuals in some respects intermediate between male and female. Certain men take on a feminine aspect because the development of their masculine organs is delayed: thus we occasionally see supposed girls —especially some devoted to sports—become changed into boys. Helene Deutsch [2] gives the case history of a young girl who paid ardent court to a married woman, wishing to abduct her and live with her. It turned out that she was in fact a hermaphrodite, and she was able to marry her divorced inamorata and have children, after a surgical operation had made her condition normally masculine. But it is by no means to be supposed that every woman invert is biologically a man sailing under false colors. The hermaphrodite, who has elements of the genital systems of both sexes, may display a feminine sexuality: I myself knew one such, exiled from Vienna by the Nazis,

---

[1] See pp. 10–11.
[2] *Psychology of Women*, Vol. I, p. 328.

who regretted her inability to appeal either to heterosexual men or to homosexuals, she herself being attracted by males only.

Under the influence of male hormones, women called "viriloid" show masculine secondary sex characteristics such as a growth of hair on the face; in women of infantile type the female hormones may be deficient and development therefore not completed. Such peculiarities may more or less directly give rise to lesbian leanings. A female of vigorous, aggressive, exuberant vitality prefers to exert herself actively and commonly spurns passivity; ill-favored, malformed, a woman may try to compensate for her inferiority by assuming virile qualities; if her erotic sensitivity is undeveloped, she does not desire masculine caresses.

But anatomy and the hormones only establish a situation and do not set the object toward which the situation is to be transcended. Helene Deutsch [3] cites also the case of a young Polish legionnaire in the First World War who, when wounded, came under her care and who was in fact a girl with pronouncedly masculine secondary sex characteristics. She had joined the army as a nurse, and then had succeeded in concealing her sex and becoming a soldier. She fell in love with a comrade, however, and later she made a favorable adjustment. Her behavior caused her comrades to regard her as a male homosexual, but in reality it was her femininity reasserting itself despite her masculine pretensions. A male does not necessarily desire woman; the fact that the homosexual male may have a perfectly masculine physique implies that a woman with viriloid characteristics is not necessarily doomed to homosexuality.

Even in women of quite normal physiology it has sometimes been asserted that "clitorid" and "vaginal" types can be distinguished, the first being fated for sapphic love. But we have seen that all childhood eroticism is clitorid; whether it remains fixed at this level or becomes transformed is not a matter of anatomy; nor is it true, as often maintained, that childish masturbation explains the later primacy of the clitoris: sexology today regards the masturbation of the child as a quite normal and prevalent phenomenon. The development of feminine eroticism, as we have seen, is a psychological process which is influenced by physiological factors but which depends upon the subject's total attitude toward existence. Marañon held that sexuality is a unitary quality and that in man it attained full development, whereas

---

[3] Ibid., p. 327.

in woman it remained at a kind of halfway stage; only the lesbian could have as rich a libido as that of the male, and she would therefore represent a "superior" feminine type. But the truth is that feminine sexuality has a structure of its own, and it is therefore absurd to speak of superiority or inferiority in connection with the male and female libidos; the choice of sexual object in no way depends on the amount of energy at the disposal of the woman.

The psychoanalysts have had the great merit of seeing in inversion a psychic and not an organic phenomenon; to them, however, it still seems to be determined by outside circumstances. But then, they have devoted little study to it. According to Freud, the maturing of feminine eroticism requires change from the clitorid stage to the vaginal stage, a change symmetrical with that which transfers to the father the love the little girl has felt for her mother. Various causes may check this developmental process; the woman may not become resigned to her "castrated" state, hiding from herself the absence of the penis and remaining fixed on her mother, for whom she is ever seeking substitutes.

In Adler's view, this arrest of development is not an accident, passively suffered: it is desired by the subject who, through the will to power, deliberately rejects her mutilation and seeks to identify herself with the male while refusing his domination. Whether a matter of infantile fixation or of masculine protest, homosexuality is thus regarded as an arrest of development. But as a matter of fact the lesbian is no more an "undeveloped" woman than a "superior" one. The history of an individual is not a fatalistically determined progression: at each moment the past is re-appraised, so to speak, through a new choice, and the "normality" of the choice gives it no preferred value—it must be evaluated according to its authenticity. Homosexuality can be for woman a mode of flight from her situation or a way of accepting it. The great mistake of the psychoanalysts is, through moralistic conformity, to regard it as never other than an inauthentic attitude.

Woman is an existent who is called upon to make herself object; as subject she has an aggressive element in her sensuality which is not satisfied on the male body: hence the conflicts that her eroticism must somehow overcome. The system is considered normal or "natural" which, abandoning her as prey to some male, restores her sovereignty by putting a child in her arms: but this supposed "normality" is enjoined by a more or less clearly comprehended social interest. Even heterosexuality permits of other solutions. Woman's homosexuality is one attempt among others to reconcile her autonomy with the passivity of her flesh. And if nature is to be invoked, one can say that all women are naturally homosexual. The lesbian, in fact, is distinguished by her refusal of the male and her liking for feminine flesh; but every adolescent female fears penetration and masculine domination, and she feels a certain repulsion for the male body; on the other hand, the female body is for her, as for the male, an object of desire.

As I have already pointed out, when men set themselves up as subjects, they also set themselves apart; when they regard the other as a thing to be taken, they make a deadly attack upon the virile ideal in the other and likewise in themselves. And when woman regards herself as object, she sees her kind and herself as prey. The male homosexual, the pederast, arouses hostility in heterosexual males and females, for both these require man to be a dominating subject; [4] both sexes, on the contrary, spontaneously view lesbians with indulgence. "I avow," said Count de Tilly, "that it is a rivalry which in no way disturbs me; on the contrary, it amuses me and I am immoral enough to laugh at it." [5] Colette attributes the same amused indifference to Renaud faced with the couple formed by the girls Claudine and Rézi.[6]

A man is more annoyed by an active and independent heterosexual woman than by an unaggressive lesbian; only the first assaults the masculine prerogatives; sapphic love affairs by no means run counter to the traditional distinction of the sexes; they involve in most cases an acceptance of femininity, not its denial. We have seen that they often appear among adolescent girls as a substitute for the heterosexual relations that such girls as yet have neither the opportunity nor the hardihood to enter upon. The homosexual affair represents a stage, an apprenticeship, and a girl who engages in it most ardently may well become tomorrow the most ardent of wives, mistresses, or mothers. What must be explained in the female invert is not, then,

---

[4] A heterosexual woman may easily be on terms of friendship with certain pederasts, because she finds security and amusement in such nonsexual relationships. But in general she feels hostile toward these men who in themselves or in others degrade the sovereign male to the status of a passive thing.

[5] In his *Memoirs* Casanova often confesses to a similar amusement at female homosexuality, calling it "a trifling matter," very different from male homosexuality.—TR.

[6] It is noteworthy that English law punishes male homosexuality, while regarding the same behavior in women as no crime.

the positive aspect of her choice, it is the negative: she is distinguished not by her taste for women but by the exclusive character of this taste.

Two types of lesbians are often distinguished (as by Jones and Hesnard): the "masculine," who "wish to imitate the male," and the "feminine," who "are afraid of the male." It is true that one can, on the whole, discern two tendencies in inversion; certain women decline passivity, whereas others choose feminine arms in which to abandon themselves passively. But these attitudes react the one on the other; the relations to the object chosen, to the object rejected, are explained the one by the other. For many reasons, as will appear, the distinction made above seems to me to be rather arbitrary.

To define the "masculine" lesbian by her will to "imitate the male" is to stamp her as inauthentic. I have already noted how many ambiguities the psychoanalysts create by accepting the masculine-feminine categories as society currently defines them. The truth is that man today represents the positive and the neutral—that is to say, the male and the human being—whereas woman is only the negative, the female. Whenever she behaves as a human being, she is declared to be identifying herself with the male. Her activities in sports, politics, and intellectual matters, her sexual desire for other women, are all interpreted as a "masculine protest"; the common refusal to take account of the values toward which she aims, or transcends herself, evidently leads to the conclusion that she is, as subject, making an inauthentic choice.

The chief misunderstanding underlying this line of interpretation is that it is *natural* for the female human being to make herself a *feminine* woman: it is not enough to be a heterosexual, even a mother, to realize this ideal; the "true woman" is an artificial product that civilization makes, as formerly eunuchs were made. Her presumed "instincts" for coquetry, docility, are indoctrinated, as is phallic pride in man. Man, as a matter of fact, does not always accept his virile vocation; and woman has good reasons for accepting with even less docility the one assigned to her. The concepts of the "inferiority complex" and the "masculine complex" remind me of the story told by Denis de Rougemont in the *Part du Diable:* a woman believed that the birds attacked her when she strolled in the country; after some months of psychoanalytic treatment, which failed to cure the obsession, the doctor went into the garden of the clinic with his patient and saw that the birds actually *did* attack her! Woman feels inferior because, in fact, the requirements of femininity *do* belittle her. She spontaneously chooses to be a complete person, a subject and a free being with the world and the future open before her; if this choice has a virile cast, it is so to the extent that femininity today means mutilation. Various statements made by female inverts to physicians clearly show that what outrages them, even in childhood, is to be regarded as feminine. They feel contempt for girlish pursuits, demand boys' games and playthings; they feel sorry for women, they are afraid of becoming effeminate, they object to being put in girls' schools.[7]

This revolt by no means implies a predetermined homosexuality; most little girls feel the same sense of outrage and the same desperation when they learn that the chance conformation of their bodies renders their tastes and aspirations blameworthy. Colette Audry [8] was enraged to discover at twelve that she could never become a sailor. It is perfectly natural for the future woman to feel indignant at the limitations imposed upon her by her sex. The real question is not why she should reject them: the problem is rather to understand why she accepts them. She conforms through docility and timidity; but this resignation will easily become transformed into revolt if the compensations offered by society seem inadequate. This is what will happen in cases where the adolescent girl feels she is unattractive, as a woman; it is in this way particularly that anatomical endowments are important; ugly of face and figure, or believing herself to be so, woman rejects a feminine destiny for which she feels poorly equipped. But it would be erroneous to say that a mannish bent is acquired in order to compensate for a lack of feminine attributes; the truth is rather that the opportunities offered to the adolescent girl seem too meager to be a fair exchange for the required sacrifice of masculine advantages. All little girls who are brought up conventionally envy the convenient clothing worn by boys; their reflections in the mirror and the promising futures they foresee for themselves are what make them come little by little to value their furbelows; if the harshly truthful mirror reflects an ordinary face, if it holds no promise, laces and ribbons continue to seem an irksome livery, even a ridiculous one, and the *"garçon manqué"* stubbornly retains her boyishness.

Even when she has a good figure and a pretty face, a woman who is absorbed in ambitious projects of her own or one who simply wants

---

[7] As in cases reported by Ellis and Stekel.
[8] *Aux yeux du souvenir.*

liberty in general will decline to abdicate in favor of another human being; she perceives herself in her activities, not merely in her immanent person: the masculine desire that reduces her to the confines of her body shocks her as much as it shocks the young boy; she feels the same disgust for submissive females as does the virile man for the passive pederast. She adopts a masculine attitude in part to repudiate any appearance of complicity with such women; she assumes masculine attire, manner, language, she forms with a feminine woman companion a couple in which she represents the male person: play-acting that is, indeed, a "masculine protest." But it is a secondary phenomenon; what is primary is the shamed repugnance of the conquering and sovereign subject at the thought of being transformed into fleshly prey. Many athletic women are homosexual; they do not regard as passive flesh a body that denotes muscle, activity, reactiveness, dash; it does not magically inspire caresses, it is a means for dealing with the world, not a mere objective thing in the world: the gulf existing between the body-for-the-self and the body-for-others seems in this case to be impassable. Analogous resistance is to be found in women of executive and intellectual types, for whom submission, even of the body, is impossible.

If the equality of the sexes were actually brought about, the obstacle just referred to would in many cases be done away with; but man is still imbued with a sense of superiority, and that state of mind is annoying for woman if she does not share it. It should be said, however, that the most willful and domineering women show little hesitation in confronting the male: the "virile" woman is often perfectly heterosexual. She does not wish to relinquish her claims as a human being; but she is no more willing to be deprived of her femininity; she chooses to join the masculine world, even to make use of it. Her strong sensuality has no fear of male violence; in seeking pleasure from the male body, she has less inner resistance to overcome than the timid virgin has. A very rough, very animal nature will not feel the humiliation of coitus; an intellectual of intrepid spirit will deny it; if sure of herself and pugnaciously inclined, woman will cheerfully engage in a duel in which she is bound to win. George Sand had a taste for young men and "effeminate" types; but Mme de Staël looked for youth and beauty in her lovers only late in life: dominating the men through her vigorous mentality and accepting their admiration with pride, she could hardly feel like prey in their arms. Such a sovereign as Catherine the Great could even permit herself masochistic debauches: in these sports she remained sole ruler. Isabelle Eberhardt, who in male costume rode horseback over the Sahara, felt in no way belittled when she gave herself to some vigorous sharpshooter. The woman who does not wish to be man's vassal is by no means one who always avoids him: she endeavors rather to make him the instrument of her pleasure. In favorable circumstances—dependent in large part on her partner—the very notion of competition disappears, and she enjoys experiencing to the full her womanly situation just as he enjoys his masculine estate.

But this reconciliation between the active personality and the sexual role is, in spite of any favorable circumstances, much more difficult for woman than for man; and there will be many women who will avoid the attempt, rather than wear themselves out in making the effort involved. Among women artists and writers there are many lesbians. The point is not that their sexual peculiarity is the source of the creative energy or that it indicates the existence of this superior type of energy; it is rather that, being absorbed in serious work, they do not propose to waste time in playing a feminine role or in struggling with men. Not admitting male superiority, they do not wish to make a pretense of recognizing it or to weary themselves in contesting it. They are looking for relaxation, appeasement, and diversion in sexual pleasure: they do better to avoid a partner who appears in the guise of an adversary; and in this way they rid themselves of the fetters implied in femininity. Very often, of course, it is the nature of her heterosexual experiences that leads the active "virile" woman to make the choice between assuming and repudiating her normal sexuality. Masculine disdain confirms the homely woman in her feeling that she is unattractive; a woman of pride will be wounded by a lover's arrogance. Here we encounter again all the reasons for frigidity already noted: resentment, spite, fear of pregnancy, the trauma of a previous abortion, and so on. The more mistrustful woman is in her approach to man, the more weighty these reasons become.

Homosexuality, however, does not always seem to be an entirely satisfactory solution when a woman of dominating personality is concerned. Since she seeks self-affirmation, it is displeasing for her not to realize wholly her feminine possibilities; heterosexual relations seem to her at once belittling and enriching; in repudiating the limitations implied by her sex, it appears that she limits herself in another way. Just as the frigid woman wants sexual pleasure while she refuses it, so the lesbian may often wish she were a normal and complete woman while preferring not to be. This indecision is evident in the case of the transvestite studied by Stekel [9] and referred to above. At sixteen this patient began lesbian affairs, feeling contempt and disgust for girls who yielded to her. She took up serious studies and began to drink. She married, and though she took the aggressive role, she failed to find sexual satisfaction. She shortly left her husband, whom she said she "loved madly," and resumed relations with women. During creative periods she felt completely male and consorted with females; at other times she felt she was feminine and had male lovers. She underwent analysis because she was sexually dissatisfied either way.

The lesbian could readily accept the loss of her femininity if in doing so she gained a successful virility; though she can employ artificial means for deflowering and possessing her loved one, she is none the less a castrate and may suffer acutely from the realization of that fact. She is unfulfilled as a woman, impotent as a man, and her disorder may lead to psychosis. One patient said to Dalbiez: [1] "If I only had something to penetrate with, it would be better." Another wished that her breasts were rigid. The lesbian will often try to compensate for her virile inferiority by an arrogance, an exhibitionism, by which, in fact, an inner disequilibrium is betrayed. Sometimes, again, she will succeed in establishing with other women a type of relation quite analogous to those which a "feminine" man or a youth still uncertain of his virility might have with them. A very striking case of this kind is that of "Count Sandor" reported by Krafft-Ebing. [2] By means of the expedient just mentioned, this woman had attained a state of equilibrium, which was destroyed only by the intervention of society.

Sarolta came of a titled Hungarian family known for its eccentricities. Her father had her reared as a boy, calling her Sandor; she rode horseback, hunted, and so on. She was under such influences until, at thirteen, she was placed in an institution. A little later she

---

[9] Reported at length in *Frigidity in Woman*, Vol. II, Ch. xiv.

[1] *La Méthode psychanalytique et la doctrine freudienne.*

[2] *Psychopathia Sexualis* (English translation, Physicians and Surgeons Book Co., 1931), p. 428.

fell in love with an English girl, pretending to be a boy, and ran away with her. At home again, later, she resumed the name Sandor and wore boy's clothing, while being carefully educated. She went on long trips with her father, always in male attire; she was addicted to sports, drank, and visited brothels. She felt particularly drawn toward actresses and other such detached women, preferably not too young but "feminine" in nature. "It delighted me," she related, "if the passion of a lady was disclosed under a poetic veil. All immodesty in a woman was disgusting to me. I had an indescribable aversion to female attire—indeed, for everything feminine, but only in so far as it concerned me; for, on the other hand, I was all enthusiasm for the beautiful sex." She had numerous affairs with women and spent a good deal of money. At the same time she was a valued contributor to two important journals.

She lived for three years in "marriage" with a woman ten years older than herself, from whom she broke away only with great difculty. She was able to inspire violent passions. Falling in love with a young teacher, she was married to her in an elaborate ceremony, the girl and her family believing her to be a man; her father-in-law on one occasion noticed what seemed to be an erection (probably a priapus); she shaved as a matter of form, but servants in the hotel suspected the truth from seeing blood on her bedclothes and from spying through the keyhole.

Thus unmasked, Sandor was put in prison and later acquitted, after thorough investigation. She was greatly saddened by her enforced separation from her beloved Marie, to whom she wrote long and impassioned letters from her cell.

The examination showed that her conformation was not wholly feminine: her pelvis was small and she had no waist. Her breasts were developed, her sexual parts quite feminine but not maturely formed. Her menstruation appeared late, at seventeen, and she felt a profound horror of the function. She was equally horrified at the thought of sexual relations with the male; her sense of modesty was developed only in regard to women and to the point that she would feel less shyness in going to bed with a man than with a woman. It was very embarrassing for her to be treated as a woman, and she was truly in anguish at having to wear feminine clothes. She felt that she was "drawn as by a magnetic force toward women of twenty-four to thirty." She found sexual satisfaction exclusively in caressing her loved one, never in being caressed. At times she made use of a stocking stuffed with oakum as a priapus. She detested men. She was very sensitive to the moral esteem of others, and she had much literary talent, wide culture, and a colossal memory.

Sandor was not psychoanalyzed, but a number of salient points emerge from the simple statement of the facts. It would appear that without a "masculine protest," quite spontaneously, she always thought of herself as a man, thanks to her upbringing and her natural constitution; the manner in which her father included her in his traveling and in his life evidently had a decisive influence. Her mannishness was so well established that she showed no ambivalence in regard to women; loving them like a man, she did not feel herself compromised by them; she loved them in a purely dominating, active way, without accepting reciprocal attentions. But it is remarkable that she "detested men" and that she liked older women especially. This suggests that she had a *masculine* Œdipus complex in regard to her mother; she retained the childish attitude of the very little girl who, forming a couple with her mother, nourishes the hope of protecting her and some day dominating her.

It often happens that when the child has felt a lack of maternal affection, she is haunted all her life by the need for it: reared by her father, Sandor must have dreamed of a loving and dear mother, whom she sought, later, in other women; that explains her profound envy of other men, bound up with her respect, her "poetic" love, for detached women and older women, who seemed in her eyes to bear a sacred character. Her attitude toward women was precisely that of Rousseau with Mme de Warens, of the young Benjamin Constant with Mme de Charrière: sensitive and "feminine" adolescents, they also turned to motherly mistresses. We frequently meet with the lesbian, more or less markedly of this type, who has never identified herself with her mother—because she either admired or detested her too much—but who, while declining to be a woman, wishes to have around her the soft delight of feminine protection; from the warm shelter of that womb she can emerge into the outer world with mannish boldness; she behaves like a man, but as a man she is fragile, weak, and this makes her desire an older mistress; the pair will correspond to that well-known heterosexual couple: matron and adolescent.[3]

The psychoanalysts have strongly emphasized the importance of the early relations established between the homosexual woman and her mother. There are two cases in which the adolescent girl finds difficulty in escaping her mother's influence: if she has been too lovingly watched over by an anxious mother, or if she has been maltreated by a "bad mother," who has inspired in the girl a deep sense of guilt. In the first case their relation often verges upon homosexuality: they sleep together, caress each other, or indulge in breast kisses; the young girl will later seek the same happiness in other arms. In the second case she will feel keenly the need for a "good mother," who will protect her from the first and ward off the curse she feels has been placed upon her. One of Havelock Ellis's subjects, who had detested her mother throughout her childhood, describes the love she felt at sixteen for an older woman, as follows: [4]

> I felt like an orphaned child who had suddenly acquired a mother, and through her I began to feel less antagonistic to grown people and to feel the first respect I had ever felt for what they said. . . . My love for her was perfectly pure, and I thought of hers as simply maternal. . . . I liked her to touch me and she sometimes held me in her arms or let me sit on her lap. At bedtime she used to come and say good-night and kiss me upon the mouth.

If the older woman is so inclined, the younger will be delighted to abandon herself to more ardent embraces. She will ordinarily assume the passive role, for she wishes to be dominated, protected, cradled, and caressed like a small child. Whether such relations remain platonic or become physical, they frequently have the character of a true amorous passion. But from the very fact that they form a classic stage in adolescent development, it is clear that they are insufficient to explain a definite choice of homosexuality. In them the young girl seeks at once a liberation and a security that she could find also in masculine arms. After having passed through the period of amorous enthusiasm, the younger woman often feels toward the older the same

---

[3] Like the Marschallin and Octavian in Richard Strauss's opera *Der Rosenkavalier.*—TR.

[4] *Studies in the Psychology of Sex*, Vol. II, Part 2. p. 238.

ambivalent sentiment that she felt toward her mother; she submits to her influence while desiring to escape from it; if her friend insists on holding her, she will remain for a time her "captive"; [5] but she finally escapes, after bitter scenes or in friendly fashion; having done with adolescence, she feels ripe for the life of a normal woman. To become a confirmed lesbian she must either refuse—like Sandor—to accept her femininity or let it flower in feminine arms. This is to say that fixation on the mother is not by itself enough to explain inversion. And this condition may indeed be chosen for quite other reasons. The woman may discover or foresee through complete or partial experiences that she will not derive pleasure from heterosexual relations, that only another woman can fully provide it: to the woman who makes a religion of her femininity, especially, the homosexual embrace may prove most satisfying.

It is most important to emphasize the fact that refusal to make herself the object is not always what turns woman to homosexuality; most lesbians, on the contrary, seek to cultivate the treasures of their femininity. To be willing to be changed into a passive object is not to renounce all claim to subjectivity: woman hopes in this way to find self-realization under the aspect of herself as a thing; but then she will be trying to find herself in her otherness, her alterity. When alone she does not succeed in really creating her double; if she caresses her own bosom, she still does not know how her breasts seem to a strange hand, nor how they are felt to react under a strange hand; a man can reveal to her the existence of her flesh *for herself*—that is to say, as she herself perceives it, but not what it is *to others*. It is only when her fingers trace the body of a woman whose fingers in turn trace her body that the miracle of the mirror is accomplished. Between man and woman love is an act; each torn from self becomes other: what fills the woman in love with wonder is that the languorous passivity of her flesh should be reflected in the male's impetuosity; the narcissistic woman, however, recognizes her enticements but dimly in the man's erected flesh. Between women love is contemplative; caresses are intended less to gain possession of the other than gradually to re-create the self through her; separateness is abolished, there is no struggle, no victory, no defeat; in exact reciprocity each is at once subject and object, sovereign and slave; duality becomes mutuality. Says Colette in *Ces plaisirs*: "The close resemblance gives certitude of

---

[5] As in Dorothy Baker's novel *Trio*, otherwise quite superficial.

pleasure. The lover takes delight in being sure of caressing a body the secrets of which she knows, and whose preferences her own body indicates to her." And Renée Vivien's poem (from *Sortilèges*) expresses the same idea: "Our bodies are made alike . . . Our destiny the same . . . In you I love my child, my darling, and my sister."

This mirroring may assume a maternal cast; the mother who sees herself and projects herself in her daughter often has a sexual attachment for her; she has in common with the lesbian the longing to protect and cradle a soft carnal object in her arms. Colette brings out this analogy when she writes in *Vrilles de la vigne* as follows: "You will delight me, bending over me, when, with your eyes filled with maternal concern, you seek in your passionate one the child you have not borne"; and Renée Vivien enlarges on the same sentiment in another of her poems: ". . . And my arms were made the better to shelter you . . . Like a warm cradle where you shall find repose."

In all love—sexual or maternal—exist at once selfishness and generosity, desire to possess the other and to give the other all; but the mother and the lesbian are similar especially in the degree to which both are narcissistic, enamored respectively in the child or the woman friend, each of her own projection or reflection.

But narcissism—like the mother fixation—does not always lead to homosexuality, as is proved, for example, in the case of Marie Bashkirtsev, in whose writings no trace of affection for women is to be found. Cerebral rather than sensual, and extremely conceited, she dreamed from childhood of being highly regarded by men: she was interested only in what could add to her renown. A woman who idolizes herself alone and whose aim is success in general is incapable of a warm attachment to other women; she sees in them only enemies and rivals.

The truth is that there is never a single determining factor; it is always a matter of a choice, arrived at in a complex total situation and based upon a free decision; no sexual fate governs the life of the individual woman: her type of eroticism, on the contrary, expresses her general outlook on life.

Environmental circumstances, however, have a considerable influence on the choice. Today the two sexes still live largely separated lives: in boarding schools and seminaries for young women the transition from intimacy to sexuality is rapid; lesbians are far less numerous in environments where the association of girls and boys facilitates heterosexual experiences. Many women who are employed in work-shops and offices, surrounded by women, and who see little of men, will tend to form amorous friendships with females: they will find it materially and morally simple to associate their lives. The absence or difficulty of heterosexual contacts will doom them to inversion. It is hard to draw the line between resignation and predilection: a woman can devote herself to women because man has disappointed her, but sometimes man has disappointed her because in him she was really seeking a woman.

For all these reasons it is erroneous to distinguish sharply between the homosexual and the heterosexual woman. Once past the uncertain period of adolescence, the normal male no longer permits himself homosexual amusements; but the normal woman often returns to the amours—platonic or not—which have enchanted her youth. Disappointed in man, she may seek in woman a lover to replace the male who has betrayed her. Colette indicated in her *Vagabonde* this consoling role that forbidden pleasures may frequently play in woman's existence: some women, as it happens, spend their whole lives in being thus consoled. Even a woman with no lack of masculine embraces may not disdain calmer pleasures. If she is passive and sensual, she will not be repelled by the caresses of a woman friend, since she will in this case have only to give way and let herself be gratified. If she is active and fiery, she will seem "androgynous," not on account of some mysterious combination of male and female hormones, but simply because aggressiveness and lust for possession are regarded as virile qualities; Colette's Claudine, in love with Renaud, is none the less attracted by Rézi's charms; she is entirely a woman without losing for all that the wish to take and caress. Among "nice women," of course, these "perverse" desires are carefully repressed, but nevertheless they are manifested in the form of pure but intense friendships or under the cover of maternal affection; sometimes they burst forth violently during a psychosis or in the crisis of the menopause.

For still better reasons, it is useless to try to classify lesbians in two well-marked categories. Because they often are pleased to imitate a bisexual couple, superposing a social make-believe upon their true relations, they themselves suggest dividing lesbians into "virile" and "feminine" types. But the fact that one wears severe suits and the other feminine frocks should give rise to no illusion. On closer observation it is to be seen that, except in a few cases, their sexuality is ambiguous. The woman who turns lesbian because she haughtily declines male domination is often pleased to find the same proud amazon in another. Formerly lesbians flourished among the women students at Sèvres, who lived together far from men; they took pride in belonging to a feminine elite and wished to remain autonomous subjects; the common feeling that united them against the privileged caste enabled each to admire in a friend the impressive being whom she idolized in herself; in their mutual embraces each was at once man and woman and each was enchanted with the other's androgynous qualities.

On the other hand, a woman who wishes to enjoy her femininity in feminine arms can also know the pride of obeying no master. Renée Vivien dearly loved feminine beauty, and she wished to be beautiful; she adorned herself, she was proud of her long hair; but she took pleasure in feeling free, inviolate. In her poems she expresses her scorn for the women who in marriage consent to become men's serfs. Her liking for strong drink, her sometimes obscene language, showed her desire for virility. The fact is that in most couples the caresses are reciprocal. In consequence the respective roles of the two partners are by no means definitely fixed: the woman of more childish nature can play the part of the adolescent youth associated with the protective matron or that of the mistress on her lover's arm. They can enjoy their love in a state of equality. Because the partners are homologous, basically alike, all kinds of combinations, transpositions, exchanges, *comédies* are possible. Their relations become balanced according to the psychological tendencies of each of the two friends and in accordance with the total situation. If one of them helps and supports the other, she assumes male functions: tyrannical protector, exploited dupe, respected lord and master, or sometimes even pimp; a moral, social, or intellectual superiority may confer authority upon her; however, the one most loved will enjoy privileges bestowed upon her by the passionate attachment of the one who is most loving. The association of two women, like that of a man and a woman, assumes many different forms; it may be based upon sentiment, material interest, or habit; it may be conjugal or romantic; it has room for sadism, masochism, generosity, fidelity, devotion, capriciousness, egotism, betrayal: among lesbians there are prostitutes and also great lovers.

But certain circumstances give these liaisons special characteristics. They are not sanctioned by an institution or by the mores, nor are they regulated by conventions; hence they are marked by especial sincerity. Man and woman—even husband and wife—are in some degree playing a part before one another, and in particular woman, upon whom the male always imposes some requirement: virtue beyond suspicion, charm, coquettishness, childishness, or austerity. Never in the presence of husband or lover can she feel wholly herself; but with her woman friend she need not be on parade, need not pretend: they are too much of a kind not to show themselves frankly as they are. This similarity engenders complete intimacy. Frequently eroticism has but a small part in these unions; here sex pleasure is of a nature less violent and vertiginous than between man and woman, it does not bring about such overwhelming transformations; but when male and female lovers have withdrawn from the carnal embrace, they again become strangers; the male body in itself becomes repulsive to the woman; and the man often feels a kind of flat loathing for his companion's female body. Carnal affection between women is more even, has more continuity; they are not carried away in frenetic ecstasies, but they never sink back into hostile indifference; to look at each other, to touch each other is a tranquil pleasure, prolonging that of the bed. The union of Sarah Ponsonby with her woman companion lasted for almost fifty years without a cloud: apparently they were able to create a peaceful Eden apart from the ordinary world.[6]

But sincerity also exacts a price. Because they show themselves frankly as they are, unconcerned with dissimulation or self-control, a feminine couple may engage in remarkably violent scenes. A man and a woman are intimidated by the fact that they are different: he feels pity and concern for her; he feels bound to treat her with courtesy, indulgence, restraint; she respects him and fears him somewhat, she endeavors to control herself in his presence; each is careful to spare the mysterious other, being uncertain of his or her feelings and reactions. But women are pitiless toward each other; they thwart, provoke, pursue, fall upon one another tooth and nail, and drag each other down into bottomless abjection. Masculine imperturbability, whether due to indifference or self-control, is a barrier against which feminine scenes break in vain like swirling waters against a dike; but between two women tears and frenzies rise in alternate crescendo; their

---

[6] See Mary Gordon's *Chase of the Wild Goose* (London: Hogarth Press; 1937), in which the story of the lifelong association of Miss Sarah Ponsonby and Lady Eleanor Butler is beautifully—and reticently—told.—TR.

appetite for outdoing each other in reproaches and for endlessly "having it out" is insatiable. Demands, recriminations, jealousy, tyrannizing—all these plagues of married life are here let loose with redoubled intensity.

If such amours are often stormy, it is also true that they are ordinarily carried on under more threatening conditions than are heterosexual affairs. They are condemned by a society with which they can hardly be integrated successfully. The woman who assumes the virile role—through her nature, her situation, or her strength of passion—will regret not giving her loved one a normal and respectable life, not being able to marry her; and she will reproach herself for leading her friend into questionable ways: such are the sentiments that Radclyffe Hall attributes to her heroine in *The Well of Loneliness*. This remorse is manifested in a morbid anxiety and especially in a torturing jealousy. The passive or less deeply smitten partner, on her side, will in fact suffer from the weight of social censure; she will believe herself degraded, perverted, frustrated, she will feel resentment against the woman who brings all this upon her. It may happen that one of the two women wants to have a child; if so, she can sadly resign herself to her sterility, or the two can adopt a child, or the one who longs for maternity can appeal to a man; the child may serve to unite them more firmly, or it may be a new source of friction.

What gives homosexual women a masculine cast is not their erotic life, which, on the contrary, confines them to a feminine universe; it is rather the whole group of responsibilities they are forced to assume because they dispense with men. Their situation is the reverse of the courtesan's, for she sometimes takes on a virile character from living among men—as did Ninon de Lenclos—but still depends upon them. The peculiar atmosphere that surrounds lesbians comes from the contrast between the gynæceum-like climate of their private lives and the masculine freedom of their public existence. They act like men in a world without men. Woman by herself, apart from man, seems somewhat unusual; it is not true that men respect women; they respect one another through their women—wives, mistresses, or the prostitutes they pimp for. Without masculine protection woman is helpless before a superior caste that is aggressive, sneeringly amused, or hostile. As an erotic "perversion," feminine homosexuality may elicit a smile; but as implying a mode of life, it arouses contempt or scandalized disapproval. If there is a good deal of aggressiveness and affectation in the attitude of lesbians, it is because there is no way in which they can live naturally in their situation: being natural implies being unselfconscious, not picturing one's acts to oneself; but the attitude of other people constantly directs the lesbian's attention upon herself. She can go her own way in calm indifference only when she is old enough or backed by considerable social prestige.

It is difficult to state with certainty, for example, whether the lesbian commonly dresses in mannish fashion by preference or as a defense reaction. Certainly it is often a matter of spontaneous choice. Nothing is less *natural* than to dress in feminine fashion; no doubt masculine garb is artificial also, but it is simpler and more convenient, being intended to facilitate rather than to hinder activity; George Sand wore male clothing; in her last book, *Moi*, Thyde Monnier confessed her preference for trousers; every active woman likes low heels and sturdy materials. The significance of woman's attire is evident: it is decoration, and to be decorated means to be offered. The heterosexual feminists were formerly as intransigent in this matter as the lesbians: declining to make themselves into merchandise, offered for sale, they affected severe tailor-made suits and felt hats; elaborate low-necked gowns seemed to them symbolical of the social order they were fighting. Today they have succeeded in gaining the reality, and so in their eyes the symbol is of less importance. But it remains important for the lesbian to the extent that she must still assert her claim. It may happen also that severe dress is more becoming to her, if physical traits have motivated her choice of lesbianism.

It should be pointed out, further, that one function of finery is to gratify woman's tactile sensuousness; but the lesbian disdains the appeal of velvet and silk: like Sandor she enjoys them on her friends, or her friend's body itself may take their place. For similarly, also, the lesbian often likes to drink hard liquor, smoke strong tobacco, use rough language, take violent exercise: in her eroticism she gets enough soft feminine sweetness, and by way of contrast she enjoys a climate that is not so mild. Thus she may come to enjoy the company of men.

But here a new factor is involved: that is the relation—often ambiguous—which she sustains with men. A woman fully assured in her virile powers will want only men as friends and companions; but such assurance will hardly be found in any woman who does not have in-

terests in common with them, who—in business, activities, or art—
does not work and find success like a man. When Gertrude Stein entertained friends, she conversed only with the men and left to Alice
Toklas the duty of talking with the ladies.[7] But toward women the
strongly virile female homosexual will take an ambivalent attitude:
she feels contempt for them, but with them she suffers from an inferiority complex both as woman and as man. She fears that to them
she will seem at once a defective woman and an incomplete man, and
this leads her to affect a haughty superiority or to show toward them
—like Stekel's transvestite—a sadistic aggressiveness.

But such cases are rather rare. Most lesbians, as we have seen, reticently avoid men: in them, as in the frigid woman, there is a feeling
of resentment, timidity, pride; they do not feel truly men's peers; to
their feminine resentment is added a masculine inferiority complex;
men are rivals better equipped to seduce, possess, and retain their
prey; they detest the "defilement" to which men subject woman.
They are incensed also to see men holding social advantages and to
feel that they are the stronger: it is a burning humiliation to be unable to fight with a rival, to know that he is capable of knocking you
down with a blow of his fist. This complicated hostility is one of the
reasons that impel certain female homosexuals to make themselves
conspicuous; they flock by themselves; they form clubs of a sort to
show that they have no more need of men socially than sexually.
From this the descent is easy to empty bragging and all the play-
acting that springs from insincerity. The lesbians play first at being
a man; then even being a lesbian becomes a game; masculine clothing, at first a disguise, becomes a uniform; and under the pretext of
escaping male oppression, woman becomes enslaved to the character
she plays; wishing not to be confined in woman's situation, she is
imprisoned in that of the lesbian. Nothing gives a darker impression
of narrow-mindedness and of mutilation than these groups of emancipated women. It should be added that many women declare themselves to be homosexual only through self-interested compliance: they
adopt lesbianism only with their growing awareness of its equivocal
allurements, hoping moreover to entice such men as may like "vicious"

---

[7] A heterosexual woman who believes—or can convince herself—that her merits
enable her to transcend sexual differences will easily take the same attitude. So it
was with Mme de Staël.

women. These noisy zealots—who are obviously the most noticeable of the lesbians—help to cast discredit upon what common opinion regards as a vice and as a pose.

The truth is that homosexuality is no more a perversion deliberately indulged in than it is a curse of fate.[8] It is an attitude *chosen in a certain situation*—that is, at once motivated and freely adopted. No one of the factors that mark the subject in connection with this choice—physiological conditions, psychological history, social circumstances—is the determining element, though they all contribute to its explanation. It is one way, among others, in which woman solves the problems posed by her condition in general, by her erotic situation in particular. Like all human behavior, homosexuality leads to make-believe, disequilibrium, frustration, lies, or, on the contrary, it becomes the source of rewarding experiences, in accordance with its manner of expression in actual living—whether in bad faith, laziness, and falsity, or in lucidity, generosity, and freedom.

---

[8] *The Well of Loneliness* presents a heroine with a psychophysiologically determined taint. But the documentary value of this novel is very slight despite its wide repute.

PART V

SITUATION

CHAPTER XVI

The Married Woman

MARRIAGE is the destiny traditionally offered to women by society. It is still true that most women are married, or have been, or plan to be, or suffer from not being. The celibate woman is to be explained and defined with reference to marriage, whether she is frustrated, rebellious, or even indifferent in regard to that institution. We must therefore continue this study by analyzing marriage.

Economic evolution in woman's situation is in process of upsetting the institution of marriage: it is becoming a union freely entered upon by the consent of two independent persons; the obligations of the two contracting parties are personal and reciprocal; adultery is for both a breach of contract; divorce is obtainable by the one or the other on the same conditions. Woman is no longer limited to the reproductive function, which has lost in large part its character as natural servitude and has come to be regarded as a function to be voluntarily assumed; [1] and it is compatible with productive labor, since, in many cases, the time off required by a pregnancy is taken by the mother at the expense of the State or the employer. In the Soviet Union marriage was

---

[1] See Book I, pp. 117 ff.

for some years a contract between individuals based upon the complete liberty of the husband and wife; but it would seem that it is now a duty that the State imposes upon them both. Which of these tendencies will prevail in the world of tomorrow will depend upon the general structure of society, but in any case male guardianship of woman is disappearing. Nevertheless, the epoch in which we are living is still, from the feminist point of view, a period of transition. Only a part of the female population is engaged in production, and even those who are belong to a society in which ancient forms and antique values survive. Modern marriage can be understood only in the light of a past that it tends to perpetuate in part.

Marriage has always been a very different thing for man and for woman. The two sexes are necessary to each other, but this necessity has never brought about a condition of reciprocity between them; women, as we have seen, have never constituted a caste making exchanges and contracts with the male caste upon a footing of equality. A man is socially an independent and complete individual; he is regarded first of all as a producer whose existence is justified by the work he does for the group; we have seen why it is that the reproductive and domestic role to which woman is confined has not guaranteed her an equal dignity. Certainly the male needs her; in some primitive groups it may happen that the bachelor, unable to manage his existence by himself, becomes a kind of outcast; in agricultural societies a woman coworker is essential to the peasant; and for most men it is of advantage to unload certain drudgery upon a mate; the individual wants a regular sexual life and posterity, and the State requires him to contribute to its perpetuation. But man does not make his appeal directly to woman herself; it is the men's group that allows each of its members to find self-fulfillment as husband and father; woman, as slave or vassal, is integrated within families dominated by fathers and brothers, and she has always been given in marriage by certain males to other males. In primitive societies the paternal clan, the gens, disposed of woman almost like a thing: she was included in deals agreed upon by two groups. The situation is not much modified when marriage assumes a contractual form in the course of its evolution; [2] when dowered or having her share in inheritance, woman would seem to have civil standing as a person, but dowry and inherit-

---

[2] This evolution proceeded in discontinuous fashion, being repeated in Egypt, Rome, and modern civilization, as detailed in Book I, Part II, "History."

ance, still enslave her to her family. During a long period the contracts were made between father-in-law and son-in-law, not between wife and husband; only widows then enjoyed economic independence.[3] The young girl's freedom of choice has always been much restricted; and celibacy—apart from the rare cases in which it bears a sacred character—reduced her to the rank of parasite and pariah; marriage is her only means of support and the sole justification of her existence. It is enjoined upon her for two reasons.

The first reason is that she must provide the society with children; only rarely—as in Sparta and to some extent under the Nazi regime—does the State take woman under direct guardianship and ask only that she be a mother. But even the primitive societies that are not aware of the paternal generative role demand that woman have a husband, for the second reason why marriage is enjoined is that woman's function is also to satisfy a male's sexual needs and to take care of his household. These duties placed upon woman by society are regarded as a *service* rendered to her spouse: in return he is supposed to give her presents, or a marriage settlement, and to support her. Through him as intermediary, society discharges its debt to the woman it turns over to him. The rights obtained by the wife in fulfilling her duties are represented in obligations that the male must assume. He cannot break the conjugal bond at his pleasure; he can repudiate or divorce his wife only when the public authorities so decide, and even then the husband sometimes owes her compensation in money: the practice even becomes an abuse in Egypt under Bocchoris or, as the demand for alimony, in the United States today. Polygamy has always been more or less openly tolerated: man may bed with slaves, concubines, mistresses, prostitutes, but he is required to respect certain privileges of his legitimate wife. If she is maltreated or wronged, she has the right—more or less definitely guaranteed—of going back to her family and herself obtaining a separation or divorce.

Thus for both parties marriage is at the same time a burden and a benefit; but there is no symmetry in the situations of the two sexes; for girls marriage is the only means of integration in the community, and if they remain unwanted, they are, socially viewed, so much wastage. This is why mothers have always eagerly sought to arrange marriages for them. In the last century they were hardly consulted among middle-class people. They were offered to possible suitors by

---

[3] Hence the special place of the young widow in erotic literature.

means of "interviews" arranged in advance. Zola describes this custom in *Pot-Bouille*.

"A failure, it's a failure," said Mme Josserand, falling into her chair. M. Josserand simply said: "Ah!"

"But," continued Mme Josserand in a shrill voice, "you don't seem to understand, I'm telling you that there's another marriage gone, and it's the seventh that has miscarried.

"You hear," she went on, advancing on her daughter. "How did you spoil this marriage?"

Bertha realized that it was her turn.

"I don't know, Mamma," she murmured.

"An assistant department head," her mother continued, "not yet thirty, and with a great future. A man to bring you his pay every month; substantial, that's all that counts. . . . You did something stupid, the same as with the others?"

"No, Mamma, certainly not."

"When you were dancing with him you disappeared into the small parlor."

Bertha said in some confusion: "Yes, Mamma—and as soon as we were alone he wanted to act disgracefully, he hugged me and took hold of me like this. Then I got scared and pushed him against a piece of furniture."

Her mother interrupted, furious again: "Pushed him against the furniture! You wretch, you pushed him!"

"But, Mamma, he was holding on to me."

"So? He was holding on to you, fancy that! And we send these simpletons to boarding school! What do they teach you, tell me! Ah, just for a kiss behind the door! Should you really tell us about such a thing, your parents? And you push people against furniture, and you spoil chances to marry!"

She assumed a didactic air and continued:

"That's the end, I give up, you are just stupid, my dear. Since you have no fortune, understand that you have to catch men some other way. The idea is to be agreeable, to gaze tenderly, to forget about your hand, to allow little intimacies without seeming to notice; in a word, you fish for a husband. . . . What bothers me is that she is not too bad, when she feels like it. Come, now, stop crying and look at me as if I were a gentleman courting you. See, you drop your fan so that when he picks it up he will touch your fingers. . . . And don't be stiff, let your waist bend. Men don't like boards. And above all don't be a ninny if they go too far. A man who goes too far is done for, my dear."

Through the long evening of furious talk the girl was docile and resigned, but her heart was heavy, oppressed with fear and shame. . . .

In such circumstances the girl seems absolutely passive; she *is* married, *given* in marriage by her parents. Boys *get* married, they *take* a wife. They look in marriage for an enlargement, a confirmation of their existence, but not the mere right to exist; it is a charge they assume voluntarily. Thus they can inquire concerning its advantanges and disadvantages, as did the Greek and medieval satirists; for them it is one mode of living, not a preordained lot. They have a perfect right to prefer celibate solitude; some marry late, or not at all.

In marrying, woman gets some share in the world as her own; legal guarantees protect her against capricious action by man; but she becomes his vassal. He is the economic head of the joint enterprise, and hence he represents it in the view of society. She takes his name; she belongs to his religion, his class, his circle; she joins his family, she becomes his "half." She follows wherever his work calls him and determines their place of residence; she breaks more or less decisively with her past, becoming attached to her husband's universe; she gives him her person, virginity and a rigorous fidelity being required. She loses some of the rights legally belonging to the unmarried woman. Roman law placed the wife in the husband's hands *loco filiæ*, in the position of a daughter; early in the nineteenth century the conservative writer Bonald pronounced the wife to be to her husband as the child is to its mother; before 1942 French law demanded the wife's obedience to her husband; law and custom still give him great authority, as implied in the conjugal situation itself.

Since the husband is the productive worker, he is the one who goes beyond family interest to that of society, opening up a future for himself through co-operation in the building of the collective future: he incarnates transcendence. Woman is doomed to the continuation of the species and the care of the home—that is to say, to immanence.[4] The fact is that every human existence involves transcendence and immanence at the same time; to go forward, each existence must be maintained, for it to expand toward the future it must integrate the past, and while intercommunicating with others it should find self-confirmation. These two elements—maintenance and progression —are implied in any living activity, and for *man* marriage permits precisely a happy synthesis of the two. In his occupation and his political life he encounters change and progress, he senses his extension through time and the universe; and when he is tired of such roaming, he gets himself a home, a fixed location, and an anchorage in the world. At evening he restores his soul in the home, where his wife takes care of his furnishings and children and guards the things of the past that she keeps in store. But she has no other job than to maintain and provide for life in pure and unvarying generality; she perpetuates the species without change, she ensures the even rhythm of the days and the continuity of the home, seeing to it that the doors are locked. But she is allowed no direct influence upon the future nor upon the world; she reaches out beyond herself toward the social group only through her husband as intermediary.

Marriage today still retains, for the most part, this traditional form. And, first of all, it is forced much more tyrannically upon the young girl than upon the young man. There are still important social strata in which no other vista opens before her; among the workers of the land the unmarried woman is a pariah; she remains a servant of her father, of her brothers, or of her brother-in-law; she can hardly join the exodus to the cities; marriage enslaves her to a man, but it makes her mistress of a home. In certain middle-class circles, the young girl is still left incapable of making a living; she can only vegetate as a parasite in her father's home or take some menial position in the home of a stranger. Even when she is more emancipated, she is led to prefer marriage to a career because of the economic advantages held by men: she tends to look for a husband who is above her in status or who she hopes will make a quicker or greater success than she could.

It is still agreed that the act of love is, as we have seen, a *service* rendered to the man; he *takes* his pleasure and owes her some payment. The woman's body is something he buys; to her he represents

---

[4] See Book I. We find this view expressed by St. Paul, the Church Fathers, Rousseau, Proudhon, August Comte, D. H. Lawrence, and others.

capital she is authorized to exploit. Sometimes she may bring a dowry; or, often, she undertakes to do certain domestic work: keeping house, rearing children. In any case she has the right to accept support and is even urged to do so by traditional morality. She is naturally tempted by this relatively easy way, the more so because occupations open to women are often disagreeable and poorly paid; marriage, in a word, is a more advantageous career than many others.

The attainment of sexual freedom by the unmarried woman, further, is still made difficult by social customs. In France adultery committed by a wife has been considered, up to the present time, to be a legal offense, whereas no law forbids a woman free love; nevertheless, if she wishes to take a lover, she must first get married. Even at the present time many young middle-class women of strict behavior marry "so as to be free." A good many American young women have gained sexual freedom; but their actual experiences are rather like those of the young girls described by Malinowski in *The Sexual Life of Savages*, who practice inconsequential love-making in the "bachelors' house"; it is understood that they will marry later, when they will be regarded as fully adult. A single woman in America, still more than in France, is a socially incomplete being even if she makes her own living; if she is to attain the whole dignity of a person and gain her full rights, she must wear a wedding ring. Maternity in particular is respectable only for a married woman; the unwed mother remains an offense to public opinion, and her child is a severe handicap for her in life.

For all these reasons a great many adolescent girls—in the New World as in the Old—when asked about their plans for the future, reply today as formerly: "I want to get married." But no young man considers marriage as his fundamental project. Economic success is what will bring him adult standing; such success may imply marriage —especially for the peasant—but it can also preclude it. The conditions of modern life—less stable, more uncertain than in the past— make the responsibilities of marriage especially heavy for the young man. Its benefits, on the other hand, have decreased, since it is easily possible for him to obtain board and room and since sexual satisfaction is generally available. No doubt marriage can afford certain material and sexual conveniences: it frees the individual from loneliness, it establishes him securely in space and time by giving him a home and children; it is a definitive fulfillment of his existence. But, for all that, the masculine demand is on the whole less than the feminine supply. A father can be said less to give his daughter than to get rid of her; the girl in search of a husband is not responding to a masculine demand, she is trying to create one.

The arranged marriage is not a thing of the past; there is a whole bourgeois class of solid substance which is keeping it alive. Around Napoleon's tomb, at the Opera, at a ball, on the beach, at a tea, the fair aspirant, with every hair in place and wearing a new gown, timidly exhibits her physical graces and her modest conversation; her parents keep at her: "You have already cost me enough in meeting different ones; make up your mind. The next time it will be your sister's turn." The unhappy candidate knows that her chances become less and less as she approaches nearer and nearer to being an old maid; claimants to her hand are few: she has scarcely more freedom of choice than the Bedouin girl given in exchange for a flock of sheep. As Colette puts it: [5] "A girl without fortune or gainful occupation . . . can only hold her tongue, seize her opportunity when it comes, and thank God!"

Less crudely, in higher social circles, young people are allowed to meet under their mothers' watchful eyes. Somewhat more emancipated, the girls get out more, they attend classes, take up an occupation that enables them to meet men. Between 1945 and 1947 Mme Claire Leplae investigated the problem of matrimonial choice in the Belgian middle class.[6] I will cite a few of the results she obtained: arranged marriages, frequent before 1945, had almost disappeared; a few were negotiated through priests or by correspondence. Social contacts accounted for 48 per cent of engagements; studies and work done in common, 22 per cent; personal acquaintance and visits, 30 per cent; childhood friendships, very few. Money played a leading part in 30 to 70 per cent of marriages, according to various answers. Parents were said to be anxious to get their daughters married by 48 per cent of those answering; 17 per cent wished to keep their daughters. Girls were reported as being very eager to marry by 36 per cent; desirous of marrying, 38 per cent; preferred not to marry rather than to make a bad marriage, 26 per cent. There was general agreement that girls expected marriage to increase their freedom. A great

---

[5] In *La Maison de Claudine.*
[6] See Claire Leplae: *Les Fiançailles.*

majority said that girls were more active than young men in seeking marriage and taking the initiative in the matter.

There is no similar document concerning France, but middle-class conditions are similar, and no doubt corresponding conclusions would be reached. Arranged marriages have always been more numerous in France than elsewhere, and clubs devoted to such matters still flourish. Matrimonial notices occupy much space in newspapers. In France, as in America, mothers, older friends, and women's magazines cynically teach young women the art of "catching" husbands, as flypaper catches flies; it is a kind of "fishing" or "hunting" that requires great skill: "Don't aim too high or too low; be realistic, not romantic; mix coquettishness with modesty; don't demand too much or too little." Young men mistrust women who "want to get married." Mme Leplae reports a young Belgian's remark: "Nothing is more disagreeable to a man than to feel himself pursued, to realize that a woman is trying to hook him." And men endeavor to avoid such efforts to ensnare them. The girl's choice is usually quite limited; and it could not be really free unless she felt free also not to marry. Her decision is ordinarily marked by calculation, disgust, resignation, rather than by enthusiasm. If the man is reasonably eligible in such matters as health and position, she accepts him, love or no love.

While desiring marriage, however, the girl frequently fears it. It is of greater benefit to her than to the man, and hence she is more eager for it than he is; but it also means greater sacrifices for her, in particular because it implies a more drastic rupture with the past. We have seen that many adolescent girls feel anguish at the thought of leaving the paternal home; this anxiety increases as the event draws near. Here is the moment when many neuroses originate; the same thing may happen with young men who fear the new responsibilities they are about to assume; but it is much commoner with young girls for reasons already discussed, reasons that are most weighty at this critical time. I cite briefly a single case borrowed from Stekel, that of a girl of good family whom he had under treatment for several neurotic symptoms.

She suffered from vomiting, took morphine every night, flew into rages, refused to bathe, stayed in her room. She was engaged, said she loved her fiancé and had given herself to him, but later admitted she had felt no pleasure and recalled his kisses with disgust. She adored her mother but felt herself not loved enough; she could not bear the thought of marrying and leaving home, fell sick, offended her fiancé, and declared she wished to give up all thought of marriage and remain at home, always, like a child. Her mother insisted, but a week before the wedding day she committed suicide.

In other instances, the girl remains obstinately ill, pretending to be in despair at not being able to marry the man she "adores," though in reality being ill to avoid marrying him; she recovers on breaking the engagement. Sometimes the fear of marriage originates in earlier erotic experiences of traumatic nature, and it often arises from dread that her loss of virginity will be discovered. But frequently what makes unbearable the idea of giving herself over to a strange male is the girl's strong attachment to family and home. And many of those who decide to marry—because it is the thing to do, because of pressure put on them, because it is the only sensible solution, because they want a normal existence as wife and mother—none the less retain secret and deep-seated feelings of resistance which make the beginnings of married life difficult, which may even prevent forever the attainment of a happy equilibrium.

Marriages, then, are not generally founded upon love. As Freud put it: "The husband is, so to speak, never more than a substitute for the beloved man, not that man himself." And this dissociation is in no way accidental. It is implied in the very nature of the institution, the aim of which is to make the economic and sexual union of man and woman serve the interest of society, not assure their personal happiness. In patriarchal regimes—as today among certain Mohammedans—it may happen that engaged persons chosen by parental authority have not even seen each other's faces before the wedding day. There could be no question of founding a lifelong enterprise, viewed in its social aspect, on a sentimental or erotic fancy.

In this discreet arrangement [says Montaigne], the appetites are not usually so wanton; they are sober and more blunted. Love hates that people should be bound by ties other than his own and goes faintly to work in intimacies that are arranged and maintained under another title, as marriage is. Connections and substance there rightly count for as much or more than charms and beauty. Men do not marry for themselves, whatever they may say; they marry as much, or more, for their posterity, their family.[7]

Because it is the man who "takes" the woman, he has somewhat more possibility of choosing—especially when feminine offers are numerous. But since the sexual act is regarded as a *service* assigned to woman, on which are based the advantages conceded to her, it is logical to ignore her personal preferences. Marriage is intended to deny her a man's liberty; but as there is neither love nor individuality without liberty, she must renounce loving a specific individual in order to assure herself the lifelong protection of some male. I have heard a pious mother of a family inform her daughters that "love is a coarse sentiment reserved for men and unknown to women of propriety." In naïve form, this is the very doctrine enunciated by Hegel [8] when he maintains that woman's relations as mother and wife are basically general and not individual. He maintains, therefore, that for her it is not a question of *this husband* but of *a husband* in general, of children in general. Her relations are not based on her individual feeling but on a universal; and thus for her, unlike man, individualized desire renders her ethic impure.

That is, woman is not concerned to establish individual relations with a chosen mate but to carry on the feminine functions in their generality; she is to have sex pleasure only in a specified form and not individualized. In regard to her erotic fate, two essential consequences follow: first, she has no right to any sexual activity apart from marriage; sexual intercourse thus becoming an institution, desire and gratification are subordinated to the interest of society for both sexes; but man, being transcended toward the universal as worker and citizen, can enjoy contingent pleasures before marriage and extramaritally. In any case man's justification is reached by other roads; whereas in a world in which woman is essentially defined as female, it is as female alone that she can find justification. In the second place, we have seen that the connection between the general and the individual is biologically different in male and female: in accomplish-

---

[7] Michel de Montaigne: *Essays* (Alfred A. Knopf, 1936), Vol. III, p. 58.

[8] *The Phenomenology of Mind* (Baillie trans., London: Allen & Unwin, 1931), p. 476.

ing his specific task as husband and as reproductive agent, the former is sure of obtaining at least some sexual pleasure; [9] in the female, on the contrary, the reproductive function is very often dissociated from erotic pleasure. So that, while being supposed to lend ethical standing to woman's erotic life, marriage is actually intended to suppress it.

This sexual frustration of woman has been deliberately accepted by men; as we have seen, depending upon an optimistic philosophy that nature is responsible, they have easily resigned themselves to woman's tribulations: it is her lot; the Biblical curse confirms them in this convenient opinion. The painful burden of pregnancy—that heavy payment exacted from woman in exchange for a brief and uncertain pleasure—has even been the subject of much facetiousness. "Five minutes' pleasure: nine months' pain," and "it goes in easier than it comes out"—an amusing contrast. But there is sadism in this philosophy. Many men enjoy feminine misery and repudiate the idea that it is desirable to ameliorate it.[1] It is understandable, then, that males have had no scruple at all in denying their mates sexual happiness; they have even found it advantageous to deny them the temptations of desire along with the independence of enjoyment.[2]

Montaigne expresses this idea with charming cynicism, remarking that it is a kind of incest to practice the extravagances of amorous license in "this sacred and venerable business of parenthood," and asserting that he has seen no marriages more troublous or early to fail than those infused with beauty and amorous desires. "Marriage is a holy union, and any pleasure taken in it should be restrained, serious, and mixed with some severity."

It is true enough that if the husband awakens feminine sensuality,

---

[9] Of course the adage "any port in a storm" is grossly cynical; man seeks something more than brute sexual pleasure; nevertheless the prosperity of houses of prostitution is enough to prove that man can obtain some satisfaction from whatever woman is available.

[1] There are those, for example, who hold that the pain of childbirth is necessary for the appearance of the maternal instinct: hinds that have given birth under anesthesia have abandoned their fawns. The alleged facts are by no means clear; and in any case women are not hinds. The truth is that some men find it shocking to lighten the burdens of femininity.

[2] Even in our time, woman's claim to sexual pleasure still arouses male anger. In a small work on the female orgasm, a Dr. Grémillon, taking issue with Stekel, declares that the normal, fertile woman has no orgasm. He goes on to say that erotogenic zones are artificial, not natural, they are signs of degeneration; to create them is unhygienic and foolish, for women thus become insatiable, new and terrible creatures, capable of crime, and so on.

he awakens it in its general form, for he has not been chosen as an individual; he is making his wife ready to seek pleasure in other arms. Montaigne agrees, but is honest enough to acknowledge that masculine prudence puts woman in a thankless situation: "we want them healthy, vigorous, plump, and chaste, all at once—that is to say, both hot and cold." Proudhon is less candid: according to him, it is a matter of "righteousness" to eliminate love from marriage; "all amorous conversation is unseemly, even between the engaged or the married; it is destructive of domestic respect, love of work, and the performance of social duty."

During the nineteenth century, however, middle-class conceptions became somewhat modified; there was an ardent effort to defend and preserve marriage; and, on the other hand, the progress of individualism made impossible the simple suppression of feminine claims; Saint-Simon, Fourier, George Sand, and all the romantics had too vigorously proclaimed the right to love. The problem was posed of integrating with marriage the personal sentiments that had hitherto been calmly excluded. At this time was invented the equivocal concept of "conjugal love," that miraculous fruit of the traditional marriage of convenience. Balzac expresses the ideas of the conservative middle class in all their lack of logic. He recognizes that in principle marriage and love have nothing in common; but he finds it repugnant to equate a respectable institution with a simple business deal in which woman is treated as a thing. He thus arrives at the disconcerting incoherencies of his *Physiologie du mariage*, where he speaks of marriage as a contract, entered into by most men to legalize reproduction and in which love is an absurdity, and then goes on to speak of a "perfect concord of souls" and "happiness" attained by the man's adherence to "rules of honor and delicacy." He urges, further, obedience to the "secret laws of nature which make sentiment bloom," calls for "sincere love," and asserts that passion for one's wife, thus cultivated, can permanently endure.

He then proceeds with his exposition of the science of marriage. But it is soon evident that in Balzac's view the question for the husband is not to be loved but to avoid being deceived: he is to have no hesitation in keeping his wife uncultured, weak, and stupid solely to safeguard his honor. If there is any sense in these vague ideas, it would seem to be that a man marries for convenience, takes his pleasure impersonally, and later arouses love in his wife by following certain formulas. But can Balzac honestly believe that love, rather than disgust, is aroused by amorous manipulations when love is not shared in the first place? The truth is that in his various discussions he cynically evades the problem. He fails to grasp the fact that there are no neutral sentiments and that the lack of love, constraint, ennui are less likely to arouse tender feelings than to cause resentment, impatience, and hostility.

To reconcile marriage and love is such a *tour de force* that nothing less than divine intervention is required for success; this is the solution reached through devious ways by Kierkegaard.[3] Love, he says, is spontaneous; marriage is a decision; the amorous inclination, however, is to be aroused by marriage or by the decision to wish to marry. Something so mysterious as to be explained only by divine action paradoxically occurs in virtue of reflection and decision, and the whole process must be simultaneous. This is to say that to love is not to marry and that it is hard to see how love can become duty. But the paradox does not dismay Kierkegaard. He agrees that "reflection is the destroying angel of spontaneity," but says that the decision is a new spontaneity based on ethical principles, it is a "religious conception" which "should open the way to amorous inclination" and protect it from all danger. A real husband, he says, "is a miracle." As for the wife, reason is not for her, she is without "reflection"; "she passes from the immediacy of love to the immediacy of the religious." In plain language this means that a man in love decides on marriage by an act of faith in God, which should guarantee the harmony of feeling and obligation; and that when a woman is in love she wishes to marry. I once knew an old lady of Catholic faith who more naïvely believed in the "sacramental thunderclap"; she declared that when the pair say the definitive "I do" at the foot of the altar, they feel their hearts flame miraculously with mutual love. Kierkegaard fully admits that there should be a preceding "inclination"; but that this should last through life is no less miraculous.

In France, however, *fin de siècle* novelists and playwrights, less confident in the virtue of the sacrament, seek to arouse conjugal happiness by more purely human methods; more boldly than Balzac, they recognize the possibility of integrating eroticism with legitimate love. Marcel Prévost exhorts the young husband to treat his wife like a mistress, and he paints discreetly the pleasures of married life. Bern-

---

[3] *In Vino Veritas* and *Propos sur le mariage*.

stein makes himself the dramatist of legitimate love: in comparison with the amoral, lying, sensual, thieving, wayward wife, the husband seems a wise and generous being; and one feels that he is a strong and skillful lover. In reaction against the novels of adultery appear numerous romantic vindications of marriage. Even Colette yields to this wave of moralizing when, in her *Ingénue libertine*, after having described the unfortunate experiences of a young wife who was awkwardly deflowered, she decides to let her become acquainted with erotic pleasures in her husband's arms. In a novel by Martin Maurice the young wife learns the erotic arts from a lover, then she returns and gives her husband the benefit of her experiences.

For other reasons and in a different way the Americans of today, at once respecters of marriage and individualists, are multiplying their efforts to integrate sexuality and marriage. A great many books are being published on the subject of married life, intended to teach the couple how to adapt themselves to one another and in particular to teach the man how to bring about a happy harmony with his wife. Psychoanalysts and doctors act as "marriage counselors"; it is generally agreed among them that women have a right to sex pleasure and that men should know the appropriate techniques. But, as we have seen, sexual pleasure is not only a matter of technique. Even if the young man has learned by heart twenty marriage manuals, he cannot be sure, for all that, of being able to make his new wife love him. It is to the total psychological situation that she reacts. And traditional marriage is far from creating the most favorable conditions for the awakening and development of feminine eroticism.

Formerly, in matriarchal groups, virginity was not demanded of the girl at marriage; and it was even customary, for mystic reasons, for her to be deflowered before the wedding. In certain rural districts of France one may still observe the survival of this ancient license; prenuptial chastity is not required; and even those who have made a misstep—that is, unwed mothers—sometimes find a husband more easily than the others. It is also true, on the other hand, that in circles which accept the emancipation of woman, young girls are granted the same sexual freedom as boys. But the paternalistic ethics imperatively demand that the fiancée be given over to her husband in virginal condition; he wants to be sure she carries no stranger's seed; he wants single and exclusive ownership of this flesh he is making his own; [4]

---

[4] See Book I, pp. 152 ff.

virginity took on a moral, religious, and mystical value, and this value is still very generally recognized today. There are parts of France where the bridegroom's friends wait behind the door of the nuptial chamber, laughing and singing, until the husband comes out in triumph to show them the bloodstained sheet; or the parents may display it next morning to the neighbors.[5] In less crude form such wedding-night customs are very widespread.

These customs have inspired a whole literature of broad, risqué tales because they emphasize the necessarily obscene separation of human sexuality into social ceremony and animal function. A humanist morality would require that all life experience have a human meaning, that it be infused with liberty; in a genuinely moral erotic relation there is free assumption of desire and pleasure, or at least a moving struggle to regain liberty in the midst of sexuality; but this is possible only when the other is recognized *as an individual*, in love or in desire. When sexuality is no more to be redeemed by the individual, but God or society is supposed to justify it, then the relation of the two partners is no more than an animal relation. It is quite understandable that right-thinking matrons speak of carnal experiences disgustedly: they have abased them to the level of scatological functions. It is for the same reason that one hears obscene laughter at the wedding feast. There is an obscene paradox in superposing a stately ceremony upon an animal function of brutal reality. The marriage ceremony displays its universal and abstract significance: a man and a woman are united in accordance with symbolic ritual in full view of all; but in the secrecy of the marriage bed they are concrete and single individuals alone together, and all eyes are averted from their embraces. Colette at thirteen was a guest at a peasant wedding, and she was filled with confusion when a friend took her to see the nuptial chamber:

The young couple's room! The curtained bed, high and narrow, the bed stuffed with feathers, piled with goosedown pillows, the bed that will be the termination of a day steaming with sweat, incense, the breath of cattle, the smell of cooking. . . . Soon the young couple will be here. I had not thought of this. They will

---

[5] The Kinsey Report (p. 548) states that "first generation immigrants in some parts of this country today may still send the blood-stained napkin back to relatives in Europe, as evidence of the valid consummation of the marriage."

sink into this deep featherbed. . . . They will engage in that obscure struggle about which my mother's frank words and the life of the barnyard had taught me too much and too little. And then what? I was frightened by this chamber and this bed which I had never thought of.

In her childish distress the little girl felt the contrast between the trappings of the family celebration and the animal mystery of the great curtained bed. The lewdly ribald aspect of weddings scarcely appears in civilizations where woman is not individualized, as in the Orient, Greece, and Rome; the animal function seems as generalized, impersonal, as the social rites; but in our time, in the West, men and women are regarded as individuals, and the members of the wedding smirk and giggle because it is this particular man and this particular woman who are going to consummate in a quite individual experience the act that is veiled under ritual and flowers. There is, to be sure, a macabre contrast between the pomp of elaborate funerals and the decay of the tomb. But the dead does not awaken when interred; whereas the bride feels a terrible surprise when she discovers the highly personal and circumstantial nature of the *real* experience promised her by the mayor's insignia of office and the organ music of the church.

It is not only in farce and vaudeville that we see young women fleeing their wedding night to go home in tears to mother. Psychiatric books are full of histories of the kind; and I have myself been told of a number of cases: the girls concerned had been too carefully brought up, and since they had no sexual education, the sudden discovery of eroticism was too much for them. Girls have sometimes believed that the kiss was sexual union in complete form, and Stekel tells of a bride who thought her husband insane on account of his quite normal behavior on the honeymoon trip. A girl may even marry a female invert and live with her for years without suspecting anything wrong.

A poem by Michaux, *Nuits de noces*, puts the situation in a nutshell: if the bridegroom should put his wife in a well to soak overnight, she would feel with reason that her vague apprehensions were justified. "So this is marriage! No wonder they keep the actual details a great secret," she thinks; but, being vexed, she does not speak out, and the neighbors hear nothing about it. Today many young women are better informed; but their willingness remains formal, abstract; and their defloration is still in the nature of a rape. Havelock Ellis remarks that there are certainly more rapes committed in marriage than outside of it. Neugebauer [6] records more than one hundred and fifty cases of injuries to women in intercourse. Ellis reports that among six intelligent middle-class women, all said that the first marital intercourse came as a shock; two were quite ignorant, and the others, who thought they knew, were physically injured none the less. Adler also emphasized the psychological importance of defloration, declaring that the moment may affect a lifetime, for the efforts of a maladroit husband may lead to permanent frigidity. A few of many illustrative cases have been cited in a preceding chapter.

We have already considered the many inhibitions and difficulties that the virgin must overcome if she is to accomplish her sexual destiny: her initiation requires a real travail at once physiological and psychic. The attempt to crowd it all into one night is stupid and barbarous; it is absurd to make a duty of such a delicate and difficult matter as the first intercourse. The woman is the more frightened because the strange operation she must undergo is sacred, because society, religion, family, and friends have solemnly handed her over to her husband as if to a master; and also because the act seems to her to involve her whole future, marriage being still regarded as a definitive step taken once for all. At this moment she feels herself truly revealed in the absolute: this man to whom she is vowed forever incarnates Man as a whole in her eyes; and now he is revealed to her also as an unknown, but one who is of frightful importance, since he is to be her lifelong companion. Then, too, the man himself is filled with anxiety by the assignment that now weighs upon him; he has his own difficulties, his own complexes, which may make him either timid and clumsy or rough; and sometimes he is rendered impotent on his wedding night by the very solemnity of it all. The psychologist Janet reports cases of this nature, one a tragicomic affair in which an enraged father-in-law demanded medical testimony for use in divorce proceedings. The unfortunate son-in-law asserted his former powers, but admitted that since his marriage a feeling of embarrassment and shame had made him ineffectual.

Too much impetuosity frightens the virgin, too much respectfulness humiliates her; women hate forever a man who selfishly takes

---

[6] *Monatsschrift für Geburtshilfe*, Vol. IX (1889).

his pleasure at the price of their suffering; but they feel eternal resentment against men who have seemed to disdain them (as in some of Stekel's cases already cited), and often against those who have not attempted to deflower them during the first night or have been unable to do so. Helene Deutsch refers to certain husbands who, lacking strength or courage, prefer to have a physician deflower their brides, asserting that the partner's hymen is unusually resistant, which is usually untrue. In such cases, she says, the woman feels a contempt difficult to overcome for the man who was unable to penetrate her in normal fashion.[7] One of Freud's observations (quoted by Stekel) shows that a husband's impotence can act as a trauma, giving rise to an obsession in the wife. In this case she constantly rearranged a table cover so that the maid might see a spot on it. This was traced to the husband's efforts on the wedding night to conceal his inability by spotting the sheets with red ink so that the chambermaid might not suspect the truth.

The wedding night transforms the erotic act into a test that both parties fear their inability to meet, each being too worried by his or her own problems to be able to think generously of the other. This gives the occasion a formidable air of solemnity, and it is not surprising if it dooms the woman to lasting frigidity. The difficult problem facing the husband is this: if, in Aristotle's phrase, "he titillates his wife too lasciviously," she may be scandalized and outraged; it would appear that the fear of this outcome paralyzes American husbands, for example, especially in couples of college education who have practiced extreme premarital restraint, as the Kinsey Report states (p. 544), because the women of this group are deeply inhibited and unable to "participate with the abandon which is necessary for the successful consummation of any sexual relation." But if, on the other hand, the husband "respects" his wife, he fails to awaken her sensuality. This dilemma is created by the ambiguity of the feminine attitude: the young woman simultaneously desires and declines sex pleasure; she demands a reserve from which she suffers. Unless exceptionally fortunate, the young husband will of necessity seem either a libertine or a bungler. It is not astonishing, therefore, that "conjugal duties" may often seem boring and repugnant to the wife.

As a matter of fact, many women become mothers and grandmothers without ever having experienced the orgasm or even any sex

---

[7] *Psychology of Women*, Vol. II. p. 82.

excitement at all; in some cases they endeavor to escape the demean-
ing "duty" through a doctor's recommendation or on other pretexts.
Kinsey states (p. 571) that there are many wives "who report that
they consider their coital frequencies already too high and wish that
their husbands did not desire intercourse so often. A very few wives
wish for more frequent coitus." But as we have seen, woman's erotic
capabilities are almost unlimited. This contradiction clearly indicates
that marriage kills feminine eroticism in the effort to regularize it.

The period of engagement would seem precisely adapted for making the girl's initiation gradual; but custom often imposes strict chastity upon the couple. When the virgin does "know" her future husband during the engagement, her situation is not very different from
that of the young married woman; she yields only because her engagement seems about as definitive as marriage, and her first intercourse
is still an ordeal. Once she has given herself—even if she does not become pregnant, which would surely be binding—it is rare indeed that
she ventures to change her mind.

The difficulties of the first experiences are readily overcome if love
or desire evokes the full consent of both partners; the delight the
lovers give and take in mutual recognition of their freedom is what
lends strength and dignity to physical passion; under these circumstances nothing they do is degrading, since nothing is a matter of
submission, everything a matter of willing generosity. Marriage is
obscene in principle in so far as it transforms into rights and duties
those mutual relations which should be founded on a spontaneous
urge; it gives an instrumental and therefore degrading character to
the two bodies in dooming them to know each other in their general
aspect *as* bodies, not as persons. The husband is often chilled by the
idea that he is doing a duty, and the wife is ashamed to find herself
given to someone who is exercising a right over her. It may happen,
of course, that at the beginning of married life their relations become
individualized; the sexual apprenticeship proceeds sometimes by slow
gradations; from the first night a happy physical attraction may show
itself. Marriage promotes a carefree abandon in woman by eliminating the notion of sin still commonly associated with the flesh; regular
and frequent intercourse engenders a carnal intimacy that favors
sexual maturation. For these reasons there are wives who find full
gratification during the first years of marriage. It is to be noted that
they feel toward their husbands a gratitude that inclines them to

pardon later on such faults as they may have. Stekel remarks that "wives who are unable to free themselves from an unhappy marriage have always been those who are sexually satisfied by their husbands," though, one supposes, otherwise displeased. Nevertheless the girl runs a great risk when she undertakes to sleep all her life and exclusively with a man with whom she is sexually unacquainted, since her erotic fate depends essentially on her partner's personality; this is the paradoxical situation that Léon Blum quite rightly attacked in his book on marriage.[8]

It is sheer hypocrisy to hold that a union based on convenience has much chance of inducing love; it is pure absurdity to maintain that two married persons, bound by ties of practical, social, and moral interest, will provide each other with sex satisfaction as long as they live. But the proponents of the marriage of reason have no difficulty in showing that the love-match, also, is not especially likely to assure the happiness of the couple. In the first place, the idealistic love often felt by the young girl does not always incline her toward sexual love; her platonic idolizations, her daydreams, her passions projecting childish or juvenile obsessions, are not suited to the test of everyday life nor will they endure for long. Even if a strong and sincere erotic attraction exists between her and her fiancé, this is not a solid foundation for a lifelong enterprise. As Colette writes in *La Vagabonde*:

Sensual pleasure occupies a very small and fiery place in the illimitable desert of love, glowing so brightly that at first nothing else is to be seen. Around this inconstant campfire is danger, is the unknown. When we arise from a short embrace or even a long night, comes again the necessity of living near each other, for each other.

But further, even when sexual love exists before the marriage or awakens during the honeymoon, it very rarely persists through the long years to come. No doubt fidelity is necessary for sexual love, because the desire felt by two people in love concerns them as individuals; they are unwilling for this to be contradicted by experiences with out-

---

[8] *Du mariage*, recently referred to in *The New Yorker*, March 31, 1951, p. 68. Genêt says that Blum's advocacy of premarital experiences for woman, as making for more solid marriages, came as a shock to the French, "especially French mothers."—TR.

siders; they want each one to be irreplaceable for the other; but such fidelity has meaning only in so far as it is spontaneous, and the magic of eroticism spontaneously evaporates rather rapidly. The miracle is that to each lover it entrusts, for the moment and in the flesh, a being whose existence reaches out in unlimited transcendence; the possession of this being is no doubt impossible, but at least contact is made in an especially privileged and poignant way. But when the individuals no longer desire such contact because of hostility, disgust, or indifference between them, erotic attraction disappears. And it dies almost as surely in an atmosphere of esteem and friendship, for two human beings associated in their transcendence, out into the world and through their common projects, no longer need carnal union; and because this union has lost its meaning they even find it repugnant.

Montaigne's word *incest* is profoundly significant. Eroticism is a movement toward the *Other*, this is its essential character; but in the deep intimacy of the couple, husband and wife become for one another the *Same*; no exchange is any longer possible between them, no giving and no conquering. Thus if they do continue to make love, it is often with a sense of shame: they feel that the sexual act is no longer an intersubjective experience in which each goes beyond self, but rather a kind of joint masturbation. That they each regard the other as a utensil necessary for the satisfaction of their needs is a fact that conjugal politeness ignores but that springs to view if this politeness fails, as, for example, in the observations reported by Dr. Lagache.[9] The jealous wife regards the male member as an article providing pleasure that belongs to her and of which she is as niggardly as she is of the preserves stored in her cupboards—if the husband is generous with a neighbor, none will remain for the wife; she scrutinizes his underwear to see if he has squandered the precious seed. As for the husband, he satisfies his desires on her without consulting her opinion.

This brutish satisfying of a need, be it said again, is not enough to satisfy human sexuality, and that is why there is often an aftertaste of vice in what would seem to be the most legitimate embraces. Frequently the wife finds assistance in erotic fantasies. Stekel cites the case of a woman of twenty-five who could attain a slight orgasm with her husband if she imagined a powerful older man was taking her by force. Thus the wife imagines that she is being raped, that her hus-

---

[9] In his *Nature et forme de la jalousie*.

band is not himself but an *other*. The husband enjoys the same dream; in his wife he is possessing the legs of some dancer he has seen on the stage, the bosom of a pin-up girl whose picture he has looked at, a memory, an image. Or he may fancy his wife desired, possessed, violated, which is a way of restoring her lost alterity. As Stekel says, marriage gives rise to fantastic comedies and play-acting between the partners, which may threaten to destroy the boundary between appearance and reality; and indeed in extreme cases definite perversion does appear. The husband becomes a voyeur: he must needs see his wife in intercourse with a lover, or know of it, to feel again a little of the old magic; or he makes sadistic efforts to elicit remonstrances so that finally he becomes aware of her consciousness and freedom as an individual, and he feels that it is really a human being whom he is possessing. Inversely, masochistic behavior appears in the wife who seeks to arouse in her husband the master, the tyrant, that he is not in reality. I once knew a convent-bred and pious woman, authoritative and domineering during the daytime, who at night passionately demanded to be whipped by her husband; he was horrified, but acceded to her wish. Even vice itself takes on in marriage a cold, prearranged, and grim aspect that makes it dismal indeed as a last resource.

The fact is that physical love can be treated neither as an end in itself nor as a mere means to an end; it cannot serve as a justification of existence; but neither can it be justified extraneously. That is, it should play in any human life an episodic and independent role. Which is to say that above all it must be free.

Thus what bourgeois optimism has to offer the engaged girl is certainly not love; the bright ideal held up to her is that of happiness, which means the ideal of quiet equilibrium in a life of immanence and repetition. In certain periods of prosperity and security this has been the ideal of the middle class as a whole and especially of landed proprietors; their aim has been not the conquest of the future and of the world but the peaceful conservation of the past, the maintenance of the *status quo*. A gilded mediocrity lacking ambition and passion, aimless days indefinitely repeated, life that slips away gently toward death without questioning its purpose—this is what they meant by "happiness." This false wisdom, vaguely inspired by Epicurus and Zeno, is today discredited: to conserve and continue the world as it

is seems neither desirable nor possible. The male is called upon for
action, his vocation is to produce, fight, create, progress, to transcend
himself toward the totality of the universe and the infinity of the
future; but traditional marriage does not invite woman to transcend
herself with him; it confines her in immanence, shuts her up within
the circle of herself. She can thus propose to do nothing more than
construct a life of stable equilibrium in which the present as a con-
tinuance of the past avoids the menaces of tomorrow—that is, construct precisely a life of happiness. In place of love, she will feel a
tender and respectful sentiment known as conjugal love, wifely affection; within the walls of the home she is to manage, she will enclose
her world; she will see to the continuation of the human species
through time to come.

But no existent ever relinquishes his transcendence, even when he
stubbornly forswears it. The old-time bourgeois thought that in preserving the established order, in showing its virtues through his own
prosperity, he was serving God, his country, a regime, a civilization:
to be happy was to fulfill his function as a man. Woman, too, must
envisage purposes that transcend the peaceful life of the home; but
it is man who will act as intermediary between his wife as an individuality and the universe, he will endue her inconsequential life of
contingency with human worth. Obtaining in his association with his
wife the strength to undertake things, to act, to struggle, he is her
justification: she has only to put her existence in his hands and he
will give it meaning. This presupposes a humble renunciation on her
part; but she is compensated because, under the guidance and protection of masculine strength, she will escape the effects of the original
renunciation; she will once more become essential. Queen in her hive,
tranquilly at rest within her domain, but borne by man out into limitless space and time, wife, mother, mistress of the home, woman finds
in marriage at once energy for living and meaning for her life. We
must now see how this ideal works out in reality.

The ideal of happiness has always taken material form in the house,
whether cottage or castle; it stands for permanence and separation
from the world. Within its walls the family is established as a discrete cell or a unit group and maintains its identity as generations
come and go; the past, preserved in the form of furnishings and ancestral portraits, gives promise of a secure future; in the garden the

seasons register their reassuring cycle in the growth of edible vegetables; each year the same springtime with the same flowers foretells
the return of immutable summer, of autumn with its fruits no different from the fruits of any other autumn: neither time nor space
fly off at a tangent, they recur in their appointed cycles. In every civilization based on landed property an ample literature sings the poetry
of hearth and home; in such a work as Henry Bordeaux's *La Maison*
it sums up all the middle-class values: fidelity to the past, patience,
economy, foresight, love of family and of the native soil, and so on.
It often happens that the poets of the home are women, since it is
woman's task to assure the happiness of the family group; her part,
as in the time when the Roman *domina* sat in the atrium, is to be
"lady of the house."

Today the house has lost its patriarchal splendor; for the majority
of men it is only a place to live in, no longer freighted with the
memory of dead generations, no longer encompassing the centuries
to come. But still woman is all for giving her "interior" the meaning
and value that the true house and home once had. In *Cannery Row*
Steinbeck describes a vagrant woman who was determined to decorate
with rugs and curtains the discarded engine boiler in which she lived
with her husband; he objected in vain that the curtains were useless—
"We got no windows."

This concern is specifically feminine. A normal man regards the
objects around him as instruments; he arranges them in accordance
with the purposes for which they are intended; to him "order"—
where a woman will often see only disorder—means to have his cigar-
ettes, his papers, his tools, within easy reach. Among others, artists
who can re-create the world through their chosen material—painters
and sculptors—are quite careless of the surroundings in which they
live. Rilke writes of Rodin:

> When I first came to Rodin . . . I knew that his house was
> nothing to him, a paltry little necessity perhaps, a roof for time of
> rain and sleep; and that it was no care to him and no weight upon
> his solitude and composure. Deep in himself he bore the darkness,
> shelter, and peace of a house, and he himself had become sky above
> it, and wood around it, and distance and great stream always
> flowing by.[1]

---

[1] Letter to Lou Andreas-Salomé, August 8, 1903.

But in order to find a hearth and home within oneself, one must first have found self-realization in works or in deeds. Man is but mildly interested in his immediate surroundings because he can find self-expression in projects. Whereas woman is confined within the conjugal sphere; it is for her to change that prison into a realm. Her attitude toward her home is dictated by the same dialectic that defines her situation in general: she takes by becoming prey, she finds freedom by giving it up; by renouncing the world she aims to conquer a world.

It is not without some regret that she shuts behind her the doors of her new home; when she was a girl, the whole countryside was her homeland; the forests were hers. Now she is confined to a restricted space; Nature is reduced to the dimensions of a potted geranium; walls cut off the horizon. But she is going to set about overcoming these limitations. In the form of more or less expensive bric-a-brac she has within her four walls the fauna and flora of the world, she has exotic countries and past times; she has her husband, representing human society, and she has her child, who gives her the entire future in portable form.

The home becomes the center of the world and even its only reality; "a kind of counter-universe or universe in opposition" (Bachelard); refuge, retreat, grotto, womb, it gives shelter from outside dangers; it is this confused outer world that becomes unreal. And particularly at evening, with shutters closed, the wife feels herself queen; she is disturbed by the light shed abroad at noonday by the sun that shines for all; at night she is no longer dispossessed, for she does away with what are not her possessions; from under the lampshade she sees shining a light that is her own and that illuminates her dwelling exclusively: nothing else exists. Reality is concentrated inside the house, while outer space seems to collapse.

Thanks to the velvets and silks and porcelains with which she surrounds herself, woman can in some degree satisfy that tactile sensuality which her erotic life can seldom assuage. These decorations will also provide an expression of her personality; she is the one who has chosen, made, hunted out furnishings and knick-knacks, who has arranged them in accordance with an æsthetic principle in which regard for symmetry is usually an important element; they reflect her individuality while bearing public witness to her standard of living. Her home is thus her earthly lot, the expression of her social value and of her truest self. Because she *does* nothing, she eagerly seeks self-realization in what she *has*.

In domestic work, with or without the aid of servants, woman makes her home her own, finds social justification, and provides herself with an occupation, an activity, that deals usefully and satisfyingly with material objects—shining stoves, fresh, clean clothes, bright copper, polished furniture—but provides no escape from immanence and little affirmation of individuality. Such work has a negative basis: cleaning is getting rid of dirt, tidying up is eliminating disorder. And under impoverished conditions no satisfaction is possible; the hovel remains a hovel in spite of woman's sweat and tears: "nothing in the world can make it pretty." Legions of women have only this endless struggle without victory over the dirt. And for even the most privileged the victory is never final.

Few tasks are more like the torture of Sisyphus than housework, with its endles repetition: the clean becomes soiled, the soiled is made clean, over and over, day after day. The housewife wears herself out marking time: she makes nothing, simply perpetuates the present. She never senses conquest of a positive Good, but rather indefinite struggle against negative Evil. A young pupil writes in her essay: "I shall never have house-cleaning day"; she thinks of the future as constant progress toward some unknown summit; but one day, as her mother washes the dishes, it comes over her that both of them will be bound to such rites until death. Eating, sleeping, cleaning—the years no longer rise up toward heaven, they lie spread out ahead, gray and identical. The battle against dust and dirt is never won.

Washing, ironing, sweeping, ferreting out rolls of lint from under wardrobes—all this halting of decay is also the denial of life; for time simultaneously creates and destroys, and only its negative aspect concerns the housekeeper. Hers is the position of the Manichæist, regarded philosophically. The essence of Manichæism is not solely to recognize two principles, the one good, the other evil; it is also to hold that the good is attained through the abolition of evil and not by positive action. In this sense Christianity is hardly Manichæist in spite of the existence of the devil, for one fights the demon best by devoting oneself to God and not by endeavoring to conquer the evil one directly. Any doctrine of transcendence and liberty subordinates the defeat of evil to progress toward the good. But woman is not called upon to build a better world: her domain is fixed and she has only to keep up the never ending struggle against the evil principles that creep into it; in her war against dust, stains, mud, and dirt she is fighting sin, wrestling with Satan.

But it is a sad fate to be required without respite to repel an enemy instead of working toward positive ends, and very often the housekeeper submits to it in a kind of madness that may verge on perversion, a kind of sado-masochism. The maniac housekeeper wages her furious war against dirt, blaming life itself for the rubbish all living growth entails. When any living being enters her house, her eye gleams with a wicked light: "Wipe your feet, don't tear the place apart, leave that alone!" She wishes those of her household would hardly breathe; everything means more thankless work for her. Severe, preoccupied, always on the watch, she loses *joie de vivre*, she becomes overprudent and avaricious. She shuts out the sunlight, for along with that come insects, germs, and dust, and besides, the sun ruins silk hangings and fades upholstery; she scatters naphthalene, which scents the air. She becomes bitter and disagreeable and hostile to all that lives: the end is sometimes murder.

The healthy young woman will hardly be attracted by so gloomy a vice. Such nervousness and spitefulness are more suited to frigid and frustrated women, old maids, deceived wives, and those whom surly and dictatorial husbands condemn to a solitary and empty existence. I knew an old beldame, once gay and coquettish, who got up at five each morning to go over her closets; married to a man who neglected her, and isolated on a lonely estate, with but one child, she took to orderly housekeeping as others take to drink. In this insanity the house becomes so neat and clean that one hardly dares live in it; the woman is so busy she forgets her own existence. A household, in fact, with its meticulous and limitless tasks, permits to woman a sado-masochistic flight from herself as she contends madly with the things around her and with herself in a state of distraction and mental vacancy. And this flight may often have a sexual tinge. It is noteworthy that the rage for cleanliness is highest in Holland, where the women are cold, and in puritanical civilizations, which oppose an ideal of neatness and purity to the joys of the flesh. If the Mediterranean Midi lives in a state of joyous filth, it is not only because water is scarce there; love of the flesh and its animality is conducive to toleration of human odor, dirt, and even vermin.

The preparation of food, getting meals, is work more positive in nature and often more agreeable than cleaning. First of all it means marketing, often the bright spot of the day. And gossip on doorsteps, while peeling vegetables, is a gay relief for solitude; to go for water is a great adventure for half-cloistered Mohammedan women; women in markets and stores talk about domestic affairs, with a common interest, feeling themselves members of a group that—for an instant—is opposed to the group of men as the essential to the inessential. Buying is a profound pleasure, a discovery, almost an invention. As Gide says in his *Journal*, the Mohammedans, not knowing gambling, have in its place the discovery of hidden treasure; that is the poetry and the adventure of mercantile civilizations. The housewife knows little of winning in games, but a solid cabbage, a ripe Camembert, are treasures that must be cleverly won from the unwilling storekeeper; the game is to get the best for the least money; economy means not so much helping the budget as winning the game. She is pleased with her passing triumph as she contemplates her well-filled larder.

Gas and electricity have killed the magic of fire, but in the country many women still know the joy of kindling live flames from inert wood. With her fire going, woman becomes a sorceress; by a simple movement, as in beating eggs, or through the magic of fire, she effects the transmutation of substances: matter becomes food. There is enchantment in these alchemies, there is poetry in making preserves; the housewife has caught duration in the snare of sugar, she has enclosed life in jars. Cooking is revelation and creation; and a woman can find special satisfaction in a successful cake or a flaky pastry, for not everyone can do it: one must have the gift.

Here again the little girl is naturally fond of imitating her elders, making mud pies and the like, and helping roll real dough in the kitchen. But as with other housework, repetition soon spoils these pleasures. The magic of the oven can hardly appeal to Mexican Indian women who spend half their lives preparing tortillas, identical from day to day, from century to century. And it is impossible to go on day after day making a treasure-hunt of the marketing or ecstatically viewing one's highly polished faucets. The male and female writers who lyrically exalt such triumphs are persons who are seldom or never engaged in actual housework. It is tiresome, empty, monotonous, as a career. If, however, the individual who does such work is also a producer, a creative worker, it is as naturally integrated in life as are the organic functions; for this reason housework done by men seems much less dismal; it represents for them merely a negative and inconsequential moment from which they quickly escape. What makes the lot of the wife-servant ungrateful is the division of labor which dooms her completely to the general and the inessential. Dwelling-place and food are useful for life but give it no significance: the immediate goals of the housekeeper are only means, not true ends. She endeavors, naturally, to give some individuality to her work and to make it seem essential. No one else, she thinks, could do her work as well; she has her rites, superstitions, and ways of doing things. But too often her "personal note" is but a vague and meaningless rearrangement of disorder.

Woman wastes a great deal of time and effort in such striving for originality and unique perfection; this gives her task its meticulous, disorganized, and endless character and makes it difficult to estimate the true load of domestic work. Recent studies show that for married women housework averages about thirty hours per week, or three fourths of a working week in employment. This is enormous if done in addition to a paid occupation, little if the woman has nothing else to do. The care of several children will naturally add a good deal to woman's work: a poor mother is often working all the time. Middle-class women who employ help, on the other hand, are almost idle; and they pay for their leisure with ennui. If they lack outside interests, they often multiply and complicate their domestic duties to excess, just to have something to do.

The worst of it all is that this labor does not even tend toward the creation of anything durable. Woman is tempted—and the more so the greater pains she takes—to regard her work as an end in itself. She sighs as she contemplates the perfect cake just out of the oven: "it's a shame to eat it!" It is really too bad to have husband and children tramping with their muddy feet all over her waxed hardwood floors! When things are used they are soiled or destroyed—we have seen how she is tempted to save them from being used; she keeps preserves until they get moldy; she locks up the parlor. But time passes inexorably; provisions attract rats; they become wormy; moths attack blankets and clothing. The world is not a dream carved in stone, it is made of dubious stuff subject to rot; edible material is as equivocal as Dali's fleshy watches: it seems inert, inorganic, but hidden larvæ may have changed it into a cadaver. The housewife who loses herself in things becomes dependent, like the things, upon the whole world:

linen is scorched, the roast burns, chinaware gets broken; these are absolute disasters, for when things are destroyed, they are gone forever. Permanence and security cannot possibly be obtained through them. The pillage and bombs of war threaten one's wardrobes, one's house.

The products of domestic work, then, must necessarily be consumed; a continual renunciation is required of the woman whose operations are completed only in their destruction. For her to acquiesce without regret, these minor holocausts must at least be reflected in someone's joy or pleasure. But since the housekeeper's labor is expended to maintain the *status quo*, the husband, coming into the house, may notice disorder or negligence, but it seems to him that order and neatness come of their own accord. He has a more positive interest in a good meal. The cook's moment of triumph arrives when she puts a successful dish on the table: husband and children receive it with warm approval, not only in words, but by consuming it gleefully. The culinary alchemy then pursues its course, food becomes chyle and blood.

Thus, to maintain living bodies is of more concrete, vital interest than to keep a fine floor in proper condition; the cook's effort is evidently transcended toward the future. If, however, it is better to share in another's free transcendence than to lose oneself in things, it is not less dangerous. The validity of the cook's work is to be found only in the mouths of those around her table; she needs their approbation, demands that they appreciate her dishes and call for second helpings; she is upset if they are not hungry, to the point that one wonders whether the fried potatoes are for her husband or her husband for the fried potatoes. This ambiguity is evident in the general attitude of the housekeeping wife: she takes care of the house for her husband; but she also wants him to spend all he earns for furnishings and an electric refrigerator. She desires to make him happy; but she approves of his activities only in so far as they fall within the frame of happiness she has set up.

There have been times when these claims have in general found satisfaction: times when such felicity was also man's ideal, when he was attached above all to his home, to his family, and when even the children chose to be characterized by their parents, their traditions, and their past. At such times she who ruled the home, who presided at the dinner table, was recognized as supreme; and she still plays this resplendent role among certain landed proprietors and wealthy peasants who here and there perpetuate the patriarchal civilization.

But on the whole marriage is today a surviving relic of dead ways of life, and the situation of the wife is more ungrateful than formerly, because she still has the same duties but they no longer confer the same rights, privileges, and honors. Man marries today to obtain an anchorage in immanence, but not to be himself confined therein; he wants to have hearth and home while being free to escape therefrom; he settles down but often remains a vagabond at heart; he is not contemptuous of domestic felicity, but he does not make of it an end in itself; repetition bores him; he seeks after novelty, risk, opposition to overcome, companions and friends who take him away from solitude *à deux*. The children, even more than their father, want to escape beyond family limits: life for them lies elsewhere, it is before them; the child always seeks what is different. Woman tries to set up a universe of permanence and continuity; husband and children wish to transcend the situation she creates, which for them is only a given environment. This is why, even if she is loath to admit the precarious nature of the activities to which her whole life is devoted, she is nevertheless led to impose her services by force: she changes from mother and housewife into harsh stepmother and shrew.

Thus woman's work within the home gives her no autonomy; it is not directly useful to society, it does not open out on the future, it produces nothing. It takes on meaning and dignity only as it is linked with existent beings who reach out beyond themselves, transcend themselves, toward society in production and action. That is, far from freeing the matron, her occupation makes her dependent upon husband and children; she is justified through them; but in their lives she is only an inessential intermediary. That "obedience" is legally no longer one of her duties in no way changes her situation; for this depends not on the will of the couple but on the very structure of the conjugal group. Woman is not allowed to *do* something positive in her work and in consequence win recognition as a complete person. However respected she may be, she is subordinate, secondary, parasitic. The heavy curse that weighs upon her consists in this: the very meaning of her life is not in her hands. That is why the successes and the failures of her conjugal life are much more gravely important for her than for her husband; he is first a citizen, a producer, secondly a husband; she is before all, and often exclusively, a wife; her work does not take her out of her situation; it is from the latter, on the contrary, that her work takes its value, high or low. Loving, generously devoted, she will perform her tasks joyously; but they will seem to her mere dull drudgery if she performs them with resentment. In her destiny they will never play more than an inessential role; they will not be a help in the ups and downs of conjugal life. We must go on to see, then, how woman's condition is concretely experienced in life —this condition which is characterized essentially by the "service" of the bed and the "service" of the housekeeping and in which woman finds her place of dignity only in accepting her vassalage.

The young girl meets one crisis in passing from childhood to adolescence; it is another and a more violent crisis that plunges her into adult life. To the disturbances easily provoked in woman by a too abrupt sexual initiation are added the anxieties inherent in all transition from one state to another. Nietzsche puts it as follows:

> To be hurled by marriage as by a frightful stroke of lightning into reality and knowledge, to discover love and shame in contradiction, to have to feel in regard to a single object ravishment, sacrifice, duty, pity, and terror, because of the unexpected propinquity of God and the beast—here is created a confusion of soul which seeks in vain its equal.

The excitement of the traditional wedding trip was intended in part to mask this confusion: torn for some weeks out of her everyday world, with all social ties temporarily broken, the young woman lost her position in space, in time, and in reality.[2] But sooner or later she has to resume that position; and she never finds herself in her new home without some disquiet. Her ties with her parental home are much closer than the young man's, and when she breaks away she feels that anguish of abandonment and the vertigo of liberty more or less painfully. If she has already gained some freedom, or if, still under family domination, she can still count on some protection, the change will be less noticeable; but as a rule, even if she wants to be free, she will be upset by the separation from all she has hitherto known and trusted.

---

[2] The *fin de siècle* literature commonly put the scene of defloration in a sleeping-car, which is a way of putting it "nowhere."

Only a full and ardent erotic life could restore her to an atmosphere of peaceful immanence; but usually she is more upset than gratified at first. Her reactions are much like those following her first menstruation: distaste for this revelation of her femininity, repulsion at the thought of its repetition. With menses established, the young girl was sadly aware that she was still not an adult; deflowered, married, she is an adult, the last step has been taken—and now what? There is alarming disappointment attached to marriage itself as well as to defloration: a woman who has "known" her fiancé or other men already but for whom marriage represents full accession to adult life will often have the same reaction. There is exaltation in beginning an enterprise, but nothing is more depressing than to become aware of a fate over which one has no control. Upon this definitive, immutable background liberty seems intolerably gratuitous. Formerly, when still sheltered by her family, the young girl used what liberty she had in revolt and hope for change, in gaining marriage itself; now she *is* married, and before her there is no *other* future, this is to be her whole lot on earth. She knows just what her tasks are to be: the same as her mother's. Day after day the same rites will be repeated. As a girl she had nothing, but in dreams she hoped for everything. Now she has her bit of the earth, and she thinks in anguish: "Only this, forever! Forever this husband, this dwelling." She has nothing to await, nothing important to wish for.

And yet she fears her new responsibilities. Even if her husband is a man of maturity and authority, the fact that she has sexual relations with him robs him of prestige: he could not replace a father, much less a mother; he cannot deliver her from her freedom. In the solitude of her new home, bound to a man who is more or less a stranger to her, no longer a child but a wife and destined to become a mother in her turn, she feels a chill; parted forever from the maternal bosom, lost in a world where no future calls, abandoned in an icy present, she becomes aware of the ennui and the flat dullness of pure and empty sham. All this distress is depicted with startling clarity in the diary of the young Countess Tolstoy, married with girlish enthusiasm to the great writer, to whose past and to whose interests she found herself a total stranger. She was not the first woman in his life, she could not penetrate his inner consciousness, carnal relations were repugnant, he was often in a bad humor and unloving, she was going to die, what use to live? Why did she ever leave home? She had nothing to do, no inner resources, nothing to long for, life was boring. The novelists Colette and Marcel Prévost describe the same sad boredom and disappointment; and psychiatrists like Janet [3] report the neurotic consequences that sometimes follow in extreme cases.

Marriage is often a crisis also for the man, as is shown by the fact that mental disorders sometimes originate during his engagement and the early days of conjugal life. Less attached to his family than are his sisters, the young man belongs to some confraternity—high school, college, apprentice workshop, team, gang—which protects him against loneliness; this he quits when he begins his true adult existence; he fears his approaching solitude and often marries to avert it. But he is the dupe of that common illusion in which the couple is seen as a "conjugal *society*." Save during the brief flare of an amorous passion, two individuals cannot constitute a world that protects each of them against the world: this is what they both realize the day after their marriage. Before long the wife, becoming familiar and submissive, does not mask from her husband his state of isolation; she is a charge, not a way of escape; she does not deliver him from the weight of his responsibilities but on the contrary increases them. Difference in sex often implies differences in age, education, situation, which allow of no real mutual understanding: intimates, the two are yet strangers. Formerly a veritable abyss yawned between them: the girl, brought up in a state of ignorance and innocence, had no "past," while her fiancé had "lived"; it was for him to introduce her to the facts of life. Some males were agreeably impressed by this delicate role; others, more clear-sighted, surveyed uneasily the distance that separated them from their future mates. In *The Age of Innocence* [4] Edith Wharton notes the misgivings aroused in a young American of 1870 by his fiancée:

With a new sense of awe he looked at the frank forehead, serious eyes and gay innocent mouth of the young creature whose soul's custodian he was to be. That terrifying product of the social system he belonged to and believed in, the young girl who knew nothing and expected everything, looked back at him like a stranger. . . . What could he and she really know of each other, since it was his

---

[3] *Les Obsessions de la psychasthénie.*

[4] See A. H. Quinn (ed.): *An Edith Wharton Treasury* (Appleton-Century-Crofts, 1950), pp. 28, 29, 30.

duty, as a "decent" fellow, to conceal his past from her, and hers, as a marriageable girl, to have no past to conceal? . . . The young girl who was the centre of this elaborate system of mystification remained the more inscrutable for her very frankness and assurance. She was frank, poor darling, because she had nothing to conceal, assured because she knew of nothing to be on her guard against; and with no better preparation than this, she was to be plunged overnight into what people evasively called "the facts of life." . . . But when he had gone the brief round of her he returned discouraged by the thought that all this frankness and innocence were only an artificial product . . . a creation of factitious purity, so cunningly manufactured by a conspiracy of mothers and aunts and grandmothers and long-dead ancestresses, because it was supposed to be what he wanted, what he had a right to, in order that he might exercise his lordly pleasure in smashing it like an image made of snow.

Today the chasm is not so deep, because the young girl is not so artificial a being; she is better informed, better equipped for life. But often she is still much younger than her husband. This is a point that has not been sufficiently emphasized; very often what are really matters of unequal maturity have been taken for differences in sex characteristics; in many cases the woman is a child, not because she is a woman but because she is in fact very young. The sober-mindedness of her husband and his friends is stifling, it weighs her down. Tolstoy's wife, Sophie, writes a year after her marriage:

> He is old, he is too absorbed, and as for me, I feel so young and inclined to folly! Instead of going to bed I should like to dance madly, but with whom?
>
> An atmosphere of old age surrounds me, everyone around is old. I force myself to repress every youthful urge, so out of place does it seem in this restrained environment.

For his part, the husband sees in his wife a "baby"; she is not the companion for him that he expected she would be and he lets her feel it, much to her humiliation. No doubt she is glad to find a new guide when she leaves home, but she also wishes to be regarded as a "grown-up"; she wants to remain a child, she wishes to become a woman; an older husband can never treat her in a wholly satisfactory manner.

When, however, the age difference is slight, the fact remains that the young man and the young woman have been brought up quite differently; she comes out of a feminine world in which she has been taught feminine good deportment and a respect for feminine values, whereas he has been trained in the principles of male ethics. It is often very hard for them to understand each other, and conflicts soon arise.

Because marriage normally subordinates wife to husband, the problem of their mutual relations is posed most sharply to the female. The paradox of marriage lies in that fact that it has at once an erotic and a social function: this ambivalence is reflected in the figure presented by the husband in the eyes of the young woman. He is a demigod endued with virile prestige and destined to replace her father: protector, provider, teacher, guide; the wife's existence is to unfold in his shadow; he is the custodian of values, the sponsor of truth, the ethical vindication of the couple. But he is also a male with whom she must share an experience that is often shameful, grotesque, objectionable, or upsetting, in any case incidental; he invites his wife to revel with him in sensual indulgence while he leads her firmly toward the ideal. This scene from Mauriac's *Thérèse Desqueyroux* illustrates the point:

> One evening in Paris, Bernard made a conspicuous exit from a music hall where the show had shocked him. "Just think of foreigners seeing that! It's a shame, and we will be judged on that sort of thing." Thérèse was amazed that this modest soul was none other than the man to whose prolonged nocturnal ingenuities she would be subjected in less than an hour.

Many hybrid forms between mentor and faun are possible. Sometimes the man is at once father and lover, the sexual act becomes a sacred orgy and the adoring wife finds ultimate salvation at the price of total submission. This loving passion is very rare in married life. Sometimes, again, the wife will love her husband platonically, but she will decline to abandon herself in the arms of a man she respects too much, as in the case of a woman married to a great artist whom she adored but with whom she was completely frigid, as reported by

Stekel. On the contrary, she may enjoy with him a pleasure that she feels as a common depravity and that is fatal to her esteem and respect. Again, an erotic frustration may relegate her husband forever to the rank of brute: hated as flesh, he will be despised as spirit; inversely, we have seen how scorn, antipathy, resentment doom a woman to frigidity. What happens rather often is for the husband to remain, after their sexual experience, a respected superior whose animal weaknesses are excusable; for one example, this seems to have been the case with Victor Hugo's wife, Adèle. Or he may be simply an agreeable partner without particular prestige, at once loved and detested. Katherine Mansfield has described one of the forms of this ambivalence in her story entitled *Prelude:* [5]

> For she really was fond of him; she loved and admired and respected him tremendously. Oh, better than anyone else in the world. She knew him through and through. He was the soul of truth and decency, and for all his practical experience he was awfully simple, easily pleased and easily hurt.
>
> If only he wouldn't jump at her so, and bark so loudly, and watch her with such eager, loving eyes. He was too strong for her; she had always hated things that rush at her, from a child. There were times when he was frightening—really frightening. When she just had not screamed at the top of her voice: "You are killing me." And at those times she had longed to say the most coarse, hateful things. . . . Yes, yes, it was true. . . . For all her love and respect and admiration she hated him. . . . It had never been so plain to her as it was at this moment. There were all her feelings for him, sharp and defined, one as true as the other. And there was this other, this hatred, just as real as the rest. She could have done her feelings up in little packets and given them to Stanley. She longed to hand him that last one, for a surprise. She could see his eyes as he opened that.

The young wife very seldom admits her feelings to herself with such sincerity. To love her husband and to be happy is a duty she owes to herself and to society; it is what her family expects of her; or if her parents have opposed her marriage, it is a way of showing how wrong they were. She commonly begins by living her married life in

---

[5] In *The Short Stories of Katherine Mansfield.*

bad faith; she readily persuades herself that she feels a great love for her husband; and this passion assumes a form more mad, more possessive, and more jealous the less satisfied the wife is sexually. To compensate for the disappointment that at first she will not admit even to herself, she feels an insatiable desire for her husband to be with her. Stekel gives many examples of these unwholesome attachments; and Sophie Tolstoy's journal reflects her vain effort to compensate by moral or "poetic" exaltation and by anxious and jealous demands for the absence of a true love for her husband.

Very often the wife persists in her pretense of love through morality, hypocrisy, pride, or timidity. Her real hostility may be expressed by the young woman's more or less violent efforts to avoid the domination of her husband. After the honeymoon and the period of disturbance that often follows, she endeavors to regain her independence, which is no easy matter. Often older, with masculine prestige, legally "head of the family," her husband has a position of moral and social superiority; very often he seems, at least, to be intellectually superior also. He has the advantage of superior culture or, at any rate, professional training; since adolescence he has taken an interest in world affairs—they are his affairs—he knows something of law, he keeps up with politics, he belongs to a party, to a union, to social organizations; as worker and citizen his thinking is related to action. He knows the test of stern reality: that is, the average man has the technique of reasoning, a feeling for facts and experience, some critical sense.

This is what a great many young women lack. Even if they have read, listened to lectures, toyed with accomplishments, their miscellaneous information does not constitute culture; it is not that through mental defect they are unable to reason properly, it is rather that experience has not held them to strict reasoning; for them thought is an amusement rather than an instrument; even though intelligent, sensitive, sincere, they are unable to state their views and draw conclusions, for lack of intellectual technique. That is why their husbands, even though of comparatively mediocre ability, will easily dominate them and prove themselves to be in the right even when in the wrong. In masculine hands logic is often a form of violence, a sly kind of tyranny: the husband, if older and better educated than his wife, assumes on the basis of this superiority to give no weight at all to her opinions when he does not share them; he tirelessly *proves* to her that he is right. For her part, she becomes obstinate and refuses to see anything in her husband's arguments; he simply sticks to his own notions. And so a deep misunderstanding comes between them. He makes no effort to comprehend the feelings and reactions she is not clever enough to justify, though they are deeply rooted in her; she does not grasp what is vital behind the pedantic logic with which her husband overwhelms her. She has no recourse save silence, or tears, or violence, and in the end throws something at him.[6]

Sometimes a wife will try to continue the struggle. But frequently she gives up with good or bad grace, like Nora in Ibsen's play A *Doll's House*, and lets her husband think for her—at least for a time. She says to her husband: "You settled everything according to your taste —and I got the same tastes as you, or I pretended to—I don't know which—both ways, perhaps—sometimes one, sometimes the other." [7] Through timidity, or awkwardness, or laziness a wife may leave it to her husband to form their common opinions on all general and abstract subjects. An intelligent, cultivated, independent woman, who, however, had for fifteen years looked up to a husband whom she thought superior, told me how disturbed she felt, after his death, when she found she was compelled to decide for herself regarding her beliefs and conduct; she still tried to determine what he would have thought in each case.

As a rule the husband takes pleasure in this role of mentor and guide. Nora's husband assures her: "Only lean on me—let me counsel and guide you! I wouldn't be a true man if this very, womanly helplessness didn't make you doubly attractive in my eyes. . . . I have broad wings to shield you." [8] Home for the evening after a hard day of struggle with his equals, of yielding to his superiors, he likes to feel himself an absolute superior and a dispenser of undeniable truths. He relates the events of the day, explains how right he has been in arguments with opponents, happy to find in his wife a double who bolsters his self-confidence; he comments on the papers and the political news, he willingly reads aloud to her so that even her contact

---

[6] As with the couple described in Chardonne's *Épithalame*.

[7] Edition of 1909, p. 126, edited by H. L. Mencken. In his Introduction Mencken says: "The play was remarkable for two reasons: first, because it conveyed a sense of photographic reality; and secondly, because it presumed to criticize an institution which the vast majority of human beings held to be impeccable."—TR.

[8] A *Doll's House*, p. 122.

with culture may not be independent. To increase his authority, he tends to exaggerate feminine incapacity; she accepts this subordinate role with more or less docility. Women left to their own resources for a time, though they may sincerely regret their husbands' absence, are often surprised and pleased to discover that in such circumstances they have unsuspected possibilities; they take charge, raise children, make decisions, carry on without help. They find it irksome when the return of their men dooms them again to incompetence.

Marriage incites man to a capricious imperialism: the temptation to dominate is the most truly universal, the most irresistible one there is; to surrender the child to its mother, the wife to her husband, is to promote tyranny in the world. Very often it is not enough for the husband to be approved of and admired, for him to be counselor and guide; he issues commands, he plays the lord and master. All the resentments accumulated during his childhood and his later life, those accumulated daily among other men whose existence means that he is browbeaten and injured—all this is purged from him at home as he lets loose his authority upon his wife. He enacts violence, power, unyielding resolution; he issues commands in tones of severity; he shouts and pounds the table: this farce is a daily reality for his wife. He is so firm in his rights that the slightest sign of independence on her part seems to him a rebellion; he would fain stop her breathing without his permission.

But she does rebel. Even if at first she was impressed by male prestige, her bedazzlement soon evaporates. The child one day perceives that his father is a contingent individual; the wife soon discovers that she has before her not the lofty figure of lord and master but a man; she sees no reason to be under his thumb; he seems to her to represent no more than an unpleasant and unjust duty. Sometimes she submits with masochistic pleasure: she assumes the role of victim and her resignation is only a long, silent reproach; but it may often happen also that she engages in open battles with her master and insists on tyrannizing over him in return.

Only a naïve husband can suppose that he will easily subdue his wife to his will and "shape" her as he pleases. "A wife is what her husband makes her," says Balzac; but he says just the opposite a few pages later. In the abstract and logical field the wife often yields to the male's authority; but when it comes to matters she really cares about, she opposes him with covert tenacity. The influences of childhood and youth affect her much more deeply than they do a man, for she is more closely confined within the boundaries of her individual history. Most often she never rids herself of what she has acquired in early life. A husband may impose his political views on his wife, but he will never change her religious convictions nor shake her superstitious beliefs.

In spite of new opinions she has acquired, in spite of principles she echoes like a parrot, she retains her own peculiar view of things. This resistance may make her incapable of understanding a husband more intelligent than she is; or, on the contrary, it may elevate her above dull masculine sobriety, as happens with the heroines of Stendhal, Ibsen, and Shaw. Sometimes out of hostility to her husband—whether because he has disappointed her sexually or, on the contrary, because he domineers over her and she wants revenge—she deliberately clings to values other than his; she relies upon the authority of a mother, a father, a brother, of some masculine personality who seems to her to be "superior," of a confessor, or of a sister, in order to get the better of him. Or, without offering anything positive in opposition, she strives to contradict him systematically, to attack and to wound him; she endeavors to give him an inferiority complex. If she has the necessary resources, she will, of course, take delight in dazzling her husband, in imposing her judgment, her opinions, her commands; she will assume complete moral authority.

Where it is impossible for her to contest the mental superiority of her husband, she will try to take her revenge on the sexual level, by refusing to permit her husband's embraces until she gets what she wants, or by insulting him with a show of frigidity, or by reducing him to the position of a suppliant for her favors, through capricious and coquettish behavior; through flirting, making him jealous, deceiving him in one way or another, she tries to humiliate him as a virile man. If she does not dare to push things too far, she proudly nurses in her heart the secret of her haughty frigidity; she often confides it to her diary, more often to her friends. Many married women find amusement in confiding to one another the "tricks" they use in simulating a pleasure that they deny feeling in reality; and they laugh cruelly at the conceited simplicity of their dupes. Such confidences may often represent still more play-acting, for the boundary between frigidity and the will to frigidity is an uncertain one. In any case they consider themselves to lack sex feeling and thus they satisfy their resentment.

There are women, sometimes likened to the praying mantis, who wish to triumph both by night and by day: they are cold in love-making, scornful in conversation, tyrannical in conduct. According to Mabel Dodge Luhan,[9] Frieda, the wife of D. H. Lawrence, was of this type. Unable to deny his mental superiority, she asserted that she imposed upon him her own vision of the world, in which only sexual values counted. "He has to get it all from me. . . . Nobody knows that. Why, I have done pages of his books for him," she declared. But she felt a constant need to prove how necessary she was to him and never let their marriage become a calm routine. She always had a new bombshell to explode, and their married life became a series of scenes in which neither would yield. Other women may display a similar will to domination by constant belittling of their husbands' appearance, ability, and earning power, or by evaluating their works only in terms of cash income. Such tactics are used against the male, as essential subject, in an effort to deny his transcendence. Men readily suppose that woman entertains dreams of castration regarding them, but in truth her attitude is ambiguous: she desires rather to humiliate the male sex than to do away with it. More exactly, she wishes to deprive man of his projects, of his future. She triumphs when husband or child is ill, weary, reduced to mere flesh, appearing then to be no more than one object among others, something to be cared for efficiently, like the pots and pans. The heavy, fleshly hand on the sick man is intended to make him feel that he, too, is but a fleshly thing.

Woman wants man to be not a body expressing a subject, but mere passive flesh. Against existence she affirms mere life; against the things of the spirit, the things of the flesh; she is prone to take Pascal's whimsical attitude toward male enterprises, believing with him that "all of man's woe comes from one thing only, not being able to remain quietly in his room"; she would gladly keep him shut up at home. All activity that does not directly benefit the life of the family provokes her hostility; the wife of Bernard Palissy [1] was indignant when be burned the family furniture for fuel in his efforts to invent

---

[9] *Lorenzo in Taos*, (Alfred A. Knopf, 1932), p. 50.

[1] Sixteenth-century writer, chemist, artist in ceramics and enamel.—TR.

a new enamel, which the world had been well able to do without up to that time; Racine's wife wanted him to take an interest in the currants in her garden but would not read his tragedies.

These conflicts may go so far as to cause a rupture, but as a rule woman wants to "hold" her husband, while resisting his domination. She struggles with him in the effort to uphold her independence, and she battles with the rest of the world to preserve the "situation" that dooms her to dependence. This double game is difficult to play, explaining in part the disturbed and nervous state in which many women spend their lives.

To "catch" a husband is an art; to "hold" him is a job—and one in which great competence is called for. A wise sister said to a peevish young wife: "Be careful, making scenes with Marcel is going to cost you your *job*." What is at stake is extremely serious: material and moral security, a home of one's own, the dignity of wifehood, a more or less satisfactory substitute for love and happiness. A wife soon learns that her erotic attractiveness is the weakest of her weapons; it disappears with familiarity; and, alas, there are other desirable women all about. Still, she endeavors to make herself seductive, to please; she is often torn between the pride that inclines her toward frigidity and the hope that her sensual ardor will flatter her husband and endear her to him. She also counts on force of habit, on the charm of a pleasant abode, his liking for good food, his affection for his children; she makes an effort to "do him credit" by the way she entertains and dresses, and she tries to influence him by her advice and counsel; in so far as she can, she will make herself indispensable to his social success and to his work.

But, above all, a whole tradition enjoins upon wives the art of "managing" a man; one must discover and humor his weaknesses and must cleverly apply in due measure flattery and scorn, docility and resistance, vigilance and leniency. This last mixture of attitudes is an especially delicate matter. A husband must be granted neither too much nor too little freedom. If she is too obliging, a wife finds her husband escaping her; whatever money and passion he devotes to other women is taken from her; and she runs the risk of having a mistress get enough power over him to make him divorce her or at least to take first place in his life. But if she denies him any adventures whatever, if she annoys him with her watchfulness, her scenes, her demands, she is likely to turn him definitely against her. It is a matter of knowing how to "make concessions" designedly; if one's husband "cheats" a little, one will close one's eyes; but at other times one must keep them wide open. In particular, a married woman is on her guard against young women who would be only too happy, she thinks, to steal her "job." In order to tear her husband away from an alarming rival, she will take him on a trip, try to offer him diversion; if necessary—following Mme de Pompadour as a model— she will provide a new and less dangerous rival. If nothing succeeds, she will resort to bursts of weeping, nervous outbreaks, attempts at suicide, and the like; but too many scenes and recriminations will drive her husband out of the house. The wife thus runs the risk of making herself unbearable at the moment when she most needs to be seductive; if she wants to win the game she will contrive a skillful mixture of affecting tears and brave smiles, of blackmail and coquetry.

This is indeed a melancholy science—to dissimulate, to use trickery, to hate and fear in silence, to play on the vanity and the weaknesses of a man, to learn to thwart him, to deceive him, to "manage" him. But woman's good excuse for it all is that she has been required to involve herself wholly in her marriage. She has no gainful occupation, no legal capacities, no personal relations, even her name is hers no longer; she is nothing but her husband's "half." If he leaves her, she can usually count on help neither from her own inner resources nor from without. It is easy to criticize Tolstoy's wife, Sophie; but if she had refused to practice the hypocrisy of married life, where could she have gone, what would have been her lot? To be sure, she seems to have been a hateful shrew; but could she have been asked to love her tyrant and bless her enslavement? For loyalty and friendship to exist between man and wife, the essential condition is that they both be free with relation to each other and be equal in concrete matters. Since man alone possesses economic independence and since he holds —by law and custom—the advantages attached to masculinity, it is natural enough for him often to appear a tyrant, and this drives woman to revolt and dissimulation.

No one dreams of denying the tragedies and the shabby imperfections of married life; but the defenders of marriage find support in the idea that conflict arises from the ill will of individuals, not from the institution itself. Tolstoy, for one example, described the ideal couple in the epilogue of *War and Peace*: that of Pierre and Natasha. She had been a coquettish and romantic girl, but when she married she astounded everyone by giving up dress, society, and all amusements to devote herself exclusively to her husband and her children. She became the very type of the matron, losing "that flame of life which had once been her charm" and acquiring a jealous and exigent attitude toward Pierre, who in turn abandoned his former companions and devoted himself to business and family.

This idyllic picture deserves closer scrutiny. The couple were united, says Tolstoy, like soul and body; but when a soul leaves its body, only one corpse remains; what would happen if Pierre should ever cease to love Natasha? D. H. Lawrence, too, declines to accept the hypothesis of masculine inconstancy: Don Ramón will always love the Indian girl, Teresa, who has given him her soul.[2] However, one of the most ardent zealots of love unique, absolute, eternal, the poet André Breton,[3] has to admit that at least under existing circumstances this love may be mistaken in its object: error or fickleness, whichever it may be, it is still man's desertion as far as the woman is concerned. Pierre, a robust and sensual man, will be carnally attracted by other women; Natasha will show her jealousy, and before long their relations will become embittered; he will leave her, which will ruin life for her, or he will lie to her and put up with her resentfully, which will spoil life for him, or they will go on in an existence of compromise and half-measures, which will make them both unhappy.

It may be objected that Natasha will at least have her children; but children are a source of delight only within a balanced frame of reference which includes their father; for the neglected, jealous wife they become a heavy burden. Tolstoy admires Natasha's blind devotion to Pierre's ideas; but another man, Lawrence, who also demands a blind devotion from woman, holds both Pierre and Natasha in derision; in the opinion of other men, a man may be an idol of clay and not a genuine god; in worshipping him, one loses one's life instead of saving it; how is one to know? Masculine claims are contradictory: authority no longer works. Woman must judge and be critical, she cannot remain a mere docile echo. Moreover, it is debasing her to impose upon her principles and values that she has not freely reached by her own effort; what she is able to agree with in her husband's way of thinking she should agree with only through an in-

[2] See Book I, p. 222.
[3] See Book I, p. 233.

dependent act of judgment; what is foreign to her in his ideas she should not be called on either to approve or to deny; she cannot borrow from another her own reasons for existing.

The most damning judgment against the Pierre-Natasha myth is to be found in the Tolstoy couple, Leo and Sophie, which gave origin to it. Sophie feels a deep repulsion for her husband, she finds him "frightfully dull"; he deceives her with every peasant woman in the neighborhood, she is jealous and bored to death; she goes neurotically through her many pregnancies, and her children neither fill the void in her heart nor occupy the emptiness of her days; home is for her an arid desert; for her husband it is a hell on earth. And it all ends with Sophie, a hysterical old woman, sleeping half naked in the damp night of the forest, and with Leo, a harried old man, running away and disowning finally their "union" of a lifetime.

Tolstoy's case is, of course, exceptional; there are many marriages that "go well"—that is to say, in which man and wife reach a compromise. They live side by side without too much mutual torment, too much lying to each other. But there is one curse they very rarely escape: it is boredom. Whether the husband succeeds in making his wife an echo of himself or each one is entrenched within a private universe, after some months or years they have nothing left to say to one another. The couple is a community the members of which have lost their independence without escaping loneliness; they are statically united, they are "one," instead of maintaining a dynamic and living relation. This is the reason why they can give each other nothing, exchange nothing, whether in the realm of ideas or on the erotic plane. A thousand evenings of vague small talk, blank silences, yawning over the newspaper, retiring at bedtime! [4]

It is sometimes said that these very silences give evidence of an intimacy too deep for words, and surely no one will deny that married life creates intimacy; this, however, is true of all family relations, which none the less conceal hate, jealousy, and resentment. There is a great difference between such intimacy and a true human fellow feeling. [5]

---

[4] Pictured to the life in Dorothy Parker's short story *Too Bad* (reprinted in the Modern Library, No. 123, 1943).

[5] Jouhandeau says in his *Chroniques maritales:* "You realize that you are the victim of a poison, but you have become habituated to it. How renounce it without renouncing yourself? . . . When I think of her I feel that conjugal love has nothing to do with sympathy, nor with sensuality, nor with passion, nor with

The proponents of conjugal love [6] are quite prepared to agree that it is not a love affair and that this is precisely what gives it a marvelous character. For the middle class has in recent years invented an epic style of expression in which routine takes on the cast of adventure, fidelity, that of a sublime passion; ennui becomes wisdom, and family hatred is the deepest form of love. The truth is, however, that when two individuals detest each other, while being unable to get along without each other, it is not of all human relations the truest and most moving, but rather the most pitiable.

The ideal, on the contrary, would be for entirely self-sufficient human beings to form unions one with another only in accordance with the untrammeled dictates of their mutual love. It seemed admirable to Tolstoy that the bond between Natasha and Pierre should be something "indefinable, but firm and strong as was the union of his own soul with his body." If we accept the dualistic hypothesis, the body represents, for the soul, something purely incidental; and thus in the conjugal union each person would have for the other the inevitable, dull tediousness of the contingent—the senseless fact that happens to be so; it is as an irrational and unchosen presence, as an unavoidable and material condition, even, of existence, that the partner must be accepted and loved. These two words are deliberately confused in the view we are considering, and hence comes the mystification: what one accepts is not what one loves. One accepts—assumes, has to put up with—one's body, one's past, one's present situation; but love is an outgoing movement, an impulse toward another person, toward an existence separate and distinct from one's own, toward an end in view, a future; accepting a burden, a tyranny, involves not love but repulsion.

A human relation has value only in so far as it is directly experienced; the relations of children to parents, for example, take on value only when they are consciously realized; it is not to be wondered at that conjugal relations tend to relapse from the condition of directly experienced emotion, and that the husband and wife lose their liberty

---

friendship, nor with love. Sufficient unto itself, reducible to none of these various sentiments, it has its own nature, its particular essence, and its unique character, according to the couple it unites."

[6] There can be love in marriage; but then one does not speak of "conjugal love"; when one uses these words, love is absent; just as when one calls a man "very communistic," one means that he is not a Communist; a "fine, honest man" is a man who does not belong to the simple category of honest men.

of feeling in the process. This complex mixture of affection and resentment, hate, constraint, resignation, dullness, and hypocrisy called conjugal love is supposedly respected only by way of extenuation, whitewash. But the same is true of affection as of physical love: for it to be genuine, authentic, it must first of all be free.

Liberty, however, does not mean fickleness: a tender sentiment is an involvement of feeling which goes beyond the moment; but it is for the individual alone to determine whether his will in general and his behavior in detail are to be such as to maintain or, on the contrary, to break off the relation he has entered upon; sentiment is free when it depends upon no constraint from outside, when it is experienced in fearless sincerity. The constraint of "conjugal love" leads, on the other hand, to all kinds of repressions and lies. And first of all it prevents the couple from really knowing each other. Daily intimacy creates neither understanding nor sympathy. The husband respects his wife too much to take an interest in the phenomena of her psychic life: that would be to recognize in her a secret autonomy that could prove disturbing, dangerous; does she really find pleasure in the marriage bed? Does she truly love her husband? Is she actually happy to obey him? He prefers not to ask; to him these questions even seem shocking.

For he has married a "good woman"; by her very nature she is virtuous, devoted, faithful, pure, and happy, and she thinks what is proper for her to think. A man who has been sick, after thanking his friends, his relatives, and his nurses for their attentions, then says to his young wife, who for six months has not left his bedside: "You I do not thank, you have only done your duty." A husband regards none of his wife's good qualities as particularly meritorious; they are guaranteed by society, they are implied by the institution of marriage itself; he fails to realize that his wife is no character from some pious and conventional treatise, but a real individual of flesh and blood; he takes for granted her fidelity to the strict regimen she assumes, not taking into account that she has temptations to vanquish, that she may yield to them, that in any case her patience, her chastity, her propriety, are difficult conquests; he is still more profoundly ignorant of her dreams, her fancies, her nostalgic yearnings, of the emotional climate in which she spends her days. He may think and speak of her with delicacy and affection, without regarding her as a free individual. Thus the simple and loyal man is often described as disillusioned by feminine perfidy when he learns all of a sudden that his wife does not love him and is leaving him. The husbands in Bernstein's plays, for example, are scandalized when they discover that their consorts are thievish, wicked, adulterous; they take the blow with masculine courage, but the author fails none the less to make them seem generous and strong; they seem to us, on the contrary, mere dolts without real feeling and good will. Man may reproach women for their dissimulation, but his complacency must be great indeed for him to be so constantly duped.

Woman is doomed to immorality, because for her to be moral would mean that she must incarnate a being of superhuman qualities: the "virtuous woman" of Proverbs, the "perfect mother," the "honest woman," and so on. Let her but think, dream, sleep, desire, breathe without permission and she betrays the masculine ideal. This is why many wives let themselves go, "are themselves," only in the absence of their husbands. On the other hand, the wife does not know her husband; she thinks she perceives his true aspect because she sees him in his daily round of inessential circumstances; but man is first of all what he *does* in the world among other men. To fail to comprehend the flight of his transcendence is to denature him. As a woman has said: "One marries a poet, and when one is his wife the first thing to be noticed is that he forgets to pull the chain in the toilet." He remains none the less a poet, and the wife who is not interested in his work knows him not so well as some distant reader. Nor is it, very often, the wife's fault if such participation is denied her: she cannot be in touch with her husband's doings, she has neither the experience nor the culture needed to "follow" his work; she fails to join him in the undertakings that are much more essential in his eyes than the monotonous round of daily life.

In certain privileged cases the wife may succeed in becoming her husband's true companion, discussing his projects, giving him counsel, collaborating in his works. But she is lulled in illusion if she expects in this way to accomplish work she can call her own, for he remains alone the free and responsible agent. She must love him if she is to find joy in his service; otherwise she will find only vexation, because she will feel herself robbed of the fruit of her efforts. Men—faithful as they are to Balzac's injunction to treat woman as slave while persuading her that she is queen—exaggerate to the full the influence exercised by women; but at bottom they know very well that they lie.

Georgette Le Blanc was the dupe of this hoax when she demanded
that Maeterlinck inscribe both their names on the book that, she
thought, they had written together. In his preface to the singer's
Souvenirs, Grasset told Mme Le Blanc quite plainly that each man
readily salutes in the woman who shares his life a colleague and an
inspiration, but that none the less he regards his work as entirely his
own—and with reason. In every act, in every work, it is the factor of
choice and decision that counts. Woman usually plays the part of
the crystal ball of the fortune-teller: another would do as well. And
the proof is that very often the man does accept another counselor,
another collaborator, with equal confidence, as Tolstoy accepted one
of his daughters as copyist and corrector of his manuscripts, when
his wife thought herself indispensable for this work. Only independent work of her own can assure woman's genuine independence.[7]

Married life assumes different forms in different cases. But for a
great many women the day passes in much the same fashion. The
husband leaves in the morning and the wife is glad to hear the door
close behind him. She is free; the children go to school; she is alone;
she attends to a thousand small tasks; her hands are busy, but her
mind is empty; what plans she has are for the family; she lives only
for them; it relieves her ennui when they return. Her husband used
to bring her flowers, a little present, but how foolish this would seem
now! He is in no hurry to get home, dreading the all too frequent
scene in which she takes a small revenge for her boredom and expresses her anticipated disappointment in an appearance hardly
worth waiting for. And the husband is disappointed, too, even if she
keeps silence on her wrongs. He is tired from his work and has a
contradictory desire for rest and stimulation, which she fails to satisfy. The evening is dull: reading, radio, desultory talks; each remains
alone under cover of this intimacy. The wife wonders, with hope or
apprehension, whether tonight—at last—"something will happen."
She goes to sleep disappointed, vexed, solaced, as the case may be;
and it is with pleasure that she will hear him slam the door next
morning. Woman's lot is harder to bear in poverty and toil; it is

---

[7] Sometimes a *true* collaboration exists between a man and a woman: as with
the Joliot-Curie couple, for example, famous French physicists. But then the
woman, as competent as the man, steps out of her role as wife; their relation is
no longer of the conjugal type. There are also women who make use of a man
to attain their personal ends; they, too, are outside the situation of the married
woman.

lighter with leisure and diversion; but this design for living—ennui, waiting, disappointment—recurs in innumerable cases.

Certain avenues of escape [8] are open to women; but in practice they are not available to all. In the country, especially, the chains of marriage are heavy, and the wife must somehow accommodate herself to a situation from which she cannot escape. Some, full of importance, become tyrannical and shrewish matrons; some become complaisant, masochistic victims and slaves of their families. Some continue the narcissistic behavior we have seen in the young girl, still doing and being really nothing, feeling "misunderstood" in the melancholy cult of self, seeking refuge in romantic dreams, pretenses, invalidism, scenes, imaginary dramas, flowers, clothes. This symbolic behavior through which women seek escape can lead to mental decay, obsessions, even crimes. An odious husband may finally be murdered as the only way out of an intolerable situation.

A woman determined, in spite of her condition, to go on living in a clear-sighted and genuine manner may have no other resort than a stoic pride. Being in every material way dependent, she can know only an inner, abstract freedom; she refuses to accept ready-made principles and values, she uses her judgment, she questions, and thus she escapes conjugal slavery; but her aloofness, her fidelity to the rule: "Bear and abstain," constitute but a negative attitude. Immobilized, in renunciation and cynicism, she lacks positive employment for her power; she aids others, consoles, protects, gives, does this and that; but she suffers from finding no truly demanding task, no real aim. Consumed in her solitude and sterility, she may deny and destroy herself.

A remarkable example of such a fate is furnished us by "Zélide," Mme de Charrière, brilliant eighteenth-century woman of letters, [9] whose love of reason, penetrating intelligence, and vivacious "flame of life" were not enough to save her from the slow assassination of a dull marriage. She could not marry the man who really interested her as a young girl, and at thirty she espoused M. de Charrière, an estimable, learned, phlegmatic, honest mathematician, who remained

---

[8] See Ch. xviii.

[9] Geoffrey Scott tells her story with beauty, sympathy, and wit in his *The Portrait of Zélide* (Charles Scribner's Sons, 1925). Boswell knew her in Holland when she was the brilliant young beauty of Zuilen, Mlle van Tuyll; the story of the flirtation and the letters later exchanged are given in F. A. Pottle's *Boswell in Holland*, 1763–1764 (McGraw-Hill Book Company, 1952).—Tr.

just that in spite of her ardor and good will, taking her to live in a gloomy household in the small Swiss town of Colombier. She killed some time with domestic work, and "taking ennui for Muse," she wrote four novels on the life and customs of near-by Neuchâtel, which aroused local enmity, and one depicting the prolonged misery of a marriage (like her own) between a lively and sensitive woman and a man who was good, but cold and ponderous: a conjugal life of misunderstandings, disappointments, and small resentments. Then Benjamin Constant appeared and was her passionate concern for eight years. When he became attached to the train of Mme de Staël, she shut herself up at home for fifteen years, "accepting the presence of M. de Charrière at her side as she accepted the Alps," and giving charitable aid, advice, and instruction to refugees and the local peasantry. She wrote letters and a few more books, but most of her life was consumed in the desperately small and dull details of what seemed to occasional visitors a living tomb.

One may say, perhaps, that M. de Charrière's life was no·gayer than his wife's; but at least it was his own choice and seems to have been appropriate to his mediocrity. And if we imagine a man with Zélide's gifts, we can be certain that he would not have wasted away in the arid solitude of Colombier. He would have made his place in the world of enterprise, struggle, action, life. How many women of talent, engulfed in marriage, have been (in Stendhal's phrase) "lost to humanity"! It has been said that marriage diminishes man, which is often true; but almost always it annihilates woman.

In the early years of marriage the wife often lulls herself with illusions, she tries to admire her husband wholeheartedly, to love him unreservedly, to feel herself indispensable to him and the children. And then her true sentiments become clear; she sees that her husband could get along very well without her, that her children are bound to get away from her and to be always more or less ungrateful. The home no longer saves her from empty liberty; she finds herself alone, forlorn, a subject; and she finds nothing to do with herself. Affectionate attachments and habitual ways may still be a great help, but not salvation. All sincere women writers have noted the melancholy in the heart of "the woman of thirty"; it is a trait common to the heroines of Katherine Mansfield, Dorothy Parker, Virginia Woolf. They sing gaily at the beginning of married life and maternity, but later on they manifest a certain distress. It is a remarkable fact that in

France suicide is less common in married than in unmarried women up to age thirty, but not therafter.[1]

The tragedy of marriage is not that it fails to assure woman the promised happiness—there is no such thing as assurance in regard to happiness—but that it mutilates her; it dooms her to repetition and routine. The first twenty years of woman's life are extraordinarily rich, as we have seen; she discovers the world and her destiny. At twenty or thereabouts mistress of a home, bound permanently to a man, a child in her arms, she stands with her life virtually finished forever. Real activities, real work, are the prerogative of her man: she has mere things to occupy her which are sometimes tiring but never fully satisfying. Her renunciation and devotion have been lauded, but it often seems to her bootless indeed to busy herself "with the care of two persons for life." It is all very fine to be forgetful of self, but still one must know for whom, for what. And the worst of it is that her very devotion often seems annoying, importunate; it is transformed for the husband into a tyranny from which he tries to escape; and yet he it is who imposes it upon his wife as her supreme, her unique justification. In marrying her he obliges her to give herself entirely to him; but he does not assume the corresponding obligation, which is to accept this gift and all its consequences.

It is the duplicity of the husband that dooms the wife to a misfortune of which he complains later that he is himself the victim. Just as he wants her to be at once warm and cool in bed, he requires her to be wholly his and yet no burden; he wishes her to establish him in a fixed place on earth and to leave him free, to assume the monotonous daily round and not to bore him, to be always at hand and never importunate; he wants to have her all to himself and not to belong to her; to live as one of a couple and to remain alone. Thus she is betrayed from the day he marries her. Her life through, she measures the extent of that betrayal. What D. H. Lawrence says of sexual love is generally valid: the union of two human beings is doomed to frustration if it is an attempt at a mutual completion which supposes an original mutilation; marriage should be a combining of two whole, independent existences, not a retreat, an annexation, a flight, a remedy. Ibsen's Nora [2] understands this when she makes up her mind that before she can be a wife and mother she

---

[1] Halbwachs: *Les Causes du suicide*, pp. 195–239.
[2] Heroine of *A Doll's House*.

must first become a complete person. The couple should not be regarded as a unit, a closed cell; rather each individual should be integrated as such in society at large, where each (whether male or female) could flourish without aid; then attachments could be formed in pure generosity with another individual equally adapted to the group, attachments that would be founded upon the acknowledgment that both are free.

This balanced couple is not a utopian fancy: such couples do exist, sometimes even within the frame of marriage, most often outside it. Some mates are united by a strong sexual love that leaves them free in their friendships and in their work; others are held together by a friendship that does not preclude sexual liberty; more rare are those who are at once lovers and friends but do not seek in each other their sole reasons for living. Many nuances are possible in the relations between a man and a woman: in comradeship, pleasure, trust, fondness, co-operation, love, they can be for each other the most abundant source of joy, richness, and power available to human beings. Individuals are not to be blamed for the failure of marriage: it is—counter to the claims of such advocates as Comte and Tolstoy—the institution itself, perverted as it has been from the start. To hold and proclaim that a man and a woman, who may not even have chosen each other, *are in duty bound* to satisfy each other in every way throughout their lives is a monstrosity that necessarily gives rise to hypocrisy, lying, hostility, and unhappiness.

The traditional form of marriage is now undergoing modification, but it still involves oppression, which the two spouses feel in different ways. With regard only to the abstract, theoretical rights they enjoy, they are today almost equals; they are more free to choose one another than formerly, they can separate much more easily, especially in America, where divorce is no rarity; differences in age and culture between them are commonly less marked than they once were; the husband recognizes more willingly the independence his wife demands; they may share the cares of housekeeping equally; their diversions are enjoyed together: camping, bicycling, swimming, automobiling, and so on. The wife does not necessarily spend her days awaiting her husband's return; she may go in for sports, belong to clubs, associations, musical organizations, and the like, she is often busy outside the home, she may even have an occupation that brings her more or less money.

Many young households give the impression of being on a basis of perfect equality. But as long as the man retains economic responsibility for the couple, this is only an illusion. It is he who decides where they will live, according to the demands of his work; she *follows* him from city to country or vice versa, to distant possessions, to foreign countries; their standard of living is set according to his income; the daily, weekly, annual rhythms are set by his occupation; associations and friendships most often depend upon his profession. Being more positively integrated in society than his wife, he guides the couple in intellectual, political, and moral matters.[3] Divorce is only a theoretical possibility for the woman who cannot earn her own living; if in America alimony is a heavy charge upon the man, in France the lot of the abandoned wife or mother, dependent upon a ridiculously small pension, is a scandal.

But the basic inequality still lies in the fact that the husband finds concrete self-realization in work and action, whereas for the wife, as such, liberty has only a negative aspect; the situation of young American women, among others, recalls that of the emancipated Roman women of the decadent period.[4] As we have seen, the Roman women could choose between two types of conduct: some carried on the mode of life and retained the virtues of their grandmothers, the rest passed their time in vain disorders. Similarly, many American wives remain "home-bodies," in conformity with the traditional model; the rest for the most part only waste their time and energy. In France, even with the best will in the world on the part of the husband, once the young woman becomes a mother, the duties of the household overwhelm her no less surely than of yore.

It is a commonplace to say that in modern families, and especially in the United States, woman has reduced man to slavery. And this is nothing new. Since the times of the ancient Greeks males have always complained about Xantippe's tyranny. It is true, however, that woman now interferes in masculine domains that were formerly forbidden territory; I know, for example, university student couples in which the woman struggles madly for the success of her male, regu-

---

[3] The reader should constantly remind himself—and especially herself!—that the author often—though by no means always—has France in mind; but there are few indeed of her statements, however sweeping, for which no concrete illustrations could be found in the United States, and elsewhere.—TR.

[4] See Book I, p. 95.

lating his time schedule and diet and watching over his work in general; she deprives him of all amusement, almost puts him under lock and key. It is also true that the man is more defenseless than formerly against this despotism; he recognizes woman's theoretical rights and knows that she can concretely realize them only through him; he must compensate at his own expense for the impotence and sterility to which woman is condemned. In order to achieve an apparent equality in their association, it must be he who gives the most because he has more. But, precisely, if she receives, demands, it is because she is the poorer. The dialectic of master and slave [5] here finds its most concrete application: in oppressing, one becomes oppressed. Men are enchained by reason of their very sovereignty; it is because they alone earn money that their wives demand checks, it is because they alone engage in a business or profession that their wives require them to be successful, it is because they alone embody transcendence that their wives wish to rob them of it by taking charge of their projects and successes.

Inversely, the tyranny exercised by woman only goes to show her dependence: she knows that the success of the couple, its future, its happiness, its justification rest in the hands of the other; if she seeks desperately to bend him to her will, it is because she is alienated in him—that is, her interests as an individual lie in him. She makes a weapon of her weakness; but the fact remains that she is weak. Conjugal slavery is chiefly a matter of daily irritation for the husband; but it is something more deep-seated for the woman; a wife who keeps her husband at her side for hours because she is bored certainly bothers him and seems burdensome; but in the last analysis he can get along without her much more easily than she can without him; if he leaves her, she is the one whose life will be ruined. The great difference is that with woman dependency is interiorized: she *is* a slave even when she behaves with apparent freedom; while man is essentially independent and his bondage comes from without. If he seems to be the victim, it is because his burdens are most evident: woman is supported by him like a parasite; but a parasite is not a conquering master. The truth is that just as—biologically—males and females are never victims of one another but both victims of the species, so man and wife together undergo the oppression of an institution they did not create. If it is asserted that *men* oppress

---

[5] See Book I, pp. xx, 64, 78.

women, the husband is indignant; he feels that *he* is the one who is oppressed—and he is; but the fact is that it is the masculine code, it is the society developed by the males and in their interest, that has established woman's situation in a form that is at present a source of torment for both sexes.

It is for their common welfare that the situation must be altered by prohibiting marriage as a "career" for woman. Men who declare themselves antifeminists, on the ground that "women are already bad enough as it is," are not too logical; it is precisely because marriage makes women into "praying mantises," "leeches," "poisonous" creatures, and so on, that it is necessary to transform marriage and, in consequence, the condition of women in general. Woman leans heavily upon man because she is not allowed to rely on herself; he will free himself in freeing her—that is to say, in giving her something to *do* in the world.

There are young women who are already endeavoring to win this positive, active independence; but there are few who persevere for long in their studies or profession. Usually they know very well that their interests in connection with their work will be sacrificed to their husbands' careers; they bring home merely supplementary income; they involve themselves only superficially in enterprises that do not free them from conjugal servitude. Even those who have a serious profession fail to draw from it the same social benefits as do men: the wives of French lawyers, for example, are entitled to a pension on the death of their husbands; but a corresponding pension will not be paid to the husbands of women lawyers on the decease of the latter. This means, in other words, that the woman who works is not regarded as supporting the couple in the same sense as does a man. There are women who find true independence in a profession; but there are a great many for whom "outside work" represents within the frame of marriage only a matter of added fatigue. Besides, it usually happens that the birth of a child compels them to limit themselves to their role as matron; it is very difficult to reconcile work and maternity under present conditions.

Now, it is precisely the child that according to tradition should assure to woman a real independence in which she is relieved of devoting herself to any other end. If as wife she is not a complete individual, she becomes such as mother: the child is her happiness and her justification. Through the child she is supposed to find self-realization sexually and socially; through childbearing, then, the institution of marriage gets its meaning and attains its purpose. It will be well, therefore, for us to examine this supreme stage in woman's life history.

CHAPTER XVII

The Mother

IT is in maternity that woman fulfills her physiological destiny; it is her natural "calling," since her whole organic structure is adapted for the perpetuation of the species. But we have seen already that human society is never abandoned wholly to nature. And for about a century the reproductive function in particular has no longer been at the mercy solely of biological chance; it has come under the voluntary control of human beings.[1] Certain countries have officially adopted scientific methods of contraception; in nations under Catholic influence it is practiced in a clandestine manner: either the man uses *coitus interruptus* or the woman rids her body of the sperm after intercourse. These forms of contraception are frequently a source of conflict and resentment between lovers or married couples; the man dislikes having to be on his guard at the moment of enjoyment; the woman detests the disagreeable task of douching; he is resentful of the woman's too fertile body; she dreads the germs of life that he risks placing within her. And both are appalled when in spite of all precautions she finds herself "caught." This happens frequently in countries where contraceptive methods are primitive. Then resort is had to an especially desperate remedy: that is, abortion. No less illegal in countries that permit contraception, it is far less often needed. But in France it is an operation to which many women are forced to resort and which haunts the love-life of most of them.

There are few subjects on which bourgeois society displays greater hypocrisy; abortion is considered a revolting crime to which it is indecent even to refer. For an author to describe the joy and the suffering of a woman in childbirth is quite all right; but if he depicts a case of abortion, he is accused of wallowing in filth and presenting humanity in a sordid light. Now, there are in France as many abortions per year as there are births. It is thus a phenomenon so widespread that it must in fact be regarded as one of the risks normally implied in

---

[1] See Book I, pp. 118 ff., where the reader will find a historical account of birth control and abortion.

woman's situation. The law persists, however, in making it a misdemeanor and so requires that this delicate operation be performed
in secret. Nothing could be more absurd than the arguments brought
forward against the legalization of abortion. It is maintained that
the operation is a dangerous one. But honest physicians recognize
with Magnus Hirschfeld [2] that "abortion performed by a competent
specialist in a hospital, and with proper precautions, does not involve
the grave dangers asserted by the penal code." On the contrary, what
makes it a serious risk for women is the way in which it is actually
done under present conditions. The lack of skill on the part of abor-
tionists and the bad conditions under which they operate cause many
accidents, some of them fatal.

Enforced maternity brings into the world wretched infants, whom
their parents will be unable to support and who will become the victims of public care or "child martyrs." It must be pointed out that
our society, so concerned to defend the rights of the embryo, shows
no interest in the children once they are born; it prosecutes the abor-
tionists instead of undertaking to reform that scandalous institution
known as "public assistance"; those responsible for entrusting the
children to their torturers are allowed to go free; society closes its eyes
to the frightful tyranny of brutes in children's asylums and private
foster homes. And if it is not admitted that the fetus belongs to the
woman who carries it, it is on the other hand agreed that the child is
a thing belonging to its parents and at their mercy. Within a single
week we have lately seen a surgeon commit suicide because he was
convicted of practicing abortion, and a father who had beaten his
son almost to death given three months in prison, with sentence sus-
pended. Recently a father let his son die of croup, for lack of care; a
mother refused to call a doctor for her daughter, because of her complete submission to God's will: at the cemetery children had thrown
stones at her; but when certain journalists expressed their indignation, a number of worthy people protested that children belong to
their parents, that no interference by outsiders is allowable. Published reports indicate that as a result of this attitude a million French
children are in physical and moral danger. Arab women in North
Africa cannot resort to abortion, and seven or eight out of ten children
born to them die; yet no one is disturbed because this pitiable and

---

[2] Late director of the Institute for Sexual Research in Berlin. Some of his work
is presented in *Sexual Anomalies and Perversions* (Emerson Books, 1944).—Tr.

absurd excess of maternities kills their maternal feeling. If all this favors morality, what is to be the thought of such a morality? It must be said in addition that the men with the most scrupulous respect for embryonic life are also those who are most eagerly officious when it comes to condemning adults to death in war.

The practical considerations advanced against abortion are without weight; as for the moral considerations, they amount in the end to the old Catholic argument: the unborn child has a soul, which is denied access to paradise if its life is interrupted without baptism. It is remarkable that the Church at times authorizes the killing of adult men, as in war or in connection with legal executions; it reserves an uncompromising humanitarianism for man in the fetal condition. Here redemption by baptism is lacking; but in the times of the Holy Wars the infidels were equally unbaptized, and yet their slaughter was heartily encouraged. Doubtless the victims of the Inquisition were not all in a state of grace, any more than is the criminal who is guillotined today and the soldiers dead on the field of battle. In all these cases the Church leaves the matter to the grace of God; it admits that man is only an instrument in His hands and that the salvation of a soul is settled between that soul and God. Why then should God be forbidden to receive the embryonic soul in heaven? If a Church council should authorize it, He would no more object than He did in the glorious epochs when heathens were piously slaughtered.

The fact is that here the stumbling-block is an old, obstinate tradition that has nothing to do with morality. We must also reckon with that masculine sadism of which I have already had occasion to speak.[3] A striking example is a book by Dr. Roy, dedicated in 1943 to Pétain; it is a monumental instance of bad faith. The author insists with paternal solicitude upon the dangers of abortion, but nothing seems to him more hygienic than a Cæsarian delivery. He favors regarding abortion as a crime rather than a misdemeanor; and he would have it forbidden even as a therapeutic measure—that is, when the pregnancy threatens the life or health of the mother. It is immoral to make a choice between one life and another, he declares, and, fortified by this argument, he advises sacrificing the mother. He asserts that the fetus does not belong to the mother, it is an independent being. When these "right-thinking" physicians are lauding maternity, however, they state that the fetus forms a part of the mother's body, that

[3] P. 436.

it is not a parasite living at the latter's expense. How lively anti-feminism still is can be judged by the eagerness of certain men to reject everything favorable to the emancipation of women.

Moreover, the law—which dooms many young women to death, sterility, invalidism—is quite powerless to assure an increase in the number of births. One thing that friends and enemies of legal abortions agree on is the radical failure of repressive legislation. In France, according to good authorities, abortions have averaged about one million per year in recent times.[4] And of these about two thirds are attributed to married women. An unknown but large number of deaths and injuries result from these clandestine and often improperly performed operations.

Sometimes abortion is referred to as a "class crime," and there is much truth in this. Contraceptive knowledge is widespread in the middle class, and the existence of the bathroom makes practical application easier than in the homes of workers and peasants without running water; middle-class young women are more prudent than others; and among people in easy circumstances the infant is not so heavy a charge. Poverty, crowded quarters, and the need for women to work outside the home are among the most frequent causes of abortion. It would seem that most often the couple decides to limit births after two maternities; and so it is that the repulsive aborted woman is also the splendid mother cradling two blond angels in her arms: one and the same person. But in lower-income groups miscarriage and abortion, however desperately needed, usually mean the resignation of despair and much suffering for each woman concerned.

The severity of this ordeal varies greatly according to circumstances. The woman conventionally married or comfortably "kept," sure of a man's support, having money and relatives, enjoys great advantages. In the first place, she finds it easier than do others to obtain recommendation for a "therapeutic abortion"; if necessary she can afford a trip to some place where the attitude toward abortion is one of liberal toleration, such as Switzerland. In the present state of gynecological knowledge the operation involved is not dangerous when performed by a specialist with all the advantages of sterile technique and, if needed, the resources of anesthesia; in the absence of official col-

---

[4] Dr. R. L. Dickinson suggests "two-thirds of a million" as the probable number of abortions performed annually in the United States. *Control of Conception* (1938), p. 286.—TR.

lusion, she can find unofficial help that is equally safe: she knows good addresses, she has enough money to pay for conscientious care, and she need not wait until her pregnancy is advanced; she will be treated with consideration. Some of these privileged persons assert that the little accident is good for the health and improves the complexion.

But, on the other hand, few distressful situations are more pitiable than that of an isolated young girl, without money, who finds herself driven to a "criminal" act in order to undo a "mistake" that her group considers unpardonable. Just this is the case each year in France with about 300,000 employees, secretaries, students, workers, and peasant women; illegitimate motherhood is still so frightful a fault that many prefer suicide or infanticide to the status of unmarried mother: which means that no penalty could prevent them from "getting rid" of the unborn baby. The common story is one of seduction, in which a more or less ignorant girl is led on by her irresponsible lover until the almost inevitable happens, with concealment from family, friends, and employer a necessity, and an abortion the dreaded but only conceivable means of escape.

It is often the seducer himself who convinces the woman that she must rid herself of the child. Or he may have already abandoned her when she finds herself pregnant, or she may generously wish to hide her disgrace from him, or she may find him incapable of helping her. Sometimes she declines to bear the infant not without regret; for some reason—it may be because she does not decide immediately to do away with it, or because she knows no good address, or because she does not have ready money and has lost time in trying useless drugs— she has reached the third, fourth, or fifth month of her pregnancy when she undertakes to get rid of it; the abortion will then be far more dangerous, painful, and compromising than in earlier months. The woman is aware of this; she attempts her deliverance in anguish and despair. In rural districts the use of the probe is hardly known; the countrywoman who has made a "slip" lets herself fall off the ladder in the barn or she falls downstairs, and very often she gets hurt in vain; and it may also happen that a small strangled corpse is found under a hedge or in a ditch.

In the cities women help one another out. But it is not always easy to locate a lay abortionist, still less to get the necessary money together. So the pregnant woman appeals to a woman friend, or operates on herself. These nonprofessional surgeons are often incompetent; they are prone to cause perforation by probe or knitting-needle. A doctor told me about an ignorant cook who, in the attempt to inject vinegar into the uterus, injected it into the bladder, which was atrociously painful. Crudely begun and poorly cared for, the abortion is often more painful than normal childbirth, it may be accompanied by nervous upsets that can verge on an epileptic fit, it is capable of giving rise to serious internal disorders, and it can induce a fatal hemorrhage.

Colette has described in *Gribiche* the harsh agony endured by a music-hall dancer in the ignorant hands of her mother; a standard remedy, said the latter, is to drink a concentrated soap solution and then to run for a quarter of an hour. Such treatments often kill the mother in the attempt to get rid of the baby. I was told of a stenographer who remained for four days in her room, bathed in her own blood, without food or water, because she had not dared to call for help.

It is difficult to imagine abandonment more frightful than that in which the menace of death is combined with that of crime and shame. The ordeal is less savage in the case of poor but married women who act with the agreement of their husbands and without being tormented by useless scruples. A social worker told me, in connection with this last point, that in her area the women exchanged advice, lent one another instruments, and assisted one another, as simply as if it were a matter of removing corns from the feet. But they have to endure severe physical pain; the hospitals are obliged to receive a woman whose miscarriage has begun, but she is *punished* sadistically by the withholding of all sedatives during her pains and during the final operation of curetting. It appears that this persecution does not arouse the indignation of women only too habituated to pain; but they are sensitive to the humiliations heaped upon them. The fact that the operation they have undergone is clandestine and criminal multiplies its dangers and gives it an abject and agonizing character. Pain, illness, and death take on the appearance of a chastisement: we know how great is the difference between suffering and torture, accident and punishment; through all the risks she takes, the woman feels herself to be blameworthy, and this interpretation of anguish and transgression is peculiarly painful.

This moral aspect of the drama is more or less intensely felt according to circumstances. It hardly comes in question for women who are highly "emancipated," thanks to their means, their social position, and the liberal circles to which they belong, or for those schooled by poverty and misery to disdain bourgeois morality. There is a more or less disagreeable moment to live through, and it must be lived through, that is all. But many women are intimidated by a morality that for them retains its prestige even though they are unable to conform to it in their behavior; they inwardly respect the law they transgress, and they suffer from this transgression; they suffer still more from having to find accomplices.

First of all they undergo the humiliation of begging and cringing: they beg for an address, they beg a doctor and a midwife to take care of them; they risk being haughtily turned down, or they expose themselves to a degrading complicity. The deliberate invitation of another to commit an illegal act is an experience unknown to most men, and one that a woman undergoes in a confusion of fear and shame. In her heart she often repudiates the interruption of pregnancy which she is seeking to obtain. She is divided against herself. Her natural tendency can well be to have the baby whose birth she is undertaking to prevent; even if she has no positive desire for maternity, she still feels uneasy about the dubious act she is engaged in. For if it is not true that abortion is murder, it still cannot be considered in the same light as a mere contraceptive technique; an event has taken place that is a definite beginning, the progress of which is to be stopped.

Some women will be haunted by the memory of this child which has not come into being. Helene Deutsch [5] cites the case of a married woman, otherwise psychologically normal, who was twice compelled, because of her physical condition, to lose a fetus of three months and who felt obliged to erect a small tombstone for each of them. She piously tended these memorials, though she later produced several children. If the miscarriage has been voluntarily induced, the woman will have more reason to entertain the feeling that she has committed a sin. The remorse that in childhood may have followed the jealous wish for the death of a newborn brother is revived, and the woman feels herself guilty of having really killed a baby. Pathological states of melancholy may express this feeling of culpability. Other women may gain from abortion the sense of having destroyed a part of themselves and feel resentment against the man who has agreed to or requested this mutilation. In another case cited by Mrs.

[5] *Psychology of Women*, Vol. II, p. 182.

Deutsch, the girl was deeply in love and insisted on having an abortion for the sake of her lover's career; but afterward she refused to see him, feeling that she had sacrificed too much. If such a definite rupture of relations is rare, the woman may, on the other hand, become frigid, either with men in general or with the one who made her pregnant.

Men tend to take abortion lightly; they regard it as one of the numerous hazards imposed on women by malignant nature, but fail to realize fully the values involved. The woman who has recourse to abortion is disowning feminine values, her values, and at the same time is in most radical fashion running counter to the ethics established by men. Her whole moral universe is being disrupted. From infancy woman is told over and over that she is made for childbearing, and the splendors of maternity are forever being sung to her. The drawbacks of her situation—menstruation, illnesses, and the like—and the boredom of household drudgery are all justified by this marvelous privilege she has of bringing children into the world. And now here is man asking woman to relinquish her triumph as female in order to preserve his liberty, so as not to handicap his future, for the benefit of his profession!

The child is no longer a priceless treasure at all, to give birth is no longer a sacred function; this proliferation of cells becomes adventitious and troublesome; it is one more feminine defect. In comparison, the monthly bother seems a blessing: now the return of the red flow is anxiously watched for, that flow which had seemed horrifying to the young girl and for which she was consoled by the promised joys of motherhood. Even when she consents to abortion, even desires it, woman feels it as a sacrifice of her femininity: she is compelled to see in her sex a curse, a kind of infirmity, and a danger. Carrying this denial to one extreme, some women become homosexual after the trauma of abortion.

Furthermore, when man, the better to succeed in fulfilling his destiny as man, asks woman to sacrifice her reproductive possibilities, he is exposing the hypocrisy of the masculine moral code. Men universally forbid abortion, but individually they accept it as a convenient solution of a problem; they are able to contradict themselves with careless cynicism. But woman feels these contradictions in her wounded flesh; she is as a rule too timid for open revolt against masculine bad faith; she regards herself as the victim of an injustice that makes her a criminal against her will, and at the same time she feels soiled and humiliated. She embodies in concrete and immediate form, in herself, man's fault; he commits the fault, but he gets rid of it by putting it off on her; he merely says some words in a suppliant, threatening, sensible, or furious tone: he soon forgets them; it is for her to interpret these words in pain and blood. Sometimes he says nothing, he just fades away; but his silence and his flight constitute a still more evident breach of the whole moral code established by males.

The "immorality" of women, favorite theme of misogynists, is not to be wondered at; how could they fail to feel an inner mistrust of the presumptuous principles that men publicly proclaim and secretly disregard? They learn to believe no longer in what men say when they exalt woman or when they exalt man: the one thing they are sure of is this rifled and bleeding womb, these shreds of crimson life, this child that is not there. It is at her first abortion that woman begins to "know." For many women the world will never be the same. And yet, for lack of widely available contraceptives, abortion is today in France the only recourse for women unwilling to bring into the world children doomed to misery and death. As Stekel very justly says: "The law forbidding abortion is unmoral, since it is necessarily bound to be violated every day, every hour."

Contraception and legal abortion would permit woman to undertake her maternities in freedom. As things are, woman's fecundity is decided in part voluntarily, in part by chance. Since artificial insemination has not come into common use at present, it may happen that a woman desires maternity without getting her wish—because she lacks contact with men, or because her husband is sterile, or because she is herself unable to conceive. And, on the other hand, a woman often finds herself compelled to reproduce against her will. Pregnancy and motherhood are very variously experienced in accordance with the woman's true attitude, which may be one of revolt, resignation, satisfaction, or enthusiasm. It must be realized that the avowed decisions and sentiments of the young mother do not always correspond with her deeper desires. A young unmarried mother may be overwhelmed by the material burdens suddenly forced upon her and may be overtly in despair, and yet find in her baby the realization of her secret dreams. On the other hand, a young married woman who welcomes her pregnancy with joy and pride may inwardly fear and dislike it under the influence of obsessions, fantasies, and memories of infancy that she declines to recognize openly. This is one of the reasons that account for women's secrecy on this subject. Their silence comes in part from their delight in surrounding with mystery an experience that belongs exclusively to them; but in addition they are baffled by inner contradictions and conflicts they are aware of at this time. As Nancy Hale says: "The preoccupations of pregnancy are a dream that is forgotten as entirely as the dream of birth pains." These are complex truths, clear to them then, which they try to bury in forgetfulness.

During childhood and adolescence, as we have seen, woman passes through several phases in her attitude toward maternity. To the little girl it is a miracle and a game, the doll representing a future baby to possess and domineer over; to the adolescent girl maternity seems a threat to the integrity of her precious person, sometimes savagely repudiated. Sometimes she at once fears and longs for it, with hallucinations of pregnancy and all sorts of anxieties. Some girls enjoy exercising a maternal authority over children in their care, without being disposed to assume all its responsibilities. And some women have this attitude throughout life, fearing pregnancy for themselves and becoming midwives, nurses, governesses, and devoted aunts. Others, not repelled by maternity, are too much preoccupied with love-life or career to undertake it. Or they fear the burden a child would be for them or their husbands.

Very often women deliberately make sure of not conceiving, either by avoiding all sexual relations or by using contraceptives; but there are also cases where fear of childbirth is not admitted, and a psychic defense reaction prevents conception; [6] functional disorders of nervous origin are often disclosed on medical examination. The acceptance or avoidance of conception depends upon the same factors as the attitude toward pregnancy in general. During pregnancy the woman's childbirth dreams and adolescent anxieties reappear; it is experienced in very diverse ways according to the relations that exist between the subject and her mother, her husband, and herself.

Becoming a mother in her turn, the woman in a sense takes the place of her own mother: it means complete emancipation for her. If she sincerely desires it, she will be delighted with her pregnancy

---

[6] A number of such cases are described by Helene Deutsch: *Psychology of Women*, Vol. II, pp. 106 ff.—TR.

and will have the courage to go through with it by herself; but if she is still under maternal domination, and willingly, she, on the contrary, puts herself in her mother's hands; her newborn child will seem to her like a brother or sister rather than her own offspring. If she at once wishes yet does not dare to free herself, she is apprehensive lest the child, instead of saving her, will bring her again under the yoke, and this anxiety may even bring on a miscarriage.[7] Guilt feelings in regard to a mother hated in childhood may also affect pregnancy more or less unfavorably.

Not less important is the relation between the woman and the father of her child. An already mature, independent woman may want to have a child belonging wholly to herself. I have known one whose eyes lighted up at the sight of a fine male, not with sexual desire but because she judged him a good begetter; such are the maternally minded amazons who are enthusiastic over the miraculous possibilities of artificial insemination. If a woman of this type is married to the father of her child, she denies him any rights in their offspring; she endeavors (like Paul's mother in Lawrence's *Sons and Lovers*) to develop an exclusive association between herself and their common progeny. But in most cases the woman needs masculine support in accepting her new responsibilities; she will gladly devote herself to her newborn only if a man devotes himself to her.

The more childish and timid the wife, the greater is this need. Sometimes a very young wife becomes panicky after having one or two babies, and her demands on her husband become excessive. She is in a state of constant anxiety, wants him to stay at home much of the time, interferes with his work, exaggerates the importance of minor incidents, and often calls for so much assistance that she drives him out of the house.

If she loves her husband, a wife will often model her feelings on his: she accepts pregnancy and maternity with delight or the contrary according to his attitude of pride or annoyance. Sometimes the child is wished for to fortify a liaison or a marriage, and the strength of the mother's attachment to her baby depends on the success or failure of her plans. If she is hostile to her husband, the situation is still different: she may devote herself fiercely to her child and withhold it from her husband or, on the contrary, hate it as being the offspring of the man she detests. A brutal wedding night may cause the resulting child

---

[7] This situation is described by Helene Deutsch, op. cit., Vol. II, pp. 142 ff.

to be hated before and after birth. Tolstoy's wife reports in her journal that her first pregnancy made her ill in mind and body, reflecting her ambivalent feelings toward her husband.

But pregnancy is above all a drama that is acted out within the woman herself. She feels it as at once an enrichment and an injury; the fetus is a part of her body, and it is a parasite that feeds on it; she possesses it, and she is possessed by it; it represents the future and, carrying it, she feels herself vast as the world; but this very opulence annihilates her, she feels that she herself is no longer anything. A new life is going to manifest itself and justify its own separate existence, she is proud of it; but she also feels herself tossed and driven, the plaything of obscure forces. It is especially noteworthy that the pregnant woman feels the immanence of her body at just the time when it is in transcendence: it turns upon itself in nausea and discomfort; it has ceased to exist for itself and thereupon becomes more sizable than ever before. The transcendence of the artisan, of the man of action, contains the element of subjectivity; but in the mother-to-be the antithesis of subject and object ceases to exist; she and the child with which she is swollen make up together an equivocal pair overwhelmed by life. Ensnared by nature, the pregnant woman is plant and animal, a stock-pile of colloids, an incubator, an egg; she scares children proud of their young, straight bodies and makes young people titter contemptuously because she is a human being, a conscious and free individual, who has become life's passive instrument.

Ordinarily life is but a condition of existence; in gestation it appears as creative; but that is a strange kind of creation which is accomplished in a contingent and passive manner. There are women who enjoy the pleasures of pregnancy and suckling so much that they desire their indefinite repetitions; as soon as a baby is weaned these mothers feel frustrated. Such women are not so much mothers as fertile organisms, like fowls with high egg-production. And they seek eagerly to sacrifice their liberty of action to the functioning of their flesh: it seems to them that their existence is tranquilly justified in the passive fecundity of their bodies. If the flesh is purely passive and inert, it cannot embody transcendence, even in a degraded form; it is sluggish and tiresome; but when the reproductive process begins, the flesh becomes root-stock, source, and blossom, it assumes transcendence, a stirring toward the future, the while it remains a gross and present reality. The disjunction previously suffered by the woman in the weaning of an earlier child is compensated for; she is plunged anew into the mainstream of life, reunited with the wholeness of things, a link in the endless chain of generations, flesh that exists by and for another fleshly being. The fusion sought in masculine arms—and no sooner granted than withdrawn—is realized by the mother when she feels her child heavy within her or when she clasps it to her swelling breasts. She is no longer an object subservient to a subject; she is no longer a subject afflicted with the anxiety that accompanies liberty, she is one with that equivocal reality: life. Her body is at last her own, since it exists for the child who belongs to her. Society recognizes her right of possession and invests it, moreover, with a sacred character. Her bosom, which was previously an erotic feature, can now be freely shown, for it is a source of life; even religious pictures show us the Virgin Mother exposing her breast as she beseeches her Son to save mankind. With her ego surrendered, alienated in her body and in her social dignity, the mother enjoys the comforting illusion of feeling that she is a human being *in herself*, a *value*.

But this is only an illusion. For she does not really make the baby, it makes itself within her; her flesh engenders flesh only, and she is quite incapable of establishing an existence that will have to establish itself. Creative acts originating in liberty establish the object as value and give it the quality of the essential; whereas the child in the maternal body is not thus justified; it is still only a gratuitous cellular growth, a brute fact of nature as contingent on circumstances as death and corresponding philosophically with it. A mother can have *her* reasons for wanting *a* child, but she cannot give to *this* independent person, who is to exist tomorrow, his own reasons, his justification, for existence; she engenders him as a product of her generalized body, not of her individualized existence. Colette Audry's heroine [8] understands this when she says;

I had never thought that he could give meaning to my life. . . . His life had germinated within me, and, whatever might happen, I had to bring his development to term, without being able to hurry things even if it meant my death. Then he was there, born of me; thus he was like a piece of work that I might have done in life . . . but after all he was nothing of the kind.

---

[8] In *On joue perdant*, "*L'Enfant*."

In a sense the mystery of the Incarnation repeats itself in each mother; every child born is a god who is made man: he cannot find self-realization as a being with consciousness and freedom unless he first comes into the world; the mother lends herself to this mystery, but she does not control it; it is beyond her power to influence what in the end will be the true nature of this being who is developing in her womb. She gives expression to this uncertainty in two contradictory fantasies: every mother entertains the idea that her child will be a hero, thus showing her wonderment at the thought of engendering a being with consciousness and freedom; but she is also in dread of giving birth to a defective or a monster, because she is aware to what a frightening extent the welfare of the flesh is contingent upon circumstances—and this embryo dwelling within her is only flesh. There are cases in which one or the other of the myths bemuses her; but frequently the woman oscillates between the two. She also feels another ambiguity. Caught up in the great cycle of the species, she affirms life in the teeth of time and death: in this she glimpses immortality; but in her flesh she feels the truth of Hegel's words: "The birth of children is the death of parents." The child, he says, again, is "the very being of their love which is external to them," and, inversely, the child will attain his own being "in separating from its source, a separation in which that source finds its end." This projection of herself is also for the woman the foreshadowing of her death. She expresses this truth in the fear she feels when she thinks of childbirth: she fears that it will mean the loss of her own life.

The significance of pregnancy being thus ambiguous, it is natural that woman should assume an ambivalent attitude toward it; moreover her attitude changes with the various stages in fetal development. It should first be emphasized that at the beginning of the process the baby is not present; it has as yet only an imaginary existence; the mother-to-be can muse upon the little being who is to be born some months hence and busy herself with the preparation of his cradle and layette; she experiences concretely no more than the disturbing organic phenomena taking place within her. Certain high priests of Life and of Fecundity mystically proclaim that a woman knows by the kind of pleasure she feels that the man has just impregnated her: a myth that must be discarded. She never has a reliable intuition at the time of the event; she infers it later from more or less uncertain signs. Her menstruation ceases, she grows stout, her breasts become heavy and tender, she suffers from vertigo and nausea; sometimes she believes simply that she is ill and a doctor informs her of her true condition. Then she knows that her body is destined to transcend itself; day after day a growth arising from her flesh but foreign to it is going to enlarge within her; she is the prey of the species, which imposes its mysterious laws upon her, and as a rule this subjection to strange outer forces frightens her, her fright being manifested in morning sickness and nausea. These are in part brought on by modification of the gastric secretions produced at this time; but if this reaction, unknown in other mammals, is an important one in woman, the cause of it is psychic; it expresses the sharpness that at this time marks the conflict, in the human female, between the species and the individual.[9] Even if the woman deeply desires to have a child, her body vigorously revolts when obliged to undergo the reproductive process. Stekel says that "in states of nervous anxiety" the vomiting of a pregnant woman always expresses a certain refusal of the infant; and if the woman is hostile—for reasons often unavowed—the digestive troubles are exaggerated.

"Psychoanalysis has taught us that psychogenic intensification of the oral pregnancy symptom of vomiting takes place only when the oral expulsion tendencies are accompanied by . . . emotions of hostility to pregnancy or to the fœtus," says Helene Deutsch;[1] and she adds: "Often the psychologic content in pregnancy vomiting is exactly the same as that in the hysterical vomiting of young girls that is induced by an unconscious pregnancy fantasy." In both cases there is a revival of the ancient idea of fecundation by way of the mouth, which children often entertain. By childish women in particular, pregnancy is considered, as in former times, to be an illness of the digestive apparatus. Helene Deutsch cites the case of a patient who carefully examined her vomit for fragments of the embryo, though she said she *knew* that this was an absurd obsession. Morbid hunger, lack of appetite, and feelings of disgust indicate the same hesitation between the wish to preserve and the wish to destroy the embryo. I once knew a young woman who suffered at the same time from excessive vomiting and severe constipation; she once told me of her own accord that she had the impression simultaneously of trying to expel the fetus and

---

[9] See Book I, Ch. i.
[1] Op. cit., Vol. II, p. 128.

forcing herself to retain it, which corresponded exactly to her conscious wishes.

In his work *Le Mariage*, Dr. Arthus describes a case that I summarize as follows:

> Mme T— manifests serious disorders of pregnancy accompanied by uncontrollable vomiting. . . . Her condition is so alarming as to suggest a therapeutic abortion. . . . The patient is distressed at the thought. . . . The brief analysis possible reveals that Mme T— has subconsciously identified herself with a former school friend who had played a large part in her affective life and who died as a result of her first pregnancy. As soon as this background is brought into consciousness, the symptoms are relieved; after two weeks the vomiting still occurs but is no longer dangerous.

Constipation, diarrhea, and expulsive efforts always represent the same mixture of desire and anxiety; sometimes the result is miscarriage: almost all spontaneous miscarriages are of psychic origin. The disorders mentioned are the more accentuated the more the woman regards them as important and the more self-centered she is. In particular, the well-known special longings of pregnant women are obsessions of childish origin, self-indulgently retained; they always have reference to things to eat, in consequence of the childish idea of alimentary fecundation; the woman, feeling herself physically upset, expresses this sensation of strangeness through a longing with which she is sometimes obsessed, as often happens in psychic disorder. There is, moreover, a cultivation of these longings as a matter of tradition, just as there used to be a cultivation of hysteria; the woman expects to have them, she is on the watch for them, she invents them. I have heard of a young unmarried pregnant woman who had such a mad longing for spinach that she ran to the market to buy some and tapped her foot with impatience waiting for it to cook. In this way she expressed her anxiety at being alone; knowing that she could depend on herself only, she went about satisfying her longings in feverish haste. In her *Memoirs* the Duchess of Abrantès amusingly describes the kind of case in which the longing is insistently suggested by those around the woman. She complains that she was surrounded by too much solicitude during her pregnancy.

These cares and kind attentions increased the discomfort, nausea, nervousness, and numerous other sufferings which almost always accompany first pregnancies, I found it so. . . . It was my mother who made the beginning, one day when I was having dinner with her. . . . "Good heavens," she cried suddenly, "good heavens! I forgot to ask you what you especially *longed* for."

"But there is nothing in particular," I replied.

"You have no special longing," exclaimed my mother, "nothing! But that is unheard of. You must be wrong. You haven't noticed. I'll speak to your mother-in-law about it."

And so there were my two mothers in consultation. And so there was Junot, afraid I would bear him a child with a wild boar's head . . . asking me every morning: "Laura, what do you long for?" My sister-in-law added her voice . . . saying that she had seen innumerable people disfigured because of unsatisfied longings. . . . I finally got frightened myself. . . . I tried to think of what would please me most and couldn't think of a thing. One day, when I was eating pineapple lozenges, it finally occurred to me that a pineapple ought to be just the thing. Once I had convinced myself that I had a *longing* for a pineapple, I felt at first a very lively desire, increased when I found they were not in season. Ah, then I felt that mad desire which makes you feel that you will die if it is not satisfied. [Finally a pineapple was obtained and served.] I pushed the plate away. "But—I don't know what is the matter with me, I can't eat pineapple." . . . They not only had to take it away but also to open the windows and perfume my room in order to remove the least traces of an odor that had become hateful to me in an instant. The strangest part of it is that since then I have never been able to eat pineapple without practically forcing myself.

Women who are treated with most concern, or who are most concerned with themselves, are the ones who show the greatest number of morbid symptoms. Those who undergo the ordeal of pregnancy with greatest ease are, on the one hand, the matrons who are wholly consecrated to their reproductive function, and, on the other, those mannish women who are not particularly fascinated by the adventures of their bodies and are quite ready and willing to go through them without fuss: Mme de Staël carried on a pregnancy as readily as a conversation.

While pregnancy advances, the relation between mother and fetus changes. The latter is firmly settled in the mother's womb; the two organisms are mutually adapted, and between them biological exchanges take place that enable the woman to regain her balance. She no longer feels herself possessed by the species; it is she who possesses the fruit of her body. During the first months she was an ordinary woman, and one the worse for the secret activity going on within her; later she is recognizably a mother-to-be, and her infirmities are but the other side of her glory. As her weakness becomes more pronounced, it excuses everything. Many women find in their later pregnancy a marvelous peace: they feel justified. Previously they had always felt a desire to observe themselves, to scrutinize their bodies; but they had not dared to indulge this interest too freely, from a sense of social propriety. Now it is their right; everything they do for their own benefit they are doing also for the child. They are no longer called upon for work or effort; they no longer have to think of others; the dreams of the future they cherish lend meaning to the present moment; they have only to let themselves live: they are on vacation:

The pregnant woman's *raison de'être* is there, in her womb, and gives her a perfect sense of rich abundance. A patient of Helene Deutsch said: "It is like a stove in the winter that is always lit, that is there for you alone, entirely subject to your will. It is also like a constantly gushing cold shower in the summer, refreshing you. It is there." [2] Thus fulfilled, the woman has also the satisfaction of feeling that she is "interesting," something that has been her deepest wish since adolescence; as wife she suffered from her dependency with regard to man; now she is no longer in service as a sexual object, but she is the incarnation of the species, she represents the promise of life, of eternity. Her entourage respects her; her very caprices become sacred, and this, as we have seen, is what encourages her to invent "longings." As Helene Deutsch says, "Pregnancy permits woman to rationalize performances which otherwise would appear absurd." Justified by the presence of an other in her womb, she at last enjoys the privilege of being wholly herself.

In *L'Étoile Vesper* Colette describes that phase of her pregnancy.

[2] Op. cit., Vol. II, p. 157.

Insidiously, slowly, the bliss of women big with child spread through me. I was no longer subject to any discomfort, any misery whatever. Euphoria, the purr of contentment—by what name, scientific or common, should I call this sense of protection from harm? The feeling must have been quite overwhelming, since I do not forget it. I am tired of hiding what was never mentioned— namely, the state of pride, of vulgar grandeur, which I enjoyed while ripening my fruit. . . . Each night I said a little farewell to one of the good days of my life. I well knew that I would look back upon it with regret. But cheerfulness, contentment, euphoria, submerged everything, and over me reigned the gentle animality, the sluggishness that came from increasing weight and the voiceless demands of the creature that was developing within me.

Sixth, seventh month. . . . The first strawberries, the first roses. Can I call my pregnancy anything less than a long holiday? The pangs of childbirth are forgotten, but not so a long, unique holiday: I remember it all. I recall especially that slumber overcame me at odd times, and that I felt again, as in childhood, the need to sleep on the ground, on the grass, on the warm earth. It was my sole "longing," and a wholesome one. Toward the end I was like a rat trying to make off with a stolen egg. An inconvenience to myself, I became too fatigued to go to bed. . . . For all my weight and my fatigue, my holiday still continued. I was borne on a shield of privileges and attentions.

Colette tells us that one of her friends called this pleasant pregnancy "a man's pregnancy." And in fact she seems typical of those women who bear their condition valiantly because they are not absorbed in it. At the same time she continued her work as a writer. "The baby indicated that he would be finished first, and I put the cap on my fountain pen."

Other women feel the weight of it more; they muse endlessly on their new importance. With the slightest encouragement they revive in their own cases the masculine myths: against the light of the mind they oppose the fecund darkness of Life; against the clarity of consciousness, the mysteries of inwardness; against productive liberty, the weight of this belly growing there enormously without human will. The mother-to-be feels herself one with soil and sod, stock and root; when she drowses off, her sleep is like that of brooding chaos with worlds in ferment. Some, those more forgetful of self, are delighted above all with the living treasure growing within them. This delight is given expression in Cécile Sauvage's poems, *L'Ame en bourgeon:*

> You belong to me as the dawn to the plain
> Around you my life is like warm wool
> In which your delicate members grow in secret.

And farther on:

> Little soul in bud joined to my flower
> Your heart I fashion from a bit of mine.

And in a letter to her husband:

It's queer, I feel as if I were in attendance at the formation of a very tiny planet and were shaping the fragile orb. I have never been so close to life. Never have I so clearly felt that I am sister to the earth, with its vegetation and vital sap. My feet tread on the earth as if it were a living thing. I dream in broad daylight of flutes, awakened bees, and dew, for now he kicks and stirs within me. Could you but know how this budding soul fills my heart with the freshness of springtime and with youth! And to think that it is the infant soul of Pierrot, and that in the darkness inside me this soul is perfecting two great eyes of infinite depth like his.

On the other hand, women who are primarily interested in pleasing men, who see themselves essentially as erotic objects, who are in love with their own bodily beauty, are distressed to see themselves deformed, disfigured, incapable of arousing desire. Pregnancy seems to them no holiday, no enrichment at all, but rather a diminution of the ego. Isadora Duncan writes as follows: [3]

The child asserted itself now, more and more. It was strange to see my beautiful marble body softened and broken and stretched and deformed. . . . As I walked beside the sea, I sometimes felt an excess of strength and prowess, and I thought this creature would be mine, mine alone, but on other days . . . I felt myself some poor animal in a mighty trap. . . . With alternate hope and despair, I often thought of the pilgrimage of my childhood, my youth, my wanderings in distant countries, my discoveries in Art, and they were as a misty, far-away Prologue, leading up to this—

---

[3] *My Life*, pp. 191 ff.

the before-birth of a child. What any peasant woman could have!
. . . I began to be assailed with all sorts of fears. In vain I told
myself that every woman had children. . . . It was all in the
course of life, etc. I was, nevertheless, conscious of fear. Of what?
Certainly not of death, nor even of pain—some unknown fear, of
what I did not know. . . . More and more my lovely body bulged
under my astonished gaze. . . . Where was my lovely, youthful
Naiad form? Where my ambition? My fame? Often, in spite of
myself, I felt very miserable and defeated. This game with the
giant Life was too much. But then I thought of the child to come,
and all such painful thoughts ceased. . . . Cruel hours of tender
waiting in the night. . . . With what a price we pay for the glory
of motherhood.

In the last stage of pregnancy there are indications of the break
between mother and child. Women perceive the child's first movement with varied feelings, this kick delivered at the portals of the
world, against the uterine wall that shuts him off from the world.
One woman is lost in wonder at this signal announcing the presence
of an independent being; another may feel repugnance at containing a stranger. Once more the union of fetus and maternal body is
disturbed: the uterus descends, the woman has sensations of pressure, tension, and difficult breathing. She is now in the possession
not of the species in general but of this infant who is about to be
born; up to this time he has been only a mental image, a hope; now
he becomes a solid, present reality, and his reality creates new problems. Every transition is fraught with anxiety: childbirth appears especially terrifying. When the woman approaches her term, all her
childish terrors come to life again; if through feelings of guilt she
believes she is under her mother's curse, she persuades herself that
she is going to die or that the child will die. In *War and Peace* Tolstoy depicts in the young Lise one of these infantile women who see
childbirth as a sentence of death; and in fact she does die.

The significance of childbirth varies greatly in different cases: the
mother desires at the same time to retain the precious flesh that is
a treasured portion of her ego and to rid herself of an intruder; she
wants to have her dream actually in her hands at last, but she dreads
the new responsibilities that this material realization is going to
create. Either desire may predominate, but she is often torn between

them. It frequently happens, also, that she is of two minds in her approach to the agonizing ordeal: she means to prove to herself and to her entourage—to her mother, to her husband—that she can weather the storm without assistance; but at the same time she bears a grudge against the world, against life, against her family, for the sufferings inflicted upon her, and in protest she remains passive. Women of independent character—matrons or mannish women— are disposed to play an active part just before and even during the birth; those of very childish nature are passive in hands of midwife or mother; some take pride in making no outcry; others refuse to obey any directions.

On the whole we may say that in this crisis women give expression to their fundamental attitude toward the world in general and toward their own maternity in particular: they may be stoical, resigned, demanding, domineering, rebellious, passive, or tense. These psychological bents have an enormous influence on the duration and difficulty of childbirth (which is also affected, of course, by purely organic factors). It is significant that woman—like the females of certain domesticated animals—requires help in performing the function assigned to her by nature; there are peasants living in harsh circumstances and shamefaced unmarried mothers who give birth alone, but their being alone at this time often results in death for the baby or incurable illness for the mother. At just the time when woman attains the realization of her feminine destiny, she is still dependent: proof again that in the human species nature and artifice are never wholly separated. In natural circumstances the conflict between the interest of the feminine individual and that of the species is so acute that it often brings about the death of either the mother or the child: it is human intervention, medical or surgical, that has considerably reduced—and even almost eliminated—the formerly frequent mishaps. Anesthetic techniques are doing much to nullify the Biblical pronouncement: "In sorrow thou shalt bring forth children"; their use is common in America and is beginning to spread in France; a law passed in May 1949, has made them obligatory in England.[4] It

---

[4] I have already noted that some antifeminists are indignant in the name of nature and the Bible at any proposal to eliminate labor pains, which they regard as one of the sources of the maternal "instinct." Helene Deutsch seems somewhat drawn to this view, remarking that a mother who has not suffered from her labor pains does not feel the baby profoundly hers when it is placed in her arms. She agrees, however, that the same feelings of emptiness and estrangement are some-

is difficult to determine just how much relief from suffering woman obtains through these methods. The fact that the duration of delivery may vary from twenty-four to two or three hours forbids generalization. For some women childbirth is a martyrdom. So it was for Isadora Duncan; she had gone through her pregnancy in agony, and no doubt her delivery pains were intensified by her psychological resistance. She writes as follows:

> Talk about the Spanish Inquisition! No woman who has borne a child would have to fear it. It must have been a mild sport in comparison. Relentless, cruel, knowing no release, no pity, this terrible, unseen genie had me in his grip, and was, in continued spasms, tearing my bones and my sinews apart. They say such suffering is soon forgotten. All I have to reply is that I have only to shut my eyes and I hear again my shrieks and groans as they were then.[5]

Some women, on the contrary, consider the ordeal a relatively easy one to bear. A few find sensual pleasure in it. One of Stekel's patients, already referred to, wrote in her confession that she was so sexual a being that for her childbirth was a sexual act. Her attractive nurse administered baths and douches, which were highly exciting and gave her nervous spasms.

There are some women who say that childbirth gives them a sense of creative power; they have really accomplished a voluntary and productive task. Many, at the other extreme, have felt themselves passive—suffering and tortured instruments.

The first relations of the mother with her newborn child are equally variable. Some women suffer from the emptiness they now feel in their bodies: it seems to them that their treasure has been stolen. In her poems Cécile Sauvage expresses this feeling: "I am the hive whence the swarm has departed"; and also: "He is born, I have lost my young beloved, now he is born, I am alone."

---

times to be observed in women who have experienced the pangs of delivery; and she maintains throughout her book that maternal love is a sentiment, a conscious attitude, not an instinct, and that it is not necessarily connected with pregnancy. According to her, a woman may feel maternal love for an adopted child, for one her husband has had by a former wife, and so on. This contradiction evidently stems from the fact that she regards woman as doomed to masochism, her thesis compelling her to assign a high value to feminine suffering.

[5] *My Life*, pp. 194–5.

At the same time, however, there is an amazed curiosity in every young mother. It is strangely miraculous to see and to hold a living being formed within oneself and issued forth from oneself. But just what part has the mother had in the extraordinary event that brings into the world a new existence? She does not know. The newborn would not exist had it not been for her, and yet he leaves her. There is an astonished melancholy in seeing him outside, cut off from her. And almost always disappointment. The woman would like to feel the new being as surely *hers* as is her own hand; but everything he experiences is shut up inside him; he is opaque, impenetrable, apart; she does not even recognize him because she does not know him. She has experienced her pregnancy without him: she has no past in common with this little stranger. She expected that he would be at once familiar; but no, he is a newcomer, and she is surprised at the indifference with which she receives him. In the reveries of her pregnancy he was a mental image with infinite possibilities, and the mother enjoyed her future maternity in thought; now he is a tiny, finite individual, and he is there in reality—dependent, delicate, demanding. Her quite real joy in his finally being there is mingled with regret to find him no more than that.

Many young mothers regain through nursing an intimate animal relationship with their infants, after the birth-separation has occurred; it is more tiring than pregnancy, but it enables the nursing mother to prolong the state of being on vacation, in peace and plenitude, enjoyed in pregnancy. Colette Audry says of one of her heroines: [6]

> When she was nursing the baby, there was quite rightly nothing else for her to do, and it could last for hours; she did not even think of what would come afterward. She had only to wait until he left her breast like a big bee.

But there are women who cannot nurse and whose first surprised indifference continues until they find definite new bonds with the infant. This was the case with Colette, for one, who was unable to nurse her baby daughter and who describes her first maternal feeling with her customary sincerity in *L'Étoile Vesper:*

---

[6] In *On joue perdant.*

Then followed the contemplation of an arrival in the house who had not come in through the door. . . . Did I put enough love into my contemplation? I fear I cannot say so. I was, to be sure, accustomed to marvel at things—I still am. So I marveled at the assemblage of prodigies that is the newborn child: her finger-nails, transparent as the pink shrimp's convex shell, the soles of her feet, which had come to us without touching the ground. The feathery lightness of her eyelashes, lowered on her cheeks or inter-posed between the scenery of earth and the pale-blue dream in her eyes. Her tiny sex, a faintly grooved almond, bivalved, precisely closed, lip to lip. But I gave no name to this minutely detailed admiration of my daughter, I did not feel it as love. I watched and waited. . . . From these sights, long awaited in my life, I did not acquire the usual bedazzled mother's watchfulness and rivalry. When, I wondered, would come the sign that for me would be-token a second and more difficult entrance into my life? I had to conclude that in the end I would be transformed into an ordinary mother through many admonitions, furtive upheavals of jealousy, erroneous forewarnings and even right ones, pride in controlling a life that I had humbly created, and the somewhat insincere con-sciousness of giving the other a lesson in modesty. Yet I shall re-cover my serenity only when intelligible language comes from her sweet lips, when consciousness, mischievousness, and even affection make a baby like any other into a daughter, and *a* daughter into *my* daughter!

There are also many mothers who are alarmed at their new respon-sibilities. During her pregnancy such a woman had only to abandon herself to her flesh; no initiative was called for. Now she is con-fronted by a person who has rights to be considered. There are some women who, still gay and carefree, gaily pet their babies while still in the hospital, but on returning home begin to regard them as bur-densome. Even nursing affords such a woman no pleasure; on the contrary, she is apprehensive of ruining her bosom; she resents feel-ing her nipples cracked, the glands painful; suckling the baby hurts; the infant seems to her to be sucking out her strength, her life, her happiness. It inflicts a harsh slavery upon her and it is no longer a part of her: it seems a tyrant; she feels hostile to this little stranger, this individual who menaces her flesh, her freedom, her whole ego.

Many other factors are involved. The woman's relations with her mother retain all their importance. Helene Deutsch reports the case of a young nursing mother whose milk failed each time her mother came to visit; her nervousness was like that of a schoolgirl faced with examinations.[7] The young mother often asks for help, but she is jealous of the care given the baby by the other person and takes a sullen attitude toward her. Her relations with the baby's father and his own feelings in the matter also exert a large influence. A whole complex of economic and sentimental considerations makes the baby seem either a burden and a hindrance or a jewel, a means of liberation and security. There are cases in which hostility becomes open hatred, expressed by extreme neglect or bad treatment. Usually the mother, mindful of her duty, tries to combat this hostility; the remorse she feels gives rise to anxiety states in which the apprehensions of pregnancy are continued. Psychoanalysts agree that mothers who are obsessed with the idea of harming their infants and who imagine horrible accidents feel toward them an enmity that they force themselves to repress.

What is in any case remarkable and distinguishes this relation of mother and baby from all other human relations is the fact that at first the baby itself takes no active part in it: its smiles, its babble, have no sense other than what the mother gives them; whether it seem charming and unique, or tiresome, commonplace, and hateful, depends upon her, not upon the baby. This is the reason why cold, unsatisfied, melancholy women who expect to find a companionship, a warmth, a stimulation in the infant which will draw them out of themselves are always deeply disappointed. Like the transitions of puberty, sexual initiation, and marriage, that of maternity gives rise to a feeling of morose disappointment in subjects who hope that an outward event can renovate and justify their lives. Sophie Tolstoy writes that those nine months were the most terrible in her life, and the less said about the tenth the better. In her journal she tries in vain to express the conventional joy, but we are struck by her sadness and her fear of new responsibilities, though she avows a strong maternal feeling and says she loves her husband because the child is his. But it is clear that she thus parades her love for her husband only because she actually did not love him. This dislike was in reality reflected upon the child conceived in loathsome embraces.

---

[7] Op. cit., Vol. II, p. 281.

Katherine Mansfield has described the uncertain attitude of a young mother who though fond of her husband is repelled by his embraces. With her children she feels affectionate and at the same time has an impression of emptiness, which she gloomily interprets as complete indifference. Reclining at ease in the garden, with her lately born son close by, Linda is thinking of her husband, Stanley.[8]

Well, she was married to him. And what was more she loved him. Not the Stanley whom everyone saw, not the everyday one; but a timid, sensitive, innocent Stanley who knelt down every night to say his prayers. . . . But the trouble was . . . she saw *her* Stanley so seldom. There were glimpses, moments, breathing spaces of calm, but all the rest of the time it was like living in a house that couldn't be cured of the habit of catching on fire, on a ship that got wrecked every day. And it was always Stanley who was in the thick of the danger. Her whole time was spent in rescuing him, and restoring him, and calming him down, and listening to his story. And what was left of her time was spent in the dread of having children. . . . It was all very well to say that it was the common lot of women to bear children. It wasn't true. She, for one, could prove that wrong. She was broken, made weak, her courage was gone, through childbearing. And what made it doubly hard to bear was, she did not love her children. It was useless pretending. . . . No, it was as though a cold breath had chilled her through and through on each of those awful journeys; she had no warmth left to give them. As to the boy—well, thank Heaven, mother had taken him; he was mother's, or Beryl's, or anybody's who wanted him. She had hardly held him in her arms. She was so indifferent about him that as he lay there . . . Linda glanced down. . . .

There was something so quaint, so unexpected about that smile that Linda smiled herself. But she checked herself and said to the boy coldly, "I don't like babies."

"Don't you like babies?" The boy couldn't believe her. "Don't like *me*?" He waved his arms foolishly at his mother.

Linda dropped off her chair on to the grass.

"Why do you keep on smiling?" she said severely. "If you knew what I was thinking about, you wouldn't." . . . Linda was so

---

[8] "At the Bay," in *The Short Stories of Katherine Mansfield*, pp. 279–80.

astonished at the confidence of this little creature. . . . Ah no, be sincere. That was not what she felt; it was something far different, it was something so new, so . . . The tears danced in her eyes; she breathed in a small whisper to the boy, "Hallo, my funny!"

These examples all show that no maternal "instinct" exists: the word hardly applies, in any case, to the human species. The mother's attitude depends on her total situation and her reaction to it. As we have just seen, this is highly variable.

But the fact remains that unless the circumstances are positively unfavorable the mother will find her life enriched by her child. Concerning one young mother Colette Audry remarks that her child was like a proof of the reality of her own existence, through him she had a hold on things in general and on herself to begin with. And this author makes another woman say:

> He was heavy in my arms and on my bosom like the heaviest thing in the world, to the limit of my strength. He buried me in silence and darkness. All at once he had put the weight of the world on my shoulders. That was indeed why I wanted to have him. I was too light by myself.

If certain women who are fecund rather than motherly lose interest in their offspring at weaning or at birth and desire only a new pregnancy, many, on the contrary, feel that the separation is what gives them the child; it is no longer an indistinguishable part of themselves but a portion of the outer world; it no longer vaguely haunts their bodies, but can be seen and touched. After the pain of birth, Cécile Sauvage expresses the joy of motherly possession in a poem where she refers to the baby as her "little lover," her little double, whom she can hold and kiss and greet with happiness and excitement; it is her "little statue of blood, joy, and naked flesh."

It has been asserted time and again that woman is pleased to acquire in the infant an equivalent of the penis, but this is by no means an exact statement. The fact is that the grown man no longer sees in his penis a wonderful toy as in childhood; the value it has for the adult lies in the desirable objects it enables him to possess. Similarly, the adult woman envies the male the prey he takes possession of, not the instrument by which he takes it. The infant satisfies that aggressive eroticism which is not fully satisfied in the male embrace: the infant corresponds, for the woman, to the mistress whom she leaves to the male and whom he does not represent for her. The correspondence is not exact, of course; every relation is *sui generis*, unique; but the mother finds in her infant—as does the lover in his beloved—a carnal plenitude, and this not in surrender but in domination; she obtains in her child what man seeks in woman: an other, combining nature and mind, who is to be both prey and *double*. The baby incarnates all nature. Colette Audry's heroine tells us that she found in her child "a skin for the touch of my fingers that fulfilled the promise of all kittens, all flowers." The infant's flesh has that softness, that warm elasticity, which the woman, when she was a little girl, coveted in her mother's flesh and, later, in things everywhere. The baby is plant and animal, in its eyes are rains and rivers, the azure of sea and sky; its fingernails are coral, its hair a silky growth; it is a living doll, a bird, a kitten; "my flower, my pearl, my chick, my lamb." The mother murmurs almost a lover's words, and like a lover she makes avid use of the possessive case; she employs the same gestures of possession: caresses, kisses; she hugs her child to her bosom, she keeps him warm in her arms and in her bed. Sometimes these relations are of a clearly sexual kind. In the confession already cited from Stekel, the mother says she felt ashamed because her nursing had a sexual tinge and her baby's touches made her shiver delightfully; when two years old he caressed her like a lover, almost irresistibly, and she had to fight the temptation to toy with his penis.

Maternity takes on a new aspect when the child grows older; at first it is only a baby like any other, it exists only in its generality, one example of a class; then little by little it takes on individuality. Women of very domineering or very sensual disposition then grow cool toward the child; and at this time, on the contrary, certain others—like Colette—begin to take a real interest in their offspring. The relation of mother to child becomes more and more complex: the child is a double, an *alter ego*, into whom the mother is sometimes tempted to project herself entirely, but he is an independent subject and therefore rebellious; he is intensely real today, but in imagination he is the adolescent and adult of the future. He is a rich possession, a treasure, but also a charge upon her, a tyrant. The mother's joy in him is one of generosity; she must find her pleasure in serving, giving, making him happy, like the mother described by Colette Audry:

> So he enjoyed a happy childhood, such as one reads of in books; but it was like the childhood of books as real roses resemble roses on postcards. And this happiness of his flowed from me as did the milk on which I had fed him.

Like the woman in love, the mother is delighted to feel herself necessary; her existence is justified by the wants she supplies; but what gives mother love its difficulty and its grandeur is the fact that it implies no reciprocity; the mother has to do not with man, a hero, a demigod, but with a small, prattling soul, lost in a fragile and dependent body. The child is in possession of no values, he can bestow none, with him the woman remains alone; she expects no return for what she gives, it is for her to justify it herself. This generosity merits the laudation that men never tire of conferring upon her; but the distortion begins when the religion of Maternity proclaims that all mothers are saintly. For while maternal devotion may be perfectly genuine, this, in fact, is rarely the case. Maternity is usually a strange mixture of narcissism, altruism, idle daydreaming, sincerity, bad faith, devotion, and cynicism.

The great danger which threatens the infant in our culture lies in the fact that the mother to whom it is confided in all its helplessness is almost always a discontented woman: sexually she is frigid or unsatisfied; socially she feels herself inferior to man; she has no independent grasp on the world or on the future. She will seek to compensate for all these frustrations through her child. When it is realized how difficult woman's present situation makes her full self-realization, how many desires, rebellious feelings, just claims she nurses in secret, one is frightened at the thought that defenseless infants are abandoned to her care. Just as when she coddled and tortured her dolls by turns, her behavior is symbolic; but symbols become grim reality for her child. A mother who whips her child is not beating the child alone; in a sense she is not beating it at all: she is taking her vengeance on a man, on the world, or on herself. Such a mother is often remorseful and the child may not feel resentment, but it feels the blows.

This cruel aspect of maternity has always been known, but it has in the past been hypocritically attributed to the figure of the cruel stepmother, punishing the offspring of a "good" mother who is dead. In recent literature the "bad" mother has been frequently portrayed, and if such types seem somewhat exceptional, it is because most women have the morality and decency to repress their spontaneous impulses; nevertheless these impulses suddenly flash out at times in angry scenes, slaps, punishments, and the like. Along with the mothers who are frankly sadistic, there are many who are especially capricious and domineering; now they treat the child as a doll, now as an obedient little slave; if vain, they show it off; if jealous, they hide it away. Frequently they expect too much in the way of gratitude for their care. When Cornelia displayed her children and said "these are my jewels," she set an evil example for posterity; too many mothers hope to repeat this proud gesture and do not hesitate to sacrifice the ordinary little individual who is not fulfilling their hopes. They try to make him like, or unlike, their husbands, or they wish him to resemble other admired relatives; they try to make him in the image of some hero. Such tyranny is harmful to the child and always disappointing to the mother. This educational obstinacy and the capricious sadism already referred to are often combined; the mother excuses her outbursts of anger by the pretext that she wants to "train" the child; and her lack of success in this enterprise increases her hostility.

Another common attitude, and one not less ruinous to the child, is masochistic devotion, in which the mother makes herself the slave of her offspring to compensate for the emptiness of her heart and to punish herself for her unavowed hostility. Such a mother is morbidly anxious, not allowing her child out of her sight; she gives up all diversion, all personal life, thus assuming the role of victim; and she derives from these sacrifices the right to deny her child all independence. This renunciation on the mother's part is easily reconciled with a tyrannical will to domination; the *mater dolorosa* forges from her sufferings a weapon that she uses sadistically; her displays of resignation give rise to guilt feelings in the child which often last a lifetime: they are still more harmful than her displays of aggression. Tossed this way and that, baffled, the child can find no defensive position: now blows, now tears, make him out a criminal.

The main excuse of the mother is that her child by no means provides that happy self-fulfillment which has been promised her since her own childhood; she blames him for the deception of which she has been the victim and which he innocently exposes. She did as she pleased with her dolls; when she helped a sister or a friend with a baby, the responsibility was not hers. But now society, her husband, her mother, and her own pride hold her to account for that little strange life, as if it were all her doing. Her husband, in particular, is irritated by the child's faults as he is by a spoiled dinner or the misconduct of his wife; his unreasonable demands often affect adversely the relation of mother to child. An independent woman—thanks to her solitary state, her freedom from care, or her authority in the house—will be much more serene in mind than one subject to domineering demands to which she must accede willy-nilly in forcing the child to accede.

For the great difficulty is to bring within preconceived patterns an existence as mysterious as that of an animal, as turbulent and disorderly as natural forces, and yet human. One can neither train a child without talking, as one trains a dog, nor make him listen to reason through the use of adult words; and he takes advantage of this situation by answering words with animal-like sobs or tantrums and by opposing restraints with impertinent words.

The problem thus offered is certainly challenging, and the mother who has time for it enjoys her educational function: quietly settled in the park, she finds the child still as good an excuse for taking her ease as he was during pregnancy; often, being more or less infantile herself, she is very well pleased to be silly along with him, renewing the games and words, the interests and joys, of her own early days. But when the mother is busy with washing, cooking, nursing another baby, marketing, and entertaining guests, and particularly when she is occupied with her husband, the child is merely harassing and bothersome. She has no leisure for "training" him; the main thing is to prevent him from getting into trouble; he is always breaking or tearing or dirtying and is a constant danger to objects and to himself; he is on the go, he cries, he talks, he makes a noise. He is living his life on his own account, and this life of his disturbs that of his parents. Their interests and his do not mesh, and that causes all the trouble. Forever burdened with him, his parents constantly impose sacrifices he does not understand: he is sacrificed to their peace and quiet and also to his own future. Quite naturally he rebels. He does not comprehend the explanations his mother tries to give him, for she cannot penetrate into his consciousness; his dreams, his fears, his obsessions, his desires, make up a world into which she cannot see: the mother can only regulate from outside, blindly, an individual who finds her irrelevant rules an absurd imposition.

When the child grows older, this lack of comprehension remains: he enters a world of interests and values from which his mother is excluded; often enough he scorns her on that account. The boy especially, proud of his masculine prerogatives, laughs at orders from a woman: she insists on his attending to his duties, but she does not know how to solve his assigned problems or translate his Latin: she cannot keep up with him. The mother sometimes wears herself out to the point of tears in this thankless task. Its difficulty is seldom realized by her husband: it is the attempt to control a being with whom you are not in communication and who is none the less a human being, to obtrude yourself upon an independent stranger who is defined and affirmed only in revolting against you.

The situation varies according to the sex of the child; and though it is more difficult when a boy is concerned, the mother normally makes a better adjustment to it. Because of the prestige attributed to men by women, as well as the advantages they actually have, many women prefer to have sons. "How wonderful to bring a man into the world!" they say; we have seen that they dream of engendering a "hero," and the hero is obviously of the male sex. A son will be a leader of men, a soldier, a creator; he will bend the world to his will, and his mother will share his immortal fame; he will give her the houses she has not constructed, the lands she has not explored, the books she has not read. Through him she will possess the world—but only on condition that she possess her son. Thence comes the paradox of her attitude.

Freud holds that the relation between mother and son is the one of least ambivalence; but the fact is that in maternity, as in marriage and the love affair, woman takes an equivocal attitude toward masculine transcendence. If her experience in marriage or in love has made her hostile to man, it will give her satisfaction to domineer over the male reduced to his childish form; she will treat the arrogant sex in an ironical and unceremonious fashion. Sometimes, for example, she will frighten the child by threatening that the mark of his maleness will be cut off unless he behaves. Even if she is humbler, more gentle, and respects in her son the hero of the future, she is forced to reduce him to his present, immanent reality in order to make him really hers: just as she treats her husband as a child, so she treats her child as a baby. It is too rational, too simple, to believe that she would like to castrate her son; her dream is more contradictory: she would have him of unlimited power, yet held in the palm of her hand, dominating the world, yet on his knees before her. She encourages him to be soft, greedy, generous, timid, quiet, she forbids sport and playmates, she makes him lack self-confidence, because she intends to *have him* for herself; but she is disappointed if at the same time he fails to become an adventurer, a champion, a genius worthy of her pride. There is no doubt her influence is often injurious—as Montherlant and other writers have represented it to be. Fortunately for the boy, he can rather easily escape the toils: he is encouraged to do so by tradition and the social group. And the mother herself is resigned to it, for she knows very well that the struggle against man is an unequal one. She consoles herself by playing the part of *mater dolorosa* or by thinking how proud she is to have engendered one of her conquerors.

The little girl comes nearer to being wholly given over to her mother, and the claims of the latter are therefore increased. Their relations are much more dramatic. In her daughter the mother does not hail a member of the superior caste; in her she seeks a double. She projects upon her daughter all the ambiguity of her relation with herself; and when the otherness, the alterity, of this *alter ego* comes to be affirmed, the mother feels herself betrayed. It is between mother and daughter that the conflicts of which I have spoken take aggravated form.

There are women sufficiently satisfied with life to desire reincarnation in a daughter or at least to accept a daughter without disappointment; they will want to give the child the opportunities they have had and also those they have missed; they will make her youth a happy one. Colette has given us the portrait of one of these well-balanced and generous mothers: Sido dearly loved her daughter without infringing on her freedom; she filled her life with joy without making any demands, because she drew her happiness from her own heart. It may happen that the mother, in her devotion to this double in which she recognizes and transcends herself, will end by projecting herself totally upon her daughter; renouncing her ego, she makes her child's happiness her only care; she may even be egotistical and hard toward the rest of the world. The danger she runs is that of becoming annoying to the one she adores, as did Mme de Sévigné to her daughter, Mme Grignan; the girl will angrily try to rid herself of a devotion that is tyrannical; often she has poor success in this effort and all her life remains infantile, timid in facing her responsibilities, because she has been too carefuly watched over. But it is above all a certain masochistic type of motherliness that threatens to weigh offensively upon the young girl. Some women feel their femininity as an absolute curse; such a woman wishes for or accepts a daughter with the bitter pleasure of self-recognition in another victim, and at the same time she feels guilty for having brought her into the world. Her remorse and the pity she feels through her daughter for herself are manifested in endless anxieties; she will hardly go a step away from her child; she will sleep in the same room with her for fifteen or twenty years; the little girl will be destroyed in the fire of that restless passion.

Most women simultaneously demand and detest their feminine condition; they live it through in a state of resentment. The disgust they have for their sex might well lead them to give their daughters a man's education, but they are rarely large-minded enough. Vexed at having produced a woman, the mother greets her with this ambiguous curse: "You shall be a woman." She hopes to compensate for her inferiority by making a superior creature out of one whom she regards as her double; and she also tends to inflict upon her the disadvantages from which she has suffered. Sometimes she tries to impose on the child exactly her own fate: "What was good enough for me is good enough for you; I was brought up this way, you shall share my lot." Sometimes, on the contrary, she grimly forbids the child to resemble her; she wants her experience to be of some use, it is one way of having a second chance. The prostitute sends her daughter to a convent, the ignorant woman has hers educated. In S. de Tervagne's *Asphyxie*, the mother, who sees in her daughter the detested consequence of a youthful error, furiously admonishes her:

> Try to understand. If such a thing should happen to you, I would disown you. As for me, I didn't know a thing. A sin! A vague idea, sin. If a man calls out to you, don't go to him. Con-

tinue on your way. Don't turn around. You understand me? You are forewarned; that mustn't happen to you, and if it should happen, I would have no pity on you, I would leave you in the gutter.

Real conflicts arise when the girl grows older; as we have seen, she wishes to establish her independence from her mother. This seems to the mother a mark of hateful ingratitude; she tries obstinately to checkmate the girl's will to escape; she cannot bear to have her double become *an other*. The pleasure of feeling absolutely superior—which men feel in regard to women—can be enjoyed by woman only in regard to her children, especially her daughters; she feels frustrated if she has to renounce her privilege, her authority. Whether a loving or a hostile mother, the independence of her child dashes her hopes. She is doubly jealous: of the world, which takes her daughter from her, and of her daughter, who in conquering a part of the world robs her of it.

This jealousy is at first concerned with relations between the little girl and her father. Sometimes the mother makes use of the child to bind her husband to the home; if she fails she is naturally vexed, but if the scheme succeeds, she at once revives her childish complex in inverse form: that is, she is incensed against her daughter as she was formerly against her mother; she sulks, she feels abandoned and misunderstood. A Frenchwoman, married to a foreigner who dearly loved his daughters, one day cried angrily: "I have had enough of this living with aliens!"

Frequently the oldest girl, her father's favorite, is the special object of the mother's persecution. She loads her with disagreeable tasks, requires of her a sobriety beyond her age: since she is a rival, she will be treated as an adult; she, too, will have to learn that "life is no novel, no bed of roses; you can't do as you please, you are not on earth just to have a good time," and so on. Very often the mother slaps the child without rhyme or reason: "That will teach you." For one thing, she means to show that she still has the upper hand—for what is most vexatious is that the mother has no real superiority to oppose to a girl of eleven or twelve; the latter is already able to perform household tasks perfectly, she is "quite a little woman"; she even has a vivacity, a curiosity, and a clear-sightedness that make her in many ways superior to adult women. The mother likes to rule alone over her feminine universe; she wants to be unique, irreplaceable; and now she finds herself reduced by her young helper to the status of one among many who merely perform a general function. She scolds her daughter severely if, after two days' absence, she finds the house in disorder; but she is filled with anger and fear if she finds that the life of the family goes on perfectly well without her. She cannot bear to have her daughter become really her double, a substitute for herself.

It is even more intolerable, however, for her to have her daughter boldly assert herself as an *other*, an independent person. She systematically takes a dislike to the friends among whom her daughter seeks help against family oppression and who "work on her feelings"; she criticizes them, forbids her daughter to see them too often or even to be with them at all, on the pretext that they "have had a bad influence" on her. Any influence that is not hers is bad, but she feels a special animosity toward women of her own age—teachers, mothers of companions—with whom the little girl becomes affectionate; such feelings, she says, are ridiculous or morbid. Sometimes the child's gaiety, heedlessness, games, laughter, are enough to exasperate her. These things are more easily pardoned in boys, for they are enjoying their masculine privileges, as is natural; and she has long since given up a hopeless struggle. But why should her daughter, this other woman, enjoy advantages denied to her? Ensnared in "serious" matters herself, she is envious of all the occupations and amusements that take the girl out of the boredom of the home; this escape gives the lie to all the values to which she has sacrificed herself.

The older the child gets, the more does resentment gnaw at the mother's heart; each year brings her nearer her decline, but from year to year the young body develops and flourishes; it seems to the mother that she is robbed of this future which opens before her daughter. Here is the source of the irritation some women feel when their daughters first menstruate: they begrudge them their being henceforth real women. In contrast with the repetition and routine that are the lot of the older woman, this newcomer is offered possibilities that are still unlimited: it is these opportunities that the mother envies and hates; being unable to obtain them for herself, she often tries to decrease or abolish them. She keeps the girl in the house, watches her, tyrannizes over her; she purposely dresses her like a fright, gives her no leisure time, gets savagely angry if the girl uses make-up, if she "goes out"; all her resentment against life she turns against this young life which is springing toward a new future. She endeavors to humiliate the young girl, she ridicules her ventures, she nags her. Open war is often declared between them. Normally the younger wins, for time works with her; but her victory is tinged with wrongdoing. Her mother's attitude gives rise at the same time to revolt and remorse; the mere presence of her mother makes her a culprit. We have seen how heavily this feeling of guilt can burden her future. Willy-nilly, the mother accepts defeat in the end; when her daughter becomes an adult, a more or less uneasy friendship is established between them. But the one remains forever disappointed and frustrated; the other will often believe that she is under a curse.

We shall turn later to the relation between the mother of advanced age and her older children, but it is evidently during the first twenty years that children occupy the most important place in their mother's life. The dangerous falsity of two currently accepted preconceptions is clearly evident from what I have just been saying about these early relations.

The first of these preconceptions is that maternity is enough in all cases to crown a woman's life. It is nothing of the kind. There are a great many mothers who are unhappy, embittered, unsatisfied. Tolstoy's wife is a significant example; she was brought to childbed more than twelve times and yet writes constantly in her journal about the emptiness and uselessness of everything, including herself. She tells of calm and happy moments, when she enjoyed being indispensable to her children, and she speaks of them as her sole weapon against the superiority of her husband; but all this was absolutely insufficient to give meaning to her boresome existence. At times she felt capable of anything, but there was nothing for her beyond caring for the children, eating, drinking, sleeping; what should have brought happiness made her sad. She wished ardently to bring her children up well, but the eternal struggle with them made her impatient and angry.

The mother's relation with her children takes form within the totality of her life; it depends upon her relations with her husband, her past, her occupation, herself; it is an error as harmful as it is absurd to regard the child as a universal panacea. This is also Helene Deutsch's conclusion in the work, often quoted above, in which she examines the phenomena of maternity in the light of her psychiatric experience. She gives this function a high importance, believing that through it woman finds complete self-realization—but on condition that it is freely assumed and *sincerely* wanted; the young woman must be in a psychological, moral, and material situation that allows her to bear the effort involved; otherwise the consequences will be disastrous. In particular, it is criminal to recommend having a child as a remedy for melancholia or neurosis; that means the unhappiness of both mother and child. Only the woman who is well balanced, healthy, and aware of her responsibilities is capable of being a "good" mother.

As we have seen, the curse which lies upon marriage is that too often the individuals are joined in their weakness rather than in their strength—each asking from the other instead of finding pleasure in giving. It is even more deceptive to dream of gaining through the child a plenitude, a warmth, a value, which one is unable to create for oneself; the child brings joy only to the woman who is capable of disinterestedly desiring the happiness of another, to one who without being wrapped up in self seeks to transcend her own existence. To be sure, the child is an enterprise to which one can validly devote oneself; but it represents a ready-made justification no more than any other enterprise does; and it must be desired for its own sake, not for hypothetical benefits. As Stekel well says: [9]

Children are not substitutes for one's disappointed love, they are not substitutes for one's thwarted ideal in life, children are not mere material to fill out an empty existence. Children are a responsibility and an opportunity. Children are the loftiest blossoms upon the tree of untrammeled love. . . . They are neither playthings, nor tools for the fulfillment of parental needs or ungratified ambitions. Children are obligations; they should be brought up so as to become happy human beings.

There is nothing *natural* in such an obligation: nature can never dictate a moral choice; this implies an engagement, a promise to be carried out. To have a child is to undertake a solemn obligation; if the mother shirks this duty subsequently, she commits an offense against an existent, an independent human being; but no one can impose the engagement upon her. The relation between parent and offspring, like that between husband and wife, ought to be freely

---

[9] *Frigidity in Woman*, Vol. II, pp. 305, 306.

willed. And it is not true, even, that having a child is a privileged accomplishment for woman, primary in relation to all others; it is often said of a woman that she is coquettish, or amorous, or lesbian, or ambitious, "for lack of a child"; her sexual life, the aims, the values she pursues, would in this view be substituted for a child. In fact, the matter is originally uncertain, indeterminate: one can say as well that a woman wants a child for lack of love, for lack of occupation, for lack of opportunity to satisfy homosexual tendencies. A social and artificial morality is hidden beneath this pseudo-naturalism. That the child is the supreme aim of woman is a statement having precisely the value of an advertising slogan.

The second false preconception, directly implied by the first, is that the child is sure of being happy in its mother's arms. There is no such thing as an "unnatural mother," to be sure, since there is nothing natural about maternal love; but, precisely for that reason, there are bad mothers. And one of the major truths proclaimed by psychoanalysis is the danger to the child that may lie in parents who are themselves "normal." The complexes, obsessions, and neuroses of adults have their roots in the early family life of those adults; parents who are themselves in conflict, with their quarrels and their tragic scenes, are bad company for the child. Deeply scarred by their early home life, their approach to their own children is through complexes and frustrations; and this chain of misery lengthens indefinitely. In particular, maternal sado-masochism creates in the daughter guilt feelings that will be expressed in sado-masochistic behavior toward her children, and so on without end.

There is an extravagant fraudulence in the easy reconciliation made between the common attitude of contempt for women and the respect shown for mothers. It is outrageously paradoxical to deny woman all activity in public affairs, to shut her out of masculine careers, to assert her incapacity in all fields of effort, and then to entrust to her the most delicate and the most serious undertaking of all: the molding of a human being. There are many women whom custom and tradition still deny the education, the culture, the responsibilities and activities that are the privilege of men, and in whose arms, nevertheless, babies are put without scruple, as earlier in life dolls were given them to compensate for their inferiority to little boys. They are permitted to play with toys of flesh and blood.

Woman would have to be either perfectly happy or a saint to resist the temptation to abuse her privileges. Montesquieu was perhaps right when he said that it would be better to turn over to women the government of the State rather than that of the family; for if she is given opportunity, woman is as rational, as efficient, as a man; it is in abstract thought, in planned action, that she rises most easily above her sex. It is much more difficult, *as things are*, for her to escape from her woman's past, to attain an emotional balance that nothing in her situation favors. Man, also, is much more balanced and rational at work than at home; he makes his business calculations with mathematical precision, but he becomes illogical, lying, capricious, at home with his wife, where he "lets down." In the same way she "lets down" with her child. And her letting down is more dangerous because she can better defend herself against her husband than can the child against her. It would clearly be desirable for the good of the child if the mother were a complete, unmutilated person, a woman finding in her work and in her relation to society a self-realization that she would not seek to attain tyrannically through her offspring; and it would also be desirable for the child to be left to his parents infinitely less than at present, and for his studies and his diversions to be carried on among other children, under the direction of adults whose bonds with him would be impersonal and pure.

Even when the child seems a treasure in the midst of a happy or at least a balanced life, he cannot represent the limits of his mother's horizon. He does not take her out of her immanence; she shapes his flesh, she nourishes him, she takes care of him. But she can never do more than create a situation that only the child himself as an independent being can transcend; when she lays a stake on his future, her transcendence through the universe and time is still by proxy, which is to say that once more she is doomed to dependency. Not only her son's ingratitude, but also his failure will give the lie to all her hopes: as in marriage or love, she leaves it to another to justify her life, when the only authentic course is freely to assume that duty herself.

We have seen that woman's inferiority originated in her being at first limited to repeating life, whereas man invented reasons for living more essential, in his eyes, than the not-willed routine of mere existence; to restrict woman to maternity would be to perpetuate this situation. She demands today to have a part in that mode of activity in which humanity tries continually to find justification through transcendence, through movement toward new goals and accomplishments; she cannot consent to bring forth life unless life has meaning; she cannot be a mother without endeavoring to play a role in the economic, political, and social life of the times. It is not the same thing to produce cannon fodder, slaves, victims, or, on the other hand, free men. In a properly organized society, where children would be largely taken in charge by the community and the mother cared for and helped, maternity would not be wholly incompatible with careers for women. On the contrary, the woman who works—farmer, chemist, or writer—is the one who undergoes pregnancy most easily because she is not absorbed in her own person; the woman who enjoys the richest individual life will have the most to give her children and will demand the least from them; she who acquires in effort and struggle a sense of true human values will be best able to bring them up properly. If too often, today, woman can hardly reconcile with the best interests of her children an occupation that keeps her away from home for hours and takes all her strength, it is, on the one hand, because feminine employment is still too often a kind of slavery, and, on the other, because no effort has been made to provide for the care, protection, and education of children outside the home. This is a matter of negligence on the part of society; but it is false to justify it on the pretense that some law of nature, God, or man requires that mother and child belong exclusively to one another; this restriction constitutes in fact only a double and baneful oppression.

It is fraudulent to maintain that through maternity woman becomes concretely man's equal. The psychoanalysts have been at great pains to show that the child provides woman with an equivalent of the penis; but enviable as this manly attribute may be, no one pretends that its mere possession can justify or be the supreme end of existence. There has also been no dearth of talk about the sacred rights of the mother; but it is not as mothers that women have gained the right to vote, and the unwed mother is still in disrepute; it is only in marriage that the mother is glorified—that is, only when she is subordinated to a husband. As long as the latter remains the economic head of the family, the children are much more dependent on him than on her, though she is much more occupied with them than he is. That is the reason, as we have seen, why the relation of the mother to her children is intimately affected by that which she maintains with her husband.

Thus the relations between husband and wife, the tasks of housekeeping, and maternity, form a whole in which all the factors affect each other. Affectionately united with her husband, the wife can cheerfully carry the housekeeping load; happy in her children, she will be forbearing with her husband. But such harmony is not easy to attain, for the various functions assigned to woman are out of tune with one another. The women's magazines are full of advice to the housekeeper on the art of preserving her sexual attractiveness while washing dishes, of continuing to be well dressed during pregnancy, of reconciling coquetry, maternity, and economy. But even the wife who follows such counsel unswervingly will soon be distracted and disfigured by her cares; it is very difficult to remain desirable with dishpan hands and a body deformed by maternities. This is why the amorous type of woman feels resentment toward the children who ruin her seductiveness and deprive her of her husband's attentions. If, on the other hand, she is of the deeply maternal type, she is made jealous by her husband's claim to own the children along with everything else.

Then again, the "good" housekeeper is in opposition to the activities of life, as we have seen: the child is the foe of waxed floors. Maternal love often loses itself in the angry scolding that goes with the care of a well-kept home. It is not surprising that the woman who struggles among these contradictions very often passes her days in a state of nervousness and acrimony; she always loses in one way or another, and her gains are precarious, they are not registered in any surely successful outcome. She can never find salvation in her work itself; it keeps her busy but it does not justify her existence, for her justification rests with free personalities other than her own. Shut up in the home, woman cannot herself establish her existence; she lacks the means requisite for self-affirmation as an individual; and in consequence her individuality is not given recognition. Among the Arabs and the Indians and in many rural populations a woman is only a female domesticated animal, esteemed according to the work she does and replaced without regret if she disappears. In modern civilization she is more or less individualized in her husband's eyes; but unless she completely renounces her ego, engulfing herself like the Natasha of *War and Peace* in a passionate and tyrannical devotion to her family, she suffers from being reduced to pure generality. She is *the* housekeeper, *the* wife, *the* mother, unique and undiscriminated; Natasha delights in this supreme self-abasement and, by rejecting all comparisons, denies the existence of *others*. But modern Western woman wants, on the contrary, to feel that people distinguish her as *this* housekeeper, *this* wife, *this* mother, *this* woman. That is the satisfaction she will seek in social life.

CHAPTER XVIII

Social Life

THE FAMILY is not a closed community: its isolation is qualified by communications set up with other social units; the home is not merely an "interior" within which the couple is shut away; it is also the expression of that couple's standard of life, its financial status, its taste, and thus the home must needs be on view to other people. It is essentially the woman's part to direct this social life. The man is joined to the community, as producer and citizen, by bonds of an organic solidity based upon the division of labor; the couple is a social person, defined by the family, the class, the circle, and the race to which it belongs, attached by bonds of a mechanical solidity to groups of corresponding social situation; the wife can embody this relation most purely, for the husband's professional associations are often out of tune with his social standing, whereas the wife, with no occupational demands, can confine herself to the society of her equals. Furthermore, she has the leisure to keep up, by "paying calls" and having "at-homes," those relations which are of no practical use and which, of course, are important only in classes whose members are intent upon holding their rank in the social scale—that is to say, who consider themselves superior to certain others. She delights in the display of her "interior," even of her own appearance, which her husband and children do not notice because they are familiar with them. Her social duty, which is "to make a good showing," combines with her pleasure in letting herself be seen.

And, in the first place, she must "make a good showing" where she is herself concerned; in the house, attending to her work, she is merely clothed; to go out, to receive, she "dresses up." Formal attire has a double function: it is intended to indicate the social standing of the woman (her standard of living, her wealth, the social circles to which she belongs), but at the same time it puts feminine narcissism in concrete form; it is a uniform and an adornment; by means of it the woman who is deprived of *doing* anything feels that she expresses what she *is*. To care for her beauty, to dress up, is a kind of work that enables her to take possession of her person as she takes possession of her home through housework; her ego then seems chosen and re-created by herself. Social custom furthers this tendency to identify herself with her appearance. A man's clothes, like his body, should indicate his transcendence and not attract attention; [1] for him neither elegance nor good looks call for his setting himself up as object; moreover, he does not normally consider his appearance as a reflection of his ego.

Woman, on the contrary, is even required by society to make herself an erotic object. The purpose of the fashions to which she is enslaved is not to reveal her as an independent individual, but rather to cut her off from her transcendence in order to offer her as prey to male desires; thus society is not seeking to further her projects but to thwart them. The skirt is less convenient than trousers, high-heeled shoes impede walking; the least practical of gowns and dress shoes, the most fragile of hats and stockings, are most elegant; the costume may disguise the body, deform it, or follow its curves; in any case it puts it on display. This is why dressing up is an enchanting game for the little girl, who loves to contemplate herself; later her childish independence rises in rebellion against the constraint imposed by light-colored muslins and patent-leather shoes; at the awkward age the girl is torn between the wish and the refusal to display herself; but when she has once accepted her vocation as sexual object, she enjoys adorning herself.

Through adornment, as I have pointed out,[2] woman allies herself to nature while bringing to nature the need of artifice; for man she becomes flower and gem—and for herself also. Before bestowing upon him the undulations of water, the warm softness of furs, she takes them herself. Her relation to her knickknacks, her rugs, her cushions, and her bouquets is much less intimate than to the feathers, pearls, brocades, and silks she blends with her flesh; their iridescent hues and their soft textures make up for the harshness of the erotic universe that is her lot; she values them the more, the less her sensuality finds satisfaction. If many lesbians dress in mannish fashion, it is not only by way of imitation of the males and defiance to society; they are in no need of the caresses of velvet and satin because they find the same

---

[1] As noted in Book I. Exception must be made for homosexuals, since they regard themselves, precisely, as sexual objects; and also for fops, who call for separate study. In particular, the current "zoot-suitism" of American Negroes, with their bright-colored and showily tailored garb, has very complex causes.

[2] Book I, pp. 158 ff.

passive qualities upon a feminine body.[3] The heterosexual woman, dedicated to the crude masculine embrace—even if she likes it and all the more if she does not—has no fleshly prey to embrace other than her own body, so she perfumes it to change it into a flower, and the gleam of diamonds in her necklace mingles with the luster of her skin; in order to possess them, she identifies herself with all the riches of the world. She covets not only their sensuous delights, but sometimes their sentimental and ideal values also. This jewel is a souvenir, that one a symbol. There are women who make of themselves a nosegay, a cage of birds; there are others who are museums, still others who are hieroglyphics. Georgette Leblanc writes as follows in her *Mémoires*, recalling her youthful years:

> I was always dressed like a picture. I would go for a week as a Van Eyck, as one of Rubens's allegories, or as Memling's *Virgin*. I can still see myself crossing a Brussels street one winter's day in a dress of amethyst velvet, trimmed with silver braid borrowed from some chasuble. Dragging a long train which I scorned to lift, I conscientiously swept the sidewalks. My yellow fur hood framed my blond hair, but the most unusual item was the diamond set on a frontlet in the middle of my forehead. The reason for all this? Simply that I enjoyed it and it made me feel I was living quite unconventionally. The more I was laughed at, the more burlesque my attire became. I would have been ashamed to change any detail of my appearance because it was made fun of. That would have seemed a degrading surrender. . . . At home it was different. My models were the angels of Gozzoli and Fra Angelico, the figures of Burne-Jones and Watts. I was always dressed in azure and gold; my flowing robes spread about me in manifold trains.

The best examples of this magical appropriation of the universe are found in asylums for the insane. The woman who fails to control her love for precious objects and for symbols forgets her own true appearance and ventures to dress extravagantly. Thus the little girl regards dressing up as a disguise that changes her into a fairy, a queen, or a flower; she thinks herself beautiful when she is loaded with wreaths and ribbons, because she identifies herself with this marvelous finery.

[3] Sandor, a homosexual described by Krafft-Ebbing, adored well-dressed women, but she never "dressed up." (See page 412 above.)

The naïve young girl, charmed by the color of some material, does not notice the sallow tint reflected in her complexion. This lush bad taste is found also in adult artists and intellectuals more fascinated with the external world than conscious of their own appearance; enchanted with these antique fabrics, these ancient jewels, they delight in evoking China or the Middle Ages and take but a hasty and biased glance in the mirror. At times one wonders at the strange trappings affected by older women: diadems, laces, gaudy dresses, and odd necklaces; these unfortunately attract attention to their ravaged features. Having lost their power of seduction, many of these women have come to the point where dressing up is an idle game, as in their early youth. A woman of elegance, on the contrary, can if need be seek sensuous or æsthetic pleasure in her toilette, but she will certainly keep it appropriate to her appearance; the color of her gown will favor her complexion, its cut will emphasize or improve her figure. What she treasures is herself adorned, and not the objects that adorn her.

The toilette is not only adornment; as I have said, it also indicates woman's social situation. Only the prostitute, functioning exclusively as an erotic object, should display herself as this and no more; like the saffron-dyed hair and the flower-strewn robe of antiquity, the high heels, clinging satin, heavy make-up, and strong perfumes of today advertise her profession. Any other kind of woman is subject to criticism if she "dresses like a streetwalker." Her erotic capacities are integrated with the life of society and should be evident only in this sober light. But let it be emphasized that decency by no means consists in dressing with strict modesty. A woman who appeals too obviously to male desire is in bad taste; but one who seems to reject it is no more commendable. People think that she wants to be mannish and is probably a lesbian, or that she wants to render herself conspicuous and is doubtless an eccentric. In refusing her role as object, she is defying society; she is perhaps an anarchist. If she simply wants to be inconspicuous, she must remain feminine. Custom regulates the compromise between exhibitionism and modesty; at one time it is the bosom that the "decent woman" must cover, at another time the ankles; sometimes the young girl may emphasize her charms to attract prospects, while the married woman gives up all adornment, as in many peasant cultures; at other times young girls are obliged to wear filmy, candy-colored frocks of conservative cut, while older women are permitted clinging gowns, heavy materials, rich colors, and provocative styles; on a sixteen-year-old, black seems showy because it is not worn at that age.[4]

These rules are not to be disregarded, of course; but in all cases, even in the most conventional circles, the sexual aspect of woman will be emphasized; a clergyman's wife, for example, has her hair waved, wears light make-up, and follows the mode discreetly, indicating by the care she takes of her physical attractiveness that she accepts her role as female. This integration of the erotic with social life is especially evident in the evening gown. To indicate that it is a social occasion, marked, that is, by luxury and conspicuous waste, these gowns should be costly and fragile; they should also be as inconvenient as possible; the skirts are long and so wide or so hobble-like as almost to prohibit walking; beneath her jewels, flounces, spangles, flowers, feathers, and false hair, a woman is changed into a doll of flesh. Even this flesh is on show; like open, blooming flowers, women display their shoulders, backs, and bosoms. Except in orgies, men are not supposed to show too much interest in all this; they are limited to casual glances and the embraces of the dance; but each can find enchantment in being the king of a world full of such delicate treasures. As regards the men, the party here takes on the aspect of a potlatch, a ceremonial in which gifts are exchanged; each one offers, as a gift to all the others, the spectacle of the feminine body that is his property. In evening costume the wife is disguised as a woman, to serve the pleasure of all the males and gratify the pride of her proprietor.

This social significance of the toilette allows woman to express, by her way of dressing, her attitude toward society. If she is submissive to the established order, she will assume a discreet and stylish personality. Here there are many possible nuances: she can present herself as fragile, childlike, mysterious, frank, austere, gay, sedate, rather bold, demure. Or if, on the contrary, she scorns the conventions, she will make it evident by her originality. It is noteworthy that in many novels the "emancipated woman" differentiates herself by an audacity of dress that emphasizes her nature as sexual object, therefore her dependence. For example, in Edith Wharton's *The Age of Innocence* the young divorcee, who has an adventurous past and an audacious heart, appears first in extreme décolleté; the ripple of scandal that she

---

[4] In an otherwise stupid film set in the last century, Bette Davis created a scandal by wearing a red dress to a ball, when white was the proper thing for unmarried girls. Her action was looked upon as a revolt against the established order.

arouses is for her a clear reflection of her disdain for conformity. Similarly, the young girl will enjoy dressing like a mature woman, the older woman like a little girl, the courtesan like a woman of good society, and the latter like a "vamp."

Even if each woman dresses in conformity with her status, a game is still being played: artifice, like art, belongs to the realm of the imaginary. It is not only that girdle, brassiere, hair-dye, make-up, disguise body and face; but that the least sophisticated of women, once she is "dressed," does not present *herself* to observation; she is, like the picture or statue, or the actor on the stage, an agent through whom is suggested someone not there—that is, the character she represents, but is not. It is this identification with something unreal, fixed, perfect as the hero of a novel, as a portrait or a bust, that gratifies her; she strives to identify herself with this figure and thus to seem to herself to be stabilized, justified in her splendor.

In just this way, in Marie Bashkirtsev's *Écrits intimes* we see her tirelessly multiplying her image in page after page. She spares us no one of her costumes; with each new toilette, she believes herself quite transformed, and she renews her self-adoration.

I took a large shawl of Mother's, I cut a hole for my head and sewed the sides together. This shawl, falling in classic folds, gave me an Oriental, Biblical, exotic air.

I go to Laferrière's and Caroline in three hours makes me a gown in which I seem enveloped in a cloud. It is just a piece of English crepe which she drapes on me and which makes me thin, elegant, tall.

Enveloped in a flowing robe of warm wool, I was a figure of Lefebvre, who knows so well how to bring out his young and lissome bodies under modest draperies.

She repeats this refrain day after day: "I was charming in black. . . . In gray I was charming. . . . I was in white, charming."

Mme de Noailles gave great importance to dress, and in her *Mémoires* she sadly relates the drama of a gown that failed.

I loved lively colors, their bold contrasts; a gown seemed like a landscape, a start on the road of destiny, a promise of adventure. But when I put on one that had been poorly made, I did not fail to suffer on account of the defects that then appeared.

If the toilette has so much importance for many women, it is because in illusion it enables them to remold the outer world and their inner selves simultaneously. A German novel, *The Young Girl in Artificial Silk*, by I. Keun, describes the passion of a young girl for a cloak of white fur. She loved its sensuous warmth and, enveloped in its precious folds, she experienced a feeling of beatitude and security; and in it she possessed a world of beauty and a destiny quite beyond her in reality.

Since woman is an object, it is quite understandable that her intrinsic value is affected by her style of dress and adornment. It is not entirely futile for her to attach so much importance as she does to silk or nylon stockings, to gloves, to a hat, because it is an imperative obligation for her to keep up her position. In America a large part of the working girl's budget is assigned to beauty care and clothes. In France this expense is lighter; none the less the better showing a woman makes, the more she is respected; the more necessary it is for her to work, the more advantageous it is for her to appear prosperous; smart appearance is a weapon, a flag, a defense, a letter of recommendation.

Elegance is also a bondage; its benefits have to be paid for; and the cost is so dear that, now and then, a department-store detective catches a society woman or an actress in the act of stealing perfumes, silk stockings, underwear, or the like. Many women engage in prostitution or accept financial "assistance" in order to be well dressed; it is the toilette that makes them need extra money. Being well dressed also takes time and care; but it is a task that sometimes affords positive joys; in this sphere, as in family marketing, there are possible discoveries of hidden treasure, bargain-hunting, stratagems, schemes, and ingenuities. If she is clever, a woman can even run up sartorial creations for herself. Bargain days are made adventures. A new dress is a celebration. Make-up or hair-do can substitute for creating a work of art. Today, more than formerly,[5] woman knows the joy of developing her body through sports, gymnastics, baths, massage, and health diets; she decides what her weight, her figure, and the color of her skin shall be. Modern æsthetic concepts permit her to combine beauty

---

[5] It would seem, however, that according to recent surveys the women's gymnasia in France are today almost deserted; it was especially in the period between 1920 and 1940 that Frenchwomen were addicted to physical culture. In recent years the difficulties of housekeeping have been too severe.

and activity: she has a right to trained muscles, she declines to get fat; in physical culture she finds self-affirmation as subject and in a measure frees herself from her contingent flesh; but this liberation easily falls back into dependence. The Hollywood star triumphs over nature, but she becomes a passive object again in the producer's hands.

Besides these victories, in which woman may rightly rejoice, keeping attractive implies—like the upkeep of the home—a struggle against duration; for her body also is an object that deteriorates with time. In *On joue perdant* Colette Audry has described this combat, comparable with the housekeeper's battle with dust:

> Already it was no longer the solid flesh of youth; the shapes of her muscles along arm and thigh showed under a layer of fat covered with slackened skin. Worried, she again revised her schedule: in the morning a half-hour of setting-up exercises, and at night, before going to bed, fifteen minutes of massage. She began to consult medical books and fashion magazines, to watch her waistline. She made fruit juices to drink, she took laxatives occasionally, and she wore rubber gloves for washing the dishes. Her two concerns— to rejuvenate her body and to furbish her house—finally became one, so that in the end she reached a kind of dead center. . . . The world was as if stopped, suspended outside aging and decay. . . . At the swimming pool she now took serious lessons to improve her style, and the beauty magazines held her attention with their oft repeated recipes. Ginger Rogers confides: "I use a hundred strokes of my hairbrush every morning; it takes exactly two minutes and a half, and my hair is silken. . . ." How to slenderize your ankles: every day raise yourself thirty times on tiptoe without touching the heels to the floor; this exercise takes only a minute, and what is a minute out of a whole day? Another time it was an oil bath for fingernails, or a lemon for the hands, or crushed strawberries for the cheeks.

Here again routine makes drudgery of beauty care and the upkeep of the wardrobe. Horror at the depreciation that all living growth entails will arouse in certain frigid or frustrated women a horror of life itself: they endeavor to preserve themselves as others preserve furniture or canned food. This negative obstinacy makes them enemies of their own existence and hostile to others: good meals spoil the figure, wine injures the complexion, too much smiling brings wrinkles, the sun damages the skin, sleep makes one dull, work wears one out, love puts rings under the eyes, kisses redden the cheeks, caresses deform the breasts, embraces wither the flesh, maternity disfigures face and body. We know how angrily the young mother wards off a child attracted by her ball gown: "Don't touch me with your clammy hands, you'll spoil my dress!" The coquette similarly rebuffs the eager attention of husband or lover. She would like to shield herself from men, from the world, from time, as one protects furniture with slip-covers.

But all these precautions do not prevent the appearance of gray hairs and crow's-feet. Woman knows from youth that this fate is unavoidable. And in spite of all her prudence, accidents will happen: wine is spilled on her dress, a cigarette burns it; this marks the disappearance of the luxurious and festive creature who bore herself with smiling pride in the ballroom, for she now assumes the serious and severe look of the housekeeper; it becomes all at once evident that her toilette was not a set piece like fireworks, a transient burst of splendor, intended for the lavish illumination of a moment. It is rather a rich possession, capital goods, an investment; it has meant sacrifice; its loss is a real disaster. Spots, rents, botched dressmaking, bad hairdo's are catastrophes still more serious than a burnt roast or a broken vase; for not only does the woman of fashion project herself into things, she has chosen to make herself a thing, and she feels directly threatened in the world. Her relations with dressmaker and milliner, her fidgeting, her strict demands—all these manifest her serious attitude and her sense of insecurity. A successful gown makes her the personage of her dreams; but in a twice-worn toilette, or in one that is a failure, she feels herself an outcast. Marie Bashkirtsev tells us that her humor, deportment, and facial expression, all depended on her gown; when she was not appropriately dressed she felt awkward, common, and therefore humiliated. Many women would rather miss an occasion than go badly dressed, even if they are not going to be noticed as individuals.

While some women, however, assert that they "dress for themselves," we have seen that even in narcissism being observed by others is implied. Women fond of dress are hardly ever entirely satisfied not to be seen, except among the insane; usually they want witnesses. After ten years of marriage Tolstoy's wife still wished to be admired and to have her husband see she did. She liked ribbons and ornaments and wanted to have her hair waved; and if no one noticed, what matter? But she felt like crying.

A husband is not good in this role of witness. Here again his requirements are equivocal. If his wife is too attractive he gets jealous; but every husband is more or less of a King Candaules; [6] he wants his wife to do him credit, to be elegant, pretty, or at least "passable"; if not, he is likely to be ill-humored and sarcastic when they have company. We have seen that in marriage erotic and social values are not well reconciled, and this antagonism is reflected here. The wife who emphasizes her sex appeal shows bad taste, in her husband's opinion; he disapproves audaciousness that he would find seductive in another woman, and this disapproval kills any desire he might otherwise feel. If his wife dresses modestly, he approves, but without enthusiasm: he does not find her attractive and feels vaguely reproachful. Because of this he seldom inspects her on his own account; he views her through the eyes of others. "What will people say about her?" His conjectures are not likely to be right, for he credits others with his husbandly point of view.

Nothing irritates a woman more than to see her husband admire in another woman the clothes and behavior which he criticizes in her case. It should be said, moreover, that he is too close to her to see her; to him her face is always the same; he does not notice either her new toilette or her changes in hair-do. Even a loving husband or an ardent lover will often be indifferent to a woman's clothes. If they love her intensely in the nude, even the most becoming costumes do no more than conceal her; and she will be as dear to them when poorly dressed or tired out as when dazzling. If they no longer love her, the most flattering clothes will not do any good. Dress can be a weapon of conquest, but not a defensive weapon; its art is to create mirages, it presents an imaginary object to the eye; but in the carnal embrace, as in the familiarity of everyday life, all mirages fade from view; conjugal sentiment, like physical love, exists on the plane of reality. Woman does not dress for the man she loves. In one of her

---

[6] A king of ancient Lydia, who was so proud of his wife that he showed her naked to one of his ministers.—TR.

novels [7] Dorothy Parker describes a young wife impatiently awaiting her husband's visit on leave; she decides to make herself beautiful for the event:

> She bought a new dress; black—he liked black dresses—simple—he liked plain dresses—and so expensive that she would not think of its price. . . .
> "Do you really like my dress?"
> "Oh, yes," he said. "I always liked that dress on you."
> It was as if she turned to wood. "This dress," she said, enunciating with insulting distinctness, "is brand new. I have never had it on before in my life. In case you are interested, I bought it especially for this occasion."
> "I'm sorry, honey," he said. "Oh, sure, now I see it's not the other one at all. I think it's great. I like you in black."
> "At moments like this," she said, "I almost wish I were in it for another reason."

It has often been said that woman dresses to inspire jealousy in other women, and such jealousy is in fact a clear sign of success; but it is not the only thing aimed at. Through the envious or admiring approval obtained, she seeks to gain an absolute affirmation of her beauty, her elegance, her taste—herself; she shows herself to bring herself into being. In this she submits to a painful dependence; the devotion of the housekeeper is useful even if it fails of recognition; the coquette's efforts are in vain if they attract no one's attention. She seeks a definite valuation of herself, and it is this demand for the absolute that makes her quest so harassing; condemned by one single voice, this hat *is* ugly; a compliment pleases her but a failure ruins her; and as the absolute is manifested only in an infinite series of cases, she will never obtain final success. This is why the woman of fashion, the coquette, is highly vulnerable; it also explains why some pretty and much admired women can be sadly convinced that they are neither beautiful nor elegant, that what they lack is precisely the final approbation of an unknown judge; for they aim at a permanent state of being (the *en-soi*) which is not capable of realization. Rare indeed are those superb women of fashion who in themselves embody the laws of elegance, whom no one can find in error because it is they who define

---

[7] *The Lovely Leave* (Viking Press, 1944), pp. 25, 32.

success and failure by fiat; while their rule endures, they can be re-garded as models of success. Unfortunately this success is of no use to anybody.

The toilette simultaneously implies going out and entertaining; for that matter, this was its original purpose. A woman parades her new costume from one drawing-room to another and invites other women to see her preside over her own. On certain especially formal occasions her husband accompanies her on her calls; but usually he is at work when she attends to her "social duties." The deadly ennui that afflicts these functions has been described a thousand times. It is explained by the fact that women brought together by social "obligations" have nothing worth while to say to each other. No common interest unites the wives of lawyer and doctor—or the wives of Dr. Doe and Dr. Roe. It is bad form in general conversation to talk about the children's pranks or domestic difficulties. So the women are reduced to com-ments on the weather and the latest best-seller, or perhaps to some general ideas borrowed from their husbands. The custom of holding at-homes is gradually dying out; but in various forms the tiresome duty of paying calls survives in France. In America bridge frequently re-places conversation, an advantage only for women who enjoy the game.

But social life does have aspects more attractive than this tiresome performance of conventional duties. A reception involves something more than merely welcoming others into a woman's own home; it changes this dwelling into a domain of enchantment; the social func-tion is at once a party and a ceremony. The hostess displays her treas-ures: silver, linen, glassware; she arranges cut flowers. Ephemeral and useless, flowers typify the needless extravagance of parties marked by expense and luxury; open in their vases, doomed to early death, they take the place of bonfires, incense and myrrh, libations, offerings. The table is laden with fine food and precious wines. The idea is to devise gracious gifts, which, while supplying the needs of the guests, antici-pate their desires; the repast is changed into a mysterious ceremony. Virginia Woolf emphasizes this aspect in a passage from *Mrs. Dallo-way:* [8]

And so there began a soundless and exquisite passing to and fro through swing doors of aproned white-capped maids, handmaidens

[8] New York: Harcourt, Brace & Co. (1925); pp. 157–8, 184–5, 259.

not of necessity, but adepts in a mystery or grand deception prac-
tised by hostesses in Mayfair from one-thirty to two, when, with a
wave of the hand, the traffic ceases, and there rises instead this
profound illusion in the first place about the food—how it is not
paid for; and then that the table spreads itself voluntarily with glass
and silver, little mats, saucers of red fruit; films of brown cream
mask turbot; in casseroles severed chickens swim; coloured, un-
domestic, the fire burns; and with the wine and the coffee (not
paid for) rise jocund visions before musing eyes; gently speculative
eyes; eyes to whom life appears, musical, mysterious.

The woman who presides over these mysteries is proud to feel herself the creator of a perfect moment, the bestower of happiness and
gaiety. It is through her that the guests have been brought together,
an event has taken place; she is the gratuitous source of joy and harmony.

This is exactly what Mrs. Dalloway feels:

But suppose Peter said to her, "Yes, yes, but your parties—what's
the sense of your parties?" all she could say was (and nobody could
be expected to understand): They're an offering. . . . Here was
So-and-so in South Kensington; some one up in Bayswater; and
somebody else, say, in Mayfair. And she felt quite continuously a
sense of their existence; and she felt what a waste; and she felt what
a pity; and she felt if only they could be brought together; so she
did it. And it was an offering; to combine, to create; but to whom?

An offering for the sake of offering, perhaps. Anyhow, it was her
gift. Nothing else had she. . . .

Anybody could do it; yet this anybody she did a little admire,
couldn't help feeling that she had, anyhow, made this happen.

If there is pure generosity in this service rendered to others, the
party is truly a party. But social routine has had the effect of quickly
changing celebration into institution, gift into obligation, and of ele-
vating the party to the status of a rite. While enjoying the dinner-party,
the guest is forcibly reminded that she must give one in return: she
complains at times of being entertained too lavishly. "The X's just
wanted to impress us," she tells her husband sourly. I was informed,
for example, that during the last war the teas in a small Portuguese

city became very expensive parties, for at each gathering the hostess felt obliged to outdo the last in the variety and quantity of her cakes; this became so costly that one day all the women agreed not to provide anything to eat with the tea.

In such circumstances giving parties loses its generous magnificence and becomes one more burdensome duty; festive articles only give trouble: the glassware and tablecloth must be looked after, the champagne and sweets made ready in due quantity; a cup broken, the upholstery of a chair burned, mean disaster; next day it is necessary to clean up, put things in order. The wife dreads this additional work. She experiences that multifarious subjection which marks the lot of the housekeeper: she is subject to the soufflé, the roast, the butcher, the cook, the extra help; she is subject to her husband, frowning at some hitch; she is subject to the guests, sizing up the furniture and the wines and deciding whether or not the party has been a success.

Only women who are generous and sure of themselves will serenely undergo such an ordeal. A success can give them much satisfaction. But many are in this respect like Mrs. Dalloway, who loved these triumphs, these semblances, with their brilliance and excitement, yet felt their hollowness. A woman cannot really enjoy them if she takes them too seriously; otherwise she will know the torments of vanity forever unsatisfied. There are, moreover, few women fortunate enough to find in social functions full occupation for their lives. Those who devote themselves entirely to society usually try not only to make it a cult of self-worship but also to go beyond this party life toward certain loftier aims: the true salons have a literary or political cast. Women endeavor in this way to gain ascendancy over men and to play a personal role. They get away from the condition of the married woman. The latter seldom finds full self-realization in the ephemeral pleasures and triumphs sometimes vouchsafed her, which indeed often mean fatigue for her as much as diversion. The life of society demands that she "make a showing," that she put herself on exhibition, but not that she establish any true communication between herself and others. It does not take her out of her isolation.

"It is sad to think," writes Michelet,[9] "that woman, the relative being who can live only as a member of a couple, is more often alone than is

---

[9] French historian and man of letters, and author of a famous treatise on love.—TR.

man. He finds company everywhere, constantly makes new contacts. She is nothing without the family. And the family is a crushing burden; all its weight rests on her." And, in truth, woman in her confinement and isolation does not know the joys of the comradeship implied in the common pursuit of certain aims; her work does not occupy her mind, her training has given her neither a desire for independence nor any experience in using it, and yet she passes her days in solitude. Marriage may have taken her far from her family and the friends of her youth, and it is difficult to compensate for this uprooting through new acquaintances and letters from home. And there may often exist no true intimacy between the young wife and her family, even when close by: neither her mother nor her sisters are real friends. At the present time many young couples live with their in-laws, for lack of housing; but this enforced association is by no means always a source of real companionship for the bride.

The feminine friendships that she succeeds in keeping or forming are precious to a woman, but they are very different in kind from relations between men. The latter communicate as individuals through ideas and projects of personal interest, while women are confined within their general feminine lot and are bound together by a kind of immanent complicity. And what they look for first of all among themselves is the affirmation of the universe they have in common. They do not discuss opinions and general ideas, but exchange confidences and recipes; they are in league to create a kind of counteruniverse, the values of which will outweigh masculine values. Collectively they find strength to shake off their chains; they negate the sexual domination of the males by admitting their frigidity to one another, while deriding the men's desires or their clumsiness; and they question ironically the moral and intellectual superiority of their husbands and of men in general.

They compare experiences; pregnancies, births, their own and their children's illnesses, and household cares become the essential events of the human story. Their work is not a technique; by passing on recipes for cooking and the like, they endow it with the dignity of a secret science founded on oral tradition. Sometimes they discuss moral problems. The correspondence columns of women's magazines provide good examples of what they talk about; one can hardly imagine a "lonely hearts" column for men only; men meet in *the* world, which is their world, while women have to define, measure, and ex-

plore their special domain; their correspondence deals especially with
beauty counsel, recipes for cooking, directions for knitting; and they
ask for advice; through their propensity for chatter and self-display
genuine anxiety sometimes emerges.

Woman knows that the masculine code is not hers, that man takes
for granted she will not observe it since he urges her to abortion,
adultery, wrongdoing, betrayals, and lies, which he condemns officially. She therefore calls upon other women to help define a set of
"local rules," so to speak, a moral code specially for the female sex.
It is not merely through malevolence that women comment on and
criticize the behavior of their friends interminably; in order to pass
judgment on others and to regulate their own conduct, women need
much more moral ingenuity than do men.

What gives value to such relations among women is the truthful-
ness they imply. Confronting man, woman is always play-acting; she
lies when she makes believe that she accepts her status as the inessential other, she lies when she presents to him an imaginary personage
through mimicry, costumery, studied phrases. These histrionics require a constant tension; when with her husband, or with her lover,
every woman is more or less conscious of the thought: "I am not being myself"; the male world is harsh, sharp-edged, its voices are too
resounding, the lights too crude, the contacts rough. With other
women, a woman is behind the scenes; she is polishing her equipment,
but not in battle; she is getting her costume together, preparing her
make-up, laying out her tactics; she is lingering in dressing-gown and
slippers in the wings before making her entrance on the stage; she
likes this warm, easy, relaxed atmosphere. In *Le Képi* Colette shows
us two friends peacefully sewing and discussing little details of the
work, exchanging small confidences, practicing new make-ups. And
in contrast with this quiet scene is one in which preparations are being made for one of the friends to meet a young man. The atmosphere
is more serious; there are to be no tears: the make-up! An unbought
dress is regretted; fine silk stockings must be borrowed; to wear or not
to wear a flower must be decided; there are so many questions! In such
circumstances women help one another, discuss their social problems,
each creating for the others a kind of protecting nest; and what they
do and say is genuine.

For some women this warm and frivolous intimacy is dearer than
the serious pomp of relations with men. The narcissist finds, as in her

adolescence, a privileged double in another woman; it is through the other's attentive and competent eyes that she can admire her well-cut gown, her exquisite "interior." After her marriage her best friend remains a favorite witness; and she may also continue to seem a desirable object, and a desired one. As I have said, there are homosexual tendencies in almost every young girl, and the often awkward embraces of a husband do not efface them; this is the source of that sensual sweetness felt by a woman when with her intimates—a feeling without equivalent in normal men. Between woman friends this sensual attachment may be sublimated in lofty sentimentality, or it may be expressed through caresses of diffuse or specific nature. Their dalliance can also be only an amusement for leisure moments—as with women of the harem, whose main concern is to kill time—or it can have primary importance.

Women's fellow feeling rarely rises to genuine friendship, however. Women feel their solidarity more spontaneously than men; but within this solidarity the transcendence of each does not go out toward the others, for they all face together toward the masculine world, whose values they wish to monopolize each for herself. Their relations are not constructed on their individualities, but immediately experienced in generality; and from this arises at once an element of hostility. Natasha, in *War and Peace*, while deeply attached to the women of her family because she could have them witness the births of her babies, nevertheless had jealous feelings toward them, for to Pierre each one of them might embody *woman*. Women's mutual understanding comes from the fact that they identify themselves with each other; but for the same reason each is against the others. A housewife has more intimate relations with her maid than any man—unless he be homosexual—ever has with his valet or chauffeur; they exchange confidences, at times they are accomplices; but there exists also a hostile rivalry between them, for the mistress, while avoiding the actual work, wishes to have responsibility and credit for it; she wants to be thought irreplaceable, indispensable. "If I'm not there, everything goes wrong." She harshly finds her servant at fault, or tries to; if the latter does her tasks too well, the mistress loses her satisfaction of feeling herself unique. In the same way she is continually at odds with the teachers, governesses, nurses, and nursemaids who attend to her children, and with the relatives and friends who help with her work; her pretext is that they do not respect her "wishes," do not follow her "ideas." The truth is that she has neither wishes nor ideas peculiar to her; what vexes her is that, on the contrary, others perform her function precisely as she would. This is one of the main sources of all the domestic arguments that poison family life: every woman demands to be sovereign the more insistently as she lacks means for making her peculiar qualifications known.

But it is above all in the sphere of coquetry and love that each woman sees in every other an enemy. I have referred to that type of rivalry in young girls; it often continues for life. We have seen that the ideal of the woman of fashion, the "socialite," is an absolute valuation; she suffers if ever the aura of glory is missing; she hates to see the least halo crowning another, any approbation received by another she takes away; if an absolute is not unique, what is it? A woman sincerely in love is content to reign in the heart of her lover; she will not feel envious of her friends' superficial successes, but she feels that danger threatens her own affair. In fact, the theme of woman betrayed by her best friend is not a mere literary convention; the more friendly two women are, the more dangerous their duality becomes. The confidante is invited to see through the eyes of the woman in love, to feel through her heart, her flesh; she is attracted by the lover, fascinated by the man who has seduced her friend. She thinks that her loyalty protects her well enough to permit her giving free rein to her feelings, but she also dislikes playing a merely inessential role, and before long she is ready to yield, to make advances. Many women prudently avoid intimates once they are in love. This ambivalence makes it hardly possible for women to repose much confidence in their mutual feelings. The shadow of the male always hangs darkly over them. Even when he goes unmentioned, the line of St. John Perse [1] is applicable: "And the sun is not mentioned, but his presence is among us."

When by themselves, women take their revenge upon man, prepare their traps for him, curse and insult him—but they are awaiting him. As long as they are stagnating where no man is, they are sunk in contingence, in vapidity and ennui. This limbo still keeps a little of the warmth of the maternal bosom—but it is limbo. Woman dallies there with pleasure only on condition that she can anticipate an early emergence. Thus she takes pleasure in the moist warmth of her bathroom only if she imagines the brightly lighted drawing-room where she will soon make her entrance. Women are comrades in captivity

---

[1] Pen name of Alexis St.-J. Léger Léger, contemporary French poet.—TR.

for one another, they help one another endure their prison, even help one another prepare for escape; but their liberator will come from the world of men.

For most women this masculine world retains its glamour after they are married; only the husband loses his prestige; the wife discovers that in her specimen the pure essence of man is degraded. But man none the less remains the truth of the universe, the supreme authority, the marvelous, master, eye, prey, pleasure, adventure, salvation; he still incarnates transcendence, he is the answer to every question. The most loyal wife never consents to renounce this marvel and shut herself away in dull communion with a contingent, limited individual. From her childhood she retains the imperious need for a guiding hand; when her husband fails to fill this role, she turns to some other man. Sometimes her father, a brother, an uncle, or other relative, an old friend, has kept his prestige; she will lean on him.

But there are two categories of men especially destined by profession to become confidants and mentors: priests and doctors. The first enjoy the great advantage of not charging for consultation; the confessional lays them open without defense to the idle talk of devotees; they shun known pests as well as they can, but it is their duty to lead their sheep along the paths of morality, and this duty becomes the more urgent as women take on more social and political importance and as the Church endeavors to make instrumental use of them. The "director of conscience" dictates the political opinions of his penitent and governs her vote. And many husbands are angered by his interference with their married life, for it is for the confessor to say what private practices of the bedchamber are right or wrong. He shows an interest in the children's education; he advises the wife on how she shall conduct herself with her husband. The woman who has always looked up to a god in man kneels in ecstasy at the feet of the male who is the earthly substitute for God.

The doctor is better protected because he demands payment; and he can close his door to clients who are too obtrusive. But he is the object of more specific and obstinate attack; three fourths of the men pursued by overerotic women are doctors; unveiling the body in a man's presence represents for many women a great exhibitionistic pleasure. Stekel reports many cases of this kind: especially old maids who come to the doctor for trifling reasons and ask for "a very thorough examination," or go from one gynecologist to another in quest of "massage" or "treatment"; some frigid wives experience orgasm during medical examination only.[2]

The woman readily imagines that the man to whom she has exposed herself has been impressed by her physical charms or by the beauty of her soul, and thus she persuades herself, in pathological cases, that she is loved by the doctor or priest. Even if she is normal, she feels that a subtle bond exists between the man and herself; she takes pleasure in respectful obedience to his injunctions; sometimes, what is more, she gains a sense of security that helps her to accept the life she has to live.

There are wives, however, who are not content with moral authority as a prop for existence; there is a deep need in their lives for the exaltation of romance. If they wish neither to deceive nor to leave their husbands, they will take the same course as does the young girl who fears males of flesh and blood: they abandon themselves to imaginary passions. Stekel also gives various examples of this. A respectable married woman of good position falls in love with an opera tenor. She sends him flowers and notes, buys pictures of him, dreams of him. But when she has a chance to meet him she does not go; she does not want him in person, but desires merely to love him while remaining a faithful wife. Another woman loved a celebrated actor and had a room full of his pictures and references to him in print. When he died she went into mourning for a year.

We well remember the tears shed when Rudolph Valentino died. Married women and girls worship the heroes of the movies. Their images are evoked in solitary pleasure or in the fantasies of conjugal intercourse. And they may revive some childhood memory, playing the part of a grandfather, brother, teacher, or the like.

But there are also real, living men in the wife's environment; whether she is sexually satisfied or frigid or frustrated—save in the very rare case of a love that is complete, absolute, exclusive—she prizes their approbation very highly. The accustomed glance of her husband has no longer the power to animate her image of herself; her need is for eyes still full of mystery to discover her as mystery; she must be in the presence of a sovereign consciousness to receive

---

[2] Dr. R. L. Dickinson, famous American gynecologist, reports a number of cases of the same kind in his works (with Lura Beam) A *Thousand Marriages* (1931), and *The Single Woman* (1934). Many patients simply displayed more or less eroticism, but others made such pests of themselves that the doctor would refuse further treatment, or he would cool their ardor by hurting them intentionally.—TR.

her confidences, to revive her faded photographs, to bring back that dimple near the corner of her mouth and that quiver of the eyelashes that were hers alone; she is desirable, lovable, only if she is desired and loved. If she is pretty well adjusted in marriage, she seeks from other men chiefly the satisfactions of vanity; she invites them to join in her cult of self; she is seductive and pleasing, content to dream of forbidden loves, to think: "If I wished . . ." She prefers to charm many admirers rather than to become deeply attached to one of them; more ardent, less shy than the young girl, her coquetry requires males to confirm her in her consciousness of her value and power; she is often all the bolder since, being anchored in her home and having succeeded in conquering one man, she carries on the game without any great expectations and without much risk.

It may happen that after a longer or shorter period of fidelity the wife ceases to confine herself to this merely flirtatious or coquettish behavior. Her decision to deceive her husband is often born of resentment. Adler maintains that woman's infidelity is always a mode of revenge. That is going too far, but unquestionably she often yields less to the seduction of her lover than to a desire to defy her husband: "He is not the only man in the world—others can find me attractive —I am not his slave; he thinks he is pretty clever, but he can be fooled." It may be that the flouted husband retains primary importance in the wife's eyes; just as the young girl sometimes takes a lover by way of revolt against her mother, in order to find fault with her parents, to disobey them, to assert herself, so a wife whose very resentment attaches her to her husband seeks in her lover a confidant, a witness of her pose as victim, an accomplice in the disparagement of her husband. She talks to him continually about her husband, pretending to feed her lover's scorn; and unless the lover plays his part well, she will turn her back on him in a bad temper and either return to her husband or seek another consoler. But very often it is less resentment than disappointment that throws her into the arms of a lover; she has not found love in marriage, and she finds it difficult to resign herself to never knowing the delights and joys that in expectation charmed her youth. In frustrating women, by depriving them of all erotic satisfaction, in denying them liberty and individuality of feeling, marriage leads them toward adultery by an inevitable and ironical dialectic. In his essay "On Some Verses of Virgil" Montaigne says:

We train them from childhood for the business of love. Their charm, their dressing, their knowledge, their language, all their instruction, tend to no other end. Their governesses imprint nothing in them but the idea of love, if for no other reason than to disgust them with it by holding it constantly before them. . . .

It is folly then to attempt to bridle in women a desire that is so burning and so natural to them.

And Engels says:

With monogamy becoming permanent, two characteristic social figures appear: the wife's lover and the cuckold. . . . Along with monogamy and hetairism, adultery becomes an inevitable social institution, proscribed, severely punished, but impossible to suppress.

If conjugal love-making has excited the wife's curiosity without satisfying her senses, she is likely to finish her education in some other bed. If her husband has succeeded in awakening her sexuality, she will want to enjoy the same pleasures with others because she has no special feeling of attachment for him.

Moralists deplore the preference shown the lover, and I have described the attempt in bourgeois literature to rehabilitate the figure of the husband; but it is absurd to defend him by showing that in the eyes of society—that is, of other men—he is often superior to his rival. What counts here is how he looks to his wife. Now, there are two characteristics that make him odious to her. In the first place, he is the one who undertakes the ungrateful role of initiator; the contradictory requirements of the traditional virgin, who dreams of being at once violated and respected, condemns him almost necessarily to failure; she therefore remains forever frigid in his arms. With her lover she experiences neither the terror of defloration nor the first humiliation of outraged modesty; she is spared the trauma of surprise: she knows about what to expect; more frank, less easily offended, less naïve than on her wedding night, she is no longer confused between ideal love and physical desire, sentiment and sex feeling. When she takes a lover, a lover is what she really wants.

This clear-sightedness is one aspect of the freedom of the choice she makes. For here is the second objectionable characteristic that handicaps the husband: he has usually been imposed, not chosen. His wife either accepted him as a last resort or was turned over to him by her family; in any case, even if she married him for love, she has made him her master in marrying him; their relations have become a duty, and often enough he has come to seem to her a tyrant. Doubtless the choice of a lover is also limited by circumstances, but there is an element of liberty in this relation; to marry is an obligation, to take a lover is a luxury. The wife yields because her lover begs her to, and so she is certain at least of his desire, if not of his love; what takes place is not a matter of obeying the laws. The lover also has an advantage in that his allurements and his prestige are not dulled by the friction of everyday life: he remains apart, an other. Then too, she feels that in their meetings she is getting out of her ordinary self, finding a new opulence in life: she feels herself an other, a new woman. This is what some women seek above all in a liaison: to be engrossed, surprised, taken out of themselves by the other. When a break comes, they feel a despairing sense of emptiness. Janet reports [3] some of his psychiatric cases that show us, in the losses sustained, what woman seeks and finds in her lover:

> One woman of thirty-nine, in despair at being abandoned by a writer who had let her share in his work for five years, wrote that his life was so rich and he was so despotic that she was completely taken up with him and could think of nothing else. Another, aged thirty-one, was ill from the break; she wished she were an inkwell on his desk, just to see him. She explained that she had been bored; her husband knew nothing, gave her no mental occupation, understood nothing, didn't *surprise* her; his common sense was deadening. But her lover was an *astonishing* man, never emotional, cold enough to make one die of chagrin. And with that a boldness, *sang-froid*, wit, a quickness of mind, which turned her head.

There are women who get this feeling of plenitude and joyous excitement only at the beginning of a liaison; if her lover does not give her pleasure immediately—which often happens, the partners being frightened at first and not yet adapted to each other—she feels resentment and disgust; she may become a Messalina and engage in many affairs, quitting one lover after another. But it also happens that a woman, enlightened by the failure of her marriage, is attracted this

---

[3] In *Les Obsessions et la psychasthénie.*

time by just the kind of man to suit her, and in consequence a durable attachment is created between them. She often finds him attractive because he is of a type quite opposite to that of her husband. It was no doubt the contrast Sainte-Beuve offered to Victor Hugo that attracted Adèle, the latter's wife. Stekel cites the case of a woman married to a rough, brutal, athletic husband whose attentions caused her only pain. She met a lawyer's secretary who was frail, gentle, and amiable. He showed her delicate attentions, and they found they had spiritual interests in common. Closer intimacy revealed that his relatively feeble powers banished her frigidity. Following her divorce, they were married and lived happily ever after; he could bring her to orgasm with kisses and caresses alone, she who had been accused of frigidity by a very potent husband!

Not all liaisons thus turn out like a fairy tale. It may be that just as the young girl dreams of a liberator who will take her away from her family, so the wife awaits the lover who will take her from under the marital yoke. An oft-exploited theme is that of the ardent lover who cools off and departs when his mistress begins to speak of marriage; she is often hurt by his cautious reserve on this point, and the relations they do have are perverted by resentment and hostility. If a liaison becomes stabilized, it often takes on a familiar, conjugal character in the end; there will again be found in it all the vices of marriage: ennui, jealousy, calculation, deception, and the like. And the woman will dream of still another man to rescue her from this routine.

Adultery, further, takes on very different aspects, according to circumstances and customs. Marital infidelity in our civilization, where patriarchal traditions survive, still seems much more heinous for the wife than for the husband. Montaigne remarks:

> What an iniquitous appraisal of vices! . . . We commit and weigh our vices not according to nature but according to our interest, whereby they take on such unequal shapes. The severity of our decrees makes the addiction of women to this vice a sorer fault than its nature warrants, and involves it in consequences that are worse than their cause.

We have considered the original reasons for this severity: woman's adultery risks bringing the son of a stranger into the family, and thus defrauding legitimate heirs; the husband is master; the wife his property. Social changes, the practice of birth control, have robbed these motivations of much of their force. But the continuing will to keep woman in a state of dependency perpetuates the prohibitions that still surround her. She frequently interiorizes them; she closes her eyes to her husband's marital vagaries, though her religion, her morality, her "virtue," forbid the same behavior on her part. The restraint imposed by her entourage—especially in the small towns of the Old World as well as the New—is much more severe for her than for her husband: he goes out more, he travels, and there is more indulgence for his defections; she risks losing her reputation and her status as a married woman. The stratagems by which women succeed in foiling this watchfulness have often been described, and I myself knew a little Portuguese town of old-fashioned austerity where the young wives never go out unless accompanied by a mother-in-law or a sister-in-law; but the hairdresser rents rooms in which lovers can enjoy brief meetings. In a large city the wife has far fewer jailers; but a small circle of recent acquaintances is hardly more favorable to the growth of illicit sentiment. Hasty and clandestine, adultery does not create humane and free relationships; the falsehoods it involves end by destroying all dignity in marriage.

In many circles women have today gained some degree of sexual liberty; but it remains a difficult problem for them to reconcile their life in marriage with erotic satisfaction. Since marriage does not generally involve physical love, it would seem reasonable to separate them quite candidly. Admittedly a man can make an excellent husband and yet be inconstant: his sexual episodes do not in fact prevent him from carrying on the enterprise of a joint life in amity with his wife; this amity will even be the purer, the less ambivalent, if she does not represent a chain. We could concede the same for the wife; and, indeed, she often wishes to share her husband's life, to make a home for their children, and yet experience other loves. What makes adultery degrading is the compromise of character made necessary by hypocrisy and caution; an agreement based on liberty and sincerity would do away with one of the defects of marriage.

It must be recognized, however, that *today* the annoying formula: "It's not the same thing for a woman," still retains some truth. There is nothing *natural* about the difference referred to. It has been maintained that woman has less need of sexual activity than man, but nothing is less certain; repressed women make shrewish wives, sadistic mothers, fanatical housekeepers, unhappy and dangerous creatures. But in any case, even if woman's desires were less frequent, that would be no reason to consider their satisfaction superfluous.

The difference lies in the total erotic situation of man and woman, as defined by tradition and present-day society. The act of love for woman is still considered a *service* she renders to man, which therefore makes him seem her master. As we have seen, he can always *take* a woman who is an inferior, but it is degrading if a woman *gives herself* to a male who is socially beneath her; her consent is in either case in the nature of a surrender, a fall. A wife often accepts with good grace the fact that her husband possesses other women; she may even feel flattered: some women go so far as to imitate Mme de Pompadour and act the procuress.[4] On the other hand, in her lover's embrace the woman is changed into object, prey; it seems to the husband that she is possessed by a foreign mana, she has ceased to be his, he has been robbed of her. And the fact is that in bed the woman often feels herself, wishes herself, and, in consequence, *is* dominated. The fact is also that, because of masculine prestige, she tends to approve and to imitate the other male who, having possessed her completely, embodies in her eyes man in general. The husband is annoyed—and not without reason—to hear her familiar mouth echo a stranger's thought —he almost feels that he has himself been possessed, violated. If Mme de Charrière broke with young Benjamin Constant, who, as we have seen, played the feminine role in relation to two masculine women, it was because she could not bear to feel him marked by the hated influence of Mme de Staël. As long as woman makes herself a slave and reflects the man to whom she "gives herself," she must needs recognize the fact that her infidelities are more seriously disruptive than those of her husband.

If she does preserve her integrity, she still risks compromising her husband in her lover's mind. A wife may even be likely to feel that in yielding to another man—if only once, in haste, on a sofa—she has gained a certain superiority over her legitimate spouse. With still better reason a man who believes that he has gained possession of his mistress may think that he has made a fool of her husband. This is why an author sometimes represents his heroine as deliberately choos-

---

[4] I am speaking here of marriage. As we shall see, the attitude of the couple is reversed in the liaison.

ing a lover of lower social class; she seeks sensual satisfaction from him, but she does not wish to give him the advantage over a respected husband. In *Man's Fate* Malraux shows us a couple who have made an agreement to accord each other full liberty; yet when May tells Kyo that she has slept with a friend, he is pained at the thought that the man will imagine he has "had" her; Kyo made his decision to respect her independence because he well knew that no one ever *has* anybody; but the complacent notions entertained by another man hurt and humiliate him through May. People confuse the free woman with the loose woman. The lover himself is prone to mistake the freedom from which he profits; he prefers to believe that his mistress has yielded, has let herself be led on, that he has conquered, seduced her. A woman of pride can resign herself to the vanity of her partner, but she will find it odious for an esteemed husband to have to put up with his arrogance. It is difficult indeed for a woman to act on a plane of equality with men as long as this equality is not universally recognized and concretely realized.

In any case, adultery, friendships, society, are only diversions in married life; they can be of help in bearing its constraints but do not break them. They are unsound evasions, which by no means enable woman to take the control of her fate truly into her own hands.

CHAPTER XIX

Prostitutes and Hetairas

MARRIAGE, as we have seen,[1] is directly correlated with prostitution, which, it has been said, follows humanity from ancient to modern times like a dark shadow over the family. Man, for reasons of prudence, vows his wife to chastity, but he is not himself satisfied with the regime imposed upon her. Montaigne tells us with approval:

> The kings of Persia were wont to invite their wives to join them in their banquets; but when the wine began to excite them in good earnest and they felt impelled to give the reins to sensuality, they sent them away to their private apartments, that they might not make them partake of their immoderate lust, and caused other women to come in their stead, toward whom they did not feel such an obligation of respect.

Sewers are necessary to guarantee the wholesomeness of palaces, according to the Fathers of the Church. And it has often been remarked that the necessity exists of sacrificing one part of the female sex in order to save the other and prevent worse troubles. One of the arguments in support of slavery, advanced by the American supporters of the institution, was that the Southern whites, being all freed from servile duties, could maintain the most democratic and refined relations among themselves; in the same way, a caste of "shameless women" allows the "honest woman" to be treated with the most chivalrous respect. The prostitute is a scapegoat; man vents his turpitude upon her, and he rejects her. Whether she is put legally under police supervision or works illegally in secret, she is in any case treated as a pariah.

Viewed from the standpoint of economics, her position corresponds with that of the married woman. In *La Puberté* Marro says: "The only difference between women who sell themselves in prosti-

---

[1] Book I, Part 2.

tution and those who sell themselves in marriage is in the price and
the length of time the contract runs." For both the sexual act is a
service; the one is hired for life by one man; the other has several
clients who pay her by the piece. The one is protected by one male
against all others; the other is defended by all against the exclusive
tyranny of each. In any case the benefits received in return for the
giving of their bodies are limited by existing competition; the husband knows that he could have secured a different wife; the performing of "conjugal duties" is not a personal favor, it is the fulfilling of
a contract. In prostitution, male desire can be satisfied on no matter
what body, such desire being specific but not individualized as to
object. Neither wife nor hetaira succeeds in exploiting a man unless
she achieves an individual ascendancy over him. The great difference
between them is that the legal wife, oppressed as a married woman,
is respected as a human being; this respect is beginning definitely to
check the oppression. So long as the prostitute is denied the rights
of a person, she sums up all the forms of feminine slavery at once.

It is naïve to wonder what motives drive woman to prostitution;
today we no longer accept Lombroso's theory that lumps prostitutes
and criminals together and sees degenerates in both; it may be, as
statistics show, that the mental level of prostitutes is slightly below
the average and that some are definitely feeble-minded, for mentally
retarded women would be likely to choose a profession that demands
no special training; but the majority are normal, some highly intelligent. No fatal hereditary factor, no physiological defect, weighs upon
them. The truth is that in a world where misery and unemployment
prevail, there will be people to enter any profession that is open; as
long as a police force and prostitution exist, there will be policemen
and prostitutes, more especially as these occupations pay better than
many others. It is pure hypocrisy to wonder at the supply that masculine demand stimulates; that is simply the action of an elementary
and universal economic process. "Of all the causes of prostitution,"
wrote Parent-Duchâtelet in his report of 1857, "none is more important than unemployment and the poverty inevitably resulting from
low wages." Right-thinking moralists reply sneeringly that the sob-
stories of whores are only so much romancing for the benefit of unsophisticated clients. As a matter of fact, the prostitute would often
have been able to make a living in other ways. But if the way she
has chosen does not seem to her to be the worst, that does not prove

that vice is in her blood; it rather condemns a society in which this occupation is still one of those which seem the least repellent to many women. It is often asked: why does she choose it? The question is, rather: why has she not chosen it?

It is noteworthy, for one thing, that a large proportion of harlots are former domestic servants. A glance at any maid's room is enough to explain that fact. Exploited, enslaved, treated as a thing rather than a person, the maid-of-all-work, the chambermaid, can look forward to no improvement in her lot; sometimes she has to accept the attentions of the head of the family. From such domestic slavery and sexual subjection she slips into a slavery that could not be more degrading and that she dreams will be happier. Moreover, domestics are likely to be far from home; it is estimated that eighty per cent of Parisian prostitutes are from the provinces or the country. A woman would be prevented from entering a generally discredited profession if her family were near by and she had to watch her reputation; but when she is lost in a great city and no longer integrated in society, the abstract idea of "morality" is no barrier at all.

As long as middle-class people surround the sexual act—and especially virginity—with strong taboos, just so long will they seem a matter of indifference in many peasant and working-class environments. Numerous investigations agree that a great many young girls let themselves be deflowered by the first comer and thereafter find it quite natural to yield to anyone. Dr. Bizard investigated one hundred prostitutes and obtained the following data: one had lost her virginity at the age of eleven, two at twelve, two at thirteen, six at fourteen, seven at fifteen, twenty-one at sixteen, nineteen at seventeen, seventeen at eighteen, six at nineteen; the rest after the age of twenty-one. Thus five per cent had been violated before puberty. More than half said they gave themselves for love, because they wanted to; the others had yielded through ignorance. The first seducer is often young. Usually it is a fellow worker in shop or office, or a childhood companion; next in frequency come soldiers, foremen, valets, and students; Dr. Bizard's list includes also two lawyers, an architect, a doctor, and a pharmacist. It is rather rare for the employer himself to play this role, as the popular legend has it; but it is often his son or his nephew or one of his friends. In another study Commenge mentions also forty-five young girls of ages twelve to seventeen who had been deflowered by strangers they never saw again; they yielded indifferently, without pleasure. The details of individual cases given in such reports show how frequently and under what varied conditions girls and young women yield to casual strangers, new acquaintances, and older relatives, in apparent ignorance of possible consequences or indifferent to them.

These girls who have yielded passively have none the less undergone the trauma of defloration, we may be sure; it would be desirable to know what psychological influence this brutal experience has had on their futures; but it is not customary to psychoanalyze prostitutes, and they are not good at self-description, usually taking refuge in clichés. In certain cases the readiness to give themselves to the first comer is to be explained by the prostitution-fantasies I have mentioned, for there are many very young girls who imitate prostitutes from resentment against their families, from horror of their dawning sexuality, or from a desire to act the grown-up. They use heavy make-up, associate with boys, act coquettishly and provocatively. Those who are still childish, nonsexual, cold, think they can play with fire in safety; one day some man takes them at their word, and they slip from dreams to acts.

"When a door has once been broken open, it is hard to keep it shut," said a young prostitute of fourteen, quoted by Marro. A young girl, however, rarely decides to go on the town immediately after her defloration. Sometimes she remains attached to her first lover and goes on living with him; she takes a "regular" job; when her lover abandons her, she consoles herself with another. Now that she no longer belongs to one man, she feels she can give herself to all; sometimes it is her lover—the first or the second—who suggests this way of earning money. There are also many girls who are prostituted by their parents; in certain families—like the famous American Jukes [2]—almost all the women are destined for this business. Among young female vagrants are many little girls abandoned by their relatives; they begin by begging and slip into prostitution. In his study already referred to, Parent-Duchâtelet found that of 5,000 prostitutes, 1,441 had been influenced by poverty, 1,425 seduced and abandoned, 1,255 abandoned and left without means of support by their parents. This was in 1857, but contemporary studies suggest almost

---

[2] A scientifically correct and up-to-date account of the Jukes and Kallikak families will be found in Amram Scheinfeld's *You and Heredity* (J. B. Lippincott Co., 1950), pp. 525 ff.—Tr.

the same conclusions. Sickness often drives into prostitution women who are unable to do real work or who have lost their jobs; it upsets delicately balanced budgets and compels women to find new resources quickly. Bearing an illegitimate child has the same result. More than half of the women in Saint-Lazare prison have had one child, at least. Many have raised from three to six, some more. Few abandon their children; indeed, some unmarried mothers enter prostitution in order to support their offspring. It is well known that prostitution increases during wars and subsequent social disorders.

Under the pen-name of Marie-Thérèse a prostitute has given an account of her life in the magazine *Temps modernes*; she got her start as follows:

> I was married at sixteen to a man thirteen years older than I was. I did it to get away from home. My husband's only thought was to keep me pregnant, "so as to keep me at home," he said. He objected to make-up and movies, and my mother-in-law was always around, telling me he was right. I had two babies within two years. . . . I was bored and took a course in nursing, which I liked. . . . In the hospital a brazen young nurse told me some things I did not know, but for six months I had nothing to do with men. One day a young fellow, crude but good-looking, came to my room and persuaded me that I could change my life, go to Paris with him, not work any more. . . . For a month I was really happy with him. One day he brought in a stylish-looking woman, who, he said, could look out for herself all right. At first I did not go along. I even got a job in a local clinic to show him I wouldn't go on the streets. But I couldn't resist long. He said I didn't love him or I would work for him. I cried; at the clinic I was always sad. Finally I let him take me to the hairdresser. . . . I began to do "short jobs"! Julot followed along behind me to see that I took care of myself and to warn me in case the police came.

In some ways this story conforms to the classical one of the girl put on the street by her pimp. It sometimes happens that this role is played by a husband. And sometimes by a woman. In a study [3] of 510 young prostitutes, it was found that 284 of them lived alone, 132 with a man friend, and 94 with a woman with whom they were

---

[3] L. Faivre: *Les Jeunes Prostituées vagabondes en prison* (1931).

usually in homosexual relations. A number of these girls said they had been debauched by other women, and some of them prostituted themselves to females.

Often enough a woman may consider prostitution as merely a temporary means of increasing her income, but it has often been told how she subsequently becomes enchained. If cases of "white slavery," in which she is caught in the toils through violence, false promises, deceptive offers of work, and the like, are relatively rare, it is common for her to be kept in the business against her will. The money needed for making a start has been furnished by a pimp or procurer, to whom she is obligated, who takes most of her earnings, and from whom she never gets to the point of freeing herself. Marie-Thérèse engaged in a real struggle for several years before she succeeded in getting away:

I finally grasped the fact that Julot only wanted my dough and I thought that if I could put some distance between us I could save up some money. . . . I was timid at first and a woman who knew Julot watched me and even counted my "callers." Julot wrote me to deposit my money every night with the madam "so as not to be robbed." . . . When I wanted to buy a dress, she said Julot told her not to give me any cash. I decided to get out of the house as soon as possible. But I was tricked and sent to the hospital. I had to go back to the house to earn money for my journey . . . but I stayed only a month. . . . I worked at another place, but had too much of a grudge against Julot to be able to stay in Paris: he abused me, struck me, once almost threw me out of the window. . . . I arranged with an agent to go out of the city, but when I heard Julot knew him, I did not go to the rendezvous. . . . I got away, but after six weeks I was fed up with the house. . . . Julot saw me in the street and struck me. I had had enough of Julot, and finally I made an agreement to go to Germany.

Literature has made "Julot" a well-known figure. He plays the part of protector in the life of the prostitute. He advances money to buy clothes, afterward he defends her against the competition of other women, against the police—sometimes he is a policeman himself— and against her clients, all of whom would be only too glad to use her without paying and some of whom would want to satisfy their sadism on her. In Madrid a few years ago the gilded youth of the fascists amused themselves throwing prostitutes into the river on cold nights; in France students out for a good time sometimes take girls into the country and leave them there at night, naked. To be sure of getting her money and to avoid rough treatment, the prostitute needs a man. He gives her moral support, too: "You don't work so well alone, have less heart in the work, you get slack," some say. She is often in love with him; it is through love that she got into the work, or justifies it. In her environment man is enormously superior to woman, and this setting apart favors a kind of love-religion, which explains the passionate abnegation of certain prostitutes. In her male's strength and violence such a girl sees the sign of his virility and submits to him all the more readily. With him she knows the jealousy and torments, but also the joys of the woman in love.

The prostitute, however, sometimes feels for her man only hostility and resentment; but she remains under his power through fear, because he keeps a grip on her, as we have seen in the story just quoted. So she may often console herself with a lover chosen from among her customers. Marie-Thérèse writes:

> All the girls had lovers in addition to their Julots, and I too. He was a sailor, a very fine fellow. In spite of the fact that he was a good lover, I could not tie up with him, but we were good friends. He often came upstairs with me without making love, just to talk; he said I ought to get out of there, it was no place for me.

They also turn to women. Many prostitutes are homosexual. We have noted that there has often been a homosexual experience at the beginning of the girl's career and that many continue to live with a woman friend. According to Anna Rueling, in Germany about twenty per cent of the prostitutes would seem to be homosexual. Faivre reports that in prison the young female inmates exchange pornographic letters, very passionate in tone, and signed "Yours for life." These letters correspond to those written by schoolgirls with "crushes"; the latter are less experienced, more timid; the former are unrestrained in their sentiments, in word as in act.

In the life of Marie-Thérèse—who was initiated by a woman—we see what a privileged part is played by the girl chum as compared with the despised customer and the tyrannical pimp:

Julot brought in a girl, a poor domestic who didn't even have shoes for her feet. The things she needed were all bought at the second-hand dealer's, and then she came to work with me. She was very agreeable, and as, moreover, she loved women, we got along quite well together. She reminded me of all I had learned with the nurse. We often had fun and, instead of working, went to the movies. I was glad to have her with us.

The prostitute's girl chum evidently plays much the same role as that of the male lover of the "honest" woman who lives surrounded by women: she is the companion in pleasure, she is the person with whom relations are free and disinterested, therefore quite voluntary. The prostitute, tired out by men, disgusted with them or merely looking for diversion, will often seek relaxation and pleasure in another woman's arms. In any case, the complicity I have referred to, which directly unites women, exists in greater strength here than anywhere else. Because their relations with one half of humanity are of a commercial kind and because society as a whole treats them as pariahs, prostitutes have a close solidarity among themselves; they may happen to be rivals, to feel jealous, to hurl insults at one another, to fight; but they profoundly need one another in order to form a counter-universe in which they regain their human dignity. The comrade is the preferred confidante and witness; it is she who will appreciate the dress and the coiffure intended for man's seduction but which seem like ends in themselves under the envious or admiring gaze of other women.

As to the relations of the prostitute and her clients, opinions are widely divergent and no doubt cases differ. It has often been emphatically stated that she reserves for her lover the kiss on the mouth,[4] as the expression of voluntary affection, and that she considers the embrace of love and the professional embrace two quite different things. Evidence given by men is suspect because their vanity makes them easily duped by the girl's simulated enjoyment. It must be said that things are very different when it is a matter of a rapid and fatiguing passage from one customer to another, or of repeated relations with a familiar client. Marie-Thérèse ordinarily practiced her

---

[4] See James Jones: *From Here to Eternity* (Charles Scribner's Sons, 1951), pp. 249 ff.: "The tabu said you never kissed a whore. They didn't like it. Their kiss was private, like most women's bodies. It was a rooted law."—TR.

trade with indifference, but she does recall certain nights as being delightful. It is not unknown for a girl to refuse to accept payment from a customer who has given her pleasure, and sometimes, if he is hard up, she offers to help him out.

In general, however, the woman is "cold" when professionally at work. Some of them feel toward the whole group of their customers nothing but indifference, tinged with contempt. "Ah, what saps men are! How easy it is for women to fill their heads with anything they please!" writes Marie-Thérèse. But many feel bitterly resentful toward men; they are, for one thing, sickened by men's abnormal tastes or "vices." Whether it is because they go to a brothel to indulge vicious tastes that they do not dare admit to their wives or mistresses, or because the fact of being in a brothel leads them to think up vices on the spur of the moment, the fact is that many men demand that the women join in various perversities. Marie-Thérèse complains that Frenchmen, in particular, have insatiable imaginations. Prostitutes will tell a sympathetic doctor that "all men are more or less vicious."

One of my friends talked at length with a young prostitute in Beaujon hospital; she was very intelligent, had begun as a domestic servant, and lived with a pimp, whom she adored. "Every man is vicious," she said, "except mine. That's why I love him. If he ever shows signs of any vice, I shall leave him. The first time a customer will not always dare, he will seem normal; but when he comes back, he will begin to want to do things. . . . You say your husband has no vices, but you will see. He has them all." She detested her clients on account of these vices. Another of my friends had become intimate with a prostitute at Fresnes, in 1943. The girl insisted that ninety per cent of her customers had vices, fifty per cent were disgraceful pederasts. If they were too imaginative, they frightened her. A German officer wanted her to parade naked around the room with an armful of flowers, while he imitated a bird taking flight; despite his generosity and politeness, she fled whenever she saw him coming in. Marie-Thérèse abhorred all such vagaries, though they were priced much higher than simple coitus and often gave the girl less trouble.

These three women were unusually intelligent and sensitive. Undoubtedly they felt that when they were no longer protected by business routine, when the man ceased to be just one more customer and took on individuality, they were the prey of a capricious being, con-

scious and free—it was no longer a simple purchase. Certain prostitutes, however, specialize in "vices," because of the higher pay.

There is often an element of class resentment in the hostility these
women feel toward their clients. Helene Deutsch [5] gives at some
length the history of the attractive Anna, who was usually gentle but
suffered from attacks of rage, especially against officials, which
brought her to a psychiatric clinic for treatment. Briefly, her home
life had been so unhappy that she refused ever to marry in spite of
good opportunities. She was well adjusted to her life as a prostitute,
but she was hospitalized for tuberculosis. She hated the doctors, as
she did all "respectable" men. "Why not?" she said. "Don't we know
better than anyone that these men easily drop their masks of gentility,
self-control, and importance and behave like beasts?" She was mentally well-balanced, apart from this attitude. Another young prostitute, Julia,[6] who had been promiscuous since she was fifteen, was
tender, sweet, and helpful only toward men she thought of as weak,
or poor and in need of help; "she regarded the others as wicked
beasts who deserved harsh treatment."

Most prostitutes are morally adapted to their mode of life. Not
that they are immoral congenitally or by heredity, but they feel integrated, and with reason, in a society that manifests a demand for
their services. They know very well that the edifying lecture of the
police sergeant who registers them is pure verbiage, and elevated
sentiments proclaimed by their clients outside the brothel do little
to intimidate them. Marie-Thérèse explains that paid or not, she is
equally called a whore, but if paid, an overshrewd one; when she
wants her money, the man will pretend he did not think she was *that*
kind of girl, and so on. Paid or not, it was all one to her.

It is not their moral and psychological situation that makes the
prostitutes' lot hard to bear. It is their material condition that is
most often deplorable. Exploited by their pimps and their madams,
they live in a state of insecurity, and three fourths of them are penni-
less. After five years of the life, about seventy-five per cent have
syphilis, according to doctors who have inspected thousands. Inexperienced minors, for example, are fearfully susceptible to infection;
twenty-five per cent should be operated on as a result of gonorrheal
complications. One in twenty has tuberculosis; sixty per cent become

---

[5] *Psychology of Women*, Vol. I, pp. 264 ff.
[6] Ibid., Vol. II, p. 36.

alcoholics or drug addicts; forty per cent die before age forty. It must be added that, in spite of precautions, now and then they become pregnant and that they operate on themselves, generally under bad conditions. Common prostitution is a miserable occupation in which woman, exploited sexually and economically, subjected arbitrarily to the police, to a humiliating medical supervision, to the caprices of the customers, and doomed to microbes and disease, to misery, is truly abased to the level of a thing.[7]

There are many degrees between the common prostitute and the high-class hetaira. The essential difference is that the first carries on trade in her pure generality—as woman—with the result that competition keeps her at the level of a miserable existence; whereas the second endeavors to gain recognition for herself—as an individual— and if she succeeds, she can entertain high aspirations. Beauty and charm or sex appeal are necessary here, but are not enough: the woman must be publicly *distinguished* somehow, as a person. To be sure, her qualities will often be disclosed through some man's desire; but she will have "arrived," will be launched on her career, so to speak, only when the man has brought her worth to the attention of the world. In the last century it was her town house, her carriage, her pearls, that gave witness to the influence of the "kept woman" over her protector and elevated her to the demimonde; her merit was confirmed as long as men continued to ruin themselves for her. Social and economic changes have abolished this flamboyant type. There is no longer a demimonde within which a reputation can be established. The ambitious woman now endeavors to gain renown in a different fashion. The latest incarnation of the hetaira is the movie star. Flanked by a husband—rigorously required in Hollywood —or by a responsible man friend, she is none the less in the line of Phryne and Imperia. She yields Woman over to the dreams of man, who repays her with wealth and fame.

There has always been a vague connection between prostitution and art, beause of the fact that beauty and sexual pleasure are ambiguously associated. It is not, in fact, Beauty that arouses desires;

---

[7] Evidently the situation cannot be changed by negative and hypocritical measures. Two conditions are necessary if prostitution is to disappear: all women must be assured a decent living; and custom must put no obstacles in the way of freedom in love. Prostitution will be suppressed only when the needs to which it responds are suppressed.

but the justification of lasciviousness proposed by the Platonic theory of love [8] is hypocritical. When Phryne bared her bosom before the judges of the Areopagus in Athens and obtained acquittal, she was offering them the contemplation of a pure idea. The exhibition of an unveiled body becomes a display of art; American burlesque has made undressing a drama. "The nude is chaste," declare those old gentlemen who collect obscene photographs under the name of "artistic nudes." In the brothel the initial scene of selection is already a parade of persons on show; if more complicated, such displays become "living pictures" or "art poses" for the customers.

The prostitute who wishes to acquire individual value does not limit herself to a passive show of flesh; she strives to offer special talents. The girl flute-players of ancient Greece charmed men with their music and dancing.[9] Algerian Arab women do the *danse du ventre*; the Spanish girls who dance and sing in the Barrio Chino are simply offering themselves in a delicate manner to the connoisseur. Zola's Nana appears on the stage in order to find "protectors." Certain music halls—as were formerly some night clubs—are simply brothels. All occupations in which women are on exhibition can be used for gallantry. Unquestionably there are girls—taxi dancers, fan dancers, decoy girls, pin-up girls, models, singers, actresses—who keep love-life and business apart; the more the latter involves technique and creativeness, the better it can be regarded as an end in itself; but frequently a woman who goes before the public to earn her living is tempted to trade more intimately in her charms. Inversely, the courtesan likes to have an occupation as a cover for her real trade. Few there are who, like Colette's Léa, addressed by a friend as "Dear artist," would reply: "Artist? Really, my lovers are most indiscreet!" We have noted that the hetaira's reputation is what gives her marketable value, and nowadays it is on stage or screen that a "name" can be made which will become business capital.

Cinderella does not always dream of Prince Charming; whether

---

[8] "All the forms of love, down to the primitive drives of hunger and sex, are seen to be at heart aspirations towards the eternal, which can only reach their true goal when they have raised the soul altogether out of time and becoming, and have united her with a beauty that is universal and absolute, existent in itself and lovable for itself alone." B. A. G. Fuller: *A History of Philosophy* (Henry Holt & Co., 1938), p. 84.—TR.

[9] For an imaginative account of their activities see Pierre Louÿs's novel *Aphrodite*.—TR.

husband or lover, she is afraid he may turn into a tyrant; she prefers to dream of her own laughing face posted by the doors of the big movie houses. But almost always she will attain her ambition through masculine "protection"; and it will be men—husband, lover, suitors— who will crown her triumph by letting her share their money or their fame. It is this necessity of pleasing individuals, or the crowd, that relates the "star" to the hetaira. They play a corresponding part in society.

I use the word hetaira to designate all women who treat not only their bodies but their entire personalities as capital to be exploited. Their attitude is very different from that of creative workers who, transcending themselves in the work they produce, go beyond the given and make their appeal to a freedom in others for which they open the doors of the future. The hetaira does not reveal the world, she opens no avenues to human transcendence; [1] on the contrary, she tries to captivate the world for her own profit. Offering herself for the approbation of her admirers, she does not repudiate that passive femininity which dedicates her to man: she endues it with a magical power that enables her to catch the men in the snare of her presence and batten off them; she engulfs them along with her in immanence.

If she takes this road, woman does succeed in acquiring a certain independence. Lending herself to several men, she belongs definitely to none; the money she piles up and the name she "sells," as one sells a product, assure her economic independence. The women of ancient Greece who had most freedom were neither the matrons nor the common prostitutes, but the hetairas. The courtesans of the Renaissance and the geishas of Japan enjoyed far greater liberty than other women of their times. The Frenchwoman whose independence seems to us the most like that of a man is perhaps Ninon de Lenclos, seventeenth-century woman of wit and beauty. Paradoxically, those women who exploit their femininity to the limit create for themselves a situation almost equivalent to that of a man; beginning with that sex which gives them over to the males as objects, they come to be subjects. Not only do they make their own living like men, but they exist in

---

[1] She may be *also* an artist and invent and create while seeking to please. She can then either combine these two functions or go beyond the stage of gallantry to join the category of women who are actresses, singers, dancers, and the like, to be discussed farther on.

a circle that is almost exclusively masculine; free in behavior and conversation, they can attain—like Ninon de Lenclos—to the rarest intellectual liberty. The most distinguished are often surrounded by artists and writers who are bored by "good" women.

In the hetaira men's myths find their most seductive embodiment; she is beyond all others flesh and spirit, idol, inspiration, muse; painters and sculptors will want her as model; she will feed the dreams of poets; in her the intellectual will explore the treasures of feminine "intuition." It is easier for her than for the matron to be intelligent because she is less set in hypocrisy. Those of superior gifts will not content themselves with the role of Egeria, the trusted counselor of men; they will feel the need to prove independently the worth attributed to them by the approbation of others; they will desire to transform their passive virtues into activities. Coming out into the world as sovereign subjects, they write poetry and prose, paint pictures, compose music. Imperia thus gained celebrity among Italian courtesans. It is possible, also, for woman to use man as an instrument and perform masculine functions through his agency; the favorite mistresses of men of authority have always shared, through their powerful lovers, in the government of the world.[2]

This type of feminine emancipation can be effective also on the erotic level. In the money or other benefits she gains from man, woman may find a compensation for her feminine inferiority complex; the money has a purifying role; it does away with the battle of the sexes. If many women who are not professionals insist on extracting checks and presents from their lovers, it is not from cupidity alone, for to make the man pay—and also to pay him, as we shall see—is to change him into an instrument. In this way the woman avoids being one. The man may perhaps think he "has" her, but this sexual possession is an illusion; it is she who has *him* on the much more substantial economic ground. Her pride is satisfied. She can abandon herself to her lover's embraces; she is not yielding to a will not her own; her pleasure cannot be in any sense "inflicted" upon her; it will seem rather to be an extra benefit; she will not be "taken," since she is being paid.

---

[2] Just as certain women make use of marriage to accomplish their own purposes, others employ their lovers as means for attaining some political, economic, or other aim. They transcend the situation of the hetaira as do the others that of the matron

The courtesan, however, is reputed to be frigid. It is useful to her to be able to control her heart and her sex feeling, for if sentimental or sensual, she risks coming under the sway of a man who will exploit her or monopolize her or make her suffer. Among the embraces she accepts there are many—especially at the outset of her career—which are humiliating; her revolt against male arrogance is expressed by her frigidity. Hetairas, like matrons, freely rely on the "tricks" that enable them to behave in sham fashion. This contempt, this disgust for men clearly shows that these women are not at all sure of having won at the game of exploiter-exploited. And, truth to tell, for the vast majority of them dependence is still their lot.

No man is absolutely their master. But their need of man is most urgent. The courtesan loses her means of support entirely if he ceases to feel desire for her. The beginner knows that her whole future is in men's hands; even the star, deprived of masculine support, sees her prestige grow dim. Even the most beautiful is never sure of tomorrow, for her weapons are magical, and magic is capricious. She is bound to her protector—husband or lover—almost as firmly as a "good" wife to her husband. Not only does she owe him her services as bedfellow, but she also has to put up with his presence, his conversation, his friends, and especially the demands of his vanity. In paying for her high-heeled shoes or her satin skirt, the patron of a girl makes an investment that will bring returns; the industrialist, the producer, in covering his mistress with pearls and furs, affirms through her his wealth and power; but whether the woman is a means for making money or an excuse for spending it, the servitude is the same. The gifts lavished upon her are chains. And do these gowns, these jewels that she wears, really belong to her? Sometimes the man wants them returned to him after the break, albeit in most genteel fashion.

In order to "hold" her protector without giving up her pleasures, the woman will employ the same wiles, tricks, lies, hypocrisy that dishonor married life; if she only pretends servility, this game is itself servile. As long as she retains her beauty and celebrity, she is able, if the master of the moment becomes odious, to replace him with another. But beauty is a worry, it is a frail treasure; the hetaira depends strictly on her body, which suffers pitiless depreciation with time; for her the struggle against growing old assumes its most dramatic form. If she has great prestige, she will be able to survive the ruination of her face and figure. But maintaining the renown that is her most dependable property puts her under the worst of tyrannies: that of public opinion. The subjection of Hollywood stars is well known. Their bodies are not their own; the producer decides on the color of their hair, their weight, their figure, their type; to change the curve of a cheek, their teeth may be pulled. Dieting, gymnastics, fittings, constitute a daily burden. Going out to parties and flirting are expected under the head of "personal appearances"; private life is no more than an aspect of public life. In France there is no written rule, but a shrewd and clever woman knows what her "publicity" demands of her. The star who refuses to be pliant to these requirements will experience a brutal or a slow but inevitable dethronement. The prostitute who simply yields her body is perhaps less a slave than the woman who makes a career of pleasing the public. A woman who has "arrived" and who is recognized as talented in some real profession—acting, singing, dancing—escapes the status of hetaira; she can know true independence. But most remain all their lives in a precarious position, they are under the never ending necessity of seducing the public and the men anew.

Very often the kept woman interiorizes her dependence; respectful of public opinion, she accepts its values; she admires fashionable society and adopts its manners; she wishes to be judged on the basis of bourgeois standards. A parasite upon the wealthy middle class, she accepts its ideas; she is "right-thinking"; formerly she was prone to have her daughter convent educated and herself went to Mass when she got old, after being converted with due publicity. She is on the conservative side. She is too proud of having succeeded in making her place in the world as it stands to want things changed. Her struggle to "arrive" does not dispose her to embrace the concepts of fraternity and human solidarity; she has paid for her success by too much slavish compliance to wish sincerely for universal liberty. Zola has clearly brought out this trait in the heroine of *Nana:*

Nana had very decided opinions on the subject of books and plays: she wanted works of tender and elevated style, the kind of thing to make her dream and to ennoble her soul. . . . She raged against the republicans. What did they want, those pigs who never washed? Weren't people happy, hadn't the Emperor done everything for them? A fine lot of swine, the people! She knew them, she could tell you all about them. . . . No, really, their Republic would be a great misfortune for everybody. Ah, may God preserve the Emperor as long as possible!

During wartime no one displays a more aggressive patriotism than the ladies of easy virtue; through the nobility of sentiment they affect, they hope to rise to the level of duchesses. Commonplaces, clichés, prejudices, conventional sentiments, form the basis of their public utterances, and often they have lost all inner sincerity. Between lies and exaggerations their language loses all meaning. The whole life of the hetaira is a show; her remarks, her parroting, are intended not to express her thoughts but to produce an effect. With her protector she plays a comedy of love. There are moments when she even takes it seriously. With public opinion she plays comedies of respectability and prestige, and she ends by believing herself a paragon of virtue and a sacred idol. A persistent bad faith dominates her inner life and permits her studied lies to seem the truth. Occasionally there is something spontaneous in her life; she is not completely a stranger to love; now and then she is "that way" about somebody; sometimes she even "falls hard" for some man. But if she goes in too much for caprice, sentimentality, pleasure, she will soon lose her "position." Usually she shows in such matters all the caution of the adulterous wife; she must hide what is going on from her patron and from public opinion; and therefore she cannot give much of herself to her lovers; they are only a diversion for her, a respite. Besides, she is usually too much obsessed by concern for her success to be able to forget herself in a real love affair.

As for other women, it is common enough for the hetaira to have sensual love relations with them; feeling enmity toward the men who domineer over her, she will often find both voluptuous surcease and revenge in feminine arms: so it was with Nana and her dear friend Satin. Just as she wishes to play an active role in the world so as to make positive use of her freedom, she is also inclined to possess other human beings: very young men whom she will even enjoy making her "protégés," or young women whom she will gladly support; and toward these she will in all cases be a dominating, virile personage. Homosexual or not, she will have the complex relations I have described with women in general; she needs them as critical judges and spectators, as confidantes and accomplices, in order to create that counter-universe which all women oppressed by man require. But feminine rivalry here reaches its culminating point. The prostitute who trades in her generality as woman has her competitors; but if there is enough work to go around, even in their disputes they are conscious of their solidarity. The hetaira who seeks individual fame is *a priori* hostile to any other woman who, like herself, covets a privileged position. Here the familiar theme of woman's nasty behavior toward other women is truly exemplified.

The greatest misfortune of the hetaira is not only that her independence is the deceptive obverse of a thousand dependencies, but also that this liberty is itself negative. Such actresses as Rachel, such dancers as Isadora Duncan, even though aided by men, have an occupation that requires their ability and justifies them. They attain concrete, positive freedom in work they choose and love. But for the vast majority of women an art, a profession, is only a means: in practicing it they are not engaged in genuine projects. The movies, especially, where the star is subordinated to the director, permit her no invention, no advances in creative activity. *Someone else* exploits what she *is*; she creates nothing new. Yet it is rare enough for a woman to become a star. In the field of gallantry, as strictly defined, no road whatever is open to transcendence. Here again ennui accompanies woman's confinement in immanence. Zola makes this clear concerning Nana:

> But in her luxury, in the midst of this court, Nana was bored to death. She had men for every minute of the night and money everywhere, even in her bureau drawers, but all this contented her no longer, she felt an inner emptiness, a void that made her yawn. Her life dragged on in idleness, repeating the same monotonous hours. . . . The certainty that she would be provided for left her stretched out the whole day, not bestirring herself, asleep in the depths of that fear and that convent-like submission, as if hemmed in in her profession as courtesan. She killed time with silly amusements in her sole expectation, man.

In American literature there are many descriptions of this dense ennui that overwhelms Hollywood and seizes the traveler upon arrival. The actors and extras, too, are as bored as the women whose situation they share. As in France, official parties are often in the nature of tiresome duties. The patron who directs the life of a starlet is an older man, with friends of his own age; their concerns are foreign to the young woman, their conversation deadly; there is a gulf, still deeper than in ordinary marriage, between the novice of twenty and the banker of forty-five who spend their nights together.

The Moloch to which the hetaira sacrifices pleasure, love, liberty, is her career. The ideal of the matron is a static atmosphere of well-being which envelops her relations with husband and children. The "career" extends through time, but it is none the less an immanent objective, which is summed up in a name. The name gets bigger on the billboards and in the popular mouth as higher and higher degrees are reached in the climb up the social scale. The climber carries on her enterprise with prudence or with audacity, according to her temperament. One woman will enjoy in her career the satisfactions of a housekeeper folding fine linen in her closet; another, the intoxication of adventure. Some women limit themselves to maintaining constantly in equilibrium a situation under constant threat, which sometimes crumbles; others go on endlessly building their renown, like a Tower of Babel aiming in vain toward the sky. Some, who combine gallantry with their other activities, seem to be true adventuresses: such are spies, like Mata Hari, or secret agents. In general they are not responsible for initiating their projects, they are rather instruments in masculine hands. But, on the whole, the attitude of the hetaira is more or less analogous to that of the adventurer; like him, she is often midway between *the serious* and *adventure*, properly so called; her aim is toward respectable ready-made values, such as money and fame; but she prizes the fact of their attainment as highly as their possession, and, in the end, to her the supreme value is her subjective success. She, also, justifies this individualism by a nihilism that is more or less reasoned but put into actual practice with the more conviction in that she is hostile to men and views other women as enemies. If she is sufficiently intelligent to feel the need of moral justification, in addition, she will have recourse to a more or less fully assimilated Nietzscheism: she will assert the rights of the superior being over the ordinary, the elite over the vulgar herd. Her person seems to her a treasure the mere existence of which is a gift to humanity, so much so that in being devoted to herself she will claim to serve society. The destiny of the woman dedicated to man is haunted by love; but she who exploits the male is bemused in the worship she renders to herself. If she sets great store by her renown, it is not for purely economic reasons—she seeks in fame the apotheosis of her narcissism.

CHAPTER XX

From Maturity to old Age

THE INDIVIDUAL life history of woman—because she is still bound up in her female functions—depends in much greater degree than that of man upon her physiological destiny; and the curve of this destiny is much more uneven, more discontinuous, than the masculine curve. Each period in the life of woman is uniform and monotonous; but the transitions from one stage to another are dangerously abrupt; they are manifested in crises—puberty, sexual initiation, the menopause—which are much more decisive than in the male. Whereas man grows old gradually, woman is suddenly deprived of her femininity; she is still relatively young when she loses the erotic attractiveness and the fertility which, in the view of society and in her own, provide the justification of her existence and her opportunity for happiness. With no future, she still has about one half of her adult life to live.

"The dangerous age" is marked by certain organic disturbances,[1] but what lends them importance is their symbolic significance. The crisis of the "change of life" is felt much less keenly by women who have not staked everything on their femininity; those who engage in heavy work—in the household or outside—greet the disappearance of the monthly burden with relief; the peasant woman, the workman's wife, constantly under the threat of new pregnancies, are happy when, at long last, they no longer run this risk. At this juncture, as at many others, woman's discomforts come less from her body than from the anxious concerns she feels regarding it. The moral drama commonly begins before the physiological phenomena have appeared, and it comes to an end only after they have long since been done away with.

Long before the eventual mutilation, woman is haunted by the horror of growing old. The mature man is involved in enterprises more important than those of love; his erotic ardor is less keen than in the days of his youth; and since in him the passive qualities of an

---

[1] Cf. Book I, Ch. i.

object are not called for, the changes in his face and body do not destroy his attractiveness. In woman, on the contrary, it is usually toward thirty-five, when all inhibitions have been finally overcome, that full erotic development is attained. Then it is that her sexual desires are strongest and she most keenly wishes to have them satisfied; she has gambled much more heavily than man on the sexual values she possesses; to hold her husband and to assure herself of his protection, and to keep most of her jobs, it is necessary for her to be attractive, to please; she is allowed no hold on the world save through the mediation of some man. What is to become of her when she no longer has any hold on him? This is what she anxiously asks herself while she helplessly looks on at the degeneration of this fleshly object which she identifies with herself. She puts up a battle. But hair-dye, skin treatments, plastic surgery, will never do more than prolong her dying youth. Perhaps she can at least deceive her mirror. But when the first hints come of that fated and irreversible process which is to destroy the whole edifice built up during puberty, she feels the fatal touch of death itself.

One might think that the woman most ardently enraptured with her youth and beauty would be the one to be most disturbed; but not at all: the narcissist is too concerned with her person not to have foreseen its inevitable decline and made her preparations for retreat. She will suffer, to be sure, from her mutilation, but at least she will not be taken by surprise, and she will become adapted soon enough. The woman who has been forgetful of self, devoted, self-sacrificing, will be much more upset by the sudden revelation: "I had only one life to live; think what my lot has been, and look at me now!" To the astonishment of everyone, a radical change occurs in her: what has happened is that, dislodged from her sheltering occupations, her plans disrupted, she finds herself suddenly, without recourse, put face-to-face with herself. Beyond that milestone against which she has unexpectedly stumbled, it seems to her that there will be nothing more for her to do than merely survive her better days; her body will promise nothing; the dreams, the longings she has not made good, will remain forever unfulfilled. In this perspective she reviews the past; the moment has come to draw a line across the page, to make up her accounts; she balances her books. And she is appalled at the narrow limitations life has imposed upon her.

Confronted by the brief and disappointing story that has been hers, she resumes the behavior of the adolescent on the threshold of a still inaccessible future: she rejects the notion that this is all; she compares the poverty of her existence with the vague wealth of her personality. Because, being a woman, she has suffered her fate more or less passively, it seems to her that she has been robbed of her chance, that she has been duped, that she has slipped from youth into maturity unawares. She makes the discovery that her husband, her environment, her occupations, were unworthy of her; she feels that she has not been appreciated. She withdraws from the entourage to which she feels superior; she shuts herself up with the secret she carries in her heart that is the mysterious key to her unhappy lot. She endeavors to try out in turn all the possibilities she has not exhausted. She begins to keep an intimate diary; if she finds understanding confidantes, she unbosoms herself in endless conversations; and she meditates day and night upon her regrets, her wrongs. Just as the young girl dreams of what her future *will be,* so she evokes what *might have been* her past; she pictures her lost opportunities and invents retrospective romances.[2]

The concerns of childhood and puberty are revived, the woman goes over the stories of her youth again and again, and sentiments for her parents, her brothers and sisters, long asleep, now rise anew. Sometimes she gives herself up to a dreamy and passive gloominess. But more often she suddenly undertakes to save her lost existence. She makes a show of this personality which she has just discovered in contrasting it with the meanness of her fate; she proclaims its merits, she imperiously demands that justice be done it. Matured by experience, she feels that at last she is capable of making her mark; she would like to get into action again. And first of all, she tries with pathetic urgency to turn back the flight of time. A woman of maternal type will assert that she can still have a child: she tries passionately to create life once again. A sensual woman will endeavor to ensnare one more lover. The coquette is more than ever anxious to please. One and all, they declare they never felt so young. They want to persuade others that the passage of time has never really touched them; they begin to "dress young," they assume childish airs. The aging woman

---

[2] Helene Deutsch gives the case of a woman who had been unhappily married and divorced when very young and who afterward had many years of tranquillity with a second husband; at forty-five she began to recall her first marriage with regret and to sink into a morbid state of melancholy, for which she received psychiatric treatment (op. cit., Vol. II, p. 463).

well knows that if she ceases to be an erotic object, it is not only because her flesh no longer has fresh bounties for men; it is also because
her past, her experience, make her, willy-nilly, a person; she has struggled, loved, willed, suffered, enjoyed, on her own account. This independence is intimidating; she tries to disown it; she exaggerates her
femininity, she adorns herself, she uses perfume, she makes herself
all charm, all grace, pure immanence. She babbles to men in a childish
voice and with naïve glances of admiration, and she chatters on about
when she was a little girl; she chirps instead of talking, she claps her
hands, she bursts out laughing. And she enacts this comedy with a
certain sincerity. For her new interests, her desire to get out of the
old routine and begin anew, make her feel that she is starting life
again.

But in fact there is no question of a real start; she sees in the world
no objectives toward which she might reach out in a free and effective
manner. Her activity takes an eccentric, incoherent, and fruitless form,
because she can compensate only in a symbolic way for the mistakes
and failures of the past. For one thing, the woman of the age we are
considering will try to realize all her wishes of childhood and adolescence before it is too late: she may go back to her piano, take up
sculpture, writing, travel, she may learn skiing or study foreign languages. She now welcomes with open arms—still before it is too late—
everything she has previously denied herself. She admits her aversion
for a spouse she formerly could tolerate and becomes frigid with him;
or, on the contrary, she gives rein to ardors she formerly restrained
and overwhelms her husband with her demands; she takes up masturbation, a practice abandoned since childhood. Homosexual tendencies—which exist in masked form in almost all women—now
become manifest. She often turns them toward her daughter; but
sometimes these unaccustomed sentiments are directed toward a
woman friend. In *Sex, Life, and Faith*, Rom Landau tells the following story, as confided to him by the person concerned:

Mrs. X . . . was approaching fifty; she had been married for
twenty-five years, had three grown-up children, and was prominent
in social and charitable affairs. She met in London a woman ten
years younger who had similar interests, Mrs. Y, who invited her
for a visit. On the second evening of the visit Mrs. X suddenly
found herself passionately embracing her hostess; she declared her

astonishment and spent the night with her, then returned home terrified. Hitherto she had been quite ignorant about homosexuality, not knowing that "such things" existed. She thought of Mrs. Y with passion and for the first time in her life found the accustomed kisses and caresses of her husband rather disagreeable. She decided to see her friend again "to clear up things," and her passion only increased; their relations were more delightful than anything she had experienced up to that time. She was tortured by the notion that she had sinned and consulted a doctor to find out if there was any "scientific explanation" for her condition and if it could be justified on any moral grounds.

In this case the subject had yielded to a spontaneous impulse and was herself deeply upset by it. But often the woman deliberately seeks to experience in actuality the romances she has not known, which soon she will no longer be able to know. She absents herself from home, at times because she feels her home unworthy of her and because she wants to be alone, and at times in search of adventure. If she finds it, she throws herself into it with avidity. So it was in one of Stekel's cases:

A woman of forty, married twenty years and with grown children, began to feel that she was unappreciated and that she had wasted her life. She took up new activities and, for one thing, went to the mountains for skiing. There she met a man of thirty and became his mistress.

The woman who is under the influence of a strong tradition of decency and honor does not always go to the extreme of definite acts. But her dreams are peopled with erotic phantoms, which she also calls up in hours of wakefulness; she displays a feverish and sensual affection toward her children; she entertains incestuous obsessions concerning her son; she falls secretly in love with one young man after another; like the adolescent girl, she is haunted by notions of being raped; she knows also the mad desire for prostitution. The ambivalence of her desires and fears creates an anxiety that may induce neurosis: then she scandalizes her relatives with strange conduct, which is in reality only the expression of her imaginary life. The frontier between the imaginary and the real is still more indistinct at this disturbed period than during puberty. One of the outstanding traits of the aging woman is a feeling of depersonalization that makes her lose all objective bearings. Individuals also who have in full health come close to death say that they experienced a curious sense of doubling; when one feels oneself a conscious, active, free being, the passive object on which the fatality is operating seems necessarily as if it were another: this is not *I* being knocked down by an automobile; this cannot be *I*, this old woman reflected in the mirror! The woman who "never felt so young in her life" and who has never seen herself so old does not succeed in reconciling these two aspects of herself; it is in a dream that time flies and duration makes its inroads upon her. Thus reality retreats and dwindles, and at the same time it is no longer clearly distinguished from illusion. The woman puts her trust in what is clear to her inner eye rather than in that strange world where time flows backward, where her double no longer resembles her, where the outcome has betrayed her. She is thus inclined to ecstasies, to inspirations, to frenzies. And since love is at this time more than ever her main concern, it is normal for her to embrace the illusion that she is loved. Nine out of ten erotomaniacs are women, and these are almost all forty to fifty years old.

It is not vouchsafed to all, however, to leap over the wall of reality so boldly. Many women, denied all human love even in their dreams, look to God for help; it is precisely at the menopause that the coquette, the woman of gallantry, the debauchee, become religious; the vague notions of destiny, mystery, and lack of appreciation indulged in by woman as her autumn begins find in religion a rational unification. The devotee regards her spoiled life as a trial put upon her by God; her soul has drawn from misfortune the exceptional merits that make her worthy of a special visitation by the grace of the Lord; she will readily believe that she receives inspiration from Heaven, or even that she has been charged by Heaven with an urgent mission.

Having more or less completely lost the sense of the real, a woman during this crisis is open to every kind of suggestion, hence a confessor is in a position to acquire a powerful influence over her soul. Moreover, she will enthusiastically accept the most debatable authorities; she is a preordained prey for religious sects, spiritualists, prophets, faith healers, for any and every charlatan. This is because she not only has lost all critical sense in losing touch with the factual world, but has also become eager for a final truth: she must have the remedy, the formula, the key that, all of a sudden, will save her while saving the universe. She scorns more than ever a logic that has evidently been inapplicable to her special case; only such evidences as are especially meant for her seem convincing: revelations, inspirations, messages, even miracles, begin to flower around her. Her discoveries sometimes lead her to action: she plunges into business, enterprises, adventures, which have been suggested by some counselor or by her inner voices. In other cases she is satisfied with consecration as the vessel of absolute truth and wisdom.

Whether active or contemplative, her attitude is accompanied by feverish exaltations. The crisis of the menopause rudely cuts the life of woman in two; the resulting discontinuity is what gives woman the illusion of a "new life"; it is *another* time that opens before her, so she enters upon it with the fervor of a convert; she is converted to love, to the godly life, to art, to humanity; in these entities she loses herself and magnifies herself. She is dead and risen again, she views the world with an eye that has penetrated the secrets of the beyond, and she thinks she is about to take flight for peaks hitherto unreached.

But the world has not been changed; the peaks remain inaccessible; the messages received—however brilliantly manifest—are hard to decipher; the inner illuminations fade; before the glass stands a woman who in spite of everything has grown one day older since yesterday. The moments of exaltation are succeeded by sad hours of depression. The organism manifests this rhythm because the decline of the female sex hormones is compensated for by an overactivity of the pituitary gland; but above all it is the psychological state that governs this alternation of mood. For the woman's restlessness, her illusions, her fervor, are only a defense reaction against the overruling fatality of what has been. Once more anguish is at the throat of the woman whose life is already done before death has taken her. Instead of fighting off despair, she often chooses to yield to its intoxication. She harps endlessly on her wrongs, her regrets, her reproaches; she imagines her relatives and neighbors guilty of dark machinations against her; if there is a sister or a friend of her own age closely associated with her life, they may together build up delusions of persecution. But in particular she begins to be morbidly jealous of her husband, with this jealousy directed toward his friends, his sisters, his business; and rightly or wrongly she holds some rival responsible for all her woes. Cases of pathological jealousy are most numerous between the ages of fifty and fifty-five.

The difficulties of the menopause continue—sometimes until death —in the woman who cannot make up her mind to grow old; if she has no other resources than the exploitation of her physical charms, she will battle step by step to preserve them; she will struggle madly also if her sexual desires remain lively, which is not at all uncommon. When asked at what age a woman ceases to feel the torments of the flesh, the Princess Metternich replied: "I do not know, I am only sixty-five." Marriage, which according to Montaigne never offers woman more than "little replenishment," becomes a more and more inefficient remedy as she becomes older; she frequently pays in maturity for the inhibitions, the coldness, of her youth; when finally she begins to know the fevers of desire, her husband has long been resigned to her indifference and has made his own adjustments. Deprived of her sex appeal by familiarity and time, the wife has small chance of reviving the conjugal flame. Vexed, determined to "live her life," she will have fewer scruples—if she has ever had any—in taking lovers; but they have still to be taken: it is a man-hunt. She uses a thousand stratagems: pretending to offer herself, she imposes herself; she turns politeness, friendship, gratitude, into traps. It is not only a liking for the freshness of youthful flesh that makes her attack young men: from them only can she expect that disinterested affection which the adolescent sometimes feels for a maternal mistress. She herself has become aggressive, and the docility of the young man often pleases the older woman as much as his handsome appearance; Mme de Staël when more than forty chose callow youths, who were overwhelmed by her prestige. And in any case a timid novice is easier to capture.

When seduction and intrigue prove quite unavailing, obstinately persevering women have one resource left: that is, to pay. The tale about little knives called *cannivets*, popular in the Middle Ages, illustrates the fate of these insatiable ogresses: A young woman, in return for her favors, asked from each of her lovers a little *cannivet*, and these she kept in her cupboard. A day came when the cupboard was full; but from this time on, it was the lovers who took pride in getting a present from her after each night of love. Soon the cupboard was empty; all the *cannivets* had been handed over, and she had to buy others to replace them. Some women take a cynical view of the situation: they have had their day, it is their turn to "give *cannivets*." Money can even play in their eyes a part opposite to that which it plays for the courtesan, but equally a purifying one: it transforms the male into an instrument and allows the woman that erotic liberty which her youthful pride once rejected.

But more romantic than clear-sighted, the mistress-benefactress often attempts to buy a mirage of affection, of admiration, of respect; she even persuades herself that she gives for the pleasure of giving, without anything being asked of her. Here the young man is again a chosen lover, for she can pride herself on a maternal generosity in his behalf; and, too, he has a little of that "mystery" which, in other circumstances, a man asks of the woman he is "helping out," because in this way the crudeness of the deal is disguised by the enigma. But it is rare for insincerity to remain lenient for long; the battle of the sexes changes into a duel between the exploiter and the exploited in which the woman, deceived and flouted, risks undergoing cruel defeats. If she is wise, she will resign herself to disarmament without too much delay, even if her fires have not wholly died down.

From the day a woman consents to growing old, her situation changes. Up to that time she was still a young woman, intent on struggling against a misfortune that was mysteriously disfiguring and deforming her; now she becomes a different being, unsexed but complete: an old woman. It may be considered that the crisis of her "dangerous age" has been passed. But it should not be supposed that henceforth her life will be an easy one. When she has given up the struggle against the fatality of time, another combat begins: she must maintain a place on earth.

It is in the autumn and winter of life that woman is freed from her chains; she takes advantage of her age to escape the burdens that weigh on her; she knows her husband too well to let him intimidate her any longer, she eludes his embraces, at his side she organizes a life of her own—in friendship, indifference, or hostility. If his decline is faster than hers, she assumes control of the couple's affairs. She can also permit herself defiance of fashion and of "what people will say"; she is freed from social obligations, dieting, and the care of her beauty. As for her children, they are old enough to get along without her, they are getting married, they are leaving home. Rid of her duties, she finds freedom at last. Unfortunately, in every woman's story recurs the fact we have verified throughout the history of woman: she finds this freedom at the very time when she can make no use of it. This recurrence is in no wise due to chance: patriarchal society gave all the feminine functions the aspect of a service, and woman escapes slavery only at times when she loses all effectiveness. Toward fifty she is in full possession of her powers; she feels she is rich in experience; that is the age at which men attain the highest positions, the most important posts; as for her, she is put into retirement. She has been taught only to devote herself to someone, and nobody wants her devotion any more. Useless, unjustified, she looks forward to the long, unpromising years she has yet to live, and she mutters: "No one needs me!"

She does not become resigned to this state of affairs immediately. Sometimes she clings in distress to her husband; she stifles him with her care more overbearingly than ever; but the routine of married life is too well established; either she knows that she has long since become unnecessary to her husband, or he no longer seems worthy enough to justify her efforts. Assuring the maintenance of their life together is a task as incidental as growing old alone. What she can do hopefully is turn to her children; for them the die is not yet cast; the world, the future, are yet open to them; she would fain plunge on after them. The woman who has chanced to give birth late in life has an advantage: she is still a young mother when other women become grandmothers. But as a rule a mother sees her little ones change into adults when she is between forty and fifty. It is just as they are escaping her that she passionately endeavors to survive through them.

Her attitude varies according to whether she looks to a son or a daughter for her salvation; she ordinarily bases her fondest hopes upon the former. Here he is, come to her at last from the depths of the past, the man for whose glorious advent she once scanned the distant horizon; since the first wail of her newborn son, she has awaited this day when he would pour out all the treasures with which his father has been unable to shower her. In the meantime she has given him slaps and purges, but these are forgotten; this man whom she carried under her heart was already one of those demigods who govern the world and control the destiny of women; now he is going to recognize her in the full glory of her motherhood. He is going to defend her against the domination of her husband, avenge her for the lovers she has had and has not had; he will be her liberator, her savior. She resumes toward him the seductive and ostentatious behavior of the young girl keeping an eye out for Prince Charming; as she walks at his side, elegant, still attractive, she thinks she seems his elder sister; she is enchanted if—modeling himself upon the heroes in American films—he teases and jostles her about, laughing and respectful. With proud humility she recognizes the virile superiority of this man who was once her baby.

To what extent can these sentiments be considered incestuous? There is no doubt that when she pictures herself with self-satisfaction on her son's arm, the term *elder sister* is but a modest shield for equivocal fancies; when she is asleep, when she is off guard, in her reveries, she sometimes goes rather far; but I have already remarked that dreams and fantasies are by no means invariably the expression of hidden desire for a real act. They are often sufficient in themselves, they are the fulfillment of a desire that demands no more than imaginary satisfaction. When a mother plays in a more or less disguised manner at seeing a lover in a son, it is only a game. Eroticism in the true sense of the word usually has little place in this couple.

But these two do form a couple; it is from the depths of her femininity that the mother hails the sovereign male in her son; she puts herself in his hands with all the fervor of the woman in love, and, in return for this gift, she anticipates being elevated to a seat at the right hand of God. To gain this Assumption, the woman in love makes her appeal to the free action of her lover; she gallantly assumes a risk, and her reward lies in his eager demands. The mother, on the other hand, feels that she has acquired inviolable rights through the mere fact of having given birth; she does not wait to have her son acknowledge his obligation to her, in order to regard him as her creature, her property. She is less demanding than the woman in love because she is of a more tranquil insincerity; that is, her self-abdication is less anxiety-ridden; having made a carnal being, she takes over as her own an existence: she appropriates its acts, its works, its merits. In exalting the fruit of her womb, she elevates her own person to the skies.

Living by proxy is always a precarious expedient. Things may not turn out as wished. It often happens that the son is only a good-for-nothing, a rowdy, a failure, a dunce, an ingrate. The mother has her own ideas about the hero he is supposed to embody. Nothing is rarer than the mother who sincerely respects the human person in her child, who recognizes his liberty even in failure, who accepts with him the hazards of all dedication to accomplishment. We much more often encounter mothers who emulate that overpraised Spartan who cheerfully consigned her son to victory or death; the son's business on earth, it would seem, is to justify the existence of his mother in gaining such things, to their common profit, as she considers valuable. The mother demands that the projects of the child-god be conformable to her own ideals and that his success in them be assured. Every woman wants to give birth to a hero, a genius; but all the mothers of actual heroes and geniuses have at first complained that their sons were breaking their hearts. The fact is that a man most often wins against his mother's will the trophies which she dreamed of gaining as personal adornments and which she does not even recognize when he lays them at her feet. Even though she approves the enterprises of her son in principle, she is torn by a contradiction corresponding to that which tortures the woman in love. In order to justify his life—and that of his mother—he must go onward, transcend his life, toward certain ends and aims; and to attain them he is led to risk his health, to court danger. But he is putting in question the value of his mother's gift when he puts certain aims above the mere fact of living. She is shocked at this; she is sovereign over man only if this flesh she has engendered is for him the supreme good. He has no right to destroy what she has produced in travail. "You are going to wear yourself· out, you will get sick, something is going to happen," she dins into his ears.

She knows very well, however, that merely to live is not enough, else procreation would itself be superfluous. She is the first to object if her offspring is an idler, a poltroon. Her mind is never at rest. When he departs for the wars, she wants him to return alive—but decorated. She wants him to succeed in his career, but fears lest he overwork. Whatever he does, she always feels concern, looking on helplessly at a career that is his and over which she has no control. She fears lest he lose his way, lest he fail, lest in succeeding he ruin his health. Even if she has confidence in him, the difference in age and sex prevents any real co-operation between mother and son; she is not conversant with his work; she is not asked to collaborate.

This explains why the mother remains dissatisfied, even if she takes inordinate pride in her son. Believing that she has not only engendered a living body but also founded an absolutely necessary existence, she feels justified in retrospect; but her justification is not an occupation: she needs to continue her beneficent activity in order to occupy her days; she wants to feel that she is indispensable to her god. The hoax played on the devotee is in this case exposed in the most merciless manner: his wife is going to deprive her of her functions. The hostility she feels toward this strange woman who "takes away" her child has often been described. The mother has elevated the brute, involuntary process of parturition [3] to the height of a divine mystery, and she declines to admit that a human decision can have more weight. In her eyes the values are already established, they originate in nature, in the past: she misunderstands the worth of an obligation freely undertaken. Her son is indebted to her for his life; what does he owe this woman who was yesterday still unknown to him? It must be some kind of witchcraft that has enabled her to persuade him of the existence of a bond which up to now *did not exist*; she is scheming, not disinterested, dangerous. The mother waits impatiently for the imposture to be exposed; encouraged by the old myth of the good mother who with healing in her hands binds up the wounds inflicted by the bad woman, she watches her son's face for signs of unhappiness—and she finds them regardless of his denials. She pities him when he has no complaints to make; she spies on her daughter-in-law, she criticizes her; to each of her innovations, the mother opposes the past and its accustomed ways, which condemn the very presence of the interloper.

Each woman understands the happiness of the beloved in her own fashion: the wife wants to see in him a man through whom she will conquer society; the mother tries to protect him by taking him back to his childhood. To the plans of the young wife who expects her husband *to become* rich or eminent, the mother opposes the laws of his unchangeable nature: he *is* delicate, he must not overwork. The conflict between past and future is heightened when the newcomer gets pregnant in her turn. "The birth of children is the death of parents"; this is the time when that truth is revealed in all its cruel force: the mother who was hoping to live on in her son understands that he is condemning her to death. She gave life; life is to go on

---

[3] Put in existentialist terms by the author as *"la facticité contingente de la parturition."*—TR.

without her; she is no longer *the* Mother—merely a link. She falls from the heaven of timeless idols; she is no longer anything more than a finished, outdated individual. This is the time when in pathological cases her hatred increases to such an extent as to bring on a neurosis or drive her to the commission of a crime, as in that of Mme Lefevbre.[4]

Normally the grandmother gets over her hostility; sometimes she obstinately regards the baby as her son's only, and she loves him tyrannically; but usually the young mother claims her child for herself; the grandmother is jealous and has for the infant an ambiguous affection of the type where hostility is concealed under the appearance of anxiety.

The mother's attitude toward her grown-up daughter is most ambivalent: in her son she looks for a god; in her daughter she finds a double. The double is a dubious personage, who assassinates his original, as we see in Poe's tales and in Wilde's *The Picture of Dorian Gray*, for example. Thus in becoming a woman the daughter condemns her mother to death; and yet she lets her live on. The mother's behavior varies greatly according to whether she sees a promise of ruin or resurrection in the blossoming forth of her child.

Many a mother hardens into hostility; she does not accept being supplanted by the ingrate who owes her her life. The jealousy felt by the coquette toward the fresh adolescent girl who shows up her artifice has often been noted: she who has seen a hated rival in every woman will see the same even in her own child; she sends her away or keeps her out of sight, or she contrives to deprive her of social opportunities. She who took pride in being the Wife, the Mother, in exemplary and unique fashion, none the less fights dethronement fiercely. She goes on saying her daughter is only a child, she regards her undertakings as juvenile games; she is too young to marry, too delicate to procreate. If she persists in wanting a husband, a home,

---

[4] In 1925 this woman of sixty killed her daughter-in-law, who was six months pregnant. Condemned to death and reprieved, she spent the rest of her life in an institution, showing no remorse. She believed God approved when she killed her daughter-in-law "as you would pull up a weed or kill a savage animal." She gave as the only proof of this "savagery" the young woman's remark: "You have me now, so you will have to reckon with me." When she suspected the pregnancy, she bought a revolver "for robbers." After the menopause she clung desperately to her maternity: for twelve years she felt discomforts that were the symbolic expression of an imaginary pregnancy.

children, all this will never be more than make-believe. The mother never wearies of criticizing, deriding, or predicting trouble. If allowed to do so, she condemns her daughter to eternal childhood; if not, she tries to ruin the adult life the other is bold enough to claim. We have seen that in this she often succeeds: many a young woman remains sterile, miscarries, fails to nurse and raise her child or to take charge of her household, because of this baneful influence. Conjugal life is made impossible. Unhappy, alone, she will find refuge in her mother's sovereign arms. Should she resist, they will stand opposed in perpetual conflict; the frustrated mother transfers to her son-in-law most of the irritation aroused in her by the insolent independence of her daughter.

The mother who identifies herself passionately with her daughter is no less tyrannical; what she wants is to live her youth over again with the benefit of her ripe experience, thus rescuing her past while saving herself from it. She will herself select a son-in-law in conformity with the husband she dreamed of but never had; coquettish, affectionate, she will easily imagine that it is she whom he is marrying in some secret corner of his heart; through her daughter she will satisfy her old desires for wealth, success, and fame. Those women have often been portrayed who ardently push their children along the roads of gallantry, the movies, or the theater; under the pretext of watching over them, they take over their lives. I have been told of some who will go so far as to take the young girl's suitors into their own beds. But it is rare for the daughter to put up with this guardianship for long; once she has found a husband or a responsible protector, she will rebel. The mother-in-law who began by cherishing her son-in-law then becomes hostile; she groans over human ingratitude, poses as a martyr; she becomes in her turn an inimical mother.

Foreseeing these disappointments, many women assume an attitude of indifference when they see their daughters growing up; but if so, they get little enjoyment from them. A mother needs a rare combination of generosity and detachment in order to find enrichment in her children's lives without becoming their tyrant or making them her tormentors.

The feelings of the grandmother toward her grandchildren are extensions of those she feels toward her daughter, and she frequently transfers her hostility to them. It is not only to prevent scandal that many women compel a seduced daughter to have an abortion, or to abandon her infant, or even to do away with it: they are only too happy to deprive her of maternity, obstinately desiring to keep the privilege for themselves. They are prepared to advise even a legitimate mother to induce a miscarriage, not to nurse the baby, to send it away. On their part, they will nullify this impudent little existence by appearing indifferent to it; or more likely they will continually scold the child, punish it, and even maltreat it.

The mother who, on the contrary, identifies herself with her daughter, often accepts her children more eagerly than does the young woman. The latter is upset by the arrival of the little unknown; but to the grandmother it is an old story: she goes back twenty years in time, she is again a young woman in childbed; she regains all the joys of possession and domination which her children have not given her for a long time. All the desires for maternity which she renounced at the menopause are miraculously fulfilled; she is the real mother, she authoritatively takes charge of the baby, and if it is turned over to her, she will devote herself passionately to it. Unfortunately for her, the young mother is likely to assert her rights; then the grandmother is authorized only to play the part of assistant, which her elders formerly played in her case; she feels dethroned, and in addition she must reckon with her son-in-law's mother, of whom she is naturally jealous. Spite often perverts the love she spontaneously felt for the child at first. The anxiety shown by many grandmothers expresses the ambivalence of their feelings: they are fond of the baby in that he belongs to them, but they are also hostile to him as a little stranger; and they are ashamed of this enmity. Yet if the grandmother retains a warm affection for her grandchildren while renouncing complete possession, she can play the privileged role of guardian angel in their lives. Recognizing neither rights nor responsibilities, she loves them in pure generosity; she does not indulge in narcissistic dreams through them, she demands nothing of them, she does not sacrifice to them a future she is never to see. What she loves is simply the little beings of flesh and blood who are present here and now in their dependence and gratuitousness; she is not their educator; she need not embody abstract justice, the law. This, by the way, may be the source of conflicts that can embroil her with her grandchildren's parents.

It may happen that a woman has no descendants or is not interested in her posterity; in default of natural bonds with children or grandchildren, she sometimes endeavors to create corresponding ties artificially. She offers a maternal affection to young people; whether or not her love remains platonic, she is not entirely hypocritical in saying that she loves a protégé "like a son": the feelings of a mother, for that matter, are more or less amorous. It is true that those who emulate Mme de Warens [5] take pleasure in generously benefiting, helping, molding a man: they wish to be the source, the indispensable condition, the foundation of an existence that transcends them; they make themselves mothers and regard themselves, in respect to their lovers, much more in that light than as mistresses. And very often the maternal type of woman adopts a girl. Here again the relations take on forms more or less clearly sexual; but whether it be platonically or carnally, what is sought in the protégée is a double, miraculously rejuvenated.

The actress, the dancer, the singer become teachers: they mold pupils; the intellectual—like Mme de Charrière in her Colombier retreat [6]—indoctrinates disciples; the devotee gathers spiritual daughters about her; the woman of gallantry becomes a madam. If they bring an ardent zeal to their proselyting, it is never through pure interest in the field of effort; what they are passionately seeking is reincarnation in their protégées. Their tyrannical generosity gives rise to almost the same conflicts as those between mothers and daughters united by ties of blood. It is also possible to adopt grandchildren; and grandaunts and godmothers readily play a role like that of the grandmother. But in any case it is very rare for a woman to find in her posterity—natural or adopted—a justification for her declining years: she fails to make the career of a single one of these young existences truly hers. Either she persists in the effort to take it over and is consumed in struggles and scenes that leave her disappointed and exhausted; or she resigns herself to no more than a modest participation, as usually happens. The older mother and the grandmother repress their ideas of domination, they conceal their resentments; they content themselves with whatever their children finally give them. But in that case they get little help from them. They are left to face the desert of the future without occupation, a prey to loneliness, regret, and boredom.

Here we come upon the sorry tragedy of the aged woman: she

---

[5] See Rousseau's *Confessions*.—TR.
[6] See page 476.

realizes she is useless; all her life long the middle-class woman has often had to solve the ridiculous problem of how to kill time. But when the children are grown, the husband a made man or at least settled down, the time must still be killed somehow. Fancywork was invented to mask their horrible idleness; hands embroider, they knit, they are in motion. This is no real work, for the object produced is not the end in view; its importance is trifling, and to know what to do with it is often a problem—one can get rid of it, perhaps, by giving it to a friend or to a charitable organization, or by cluttering the mantelpiece or center table. This is no longer a game that in its use-lessness expresses the pure joy of living; and it is hardly an escape, since the mind remains vacant. It is the "absurd amusement" described by Pascal; with the needle or the crochet-hook, woman sadly weaves the very nothingness of her days. Water-colors, music, reading serve in much the same way; the unoccupied woman, in applying herself to such matters, is not trying to extend her grasp on the world, but only to relieve her boredom. An activity that does not open the future falls back into vain immanence; the idle woman opens a book and throws it aside, opens the piano only to close it, resumes her embroidering, yawns, and finally takes up the telephone.

In fact, she is most likely to seek relief in social life; she goes out, pays calls; like Mrs. Dalloway she attaches great importance to her entertaining; she goes to every wedding, every funeral; having no longer any existence of her own, she encourages company. Once a coquette, she becomes a gossip; she watches people, comments on their behavior; she compensates for her inaction by scattering criticisms and advice all around her, offering the benefit of her experience, unasked, to one and all. If she has means, she begins to hold a salon, hoping thus to appropriate the undertakings and successes of others; sometimes she sets up a despotic rule over her subjects in this way, like Mme du Deffand and Mme Verdurin. It is indeed a substitute for action to be a center of attraction, an inspiration, to create a crossroads, an "atmosphere."

There are other and more direct ways of intervening in worldly affairs; in France charitable organizations and a few "associations" exist, but particularly in America women associate in clubs, where they play bridge, read book reviews, offer literary prizes, and promote social improvements. What characterizes most of these organizations, on both continents, is that they are in themselves their own reason for existence: the ends they are supposed to have in view only serve as pretexts. The state of affairs is exactly like that described in Kafka's fable: [7] no one bothered with building the Tower of Babel; around its proposed site grew up a vast town that used up all its resources in administration, enlargement, and internal dissension. In just this way the women of the associations for this and that use up the best part of their time in organizing their organizations; they elect officers, frame a constitution, carry on disputes among themselves, and struggle with their rival association for prestige: no one must steal *their* paupers, *their* sick, *their* wounded, *their* orphans; they would rather see them die than yield them to another group. And these ladies are far from wanting a social regime that, in doing away with injustices and abuses, would make their devotion useless; they bless the wars and famines which transform them into benefactresses of humanity. It is quite clear that in their eyes the knitted goods and the packages are not for the soldiers and for the famished, but rather that these exist just for the purpose of receiving flying-helmets and bundles.

In spite of everything, some of these groups do get positive results. In the United States the influence of the venerable "moms" is powerful; this is to be explained by the leisure accorded them by their parasitic mode of life: hence its banefulness. In *Generation of Vipers* [8] Philip Wylie has this to say of the American mom: "Knowing nothing about medicine, art, science, religion, law, sanitation . . . she seldom has any special interest in *what*, exactly, she is doing as a member of any of these endless organizations, so long as it is *something*." Their effort is not integrated in a coherent and constructive plan, it does not aim at objective goals; it tends only to make their tastes and prejudices imperiously clear or to serve their interests. For example, they play a considerable role in the domain of culture, since they buy most of the books; but they read as one plays solitaire. Literature assumes sense and dignity when it makes its appeal to persons engaged in projects, when it helps them go on toward ever wider horizons; it must be integrated with the movement of human transcendence. Instead, woman abuses books and works of art, engulfing them in her immanence; the picture becomes a knickknack, music tiresome repetition, the novel a reverie of no more value than a cro-

---

[7] *Les Armes de la ville.*

[8] Ch. xi, "Common Women," p. 191.

cheted antimacassar. It is the American woman who is responsible
for the degradation of the best-sellers; these books are intended not
only merely to entertain, but worse, to entertain idle women in search
of escape. As for the general effect of the moms' activities, Philip
Wylie puts it as follows:

> They frighten politicians into sniveling servility and they terrify
> pastors; they bother bank presidents and they pulverize school
> boards. Mom has many such organizations, the real purpose of
> which is to compel an abject compliance of her environs to her
> personal desires . . . she drives out of the town and the state, if
> possible, all young harlots . . . she causes bus lines to run where
> they are convenient for her rather than for the workers . . . she
> throws prodigious fairs and parties for charity and gives the pro-
> ceeds . . . to the janitor to buy the committee some beer for its
> headache on the morning after. . . . The clubs afford mom an
> infinite opportunity for nosing into other people's business.

There is much truth in this aggressive satire. Not being specialists
in politics, or in economics, or in any technical branch, the old ladies
have no concrete grasp upon society; they are ignorant of the problems that call for action; they are incapable of working out any constructive program. Their morality is as abstract and formal as a
Kantian imperative; they issue prohibitions instead of seeking to discover avenues of progress; they do not try positively to create new
conditions. They attack what does exist in order to eliminate evils.
This explains why they always unite *against* something: alcohol,
prostitution, pornography. They do not realize that a purely negative
effort is doomed to failure, as was proved in America by the failure
of prohibition, in France by that of the law which Marthe Richard [9]
put through the Chamber of Deputies, closing the brothels. As long
as woman remains a parasite, she cannot take part effectively in
making a better world.

But it does happen that, in spite of everything, certain of the
women we are considering are entirely committed to some enterprise
and become truly effective; these women are no longer seeking merely

---

[9] It has recently been reported that Marthe Richard is now recommending that
the brothels of Paris be opened again because vice has simply been driven underground, not suppressed.—TR.

to occupy their time, they have goals in view; producers in their own right, they are outside the parasitic category we are considering here. But this about-face is rare. The majority of these women, in their private or public activities, do not have in mind a result to be achieved, but merely some way of occupying themselves—and no occupation is worth while when it is only a means of killing time. Many of them are adversely affected by this; having behind them a life already finished, they are confused in much the same way as adolescents before whom life is not yet open; they feel no pull, around them in both cases is the wasteland; contemplating any action, they mutter: "What's the use?" But the adolescent male is drawn willy-nilly into a masculine way of life that discloses responsibilities, aims, values; he is thrown out into the world, he makes decisions, he commits himself to some enterprise. If it is suggested to the older woman that she should start out toward a new future, she will sadly reply that it is too late. Not that henceforth her time is limited, for a woman goes into retirement very early; but she lacks the spirit, the confidence, the hope, the anger, that would enable her to look around and find new goals.[1] She takes refuge in the routine that has always been her lot; repetition becomes her pattern. She becomes insanely frugal; she gets more and more deeply devout; she hardens in stoicism like Mme de Charrière. She dries up, becomes indifferent, egotistical.

The old woman commonly becomes serene toward the very end of her life, when she has given up the battle, when the approach of death frees her from all concern for the future. Her husband is often the older, and she witnesses his decline in silent content—this is her revenge. If he dies first, she bears the loss cheerfully; it has often been observed that men are much more disturbed than women by the loss of the spouse late in life; they gain more from marriage than women do, particularly in old age. For then the universe is concentrated within the limits of the home; the present no longer borders on the future. At this time the wife presides over the days and maintains their steady rhythm. When the man has given up his public functions, he becomes entirely useless; his wife at least still runs the house; she is necessary to her husband, whereas he is merely a nuisance.

Old women take pride in their independence; they begin at last to

---

[1] Few indeed are those, like Grandma Moses, the celebrated American painter, who take to new and fruitful work in their old age.—Tr.

view the world through their own eyes; they note that they have been duped and deceived all their lives; sane and mistrustful, they often develop a pungent cynicism. In particular, the woman who "has lived" knows men as no man does, for she has seen in man not the image on public view but the contingent individual, the creature of circumstance, that each man in the absence of his peers shows himself to be. She knows women also, for they show themselves without reserve only to other women: she has been behind the scenes. But if her experience enables her to unmask deceits and lies, it is not sufficient to show her the truth. Amused or bitter, the wisdom of the old woman still remains wholly negative: it is in the nature of opposition, indictment, denial; it is sterile. In her thinking as in her acts, the highest form of liberty available to the woman parasite is stoical defiance or skeptical irony. At no time of life does she succeed in being at once effective and independent.

CHAPTER XXI

Woman's Situation and Character

We can now understand why there should be so many common features in the indictments drawn up against woman, from the Greeks to our times. Her condition has remained the same through superficial changes, and it is this condition that determines what is called the "character" of woman: she "revels in immanence," she is contrary, she is prudent and petty, she has no sense of fact or accuracy, she lacks morality, she is contemptibly utilitarian, she is false, theatrical, self-seeking, and so on. There is an element of truth in all this. But we must only note that the varieties of behavior reported are not dictated to woman by her hormones nor predetermined in the structure of the female brain: they are shaped as in a mold by her situation. In this perspective we shall endeavor to make a comprehensive survey of woman's situation. This will involve a certain amount of repetition, but it will enable us to apprehend the eternal feminine in the totality of her economic, social, and historical conditioning.

Sometimes the "feminine world" is contrasted with the masculine universe, but we must insist again that women have never constituted a closed and independent society; they form an integral part of the group, which is governed by males and in which they have a subordinate place. They are united only in a mechanical solidarity from the mere fact of their similarity, but they lack that organic solidarity on which every unified community is based; they are always compelled—at the time of the mysteries of Eleusis as today in clubs, salons, social-service institutes—to band together in order to establish a counter-universe, but they always set it up within the frame of the masculine universe. Hence the paradox of their situation: they belong at one and the same time to the male world and to a sphere in which that world is challenged; shut up in their world, surrounded by the other, they can settle down nowhere in peace. Their docility must always be matched by a refusal, their refusal by an acceptance. In this respect their attitude approaches that of the young girl, but it is more difficult to maintain, because for the adult woman it is not merely a matter of dreaming her life through symbols, but of living it out in actuality.

Woman herself recognizes that the world is masculine on the whole; those who fashioned it, ruled it, and still dominate it today are men. As for her, she does not consider herself responsible for it; it is understood that she is inferior and dependent; she has not learned the lessons of violence, she has never stood forth as subject before the other members of the group. Shut up in her flesh, her home, she sees herself as passive before these gods with human faces who set goals and establish values. In this sense there is truth in the saying that makes her the "eternal child." Workers, black slaves, colonial natives, have also been called grown-up children—as long as they were not feared; that meant that they were to accept without argument the verities and the laws laid down for them by other men. The lot of woman is a respectful obedience. She has no grasp, even in thought, on the reality around her. It is opaque to her eyes.

And it is true that she lacks the technical training that would permit her to dominate matter. As for her, it is not matter she comes to grips with, but life; and life cannot be mastered through the use of tools: one can only submit to its secret laws. The world does not seem to woman "an assemblage of implements" intermediate between her will and her goals, as Heidegger defines it; it is on the contrary something obstinately resistant, unconquerable; it is dominated by fatality and shot through with mysterious caprices. This mystery of a bloody strawberry that inside the mother is transformed into a human being is one no mathematics can express in an equation, no machine can hasten or delay; she feels the strength of a continuity that the most ingenious instruments are unable to divide or to multiply; she feels it in her body, swayed by the lunar rhythm and first ripened, then corrupted, by the years. Each day the kitchen also teaches her patience and passivity; here is alchemy; one must obey the fire, the water, wait for the sugar to melt, for the dough to rise, and also for the wash to dry, for the fruits to ripen on the shelf. Household activities come close to being technical operations, but they are too rudimentary, too monotonous, to prove to a woman the laws of mechanical causation. Besides, even here things are capricious; there are materials that will stand washing and others that will not, spots that can be removed and others that persist, objects that break all by themselves, dusts that spring up like plants.

Woman's mentality perpetuates that of agricultural civilizations which worshipped the magic powers of the land: she believes in magic. Her passive eroticism makes desire seem to her not will and aggression but an attraction akin to that which causes the divining rod to dip; the mere presence of her flesh swells and erects the male's sex; why should not hidden water make the hazel rod quiver? She feels that she is surrounded by waves, radiations, mystic fluids; she believes in telepathy, astrology, radiotherapy, mesmerism, theosophy, table-tipping, clairvoyants, faith healers; her religion is full of primitive superstition: wax candles, answered prayers; she believes the saints incarnate the ancient spirits of nature: this one protects travelers, that one women in labor, this other finds lost articles; and, of course, no prodigy can surprise her. Her attitude will be one of conjuration and prayer; to obtain a certain result, she will perform certain well-tested rites.

It is easy to see why woman clings to routine; time has for her no element of novelty, it is not a creative flow; because she is doomed to repetition, she sees in the future only a duplication of the past. If one knows the word and the formula, duration allies itself with the powers of fecundity—but this is itself subject to the rhythm of the months, the seasons; the cycle of each pregnancy, each flowering, exactly reproduces the one that preceded. In this play of cyclical phenomena the sole effect of time is a slow deterioration: it wears out furniture and clothes as it ruins the face; the reproductive powers are gradually destroyed by the passing of years. Thus woman puts no trust in this relentless force for destruction.

Not only is she ignorant of what constitutes a true action, capable of changing the face of the world, but she is lost in the midst of the world as if she were at the heart of an immense, vague nebula. She is not familiar with the use of masculine logic. Stendhal remarked that she could handle it as adroitly as a man if driven to it by necessity. But it is an instrument that she hardly has occasion to use. A syllogism is of no help in making a successful mayonnaise, nor in quieting a child in tears; masculine reasoning is quite inadequate to the reality with which she deals. And in the world of men, her thought, not flowing into any project, since she *does* nothing, is indistinguishable from daydreaming. She has no sense of factual truth, for lack of effectiveness; she never comes to grips with anything but words and mental pictures, and that is why the most contradictory assertions give

her no uneasiness; she takes little trouble to elucidate the mysteries
of a sphere that is in every way beyond her reach. She is content,
for her purposes, with extremely vague conceptions, confusing parties, opinions, places, people, events; her head is filled with a strange
jumble.

But, after all, to see things clearly is not her business, for she has
been taught to accept masculine authority. So she gives up criticizing,
investigating, judging for herself, and leaves all this to the superior
caste. Therefore the masculine world seems to her a transcendent reality, an absolute. "Men make the gods," says Frazer, "women worship
them." Men cannot kneel with complete conviction before the idols
they have made; but when women encounter these mighty statues
along the roads, they think they are not made with hands, and obe-
diently bow down.[1] In particular they like to have Order and Right
embodied in a leader. In every Olympus there is a supreme god; the
magic male essence must be concentrated in an archetype of which
father, husband, lovers, are only faint reflections. It is rather satirical
to say that their worship of this grand totem is of sexual nature; but
it is true that in this worship they will fully satisfy their childhood
dream of bowing the knee in resignation. In France generals like
Boulanger, Pétain, and de Gaulle [2] have always had the support of
the women; and one recalls with what fluttering pens the lady journalists on the Communist paper *L'Humanité* formerly celebrated Tito
and his splendid uniform. The general, the dictator—eagle-eyed,
square-jawed—is the heavenly father demanded by all serious right-
thinkers, the absolute guarantor of all values. Women's ineffective-
ness and ignorance are what give rise to the respect accorded by them
to heroes and to the laws of the masculine world; they accept them
not through sound judgment but by an act of faith—and faith gets
its fanatical power from the fact that it is not knowledge: it is blind,
impassioned, obstinate, stupid; what it declares, it declares uncon-
ditionally, against reason, against history, against all denial.

This obstinate reverence can take one of two forms according to

---

[1] See Sartre's play *Les Mains sales*. "HŒDERER: They need props, you understand, they are given ready-made ideas, then they believe in them as they do in
God. We're the ones who make these ideas and we know how they are cooked up;
we are never quite sure of being right." [An English translation, *Dirty Hands*, is in
Jean-Paul Sartre: *Three Plays* (New York: Alfred A. Knopf; 1949).]

[2] "When the general passed through, the public consisted largely of women
and children." (Newspaper report of his visit to Savoy.)

circumstances: it may be either the content of the law, or merely its empty form that woman passionately adheres to. If she belongs to the privileged elite that benefits from the established social order, she wants it to be unshakable and she is notably uncompromising in this desire. Man knows that he can develop different institutions, another ethic, a new legal code; aware of his ability to transcend what is, he regards history as a becoming. The most conservative man knows that some evolution is inevitable and realizes that he must adapt his action and his thinking to it; but as woman takes no part in history, she fails to understand its necessities; she is suspiciously doubtful of the future and wants to arrest the flow of time. If the idols set up by her father, her brothers, her husband, are being torn down, she can offer no way of repopulating the heavens; she rushes wildly to the defense of the old gods.

During the War of Secession no Southerners were more passionate in upholding slavery than the women. In England during the Boer War, in France during the Commune, it was the women who were most belligerently inflamed. They seek to compensate for their inactivity by the intensity of the sentiments they exhibit. With victory won, they rush like hyenas upon the fallen foe; in defeat, they bitterly reject any efforts at conciliation. Their ideas being merely attitudes, they support quite unconcernedly the most outdated causes: they can be legitimists in 1914, czarists in 1953. A man will sometimes smilingly encourage them, for it amuses him to see their fanatical reflections of ideas he expresses in more measured terms; but he may also find it irritating to have his ideas take on such a stupid, stubborn, aspect.

Woman assumes this indomitable attitude only in strongly integrated civilizations and social classes. More generally, she respects the law simply because it is the law, since her faith is blind; if the law changes, it retains its spell. In woman's eyes, might makes right because the rights she recognizes in men depend upon their power. Hence it is that when a society breaks down, women are the first to throw themselves at the feet of the conqueror. On the whole, they accept what is. One of their distinguishing traits is resignation. When the ruins of Pompeii were dug up, it was noticed that the incinerated bodies of the men were fixed in attitudes of rebellion, defying the heavens or trying to escape, while those of the women, bent double, were bowed down with their faces toward the earth. Women feel they are powerless against things: volcanoes, police, patrons, men. "Women are born to suffer," they say; "it's life—nothing can be done about it."

This resignation inspires the patience often admired in women. They can stand physical pain much better than men; they are capable of stoical courage when circumstances demand it; lacking the male's aggressive audacity, many women distinguish themselves by their calm tenacity in passive resistance. They face crises, poverty, misfortune, more energetically than their husbands; respecting duration, which no haste can overcome, they do not ration their time. When they apply their quiet persistence to an enterprise, they are sometimes startlingly successful. "Never underestimate the power of a woman." In a generous woman resignation takes the form of forbearance: she puts up with everything, she condemns no one, because she holds that neither people nor things can be other than they are. A proud woman can make a lofty virtue of resignation, as did the stoical Mme de Charrière. But it also engenders a sterile prudence; women are always trying to conserve, to adapt, to arrange, rather than to destroy and build anew; they prefer compromise and adjustment to revolution.

In the nineteenth century, women were one of the greatest obstacles in the way of the effort to free the workers: for one Flora Tristan, one Louise Michel, how many timid housewives begged their husbands not to take any chances! They were not only afraid of strikes, unemployment, and poverty: they feared that revolt might be a mistake. It is easy to understand that, if they must suffer, they preferred what was familiar to adventuring, for they could achieve a meager welfare more easily at home than in the streets.

Women's fate is bound up with that of perishable things; in losing them they lose all. Only a free subject, asserting himself as above and beyond the duration of things, can check all decay; this supreme recourse has been denied to woman. The real reason why she does not believe in a liberation is that she has never put the powers of liberty to a test; the world seems to her to be ruled by an obscure destiny against which it is presumptuous to rise in protest. She has not herself marked out those dangerous roads she is asked to follow, and so it is natural enough for her not to plunge into them with enthusiasm.[3]

---

[3] Compare the passage in *The Journals of André Gide*, Vol. I, p. 301, translated by Justin O'Brien (Alfred A. Knopf, 1949): "Creusa or Lot's wife; one tar-

Let the future be opened to her and she will no longer cling desperately to the past. When women are called upon for concrete action, when they recognize their interest in the designated goals, they are as bold and courageous as men.[4]

Many of the faults for which women are reproached—mediocrity, laziness, frivolity, servility—simply express the fact that their horizon is closed. It is said that woman is sensual, she wallows in immanence; but she has first been shut up in it. The harem slave feels no morbid passion for rose preserves and perfumed baths: she has to kill time. When woman suffocates in a dull gynæceum—brothel or middle-class home—she is bound to take refuge in comfort and well-being; besides that, if she eagerly seeks sexual pleasure, it is very often because she is deprived of it. Sexually unsatisfied, doomed to male crudeness, "condemned to masculine ugliness," she finds consolation in creamy sauces, heady wines, velvets, the caress of water, of sunshine, of a woman friend, of a young lover. If she seems to man so "physical" a creature, it is because her situation leads her to attach extreme importance to her animal nature. The call of the flesh is no louder in her than in the male, but she catches its least murmurs and amplifies them. Sexual pleasure, like rending pain, represents the stunning triumph of the immediate; in the violence of the instant, the future and the universe are denied; what lies outside the carnal flame is nothing; for the brief moment of this apotheosis, woman is no longer mutilated and frustrated. But, once again, she values these triumphs of immanence only because immanence is her lot.

---

ries and the other looks back, which is a worse way of tarrying. . . . There is no greater cry of passion than this:

> And Phædra having braved the Labyrinth with you
> Would have been found with you or lost with you.

But passion blinds her; after a few steps, to tell the truth, she would have sat down, or else would have wanted to go back—or even would have made him carry her."

[The lines quoted are from the *Phèdre* of Racine. The Creusa referred to above was the first wife of Æneas and mother of Ascanius. As related in Virgil's *Æneid*, when Troy was taken and burned, they became separated in the confusion, Æneas escaping and Creusa remaining in the city, to be rescued by Cybele, whose priestess she became. Lot's wife, in the Bible story, looked back at burning Sodom and was punished by being turned into a pillar of salt.—Tr.]

[4] The attitude of proletarian women has changed in just this way after a century; as a particular example, during the recent strikes in mines of northern France, they gave proof of as much passion and energy as the men, demonstrating and fighting beside them.

Her frivolity has the same cause as her "sordid materialism"; she considers little things important for lack of any access to great things, and, furthermore, the futilities that fill her days are often of the most serious practical concern to her. She owes her charm and her opportunities to her dress and her beauty. She often appears to be lazy, indolent; but the occupations available to her are as empty as the pure passage of time. If she is a chatterer, a scribbler, it is to divert her idle hours: for impossible action, she substitutes words. The truth is that when a woman is engaged in an enterprise worthy of a human being, she is quite able to show herself as active, efficient, taciturn—and as ascetic—as a man.

She is accused of being servile; she is always ready, it is said, to lie down at her master's feet and kiss the hand that strikes her, and it is true that she is generally lacking in real pride. The counsel dispensed in columns of "advice to the lovelorn," to deceived wives and abandoned lovers, is full of the spirit of abject submission. Woman wears herself out in haughty scenes, and in the end gathers up the crumbs that the male cares to toss to her. But what can be done without masculine support by a woman for whom man is at once the sole means and the sole reason for living? She is bound to suffer every humiliation; a slave cannot have the sense of human dignity; it is enough if a slave gets out of it with a whole skin.

And finally, if woman is earthy, commonplace, basely utilitarian, it is because she is compelled to devote her existence to cooking and washing diapers—no way to acquire a sense of grandeur! It is her duty to assure the monotonous repetition of life in all its mindless factuality. It is natural for woman to repeat, to begin again without ever inventing, for time to seem to her to go round and round without ever leading anywhere. She is occupied without ever *doing* anything, and thus she identifies herself with what she *has*. This dependence on things, a consequence of the dependence in which men keep her, explains her frugality, her avarice. Her life is not directed toward ends: she is absorbed in producing or caring for things that are never more than means, such as food, clothing, and shelter. These things are inessential intermediaries between animal life and free existence. The sole value that appertains to the inessential means is utility; it is at the level of utility that the housekeeper lives, and she does not flatter herself that she is anything more than a person useful to her kindred.

But no existent can be satisfied with an inessential role, for that immediately makes means into ends—as may be observed, for example, in politicians—and the value of the means comes to seem an absolute value. Thus utility reigns in the housekeeper's heaven, above truth, beauty, liberty; and it is in this perspective that she envisages the entire universe. This is why she adopts the Aristotelian morality of the golden mean—that is, of mediocrity. How could one expect her to show audacity, ardor, disinterestedness, grandeur? These qualities appear only when a free being strikes forward through an open future, emerging far beyond all given actuality. Woman is shut up in a kitchen or in a boudoir, and astonishment is expressed that her horizon is limited. Her wings are clipped, and it is found deplorable that she cannot fly. Let but the future be opened to her, and she will no longer be compelled to linger in the present.

The same inconsistency is displayed when, after being enclosed within the limits of her ego or her household, she is reproached for her narcissism, her egotism, with all their train: vanity, touchiness, malice, and so on. She is deprived of all possibility of concrete communication with others; she does not experience either the appeal or the benefits of solidarity, since she is consecrated entirely to her own family, in isolation. She could hardly be expected, then, to transcend herself toward the general welfare. She stays obstinately within the one realm that is familiar to her, where she can control things and in the midst of which she enjoys a precarious sovereignty.

Lock the doors and close the shutters as she will, however, woman fails to find complete security in her home. It is surrounded by that masculine universe which she respects from afar, without daring to venture into it. And precisely because she is incapable of grasping it through technical skill, sound logic, and definite knowledge, she feels, like the child and the savage, that she is surrounded by dangerous mysteries. She projects her magical conception of reality into that male world; the course of events seems to her to be inevitable, and yet anything can happen; she does not clearly distinguish between the possible and the impossible and is ready to believe anything, no matter what. She listens to and spreads rumors and starts panics. Even when things are quiet, she feels anxious; lying half asleep at night, her rest is disturbed by the nightmare shapes that reality assumes; and thus for woman condemned to passivity, the inscrutable future is haunted by phantoms of war, revolution, famine, poverty; being unable to act, she worries. Her husband, her son, when undertaking an enterprise or facing an emergency, run their own risks; their plans, the regulations they follow, indicate a sure road through obscurity. But woman flounders in confusion and darkness; she gets used to it because she does nothing; in her imagination all possibilities have equal reality: the train may be derailed, the operation may go wrong, the business may fail. What she is endeavoring to exorcize in her gloomy ruminations is the specter of her own powerlessness.

Her anxiety is the expression of her distrust of the world as given; if it seems threatening, ready to collapse, this is because she is unhappy in it. For most of the time she is not resigned to being resigned; she knows very well that she suffers as she does against her will: she is a woman without having been consulted in the matter. She dares not revolt; she submits unwillingly; her attitude is one of constant reproach. All those in whom women confide—doctors, priests, social workers—know that the usual tone is one of complaint. Among friends, woman groans over her own troubles, and they all complain in chorus about the injustice of fate, the world, and men in general.

A free individual blames only himself for his failures, he assumes responsibility for them; but everything happens to women through the agency of others, and therefore these others are responsible for her woes. Her mad despair spurns all remedies; it does not help matters to propose solutions to a woman bent on complaining: she finds none acceptable. She insists on living in her situation precisely as she does —that is, in a state of impotent rage. If some change is proposed she throws up her hands: "That's the last straw!" She knows that her trouble goes deeper than is indicated by the pretexts she advances for it, and she is aware that it will take more than some expedient to deliver her from it. She holds the entire world responsible because it has been made without her, and against her; she has been protesting against her condition since her adolescence, ever since her childhood. She has been promised compensations, she has been assured that if she would place her fortune in man's hands, it would be returned a hundredfold—and she feels she has been swindled. She puts the whole masculine universe under indictment. Resentment is the reverse side of dependence: when one gives all, one never receives enough in return.

Woman is obliged also, however, to regard the male universe with some respect; she would feel in danger without a roof over her head,

if she were in total opposition; so she adopts the Manichæist position
—the clear separation of good and evil—which is also suggested by her
experience as a housekeeper. The individual who acts considers himself, like others, as responsible for both evil and good, he knows that
it is for him to define ends, to bring them to success; he becomes
aware, in action, of the ambiguousness of all solutions; justice and
injustice, gains and losses, are inextricably mixed. But anyone who is
passive is out of the game and declines to pose ethical problems even
in thought: the good *should* be realized, and if it is not, there must be
some wrongdoing for which those to blame must be punished. Like
the child, woman conceives good and evil in simple images, as co-
existing, discrete entities; this Manichæism of hers sets her mind at
rest by doing away with the anxiety of making difficult choices. To
decide between an evil and a lesser evil, between a present good and
a greater good to come, to have to define for herself what is defeat and
what is victory—all this involves terrible risks. For the Manichæist,
the good wheat is clearly distinct from the tares, and one has merely
to remove the tares; dust stands self-condemned and cleanliness is
complete absence of dirt; to clean house is to remove dirt and rubbish.

Thus woman thinks that "it is all the Jews' fault," or the Freemasons' or the Bolsheviks', or the government's; she is always *against*
someone or something. Among those against Dreyfus the women were
even more relentless than the men. They do not always know just
where the evil principle may lie, but what they expect of a "good
government" is to sweep it out as they sweep dust out of the house.
For fervid de Gaullists, de Gaulle is the king of sweepers; they imagine him, feather duster and mop in hand, scrubbing and polishing
to make France "nice and clean."

But these hopes are always for the uncertain future; in the meantime evil continues to corrode the good; and since she cannot get
her hands on the Jews, the Freemasons, the Bolsheviks, the woman
looks about for someone responsible against whom her indignation
can find concrete expression. Her husband is the favorite victim. He
embodies the masculine universe, through him male society has taken
charge of her and swindled her. He bears the weight of the world, and
if things go wrong, it is his fault. When he comes in at night, she
complains to him about the children, the storekeepers, the cost of living, her rheumatism, the weather—and wants him to feel to blame.
She often entertains special grievances against him; but he is guilty in

the first place of being a man. He may very well have maladies and cares of his own—"that's different"—but he holds a privilege which she constantly feels as an injustice. It is a remarkable thing that the hostility she feels toward her husband or lover attaches her to him instead of alienating her from him. A man who has begun to detest wife or mistress tries to get away from her; but woman wants to have the man she hates close at hand so she can make him pay. Recrimination is not a way to get rid of her ills but to wallow in them; the wife's supreme consolation is to pose as a martyr. Life, men, have conquered her: she will turn defeat itself into victory. This explains why she will cheerfully abandon herself to frantic tears and scenes, as in her childhood.

Certainly woman's aptitude for facile tears comes largely from the fact that her life is built upon a foundation of impotent revolt; it is also doubtless true that physiologically she has less nervous control than man and that her education has taught her to let herself go more readily. This effect of education, or custom, is indeed evident, since in the past men like Benjamin Constant and Diderot, for instance, used to pour out floods of tears, and then men ceased weeping when it became unfashionable for them. But, above all, the fact is that woman is always prepared to take an attitude of frustration toward the world because she has never frankly accepted it. A man does accept the world; not even misfortune will change his attitude, he will face it, he will not let himself "give up"; whereas it takes only a little trouble to remind a woman of the hostility of the universe and the injustice of her lot. Then she hastily retires to her surest refuge: herself. These warm traces on her cheeks, these reddened eyes, what are they but the visible presence of her grief-stricken soul? Cool to her skin, scarcely salty on her tongue, tears are also a gentle if bitter caress; her face burns under the merciful flow. Tears are at once plaint and consolation, fever and cooling appeasement. Tears are woman's supreme alibi; sudden as a squall, loosed by fits and starts, typhoon, April shower, they make woman into a plaintive fountain, a stormy sky. Her eyes are blinded, misty; unseeing, they melt in rain; sightless, she returns to the passivity of natural things. One wants her conquered, but she founders in her defeat; she sinks like a stone, she drowns, she eludes the man who is contemplating her, powerless as before a cataract. He considers this performance unfair; but she considers the struggle unfair from the start, because no other effective weapon has been put in her hands. She is resorting once more to a magic conjuration. And the fact that her sobs infuriate the male is one more reason for sobbing.

Whenever tears are insufficient to express her revolt, she will make scenes of such incoherent violence as to abash a man still more. In some circles a husband may strike his wife actual blows; in others he declines to use violence precisely because he is the stronger and his fist is an effective weapon. But a woman, like a child, indulges in symbolic outbursts: she can throw herself on a man, beating and scratching, but it is only a gesture. Yet above all she is engaged in expressing, through the pantomime of the nervous crisis, the insubordination she is unable to carry out in actuality. There are other than physiological reasons for her susceptibility to convulsive manifestations: a convulsion is an interiorization of energy which, when directed outward into the environment, fails to act there on any object; it is an aimless discharge of all the negative forces set up by the situation. The mother rarely has nervous crises with her young children, because she can punish them, strike them; it is rather with her grown son, her husband, or her lover, over whom she has no real power, that woman gives way to her furious tantrums. Mme Tolstoy's hysterical scenes are significant; no doubt she did very wrong in never trying to understand her husband, and in the light of her diary she seems ungenerous, insensitive, and insincere, far from an engaging figure. But whether she was right or wrong in no way changes the horror of her situation. All her life she did nothing but bear up, amid constant reproaches, under marital embraces, maternities, solitude, and the mode of life imposed by her husband. When new decrees of Tolstoy's heightened the conflict, she was unarmed against his inimical will, which she opposed with all her powerless will; she burst out in theatrics of refusal—feigned suicides, feigned flights, feigned maladies, and the like—which were disagreeable to those about her and wearing for herself. It is hard to see that any other outcome was possible for her, since she had no positive reason to conceal her feelings of revolt, and no effective way of expressing them.

There is a way out that is open to the woman who has reached the end of her resistance—it is suicide. But it seems less often resorted to by women than by men. Here the statistics are very ambiguous.[5] Successful suicides are much more common in men than in women, but

---

[5] See Halbwachs: *Les Causes du suicide.*

attempts to end their lives are commoner in the latter. This may be so because women are more likely to be satisfied with play-acting: they *pretend* self-destruction more often than they really *want* it. It is also, in part, because the usual brutal methods are repellent: women almost never use cold steel or firearms. They are much more likely to drown themselves, like Ophelia, attesting the affinity of woman with water, where, in the still darkness, it seems that life might find passive dissolution. In general we see here again the ambiguity I have already signalized: what woman detests she does not honestly try to renounce. She plays at breaking off but in the end remains with the man who is the cause of her woes; she pretends to quit the life which hurts her, but it is relatively rare for her to succeed in killing herself. She has no taste for definitive solutions. She protests against man, against life, against her situation, but she does not make good her escape from them.

There are many aspects of feminine behavior that should be interpreted as forms of protest. We have seen that a woman often deceives her husband through defiance and not for pleasure; and she may be purposely careless and extravagant because he is methodical and economical. Misogynists who accuse woman of always being late think she lacks a sense of punctuality; but as we have seen, the fact is that she can adjust herself very well to the demands of time. When she is late, she has deliberately planned to be. Some coquettish women think they stimulate the man's desire in this way and make their presence the more highly appreciated; but in making the man wait a few minutes, the woman is above all protesting against that long wait: her life.

In a sense her whole existence is waiting, since she is confined in the limbo of immanence and contingence, and since her justification is always in the hands of others. She awaits the homage, the approval of men, she awaits love, she awaits the gratitude and praise of her husband or her lover. She awaits her support, which comes from man; whether she keeps the checkbook or merely gets a weekly or monthly allowance from her husband, it is necessary for him to have drawn his pay or obtained that raise if she is to be able to pay the grocer or buy a new dress. She waits for man to put in an appearance, since her economic dependence places her at his disposal; she is only one element in masculine life while man is her whole existence. The husband has his occupations outside the home, and the wife has to

put up with his absence all day long; the lover—passionate as he may
be—is the one who decides on their meetings and separations in accordance with his obligations. In bed, she awaits the male's desire,
she awaits—sometimes anxiously—her own pleasure.

All she can do is arrive later at the rendezvous her lover has set,
not be ready at the time designated by her husband; in that way she
asserts the importance of her own occupations, she insists on her independence; and for the moment she becomes the essential subject
to whose will the other passively submits. But these are timid attempts at revenge; however persistent she may be in keeping men
waiting, she will never compensate for the interminable hours she
has spent in watching and hoping, in awaiting the good pleasure of
the male.

Woman is bound in a general way to contest foot by foot the rule
of man, though recognizing his over-all supremacy and worshipping
his idols. Hence that famous "contrariness" for which she has often
been reproached. Having no independent domain, she cannot oppose
positive truths and values of her own to those asserted and upheld
by males; she can only deny them. Her negation is more or less thor-
oughgoing, according to the way respect and resentment are propor-
tioned in her nature. But in fact she knows all the faults in the masculine system, and she has no hesitation in exposing them.

Women have no grasp on the world of men because their experience does not teach them to use logic and technique; inversely, masculine apparatus loses its power at the frontiers of the feminine realm.
There is a whole region of human experience which the male deliberately chooses to ignore because he fails to *think* it: this experience woman *lives*. The engineer, so precise when he is laying out his
diagrams, behaves at home like a minor god: a word, and behold, his
meal is served, his shirts starched, his children quieted; procreation
is an act as swift as the wave of Moses' wand; he sees nothing astounding in these miracles. The concept of the miracle is different from
the idea of magic: it presents, in the midst of a world of rational
causation, the radical discontinuity of an event without cause, against
which the weapons of thought are shattered; whereas magical phenomena are unified by hidden forces the continuity of which can be
accepted—without being understood—by a docile mind. The newborn child is miraculous to the paternal minor god, magical for the
mother who has experienced its coming to term within her womb.

The experience of the man is intelligible but interrupted by blanks; that of the woman is, within its own limits, mysterious and obscure but complete. This obscurity makes her weighty; in his relations with her, the male seems light: he has the lightness of dictators, generals, judges, bureaucrats, codes of law, and abstract principles. This is doubtless what a housekeeper meant when she said, shrugging her shoulders: "Men, they don't think!" Women say, also: "Men, they don't know, they don't know life." To the myth of the praying mantis, women contrast the symbol of the frivolous and obtrusive drone bee.

It is understandable, in this perspective, that woman takes exception to masculine logic. Not only is it inapplicable to her experience, but in his hands, as she knows, masculine reasoning becomes an underhand form of force; men's undebatable pronouncements are intended to confuse her. The intention is to put her in a dilemma: either you agree or you do not. Out of respect for the whole system of accepted principles she should agree; if she refuses, she rejects the entire system. But she cannot venture to go so far; she lacks the means to reconstruct society in different form. Still, she does not accept it as it is. Halfway between revolt and slavery, she resigns herself reluctantly to masculine authority. On each occasion he has to force her to accept the consequences of her halfhearted yielding. Man pursues that chimera, a companion half slave, half free: in yielding to him, he would have her yield to the convincingness of an argument, but she knows that he has himself chosen the premises on which his rigorous deductions depend. As long as she avoids questioning them, he will easily reduce her to silence; nevertheless he will not convince her, for she senses his arbitrariness. And so, annoyed, he will accuse her of being obstinate and illogical; but she refuses to play the game because she knows the dice are loaded.

Woman does not entertain the positive belief that the truth is something *other* than men claim; she recognizes, rather, that there *is not* any fixed truth. It is not only the changing nature of life that makes her suspicious of the principle of constant identity, nor is it the magic phenomena with which she is surrounded that destroy the notion of causality. It is at the heart of the masculine world itself, it is in herself as belonging to this world that she comes upon the ambiguity of all principle, of all value, of everything that exists. She knows that masculine morality, as it concerns her, is a vast hoax. Man pompously thunders forth his code of virtue and honor; but in secret he invites her to disobey it, and he even counts on this disobedience; without it, all that splendid façade behind which he takes cover would collapse.

Man gladly accepts as his authority Hegel's idea according to which the citizen acquires his ethical dignity in transcending himself toward the universal, but as a private individual he has a right to desire and pleasure. His relations with woman, then, lie in a contingent region, where morality no longer applies, where conduct is a matter of indifference. With other men he has relations in which values are involved; he is a free agent confronting other free agents under laws fully recognized by all; but with woman—she was invented for this purpose—he casts off the responsibility of existence, he abandons himself to the mirage of his *en-soi*, or fixed, lower nature, he puts himself on the plane of inauthenticity. He shows himself tyrannical, sadistic, violent, or puerile, masochistic, querulous; he tries to satisfy his obsessions and whims; he is "at ease," he "relaxes," in view of the rights acquired in his public life.

His wife is often astonished—like Thérèse Desqueyroux—at the contrast between the lofty tone of his public utterances and behavior, and "his persevering inventions in the dark." He preaches the higher birth rate, but he is skillful at begetting no more children than suits his convenience. He lauds chaste and faithful wives, but he asks his neighbor's wife to commit adultery. We have seen how hypocritically men decree that abortion is criminal, when each year in France a million women are put by men in a position to need abortion; often enough the husband or lover demands this solution; often, too, they assume tacitly that it will be adopted if necessary. They count openly on the woman's willingness to make herself guilty of a crime: her "immorality" is necessary to the harmony of the moral society respected by men.

The most flagrant example of this duplicity is the male's attitude toward prostitution, for it is his demand that creates the supply. I have told with what disgusted skepticism prostitutes regard the respectable gentlemen who condemn vice in general but view their own personal whims with indulgence; yet they regard the girls who live off their bodies as perverted and debauched, not the males who use them. An anecdote will serve to illustrate this state of mind. Around the turn of the century the police found two little girls of twelve and thirteen in a brothel; testifying at the trial, the girls referred to their clients, who were men of importance, and one of the girls was about to give a name. The judge stopped her at once: "*You must not befoul the name of a respectable man!*" A gentleman decorated by the Legion of Honor is still a respectable man when deflowering a little girl; he has his weaknesses, as who does not? Whereas the little girl who has no aspirations toward the ethical realm of the universal—who is not a magistrate, or a general, or a great Frenchman, nothing but a little girl—stakes her moral value in the contingent realm of sexuality: she is perverse, corrupted, vicious, fit only for the reformatory.

In many cases man, without besmirching his lofty image, can perpetrate with woman's connivance actions that for her are infamous. She does not understand these subtleties very well; what she does comprehend is that man does not act according to the principles he professes and asks her to disobey them; he does not wish what he says he wishes. So she does not give him what she pretends to give him. She is to be a chaste and faithful wife—and on the sly she will yield to his desires; she is to be an admirable mother—but she will carefully practice birth control and will have an abortion if necessary. Man disapproves of her officially—it's the rule of the game—but he is secretly grateful for her "easy virtue," for her sterility.

Woman plays the part of those secret agents who are left to the firing squad if they get caught, and are loaded with rewards if they succeed; it is for her to shoulder all man's immorality: not the prostitute only, but all women who serve as sewer to the shining, wholesome edifice where respectable people have their abode. When, thereupon, to these women one speaks of dignity, honor, loyalty, of all the lofty masculine virtues, it is not astonishing if they decline to "go along." They laugh in derision particularly when the virtuous males have just reproached them for not being disinterested, for play-acting, for lying.[6] They well know that no other way out is open to them. Man, too, is not "disinterested" regarding money and success, but he has the means for attaining them in his work. Woman has been assigned the role of parasite—and every parasite is an exploiter. Woman has need of the male in order to gain human dignity, to eat, to enjoy life, to procreate; it is through the service of sex that she gets these

---

[6] "All with that little air of delicacy and touch-me-not prudery, assumed in a long past of slavery, with no other means of salvation and support than that air of unintentional seductiveness biding its time." (Jules Laforgue.)

benefits; because she is confined to that function, she is wholly an instrumentality of exploitation.

As for lying, except in the case of prostitution, there is no question of a frank business deal between her and her protector. Man even demands play-acting: he wants her to be the *Other*; but all existents remain subjects, try as they will to deny themselves. Man wants woman to be object: she *makes* herself object; at the very moment when she does that, she is exercising a free activity. Therein is her original treason; the most docile, the most passive, is still a conscious being; and sometimes the fact that in giving herself to him she looks at him and judges him is enough to make him feel duped; she is supposed to be only something offered, no more than prey. He also demands, however, that this "thing" give herself over to him of her own free will: in bed he asks her to feel pleasure; in the home she must sincerely recognize his superiority and his merits. She is, then, to feign independence at the moment of obedience, although at other moments she actively plays the comedy of being passive. She lies to hold the man who provides her daily bread; there are scenes and tears, transports of love, crises of nerves—all false—and she lies also to escape from the tyranny she accepts through self-interest. He encourages her in make-believe that flatters his lordliness and his vanity; and she uses against him in return her powers of dissimulation. Thus she gains revenge that is doubly sweet, for in deceiving him she satisfies her own desires and enjoys the pleasure of treating him with derision. The wife and the courtesan lie when they feign transports they do not feel; afterward, with lovers or woman friends, they make fun of the naïve vanity of their dupes. "They not only bungle things, but they expect us to wear ourselves out showing pleasure," they say resentfully.

Such conversations are very like those of domestics talking over their employers critically in the servants' quarters. Woman has the same faults because she is a victim of the same paternalistic oppression; she has the same cynicism because she sees man from top to toe, as a valet sees his master. But it is clear that none of woman's traits manifest an originally perverted essence or will: they reflect a situation. "There is dissimulation everywhere under a coercive regime," says Fourier. "Prohibition and contraband are inseparable in love as in trade." And men know that woman's faults indicate her situation so well that, anxious to maintain the hierarchy of sexes, they encourage in their companions the very traits that merit their contempt. No doubt the husband or lover is irritated by the faults of the particular woman he lives with, and yet when they extoll the charms of femininity in general, they believe it to be inseparable from its defects. If woman is not faithless, futile, cowardly, indolent, she loses her seductiveness.

In Ibsen's *A Doll's House*, Helmer explains how strong, just, understanding, indulgent, a man feels when he pardons frail woman her childish faults. And similarly the husbands in Bernstein's plays are moved to tears—with the collusion of the author—over the thieving, malicious, adulterous wife; bending over her solicitously, they display in contrast their own virile goodness. American racists and French colonials, as we have seen, similarly want the black man to be thievish, lazy, lying: this proves his unworthiness; it puts right on the side of the oppressors; if he insists on being honest and loyal, he is regarded as a "bad actor." Woman's faults, then, are magnified the more in that she will not try to combat them but, on the contrary, will make an ornament of them.

Not accepting logical principles and moral imperatives, skeptical about the laws of nature, woman lacks the sense of the universal; to her the world seems a confused conglomeration of special cases. This explains why she believes more readily in the tittle-tattle of a neighbor than in a scientific explanation. No doubt she respects the printed book, but she respectfully skims the pages of type without getting at the meaning; on the contrary, the anecdote told by some unknown in a waiting line or drawing-room at once takes on an overwhelming authority. Within her sphere all is magic; outside, all is mystery. She is unfamiliar with the criterion of plausibility; only immediate experience carries conviction—her own experience, or that of others if stated emphatically enough. As for her own self, she feels she is a special case because she is isolated in her home and hence does not come into active contact with other women; she is always expecting that destiny and men will make an exception in her favor. She believes in her intuitions much more firmly than in universally valid reasoning; she readily admits that they come from God or from some vague world-spirit; regarding some misfortune or accident she calmly thinks: "That will not happen to me." Regarding benefits, on the other hand, she imagines that "an exception will be made in my case": she rather expects special favors. The storekeeper will give her a discount, the policeman will let her through without a pass; she has been taught to overestimate the value of her smile, and no one has told her that all women smile. It is not that she thinks herself more extraordinary than her neighbor: she does not make the comparison. And for the same reason experience rarely shows her how wrong she is: she meets with one failure after another, but she does not sum them up in a valid conclusion.

This shows why women do not succeed in building up a solid counter-universe whence they can challenge the males; now and then they rail at men in general, they tell what happens in the bedroom or at childbirth, they exchange horoscopes and beauty secrets. But they lack the conviction necessary to build this grievance-world their resentment calls for; their attitude toward man is too ambivalent. Doubtless he is a child, a necessitous and vulnerable body, he is a simpleton, a bothersome drone, a mean tyrant, a vain egotist; but he is also the liberating hero, the divinity who bestows values. His desire is gross appetite, his embrace a degrading duty; yet his fire and virile force seem like demiurgic power. When a woman says ecstatically: "He is a man!" she evokes at once the sexual vigor and the social effectiveness of the man she admires. In both he displays the same creative superiority; she does not conceive of his being a great artist, a great man of business, a general, a leader, without being a potent lover, and thus his social successes always have a sexual attractiveness; inversely, she is quick to see genius in the man who satisfies her desires.

We must add that in this she is returning to one of the masculine myths. For Lawrence, as for many others, the phallus represents both living energy and human transcendence. Thus woman can see in the pleasures of the couch a communion with the spirit of the world. In mystical worship of man she is lost and also finds herself again in her glory. The contradiction is easily explained, thanks to the variety of sexually potent individuals. Some of them—whose ineffectual contingence she knows in everyday life—are the embodiment of human paltriness; in others man's grandeur reaches its summit. But woman can even countenance the confusing of these two figures in one. "If I become famous," writes a young girl in love with a man she considers superior, "R. will surely marry me, for his vanity will be flattered; he would swell with pride, out walking with me on his arm." Yet she admired him madly. In a woman's eyes the same person may very well be stingy, mean, vain, ridiculous, and a god; after all, the gods have their weaknesses. An individual who is loved as a free being, in his humanity, is regarded with that critical, demanding severity which is the other side of genuine esteem; whereas a woman submissively kneeling before her male can very well pride herself on knowing how to "manage," to "handle" him; she complaisantly flatters his "weak side" without his losing prestige. This is proof that she does not care for his individual personality as it finds expression in actual activity; she is bowing down blindly before the generalized essence in which her idol shares. Virility is a sacred aura, a given, set value that makes itself felt in spite of the pettinesses of the individual who carries it; he does not count; on the contrary, the woman, jealous of his privileged status, finds pleasure in assuming a malicious superiority over him in various respects.

The ambiguity of woman's feelings toward man is found again in her general attitude toward herself and the world. The domain in which she is confined is surrounded by the masculine universe, but it is haunted by obscure forces of which men are themselves the playthings; if she allies herself with these magical forces, she will come to power in her turn. Society enslaves Nature; but Nature dominates it. The Spirit flames out beyond Life; but it ceases to burn when life no longer supports it. Woman is justified by this equivocation in finding more verity in a garden than in a city, in a malady than in an idea, in a birth than in a revolution; she endeavors to re-establish that reign of the earth, of the Mother, dreamed by Bachofen,[7] in order to become again the essential in face of the inessential. But as she, also, is an existent having transcendence, she can give value to that domain where she is confined only by transfiguring it: she lends it a transcendent dimension. Man lives in a consistent universe that is a reality conceivable in thought. Woman is at grips with a magical reality that defies thought, and she escapes from it through thoughts without real content. Instead of taking up her existence, she contemplates in the clouds the pure Idea of her destiny; instead of acting, she sets up her own image in the realm of imagination: that is, instead of reasoning, she dreams. Hence the fact that while being "physical," she is also artificial, and while being earthy, she makes herself etherial. Her life is passed in washing pots and pans, and it is a glittering novel; man's vassal, she thinks she is his idol; carnally humiliated, she is all for Love. Because

---

7 See reference in H. Deutsch: *Psychology of Women*, Vol. I, p. 281.—TR.

she is condemned to know only the factual contingence of life, she makes herself priestess of the Ideal.

This ambivalence is evident in the way woman regards her body. It is a burden: worn away in service to the species, bleeding each month, proliferating passively, it is not for her a pure instrument for getting a grip on the world but an opaque physical presence; it is no certain source of pleasure and it creates lacerating pains; it contains menaces: woman feels endangered by her "insides." It is a "hysteric" body, on account of the close connection of the endocrine secretions with the nervous and sympathetic systems that control the muscles and the viscera. Her body displays reactions for which the woman denies responsibility; in sobs, vomiting, convulsions, it escapes her control, it betrays her; it is her most intimate verity, but it is a shameful verity that she keeps hidden. And yet it is also her glorious double; she is dazzled in beholding it in the mirror; it is promised happiness, work of art, living statue; she shapes it, adorns it, puts it on show. When she smiles at herself in the glass, she forgets her carnal contingence; in the embrace of love, in maternity, her image is destroyed. But often, as she muses on herself, she is astonished to be at one and the same time that heroine and that flesh.

Nature similarly presents a double face to her, supplying the soup kettle and stimulating mystical effusions. When she became a housekeeper and a mother, woman renounced her free roaming of field and wood, she preferred the quiet cultivation of her kitchen garden, she tamed the flowers and put them in vases: yet she is still entranced with moonlight and sunset. In the terrestrial fauna and flora she sees food and ornament before all; but in them a sap circulates which is nobility and magic. Life is not merely immanence and repetition: it has also a dazzling face of light; in flowery meadows it is revealed as Beauty. Attuned to nature by the fertility of her womb, woman is also swept by its animating breeze, which is spirit. And to the extent that she remains unsatisfied and, like the young girl, feels unfulfilled and unlimited, her soul, too, will be lost to sight down roads stretching endlessly on, toward unbounded horizons. Enslaved as she is to her husband, her children, her home, it is ecstasy to find herself alone, sovereign on the hillsides; she is no longer mother, wife, housekeeper, but a human being; she contemplates the passive world, and she remembers that she is wholly a conscious being, an irreducible free individual. Before the mystery of water and the leap of summits, the male's supremacy fades away. Walking through the heather, dipping her hand in the stream, she is living not for others, but for herself. Any woman who has preserved her independence through all her servitudes will ardently love her own freedom in Nature. Others will find there only pretexts for refined raptures; and they will hesitate at twilight between the danger of catching cold and an ecstasy of the soul.

This double allegiance to the carnal world and to a world of "poetry" defines the metaphysics, the wisdom, to which woman more or less explicitly adheres. She endeavors to combine life and transcendence, which is to say that she rejects Cartesianism, with its formal logic, and all related doctrines. She is at home in a naturalism like that of the Stoics or the Neoplatonists of the sixteenth century. It is not surprising that women, headed by Marguerite of Navarre, should accept a philosophy at once so material and so spiritual. Socially Manichæistic, as we have seen, woman has a profound need to be ontologically optimistic—she must believe that the nature of things tends on the whole to be good. The moralities of action do not suit her, for she is not allowed to act; she is therefore subject to the given: and the given, then, must be the Good; but a good which, like that of Spinoza, is recognized by reasoning, or, like that of Leibnitz, by calculation, cannot concern her.

She craves a good that is a living Harmony in the midst of which she is placed simply by virtue of being alive. The concept of harmony is one of the keys to the feminine universe; it implies a stationary perfection, the immediate justification of each element depending on the whole and on its passive participation in the totality. In a harmonious world woman thus attains what man will seek through action: she meshes with the world, she is necessary to it, she co-operates in the triumph of the Good. The moments that women regard as revelations are those in which they discover their accord with a static and self-sufficient reality: those luminous moments of happiness which Virginia Woolf (in *Mrs. Dalloway* and *To the Lighthouse*) and Katherine Mansfield (throughout her work) bestow upon their heroines by way of supreme recompense. The joy that lies in the free surge of liberty is reserved for man; that which woman knows is a quiet sense of smiling plenitude.[8] It is understandable that a mere

---

[8] In Mrs. Luhan's *Lorenzo in Taos*, p. 74, is a passage in point: "It was a still, autumn day, all yellow and crimson. Frieda and I, in a lapse of antagonism, sat on the ground together, with the red apples piled all around us. We were warmed

state of tranquillity can take high value in her eyes, since woman normally lives in the tension of denial, resentment, exaction; and she cannot be reproached for enjoying a fine afternoon or a cool evening. But it is a delusion to seek the hidden soul of the world here. The Good cannot be considered something that *is:* the world is not harmony, and no individual has an essential place in it.

There is a justification, a supreme compensation, which society is ever wont to bestow upon woman: that is, religion. There must be a religion for woman as there must be one for the common people, and for exactly the same reasons. When a sex or a class is condemned to immanence, it is necessary to offer it the mirage of some form of transcendence. Man enjoys the great advantage of having a God endorse the codes he writes; and since man exercises a sovereign authority over woman, it is especially fortunate that this authority has been vested in him by the Supreme Being. For the Jews, Mohammedans, and Christians, among others, man is master by divine right; the fear of God, therefore, will repress any impulse toward revolt in the downtrodden female. One can bank on her credulity. Woman takes an attitude of respect and faith toward the masculine universe: God in His heaven seems to her hardly less remote than a cabinet minister, and the mystery of creation is approached by that of the electrical powerhouse. But if woman quite willingly embraces religion, it is above all because it fills a profound need.

In modern civilization, which—even for woman—has a share in promoting freedom, religion seems much less an instrument of constraint than an instrument of deception. Woman is asked in the name of God not so much to accept her inferiority as to believe that, thanks to Him, she is the equal of the lordly male; even the temptation to revolt is suppressed by the claim that the injustice is overcome. Woman is no longer denied transcendence, since she is to consecrate her immanence to God; the worth of souls is to be weighed only in heaven and not according to their accomplishments on earth. As Dostoyevsky says, here below it is just a matter of different occupa-

and scented by the sun and the rich earth—and the apples were living tokens of plenitude and peace and rich living; the rich, natural flow of the earth, like the sappy blood in our veins, made us feel gay, indomitable, and fruitful like orchards. We were united for a moment, Frieda and I, in a mutual assurance of self-sufficiency, made certain, as women are sometimes, of our completeness by the sheer force of our bountiful health." Here the passage to a total vision of the world is not explicit but is clearly suggested.

tions: shining shoes or building a bridge, all alike is vanity; above and beyond social discriminations, the equality of the sexes is restored. This is why the little girl and the adolescent are much more fervent devotees than their brothers; the eye of God, which transcends the boy's transcendence, humiliates him: under this mighty guardianship he will remain a child forever; it is a more radical castration than that threatened by his father's existence. But the "eternal child," if female, finds her salvation in this eye that transforms her into a sister of the angels. It cancels the advantage of the penis. A sincere faith is a great help to the little girl in avoiding an inferiority complex: she is neither male nor female, but God's creature.

Hence it is that we find a quite masculine firmness in many of the great female saints: St. Bridget, St. Catherine of Siena, arrogantly claim to lord it over the world; they recognize no masculine authority whatever. Catherine very severely directed even her spiritual directors; Joan of Arc and St. Theresa went their appointed ways with an intrepidity unsurpassed by any man. The Church sees to it that God never authorizes women to escape male guardianship; she has put exclusively in man's hands such powerful weapons as denial of absolution and excommunication; obstinately true to her visions, Joan of Arc was burned at the stake.

Although subordinated to the law of men by the will of God Himself, woman none the less finds in Him a mighty refuge from them. Masculine logic is confuted by holy mysteries; men's pride becomes a sin, their agitation for this and that is more than absurd, it is blameworthy: why remodel this world which God Himself created? The passivity enforced upon woman is sanctified. Telling her beads by the fire, she knows she is nearer heaven than is her husband gadding about at political meetings. There is no need to *do* anything to save her soul, it is enough to *live* in obedience. The synthesis of life and spirit is accomplished: a mother not only engenders the flesh, she produces a soul for God; and this is a greater work than penetrating the futile secrets of the atom. With the heavenly Father's connivance, woman can boldly lay claim to the glory of her femininity in defiance of man.

Thus God not alone restores the feminine sex in general to its place of dignity; but each woman will find in the heavenly absent One a special support. As a human person she has little influence, but once she acts in the name of divine inspiration, her wishes become sacred.

Mme Guyon [9] says she learned, in connection with a nun's illness, "what it is to command by the Word and to obey by the same Word"; thus the devotee disguises her authority in humble obedience. When she is bringing up her children, governing a convent, organizing a charitable society, she is only a humble tool in supernatural hands; she cannot be disobeyed without offending God Himself. Men, to be sure, do not disdain this support; but it is not too reliable when they are dealing with other men, who can claim it equally well: the conflict is so arranged as to reach a decision on the human level. Woman invokes the divine will to justify her authority absolutely in the eyes of those naturally subordinated to her already and to justify it in her own eyes. If she finds this co-operation of real use, it is because she is occupied above all by her relations with herself—even when these relations affect others; for the supreme Silence can have the force of law in these wholly inward debates alone.

The fact is that woman makes religion a pretext for satisfying her own desires. Is she frigid, masochistic, sadistic? She finds holiness in renouncing the flesh, in playing the martyr, in crushing every living impulse around her. By mutilating, annihilating herself, she rises several degrees in the hierarchy of the elect; when she martyrizes husband and children, denying them all worldly happiness, she is preparing for them a choice place in paradise. According to her pious biographer, Margaret of Cortona maltreated the offspring of her fault "to punish herself for having sinned"; she fed him only after feeding all the vagrant beggars. As we have seen, hatred of the unwanted child is common: it is a godsend—literally—to be able to give way to it with righteous anger. For her part, the woman of easy virtue easily arranges things with God; the assurance of obtaining absolution for her sins tomorrow often helps the pious woman conquer her scruples today.

Whether she has chosen asceticism or sensuality, pride or humility, the concern she feels for her salvation leads her to yield to that pleasure which she prefers to all others: namely, being occupied with herself. She listens to her heartbeats, she notes the thrills of her flesh, justified by the presence of God's grace within her as is the pregnant woman by that of her fruit. Not only does she scrutinize herself with fond vigilance, but she reports on herself to her confessor; in former

---

[9] French mystic of the early eighteenth century, who taught that the pure love of God is sufficient for salvation.—TR.

times she could even savor the ecstasy of public confession. They tell of that same Margaret of Cortona that, *to punish herself for a moment of vanity,* she stood on her terrace and began to cry out like a woman in labor: "Arise, people of Cortona, arise with candles and lanterns and come out to hear the sinner!" She rehearsed all her sins, proclaiming her woe to the stars. By this vociferous humility she satisfied that need for exhibitionism often exemplified in narcissistic women. Religion sanctions woman's self-love; it gives her the guide, father, lover, divine guardian she longs for nostalgically; it feeds her daydreams; it fills her empty hours. But, above all, it confirms the social order, it justifies her resignation, by giving her the hope of a better future in a sexless heaven. This is why women today are still a powerful trump in the hand of the Church; it is why the Church is notably hostile to all measures likely to help in woman's emancipation. There must be religion for women; and there must be women, "true women," to perpetuate religion.

It is evident that woman's "character"—her convictions, her values, her wisdom, her morality, her tastes, her behavior—are to be explained by her situation. The fact that transcendence is denied her keeps her as a rule from attaining the loftiest human attitudes: heroism, revolt, disinterestedness, imagination, creation; but even among the males they are none too common. There are many men who, like women, are restricted to the sphere of the intermediary and instrumental, of the inessential means. The worker escapes from it through political action expressing a will to revolution; but the men of the classes called precisely "middle" implant themselves in that sphere deliberately. Destined like woman to the repetition of daily tasks, identified with ready-made values, respectful of public opinion, and seeking on earth naught but a vague comfort, the employee, the merchant, the office worker, are in no way superior to their accompanying females. Cooking, washing, managing her house, bringing up children, woman shows more initiative and independence than the man slaving under orders. All day long he must obey his superiors, wear a white collar, and keep up his social standing; she can dawdle around the apartment in a wrapper, sing, laugh with her neighbors; she does as she pleases, takes little risks, tries to succeed in getting certain results. She lives less than her husband in an atmosphere of conventional concern for appearances.

The office universe which, among other things, Kafka has described, this universe of formalities, of absurd gestures, of purposeless behavior, is essentially masculine. Woman gets her teeth more deeply into reality; for when the office worker has drawn up his figures, or translated boxes of sardines into money, he has nothing in his hands but abstractions. The baby fed and in his cradle, clean linen, the roast, constitute more tangible assets; yet just because, in the concrete pursuit of these aims, she feels their contingence—and accordingly her own—it often happens that woman does not identify herself with them, and she still has something left of herself. Man's enterprises are at once projects and evasions: he lets himself be smothered by his career and his "front"; he often becomes self-important, weighty. Being against man's logic and morality, woman does not fall into these traps, which Stendhal found much to his taste in her; she does not take refuge in her pride from the ambiguity of her position; she does not hide behind the mask of human dignity; she reveals her undisciplined thoughts, her emotions, her spontaneous reactions, more frankly. Thus her conversation is much less tiresome than her husband's whenever she speaks for herself and not as her lord and master's loyal "better half." He discusses what are called general ideas—that is to say, words, formulas, to be found in the columns of his paper or in technical works—she reveals a limited but concrete experience.

The well-known "feminine sensitivity" derives somewhat from myth, somewhat from make-believe; but it is also a fact that woman is more attentive than man to herself and to the world. She lives sexually in a crude masculine climate and in compensation has a liking for "nice things," which can give rise to finical affectation, but also to real delicacy. Because her sphere is limited, the objectives she does attain seem precious; not regarding them as bound up with either concepts or projects, she simply puts their splendor on display. Her wish to escape is expressed in her love of festivity: she is enchanted by the useless charm of a bouquet of flowers, a cake, a well-set table; she enjoys turning her empty leisure into a bountiful offering. Loving laughter, song, adornments, and knickknacks, she is prepared to accept all that throbs around her: the spectacle of the street, of the sky; an invitation, an evening out, open new horizons to her. Man often declines to take part in these pleasures; when he comes into the house, the gay voices are silenced, the women of the family assume the bored and proper air he expects of them.

From the depths of her solitude, her isolation, woman gains her sense of the personal bearing of her life. The past, death, the passage of time—of these she has a more intimate experience than does man; she feels deep interest in the adventures of her heart, of her flesh, of her mind, because she knows that this is all she has on earth. And more, from the fact that she is passive, she experiences more passionately, more movingly, the reality in which she is submerged than does the individual absorbed in an ambition or a profession; she has the leisure and the inclination to abandon herself to her emotions, to study her sensations and unravel their meaning. When her imagination is not lost in empty dreams, she becomes all sympathy: she tries to understand others as individuals and to identify them with herself; with her husband or lover she is capable of making this identification complete: she makes his projects and cares hers in a way he cannot imitate.

She bestows this anxious attention upon the whole world; it seems an enigma to her, and each person, each object, can be an answer; she questions them eagerly. When she grows old, her disappointed expectation is transformed into irony and an often spicy cynicism; she declines to be fooled by man's mystifications, seeing the contingent, absurd, unnecessary inverse of the imposing structure built by the males. Her dependence forbids detachment, but from the well of her imposed self-sacrifice she sometimes draws up real generosity. She forgets herself in favor of her husband, her lover, her child; she ceases to think of herself, she is pure gift, pure offering. Being poorly adapted to man's society, she is often forced to invent her mode of behavior on the spur of the moment; she is not fully satisfied with ready-made forms and clichés; with the best will in the world, she has a sense of misgiving about them which is nearer to authenticity than is the self-important assurance of her husband.

But she will have these advantages over the male only on condition that she rejects the deceptions he offers. In the upper classes women are eager accomplices of their masters because they stand to profit from the benefits provided. We have seen that the women of the upper middle classes and the aristocracy have always defended their class interests even more obstinately than have their husbands, not hesitating radically to sacrifice their independence as human beings. They repress all thought, all critical judgment, all spontaneous impulses; they parrot accepted opinions, they confuse with the ideal whatever the masculine code imposes on them; all genuineness is dead in their hearts and even in their faces. The housekeeper regains some independence in her work, gaining a concrete if limited experience from it; but a woman whose work is done by servants has no grip on the world; she lives in dreams and abstractions, in a vacuum. She does not understand the bearing of the ideas she professes; the words she uses in discussion have lost all their meaning. The financier, the captain of industry, sometimes even the military leader, know toil and care, they assume risks; they buy their privileges in an unfair market, but at least they pay for them in person. But their wives give nothing, do nothing, in exchange for all they get; on this account they believe in their indefeasible rights with so much the blinder faith. Their vain arrogance, their radical incapability, their obstinate ignorance, make them the most useless nonentities ever produced by the human species.

It is as absurd, then, to speak of "woman" in general as of the "eternal" man. And we understand why all comparisons are idle which purport to show that woman is superior, inferior, or equal to man, for their situations are profoundly different. If we compare these situations rather than the people in them, we see clearly that man's is far preferable; that is to say, he has many more opportunities to exercise his freedom in the world. The inevitable result is that masculine accomplishment is far superior to that of women, who are practically forbidden to *do* anything. Moreover, to compare the use which, within their limitations, men and women make of their liberty is *a priori* a meaningless attempt, since precisely what they do is use it freely. Under various forms, the snares of bad faith and the deceptions of overseriousness—temptations not to be genuine—await the one sex as much as the other; inner liberty is complete in both. But simply from the fact that liberty in woman is still abstract and empty, she can exercise it only in revolt, which is the only road open to those who have no opportunity of doing anything constructive. They must reject the limitations of their situation and seek to open the road of the future. Resignedness is only abdication and flight, there is no other way out for woman than to work for her liberation.

This liberation must be collective, and it requires first of all that the economic evolution of woman's condition be accomplished. There have been, however, and there are many women trying to achieve individual salvation by solitary effort. They are attempting to justify their existence in the midst of their immanence—that is, to realize transcendence in immanence. It is this ultimate effort— sometimes ridiculous, often pathetic—of imprisoned woman to transform her prison into a heaven of glory, her servitude into sovereign liberty, that we shall observe in the narcissist, in the woman in love, in the mystic.

PART VI

JUSTIFICATIONS

CHAPTER XXII

The Narcissist

It has sometimes been maintained that narcissism is the fundamental attitude of all women; [1] but to extend this idea too broadly is to destroy it, as La Rochefoucauld destroyed that of egoism. [2] The fact is that narcissism is a well-defined process of identification, in which the ego is regarded as an absolute end and the subject takes refuge from himself in it. Many other attitudes—authentic or inauthentic—are met with in woman, some of which we have already studied. But it is true that conditions lead woman more than man to turn toward herself and devote her love to herself.

All love requires the duality of a subject and an object. Woman is led into narcissism along two converging roads. As subject she feels frustrated; when very young she lacks that *alter ego* which his penis is for the boy; later on, her aggressive sexuality remains unsatisfied. And what is much more important, masculine activities are forbidden her. She is occupied, but she *does* nothing; she does not get

---

[1] As by Helene Deutsch in *Psychology of Women*, Vol. I, p. 187.
[2] In his *Maximes* (1665), La Rochefoucauld attributed all conscious human sentiment and action to the motive of self-interest.—Tr.

recognition as an individual through her functioning as wife, mother, housekeeper. The reality of man is in the houses he builds, the forests he clears, the maladies he cures; but woman, not being able to fulfill herself through projects and objectives, is forced to find her reality in the immanence of her person. Parodying the saying of Sieyès,[3] Marie Bashkirtsev wrote: "What am I? Nothing. What would I be? Everything." It is because they are nothing that many women sullenly confine their interests merely to their egos and inflate them so greatly as to confound them with Everything. "I am my own heroine," said Marie Bashkirtsev, again. A man who acts must necessarily size himself up. Ineffective, isolated, woman can neither find her place nor take her own measure; she gives herself supreme importance because no object of importance is accessible to her.

If she can thus offer *herself* to her own desires, it is because she has felt herself an object since childhood. Her education has prompted her to identify herself with her whole body, puberty has revealed this body as being passive and desirable; it is something she can touch, like satin or velvet, and can contemplate with a lover's eye. In solitary pleasure, woman may divide herself into male subject and female object; thus Irène, a patient of Dalbiez,[4] would say to herself: "I am going to love myself," or more passionately: "I am going to have intercourse with myself," or in a paroxysm: "I am going to impregnate myself." Marie Bashkirtsev also is simultaneously subject and object when she writes: "It is too bad no one can see my arms and body, all this freshness and youth."

As a matter of fact, it is impossible to be *for one's self* actually an *other* and to recognize oneself consciously as object. The duality is merely dreamed. For the child this dream is materialized in the doll; she sees herself in the doll more concretely than in her own body, because she and the doll are actually separated from each other. This need of being two in order to hold an affectionate dialogue between self and self has been expressed by Mme Anna de Noailles, for example, in her *Livre de ma vie:*

---

[3] French politician and writer, one of the founders of the Jacobins of the Revolution, around 1789.—TR.

[4] See *La Psychanalyse*. In her childhood Irène enjoyed urinating boy-fashion; in dreams she often saw herself in the form of an undine, or water-spirit, which supports Havelock Ellis's ideas on the relationship between narcissism and what he calls "undinism"—that is, a kind of urinary eroticism. (See *The Psychology of Sex*, Vol. III, Part 2.)

I loved dolls, I imagined them as alive as I was; I would not have slept warm under my coverings unless they were well wrapped in wool and velvet. . . . I dreamed I was actually enjoying pure dual solitude. . . . This need to remain whole, to be twice myself, I felt keenly in early childhood. . . . Ah, how I wished, in tragic moments when my dreamy gentleness was the victim of bitter tears, that I had beside me another little Anna to throw her arms around my neck, to console me, to understand me! . . . In later life I found her in my heart and I kept fast hold of her; the help she gave me was not in the form of consolation, as I had hoped, but in that of courage.

The adolescent puts away her dolls. But all her life the woman is to find the magic of her mirror a tremendous help in her effort to project herself and then attain self-identification. The psychoanalyst Otto Rank has thrown light on the relation between the mirror and the double in myths and dreams. In woman particularly, the image is identified with the ego. Handsome appearance in the male suggests transcendence; in the female, the passivity of immanence; only the second is intended to arrest the gaze and can hence be captured in the motionless, silvered trap. Man, feeling and wishing himself active, subject, does not see himself in his fixed image; it has little attraction for him, since man's body does not seem to him an object of desire; while woman, knowing and making herself object, believes she really sees *herself* in the glass. A passive and given fact, the reflection is, like herself, a thing; and as she does covet female flesh, her flesh, she gives life through her admiration and desire to the imaged qualities she sees. Mme de Noailles, who knew herself in this respect, confides tó us as follows:

I was less vain of my intellectual gifts, which were too vigorous to be doubted, than of the image reflected in my oft-used mirror. . . . Physical pleasure alone fully contents the soul.

The words *physical pleasure* as used here are vague and incorrect. What contents the soul is the fact that, while the mind will have to prove itself, the contemplated countenance is there, today, a given fact, indubitable. All the future is concentrated in that sheet of light, a universe within the mirror's frame; outside these narrow limits, things are a disordered chaos; the world is reduced to this sheet of glass wherein stands resplendent an image: the Unique. Each woman, lost in her reflection, rules over space and time, alone, supreme; she has every right to men and fortune, to fame and pleasure. Marie Bashkirtsev was so enamored of her beauty that she wished it to be fixed in imperishable marble; it was herself she consigned to immortality when she wrote these words:

> When I got home I undressed and was struck with my naked beauty as if I had never seen it before. I must have my statue carved, but how? It is almost impossible unless I get married. And it absolutely must be done, before I grow ugly and spoil it all. . . . I must get a husband, if only to have the statue made.

Cécile Sorel thus depicts herself, preparing for a rendezvous:

> I am at my mirror. I would be more beautiful. I struggle with my lion's mane. Sparks fly from my comb. My head is a sun surrounded by golden rays.

I recall another young woman I saw one morning in a café powder-room; she had a rose in her hand and she seemed a little intoxicated; she put her lips to the mirror as if to drink her reflection, and she murmured with a smile: "Adorable, I'm simply adorable!" At once priestess and idol, the narcissist soars haloed with glory through the eternal realm, and below the clouds creatures kneel in adoration; she is God wrapped in self-contemplation. "I love myself, I am my God!" said Mme Mejerowsky. To become God is to accomplish the impossible synthesis of the *en-soi* and the *pour-soi*;[5] the moments when an individual imagines success in this are special moments of joy, exaltation, plenitude. The young girl who in her mirror has seen beauty, desire, love, happiness, in her own features—animated, she believes, with her own consciousness—will try all her life to exhaust the promises of that dazzling revelation. Even if the woman is not a perfect beauty she will see the special riches of her soul shine through her visage, and that will be enough to intoxicate her. "She may not be admired for her beauty, but she has a certain ideal charm. . . ."

It is not astonishing if even the less fortunate can sometimes share

---

[5] That is, to be at once the changeless Fact, the Essence, and the mutable, questing Consciousness.—Tr.

in the ecstasies of the mirror, for they feel emotion at the mere fact of being a thing of flesh, which is there; as with man, the pure bounteousness of young feminine flesh is enough to amaze them; and since they feel themselves to be individual subjects, they can, with a little self-deception, endue their specific qualities with an individual attractiveness; they will discover in face or body some graceful, odd, or piquant trait. They believe they are beautiful simply because they feel they are women.

Furthermore, the mirror is not the only means of obtaining a double, though the most favored. Everyone can try to create a twin through inward dialogue. Alone most of the day, doing boresome housework, woman has leisure to build up an appropriate figure in imagination. As a young girl she dreamed of the future; shut up in an endless present, she goes over her history; she revises it in such a way as to introduce æsthetic order, transforming her contingent life into a destiny even before her death.

Women more than men cling to childhood memories: "When I was a little girl . . ." Under parental protection they were independent, they recall, with the future open before them; now they are less safe, and they are imprisoned as servants or objects in the present; once they were to conquer the world, now they are reduced to generality: one wife and housekeeper among millions of others. The woman she has become regrets the human being she was, and she seeks to find again the dead child within herself, even to revive it. So she tries to think that her tastes, ideas, sentiments, retain an exceptional freshness, even some element of oddity and defiance of the world: "You know me"; "I'm funny that way"; "I *must* have flowers around me"; and so on. She has a special color, a favorite musician, peculiar beliefs and superstitions, rather above the general. Her unique personality is expressed in her clothes and her "interior"; she builds up a double that is often sketchy, but sometimes constitutes a definite personage whose role the woman plays for life. Many women see themselves in literary heroines already created: "She is just like me!" Such identifications may be made either with beautiful, romantic figures or with martyred heroines. A woman may obstinately incarnate Our Lady of Sorrows or the unappreciated wife: "I'm the wretchedest woman in the world." As Stekel said of a patient of this type: "She got her pleasure in playing this tragic role."

A trait such women have in common is that they feel misunderstood; people around them fail to recognize their special qualities; they translate this ignorance or indifference on the part of others into the idea that they hold some secret in their hearts. The fact is that many of them have quietly buried certain episodes of childhood or youth which have had great importance in their lives; they know that their official biographies are not to be confused with their true life stories. But most often the heroine of the narcissistic woman is only imaginary, since the latter lacks self-realization in actual life; her individuality is not conferred upon her by the concrete world: it is a hidden principle, a kind of "force" or "virtue" as obscure as phlogiston. The woman believes in her heroine's presence, but if she wanted to reveal her to others, she would be as embarrassed as the neurotic struggling to confess intangible guilt. In both the "secret" boils down to the empty conviction that they have deep within them a key for deciphering and justifying feelings and actions. It is their pathological lack of will power, their inertia, that causes this delusion in neurotics; and it is inability to express herself in everyday action that makes the woman believe that she, too, has an inexpressible mystery within her. The famous myth of the mystery of woman encourages this belief and is in turn confirmed by it.

Richly endowed with her misunderstood treasures, woman shares, in her own eyes, the tragic hero's need for a ruling destiny. Her whole life is transfigured and becomes a sacred drama. In her solemnly selected gown she stands, simultaneously a priestess in sacerdotal robes and an idol adorned by the hands of the faithful and presented for the adoration of her devotees. Her home becomes the temple where her worship is performed. The narcissistic woman will bestow as much care on the furniture and ornaments that enframe her as on her costume.

When she displays herself in company or abandons herself in a lover's arms, woman accomplishes her mission: she is Venus bestowing upon the world the treasures of her beauty. It was not herself, it was Beauty that Cécile Sorel was defending when she shattered the glass covering Bib's caricature; we see in her *Mémoires* that all her life she summoned mortals to the worship of Art. So with Isadora Duncan, as she portrays herself in *My Life* (page 254):

After a performance, in my tunic, with my hair covered with roses, I was so lovely. Why should not this loveliness be enjoyed? . . . A man who labors all day with his brain . . . why should he not be taken in these beautiful arms and find comfort for his pain and a few hours of beauty and forgetfulness?

The narcissist's generosity yields her a profit: better than in mirrors, she sees her double, haloed with glory, in the eyes of others. Failing an obliging audience, she opens her heart to a confessor, a doctor, a psychoanalyst; she will consult palmists and clairvoyants. "Not that I believe in them," said a movie starlet, "but I love to have someone talk to me about myself!" She tells her friends all about herself; she seeks a listener in her lover, more eagerly than in any other person. The woman truly in love soon forgets her ego; but many women are incapable of a genuine love affair, precisely because they never forget themselves. They prefer a larger stage to the intimacy of the alcove. Hence the importance of society to them: they need eyes to gaze at them, ears to listen to them; as personages, they need the greatest possible audiences. Describing her room yet again, Marie Bashkirtsev gives utterance to this avowal: "In this way I am *on the stage* when people come in and find me writing." And farther on: "I have decided to treat myself to *quite a stage setting*. I shall build a town house finer than Sarah's, and larger studios."

For her part, Mme de Noailles writes: "I loved and I still love the agora. . . . And I have often been able to reassure friends asking my pardon for having many guests, who they feared might annoy me, by this sincere avowal: I do not like to *play to empty seats*."

Clothes and conversation will satisfy much of this feminine taste for display. But an ambitious narcissist wishes to exhibit herself in a less common and more varied manner. In particular, she will often make her life a show presented to the plaudits of the public and go on the stage in earnest. Mme de Staël tells at length in *Corinne* how she entranced Italian throngs by reciting poems that she accompanied on the harp. At her Swiss château in Coppet, one of her favorite diversions was to declaim tragic roles; as Phèdre she liked to address ardent declarations to one or another of her young lovers, costumed as Hippolyte. If circumstances permit, nothing satisfies the narcissist so profoundly as to dedicate herself publicly to the theater. "The theater," says Georgette Leblanc, "gives me what I have long sought: a reason for exaltation. Today it seems to me *a caricature of action*; something essential for excessive temperaments."

The expression she uses is striking. For lack of action, woman invents substitutes for action; to some the theater represents a favored substitute. Actresses, moreover, can aim at a variety of goals. For certain ones acting is a means of earning a living, simply a profession; for others it leads to a fame that will be exploited for purposes of gallantry; for still others, it brings the triumph of their narcissism. The greater actresses—Rachel, Duse—are genuine artists, who transcend self in roles they create; but the third-rater, on the contrary, is concerned not for what she is accomplishing but for the glory it reflects on her; she seeks first of all to emphasize her own importance. A stubborn narcissist will be limited in art as in love for want of the ability to give herself.

This defect will have a great influence on all her activities. She will be tempted by any and every road that can lead to fame, but she will never commit herself to one wholeheartedly. Painting, sculpture, literature, all are disciplines that require a hard apprenticeship and demand solitary effort; many women try them, but they soon give up unless driven by a positive desire to create; and many who persevere never do more than play at working. They may pass hours at the easel, but they love themselves too much to have a real love for painting and so end as failures. When a woman succeeds in producing good work, like Mme de Staël and Mme de Noailles, the fact is that she has not been exclusively absorbed in self-worship; but one of the defects that plague a great many women writers is a love for themselves that poisons their sincerity, limits them, and reduces their stature.

Many women fully convinced of their superiority are incapable, however, of making it manifest to the world; their ambition will then be to use as intermediary some man whom they can impress with their merits. Such a woman does not aim through free projects at values of her own; she wishes to attach ready-made values to her ego, and so she turns to men who possess influence and fame in the hope of identifying herself with them, as inspiration, muse, Egeria. Mabel Dodge Luhan offers a striking example in her relations with Lawrence: she wished to "seduce his mind, force it to produce certain things"; she had need of his vision, his creative imagination; she felt a kind of activity in having him do things, a kind of compensation for the sadness of having *nothing to do herself*. She wanted Lawrence to conquer through *her*, to have the benefit of her Taos.[6] In the same way Georgette Leblanc wished to be "food and flame" for Maeterlinck; but she also wanted her name on his book. We have to do here not with ambitious women using men for their own ends, but with women animated by a subjective desire for *importance*, which has no objective end, and intent on stealing the transcendence of another. They are by no means always successful; but they are adroit in hiding their failure from themselves and in persuading themselves of their irresistible seductiveness. Knowing themselves to be lovable, desirable, admirable, they feel sure they are loved, desired, and admired.

These illusions can lead to real insanity, and it was not without reason that Clérambault considered erotomania "a kind of occupational disease"; to feel oneself a woman is to feel oneself a desirable object, to feel oneself desired and loved. It is significant that nine out of ten patients afflicted with the illusion of being loved are women. It is quite clear that what they seek in the imaginary lover is an apotheosis of their narcissism. They wish it given an unquestioned value, as by a priest, doctor, lawyer, or any superior man. And the unqualified truth that his behavior reveals is that his mistress-in-imagination is above all other women irresistible and full of superior qualities.

Erotomania can appear in connection with various psychoses, but its content is always the same. The subject is radiantly exalted by the love of an eminent man who has been suddenly fascinated by her charms—when she was expecting nothing of the sort—and who shows his feelings in an indirect but urgent manner. This relation sometimes remains on the ideal plane and sometimes assumes a sexual cast; but its essential feature is that the famous and mighty demigod is more in love than is the woman and manifests his passion in odd and ambiguous ways. From the numerous cases reported by psychiatrists, one that is quite typical is summarized here.[7] A woman of forty-eight makes the following confession:

This concerns the Honorable M. Achille, a former Deputy and member of the bar. I have known him since 1920, but I had ob-

---

6 See Mabel Dodge Luhan's *Lorenzo in Taos*, already cited.

7 From Ferdière's *L'Érotomanie*, case of Marie-Yvonne.

served his powerful figure from a distance before I knew who he was; that made cold shivers run up and down my back. . . . Yes, it was an affair of sentiment, and we both felt it: our glances met. I had a liking for him from the first, and the same with him. . . . Anyway, he was the first to declare himself: it was toward the end of 1922; he would receive me, always alone; one day he rose and came toward me, continuing the conversation. I understood at once that it was a surge of feeling. . . . He said things to let me know. By various polite attentions he gave me to understand that our feelings were mutual. . . One time he got rid of a man who was with him, just to be alone with me. He always clasped my hand firmly. . . . He told me he was single. . . . He watched my windows. He had the parish band march by my house. I was foolish. I should have responded to his advances. . . . He believed I was repulsing him, and he took action; he should have spoken openly; he took revenge on me. He believed I had a feeling for B. and he was jealous. . . . He worked a magic spell on my photograph to hurt me—my trouble comes from that.

This kind of insanity does in fact change easily into delusions of persecution. And the same process is seen even in normal cases. The narcissist finds it impossible to admit that others are not passionately interested in her; if she has manifest proof that she is not adored, she imagines at once that she is hated. She attributes all criticism to jealousy or spite. Her frustrations are the result of evil machinations, and this confirms her in the idea of her own importance. She slips easily into megalomania or its opposite: delusions of persecution. Being the center of her own universe and knowing no other universe than hers, she becomes the absolute center of the world.

But the comedy of narcissism is played at the expense of reality; an imaginary character solicits the admiration of an imaginary public; a woman infatuated with her ego loses all hold on the actual world, she has no concern to establish any real relation with others. Mme de Staël would have declaimed *Phèdre* with less enthusiasm if she had foreseen the mocking comments that her "admirers" would jot down in their notebooks at night. But the narcissist refuses to admit that people may see her otherwise than as she presents herself, which explains why she is a poor judge of herself, though always engaged in self-contemplation, and why she very easily becomes ridiculous. She no longer listens, she talks; and when she talks she is speaking her part.

Marie Bashkirtsev writes: "This amuses me. I do not converse with him, I *act*, and, feeling that I am before an appreciative audience, I am good at childlike and whimsical intonations and at attitudinizing."

She looks at herself too much to see anything; she understands in others only what she recognizes as like herself in them; whatever is not germane to her own case, her own history, remains outside her comprehension. She loves to multiply her experiences; she wants to know the intoxication and the torments of love, the pure joys of motherhood, of friendship, of solitude, of tears and laughter; but because she can never give herself, her emotions are manufactured. Doubtless Isadora Duncan wept real tears at the death of her children. But when she wished to cast their ashes on the sea in a grand theatrical flourish, she was only an actress; and one cannot read without uneasy qualms this passage in *My Life*, in which she evokes her sorrow:

> I feel the warmth of my own body. I look down on my bare legs—stretching them out. The softness of my breasts, my arms that are never still but continually waving about in soft undulations, and I realize that for twelve years I have been weary, this breast has harboured a never-ending ache, these hands before me have been marked with sorrow, and when I am alone these eyes are seldom dry.

The adolescent can draw from her worship of her ego the courage to face the disquieting future; but she must soon pass beyond this stage, otherwise the future becomes closed. The woman who imprisons her lover in the immanence of the couple dooms him and herself to death; and the narcissist who identifies herself with her imaginary double destroys herself. Her memories become fixed, her behavior stereotyped; she reiterates words, she repeats histrionics that have gradually lost all content, hence the poverty of many diaries and autobiographies written by women; wholly occupied in burning incense to herself, the woman who does nothing makes nothing of herself and is burning incense to a nonentity.

Her misfortune is that, despite all her insincerity, she is aware of this nothingness. There can be no real relation between an individual and her double because this double does not exist. The narcissist encounters a fundamental frustration. She cannot envisage herself as a totality, she is unable to keep up the illusion of being *pour-soi–en-soi.* Her isolation, like that of every human being, is felt as contingence and forlorn abandonment. And this is why—unless she changes—she is condemned to unresting flight from herself to the crowd, to talk, to others. It would be quite wrong to suppose that she escapes dependence in choosing herself as supreme end in view; on the contrary, she dooms herself to the most complete slavery. She does not stand on her independence but makes of herself an object that is imperiled by the world and by other conscious beings.

The difficulty is not alone that her body and her face are of flesh that time will disfigure. But from the practical point of view it is an expensive enterprise to adorn the idol, to erect its pedestal, to build its temple; we have seen that in order to preserve her form in everlasting marble, Marie Bashkirtsev had to marry money. Men's fortunes went to pay for the gold, incense, and myrrh that Isadora Duncan or Cécile Sorel heaped up around their thrones. Since woman's fate is in men's hands, she commonly measures her success by the number and worth of the men she attaches to her train. But here again reciprocity comes into play; the praying mantis who tries to make the male her instrument does not thus emancipate herself from him, for in order to enchain him she must please him. The American woman, who would be men's idol, makes herself the slave of her admirers; she dresses, lives, breathes, only through men and for them.

The narcissist, in fact, is as dependent as the hetaira. If she avoids the tyranny of an individual man, she accepts the tyranny of public opinion. This tie that binds her to others implies no reciprocity of exchange, for she would cease to be a narcissist if she sought to obtain recognition in the free estimate of others while recognizing such estimation as an end to be gained through activities. The paradox of her attitude lies in the fact that she claims to be given values by a world she must consider valueless, since she alone counts in her own opinion. The approval of others is an inhuman force, mysterious and capricious, and any attempts to gain it must be through magic. Despite her superficial arrogance, the narcissist realizes her precarious position; and this explains why she is uneasy, oversensitive, irritable, constantly on the watch; her vanity is insatiable. The older she grows, the more eagerly she seeks praise and success and the more suspicious she is of conspiracies around her; distracted, obsessed, she hides in the darkness of insincerity and often ends by forming around her a shell of delirious paranoia. There is a saying that is singularly appropriate in her case: "He that findeth his life shall lose it."

CHAPTER XXIII

The Woman in Love

THE WORD *love* has by no means the same sense for both sexes, and this is one cause of the serious misunderstandings that divide them. Byron well said: "Man's love is of man's life a thing apart; 'Tis woman's whole existence." Nietzsche expresses the same idea in *The Gay Science:*

> The single word love in fact signifies two different things for man and woman. What woman understands by love is clear enough: it is not only devotion, it is a total gift of body and soul, without reservation, without regard for anything whatever. This unconditional nature of her love is what makes it a *faith*,[1] the only one she has. As for man, if he loves a woman, what he *wants*[1] is that love from her; he is in consequence far from postulating the same sentiment for himself as for woman; if there should be men who also felt that desire for complete abandonment, upon my word, they would not be men.

Men have found it possible to be passionate lovers at certain times in their lives, but there is not one of them who could be called "a great lover";[2] in their most violent transports, they never abdicate completely; even on their knees before a mistress, what they still want is to take possession of her; at the very heart of their lives they remain sovereign subjects; the beloved woman is only one value among others; they wish to integrate her into their existence and not to squander it entirely on her. For woman, on the contrary, to love is to relinquish everything for the benefit of a master. As Cécile Sauvage puts it: "Woman must forget her own personality when she is in love. It is a law of nature. A woman is nonexistent without a master. Without a master, she is a scattered bouquet."

---

[1] Nietzsche's italics.

[2] In the sense that a woman may sometimes be called "*une grande amoureuse.*"—TR.

The fact is that we have nothing to do here with laws of nature. It is the difference in their situations that is reflected in the difference men and women show in their conceptions of love. The individual who is a subject, who is himself, if he has the courageous inclination toward transcendence, endeavors to extend his grasp on the world: he is ambitious, he acts. But an inessential creature is incapable of sensing the absolute at the heart of her subjectivity; a being doomed to immanence cannot find self-realization in acts. Shut up in the sphere of the relative, destined to the male from childhood, habituated to seeing in him a superb being whom she cannot possibly equal, the woman who has not repressed her claim to humanity will dream of transcending her being toward one of these superior beings, of amalgamating herself with the sovereign subject. There is no other way out for her than to lose herself, body and soul, in him who is represented to her as the absolute, as the essential. Since she is anyway doomed to dependence, she will prefer to serve a god rather than obey tyrants—parents, husband, or protector. She chooses to desire her enslavement so ardently that it will seem to her the expression of her liberty; she will try to rise above her situation as inessential object by fully accepting it; through her flesh, her feelings, her behavior, she will enthrone him as supreme value and reality: she will humble herself to nothingness before him. Love becomes for her a religion.

As we have seen, the adolescent girl wishes at first to identify herself with males; when she gives that up, she then seeks to share in their masculinity by having one of them in love with her; it is not the individuality of this one or that one which attracts her; she is in love with man in general.[3] "And you, the men I shall love, how I await you!" writes Irène Reweliotty. "How I rejoice to think I shall know you soon: especially You, the first." Of course the male is to belong to the same class and race as hers, for sexual privilege is in play only within this frame. If man is to be a demigod, he must first of all be a human being, and to the colonial officer's daughter the native is not a man. If the young girl gives herself to an "inferior," it is for the reason that she wishes to degrade herself because she believes she is unworthy of love; but normally she is looking for a man who represents male superiority. She is soon to ascertain

---

[3] Haenigsen's newspaper comic strip "Penny" gives never flagging popular expression to this truth.—TR.

that many individuals of the favored sex are sadly contingent and earthbound, but at first her presumption is favorable to them; they are called on less to prove their worth than to avoid too gross a disproof of it—which accounts for many mistakes, some of them serious. A naïve young girl is caught by the gleam of virility, and in her eyes male worth is shown, according to circumstances, by physical strength, distinction of manner, wealth, cultivation, intelligence, authority, social status, a military uniform; but what she always wants is for her lover to represent the essence of manhood.

Familiarity is often sufficient to destroy his prestige; it may collapse at the first kiss, or in daily association, or during the wedding night. Love at a distance, however, is only a fantasy, not a real experience. The desire for love becomes a passionate love only when it is carnally realized. Inversely, love can arise as a result of physical intercourse; in this case the sexually dominated woman acquires an exalted view of a man who at first seemed to her quite insignificant.

But it often happens that a woman succeeds in deifying none of the men she knows. Love has a smaller place in woman's life than has often been supposed. Husband, children, home, amusements, social duties, vanity, sexuality, career, are much more important. Most women dream of a *grand amour*, a soul-searing love. They have known substitutes, they have been close to it; it has come to them in partial, bruised, ridiculous, imperfect, mendacious forms; but very few have truly dedicated their lives to it. The *grandes amoureuses* are most often women who have not frittered themselves away in juvenile affairs; they have first accepted the traditional feminine destiny: husband, home, children; or they have known pitiless solitude; or they have banked on some enterprise that has been more or less of a failure. And when they glimpse the opportunity to salvage a disappointing life by dedicating it to some superior person, they desperately give themselves up to this hope. Mlle Aïssé, Juliette Drouet, and Mme d'Agoult were almost thirty when their love-life began, Julie de Lespinasse not far from forty. No other aim in life which seemed worth while was open to them, love was their only way out.

Even if they can choose independence, this road seems the most attractive to a majority of women: it is agonizing for a woman to assume responsibility for her life. Even the male, when adolescent, is quite willing to turn to older women for guidance, education, mothering; but customary attitudes, the boy's training, and his own inner imperatives forbid him to content himself in the end with the easy solution of abdication; to him such affairs with older women are only a stage through which he passes. It is man's good fortune—in adulthood as in early childhood—to be obliged to take the most arduous roads, but the surest; it is woman's misfortune to be surrounded by almost irresistible temptations; everything incites her to follow the easy slopes; instead of being invited to fight her own way up, she is told that she has only to let herself slide and she will attain paradises of enchantment. When she perceives that she has been duped by a mirage, it is too late; her strength has been exhausted in a losing venture.

The psychoanalysts are wont to assert that woman seeks the father image in her lover; but it is because he is a man, not because he is a father, that he dazzles the girl child, and every man shares in this magical power. Woman does not long to reincarnate one individual in another, but to reconstruct a situation: that which she experienced as a little girl, under adult protection. She was deeply integrated with home and family, she knew the peace of quasi-passivity. Love will give her back her mother as well as her father, it will give her back her childhood. What she wants to recover is a roof over her head, walls that prevent her from feeling her abandonment in the wide world, authority that protects her against her liberty. This childish drama haunts the love of many women; they are happy to be called "my little girl, my dear child"; men know that the words: "you're just like a little girl," are among those that most surely touch a woman's heart. We have seen that many women suffer in becoming adults; and so a great number remain obstinately "babyish," prolonging their childhood indefinitely in manner and dress. To become like a child again in a man's arms fills their cup with joy. The hackneyed theme: "To feel so little in your arms, my love," recurs again and again in amorous dialogue and in love letters. "Baby mine," croons the lover, the woman calls herself "your little one," and so on. A young woman will write: "When will he come, he who can dominate me?" And when he comes, she will love to sense his manly superiority. A neurotic studied by Janet illustrates this attitude quite clearly:

All my foolish acts and all the good things I have done have the same cause: an aspiration for a perfect and ideal love in which I can give myself completely, entrust my being to another, God, man, or woman, so superior to me that I will no longer need to think what to do in life or to watch over myself. . . . Someone to obey blindly and with confidence . . . who will bear me up and lead me gently and lovingly toward perfection. How I envy the ideal love of Mary Magdalen and Jesus: to be the ardent disciple of an adored and worthy master; to live and die for him, my idol, to win at last the victory of the Angel over the beast, to rest in his protecting arms, so small, so lost in his loving care, so wholly his that I exist no longer.

Many examples have already shown us that this dream of annihilation is in fact an avid will to exist. In all religions the adoration of God is combined with the devotee's concern with personal salvation; when woman gives herself completely to her idol, she hopes that he will give her at once possession of herself and of the universe he represents. In most cases she asks her lover first of all for the justification, the exaltation, of her ego. Many women do not abandon themselves to love unless they are loved in return; and sometimes the love shown them is enough to arouse their love. The young girl dreamed of herself as seen through men's eyes, and it is in men's eyes that the woman believes she has finally found herself. Cécile Sauvage writes:

To walk by your side, to step forward with my little feet that you love, to feel them so tiny in their high-heeled shoes with felt tops, makes me love all the love you throw around me. The least movements of my hands in my muff, of my arms, of my face, the tones of my voice, fill me with happiness.

The woman in love feels endowed with a high and undeniable value; she is at last allowed to idolize herself through the love she inspires. She is overjoyed to find in her lover a witness. This is what Colette's *Vagabonde* declares:

I admit I yielded, in permitting this man to come back the next day, to the desire to keep in him not a lover, not a friend, but an eager spectator of my life and my person. . . . One must be terribly old, Margot said to me one day, to renounce the vanity of living under someone's gaze.

In one of her letters to Middleton Murry, Katherine Mansfield wrote that she had just bought a ravishing mauve corset; she at once added: "Too bad there is no one to *see* it!" There is nothing more bitter than to feel oneself but the flower, the perfume, the treasure, which is the object of no desire: what kind of wealth is it that does not enrich myself and the gift of which no one wants? Love is the developer that brings out in clear, positive detail the dim negative, otherwise as useless as a blank exposure. Through love, woman's face, the curves of her body, her childhood memories, her former tears, her gowns, her accustomed ways, her universe, everything she is, all that belongs to her, escape contingency and become essential: she is a wondrous offering at the foot of the altar of her god.

This transforming power of love explains why it is that men of prestige who know how to flatter feminine vanity will arouse passionate attachments even if they are quite lacking in physical charm. Because of their lofty positions they embody the Law and the Truth: their perceptive powers disclose an unquestionable reality. The woman who finds favor in their sight feels herself transformed into a priceless treasure. D'Annunzio's success was due to this, as Isadora Duncan explains in the introduction to *My Life*:

When D'Annunzio loves a woman, he lifts her spirit from this earth to the divine region where Beatrice moves and shines. In turn he transforms each woman to a part of the divine essence, he carries her aloft until she believes herself really with Beatrice. . . . He flung over each favorite in turn a shining veil. She rose above the heads of ordinary mortals and walked surrounded by a strange radiance. But when the caprice of the poet ended, this veil vanished, the radiance was eclipsed, and the woman turned again to common clay. . . . To hear oneself praised with that magic peculiar to D'Annunzio is, I imagine, something like the experience of Eve when she heard the voice of the serpent in Paradise. D'Annunzio can make any woman feel that she is the centre of the universe.

Only in love can woman harmoniously reconcile her eroticism and her narcissism; we have seen that these sentiments are opposed in such a manner that it is very difficult for a woman to adapt herself to her sexual destiny. To make herself a carnal object, the prey of another, is in contradiction to her self-worship: it seems to her that embraces blight and sully her body or degrade her soul. Thus it is that some women take refuge in frigidity, thinking that in this way they can preserve the integrity of the ego. Others dissociate animal pleasure and lofty sentiment. In one of Stekel's cases the patient was frigid with her respected and eminent husband and, after his death, with an equally superior man, a great musician, whom she sincerely loved. But in an almost casual encounter with a rough, brutal forester she found complete physical satisfaction, "a wild intoxication followed by indescribable disgust" when she thought of her lover. Stekel remarks that "for many women a descent into animality is the necessary condition for orgasm." Such women see in physical love a debasement incompatible with esteem and affection.

But for other women, on the contrary, only the esteem, affection, and admiration of the man can eliminate the sense of abasement. They will not yield to a man unless they believe they are deeply loved. A woman must have a considerable amount of cynicism, indifference, or pride to regard physical relations as an exchange of pleasure by which each partner benefits equally. As much as woman —and perhaps more—man revolts against anyone who attempts to exploit him sexually;[4] but it is woman who generally feels that her partner is using her as an instrument. Nothing but high admiration can compensate for the humiliation of an act that she considers a defeat.

We have seen that the act of love requires of woman profound self-abandonment; she bathes in a passive languor; with closed eyes, anonymous, lost, she feels as if borne by waves, swept away in a storm, shrouded in darkness: darkness of the flesh, of the womb, of the grave. Annihilated, she becomes one with the Whole, her ego is abolished. But when the man moves from her, she finds herself back on earth, on a bed, in the light; she again has a name, a face: she is one vanquished, prey, object.

This is the moment when love becomes a necessity. As when the

---

[4] Lawrence, for example, in *Lady Chatterley's Lover*, expresses through Mellors his aversion for women who make a man an instrument of pleasure.

child, after weaning, seeks the reassuring gaze of its parents, so must a woman feel, through the man's loving contemplation, that she is, after all, still at one with the Whole from which her flesh is now painfully detached. She is seldom wholly satisfied even if she has felt the orgasm, she is not set completely free from the spell of her flesh; her desire continues in the form of affection. In giving her pleasure, the man increases her attachment, he does not liberate her. As for him, he no longer desires her; but she will not pardon this momentary indifference unless he has dedicated to her a timeless and absolute emotion. Then the immanence of the moment is transcended; hot memories are no regret, but a treasured delight; ebbing pleasure becomes hope and promise; enjoyment is justified; woman can gloriously accept her sexuality because she transcends it; excitement, pleasure, desire are no longer a state, but a benefaction; her body is no longer an object: it is a hymn, a flame.

Then she can yield with passion to the magic of eroticism; darkness becomes light; the loving woman can open her eyes, can look upon the man who loves her and whose gaze glorifies her; through him nothingness becomes fullness of being, and being is transmuted into worth; she no longer sinks in a sea of shadows, but is borne up on wings, exalted to the skies. Abandon becomes sacred ecstasy. When she *receives* her beloved, woman is dwelt in, visited, as was the Virgin by the Holy Ghost, as is the believer by the Host. This is what explains the obscene resemblance between pious hymns and erotic songs; it is not that mystical love always has a sexual character, but that the sexuality of the woman in love is tinged with mysticism. "'My God, my adored one, my lord and master"—the same words fall from the lips of the saint on her knees and the loving woman on her bed; the one offers her flesh to the thunderbolt of Christ, she stretches out her hands to receive the stigmata of the Cross, she calls for the burning presence of divine Love; the other, also, offers and awaits: thunderbolt, dart, arrow, are incarnated in the male sex organ. In both women there is the same dream, the childhood dream, the mystic dream, the dream of love: to attain supreme existence through losing oneself in the other.

It has sometimes been maintained that this desire for annihilation leads to masochism.[5] But as I have noted in connection with eroticism, it can be called masochism only when I essay "to be fascinated

---

[5] As by Helene Deutsch in her *Psychology of Women*.

by my own status as object, through the agency of others"; [6] that is
to say, when the consciousness of the subject is directed back toward
the ego to see it in a humiliating position. Now, the woman in love
is not simply and solely a narcissist identified with her ego; she feels,
more than this, a passionate desire to transcend the limitations of
self and become infinite, thanks to the intervention of another who
has access to infinite reality. She abandons herself to love first of all
to *save herself*; but the paradox of idolatrous love is that in trying to
save herself she *denies herself* utterly in the end. Her feeling gains a
mystical dimension; she requires her God no longer to admire her
and approve of her; she wants to merge with him, to forget herself in his arms. "I would wish to be a saint of love," writes Mme
d'Agoult.[7] "I would long for martyrdom in such moments of exaltation and ascetic frenzy." What comes to light in these words is a
desire for a complete destruction of the self, abolishing the boundaries that separate her from the beloved. There is no question here
of masochism, but of a dream of ecstatic union.

In order to realize this dream, what woman wants in the first place
is to serve; for in responding to her lover's demands, a woman will
feel that she is necessary; she will be integrated with his existence, she
will share his worth, she will be justified. Even mystics like to believe,
according to Angelus Silesius, that God needs man; otherwise they
would be giving themselves in vain. The more demands the man
makes, the more gratified the woman feels. Although the seclusion
imposed by Victor Hugo on Juliette Drouet weighed heavily on the
young woman, one feels that she is happy in obeying him: to stay
by the fireside is to do something for the master's pleasure. She tries
also to be useful to him in a positive way. She cooks choice dishes
for him and arranges a little nest where he can be at home; she
looks after his clothes. "I want you to tear your clothes as much as
possible," she writes to him, "and I want to mend and clean them
all myself." She reads the papers, clips out articles, classifies letters
and notes, copies manuscripts, for him. She is grieved when the poet
entrusts a part of the work to his daughter Léopoldine.

Such traits are found in every woman in love. If need be, she herself tyrannizes over herself in her lover's name; all she is, all she

---

[6] Sartre in *L'Être et le néant*.

[7] She eloped with Franz Liszt and became the mother of Cosima Wagner. Under the name of Daniel Stern she wrote historical and philosophical books.—Tr.

has, every moment of her life, must be devoted to him and thus gain their *raison d'être*; she wishes to possess nothing save in him; what makes her unhappy is for him to require nothing of her, so much so that a sensitive lover will invent demands. She at first sought in love a confirmation of what she was, of her past, of her personality; but she also involves her future in it, and to justify her future she puts it in the hands of one who possesses all values. Thus she gives up her transcendence, subordinating it to that of the essential other, to whom she makes herself vassal and slave. It was to find herself, to save herself, that she lost herself in him in the first place; and the fact is that little by little she does lose herself in him wholly; for her the whole of reality is in the other. The love that at the start seemed a narcissistic apotheosis is fulfilled in the bitter joys of a devotion that often leads to self-mutilation.

In the early days of a *grande passion* the woman becomes prettier, more elegant than formerly: "When Adèle does my hair, I look at my forehead, because you love it," writes Mme d'Agoult. This face, this body, this room, this I—she has found a *raison d'être* for them all, she cherishes them through the mediation of this beloved man who loves her. But a little later, quite to the contrary, she gives up all coquetry; if her lover wishes it, she changes that image which at first was more precious than love itself; she loses interest in it; what she is, what she has, she makes the fief of her lord; what he does not care for, she repudiates. She would consecrate each heartbeat to him, each drop of her blood, the marrow of her bones; and it is this that is expressed in a dream of martyrdom: she would extend her gift of herself to the point of torture, of death, of being the ground under her lover's feet, being nothing but what responds to his call. Everything useless to him she madly destroys. If the present she has made of herself is wholeheartedly accepted, no masochism appears; few traces of it are seen in, for example, Juliette Drouet. In the excess of her adoration she sometimes knelt before the poet's portrait and asked forgiveness for any faults she might have committed; she did not turn in anger against herself.

Yet the descent from generous warmth of feeling to masochistic madness is an easy one. The woman in love who before her lover is in the position of the child before its parents is also liable to that sense of guilt she felt with them; she chooses not to revolt against him as long as she loves him, but she revolts against herself. If he loves her less than she wants him to, if she fails to engross him, to make him happy, to satisfy him, all her narcissism is transformed into self-disgust, into humiliation, into hatred of herself, which drive her to self-punishment. During a more or less lengthy crisis, sometimes for life, she will make herself a voluntary victim, she will struggle furiously to hurt her ego that has been unable to gratify him to the full. At this point her attitude is genuinely masochistic.

But we must not confuse this case, in which the woman in love seeks her own suffering in order to take vengeance upon herself, with those cases in which her aim is the affirmation of her man's liberty and power. It is a commonplace—and seemingly a truth—that the prostitute is proud to be beaten by her man; but what exalts her is not the idea of her beaten and enslaved person, it is rather the strength and authority, the supremacy of the male upon whom she is dependent: she also likes to see him maltreat another male; indeed, she often incites him to engage in dangerous fighting, for she wants her master to possess and display the values recognized in the environment to which she belongs.

The woman who finds pleasure in submitting to male caprices also admires the evident action of a sovereign free being in the tyranny practiced on her. It must be noted that if for some reason the lover's prestige is destroyed, his blows and demands become odious; they are precious only if they manifest the divinity of the loved one. But if they do, it is intoxicating joy to feel herself the prey of another's free action. An existent finds it a most amazing adventure to be justified through the varying and imperious will of another; one wearies of living always in the same skin, and blind obedience is the only chance for radical transformation known to a human being. Woman is thus slave, queen, flower, hind, stained-glass window, wanton, servant, courtesan, muse, companion, mother, sister, child, according to the fugitive dreams, the imperious commands, of her lover. She lends herself to these metamorphoses with ravishment as long as she does not realize that all the time her lips have retained the unvarying savor of submission. On the level of love, as on that of eroticism, it seems evident that masochism is one of the bypaths taken by the unsatisfied woman, disappointed in both the other and herself; but it is not the natural tendency of a happy resignation. Masochism perpetuates the presence of the ego in a bruised and degraded condition; love brings forgetfulness of self in favor of the essential subject.

The supreme goal of human love, as of mystical love, is identification with the loved one.[8] The measure of values, the truth of the world, are in his consciousness; hence it is not enough to serve him. The woman in love tries to see with his eyes; she reads the books he reads, prefers the pictures and the music he prefers; she is interested only in the landscapes she sees with him, in the ideas that come from him; she adopts his friendships, his enmities, his opinions; when she questions herself, it is his reply she tries to hear; she wants to have in her lungs the air he has already breathed; the fruits and flowers that do not come from his hands have no taste and no fragrance. Her idea of location in space, even, is upset: the center of the world is no longer the place where she is, but that occupied by her lover; all roads lead to his home, and from it. She uses his words, mimics his gestures, acquires his eccentricities and his tics. "I am Heathcliffe," says Catherine in *Wuthering Heights*; that is the cry of every woman in love; she is another incarnation of her loved one, his reflection, his double: she is *he*. She lets her own world collapse in contingence, for she really lives in his.

The supreme happiness of the woman in love is to be recognized by the loved man as a part of himself; when he says "we," she is associated and identified with him, she shares his prestige and reigns with him over the rest of the world; she never tires of repeating—even to excess—this delectable "we." As one necessary to a being who is absolute necessity, who stands forth in the world seeking necessary goals and who gives her back the world in necessary form, the woman in love acquires in her submission that magnificent possession, the absolute. It is this certitude that gives her lofty joys; she feels exalted to a place at the right hand of God. Small matter to her to have only second place if she has *her* place, forever, in a most wonderfully ordered world. So long as she is in love and is loved by and necessary to her loved one, she feels herself wholly justified: she knows peace and happiness. Such was perhaps the lot of Mlle Aïsse [9] with the Chevalier d'Aydie before religious scruples troubled his soul, or that of Juliette Drouet in the mighty shadow of Victor Hugo.

But this glorious felicity rarely lasts. No man really is God. The relations sustained by the mystic with the divine Absence depend on

---

[8] See T. Reik's *Psychology of Sex Relations* (Farrar, Straus & Co., 1945).—Tr.

[9] An account of her life, with her letters, will be found in *Lettres du XVIIe et du XVIIIe Siècle*, by Eugène Asse (Paris, 1873).—Tr.

her fervor alone; but the deified man, who is not God, is present. And from this fact are to come the torments of the woman in love. Her most common fate is summed up in the famous words of Julie de Lespinasse: [1] "Always, my dear friend, I love you, I suffer and I await you." To be sure, suffering is linked with love for men also; but their pangs are either of short duration or not overly severe. Benjamin Constant wanted to die on account of Mme Récamier: he was cured in a twelvemonth. Stendhal regretted Métilde for years, but it was a regret that perfumed his life without destroying it. Whereas woman, in assuming her role as the inessential, accepting a total dependence, creates a hell for herself. Every woman in love recognizes herself in Hans Andersen's little mermaid who exchanged her fishtail for feminine legs through love and then found herself walking on needles and live coals. It is not true that the loved man is absolutely necessary, above chance and circumstance, and the woman is not necessary to him; he is not really in a position to justify the feminine being who is consecrated to his worship, and he does not permit himself to be possessed by her.

An authentic love should assume the contingence of the other; that is to say, his lacks, his limitations, and his basic gratuitousness. It would not pretend to be a mode of salvation, but a human inter-relation. Idolatrous love attributes an absolute value to the loved one, a first falsity that is brilliantly apparent to all outsiders. "*He* isn't worth all that love," is whispered around the woman in love, and posterity wears a pitying smile at the thought of certain pallid heroes, like Count Guibert. It is a searing disappointment to the woman to discover the faults, the mediocrity of her idol. Novelists, like Colette, have often depicted this bitter anguish. The disillusion is still more cruel than that of the child who sees the father's prestige crumble, because the woman has herself selected the one to whom she has given over her entire being.

Even if the chosen one is worthy of the profoundest affection, his truth is of the earth, earthy, and it is no longer this mere man whom the woman loves as she kneels before a supreme being; she is duped by that spirit of seriousness which declines to take values as inci-dental—that is to say, declines to recognize that they have their

---

[1] Famous intellectual woman of the eighteenth century, noted for her salon and her fervid correspondence with the rather undistinguished military officer and writer Count Guibert, mentioned below.—Tr.

source in human existence. Her bad faith[2] raises barriers between her and the man she adores. She offers him incense, she bows down, but she is not a friend to him since she does not realize that he is in danger in the world, that his projects and his aims are as fragile as he is; regarding him as the Faith, the Truth, she misunderstands his freedom—his hesitancy and anguish of spirit. This refusal to apply a human measuring scale to the lover explains many feminine paradoxes. The woman asks a favor from her lover. Is it granted? Then he is generous, rich, magnificent; he is kingly, he is divine. Is it refused? Then he is avaricious, mean, cruel; he is a devilish or a bestial creature. One might be tempted to object: if a "yes" is such an astounding and superb extravagance, should one be surprised at a "no"? If the "no" discloses such abject selfishness, why wonder so much at the "yes"? Between the superhuman and the inhuman is there no place for the human?

A fallen god is not a man: he is a fraud; the lover has no other alternative than to prove that he really is this king accepting adulation—or to confess himself a usurper. If he is no longer adored, he must be trampled on. In virtue of that glory with which she has haloed the brow of her beloved, the woman in love forbids him any weakness; she is disappointed and vexed if he does not live up to the image she has put in his place. If he gets tired or careless, if he gets hungry or thirsty at the wrong time, if he makes a mistake or contradicts himself, she asserts that he is "not himself" and she makes a grievance of it. In this indirect way she will go so far as to take him to task for any of his ventures that she disapproves; she judges her judge, and she denies him his liberty so that he may deserve to remain her master. Her worship sometimes finds better satisfaction in his absence than in his presence; as we have seen, there are women who devote themselves to dead or otherwise inaccessible heroes, so that they may never have to face them in person, for beings of flesh and blood would be fatally contrary to their dreams. Hence such disillusioned sayings as: "One must not believe in Prince Charming. Men are only poor creatures," and the like. They would not seem to be dwarfs if they had not been asked to be giants.

---

[2] In Sartre's existentialist terminology, "bad faith" means abdication of the human self with its hard duty of choice, the wish therefore to become a thing, the flight from the anguish of liberty.—Tr.

It is one of the curses afflicting the passionate woman that her generosity is soon converted into exigence. Having become identified with another, she wants to make up for her loss; she must take possession of that other person who has captured her. She gives herself to him entirely; but he must be completely available to receive this gift. She dedicates every moment to him, but he must be present at all times; she wants to live only in him—but she wants to live, and he must therefore devote himself to making her live. Mme d'Agoult writes to Liszt:

> I love you sometimes foolishly, and at those moments I do not understand that I could not, would not, and should not be so absorbing a thought for you as you are for me.

She is trying to curb her spontaneous wish to be everything to him. The same plaintive appeal sounds in the words of Mlle de Lespinasse:

> Ah, God! If you only knew the emptiness of my days, my life, deprived of the interest and pleasure of seeing you! Dear friend, for you amusements, occupation, action, are enough; as for me, my happiness is you, only you; I would not care to live if I were not to see you and to love you every day of my life.

At first the woman in love takes delight in gratifying her lover's desire to the full; later on—like the legendary fireman who for love of his profession started fires everywhere—she applies herself to awakening this desire so that she may have it to gratify. If she does not succeed in this enterprise, she feels so humiliated and useless that her lover will feign ardors he does not feel. In making herself a slave, she has found the surest means of enchaining him. Here we come upon another falsity of love which many men—for example, Lawrence and Montherlant—have resentfully exposed: it comes in the form of a gift, when it is really a tyranny. In *Adolphe*, Benjamin Constant describes in bitter terms the chains that the too generous passion of a woman forges around a man. "She was not circumspect in her sacrifices because she was concerned with making me accept them," he says cruelly of Eléonore.

Acceptance is in fact an obligation that is binding on the lover, without his having even the benefit of seeming to be a giver; the woman requires him to accept gratefully the burdens with which she crushes him. And her tyranny is insatiable. The man in love is tyrannical, but when he has obtained what he wants he is satisfied; whereas there are no limits to woman's exigent devotion. A lover who has confidence in his mistress feels no displeasure if she absents herself, is occupied at a distance from him; sure that she is his, he prefers to possess a free being than to own a thing. For the woman, on the contrary, the absence of her lover is always torture; he is an eye, a judge, and as soon as he looks at anything other than herself, he frustrates her; whatever he sees, he robs her of; away from him, she is dispossessed, at once of herself and of the world; even when seated at her side reading or writing or whatever, he is abandoning her, betraying her. She hates his sleep. But Baudelaire grew tender over woman in sleep: "Your beautiful eyes are weary, my poor loved one"; and Proust is enchanted in watching Albertine [3] asleep. The point is that male jealousy is simply the will to exclusive possession; the loved woman, when sleep restores the disarmed candor of childhood, belongs to no one: that certitude is enough. But the god, the master, should not give himself up to the repose of immanence; the woman views this blasted transcendence with a hostile eye; she detests the animal inertia of this body which exists no longer *for her* but *in itself*, abandoned to a contingence of which her contingence is the price.[4] Violette Leduc has given strong expression to this feeling in *Je hais les dormeurs*:

> I hate sleepers. I bend over them with evil intent. Their submissiveness irritates me. I hate the unconscious calm, the blind studious face. . . . My sleeper is hard to awaken, he has made a clean sweep of everything. . . . I hate his power to create through loss of consciousness a calm which I do not share. . . . We were in swift flight from earth . . . we took off, soared, waited, came to it, moaned, won, and lost, together. We played truant in earnest. We found a new nothingness. Now you sleep . . . I hate you when you sleep.

---

[3] If Albertine were Albert it would be the same; Proust's attitude here is mas culine in either case.

[4] That is, when he loses his independent powers, his transcendence, even in sleep, it costs her hers, because she lives in and by him.—TR.

The god must not sleep lest he become clay, flesh; he must not cease to be present, lest his creature sink into nothingness. For woman, man's sleep is selfishness and treason. The lover sometimes awakens his mistress: it is to embrace her; she wakes him up simply to keep him from sleeping, to keep him there, in the room, in the bed, in her arms—like God in the tabernacle. That is what woman wants: she is a jailer.

And yet she is not willing for him to be nothing but her prisoner. This is one of the painful paradoxes of love: a captive, the god is shorn of his divinity. Woman preserves her transcendence by transferring it to him; but he must bring it to bear upon the whole world. If two lovers sink together in the absolute of passion, all their liberty is degraded into immanence; death is then the only solution. That is one of the meanings of the *Tristan and Isolde* myth. Two lovers destined solely for each other are already dead: they die of ennui, of the slow agony of a love that feeds on itself.

Woman is aware of this danger. Save in crises of jealous frenzy, she herself demands that man be all project, all action, for he is no more a hero if he engages in no exploits. The knight departing for new adventures offends his lady, yet she has nothing but contempt for him if he remains at her feet. This is the torture of the impossible love; the woman wants to possess the man wholly, but she demands that he transcend any gift that could possibly be possessed: a free being cannot be *had*. She wants to imprison *here* an existent who is, as Heidegger puts it, "a creature of far distances," but she knows very well that this attempt is foredoomed to failure. "My dear friend, I love you as one should love, excessively, madly, with transport and despair," writes Julie de Lespinasse. Idolatrous love, if clearsighted, must partake of desperation. For the loving woman who asks her lover to be a hero, a giant, a demigod, also is asking not to be all the world to him, even though she cannot have happiness unless she possesses him completely. Says Nietzsche in *The Gay Science*:

Woman's passion, a total renunciation of all rights of her own, postulates precisely that the same feeling, the same desire for renunciation, does exist also in the other sex, for if both severally made this renunciation for love, there would result, on my word I do not know just what, shall we say, perhaps, the horror of nothingness? The woman wishes to be taken . . . she demands, therefore, someone to *take* her, someone who does not give himself, who does not abandon himself, but who wishes, on the contrary, to enrich his ego through love. . . . The woman gives herself, the man adds to himself by taking her.

At the least the woman will be able to find her joy in this enrichment which she brings to her beloved; she is not Everything to him, to be sure, but she will try to believe herself indispensable; there are no degrees in necessity. If he "cannot get along without her," she considers herself the foundation of his precious existence, and she derives her own value from that. Her joy is to serve him—but he must gratefully recognize this service; the gift becomes a demand in accordance with the usual dialectic of devotion.[5] And a woman with a scrupulous mind is bound to ask herself: does he really need *me*? The man is fond of her, desires her, with a personal tenderness and desire; but would he not have an equally personal feeling for someone else in her place? Many women in love permit themselves to be deluded; they would like to ignore the fact that the general is involved in the particular, and man furthers the illusion because he shares it at first; his desire often has a fire that seems to defy time; at the moment when he wants that woman, he wants her passionately, he wants her only. And, to be sure, that moment is an absolute—but a momentary absolute. Not realizing this, duped, the woman goes on to the eternal. Deified by the master's embrace, she believes she has always been divine and destined for the god—she and nobody else. But male desire is as ephemeral as it is imperious; once allayed, it dies rather quickly, whereas it is most often afterward that woman becomes love's captive. This is the burden of a whole fluent literature and of many facile songs. "A young man passed her way, a girl sang. . . . A young man sang, a girl wept."

And if the man is lastingly attached to the woman, that is still no sign that she is necessary to him. What she claims, however, is this: her abdication of self saves her only on condition that it restores her empire; reciprocity cannot be evaded. So she must either suffer or lie to herself. Most often she clutches at the straw of falsehood. She fancies that the man's love is the exact counterpart of the love she brings to him; in bad faith she takes desire for love, erection for de-

---

[5] Which I have attempted to set forth in mv essav *Pyrrhus et Cinéas.*

sire, love for a religion. She compels the man to lie to her: "Do you love me? As much as yesterday? Will you always love me?" and so on. She cleverly poses her questions at a moment when there is not time enough to give properly qualified and sincere answers, or more especially when circumstances prevent any response; she asks her insistent questions in the course of a sexual embrace, at the verge of a convalescence, in the midst of sobs, or on a railroad platform. She makes trophies of the extorted replies; and if there are no replies, she takes silence to mean what she wishes; every woman in love is more or less a paranoiac. I recall a friend who said in reference to a long silence on the part of her distant lover: "When one wants to break off, one writes to announce the break"; then, having finally received a quite unambiguous letter: "When one really wants to break off, one doesn't write."

In considering such confidences, it is often difficult to determine just where pathological delirium begins. As described by the frantic woman in love, the behavior of the man always seems to be fantastic: he is a neurotic, a sadist, a repressed personality, a masochist, a devil, an unstable type, a coward, or all of these put together. He defies the most searching psychological explanations. "X. adores me, he is madly jealous, he would like to have me wear a mask on the street; but he is so strange a creature and is so much on his guard against love that when I ring his doorbell, he meets me on the landing and won't even let me in." Or, again: "Z. used to adore me. But he was too proud to ask me to go and live with him in Lyon. I went there and made myself at home with him. After eight days, without any argument, he put me out. I saw him again twice. When I telephoned him for the third time, he hung up in the middle of the conversation. He is a neurotic." These mysterious stories are cleared up when the man states in explanation: "I absolutely was not in love with her," or "I was on friendly terms with her, but I wouldn't be able to live with her a month." When bad faith becomes too obstinate, it leads to the insane asylum, for one of the constant characteristics of erotomania is that the behavior of the lover seems enigmatic and paradoxical; on account of this quirk, the patient's mania always succeeds in breaking through the resistance of reality. A normal woman sometimes yields in the end to the truth and finally recognizes the fact that she is no longer loved. But so long as she has not lost all hope and made this admission, she always cheats a little.

Even in mutual love there is fundamental difference in the feelings of the lovers, which the woman tries to hide. The man must certainly be capable of justifying himself without her, since she hopes to be justified through him. If he is necessary to her, it means that she is evading her liberty; but if he accepts his liberty, without which he would be neither a hero nor even a man, no person or thing can be necessary to him. The dependence accepted by woman comes from her weakness; how, therefore, could she find a reciprocal dependence in the man she loves in his strength?

A passionately demanding soul cannot find repose in love, because the end she has in view is inherently contradictory. Torn and tortured, she risks becoming a burden to the man instead of his slave, as she had dreamed; unable to feel indispensable, she becomes importunate, a nuisance. This is, indeed, a common tragedy. If she is wiser and less intransigent, the woman in love becomes resigned. She is not all, she is not necessary: it is enough to be useful; another might easily fill her place: she is content to be the one who is there. She accepts her servitude without demanding the same in return. Thus she can enjoy a modest happiness; but even within these limits it will not be unclouded.

The woman in love, much more grievously than the wife, is one who waits. If the wife is herself exclusively of the amorous type, maternity and housewifely duties, occupations, and pleasures will have no value for her: only the presence of her husband lifts her from the limbo of ennui. "After you're gone it seems hardly worth while to look out the window; then all that happens to me is dead, I am no more than a little dress flung on a chair," writes Cécile Sauvage in the early days of her marriage.[6] And as we have seen, it is very often outside of marriage that passionate love springs up and flowers. The life of Juliette Drouet is one of the most remarkable examples of entire, lifelong devotion: it was one long wait. "I wait for you eternally," she wrote to Victor Hugo. "I wait like a squirrel in a cage. . . . I wait for you because, after all, I would rather wait for you than believe that you are not coming at all," and so on indefinitely. It is true that after making her break away from her rich protector, Prince Demidov, Hugo had confined her to a small apartment and for

---

[6] It is a different matter if the woman has found her independence in marriage; then love between husband and wife can be a free exchange by two beings who are each self-sufficient.

twelve years refused to let her go out alone, lest she get involved with any of her former friends; but even when her lot was improved, she still lived only for her lover—and saw very little of him. This did not affect her love, but it filled her heart with bitterness, as her letters show. She dreams of reconciling liberty and love: "I would be at once independent and enslaved"; but being a failure as an actress, she had to resign herself to love alone. Having nothing else to do between the master's visits, she wrote him seventeen thousand letters, at the rate of three hundred to four hundred yearly. The worst horror that afflicts the woman of the harem is that her days are deserts of boredom: when the male is not making use of the object that she is to him, she is no longer anything at all. The situation of the *amoureuse* is analogous: she does not want to be other than this loved woman, nothing else seems worth while. In order to exist, then, she must have her lover at her side, occupied with her; she awaits his coming, his desire, his awakening from sleep; and as soon as he goes out, she begins again to await his return. This curse weighs on the heroine of Fannie Hurst's *Back Street*, of Rosamond Lehmann's *The Weather in the Streets*, both priestesses and victims of sheer love. It is the harsh punishment inflicted upon the woman who has not taken her destiny into her own hands.

Waiting can be a joy; to the woman who watches for her beloved in the knowledge that he is hastening toward her, that he loves her, the wait is a dazzling promise. But with the fading of the confident exaltation that can change absence itself into presence, tormenting uneasiness begins to accompany the absence: he may never come back. I knew a woman who received her lover each time with astonishment: "I thought you wouldn't come back any more," she would say. And if he asked why: "You might not return; when I wait for you I always get the feeling that I shall never see you again."

Worst of all, he may cease to love her: he may love another woman. For the intensity of a woman's effort to create her illusion—saying to herself: "He loves me madly, he can love me alone"—does not exclude the tortures of jealousy. It is characteristic of bad faith to permit passionate and contradictory affirmations. Thus the madman who obstinately insists he is Napoleon is not embarrassed in admitting that he is also a barber. Woman rarely consents to ask herself the question: does he really love me? but she asks herself a hundred times: does he love someone else? She does not admit that the fervor of her lover can have died down little by little, nor that he values love less than she does: she immediately invents rivals.

She regards love as a free sentiment and at the same time a magic spell; and she supposes that "her" male continues, of course, to love her as a free agent while he is being "bewitched," "ensnared," by a clever schemer. A man thinks of a woman as united with him, in her immanence; that is why he readily plays the Boubouroche; [7] it is difficult for him to imagine that she is also another person who may be getting away from him. Jealousy with him is ordinarily no more than a passing crisis, like love itself; the crisis may be violent and even murderous, but it is rare for him to acquire a lasting uneasiness. His jealousy is usually derivative: when his business is going badly, when he feels that life is hurting him, then he feels his woman is flouting him. [8]

Woman, on the other hand, loving her man in his alterity and in his transcendence, feels in danger at every moment. There is no great distance between the treason of absence and infidelity. From the moment when she feels less than perfectly loved, she becomes jealous, and in view of her demands, this is always pretty much her case; her reproaches and complaints, whatever the pretexts, come to the surface in jealous scenes; she will express in this way the impatience and ennui of waiting, the bitter taste of her dependence, her regret at having only a mutilated existence. Her entire destiny is involved in each glance her lover casts at another woman, since she has identified her whole being with him. Thus she is annoyed if his eyes are turned for an instant toward a stranger; but if he reminds her that she has just been contemplating some stranger, she firmly replies: "That is not the same thing at all." She is right. A man who is looked at by a woman receives nothing; no gift is given until the feminine flesh becomes prey. Whereas the coveted woman is at once metamorphosed into a desirable and desired object; and the woman in love, thus slighted, is reduced to the status of ordinary clay. And so she is always on the watch. What is he doing? At whom is he looking? With whom is he talking? What a desire has given her, a smile can take away from her; it needs only an instant to cast her down from "the

---

[7] A naïve, easygoing character in a novel and a play by Courteline, deceived by his mistress and exploited by his friends.—Tr.

[8] This is brought out, for example, in Lagache's work: *Nature et formes de la jalousie.*

pearly light of immortality" to the dim light of the everyday. She has received all from love, she can lose all in losing it. Vague or definite, ill-founded or justified, jealousy is maddening torture for the woman, because it is radically at variance with love: if the treason is unquestionable, she must either give up making love a religion or give up loving. This is a radical catastrophe and no wonder the woman in love, suspicious and mistaken in turn, is obsessed by the desire to discover the fatal truth and the fear that she will.

Being at the same time proud and anxious, the woman may suffer constant jealousy and yet be always wrong about it: Juliette Drouet felt suspicious pangs concerning every woman who came near Hugo, forgetting to fear only Léonie Biard, who was his mistress for eight years. In a state of uncertainty, every woman is a rival, a danger. Love destroys the possibility of friendship with other women because the woman in love is shut off in her lover's universe; jealousy increases her isolation and thereby narrows her dependence. It relieves her ennui, however; keeping a husband is work, but keeping a lover is a kind of sacred ministry. The woman who neglects her person while lost in happy adoration begins to feel concerned with it again once she has a presentiment of danger. Dress, care of their rooms, appearances in society, become aspects of a battle. The struggle is a tonic activity; as long as she is reasonably sure of victory, the fighter finds a poignant pleasure in the combat.

But the anguished fear of defeat transforms a free and generous gift into a humiliating service. To defend himself, the man attacks. Even a proud woman is forced to make herself gentle and passive; maneuvering, discretion, trickery, smiles, charm, docility, are her best weapons. I can still see that young woman at the door where I unexpectedly rang one evening; I had left her two hours before, badly made up, carelessly dressed, her eyes dull; but now she was expecting *him*. When she saw me, she resumed her ordinary expression, but for an instant I had time to see her, in readiness for him, nerved up in fear and hypocrisy, prepared for whatever suffering behind her sprightly smile. Her hair was carefully done, her lips and cheeks had unaccustomed coloring, she was dressed up in a lace blouse of sparkling white. Party clothes, weapons of war! Masseurs, "beauticians," know what tragic importance their clients give to apparently futile pains: one must invent new seductions for the lover, one must become that woman he wishes to encounter and possess!

But it is all in vain: she will not revive in herself that image of the Other which attracted him in the first place and can now attract him in some other woman. The lover makes the same dual and impossible demand as does the husband: he wants his mistress to be absolutely his and yet a stranger; he wants her to conform exactly to his dream and to be different from anything he can imagine, a response to his expectation and a complete surprise. The woman is torn by this contradiction and doomed to frustration. She tries to model herself on her lover's desire; many women who bloomed at the beginning of an affair that flattered their narcissism display a mad and frightening servility when they feel they are less ardently loved; haunted and impoverished, they become an annoyance to their lovers. Giving herself blindly, woman has lost that dimension of freedom which at first made her fascinating. The lover seeks his reflection in her; but if he begins to find it altogether too faithful, he gets bored. It is, again, one of the loving woman's misfortunes to find that her very love disfigures her, destroys her; she is nothing more than this slave, this servant, this too ready mirror, this too faithful echo. When she becomes aware of this, her distress reduces her worth still further; in tears, demands, and scenes she succeeds in losing all her attractiveness. An existent is what he does; but simply to be, she has come to rely on a consciousness not her own, and she has given up doing anything. "I only know how to love," writes Julie de Lespinasse. *I am love alone* [9] is the motto of the woman in love; she is nothing but love, and when her love is robbed of its object, she is no longer anything at all.

In many cases she realizes her mistake; then she tries to reassert her liberty, to regain her alterity; she becomes flirtatious. Desired by other men, she takes on renewed interest for her indifferent lover. It is the hackneyed theme of many cynical novels; sometimes absence is enough to restore her prestige. Albertine seems insipid when she is at hand and yielding; at a distance she becomes mysterious again and the jealous Proust reappraises her.

But such maneuvers are delicate; if the man sees through them, they can only ridiculously expose the servility of his slave. And even their success is not without danger; he disdains her because she is his, but he is also attached to her because she is his; which will an infidelity do away with, the disdain or the attachment? The man may be an-

---

[9] From the title of Dominique Rollin's novel *Moi qui ne suis qu'amour.*

noyed and abandon her, now that she is indifferent to him; he wants
her free, yes; but he wants her devoted. She understands this risk,
and it paralyzes her flirtatiousness. It is almost impossible for a
woman in love to play this game well; she is too afraid of being caught
in her own trap. And to the extent that she still has regard for her
lover, she will feel it repugnant to dupe him: how could he remain
a god in her eyes? If she wins the game, she destroys her idol; if she
loses it, she loses herself. There is no salvation.

A cautious *amoureuse*—but the words clash with each other—tries
to convert her lover's passion into affection, friendship, habit; or she
undertakes to attach him to her by strong ties: a child, or marriage.
This desire for marriage haunts many liaisons: it is the desire for security. The clever mistress takes advantage of a love still young to
assure her future; but when she permits herself such speculation, she
no longer deserves the name of *amoureuse*. For the *amoureuse* dreams
madly of forever holding captive the liberty of her lover, but not of
destroying it. And this explains why love-religion leads to catastrophe,
save in the very rare event of a voluntary association lasting throughout life. With Mora, Mlle de Lespinasse had the luck to get tired of
it first, she got tired of it because she met Guibert, who, on his part,
promptly got tired of her. The love of Mme d'Agoult and Liszt died
of this implacable dialectic: the fire, the vitality, the ambition, which
made Liszt attract her love, fated him to other loves. D'Annunzio's
fascinating flame had the price of his infidelity. A break can leave its
mark on a man; but, after all, he has his man's life to live. The abandoned woman no longer is anything, no longer has anything. If she is
asked how she lived before, she does not even remember. She let her
former world fall in ashes, to adopt a new country from which she
is suddenly driven; she forswore all the values she believed in, broke
off her friendships; she now finds herself without a roof over her
head, the desert all around her. How begin a new life, since outside
her lover there is nothing? She takes refuge in delirious fancies, as
formerly in the convent; or if she is too strong-minded for that, there
is nothing left but to die: very quickly, like Mlle de Lespinasse, or
by inches; the agony may drag out interminably. When for ten years,
for twenty years, a woman has been devoted to a man body and soul,
when he has remained firmly on the pedestal where she has placed
him, to be abandoned is a sudden and terrible catastrophe. "What
can I do?" asked a woman of forty, "what can I do if he doesn't love

me any more?" She dressed and made up with minute care; but her hardened visage, already done for, could scarcely arouse a new love; and as for her, after twenty years passed in the shadow of a man, could she love any other?

Many years remain to be lived when one is forty. I see again another woman, still with fine eyes and noble features despite a face puffed with sorrow, who in public let the tears flow unheeded, blind and deaf to everything but her grief. Now the god is saying to another the words invented for her; a dethroned queen, she no longer knows whether she ever did reign over a real domain. If the woman is still young, she has a chance to recover—a new love will cure her. In some cases she will give herself with a little more reserve, realizing that what is not unique cannot be absolute; but she will often dash herself to ruin more violently than she did the first time, because she must also make up for her past defeat. The failure of absolute love is a fruitful lesson only if the woman is capable of taking herself in hand again; separated from Abélard, Héloïse was not wrecked, because she built herself an independent existence in the governing of an abbey. Colette's heroines have too much pride and too many resources within themselves to be shipwrecked by a disappointment in love; and so do many women in real life. Yet there are few crimes that entail worse punishment than the generous fault of putting oneself entirely in another's hands.

Genuine love ought to be founded on the mutual recognition of two liberties; the lovers would then experience themselves both as self and as other: neither would give up transcendence, neither would be mutilated; together they would manifest values and aims in the world. For the one and the other, love would be revelation of self by the gift of self and enrichment of the world. In his work on self-knowledge [1] George Gusdorf sums up very exactly what *man* demands of love.

Love reveals us to ourselves by making us come out of ourselves. We affirm ourselves by contact with what is foreign and complementary to us. . . . Love as a form of perception brings to light new skies and a new earth even in the landscape where we have always lived. Here is the great secret: the world is different, I myself *am different*. And I am no longer alone in knowing it.

---

[1] *La Découverte de soi* (Paris, 1948), pp. 421, 425.—TR.

Even better: someone has apprised me of the fact. Woman therefore plays an indispensable and leading role in man's gaining knowledge of himself.

This accounts for the importance to the young man of his apprenticeship in love;[2] we have seen how astonished Stendhal, Malraux, were at the miracle expressed in the phrase: "I myself, I am different." But Gusdorf is wrong when he writes: "And *similarly* man represents for woman an indispensable intermediary between herself and herself," for today her situation is not *similar*; man is revealed in a different aspect but he remains himself, and his new aspect is integrated with the sum total of his personality. It would be the same with woman only if she existed no less essentially than man as *poursoi*; this would imply that she had economic independence, that she moved toward ends of her own and transcended herself, without using man as an agent, toward the social whole. Under these circumstances, love in equality is possible, as Malraux depicts it between Kyo and May in *Man's Fate*. Woman may even play the virile and dominating role, as did Mme de Warens with Rousseau, and, in Colette's *Chéri*, Léa with Chéri.

But most often woman knows herself only as different, relative; her *pour-autrui*, relation to others, is confused with her very being; for her, love is not an intermediary "between herself and herself" because she does not attain her subjective existence; she remains engulfed in this loving woman whom man has not only revealed, but created. Her salvation depends on this despotic free being that has made her and can instantly destroy her. She lives in fear and trembling before this man who holds her destiny in his hands without quite knowing it, without quite wishing to. She is in danger through an other, an anguished and powerless onlooker at her own fate. Involuntary tyrant, involuntary executioner, this other wears a hostile visage in spite of her and of himself. And so, instead of the union sought for, the woman in love knows the most bitter solitude there is; instead of cooperation, she knows struggle and not seldom hate. For woman, love is a supreme effort to survive by accepting the dependence to which she is condemned; but even with consent a life of dependency can be lived only in fear and servility.

Men have vied with one another in proclaiming that love is

[2] See Book I, pp. 183, 247.

woman's supreme accomplishment. "A woman who loves as a woman becomes only the more feminine," says Nietzsche; and Balzac: "Among the first-rate, man's life is fame, woman's life is love. Woman is man's equal only when she makes her life a perpetual offering, as that of man is perpetual action." But therein, again, is a cruel deception, since what she offers, men are in no wise anxious to accept. Man has no need of the unconditional devotion he claims, nor of the idolatrous love that flatters his vanity; he accepts them only on condition that he need not satisfy the reciprocal demands these attitudes imply. He preaches to woman that she should give—and her gifts bore him to distraction; she is left in embarrassment with her useless offerings, her empty life. On the day when it will be possible for woman to love not in her weakness but in her strength, not to escape herself but to find herself, not to abase herself but to assert herself—on that day love will become for her, as for man, a source of life and not of mortal danger. In the meantime, love represents in its most touching form the curse that lies heavily upon woman confined in the feminine universe, woman mutilated, insufficient unto herself. The innumerable martyrs to love bear witness against the injustice of a fate that offers a sterile hell as ultimate salvation.

CHAPTER XXIV

The Mystic

LOVE has been assigned to woman as her supreme vocation, and when she directs it toward a man, she is seeking God in him; but if human love is denied her by circumstances, if she is disappointed or overparticular, she may choose to adore divinity in the person of God Himself. To be sure, there have also been men who burned with that flame, but they are rare and their fervor is of a highly refined intellectual cast; whereas the women who abandon themselves to the joys of the heavenly nuptials are legion, and their experience is of a peculiarly emotional nature. Woman is habituated to living on her knees; ordinarily she expects her salvation to come down from the heaven where the males sit enthroned. They, too, are wreathed in clouds: their majesty is revealed from beyond the veils of their fleshly presence. The loved one is always more or less absent; he communicates with his worshipper by obscure signs; she knows his heart only through an act of faith; and the more superior he seems to her, the more impenetrable his behavior appears. We have seen that in erotomania this faith resists all contradiction. Woman need neither touch nor see to feel the Presence at her side. Be it doctor, priest, or God, woman will feel the same unquestionable certainties, as handmaiden she will receive in her heart the love that comes flooding from on high. Human love and love divine commingle, not because the latter is a sublimation of the former, but because the first is a reaching out toward a transcendent, an absolute. In both cases it is a matter of the salvation of the loving woman's contingent existence through her union with the Whole embodied in a supreme Person.

This ambiguity is conspicuous in many cases—pathological or normal—in which the lover is deified, or God has human characteristics. I will cite only this instance, reported by Ferdière in his work on erotomania. The woman patient is speaking:

> I corresponded in 1923 with a writer on the *Presse*; I read between the lines of his articles, and he seemed to be replying to me, giving me advice. . . . I wrote him many love letters. . . . In 1924 it

suddenly came to me that God was seeking a woman, that he was going to come and speak to me; I felt that he had given me a mission, had chosen me to found a temple; there would be a center where doctors were taking care of women. . . . At just this time I was sent to the Clermont asylum. . . . There were young doctors who wanted to remake the world: in my dark cell I felt their kisses on my fingers; I felt their sexual organs in my hands; once they said to me: "You are not sensitive, but sensual; turn over"; I turned over and I felt them in me; it was very pleasant. . . . The head doctor, Dr. D., was like a god; I sensed that something was the matter with him when he came near my bed; he looked at me as if he were saying: "I am yours." He really loved me. . . . One day his green eyes became blue as the sky and widened astonishingly. . . . He saw their effect on me as he talked to another patient, and he smiled. . . . I was taken with him and in spite of all my lovers (I had fifteen or sixteen), I could not get away from him; he was to blame. . . . For years I kept having mental conversations with him . . . when I wished to forget him he would come back into my mind . . . he would say mockingly: "Don't be afraid, you may love others, but you will always come back to me. . . ." I often wrote to him, making appointments, which I kept; he was rather cool; I felt foolish and left. . . . I heard that he married, but he will always love me. . . . He is my husband, but the decisive act never took place. . . . "Leave everything," he would say, "with me you will always mount upwards, you will be no longer a creature of earth." You see how it is; whenever I seek God, I find a man; now I don't know what religion to turn to.

Here we have to do with a pathological case. But we encounter this inextricable confusion between man and God in many devotees. The confessor in particular occupies an ambiguous place between earth and heaven. He listens with mortal ears when the penitent bares her soul, but his gaze envelops her in a supernatural light; he is a man of God, he is God present in human form. Mme Guyon thus describes her meeting with Father La Combe: "The power of grace seemed to come from him to me through the inmost pathways of the soul and went back from me to him so that he felt the same effect." The intervention of the monk was to cure her long-borne barrenness of heart and inflame her soul with a new fervor. She lived at his side throughout her great period of mysticism. And she declares: "It was not merely a complete unity; I could not distinguish him from God." It would be an oversimplification to say that she was really in love with a man and pretended to love God; she loved the man also, because he was in her eyes something other than himself. Like Ferdière's patient, what she vaguely sought to reach was the supreme source of values. That, indeed, is the aim of any mystic. The male intermediary is sometimes of use to her in starting her flight toward the lonely sky, but he is not indispensable. Not clearly distinguishing reality from make-believe, action from magic, the objective from the imaginary, woman is peculiarly prone to materialize the absent in her own body. It is a much less dubious matter to identify mysticism and erotomania, as is sometimes done. The erotomaniac feels she is made worthy through the love of a sovereign being; he takes the initiative in the amorous relation, he loves more passionately than he is loved; he makes his sentiments known by visible but secret signs; he is jealous and he is vexed at any lack of fervor in the elect, not hesitating to impose punishment; he almost never shows himself in carnal, concrete form. All this is to be met with in mystics; in particular, God cherishes through all eternity the soul He has fired with His love, He has shed His blood for her, He has prepared many mansions for her, glorious apotheoses. All she can do is abandon herself to His fires without resistance.

It is agreed today that erotomania may appear in platonic or in sexual form. Just so, the body may play a smaller or a greater part in the feelings of the mystic toward God. Her effusions are patterned upon those of earthly lovers. While Angela of Foligno was contemplating an image of Christ holding St. Francis in his arms, he said to her: "Thus shall I hold you embraced, and much more besides, not to be seen with mortal eyes. . . . I shall never leave you if you love me." Mme Guyon writes: "Love leaves me no instant of repose. I said to him: 'Oh my beloved, enough, let me go.' . . . I long for the love that sends ineffable shivers through the soul, the love that makes me swoon. . . . O my God, if You caused the most sensual of women to feel what I feel, they would at once quit their false pleasures to enjoy such true delight." We recall the famous vision of St. Theresa:

The angel held a long golden dart in his hands. From time to time he plunged it into my heart and forced it into my entrails.

When he withdrew the dart, it was as if he were going to tear out my entrails, and it left me all inflamed with love divine. . . . I am certain that the pain penetrated my deepest entrails and it seemed as if they were torn when my spiritual spouse withdrew the arrow with which he had penetrated them.

It is sometimes piously maintained that the poverty of language compels the mystic to borrow this erotic vocabulary; but she has only one body at her disposal, also, and so she borrows from earthly love not only words but physical attitudes as well; she has the same behavior to offer to God as what she displays when she offers herself to a man. That, however, in no way diminishes the value of her sentiments. When Angela of Foligno became by turns "pale and gaunt" or "plump and florid" according to the state of her heart, when she shed such deluges of hot tears that she had to apply cold water, as one of her biographers tells us, when she fell prostrate on the ground, we can hardly regard these phenomena as purely "spiritual"; but to explain them by her excessive "emotionality" alone is to invoke the "somniferous virtue" of the poppy; the body is never the *cause* of subjective experiences, since it is the subject himself in his objective aspect: the subject lives out his attitudes in the unity of his existence.

Both admirers and adversaries of mystics think that to attribute a sexual content to the ecstasies of St. Theresa is to reduce her to the rank of a hysteric. But what degrades the hysteric is not the fact that her body actively expresses her obsessions, but that she is obsessed, that her liberty is under a spell and annulled. The mastery over his body acquired by an Indian fakir does not make him the slave of it; corporeal mimicry can be an element in the *élan* of a sane, free consciousness. St. Theresa's writings hardly leave room for doubt, and they justify Bernini's statue, which shows us the saint swooning in an excess of supreme voluptuousness. It would be no less false to interpret her emotions as a simple "sublimation of sex"; there is not first an unavowed desire that later takes the form of divine love. The *amoureuse* herself is not at first the prey of a desire without object which is later to become fixed on an individual man; it is the presence of the lover that arouses in her a desire directly oriented toward him. Similarly, St. Theresa in a single process seeks to be united with God and lives out this union in her body; she is not the slave of her nerves and her hormones: one must admire, rather, the intensity of a faith that penetrates to the most intimate regions of her flesh. The truth is, as she herself understood, that the value of a mystical experience is measured not according to the way in which it is subjectively felt, but according to its objective influence. The ecstatic phenomena are almost the same in St. Theresa and in Marie Alacoque, but their messages are of very diverse interest. St. Theresa poses in a most intellectual fashion the dramatic problem of the relation between the individual and the transcendent Being; she lived out, as a woman, an experience whose meaning goes far beyond the fact of her sex; she must be ranked with Suso and St. John of the Cross. But she is a striking exception. What her minor sisters give us is an essentially feminine vision of the world and of salvation; it is not a transcendence that they seek: it is the redemption of their femininity.[1]

Woman seeks in divine love first of all what the *amoureuse* seeks in that of man: the exaltation of her narcissism; this sovereign gaze fixed attentively, amorously, upon her is a miraculous godsend. Throughout her earlier years, as young girl and young woman, Mme Guyon had always been tormented with the desire to be loved and admired. A modern Protestant mystic, Mlle Vée, writes: "Nothing makes me so unhappy as to have no one specially interested in me or sympathetic with what is going on in me." Sainte-Beuve, writing of Mme Krüdener, relates that she imagined that God was ceaselessly concerned about her, so much so that at the most critical moments with her lover she would groan: "My God, how happy I am! I ask your pardon for the excess of my happiness!" We can understand how intoxicating it is for the narcissist when all heaven becomes her mirror; her deified reflection is infinite like God Himself, and it will never fade. And at the same time, in her burning, palpitating, love-inundated breast she feels her soul created, redeemed, cherished, by the adorable Father; it is her double, it is herself she embraces, infinitely magnified through the mediation of God. These texts of St. Angela of Foligno are especially significant in this connection. Jesus speaks to her thus:

> My sweet girl, my daughter, my loved one, my temple. My daughter, my loved one, *love me for I love you*, much, much more than you can love me. Your whole life: your eating, your drinking,

---

[1] With Catherine of Siena, however, theological preoccupations were very important. She also belongs to the rather masculine type.

your sleeping, all your life finds favor in my sight. In you I will do great deeds in the eyes of the nations; in you I will be known and in you my name will be praised by many peoples. My daughter, my sweet spouse, I love you very much.

And again:

My daughter, you who are much more dear to me than I am to you, my delight, the heart of Almighty God is now upon your heart. . . . Almighty God has given much love to you, *more than to any woman in this city*; he has made you his delight.

Once more:

I bring you such love that I give no more regard to your failings and that my eyes see them no longer. I have given you a great treasure.

The elect cannot fail to respond with passion to such fervid declarations, coming from so high a source. She tries to join her lover through the usual technique of the loving woman: through annihilation. "I have but one concern and that is to love, to forget self, and to annihilate myself," writes Marie Alacoque. Ecstasy mimics corporeally that abolition of the ego; the subject neither sees nor feels any longer, the body is forgotten, denied. The dazzling and sovereign Presence is represented in intaglio by the extremity of that abandon, by the distraught acceptance of passivity. In Mme Guyon's quietism this passivity was erected into a system: as for her, she spent a large part of her life in a kind of cataleptic trance; it was a waking sleep.

Most women mystics are not content with abandoning themselves passively to God: they apply themselves actively to self-annihilation by the destruction of their flesh. No doubt asceticism has been practiced by monks and priests, but the mad rage with which woman flouts her flesh assumes special and peculiar forms. We have noted the ambiguity of woman's attitude toward her body: through humiliation and suffering she transforms it into a glory. Given over to her lover as a thing for his pleasure, she becomes a temple, an idol; torn by the pangs of childbirth, she creates heroes. The mystic will torture her flesh to have the right to claim it; reducing it to abjection, she exalts it as the instrument of salvation. Thus are to be explained the excesses in which certain saints have indulged. St. Angela of Foligno tells us that she drank with delight the water in which she had just washed lepers' hands and feet:

> This beverage flooded us with such sweetness that the joy followed us home. Never had I drunk with such pleasure. In my throat was lodged a piece of scaly skin from the lepers' sores. Instead of getting rid of it, I made a great effort to swallow it and I succeeded. It seemed to me that I had just partaken of communion. I shall never be able to express the delight that inundated me.

We know that Marie Alacoque cleaned up the vomit of a patient with her tongue; in her biography she describes the joy she felt when she had filled her mouth with the excrement of a man sick with diarrhea; [2] Jesus rewarded her when she held her lips pressed against his Sacred Heart for three hours. Devotion assumes a carnal cast especially in countries of ardent sensuality, like Spain and Italy: even today the women of a village in the Abruzzi still lacerate their tongues licking the pebbles on the ground along a way of the cross. In all these practices the women are only imitating the Redeemer who saved the flesh by the degradation of his own flesh. Women feel this great mystery in a much more concrete manner than do males.

It is in the shape of the spouse that God is most wont to appear to woman; sometimes He shows Himself in all His glory, dazzling in His white robe and in His beauty, Lord of all; He invests her in the bridal gown, He puts a crown upon her head, He takes her by the hand and promises to exalt her to heaven. But more often He is a carnal being: the wedding ring that Jesus gave to St. Catherine and that she wore invisibly on her finger was that "ring of flesh" which was cut off in his Circumcision. Above all, he is a maltreated and bleeding body: most fervently of all, she is lost in contemplation of the Crucified One; she identifies herself with the Virgin Mother, holding in her arms the remains of her Son, or with the Magdalen, standing at the foot of the cross and sprinkled with the blood of her Well-Beloved. Thus she satisfies her sado-masochistic fantasies. In the humiliation of God she sees with wonder the dethronement of Man;

---

[2] All this frightful madness can hardly fail to remind the worldly reader of masochistic horrors reported by psychiatrists.—TR.

inert, passive, covered with wounds, the Crucified is the reversed image
of the white, bloodstained martyr exposed to wild beasts, to daggers,
to males, with whom the little girl has so often identified herself; she
is overwhelmed to see that Man, Man-God, has assumed her role. She
it is who is hanging on the Tree, promised the splendor of the Resurrection. It is she: she proves it; her forehead bleeds under the crown
of thorns, her hands, her feet, her side, have been pierced by unseen
iron. Of the 321 persons bearing stigmata recognized by the Catholic
Church, only 47 are men; the others—including some famous saints
like Jeanne de la Croix—are women, on the average beyond the menopause. The most celebrated, Catherine Emmerich, was marked prematurely. When twenty-four, she had a longing to suffer the crown
of thorns; she saw a dazzling young man approach, who pressed that
crown on her head. The next day her temples and forehead were
swollen and began to bleed. Four years later, in an ecstasy, she saw
Christ with his wounds, and from them pointed rays shot out like
fine blades, which drew blood from the hands, feet, and side of the
saint. She sweat blood and spit blood at times. And still today, on
each Good Friday, Thérèse Neumann, also, shows to visitors her face
running with the blood of Christ.

In the stigmata is fully achieved the mysterious alchemy that glorifies the flesh, since they are the very presence of divine love, in the
form of a bloody anguish. We can readily understand why women are
especially concerned with the metamorphosis of the red flow into
pure golden flame. They are obsessed with this blood flowing from
the side of the King of men. St. Catherine of Siena refers to it in
most of her letters. Angela of Foligno humbled herself in the contemplation of the heart of Jesus and the open wound in his side.
Catherine Emmerich put on a red chemise to resemble Jesus when
he was like unto a "cloth wet with blood"; she saw everything
"through the blood of Jesus." Marie Alacoque—we have seen in what
circumstances—quenched her thirst for three hours from the Sacred
Heart of Jesus. She was the one who offered to the adoration of the
faithful the great red clot, surrounded with the flaming darts of love.
That is the emblem which sums up the great feminine dream: from
blood to glory through love.

Ecstasies, visions, talks with God—this inner experience is enough
for some women. Others feel impelled to transmit it to the world
through acts. The connection between action and contemplation takes

two very different forms. There are women of action like St. Catherine, St. Theresa, Joan of Arc, who know very well what goals they have in mind and who lucidly devise means for attaining them: their visions simply provide objective images for their certitudes, encouraging these women to persist in the paths they have mapped out in detail for themselves. Then there are narcissistic women, like Mme Guyon and Mme Krüdener, who, after a period of silent fervor, suddenly feel themselves in what the former calls "an apostolic state." They are not too certain about their tasks; and—like the excitement-seeking ladies of the social-service institutes—they care little what they do provided they do *something*. This was so with Mme Krüdener, who, after displaying herself as ambassadress and novelist, interiorized her conception of her own merits: it was not to assure the triumph of certain definite ideas but to confirm herself in her role as one inspired by God that she took charge of the destiny of Alexander I. If a little beauty and intelligence often are enough to make a woman feel worthy of homage, she will with better reason think she is charged with a mission when she knows she is God's elect; she preaches vague doctrines, she often founds sects, and this enables her to effect, through the members of the groups she inspires, a thrilling multiplication of her personality.

Mystical fervor, like love and even narcissism, can be integrated with a life of activity and independence. But in themselves these attempts at individual salvation are bound to meet with failure: either woman puts herself into relation with an unreality: her double, or God; or she creates an unreal relation with a real being. In both cases she lacks any grasp on the world; she does not escape her subjectivity; her liberty remains frustrated. There is only one way to employ her liberty authentically, and that is to project it through positive action into human society.

PART VII

TOWARD LIBERATION

CHAPTER XXV

The Independent Woman

Accorping to French law, obedience is no longer included among the duties of a wife, and each woman citizen has the right to vote; but these civil liberties remain theoretical as long as they are unaccompanied by economic freedom. A woman supported by a man—wife or courtesan—is not emancipated from the male because she has a ballot in her hand; if custom imposes less constraint upon her than formerly, the negative freedom implied has not profoundly modified her situation; she remains bound in her condition of vassalage. It is through gainful employment that woman has traversed most of the distance that separated her from the male; and nothing else can guarantee her liberty in practice. Once she ceases to be a parasite, the system based on her dependence crumbles; between her and the universe there is no longer any need for a masculine mediator.

The curse that is upon woman as vassal consists, as we have seen, in the fact that she is not permitted to do anything; so she persists in the vain pursuit of her true being through narcissism, love, or religion.

When she is productive, active, she regains her transcendence; in her projects she concretely affirms her status as subject; in connection with the aims she pursues, with the money and the rights she takes possession of, she makes trial of and senses her responsibility. Many women are aware of these advantages, even among those in very modest positions. I heard a charwoman declare, while scrubbing the stone floor of a hotel lobby: "I never asked anybody for anything; I succeeded all by myself." She was as proud of her self-sufficiency as a Rockefeller. It is not to be supposed, however, that the mere combination of the right to vote and a job constitutes a complete emancipation: working, today, is not liberty. Only in a socialist world would woman by the one attain the other. The majority of workers are exploited today. On the other hand, the social structure has not been much modified by the changes in woman's condition; this world, always belonging to men, still retains the form they have given it.

We must not lose sight of those facts which make the question of woman's labor a complex one. An important and thoughtful woman recently made a study of the women in the Renault factories; she states that they would prefer to stay in the home rather than work in the factory. There is no doubt that they get economic independence only as members of a class which is economically oppressed; and, on the other hand, their jobs at the factory do not relieve them of housekeeping burdens.[1] If they had been asked to choose between forty hours of work a week in the factory and forty hours of work a week in the home, they would doubtless have furnished quite different answers. And perhaps they would cheerfully accept both jobs, if as factory workers they were to be integrated in a world that would be theirs, in the development of which they would joyfully and proudly share. At the present time, peasants apart,[2] the majority of women do not escape from the traditional feminine world; they get from neither society nor their husbands the assistance they would need to become in concrete fact the equals of the men. Only those women who have a political faith, who take militant action in the unions, who have confidence in their future, can give ethical meaning to thankless daily labor. But lacking leisure, inheriting a traditional submissiveness, women are naturally just beginning to develop a political and social

---

[1] I have indicated in Book I, p. 135, how heavy these are for women who work outside.

[2] We have examined their situation in Book I, pp. 109, 134.

sense. And not getting in exchange for their work the moral and social benefits they might rightfully count on, they naturally submit to its constraints without enthusiasm.

It is quite understandable, also, that the milliner's apprentice, the shopgirl, the secretary, will not care to renounce the advantages of masculine support. I have already pointed out that the existence of a privileged caste, which she can join by merely surrendering her body, is an almost irresistible temptation to the young woman; she is fated for gallantry by the fact that her wages are minimal while the standard of living expected of her by society is very high. If she is content to get along on her wages, she is only a pariah: ill lodged, ill dressed, she will be denied all amusement and even love. Virtuous people preach asceticism to her, and, indeed, her dietary regime is often as austere as that of a Carmelite. Unfortunately, not everyone can take God as a lover: she has to please men if she is to succeed in her life as a woman. She will therefore accept assistance, and this is what her employer cynically counts on in giving her starvation wages. This aid will sometimes allow her to improve her situation and achieve a real independence; in other cases, however, she will give up her work and become a kept woman. She often retains both sources of income and each serves more or less as an escape from the other; but she is really in double servitude: to job and to protector. For the married woman her wages represent only pin money as a rule; for the girl who "makes something on the side" it is the masculine contribution that seems extra; but neither of them gains complete independence through her own efforts.

There are, however, a fairly large number of privileged women who find in their professions a means of economic and social autonomy. These come to mind when one considers woman's possibilities and her future. This is the reason why it is especially interesting to make a close study of their situation, even though they constitute as yet only a minority; they continue to be a subject of debate between feminists and antifeminists. The latter assert that the emancipated women of today succeed in doing nothing of importance in the world and that furthermore they have difficulty in achieving their own inner equilibrium. The former exaggerate the results obtained by professional women and are blind to their inner confusion. There is no good reason, as a matter of fact, to say they are on the wrong road; and still it is certain that they are not tranquilly installed in their new realm: as yet they are only halfway there. The woman who is economically emancipated from man is not for all that in a moral, social, and psychological situation identical with that of man. The way she carries on her profession and her devotion to it depend on the context supplied by the total pattern of her life. For when she begins her adult life she does not have behind her the same past as does a boy; she is not viewed by society in the same way; the universe presents itself to her in a different perspective. The fact of being a woman today poses peculiar problems for an independent human individual.

The advantage man enjoys, which makes itself felt from his childhood, is that his vocation as a human being in no way runs counter to his destiny as a male. Through the identification of phallus and transcendence, it turns out that his social and spiritual successes endow him with a virile prestige. He is not divided. Whereas it is required of woman that in order to realize her femininity she must make herself object and prey, which is to say that she must renounce her claims as sovereign subject. It is this conflict that especially marks the situation of the emancipated woman. She refuses to confine herself to her role as female, because she will not accept mutilation; but it would also be a mutilation to repudiate her sex. Man is a human being with sexuality; woman is a complete individual, equal to the male, only if she too is a human being with sexuality. To renounce her femininity is to renounce a part of her humanity. Misogynists have often reproached intellectual women for "neglecting themselves"; but they have also preached this doctrine to them: if you wish to be our equals, stop using make-up and nail-polish.

This piece of advice is nonsensical. Precisely because the concept of femininity is artificially shaped by custom and fashion, it is imposed upon each woman from without; she can be transformed gradually so that her canons of propriety approach those adopted by the males: at the seashore—and often elsewhere—trousers have become feminine.[3] That changes nothing fundamental in the matter: the individual is still not free to do as she pleases in shaping the concept of femininity. The woman who does not conform devaluates herself sexually and hence socially, since sexual values are an integral feature of society. One does not acquire virile attributes by rejecting femi-

---

[3] If that is the word.—TR.

nine attributes; even the transvestite fails to make a man of herself
—she is a travesty. As we have seen, homosexuality constitutes a
specific attitude: neutrality is impossible. There is no negative attitude that does not imply a positive counterpart. The adolescent girl
often thinks that she can simply scorn convention; but even there
she is engaged in public agitation; she is creating a new situation
entailing consequences she must assume. When one fails to adhere
to an accepted code, one becomes an insurgent. A woman who
dresses in an outlandish manner lies when she affirms with an air
of simplicity that she dresses to suit herself, nothing more. She knows
perfectly well that to suit herself is to be outlandish.

Inversely, a woman who does not wish to appear eccentric will
conform to the usual rules. It is injudicious to take a defiant attitude
unless it is connected with positively effective action: it consumes
more time and energy than it saves. A woman who has no wish to shock
or to devaluate herself socially should live out her feminine situation
in a feminine manner; and very often, for that matter, her professional success demands it. But whereas conformity is quite natural
for a man—custom being based on his needs as an independent and
active individual—it will be necessary for the woman who also is
subject, activity, to insinuate herself into a world that has doomed
her to passivity. This is made more burdensome because women confined to the feminine sphere have grossly magnified its importance:
they have made dressing and housekeeping difficult arts. Man hardly
has to take thought of his clothes, for they are convenient, suitable
to his active life, not necessarily elegant; they are scarcely a part of
his personality. More, nobody expects him to take care of them himself: some kindly disposed or hired female relieves him of this bother.

Woman, on the contrary, knows that when she is looked at she
is not considered apart from her appearance: she is judged, respected,
desired, by and through her toilette. Her clothes were originally intended to consign her to impotence, and they have remained un-
serviceable, easily ruined: stockings get runs, shoes get down at the
heel, light-colored blouses and frocks get soiled, pleats get unpleated.
But she will have to make most of the repairs herself; other women
will not come benevolently to her assistance and she will hesitate
to add to her budget for work she could do herself: permanents,
setting hair, make-up materials, new dresses, cost enough already.
When they come in after the day's work, students and secretaries

always have a stocking with a run to be fixed, a blouse to wash, a skirt to press. A woman who makes a good income will spare herself this drudgery, but she will have to maintain a more complicated elegance; she will lose time in shopping, in having fittings, and the rest. Tradition also requires even the single woman to give some attention to her lodgings. An official assigned to a new city will easily find accommodations at a hotel; but a woman in the same position will want to settle down in a place of her own. She will have to keep it scupulously neat, for people would not excuse a negligence on her part which they would find quite natural in a man.

It is not regard for the opinion of others alone that leads her to give time and care to her appearance and her housekeeping. She wants to retain her womanliness for her own satisfaction. She can regard herself with approval throughout her present and past only in combining the life she has made for herself with the destiny that her mother, her childhood games, and her adolescent fantasies prepared for her. She has entertained narcissistic dreams; to the male's phallic pride she still opposes her cult of self; she wants to be seen, to be attractive. Her mother and her older sisters have inculcated the liking for a nest: a home, an "interior," of her own! That has always been basic in her dreams of independence; she has no intention of discarding them when she has found liberty by other roads. And to the degree in which she still feels insecure in the masculine universe, she tends to retain the need for a retreat, symbolical of that interior refuge she has been accustomed to seeking within herself. Obedient to the feminine tradition, she will wax her floors, and she will do her own cooking instead of going to eat at a restaurant as a man would in her place. She wants to live at once like a man and like a woman, and in that way she multiplies her tasks and adds to her fatigue.

If she intends to remain fully feminine, it is implied that she also intends to meet the other sex with the odds as favorable as possible. Her most difficult problems are going to be posed in the field of sex. In order to be a complete individual, on an equality with man, woman must have access to the masculine world as does the male to the feminine world, she must have access to the *other*; but the demands of the *other* are not symmetrical in the two symmetrical cases. Once attained, fame and fortune, appearing like immanent qualities, may increase woman's sexual attractiveness; but the fact that she is a being of independent activity wars against her femininity, and this she is aware of. The independent woman—and above all the intellectual, who thinks about her situation—will suffer, as a female, from an inferiority complex; she lacks leisure for such minute beauty care as that of the coquette whose sole aim in life is to be seductive; follow the specialists' advice as she may, she will never be more than an amateur in the domain of elegance. Feminine charm demands that transcendence, degraded into immanence, appear no longer as anything more than a subtle quivering of the flesh; it is necessary to be spontaneously offered prey.

But the intellectual knows that she is offering herself, she knows that she is a conscious being, a subject; one can hardly dull one's glance and change one's eyes into sky-blue pools at will; one does not infallibly stop the surge of a body that is straining toward the world and change it into a statue animated by vague tremors. The intellectual woman will try all the more zealously because she fears failure; but her conscious zeal is still an activity and it misses its goal. She makes mistakes like those induced by the menopause: she tries to deny her brain just as the woman who is growing older tries to deny her age; she dresses like a girl, she overloads herself with flowers, furbelows, fancy materials; she affects childish tricks of surprised amazement. She romps, she babbles, she pretends flippancy, heedlessness, sprightliness.

But in all this she resembles those actors who fail to feel the emotion that would relax certain muscles and so by an effort of will contract the opposing ones, forcing down their eyes or the corners of their mouths instead of letting them fall. Thus in imitating abandon the intellectual woman becomes tense. She realizes this, and it irritates her; over her blankly naïve face, there suddenly passes a flash of all too sharp intelligence; lips soft with promise suddenly tighten. If she has trouble in pleasing, it is because she is not, like her slavish little sisters, pure will to please; the desire to seduce, lively as it may be, has not penetrated to the marrow of her bones. As soon as she feels awkward, she becomes vexed at her abjectness; she wants to take her revenge by playing the game with masculine weapons: she talks instead of listening, she displays subtle thoughts, strange emotions; she contradicts the man instead of agreeing with him, she tries to get the best of him. Mme de Staël won some resounding victories: she was almost irresistible. But the challenging attitude, very common among American women, for example, irritates men more often than it conquers them; and there are some men, besides, who bring it upon themselves by their own defiant air. If they would be willing to love an equal instead of a slave—as, it must be added, do those among them who are at once free from arrogance and without an inferiority complex—women would not be as haunted as they are by concern for their femininity; they would gain in naturalness, in simplicity, and they would find themselves women again without taking so much pains, since, after all, that is what they are.

The fact is that men are beginning to resign themselves to the new status of woman; and she, not feeling condemned in advance, has begun to feel more at ease. Today the woman who works is less neglectful of her femininity than formerly, and she does not lose her sexual attractiveness. This success, though already indicating progress toward equilibrium, is not yet complete; it continues to be more difficult for a woman than for a man to establish the relations with the other sex that she desires. Her erotic and affectional life encounters numerous difficulties. In this matter the unemancipated woman is in no way privileged: sexually and affectionally most wives and courtesans are deeply frustrated. If the difficulties are more evident in the case of the independent woman, it is because she has chosen battle rather than resignation. All the problems of life find a silent solution in death; a woman who is busy with living is therefore more at variance with herself than is she who buries her will and her desires; but the former will not take the latter as a standard. She considers herself at a disadvantage only in comparison with man.

A woman who expends her energy, who has responsibilities, who knows how harsh is the struggle against the world's opposition, needs —like the male—not only to satisfy her physical desires but also to enjoy the relaxation and diversion provided by agreeable sexual adventures. Now, there are still many social circles in which her freedom in this matter is not concretely recognized; if she exercises it, she risks compromising her reputation, her career; at the least a burdensome hypocrisy is demanded of her. The more solidly she establishes her position in society, the more ready people will be to close their eyes; but in provincial districts especially, she is watched with narrow severity, as a rule. Even under the most favorable circumstances—where fear of public opinion is negligible—her situation in this respect is not equivalent to man's. The differences depend both on traditional attitudes and on the special nature of feminine eroticism.

Man has easy access to fugitive embraces that are at the worst sufficient to calm his flesh and keep him in good spirits. There have been women—not many—prepared to demand that brothels for females be provided; in a novel entitled *Le Numéro* 17 a woman proposed the establishment of houses where women could resort for "sexual appeasement" through the services of "taxi-boys." [4] It appears that an establishment of this kind formerly existed in San Francisco; the customers were prostitutes, who were highly amused to pay instead of being paid. Their pimps had the place closed. Apart from the fact that this solution is chimerical and hardly desirable, it would doubtless meet with small success, for, as we have seen, woman does not obtain "appeasement" as mechanically as does the male; most women consider the arrangement hardly conducive to voluptuous abandon. At any rate, this resource is unavailable today.

Another possible solution is to pick up in the street a partner for a night or an hour—supposing that the woman, being of passionate temperament and having overcome all her inhibitions, can contemplate it without disgust—but this solution is much more dangerous for her than for the male. The risk of venereal disease is graver, because it is the man who is responsible for taking precautions against infection; and, however careful she may be, the woman is never wholly protected against the danger of conception. But what is important above all in such relations between strangers—relations that are on a plane of brutality—is the difference in physical strength. A man has not much to fear from the woman he takes home with him; he merely needs to be reasonably on his guard. It is not the same with a woman who takes a man in. I was told of two young women, just arrived in Paris and eager to "see life," who, after a look around at night, invited two attractive Montmartre characters to supper. In the morning they found themselves robbed, beaten up, and threatened with blackmail. A more significant case is that of a woman of forty, divorced, who worked hard all day to support three children and her old parents. Still attractive, she had absolutely no

---

[4] The author—whose name I have forgotten, a slip that I see no urgent need of repairing—explains at length how they could be prepared to satisfy all kinds of clients, what regimen they should follow, and so on.

time for social life, or for playing the coquette and going through the customary motions involved in getting an affair under way, which, besides, would have caused her too much bother. She had strong feelings, however, and she believed in her right to satisfy them. So she would occasionally roam the streets at night and manage to scare up a man. But one night, after spending an hour or two in a thicket in the Bois de Boulogne, her lover of the moment refused to let her go: he demanded her name and address, he wanted to see her again, to arrange to live together. When she refused, he gave her a severe beating and finally left her covered with bruises and almost frightened to death.

As for taking a permanent lover, as a man often takes a mistress, and supporting or helping him financially, this is possible only for women of means. There are some who find this arrangement agreeable; by paying the man they make him a mere instrument and can use him with contemptuous unconstraint. But as a rule, they must be old to be able to dissociate sex and sentiment so crudely, since in feminine adolescence the two are most profoundly associated, as we have seen. There are many men, for that matter, who never accept the separation of flesh and spirit; and, with more reason, a majority of women will refuse to consider it. Moreover, it involves fraudulence, to which they are more sensitive than is man; for the paying client is also an instrument herself, since her partner uses her as means of subsistence. Masculine pride conceals the ambiguities of the erotic drama from the male: he lies to himself unconsciously. More easily humiliated, more vulnerable, woman is also more clear-sighted; she will succeed in blinding herself only at the cost of entertaining a more calculated bad faith. Even granted the means, woman will never find the purchase of a male a satisfactory solution.

For most women—and men too—it is not a mere matter of satisfying erotic desire, but of maintaining their dignity as human beings while obtaining satisfaction. When a male enjoys a woman, when he gives her enjoyment, he takes the position of sole subject: he is imperious conqueror, or lavish donor—sometimes both at once. Woman, for her part, also wishes to make it clear that she subdues her partner to her pleasure and overwhelms him with her gifts. Thus, when she imposes herself on a man, be it through promised benefits, or in staking on his courtesy, or by artfully arousing his desire in its pure generality, she readily persuades herself that she is overwhelming him with her bounty. Thanks to this advantageous conviction, she can make advances without humiliating herself, because she feels she is doing so out of generosity. Thus in the novel *Blé en herbe* the "woman in white," who covets Phil's caresses, says haughtily to him: "I love only beggars and starved people." As a matter of fact, she cleverly sees to it that he does take a suppliant attitude. Then, writes Colette, "she made haste toward that obscure and narrow region where her pride could believe that the plaint is an avowal of distress and where beggars of her kind drink the illusion of liberality." Mme de Warens is the type of those women who choose young or unfortunate lovers, or those of inferior status, to lend their appetites the appearance of generosity. But there are also intrepid ones who tackle the most sturdy men and who take delight in satisfying them in spite of the fact that they have yielded only through politeness or fright.

Inversely, if the woman who entraps a man likes to imagine that she is giving herself, she who does give herself wants it understood that she also takes. "As for me, I am a woman who takes," a young journalist told me one day. The truth of the matter is that, except in the case of rape, neither one really takes the other; but here woman doubly deceives herself. For in fact a man often does seduce through his fiery aggressiveness, actively winning the consent of his partner. Save exceptionally—Mme de Staël has already been mentioned as one instance—it is otherwise with woman: she can hardly do more than offer herself; for most men are very jealous of their role. What they want is to arouse a specific excitement in the woman, not to be chosen as the means for satisfying her need in its generality: so chosen, they feel exploited.[5] A very young man once said to me: "A woman who is not afraid of men frightens them." And I have often heard older men declare: "It horrifies me to have a woman take the initiative." If a woman offers herself too boldly, the man departs, for he is intent on conquering. Woman, therefore, can take only when she makes herself prey: she must become a passive thing, a promise of submission. If she succeeds, she will think that she performed this magic conjuration intentionally, she will be subject again. But she risks remaining in the status of un-

---

[5] This feeling is the male counterpart of that which we have noted in the young girl. She, however, resigns herself to her destiny in the end.

necessary object if the male disdains her. This is why she is deeply humiliated when he rejects her advances. A man is sometimes angered when he feels that he has lost; however, he has only failed in an enterprise, nothing more. Whereas the woman has consented to make herself flesh in her agitation, her waiting, and her promises; she could win only in losing herself: she remains lost. One would have to be very blind or exceptionally clear-sighted to reconcile oneself to such a defeat.

And even when her effort at seduction succeeds, the victory is still ambiguous; the fact is that in common opinion it is the man who conquers, who *has* the woman. It is not admitted that she, like a man, can have desires of her own: she is the prey of desire. It is understood that man has made the specific forces a part of his personality, whereas woman is the slave of the species.[6] She is represented, at one time, as pure passivity, available, open, a utensil; she yields gently to the spell of sex feeling, she is fascinated by the male, who picks her like a fruit. At another time she is regarded as if possessed by alien forces: there is a devil raging in her womb, a serpent lurks in her vagina, eager to devour the male's sperm.

In any case, there is a general refusal to think of her as simply free. Especially in France the free woman and the light woman are obstinately confused, the term *light* implying an absence of resistance and control, a lack, the very negation of liberty. Feminine literature endeavors to combat this prejudice: in *Grisélidis*, for example, Clara Malraux insists on the fact that her heroine does not yield to allurement but accomplishes an act of her own volition. In America a certain liberty is recognized in woman's sexual activity, an attitude that tends to favor it. But the disdain for women who "go to bed" affected in France by even the men who enjoy their favors paralyzes a great many women who do not. They are horrified by the protests they would arouse, the comment they would cause, if they should.

Even if a woman regards anonymous rumors with contempt, she finds concrete difficulties in her relations with her partner, for common opinion is embodied in him. Very often he views the bed as

---

[6] We have seen in Book I, ch. i, that there is a certain amount of truth in this opinion. But it is not precisely at the moment of desire that the true asymmetry appears: it is in procreation. In desire man and woman assume their natural functions identically.

the proper terrain for asserting his aggressive superiority. He is eager to take and not to receive, not to exchange but to rob. He seeks to possess the woman to an extent over and above what she gives him; he demands that her consent be a defeat and that the words she murmurs be avowals he tears from her—demands that she confess her pleasure and recognize her subjection. When Claudine challenges Renard by her prompt submission, he anticipates her: he hastens to violate her when she was going to offer herself; he obliges her to keep her eyes open so he may contemplate his triumph in their movements. Similarly in *Man's Fate* the overbearing Ferral insists on lighting the lamp that Valerie wants to put out.

If she is proud and demanding, woman meets the male as an adversary, and she is much less well armed than he is. In the first place, he has physical strength, and it is easy for him to impose his will; we have seen, also, that tension and activity suit his erotic nature, whereas when woman departs from passivity, she breaks the spell that brings on her enjoyment; if she mimics dominance in her postures and movements, she fails to reach the climax of pleasure: most women who cling to their pride become frigid. Lovers are rare who allow their mistresses to satisfy dominative or sadistic tendencies; and rarer still are women who gain full erotic satisfaction even from their docility.

There is a road which seems much less thorny for women: that of masochism. When one works all day, struggles, takes responsibilities and risks, it is a welcome relaxation to abandon oneself at night to vigorous caprices. Whether schooled in love or a tyro, woman does in fact very often enjoy annihilating herself for the benefit of a masterful will. But it is still necessary for her to feel really dominated. It is not easy for one who lives her daily life among men to believe in the unconditional supremacy of the male. I have been told of the case of a woman who was not really masochistic but very "feminine"—that is, who found deep submissive pleasure in masculine arms. She had been married several times since she was seventeen and had had several lovers, always with much satisfaction. After having successfully managed an enterprise in the course of which she had men under her direction, she complained of having become frigid. There was formerly a blissful submission that she no longer felt, because she had become accustomed to dominating over males, and so their prestige had vanished.

When a woman begins to doubt men's superiority, their pretensions serve only to decrease her esteem for them. In bed, at the time when man would like to be most savagely male, he seems puerile from the very fact that he pretends virility, and woman averts her eyes; for he only conjures up the old complex of castration, the shadow of his father, or some such phantasm. It is not always from pride that a mistress refuses to yield to the caprices of her lover: she would fain have to do with an adult who is living out a real moment of his life, not with a little boy telling himself stories. The masochist is especially disappointed: a maternal compliance, annoyed or indulgent, is not the abdication she dreams of. She, too, will have to content herself with ridiculous games, pretending to believe herself dominated and enslaved, or she will pursue men supposed to be "superior" in the hope of finding a master, or she will become frigid.

We have seen that it is possible to avoid the temptations of sadism and masochism when the two partners recognize each other as equals; if both the man and the woman have a little modesty and some generosity, ideas of victory and defeat are abolished: the act of love becomes a free exchange. But, paradoxically, it is much more difficult for the woman than for the man to recognize an individual of the other sex as an equal. Precisely because the male caste has superiority of status, there are a great many individual women whom a man can hold in affectionate esteem: it is an easy matter to love a woman. In the first place, a woman can introduce her lover into a world that is different from his own and that he enjoys exploring in her company; she fascinates and amuses him, at least for a time. For another thing, on account of her restricted and subordinate situation, all her qualities seem like high achievements, conquests, whereas her mistakes are excusable; Stendhal admires Mme de Rênal and Mme de Chasteller in spite of their detestable prejudices. If a woman has false ideas, if she is not very intelligent, clear-sighted, or courageous, a man does not hold her responsible: she is the victim, he thinks—and often with reason—of her situation. He dreams of what she might have been, of what she perhaps will be: she can be credited with any possibilities, because she *is* nothing in particular. This vacancy is what makes the lover weary of her quickly; but it is the source of the mystery, the charm, that seduces him and makes him inclined to feel an easy affection in the first place.

It is much less easy for a woman to feel affectionate friendship for a man, for he *is* what he has made himself, irrevocably. He must be loved as he is, not with reference to his promise and his uncertain possibilities; he is responsible for his behavior and ideas; for him there are no excuses. Fellowship with him is impossible unless she approves his acts, his aims, his opinions. Julien can love a legitimist, as we have seen; a Lamiel could not cherish a man whose ideas she despised. Even though prepared to compromise, woman will hardly be able to take an attitude of indulgence. For man opens to her no verdant paradise of childhood. She meets him in this world which is their world in common: he comes bearing the gift of himself only. Self-enclosed, definite, decided, he is not conducive to daydreaming; when he speaks, one must listen. He takes himself seriously: if he is not interesting, he bores her, his presence weighs heavily on her. Only very young men can be endued with facile marvels; one can seek mystery and promise in them, find excuses for them, take them lightly: which is one reason why mature women find them most seductive. The difficulty is that, for their part, they usually prefer young women. The woman of thirty is thrown back on adult males. And doubtless she will encounter among them some who will not discourage her esteem and friendship; but she will be lucky if they make no show of arrogance in the matter. When she contemplates an affair or an adventure involving her heart as well as her body, the problem is to find a man whom she can regard as an equal without his considering himself superior.

I will be told that in general women make no such fuss; they seize the occasion without asking themselves too many questions, and they manage somehow with their pride and their sensuality. True enough. But it is also true that they bury in their secret hearts many disappointments, humiliations, regrets, resentments, not commonly matched in men. From a more or less unsatisfactory affair a man is almost sure of obtaining at least the benefit of sex pleasure; a woman can very well obtain no benefit at all. Even when indifferent, she lends herself politely to the embrace at the decisive moment, sometimes only to find her lover impotent and herself compromised in a ridiculous mockery. If all goes well except that she fails to attain satisfaction, then she feels "used," "worked." If she finds full enjoyment, she will want to prolong the affair. She is rarely quite sincere when she claims to envisage no more than an isolated adventure undertaken merely for pleasure, because her pleasure, far from bringing deliverance, binds her to the man; separation wounds her even when supposedly a friendly parting. It is much more unusual to hear a woman speak amicably of a former lover than a man of his past mistresses.

The peculiar nature of her eroticism and the difficulties that beset a life of freedom urge woman toward monogamy. Liaison or marriage, however, can be reconciled with a career much less easily for her than for man. Sometimes her lover or husband asks her to renounce it: she hesitates, like Colette's Vagabonde, who ardently desires the warm presence of a man at her side but dreads the fetters of marriage. If she yields, she is once more a vassal; if she refuses, she condemns herself to a withering solitude. Today a man is usually willing to have his companion continue her work; the novels of Colette Yver, showing young women driven to sacrifice their professions for the sake of peace and the family, are rather outdated; living together is an enrichment for two free beings, and each finds security for his or her own independence in the occupation of the mate. The self-supporting wife emancipates her husband from the conjugal slavery that was the price of hers. If the man is scrupulously well-intentioned, such lovers and married couples attain in undemanding generosity a condition of perfect equality.[7] It may even be the man that acts as devoted servant; thus, for George Eliot, Lewes created the favorable atmosphere that the wife usually creates around the husband-overlord. But for the most part it is still the woman who bears the cost of domestic harmony.

To a man it seems natural that it should be the wife who does the housework and assumes alone the care and bringing up of the children. The independent woman herself considers that in marrying she has assumed duties from which her personal life does not exempt her. She does not want to feel that her husband is deprived of advantages he would have obtained if he had married a "true woman"; she wants to be presentable, a good housekeeper, a devoted mother, such as wives traditionally are. This is a task that easily becomes

---

[7] It would appear that the life of Clara and Robert Schumann attained a success of this kind for a time.

overwhelming. She assumes it through regard for her partner and out of fidelity to herself also, for she intends, as we have already seen, to be in no way unfaithful to her destiny as woman. She will be a double for her husband and at the same time she will be herself; she will assume his cares and participate in his successes as much as she will be concerned with her own fate—and sometimes even more. Reared in an atmosphere of respect for male superiority, she may still feel that it is for man to occupy the first place; sometimes she fears that in claiming it she would ruin her home; between the desire to assert herself and the desire for self-effacement she is torn and divided.

There is, however, an advantage that woman can gain from her very inferiority. Since she is from the start less favored by fortune than man, she does not feel that she is to blame *a priori* for what befalls him; it is not her duty to make amends for social injustice, and she is not asked to do so. A man of good will owes it to himself to treat women with consideration, since he is more favored by fate than they are; he will let himself be bound by scruples, by pity, and so runs the risk of becoming the prey of clinging, vampirish women from the very fact of their disarmed condition. The woman who achieves virile independence has the great privilege of carrying on her sexual life with individuals who are themselves autonomous and effective in action, who—as a rule—will not play a parasitic role in her life, who will not enchain her through their weakness and the exigency of their needs. But in truth the woman is rare who can create a free relation with her partner; she herself usually forges the chains with which he has no wish to load her: she takes toward him the attitude of the *amoureuse*, the woman in love.

Through twenty years of waiting, dreaming, hoping, the young girl has cherished the myth of the liberating savior-hero, and hence the independence she has won through work is not enough to abolish her desire for a glorious abdication. She would have had to be raised exactly [8] like a boy to be able easily to overcome her adolescent narcissism; but as it is, she continues into adult life this cult of the ego toward which her whole youth has tended. She uses her professional successes as merits for the enrichment of her image; she feels the need for a witness from on high to reveal and consecrate her worth. Even if she is a severe judge of the men she evaluates in daily life,

---

[8] That is to say, not only by the same methods but in the same climate, which is impossible today, in spite of all the efforts of educators.

she none the less reveres Man, and if she encounters him, she is ready to fall on her knees.

To be justified by a god is easier than to justify herself by her own efforts; the world encourages her to believe it possible for salvation to be *given*, and she prefers to believe it. Sometimes she gives up her independence entirely and becomes no more than an *amoureuse*; more often she essays a compromise; but idolatrous love, the love that means abdication, is devastating; it occupies every thought, every moment, it is obsessing, tyrannical. If she meets with professional disappointments, the woman passionately seeks refuge in her love; then her frustrations are expressed in scenes and demands at her lover's expense. But her amatory troubles have by no means the effect of redoubling her professional zeal; she is, on the contrary, more likely to be impatient with a mode of life that keeps her from the royal road of a great love. A woman who worked ten years ago on a political magazine run by women told me that in the office they seldom talked about politics but incessantly about love: this one complained that she was loved only for her body to the neglect of her splendid intelligence; that one moaned that only her mind was appreciated, to the neglect of her physical charms. Here again, for woman to love as man does—that is to say, in liberty, without putting her very *being* in question—she must believe herself his equal and be so in concrete fact; she must engage in her enterprises with the same decisiveness. But this is still uncommon, as we shall see.

There is one feminine function that it is actually almost impossible to perform in complete liberty. It is maternity. In England and America and some other countries a woman can at least decline maternity at will, thanks to contraceptive techniques. We have seen that in France she is often driven to painful and costly abortion; or she frequently finds herself responsible for an unwanted child that can ruin her professional life. If this is a heavy charge, it is because, inversely, custom does not allow a woman to procreate when she pleases. The unwed mother is a scandal to the community, and illegitimate birth is a stain on the child; only rarely is it possible to become a mother without accepting the chains of marriage or losing caste. If the idea of artificial insemination interests many women, it is not because they wish to avoid intercourse with a male; it is because they hope that freedom of maternity is going to be accepted by society at last. It must be said in addition that in spite of convenient day nurseries and kindergartens, having a child is enough to paralyze a woman's activity entirely; she can go on working only if she abandons it to relatives, friends, or servants. She is forced to choose between sterility, which is often felt as a painful frustration, and burdens hardly compatible with a career.

Thus the independent woman of today is torn between her pro fessional interests and the problems of her sexual life; it is difficult for her to strike a balance between the two; if she does, it is at the price of concessions, sacrifices, acrobatics, which require her to be in a constant state of tension. Here, rather than in physiological data, must be sought the reason for the nervousness and the frailty often observed in her. It is difficult to determine to what extent woman's physical constitution handicaps her. Inquiry is often made, for example, about the obstacle presented by menstruation. Women who have made a reputation through their publications or other activities seem to attach little importance to it. Is this because, as a matter of fact, they owe their success to their relatively slight monthly indisposition? One may ask whether it is not because, on the contrary, their choice of an active and ambitious life has been responsible for this advantage; the interest woman takes in her maladies tends to aggravate them. Women in sports and other active careers suffer less from them than others, because they take little notice of them. There are certainly organic factors also, and I have seen the most energetic women spend twenty-four hours in bed each month, a prey to pitiless tortures; but this difficulty never prevented their enterprises from succeeding.

I am convinced that the greater part of the discomforts and maladies that overburden women are due to psychic causes, as gynecologists, indeed, have told me. Women are constantly harassed to the limit of their strength because of the moral tension I have referred to, because of all the tasks they assume, because of the contradictions among which they struggle. This does not mean that their ills are imaginary: they are as real and destructive as the situation to which they give expression. But the situation does not depend on the body; the reverse is true. Thus woman's health will not affect her work unfavorably when the woman worker comes to have the place she should; on the contrary, work will improve her physical condition by preventing her from being ceaselessly preoccupied with it.

. . .

These facts must not be lost sight of when we judge the professional accomplishments of woman and, on that basis, make bold to speculate on her future. She undertakes a career in a mentally harassing situation and while still under the personal burdens implied traditionally by her femininity. Nor are the objective circumstances more favorable to her. It is always difficult to be a newcomer, trying to break a path through a society that is hostile, or at least mistrustful. In *Black Boy* Richard Wright has shown how the ambitions of a young American Negro are blocked from the start and what a struggle he had merely in raising himself to the level where problems began to be posed for the whites. Negroes coming to France from Africa also find difficulties—with themselves as well as around them—similar to those confronting women.

Woman first finds herself in a position of inferiority during her period of apprenticeship, a point already made with reference to the young girl, but which must now be dealt with more precisely. During her studies and in the first decisive years of her career, woman rarely uses her opportunities with simple directness, and thus she will often be handicapped later by a bad start. The conflicts I have spoken of do, in fact, reach their greatest intensity between the ages of eighteen and thirty, precisely the time when the professional future is at stake. Whether the woman lives with her family or is married, her family will rarely show the same respect for her work as for a man's; they will impose duties and tasks on her and infringe on her liberty. She herself is still profoundly affected by her bringing up, respectful of values affirmed by her elders, haunted by her dreams of childhood and adolescence; she finds difficulty in reconciling the heritage of her past with the interests of her future. Sometimes she abjures her femininity, she hesitates between chastity, homosexuality, and an aggressive virago attitude; she dresses badly or wears male attire; and in this case she wastes much time in defiance, play-acting, angry fuming. More often she wants to emphasize her feminine qualities: she is coquettish, she goes out, she flirts, she falls in love, oscillating between masochism and aggressiveness. She questions, agitates, scatters herself in every way. These outside activities alone are enough to prevent complete absorption in her enterprise; the less she profits by it, the more tempted she is to give it up.

What is extremely demoralizing for the woman who aims at self-sufficiency is the existence of other women of like social status, having at the start the same situation and the same opportunities, who live as parasites. A man may feel resentment toward the privileged, but he has solidarity with his class; on the whole, those who begin with equal chances reach about the same level in life. Whereas women of like situation may, through man's mediation, come to have very different fortunes. A comfortably married or supported friend is a temptation in the way of one who is intending to make her own success; she feels she is arbitrarily condemning herself to take the most difficult roads; at each obstacle she wonders whether it might not be better to take a different route. "When I think that I have to get everything by my own brain!" said one little poverty-stricken student to me, as if stunned by the thought. Man obeys an imperious necessity; woman must constantly reaffirm her intention. She goes forward not with her eyes fixed straight ahead on a goal, but with her glance wandering around her in every direction; and her gait is also timid and uncertain. The more she seems to be getting ahead on her own hook—as I have already pointed out—the more her other chances fade; in becoming a bluestocking, a woman of brains, she will make herself unattractive to men in general, or she will humiliate her husband or lover by being too outstanding a success. So she not only applies herself the more to making a show of elegance and frivolity, but also restrains her aspiration. The hope of being one day delivered from taking care of herself, and the fear of having to lose that hope if she assumes this care for a time, combine to prevent her from unreservedly applying herself to her studies and her career.

In so far as a woman wishes to be a woman, her independent status gives rise to an inferiority complex; on the other hand, her femininity makes her doubtful of her professional future. This is a point of great importance. We have seen that girls of fourteen declared to an investigator: "Boys are better than girls; they are better workers." The young girl is convinced that she has limited capacities. Because parents and teachers concede that the girls' level is lower than that of the boys, the pupils readily concede it also; and as a matter of fact, in spite of equal curricula, the girls' academic accomplishment in French secondary schools is much lower. Apart from some exceptions, all the members of a girls' class in philosophy, for example, stand clearly below a boys' class. A great majority of the girl pupils do not intend to continue their studies, and work very superficially; the others lack the stimulus of emulation. In fairly easy examinations

their incompetence will not be too evident, but in a serious competitive test the girl student will become aware of her weaknesses. She
will attribute them not to the mediocrity of her training, but to the
unjust curse of her femininity; by resigning herself to this inequality,
she enhances it; she is persuaded that her chances of success can lie
only in her patience and application; she resolves to be as economical
as possible of her time and strength—surely a very bad plan.

The utilitarian attitude is especially disastrous in studies and professions that call for a modicum of invention and originality, and
some lucky little finds. Discussions, extracurricular reading, a walk
with the mind freely wandering, can be much more profitable, even
for translating a Greek text, than the dull compilation of involved
points of syntax. Overwhelmed by respect for authorities and the
weight of erudition, her view restricted by pedantic blinders, the
over-conscientious student deadens her critical sense and her very intelligence. Her methodical eagerness causes tension and weariness of
spirit. In the classes, for example, where students prepare for the
Sèvres competitive examinations, a suffocating atmosphere reigns
that discourages all individualities with any semblance of life. The
candidate has no wish but to escape from her self-created prison;
once she closes her books, her mind is on quite different subjects.
Unknown to her are those fertile moments when study and diversion
fuse, when the adventures of the mind assume living warmth. Dis-
heartened by the thankless nature of her tasks, she feels more and
more inept at doing them well. I recall a girl student, preparing for
teachers' examinations, who said in reference to a competition in
philosophy open to men and women: "Boys can succeed in one or
two years; for us it takes at least four years." Another, told to read a
book on Kant, an author on the reading list, protested: "That book
is too difficult; it is a book for men students!" She seemed to think
women could go through the competition at a reduced rate. To take
that attitude was to be beaten in advance and, in effect, to concede
to the men all chances of winning.

In consequence of this defeatism, woman is easily reconciled to a
moderate success; she does not dare to aim too high. Entering upon
her profession with superficial preparation, she soon sets limits to her
ambitions. It often seems to her meritorious enough if she earns her
own living; she could have entrusted her lot, like many others, to
a man. To continue in her wish for independence requires an effort

in which she takes pride, but which exhausts her. It seems to her that she has done enough when she has chosen to do something. "That in itself is not too bad for a woman," she thinks. A woman practicing an unusual profession once said: "If I were a man, I should feel obliged to climb to the top; but I am the only woman in France to occupy such a position: that's enough for me." There is prudence in this modesty. Woman is afraid that in attempting to go farther she will break her back.

It must be said that the independent woman is justifiably disturbed by the idea that people do not have confidence in her. As a general rule, the superior caste is hostile to newcomers from the inferior caste: whites will not consult a Negro physician, nor males a woman doctor; but individuals of the inferior caste, imbued with a sense of their specific inferiority and often full of resentment toward one of their kind who has risen above their usual lot, will also prefer to turn to the masters. Most women, in particular, steeped in adoration for man, eagerly seek him out in the person of the doctor, the lawyer, the office manager, and so on. Neither men nor women like to be under a woman's orders. Her superiors, even if they esteem her highly, will always be somewhat condescending; to be a woman, if not a defect, is at least a peculiarity. Woman must constantly win the confidence that is not at first accorded her: at the start she is suspect, she has to prove herself. If she has worth she will pass the tests, so they say. But worth is not a given essence; it is the outcome of a successful development. To feel the weight of an unfavorable prejudice against one is only on very rare occasions a help in overcoming it. The initial inferiority complex ordinarily leads to a defense reaction in the form of an exaggerated affectation of authority.

Most women doctors, for example, have too much or too little of the air of authority. If they act naturally, they fail to take control, for their life as a whole disposes them rather to seduce than to command; the patient who likes to be dominated will be disappointed by plain advice simply given. Aware of this fact, the woman doctor assumes a grave accent, a peremptory tone; but then she lacks the bluff good nature that is the charm of the medical man who is sure of himself.

Man is accustomed to asserting himself; his clients believe in his competence; he can act naturally: he infallibly makes an impression. Woman does not inspire the same feeling of security; she affects a lofty air, she drops it, she makes too much of it. In business, in administrative work, she is precise, fussy, quick to show aggressiveness. As in her studies, she lacks ease, dash, audacity. In the effort to achieve she gets tense. Her activity is a succession of challenges and self-affirmations. This is the great defect that lack of assurance engenders: the subject cannot forget himself. He does not aim gallantly toward some goal: he seeks rather to make good in prescribed ways. In boldly setting out toward ends, one risks disappointments; but one also obtains unhoped-for results; caution condemns to mediocrity.

We rarely encounter in the independent woman a taste for adventure and for experience for its own sake, or a disinterested curiosity; she seeks "to have a career" as other women build a nest of happiness; she remains dominated, surrounded, by the male universe, she lacks the audacity to break through its ceiling, she does not passionately lose herself in her projects. She still regards her life as an immanent enterprise: her aim is not at an objective but, through the objective, at her subjective success. This is a very conspicuous attitude, for example, among American women; they like having a job and proving to themselves that they are capable of handling it properly; but they are not passionately concerned with the *content* of their tasks. Woman similarly has a tendency to attach too much importance to minor setbacks and modest successes; she is turn by turn discouraged or puffed up with vanity. When a success has been anticipated, one takes it calmly; but it becomes an intoxicating triumph when one has been doubtful of obtaining it. This is the excuse when women become addled with importance and plume themselves ostentatiously over their least accomplishments. They are forever looking back to see how far they have come, and that interrupts their progress. By this procedure they can have honorable careers, but not accomplish great things. It must be added that many men are also unable to build any but mediocre careers. It is only in comparison with the best of them that woman—save for very rare exceptions— seems to us to be trailing behind. The reasons I have given are sufficient explanation, and in no way mortgage the future. What woman essentially lacks today for doing great things is forgetfulness of herself; but to forget oneself it is first of all necessary to be firmly assured that now and for the future one has found oneself. Newly come into the world of men, poorly seconded by them, woman is still too busily occupied to search for herself.

There is one category of women to whom these remarks do not apply because their careers, far from hindering the affirmation of their femininity, reinforce it. These are women who seek through artistic expression to transcend their given characteristics; they are the actresses, dancers, and singers. For three centuries they have been almost the only women to maintain a concrete independence in the midst of society, and at the present time they still occupy a privileged place in it. Formerly actresses were anathema to the Church, and the very excessiveness of that severity has always authorized a great freedom of behavior on their part. They often skirt the sphere of gallantry and, like courtesans, they spend a great deal of their time in the company of men; but making their own living and finding the meaning of their lives in their work, they escape the yoke of men. Their great advantage is that their professional successes—like those of men—contribute to their sexual valuation; in their self-realization, their validation of themselves as human beings, they find self-fulfillment as women: they are not torn between contradictory aspirations. On the contrary, they find in their occupations a justification of their narcissism; dress, beauty care, charm, form a part of their professional duties. It is a great satisfaction for a woman in love with her own image to *do* something in simply exhibiting what she *is*; and this exhibition at the same time demands enough study and artifice to appear to be, as Georgette Leblanc said, a substitute for action. A great actress will aim higher yet: she will go beyond the given by the way she expresses it; she will be truly an artist, a creator, who gives meaning to her life by lending meaning to the world.

These are rare advantages, but they also hide traps: instead of integrating her narcissistic self-indulgence and her sexual liberty with her artistic life, the actress very often sinks into self-worship or into gallantry; I have already referred to those pseudo-artists who seek in the movies or in the theater only to make a name for themselves that represents capital to exploit in men's arms. The conveniences of masculine support are very tempting in comparison with the risks of a career and with the discipline implied by all real work. Desire for a feminine destiny—husband, home, children—and the enchantment of love are not always easy to reconcile with the will to succeed. But, above all, the admiration she feels for her ego in many cases limits the achievement of an actress; she has such illusions regarding the value of her mere presence that serious work seems useless. She is concerned above all to put herself in the public eye and sacrifices the character she is interpreting to this theatrical quackery. She also lacks the generous-mindedness to forget herself, and this deprives her of the possibility of going beyond herself; rare indeed are the Rachels, the Duses, who avoid this reef and make their persons the instruments of their art instead of seeing in art a servant of their egos. In her private life, moreover, the bad actress will exaggerate all the narcissistic defects: she will reveal herself as vain, petulant, theatric; she will consider all the world a stage.

Today the expressive arts are not the only ones open to women; many are essaying various creative activities. Woman's situation inclines her to seek salvation in literature and art. Living marginally to the masculine world, she sees it not in its universal form but from her special point of view. For her it is no conglomeration of implements and concepts, but a source of sensations and emotions; her interest in the qualities of things is drawn by the gratuitous and hidden elements in them. Taking an attitude of negation and denial, she is not absorbed in the real: she protests against it, with words. She seeks through nature for the image of her soul, she abandons herself to reveries, she wishes to attain her *being*—but she is doomed to frustration; she can recover it only in the region of the imaginary. To prevent an inner life that has no *useful* purpose from sinking into nothingness, to assert herself against given conditions which she bears rebelliously, to create a world other than that in which she fails to attain her being, she must resort to *self-expression*. Then, too, it is well known that she is a chatterer and a scribbler; she unbosoms herself in conversations, in letters, in intimate diaries. With a little ambition, she will be found writing her memoirs, making her biography into a novel, breathing forth her feelings in poems. The vast leisure she enjoys is most favorable to such activities.

But the very circumstances that turn woman to creative work are also obstacles she will very often be incapable of surmounting. When she decides to paint or write merely to fill her empty days, painting and essays will be treated as fancywork; she will devote no more time or care to them, and they will have about the same value. It is often at the menopause that woman decides to take brush or pen in hand to compensate for the defects in her existence; but it is rather late in the day, and for lack of serious training she will never be more than amateurish. Even if she begins fairly early, she seldom envisages art as serious work; accustomed to idleness, having never felt in her mode of life the austere necessity of discipline, she will not be capable of sustained and persistent effort, she will never succeed in gaining a solid technique. She is repelled by the thankless, solitary gropings of work that never sees the light of day, that must be destroyed and done over a hundred times; and as from infancy she has been taught trickery when learning to please, she hopes to "get by" through the use of a few stratagems. Marie Bashkirtsev admits precisely that: "Yes, I never take the trouble to paint. I watched myself today. *I cheat*." Woman is ready enough to *play* at working, but she does not work; believing in the magic virtues of passivity, she confuses incantations and acts, symbolic gestures and effective behavior. She masquerades as a Beaux-Arts student, she arms herself with her battery of brushes; as she sits before her easel, her eye wanders from the white cloth to her mirror; but the bunch of flowers or the bowl of apples is not going to appear on the canvas of its own accord. Seated at her desk, turning over vague stories in her mind, woman enjoys the easy pretense that she is a writer; but she must come to the actual putting of black marks on white paper, she must give them a meaning in the eyes of others. Then the cheating is exposed. In order to please, it is enough to create mirages; but a work of art is not a mirage, it is a solid object; in order to fashion it, one must know one's business.

It is not because of her gifts and her temperament alone that Colette became a great writer; her pen has often been her means of support, and she has had to have from it the same good work that an artisan expects from his tools. Between *Claudine* and *Naissance du jour* the amateur became a professional, and that transition brilliantly demonstrates the benefits of a severe period of training. Most women, however, fail to realize the problems posed by their desire for communication; and that is what in large part explains their laziness. They always regard themselves as given; they believe that their merits derive from an immanent grace and do not imagine that worth can be acquired by conquest. In order to seduce, they know only the method of showing themselves; then their charm either works or does not work, they have no real hand in its success or failure. They suppose that in analogous fashion it is sufficient for expression, communication, to show what one is; instead of elaborating their work with reflective effort, they rely on spontaneity. Writing or smiling is all one to them; they try their luck, success will come or it will not come. If they are sure of themselves, they take for granted that the book or picture will be a success without effort; if timid, they are discouraged by the least criticism. They are unaware that error may open the way of progress, considering it an irreparable catastrophe, like a malformation. This is why they often show a disastrous petulance: they recognize their faults only with irritation and discouragement instead of learning profitable lessons from them.

Unfortunately spontaneity is not so simple to achieve as it would seem: the paradox of the commonplace—as explained by Paulhan in *Fleurs de Tarbes*—is that it is often confused with the direct presentation of the subjective impression. Thus it is that the would-be writer, at the moment when she thinks she is most original in presenting, without taking others into account, the image formed in her own mind, actually does no more than reinvent a banal cliché. If someone tells her, she is surprised; she becomes fretful and throws her pen away; she does not understand that the public reads with eye and thought turned inward and that a wholly fresh expression can bring to mind many fond memories. It is truly a precious gift to be able to fish in oneself and bring them to the surface by a language of quite lively impressions. We admire in Colette a spontaneity that is not met with in any male writer; but in her we are concerned with a well-considered spontaneity—though the two terms may seem to clash. She retains some of her material and rejects the rest always wittingly. The amateurish woman writer, instead of regarding words as interpersonal communication, a means of appealing to others, considers them to be the direct revelation of her own feeling; it seems to her that to choose, to erase, is to repudiate a part of herself; she does not want to sacrifice any of her words, at once because she is pleased with what she *is* and because she has no hope of becoming anything else. Her sterile vanity comes from the fact that she is very fond of herself without daring to analyze herself.

Thus, of the legion of women who toy with arts and letters, very few persevere; and even those who pass this first obstacle will very often continue to be torn between their narcissism and an inferiority complex. Inability to forget themselves is a defect that will weigh more heavily upon them than upon women in any other career;

if their essential aim is the abstract affirmation of self, the formal satisfaction of success, they will not give themselves over to the contemplation of the world: they will be incapable of re-creating it in art. Marie Bashkirtsev decided to paint because she wished to become famous; her obsession with fame comes between her and reality. She really does not like to paint: art is only a means; it is not her ambitious and hollow dreams that will reveal to her the import of a color or a face. Instead of giving herself generously to a work she undertakes, woman too often considers it simply as an adornment of her life; the book and the picture are merely some of her inessential means for exhibiting in public that essential reality: her own self. Moreover, it is her own self that is the principal—sometimes the unique—subject of interest to her: Mme Vigée-Lebrun never wearied of putting her smiling maternity on her canvases. The woman writer will still be speaking of herself even when she is speaking about general topics: one cannot read certain theatrical comment without being informed about the figure and corpulence of its author, on the color of her hair, and the peculiarities of her character.

To be sure, the ego is not always odious. Few books are more thrilling than certain confessions, but they must be honest, and the author must have something to confess. Woman's narcissism impoverishes her instead of enriching her; by dint of doing nothing but contemplate herself, she annihilates herself; even her self-love is stereotyped: she reveals in her writings not her genuine experience, but an imaginary idol built up with clichés. One could hardly reproach her with projecting herself in her novels as did Constant, or Stendhal; but the trouble is that she too often sees her history as a silly fairy tale. With the aid of imaginings the young girl hides from herself the reality that frightens her with its crudity, but it is deplorable that when grown to woman she still immerses the world, her characters, and herself in poetic mists. When truth comes to light from under this disguise, delightful effects are sometimes achieved; but then for one *Poussière* and one *Constant Nymph*, how many dull and vapid novels of escape!

It is natural enough for woman to attempt escape from this world where she often feels slighted and misunderstood; but one regrets only that she does not venture upon the audacious flights of a Gérard de Nerval, an Edgar Allan Poe. There are many good reasons for her timidity. To please is her first care; and often she fears she will be displeasing as a woman from the mere fact that she writes; the term *bluestocking*, though threadbare, continues to have disagreeable connotations; she lacks, further, the courage to be displeasing as a writer. The writer of originality, unless dead, is always shocking, scandalous; novelty disturbs and repels. Woman is still astonished and flattered at being admitted to the world of thought, of art—a masculine world. She is on her best behavior; she is afraid to disarrange, to investigate, to explode; she feels she should seek pardon for her literary pretensions through her modesty and good taste. She stakes on the reliable values of conformity; she gives literature precisely that personal tone which is expected of her, reminding us that she is a woman by a few well-chosen graces, affectations, and preciosities. All this helps her excel in the production of best-sellers; but we must not look to her for adventuring along strange ways.

Not that these independent women lack originality in behavior or feelings; on the contrary, some are so singular that they should be locked up; all in all, many of them are more whimsical, more eccentric, than the men whose discipline they reject. But they exercise their genius for oddity in their mode of life, their conversation, and their correspondence; if they undertake to write, they feel overwhelmed by the universe of culture, because it is a universe of men, and so they can only stammer. On the other hand, the woman who may choose to reason, to express herself, in accordance with masculine techniques, will be bent on stifling an originality that she has cause to mistrust; like the woman student, she is very prone to be studious and pedantic; she will imitate male rigor and vigor. She can become an excellent theoretician, can acquire real competence; but she will be forced to repudiate whatever she has in her that is "different." There are women who are mad and there are women of sound method: none has that madness in her method that we call genius.

It is, above all, this reasonable modesty that has hitherto set the limits of feminine talent. Many women have avoided—and now they avoid more and more—the traps of narcissism and false magic; but none have ever trampled upon all prudence in the attempt to *emerge* beyond the given world. In the first place, there are, of course, many who accept society just as it is; they are pre-eminently the poetesses of the bourgeoisie since they represent the most conservative element in this threatened class. With well-chosen adjectives they evoke the refinements of a civilization referred to as one of "quality"; they exalt the middle-class ideal of well-being and disguise the interests of their class in poetic colors; they orchestrate the grand mystification intended to persuade women to "stay womanly." Ancient houses, sheepfolds and kitchen gardens, picturesque old folks, roguish children, washing, preserving, family parties, toilettes, drawing-rooms, balls, unhappy but exemplary wives, the beauty of devotion and sacrifice, the small discontents and great joys of conjugal love, dreams of youth, the resignation of maturity—these themes the women novelists of England, France, America, Canada, and Scandinavia have exploited to their very dregs; they have thus gained fame and wealth, but have surely not enriched our vision of the world.

Much more interesting are the insurgent females who have challenged this unjust society; a literature of protest can engender sincere and powerful works; out of the well of her revolt George Eliot drew a vision of Victorian England that was at once detailed and dramatic; still, as Virginia Woolf has made us see, Jane Austen, the Brontë sisters, George Eliot, have had to expend so much energy negatively in order to free themselves from outward restraints that they arrive somewhat out of breath at the stage from which masculine writers of great scope take their departure; they do not have enough strength left to profit by their victory and break all the ropes that hold them back. We do not find in them, for example, the irony, the ease of a Stendhal, nor his calm sincerity. Nor have they had the richness of experience of a Dostoyevsky, a Tolstoy: this explains why the splendid *Middlemarch* still is not the equal of *War and Peace*; *Wuthering Heights*, in spite of its grandeur, does not have the sweep of *The Brothers Karamazov*.

Today it is already less difficult for women to assert themselves; but they have not as yet completely overcome the agelong sex-limitation that has isolated them in their femininity. Lucidity of mind, for instance, is a conquest of which they are justly proud but with which alone they would be a little too quickly satisfied. The fact is that the traditional woman is a bamboozled conscious being and a practitioner of bamboozlement; she attempts to disguise her dependence from herself, which is a way of consenting to it. To expose this dependence is in itself a liberation; a clear-sighted cynicism is a defense against humiliations and shame: it is the preliminary sketch of an assumption. By aspiring to clear-sightedness women writers are doing the cause of women a great service; but—usually without realizing it—they are still too concerned with serving this cause to assume the disinterested attitude toward the universe that opens the widest horizons. When they have removed the veils of illusion and deception, they think they have done enough; but this negative audacity leaves us still faced by an enigma, for the truth itself is ambiguity, abyss, mystery: once stated, it must be thoughtfully reconsidered, re-created. It is all very well not to be duped, but at that point all else begins. Woman exhausts her courage dissipating mirages and she stops in terror at the threshold of reality.

It is for this reason that there are, for example, sincere and engaging feminine autobiographies; but none can compare with Rousseau's *Confessions* and Stendhal's *Souvenirs d'égotisme*. We are still too preoccupied with clearly seeing the facts to try to penetrate the shadows beyond that illuminated circle. "Women never go beyond appearances," said a writer to me. It is true enough. Still amazed at being allowed to explore the phenomena of this world, they take inventory without trying to discover meanings. Where they sometimes excel is in the observation of facts, what is given. They make remarkable reporters; no male journalist has surpassed, for example, Andrée Viollis's reports on Indochina and India. Women are able to describe atmosphere and characters, to indicate subtle relationships between the latter, to make us share in the secret stirrings of their souls. Willa Cather, Edith Wharton, Dorothy Parker, Katherine Mansfield, have clearly and sensitively evoked individuals, regions, civilizations. They rarely create masculine heroes as convincing as Heathcliffe: in man they comprehend hardly more than the male. But they have often aptly described their own inner life, their experience, their own universe; attentive to the hidden substance of things, fascinated by the peculiarities of their own sensations, they present their experience, still warm, through savory adjectives and carnal figures of speech. Their vocabulary is often more notable than their syntax because they are interested in things rather than in the relations of things; they do not aim at abstract elegance, but in compensation their words speak directly to the senses.

Nature is one of the realms they have most lovingly explored. For the young girl, for the woman who has not fully abdicated, nature represents what woman herself represents for man: herself and her negation, a kingdom and a place of exile; the whole in the guise of the other. It is when she speaks of moors and gardens that the woman novelist will reveal her experience and her dreams to us most intimately. Many of them enclose the miracles of sap and season in kettles, vases, garden beds; others do not imprison plants and animals but still endeavor to make them their own through close and loving observation, like Colette or Katherine Mansfield. Few indeed there are who face nature in its nonhuman freedom, who attempt to decipher its foreign meanings, and who lose themselves in order to make union with this other presence: hardly any save Emily Brontë, Virginia Woolf, and Mary Webb at times, venture along those roads Rousseau discovered.

With still more reason we can count on the fingers of one hand the women who have traversed the given in search of its secret dimension: Emily Brontë has questioned death, Virginia Woolf life, and Katherine Mansfield—not very often—everyday contingence and suffering. No woman wrote *The Trial, Moby Dick, Ulysses,* or *The Seven Pillars of Wisdom.* Women do not contest the human situation, because they have hardly begun to assume it. This explains why their works for the most part lack metaphysical resonances and also anger; they do not take the world incidentally, they do not ask it questions, they do not expose its contradictions: they take it as it is too seriously. It should be said that the majority of men have the same limitations; it is when we compare the woman of achievement with the few rare male artists who deserve to be called "great men" that she seems mediocre. It is not a special destiny that limits her: we can readily comprehend why it has not been vouchsafed her— and may not be vouchsafed her for some time—to attain to the loftiest summits.

Art, literature, philosophy, are attempts to found the world anew on a human liberty: that of the individual creator; to entertain such a pretension, one must first unequivocally assume the status of a being who has liberty. The restrictions that education and custom impose on woman now limit her grasp on the universe; when the struggle to find one's place in this world is too arduous, there can be no question of getting away from it. Now, one must first emerge from it into a sovereign solitude if one wants to try to regain a grasp upon it: what woman needs first of all is to undertake, in anguish and pride, her apprenticeship in abandonment and transcendence: that is, in liberty.

What I desire [writes Marie Bashkirtsev] is liberty to go walking alone, to come and go, to sit on the benches in the Tuileries Gardens. Without that liberty you cannot become a true artist. You believe you can profit by what you see when you are accompanied by someone, when you must wait for your companion, your family! . . . That is the liberty which is lacking and without which you cannot succeed seriously in being something. *Thought is shackled as a result of that stupid and continual constraint. . . . That is enough to make your wings droop.* It is one of the main reasons why there are no women artists.

In truth, to become a creative artist it is not enough to be cultivated—that is to say, to make exhibitions and bits of information a part of one's life. Culture must be apprehended through the free action of a transcendence; that is, the free spirit with all its riches must project itself toward an empty heaven that it is to populate; but if a thousand persistent bonds hold it to earth, its surge is broken. To be sure, the young girl can today go out alone and idle in the Tuileries; but I have already noted how hostile the street is to her, with eyes and hands lying in wait everywhere; if she wanders carelessly, her mind drifting, if she lights a cigarette in front of a café, if she goes alone to the movies, a disagreeable incident is soon bound to happen. She must inspire respect by her costume and manners. But this preoccupation rivets her to the ground and to herself. "Your wings droop." At eighteen T. E. Lawrence took a long bicycle tour through France by himself; no young girl would be allowed to engage in any such escapade, still less to adventure on foot in a half-desert and dangerous country, as Lawrence did a year later. Yet such experiences are of incalculable influence: through them an individual, in the intoxication of liberty and discovery, learns to regard the entire earth as his territory.

Woman is in any case deprived of the lessons of violence by her nature: I have shown how her muscular weakness disposes her to passivity. When a boy settles a dispute with his fists, he feels that he is capable of taking care of himself; at the least, the young girl should in compensation be permitted to know how it feels to take the initiative in sport and adventure, to taste the pride of obstacles overcome. But not at all. She may feel herself alone *in the midst* of the world, but she never stands up *before* it, unique and sovereign.

Everything influences her to let herself be hemmed in, dominated by existences foreign to her own—and especially in the matter of love she abnegates herself instead of asserting herself. In this connection bad luck or unattractiveness are often blessings in disguise. It was her isolation that enabled Emily Brontë to write a wild and powerful book; in the face of nature, death, and destiny, she had no other backing than her own resources. Rosa Luxemburg was ugly; she was never tempted to wallow in the cult of her own image, to make herself object, prey, trap; from her youth, she was wholly spirit and liberty. Even so, it is very seldom that woman fully assumes the anguished tête-à-tête with the given world. The constraints that surround her and the whole tradition that weighs her down prevent her from feeling responsible for the universe, and that is the deep-seated reason for her mediocrity.

The men that we call great are those who—in one way or another—have taken the weight of the world upon their shoulders; they have done better or worse, they have succeeded in re-creating it or they have gone down; but first they have assumed that enormous burden. This is what no woman has ever done, what none has ever been *able* to do. To regard the universe as one's own, to consider oneself to blame for its faults and to glory in its progress, one must belong to the caste of the privileged; it is for those alone who are in command to justify the universe by changing it, by thinking about it, by revealing it; they alone can recognize themselves in it and endeavor to make their mark upon it. It is in man and not in woman that it has hitherto been possible for Man to be incarnated. For the individuals who seem to us most outstanding, who are honored with the name of genius, are those who have proposed to enact the fate of all humanity in their personal existences, and no woman has believed herself authorized to do this.

How could Van Gogh have been born a woman? A woman would not have been sent on a mission to the Belgian coal mines in Borinage, she would not have felt the misery of the miners as her own crime, she would not have sought a redemption; she would therefore have never painted Van Gogh's sunflowers. Not to mention that the mode of life of the painter—his solitude at Arles, his frequentation of cafés and brothels, all that nourished Van Gogh's art in nourishing his sensitivity—would have been forbidden her. A woman could never have become Kafka: in her doubts and her anxieties she would never have recognized the anguish of Man driven from paradise. There is hardly any woman other than St. Theresa who in total abandonment has herself lived out the situation of humanity: we have seen why. Taking her stand beyond the earthly hierarchies, she felt, like St. John of the Cross, no reassuring ceiling over her head. There were for both the same darkness, the same flashes of light, in the self the same nothingness, in God the same plenitude. When at last it will be possible for every human being thus to set his pride beyond the sexual differentiation, in the laborious glory of free existence, then only will woman be able to identify her personal history, her problems, her doubts, her hopes, with those of humanity; then only will she be able to seek in her life and her works to reveal the whole of reality and not merely her personal self. As long as she still has to struggle to become a human being, she cannot become a creator.

Once again: in order to explain her limitations it is woman's situation that must be invoked and not a mysterious essence; thus the future remains largely open. Writers on the subject have vied with one another in maintaining that women do not have "creative genius"; this is the thesis defended by Mme Marthe Borély, an erstwhile notorious antifeminist; but one would say that she sought to make her books a living proof of feminine illogicality and silliness, so self-contradictory are they. Furthermore, the concept of a creative "instinct" must be discarded, like that of the "eternal feminine," from the old panel of entities. Certain misogynists assert, a little more concretely, that woman, being neurotic, could not create anything worth while; but they are often the same men that pronounce genius a neurosis. In any case, the example of Proust shows clearly enough that psychophysiological disequilibrium signifies neither lack of power nor mediocrity.

As for the argument drawn from history, we have just been considering what to think of that; the historical fact cannot be considered as establishing an eternal truth; it can only indicate a situation that is historical in nature precisely because it is undergoing change. How could women ever have had genius when they were denied all possibility of accomplishing a work of genius—or just a work? The old Europe formerly poured out its contempt upon the American barbarians who boasted neither artists nor writers. "Let us come into existence before being asked to justify our existence," replied Jefferson, in effect. The Negroes make the same reply to the racists who reproach them for never having produced a Whitman or a Melville. No more can the French proletariat offer any name to compare with those of Racine or Mallarmé.

The free woman is just being born; when she has won possession of herself perhaps Rimbaud's prophecy will be fulfilled: "There shall be poets! When woman's unmeasured bondage shall be broken, when she shall live for and through herself, man—hitherto detestable —having let her go, she, too, will be poet! Woman will find the unknown! Will her ideational worlds be different from ours? She will come upon strange, unfathomable, repellent, delightful things; we shall take them, we shall comprehend them." [9] It is not sure that her "ideational worlds" will be different from those of men, since it will be through attaining the same situation as theirs that she will find emancipation; to say in what degree she will remain different, in what degree these differences will retain their importance—this would be to hazard bold predictions indeed. What is certain is that hitherto woman's possibilities have been suppressed and lost to humanity, and that it is high time she be permitted to take her chances in her own interest and in the interest of all.

---

[9] In a letter to Pierre Demeny, May 15, 1871.

Conclusion

No, woman is not our brother; through indolence and depravity we have made of her a being apart, unknown, having no weapon other than her sex, which not only means constant strife but is moreover an unfair weapon of the eternal little slave's mistrust—adoring or hating, but never our frank companion, a being set apart as if in *esprit de corps* and freemasonry."

Many men would still subscribe to these words of Laforgue; many think that there will always be "strife and dispute," as Montaigne put it, and that fraternity will never be possible. The fact is that today neither men nor women are satisfied with each other. But the question is to know whether there is an original curse that condemns them to rend each other or whether the conflicts in which they are opposed merely mark a transitional moment in human history.

We have seen that in spite of legends no physiological destiny imposes an eternal hostility upon Male and Female as such; even the famous praying mantis devours her male only for want of other food and for the good of the species: it is to this, the species, that all individuals are subordinated, from the top to the bottom of the scale of animal life. Moreover, humanity is something more than a mere species: it is a historical development; it is to be defined by the manner in which it deals with its natural, fixed characteristics, its *facticité*. Indeed, even with the most extreme bad faith in the world, it is impossible to demonstrate the existence of a rivalry between the human male and female of a truly physiological nature. Further, their hostility may be allocated rather to that intermediate terrain between biology and psychology: psychoanalysis. Woman, we are told, envies man his penis and wishes to castrate him; but the childish desire for the penis is important in the life of the adult woman only if she feels her femininity as a mutilation; and then it is as a symbol of all the privileges of manhood that she wishes to appropriate the male organ. We may readily agree that her dream of castration has this symbolic significance: she wishes, it is thought, to deprive the male of his transcendence.

But her desire, as we have seen, is much more ambiguous: she wishes, in a contradictory fashion, *to have* this transcendence, which is to suppose that she at once respects it and denies it, that she intends at once to throw herself into it and keep it within herself. This is to say that the drama does not unfold on a sexual level; further, sexuality has never seemed to us to define a destiny, to furnish in itself the key to human behavior, but to express the totality of a situation that it only helps to define. The battle of the sexes is not immediately implied in the anatomy of man and woman. The truth is that when one evokes it, one takes for granted that in the timeless realm of Ideas a battle is being waged between those vague essences the Eternal Feminine and the Eternal Masculine; and one neglects the fact that this titanic combat assumes on earth two totally different forms, corresponding with two different moments of history.

The woman who is shut up in immanence endeavors to hold man in that prison also; thus the prison will be confused with the world, and woman will no longer suffer from being confined there: mother, wife, sweetheart are the jailers. Society, being codified by man, decrees that woman is inferior: she can do away with this inferiority only by destroying the male's superiority. She sets about mutilating, dominating man, she contradicts him, she denies his truth and his values. But in doing this she is only defending herself; it was neither a changeless essence nor a mistaken choice that doomed her to immanence, to inferiority. They were imposed upon her. All oppression creates a state of war. And this is no exception. The existent who is regarded as inessential cannot fail to demand the re-establishment of her sovereignty.

Today the combat takes a different shape; instead of wishing to put man in a prison, woman endeavors to escape from one; she no longer seeks to drag him into the realms of immanence but to emerge, herself, into the light of transcendence. Now the attitude of the males creates a new conflict: it is with a bad grace that the man lets her go. He is very well pleased to remain the sovereign subject, the absolute superior, the essential being; he refuses to accept his companion as an equal in any concrete way. She replies to his lack of confidence in her by assuming an aggressive attitude. It is no longer a question of a war between individuals each shut up in his or her sphere: a caste claiming its rights goes over the top and it is resisted by the privileged caste. Here two transcendences are face to face;

instead of displaying mutual recognition, each free being wishes to dominate the other.

This difference of attitude is manifest on the sexual plane as on the spiritual plane. The "feminine" woman in making herself prey tries to reduce man, also, to her carnal passivity; she occupies herself in catching him in her trap, in enchaining him by means of the desire she arouses in him in submissively making herself a thing. The emancipated woman, on the contrary, wants to be active, a taker, and refuses the passivity man means to impose on her. Thus Elise and her emulators deny the values of the activities of virile type; they put the flesh above the spirit, contingence above liberty, their routine wisdom above creative audacity. But the "modern" woman accepts masculine values: she prides herself on thinking, taking action, working, creating, on the same terms as men; instead of seeking to disparage them, she declares herself their equal.

In so far as she expresses herself in definite action, this claim is legitimate, and male insolence must then bear the blame. But in men's defense it must be said that women are wont to confuse the issue. A Mabel Dodge Luhan intended to subjugate D. H. Lawrence by her feminine charms so as to dominate him spiritually thereafter; many women, in order to show by their successes their equivalence to men, try to secure male support by sexual means; they play on both sides, demanding old-fashioned respect and modern esteem, banking on their old magic and their new rights. It is understandable that a man becomes irritated and puts himself on the defensive; but he is also double-dealing when he requires woman to play the game fairly while he denies them the indispensable trump cards through distrust and hostility. Indeed, the struggle cannot be clearly drawn between them, since woman is opaque in her very being; she stands before man not as a subject but as an object paradoxically endued with subjectivity; she takes herself simultaneously as *self* and as *other*, a contradiction that entails baffling consequences. When she makes weapons at once of her weakness and of her strength, it is not a matter of designing calculation: she seeks salvation spontaneously in the way that has been imposed on her, that of passivity, at the same time when she is actively demanding her sovereignty; and no doubt this procedure is unfair tactics, but it is dictated to her by the ambiguous situation assigned her. Man, however, becomes indignant when he treats her as a free and independent being and then realizes that she is still a trap for him; if he gratifies and satisfies her in her posture as prey, he finds her claims to autonomy irritating; whatever he does, he feels tricked and she feels wronged.

The quarrel will go on as long as men and women fail to recognize each other as peers; that is to say, as long as femininity is perpetuated as such. Which sex is the more eager to maintain it? Woman, who is being emancipated from it, wishes none the less to retain its privileges; and man, in that case, wants her to assume its limitations. "It is easier to accuse one sex than to excuse the other," says Montaigne. It is vain to apportion praise and blame. The truth is that if the vicious circle is so hard to break, it is because the two sexes are each the victim at once of the other and of itself. Between two adversaries confronting each other in their pure liberty, an agreement could be easily reached: the more so as the war profits neither. But the complexity of the whole affair derives from the fact that each camp is giving aid and comfort to the enemy; woman is pursuing a dream of submission, man a dream of identification. Want of authenticity does not pay: each blames the other for the unhappiness he or she has incurred in yielding to the temptations of the easy way; what man and woman loathe in each other is the shattering frustration of each one's own bad faith and baseness.

We have seen why men enslaved women in the first place; the devaluation of femininity has been a necessary step in human evolution, but it might have led to collaboration between the two sexes; oppression is to be explained by the tendency of the existent to flee from himself by means of identification with the other, whom he oppresses to that end. In each individual man that tendency exists today; and the vast majority yield to it. The husband wants to find himself in his wife, the lover in his mistress, in the form of a stone image; he is seeking in her the myth of his virility, of his sovereignty, of his immediate reality. "My husband never goes to the movies," says his wife, and the dubious masculine opinion is graved in the marble of eternity. But he is himself the slave of his double: what an effort to build up an image in which he is always in danger! In spite of everything his success in this depends upon the capricious freedom of women: he must constantly try to keep this propitious to him. Man is concerned with the effort to appear male, important, superior; he pretends so as to get pretense in return; he, too, is aggressive, uneasy; he feels hostility for women because he is afraid of them, he is afraid of them because he is afraid of the personage, the image, with which he identifies himself. What time and strength he squanders in liquidating, sublimating, transferring complexes, in talking about women, in seducing them, in fearing them! He would be liberated himself in their liberation. But this is precisely what he dreads. And so he obstinately persists in the mystifications intended to keep woman in her chains.

That she is being tricked, many men have realized. "What a misfortune to be a woman! And yet the misfortune, when one is a woman, is at bottom not to comprehend that it is one," says Kirkegaard.[1] For a long time there have been efforts to disguise this misfortune. For example, guardianship has been done away with: women have been given "protectors," and if they are invested with the rights of the old-time guardians, it is in woman's own interest. To forbid her working, to keep her at home, is to defend her against herself and to assure her happiness. We have seen what poetic veils are thrown over her monotonous burdens of housekeeping and maternity: in exchange for her liberty she has received the false treasures of her "femininity." Balzac illustrates this maneuver very well in counseling man to treat her as a slave while persuading her that she is a queen. Less cynical, many men try to convince themselves that she is really privileged. There are American sociologists who seriously teach today the theory of "low-class gain." In France, also, it has often been proclaimed—although in a less scientific manner—that the workers are very fortunate in not being obliged to "keep up appearances" and still more so the bums who can dress in rags and sleep on the sidewalks, pleasures forbidden to the Count de Beaumont and the Wendels. Like the carefree wretches gaily scratching at their vermin, like the merry Negroes laughing under the lash and those joyous Tunisian Arabs burying their starved children with a smile, woman enjoys that incomparable privilege: irresponsibility. Free from troublesome burdens and cares, she obviously has "the better part." But

---

[1] *In Vino Veritas.* He says further: "Politeness is pleasing—essentially—to woman, and the fact that she accepts it without hesitation is explained by nature's care for the weaker, for the unfavored being, and for one to whom an illusion means more than a material compensation. But this illusion, precisely, is fatal to her. . . . To feel oneself freed from distress thanks to something imaginary, to be the dupe of something imaginary, is that not a still deeper mockery? . . . Woman is very far from being *verwahrlost* (neglected), but in another sense she is, since she can never free herself from the illusion that nature has used to console her."

it is disturbing that with an obstinate perversity—connected no doubt with original sin—down through the centuries and in all countries, the people who have the better part are always crying to their benefactors: "It is too much! I will be satisfied with yours!" But the munificent capitalists, the generous colonists, the superb males, stick to their guns: "Keep the better part, hold on to it!"

It must be admitted that the males find in woman more complicity than the oppressor usually finds in the oppressed. And in bad faith they take authorization from this to declare that she has *desired* the destiny they have imposed on her. We have seen that all the main features of her training combine to bar her from the roads of revolt and adventure. Society in general—beginning with her respected parents—lies to her by praising the lofty values of love, devotion, the gift of herself, and then concealing from her the fact that neither lover nor husband nor yet her children will be inclined to accept the burdensome charge of all that. She cheerfully believes these lies because they invite her to follow the easy slope: in this others commit their worst crime against her; throughout her life from childhood on, they damage and corrupt her by designating as her true vocation this submission, which is the temptation of every existent in the anxiety of liberty. If a child is taught idleness by being amused all day long and never being led to study, or shown its usefulness, it will hardly be said, when he grows up, that he chose to be incapable and ignorant; yet this is how woman is brought up, without ever being impressed with the necessity of taking charge of her own existence. So she readily lets herself come to count on the protection, love, assistance, and supervision of others, she lets herself be fascinated with the hope of self-realization without *doing* anything. She does wrong in yielding to the temptation; but man is in no position to blame her, since he has led her into the temptation. When conflict arises between them, each will hold the other responsible for the situation; she will reproach him with having made her what she is: "No one taught me to reason or to earn my own living"; he will reproach her with having accepted the consequences: "You don't know anything, you are an incompetent," and so on. Each sex thinks it can justify itself by taking the offensive; but the wrongs done by one do not make the other innocent.

The innumerable conflicts that set men and women against one another come from the fact that neither is prepared to assume all the consequences of this situation which the one has offered and the other accepted. The doubtful concept of "equality in inequality," which the one uses to mask his despotism and the other to mask her cowardice, does not stand the test of experience: in their exchanges, woman appeals to the theoretical equality she has been guaranteed, and man the concrete inequality that exists. The result is that in every association an endless debate goes on concerning the ambiguous meaning of the words *give* and *take:* she complains of giving her all, he protests that she takes his all. Woman has to learn that exchanges—it is a fundamental law of political economy—are based on the value the merchandise offered has for the buyer, and not for the seller: she has been deceived in being persuaded that her worth is priceless. The truth is that for man she is an amusement, a pleasure, company, an inessential boon; he is for her the meaning, the justification of her existence. The exchange, therefore, is not of two items of equal value.

This inequality will be especially brought out in the fact that the time they spend together—which fallaciously seems to be the same time—does not have the same value for both partners. During the evening the lover spends with his mistress he could be doing something of advantage to his career, seeing friends, cultivating business relationships, seeking recreation; for a man normally integrated in society, time is a positive value: money, reputation, pleasure. For the idle, bored woman, on the contrary, it is a burden she wishes to get rid of; when she succeeds in killing time, it is a benefit to her: the man's presence is pure profit. In a liaison what most clearly interests the man, in many cases, is the sexual benefit he gets from it: if need be, he can be content to spend no more time with his mistress than is required for the sexual act; but—with exceptions—what she, on her part, wants is to kill all the excess time she has on her hands; and—like the storekeeper who will not sell potatoes unless the customer will take turnips also—she will not yield her body unless her lover will take hours of conversation and "going out" into the bargain. A balance is reached if, on the whole, the cost does not seem too high to the man, and this depends, of course, on the strength of his desire and the importance he gives to what is to be sacrificed. But if the woman demands—offers—too much time, she becomes wholly intrusive, like the river overflowing its banks, and the man will prefer to have nothing rather than too much. Then she reduces her demands; but very often the balance is reached at the cost of a double tension: she feels that the man has "had" her at a bargain, and he thinks her price is too high. This analysis, of course, is put in somewhat humorous terms; but—except for those affairs of jealous and exclusive passion in which the man wants total possession of the woman—this conflict constantly appears in cases of affection, desire, and even love. He always has "other things to do" with his time; whereas she has time to burn; and he considers much of the time she gives him not as a gift but as a burden.

As a rule he consents to assume the burden because he knows very well that he is on the privileged side, he has a bad conscience; and if he is of reasonable good will he tries to compensate for the inequality by being generous. He prides himself on his compassion, however, and at the first clash he treats the woman as ungrateful and thinks, with some irritation: "I'm too good to her." She feels she is behaving like a beggar when she is convinced of the high value of her gifts, and that humiliates her.

Here we find the explanation of the cruelty that woman often shows she is capable of practicing; she has a good conscience because she is on the unprivileged side; she feels she is under no obligation to deal gently with the favored caste, and her only thought is to defend herself. She will even be very happy if she has occasion to show her resentment to a lover who has not been able to satisfy all her demands: since he does not give her enough, she takes savage delight in taking back everything from him. At this point the wounded lover suddenly discovers the value *in toto* of a liaison each moment of which he held more or less in contempt: he is ready to promise her everything, even though he will feel exploited again when he has to make good. He accuses his mistress of blackmailing him: she calls him stingy; both feel wronged.

Once again it is useless to apportion blame and excuses: justice can never be done in the midst of injustice. A colonial administrator has no possibility of acting rightly toward the natives, nor a general toward his soldiers; the only solution is to be neither colonist nor military chief; but a man could not prevent himself from being a man. So there he is, culpable in spite of himself and laboring under the effects of a fault he did not himself commit; and here she is, victim and shrew in spite of herself. Sometimes he rebels and becomes cruel, but then he makes himself an accomplice of the injustice, and the fault becomes really his. Sometimes he lets himself be annihilated, devoured, by his demanding victim; but in that case he feels duped. Often he stops at a compromise that at once belittles him and leaves him ill at ease. A well-disposed man will be more tortured by the situation than the woman herself: in a sense it is always better to be on the side of the vanquished; but if she is well-disposed also, incapable of self-sufficiency, reluctant to crush the man with the weight of her destiny, she struggles in hopeless confusion.

In daily life we meet with an abundance of these cases which are incapable of satisfactory solution because they are determined by unsatisfactory conditions. A man who is compelled to go on materially and morally supporting a woman whom he no longer loves feels he is victimized; but if he abandons without resources the woman who has pledged her whole life to him, she will be quite as unjustly victimized. The evil originates not in the perversity of individuals—and bad faith first appears when each blames the other—it originates rather in a situation against which all individual action is powerless. Women are "clinging," they are a dead weight, and they suffer for it; the point is that their situation is like that of a parasite sucking out the living strength of another organism. Let them be provided with living strength of their own, let them have the means to attack the world and wrest from it their own subsistence, and their dependence will be abolished—that of man also. There is no doubt that both men and women will profit greatly from the new situation.

A world where men and women would be equal is easy to visualize, for that precisely is what the Soviet Revolution *promised*: women raised and trained exactly like men were to work under the same conditions [2] and for the same wages. Erotic liberty was to be recognized by custom, but the sexual act was not to be considered a "service" to be paid for; woman was to be *obliged* to provide herself with other ways of earning a living; marriage was to be based on a free agreement that the spouses could break at will; maternity was to be voluntary, which meant that contraception and abortion were to be authorized and that, on the other hand, all mothers and their chil-

---

[2] That certain too laborious occupations were to be closed to women is not in contradiction to this project. Even among men there is an increasing effort to obtain adaptation to profession; their varying physical and mental capacities limit their possibilities of choice; what is asked is that, in any case, no line of sex or caste be drawn.

dren were to have exactly the same rights, in or out of marriage; pregnancy leaves were to be paid for by the State, which would assume charge of the children, signifying not that they would be *taken away* from their parents, but that they would not be *abandoned* to them.

But is it enough to change laws, institutions, customs, public opinion, and the whole social context, for men and women to become truly equal? "Women will always be women," say the skeptics. Other seers prophesy that in casting off their femininity they will not succeed in changing themselves into men and they will become monsters. This would be to admit that the woman of today is a creation of nature; it must be repeated once more that in human society nothing is natural and that woman, like much else, is a product elaborated by civilization. The intervention of others in her destiny is fundamental: if this action took a different direction, it would produce a quite different result. Woman is determined not by her hormones or by mysterious instincts, but by the manner in which her body and her relation to the world are modified through the action of others than herself. The abyss that separates the adolescent boy and girl has been deliberately opened out between them since earliest childhood; later on, woman could not be other than what she *was made*, and that past was bound to shadow her for life. If we appreciate its influence, we see clearly that her destiny is not predetermined for all eternity.

We must not believe, certainly, that a change in woman's economic condition alone is enough to transform her, though this factor has been and remains the basic factor in her evolution; but until it has brought about the moral, social, cultural, and other consequences that it promises and requires, the new woman cannot appear. At this moment they have been realized nowhere, in Russia no more than in France or the United States; and this explains why the woman of today is torn between the past and the future. She appears most often as a "true woman" disguised as a man, and she feels herself as ill at ease in her flesh as in her masculine garb. She must shed her old skin and cut her own new clothes. This she could do only through a social evolution. No single educator could fashion a *female human being* today who would be the exact homologue of the *male human being;* if she is raised like a boy, the young girl feels she is an oddity and thereby she is given a new kind of sex specification. Stendhal understood this when he said: "The forest must be planted all at once." But if we imagine, on the contrary, a society in which the equality of the sexes would be concretely realized, this equality would find new expression in each individual.

If the little girl were brought up from the first with the same demands and rewards, the same severity and the same freedom, as her brothers, taking part in the same studies, the same games, promised the same future, surrounded with women and men who seemed to her undoubted equals, the meanings of the castration complex and of the Œdipus complex would be profoundly modified. Assuming on the same basis as the father the material and moral responsibility of the couple, the mother would enjoy the same lasting prestige; the child would perceive around her an androgynous world and not a masculine world. Were she emotionally more attracted to her father —which is not even sure—her love for him would be tinged with a will to emulation and not a feeling of powerlessness; she would not be oriented toward passivity. Authorized to test her powers in work and sports, competing actively with the boys, she would not find the absence of the penis—compensated by the promise of a child—enough to give rise to an inferiority complex; correlatively, the boy would not have a superiority complex if it were not instilled into him and if he looked up to women with as much respect as to men.[3] The little girl would not seek sterile compensation in narcissism and dreaming, she would not take her fate for granted; she would be interested in what she was *doing*, she would throw herself without reserve into undertakings.

I have already pointed out how much easier the transformation of puberty would be if she looked beyond it, like the boys, toward a free adult future: menstruation horrifies her only because it is an abrupt descent into femininity. She would also take her young eroticism in much more tranquil fashion if she did not feel a frightened disgust for her destiny as a whole; coherent sexual information would do much to help her over this crisis. And thanks to coeducational schooling, the august mystery of Man would have no occasion to

---

[3] I knew a little boy of eight who lived with his mother, aunt, and grandmother, all independent and active women, and his weak old half-crippled grandfather. He had a crushing inferiority complex in regard to the feminine sex, although he made efforts to combat it. At school he scorned comrades and teachers because they were miserable males.

enter her mind: it would be eliminated by everyday familiarity and open rivalry.

Objections raised against this system always imply respect for sexual taboos; but the effort to inhibit all sex curiosity and pleasure in the child is quite useless; one succeeds only in creating repressions, obsessions, neuroses. The excessive sentimentality, homosexual fervors, and platonic crushes of adolescent girls, with all their train of silliness and frivolity, are much more injurious than a little childish sex play and a few definite sex experiences. It would be beneficial above all for the young girl not to be influenced against taking charge herself of her own existence, for then she would not seek a demigod in the male—merely a comrade, a friend, a partner. Eroticism and love would take on the nature of free transcendence and not that of resignation; she could experience them as a relation between equals. There is no intention, of course, to remove by a stroke of the pen all the difficulties that the child has to overcome in changing into an adult; the most intelligent, the most tolerant education could not relieve the child of experiencing things for herself; what could be asked is that obstacles should not be piled gratuitously in her path. Progress is already shown by the fact that "vicious" little girls are no longer cauterized with a red-hot iron. Psychoanalysis has given parents some instruction, but the conditions under which, at the present time, the sexual training and initiation of woman are accomplished are so deplorable that none of the objections advanced against the idea of a radical change could be considered valid. It is not a question of abolishing in woman the contingencies and miseries of the human condition, but of giving her the means for transcending them.

Woman is the victim of no mysterious fatality; the peculiarities that identify her as specifically a woman get their importance from the significance placed upon them. They can be surmounted, in the future, when they are regarded in new perspectives. Thus, as we have seen, through her erotic experience woman feels—and often detests— the domination of the male; but this is no reason to conclude that her ovaries condemn her to live forever on her knees. Virile aggressiveness seems like a lordly privilege only within a system that in its entirety conspires to affirm masculine sovereignty; and woman *feels* herself profoundly passive in the sexual act only because she already *thinks* of herself as such. Many modern women who lay claim to their dignity as human beings still envisage their erotic life from the standpoint of a tradition of slavery: since it seems to them humiliating to lie beneath the man, to be penetrated by him, they grow tense in frigidity. But if the reality were different, the meaning expressed symbolically in amorous gestures and postures would be different, too: a woman who pays and dominates her lover can, for example, take pride in her superb idleness and consider that she is enslaving the male who is actively exerting himself. And here and now there are many sexually well-balanced couples whose notions of victory and defeat are giving place to the idea of an exchange.

As a matter of fact, man, like woman, is flesh, therefore passive, the plaything of his hormones and of the species, the restless prey of his desires. And she, like him, in the midst of the carnal fever, is a consenting, a voluntary gift, an activity; they live out in their several fashions the strange ambiguity of existence made body. In those combats where they think they confront one another, it is really against the self that each one struggles, projecting into the partner that part of the self which is repudiated; instead of living out the ambiguities of their situation, each tries to make the other bear the abjection and tries to reserve the honor for the self. If, however, both should assume the ambiguity with a clear-sighted modesty, correlative of an authentic pride, they would see each other as equals and would live out their erotic drama in amity. The fact that we are human beings is infinitely more important than all the peculiarities that distinguish human beings from one another; it is never the given that confers superiorities: "virtue," as the ancients called it, is defined at the level of "that which depends on us." In both sexes is played out the same drama of the flesh and the spirit, of finitude and transcendence; both are gnawed away by time and laid in wait for by death, they have the same essential need for one another; and they can gain from their liberty the same glory. If they were to taste it, they would no longer be tempted to dispute fallacious privileges, and fraternity between them could then come into existence.

I shall be told that all this is utopian fancy, because woman cannot be "made over" unless society has first made her really the equal of man. Conservatives have never failed in such circumstances to refer to that vicious circle; history, however, does not revolve. If a caste is kept in a state of inferiority, no doubt it remains inferior; but liberty can break the circle. Let the Negroes vote and they become worthy of having the vote: let woman be given responsibilities and she is able to assume them. The fact is that oppressors cannot be expected to make a move of gratuitous generosity; but at one time the revolt of the oppressed, at another time even the very evolution of the privileged caste itself, creates new situations; thus men have been led, in their own interest, to give partial emancipation to women: it remains only for women to continue their ascent, and the successes they are obtaining are an encouragement for them to do so. It seems almost certain that sooner or later they will arrive at complete economic and social equality, which will bring about an inner metamorphosis.

However this may be, there will be some to object that if such a world is possible it is not desirable. When woman is "the same" as her male, life will lose its salt and spice. This argument, also, has lost its novelty: those interested in perpetuating present conditions are always in tears about the marvelous past that is about to disappear, without having so much as a smile for the young future. It is quite true that doing away with the slave trade meant death to the great plantations, magnificent with azaleas and camellias, it meant ruin to the whole refined Southern civilization. The attics of time have received its rare old laces along with the clear pure voices of the Sistine *castrati*,[4] and there is a certain "feminine charm" that is also on the way to the same dusty repository. I agree that he would be a barbarian indeed who failed to appreciate exquisite flowers, rare lace, the crystal-clear voice of the eunuch, and feminine charm.

When the "charming woman" shows herself in all her splendor, she is a much more exalting object than the "idiotic paintings, overdoors, scenery, showman's garish signs, popular chromos," that excited Rimbaud; adorned with the most modern artifices, beautified according to the newest techniques, she comes down from the remoteness of the ages, from Thebes, from Crete, from Chichén-Itzá; and she is also the totem set up deep in the African jungle; she is a helicopter and she is a bird; and there is this, the greatest wonder of all: under her tinted hair the forest murmur becomes a thought, and words issue from her breasts. Men stretch forth avid hands toward the marvel, but when they grasp it it is gone; the wife, the mistress,

---

[4] Eunuchs were long used in the male choirs of the Sistine Chapel in Rome, until the practice was forbidden by Pope Leo XIII in 1880. The operation of castration caused the boy's soprano voice to be retained into adulthood, and it was performed for this purpose.—TR.

speak like everybody else through their mouths: their words are worth just what they are worth; their breasts also. Does such a fugitive miracle—and one so rare—justify us in perpetuating a situation that is baneful for both sexes? One can appreciate the beauty of flowers, the charm of women, and appreciate them at their true value; if these treasures cost blood or misery, they must be sacrificed.

But in truth this sacrifice seems to men a peculiarly heavy one; few of them really wish in their hearts for woman to succeed in making it; those among them who hold woman in contempt see in the. sacrifice nothing for them to gain, those who cherish her see too much that they would lose. And it is true that the evolution now in progress threatens more than feminine charm alone: in beginning to exist for herself, woman will relinquish the function as double and mediator to which she owes her privileged place in the masculine universe; to man, caught between the silence of nature and the demanding presence of other free beings, a creature who is at once his like and a passive thing seems a great treasure. The guise in which he conceives his companion may be mythical, but the experiences for which she is the source or the pretext are none the less real: there are hardly any more precious, more intimate, more ardent. There is no denying that feminine dependence, inferiority, woe, give women their special character; assuredly woman's autonomy, if it spares men many troubles, will also deny them many conveniences; assuredly there are certain forms of the sexual adventure which will be lost in the world of tomorrow. But this does not mean that love, happiness, poetry, dream, will be banished from it.

Let us not forget that our lack of imagination always depopulates the future; for us it is only an abstraction; each one of us secretly deplores the absence there of the one who was himself. But the humanity of tomorrow will be living in its flesh and in its conscious liberty; that time will be its present and it will in turn prefer it. New relations of flesh and sentiment of which we have no conception will arise between the sexes; already, indeed, there have appeared between men and women friendships, rivalries, complicities, comradeships—chaste or sensual—which past centuries could not have conceived. To mention one point, nothing could seem to me more debatable than the opinion that dooms the new world to uniformity and hence to boredom. I fail to see that this present world is free from boredom or that liberty ever creates uniformity.

To begin with, there will always be certain differences between man and woman; her eroticism, and therefore her sexual world, have a special form of their own and therefore cannot fail to engender a sensuality, a sensitivity, of a special nature. This means that her relations to her own body, to that of the male, to the child, will never be identical with those the male bears to his own body, to that of the female, and to the child; those who make much of "equality in difference" could not with good grace refuse to grant me the possible existence of differences in equality. Then again, it is institutions that create uniformity. Young and pretty, the slaves of the harem are always the same in the sultan's embrace; Christianity gave eroticism its savor of sin and legend when it endowed the human female with a soul; if society restores her sovereign individuality to woman, it will not thereby destroy the power of love's embrace to move the heart.

It is nonsense to assert that revelry, vice, ecstasy, passion, would become impossible if man and woman were equal in concrete matters; the contradictions that put the flesh in opposition to the spirit, the instant to time, the swoon of immanence to the challenge of transcendence, the absolute of pleasure to the nothingness of forgetting, will never be resolved; in sexuality will always be materialized the tension, the anguish, the joy, the frustration, and the triumph of existence. To emancipate woman is to refuse to confine her to the relations she bears to man, not to deny them to her; let her have her independent existence and she will continue none the less to exist for him *also:* mutually recognizing each other as subject, each will yet remain for the other an *other.* The reciprocity of their relations will not do away with the miracles—desire, possession, love, dream, adventure—worked by the division of human beings into two separate categories; and the words that move us—giving, conquering, uniting—will not lose their meaning. On the contrary, when we abolish the slavery of half of humanity, together with the whole system of hypocrisy that it implies, then the "division" of humanity will reveal its genuine significance and the human couple will find its true form. "The direct, natural, necessary relation of human creatures is the *relation of man to woman,*" Marx has said.[5] "The nature of this relation determines to what point man himself is to be considered as a *generic being,* as mankind; the relation of man to woman is the

---

[5] *Philosophical Works,* Vol. VI (Marx's italics).

most natural relation of human being to human being. By it is shown, therefore, to what point the *natural* behavior of man has become *human* or to what point the *human* being has become his *natural* being, to what point his *human nature* has become his *nature*."

The case could not be better stated. It is for man to establish the reign of liberty in the midst of the world of the given. To gain the supreme victory, it is necessary, for one thing, that by and through their natural differentiation men and women unequivocally affirm their brotherhood.

Index